World Development Report 1987

Published for The World Bank
Oxford University Press

Oxford University Press

NEW YORK OXFORD LONDON GLASGOW
TORONTO MELBOURNE WELLINGTON HONG KONG
TOKYO KUALA LUMPUR SINGAPORE JAKARTA
DELHI BOMBAY CALCUTTA MADRAS KARACHI
NAIROBI DAR ES SALAAM CAPE TOWN

ISBN 0-19-520562-6 clothbound
ISBN 0-19-520563-4 paperback
ISSN 0163-5085

The Library of Congress has cataloged this serial publication as follows:
World development report. 1978–
[New York] Oxford University Press.
v. 27 cm. annual.
Published for The World Bank.

1. Underdeveloped areas—Periodicals. 2. Economic development—
Periodicals I. International Bank for Reconstruction and Development.

HC59.7.W659   *330.9′172′4*   *78-67086*

This book is printed on paper that adheres to
the American National Standard for Permanence of Paper
for Printed Library Materials, Z39.48-1984.

Foreword

This Report is the tenth in the annual series assessing development issues. Part I reviews recent trends in the world economy and their implications for the future prospects of developing countries. It also examines the role of foreign trade in the industrialization of developing countries—the theme of Part II of the Report. Like its predecessors, the Report includes an annex, the World Development Indicators, which provides selected social and economic data for more than 100 countries.

The world economy continues to expand, but the expansion is modest and uneven. Many developing countries are still laboring under a large burden of debt and are unable to restore their growth momentum. In some cases, their living standards are lower today than a decade ago. Part I of the Report stresses that better economic performance is possible in both industrial and developing countries, provided the commitment to economic policy reforms is maintained and reinforced.

More vigorous growth in industrial countries is necessary to spur the growth of exports and output in the developing world and thereby alleviate debt servicing problems and reduce poverty. The large external payments imbalances among industrial countries are a source of instability and threaten to interrupt progress in reducing inflation and lowering interest rates. The Report argues for strengthened cooperation among industrial countries in the sphere of macroeconomic policy to promote smooth adjustment to these imbalances and to lay the groundwork for other reforms that would raise productivity and growth in the longer term.

Many developing countries have been making strenuous efforts to stabilize their economies, deal with a heavy debt burden, and cope with declining commodity prices and lower inflows of private capital. They have no alternative but to persevere in these efforts. Where governments are making genuine efforts at reform—frequently in the face of opposition from entrenched interests and in spite of adjustment costs—the international community has a responsibility to provide increased assistance. The Report argues for increases in official and private capital flows and, where appropriate, for debt restructuring on terms that permit a restoration of long-term growth.

Practically all societies at early stages of their development have viewed industrialization as the main vehicle for improving living standards. It is not surprising, therefore, that governments have played an active role in promoting industrialization. Part II of the Report reviews and evaluates the varied experience with government policies in support of industrialization. Emphasis is placed on policies which affect both the efficiency and sustainability of industrial transformation, especially in the sphere of foreign trade.

The Report finds that developing countries which followed policies that promoted the integration of their industrial sector into the international economy through trade have fared better than those which insulated themselves from international competition. Successful countries have typically followed policies on trade, exchange rates, and related matters that did not bias industrial production toward the domestic market. Protection has been relatively modest and its impact on exports offset through other incentives.

Better integration into the international economy

presupposes the willingness of trading partners to provide access to their markets. The economic expansion in the industrial countries since World War II was supported, and in turn made easier, by significant liberalization of trade in manufactures. Outward-oriented developing countries benefited significantly from this liberalization. Beginning in the 1970s, however, the shifting pattern of comparative advantage and the increased competition, especially from developing countries, posed a serious challenge to traditional industrial sectors in the developed world. This gave rise to the "new protectionism"—a series of actions by industrial countries aimed at controlling access to their markets, mainly through nontariff barriers. These actions undermine productivity and growth in the industrial countries and frustrate the efforts of developing countries to increase their exports at a time when such increases are critical to restoration of their economic growth.

The launching of the Uruguay Round of multilateral trade negotiations under the General Agreement on Tariffs and Trade (GATT) offers a promise to reverse protectionist pressures worldwide. A strong commitment by all governments to an open multilateral system under the leadership of the major trading countries of the world is necessary to translate this promise into a reality over the next decade.

Like all previous World Development Reports, this is a study by the staff of the World Bank, and the judgments in it do not necessarily reflect the views of the Board of Directors or the governments they represent.

Barber B. Conable
President
The World Bank

June 1, 1987

This Report has been prepared by a team led by Sarath Rajapatirana and comprising Yaw Ansu, Thorkild Juncker, Alasdair MacBean, Chong-Hyun Nam, Vikram Nehru, and Geoffrey Shepherd. The team was assisted by Josephine Bassinette, M. Shahbaz Khan, Fayez S. Omar, Subramanian S. Sriram, Silvia Torres Mendoza, John Wayem, and Deborah L. Wetzel. The Economic Analysis and Projections Department prepared the main projections and statistical materials presented in the Report. Thanks go to the production staff for the Report, including Bill Fraser, Pensri Kimpitak, and Victoria Lee, and especially to the support staff, headed by Rhoda Blade-Charest and including Trinidad Angeles, Banjonglak Duangrat, Carlina Jones, and Patricia Smith. Anne O. Krueger played a principal role in the initial stages of the Report's preparation. The work was carried out under the general direction of Benjamin B. King and Constantine Michalopoulos, with Clive Crook as the principal editor.

Contents

Text figures

Text tables

Statistical appendix tables

Acronyms and initials

ACP   African, Caribbean, and Pacific
CPE   Centrally planned economy
CVD   Countervailing duty
DUP   Directly unproductive profit seeking
EC   The European Community comprises Belgium, Denmark, France, Federal Republic of Germany, Greece, Ireland, Italy, Luxembourg, Netherlands, Portugal, Spain, and United Kingdom
EFTA   European Free Trade Association
EPZ   Export processing zone
GATT   General Agreement on Tariffs and Trade
GDP   Gross domestic product
GNP   Gross national product
GSP   Generalized System of Preferences
GSTP   Global System of Trade Preferences
IDA   International Development Association
IFC   International Finance Corporation
ILO   International Labour Organisation
IMF   International Monetary Fund
ITO   International Trade Organization
LIBOR   London interbank offered rate
LTA   Long Term Arrangement Regarding International Trade in Cotton Textiles
MFA   Multifibre Arrangement

MFN   Most favored nation
MITI   Ministry of International Trade and Industry
MNC   Multinational corporation
MTN   Multilateral trade negotiations
MYRA   Multiyear restructuring agreement
NAIC   North Atlantic industrial country
NIC   Newly industrializing country
NTB   Nontariff barrier
ODA   Official development assistance
OECD   The Organisation for Economic Co-operation and Development members are Australia, Austria, Belgium, Canada, Denmark, Finland, France, Federal Republic of Germany, Greece, Iceland, Ireland, Italy, Japan, Luxembourg, Netherlands, New Zealand, Norway, Portugal, Spain, Sweden, Switzerland, Turkey, United Kingdom, and United States
SITC   Standard International Trade Classification
SOE   State-owned enterprise
UNCTAD   United Nations Conference on Trade and Development
VCR   Videocassette recorder
VER   Voluntary export restraint
VIE   Voluntary import expansion

Definitions and data notes

The principal country groups used in the text of this Report and in the World Development Indicators are defined below. The overall classification uses GNP per capita as the main criterion.

• *Developing countries* are divided into: *low-income economies,* with 1985 GNP per person of $400 or less; and *middle-income economies,* with 1985 GNP per person of $401 or more.

• *High-income oil exporters* comprise Bahrain, Brunei, Kuwait, Libya, Qatar, Saudi Arabia, and the United Arab Emirates.

• *Industrial market economies* are the members of the Organisation for Economic Co-operation and Development, apart from Greece, Portugal, and Turkey, which are included among the middle-income developing countries. This group is commonly referred to in the text as *industrial economies* or *industrial countries.*

• *Nonreporting nonmember economies* are Albania, Angola, Bulgaria, Cuba, Czechoslovakia, German Democratic Republic, Democratic People's Republic of Korea, Mongolia, and the U.S.S.R.

For analytical purposes, a number of other overlapping classifications based predominantly on exports or external debt are used in addition to geographic country groupings:

• *Oil exporters* are middle-income developing countries with exports of petroleum and gas, including reexports, accounting for 30 percent of merchandise exports: Algeria, Arab Republic of Egypt, Cameroon, Ecuador, Gabon, Indonesia, Iraq, Islamic Republic of Iran, Mexico, Nigeria, Oman, People's Republic of the Congo, Syrian Arab Republic, Trinidad and Tobago, and Venezuela.

• *Exporters of manufactures* are developing economies with exports of manufactures (defined for this purpose as SITC 5, 6, 7, and 8, less 651, 652, 654, 655, 667, 68) accounting for more than 30 percent of exports of goods and services: Brazil, China, Hong Kong, Hungary, India, Israel, Poland, Portugal, Republic of Korea, Romania, Singapore, and Yugoslavia.

• *Highly indebted countries* are seventeen countries deemed to have encountered severe debt servicing difficulties: Argentina, Bolivia, Brazil, Chile, Colombia, Costa Rica, Côte d'Ivoire, Ecuador, Jamaica, Mexico, Morocco, Nigeria, Peru, Philippines, Uruguay, Venezuela, and Yugoslavia.

• *Sub-Saharan Africa* is made up of all countries south of the Sahara excluding South Africa.

• *Middle East and North Africa* comprise Afghanistan, Algeria, Arab Republic of Egypt, Iraq, Islamic Republic of Iran, Israel, Jordan, Kuwait, Lebanon, Libya, Morocco, Oman, People's Democratic Republic of Yemen, Saudi Arabia, Syrian Arab Republic, Tunisia, Turkey, United Arab Emirates, and Yemen Arab Republic.

• *East Asia* comprises all low- and middle-income economies of East and Southeast Asia and the Pacific, east of and including China, Mongolia, and Thailand.

• *South Asia* comprises Bangladesh, Bhutan, Burma, India, Nepal, Pakistan, and Sri Lanka.

• *Latin America and the Caribbean* comprise all American and Caribbean countries south of the United States.

Economic and demographic terms are defined in the technical notes to the World Development Indicators. The Indicators use the country groupings given above but include only countries with a population of 1 million or more.

Billion is 1,000 million.

Trillion is 1,000 billion.

Tons are metric tons, equal to 1,000 kilograms, or 2,204.6 pounds.

Growth rates are in real terms unless otherwise stated. Growth rates for spans of years in tables cover the period from the beginning of the base year to the end of the last year given.

Dollars are current U.S. dollars unless otherwise specified.

All tables and figures are based on World Bank data unless otherwise specified.

The symbol .. in tables means "not available."

The symbol — in tables means "not applicable."

Data from secondary sources are not always available through 1985. The numbers in this *World Development Report* shown for historical data may differ from those shown in previous Reports because of continuous updating as better data become available and because of recompilation of certain data for a ninety-country sample. The recompilation was necessary to permit greater flexibility in regrouping countries for the purpose of making projections.

Industrialization and foreign trade: an overview

This Report examines the role of foreign trade in industrialization. The pace and character of industrial development are not simply the result of trade policies. Many other factors matter. A country's size, its natural resources, the skills of its people, the stability of its government and institutions and their ability to promote change, the fiscal, monetary, and exchange rate policies that the government pursues—all these and still more factors influence a country's ability to industrialize.

The role of foreign trade in industrialization is an important issue for several reasons. First, although the relationship between trade policy and industrial development has concerned policymakers and economists for a long time, empirical studies over the past thirty years now make it possible for useful lessons to be drawn concerning the advantages and disadvantages of different trade policies. Second, many fear that slow world growth and rising protection in industrial countries may cloud the prospects for developing countries' exports. Third, continuing debt problems increase the developing countries' need to raise their net earnings of foreign exchange to service debt and maintain adequate growth.

This does not mean that other factors can be ignored. If, for example, a country reduces its trade barriers but fails to make appropriate changes in its fiscal, monetary, and exchange rate policies, the benefits it hoped for may not materialize. Domestic inflation and an overvalued exchange rate could discourage the investment flows needed to respond to the new price incentives. Analysts looking at the past and governments setting policies for the future have to bear in mind the complexity of the relationships among policies.

This Report stresses *efficient* industrialization because there is evidence of inefficiencies in industries in both industrial and developing countries. These industries may not show financial losses because protection allows domestic firms to sell above international prices. Overvalued exchange rates may allow them to buy machinery and intermediate goods from abroad at prices below their true cost to the economy. Such overvaluation of outputs and undervaluation of inputs will exaggerate both the industries' profits and the contribution that their output makes to the national product. At the same time, undervaluation of exports and agricultural products will disguise their potential contribution to growth. The net effect is to magnify industry's part in domestic output and growth. Simple statistics on the share of industry or manufacturing in gross domestic product (GDP) are suspect in many countries.

The term ''efficient'' begs many questions. It has meaning only in relation to specific objectives: efficiency is measured by the costs of attaining these objectives. Industrialization contributes to economic development. So the question is, What are the ultimate objectives of economic development? Different governments may have different objectives in mind and will certainly disagree about the weight to be attached to them. Generally, however, they will include faster growth of national income, alleviation of poverty, and reduction of income inequalities. How is industrialization expected to contribute to these goals?

Much of the early literature treated industrialization as the key element in economic development. The experience of the industrial economies showed a close association between development

Box 1.1 The World Bank's support for industrialization

"Excessive emphasis on industry for industry's sake, above all heavy industry, may leave an undeveloped country with the symbol of development rather than the substance. There are of course a number of instances where heavy industry may be justified . . . But, in general, capital should be applied where it brings the greatest return" (World Bank memorandum to the United Nations Economic and Employment Commission, May 14, 1949). This 1949 quote is as relevant today as it was then. The Bank has always viewed industrialization not as an end in itself, but as a means to raise productivity and incomes. And it is this view that has shaped and guided the Bank's support for industrialization in its member countries.

The Bank has supported the efforts of its member countries in building new industrial capacity, improving the efficiency of existing capacity, and providing training and technical assistance to accelerate the acquisition and mastery of new skills and new technology. Until the late 1970s, it did this by financing industrial subsector studies, project feasibility studies, project design and engineering, technical assistance, and industrial investments. It also financed industry indirectly by lending to industrial development banks; these loans served the additional purpose of deepening financial markets in developing countries. To complement these efforts, the International Finance Corporation (IFC), an affiliate of the World Bank, supports the projects of private investors through loans as well as equity participation. Last, but not least, the Bank's lending for education and physical infrastructure, in contributing to economic development, has helped build skills, transport, communications, and power—all vital inputs to modern industry.

More recently, however, the Bank's support for industrial development has added a new dimension to its emphasis on projects. It now includes support for improved policies and strengthened institutions. This was in response to the structural adjustment problems faced by developing countries following the international recession and to a growing awareness of the influence of policies and institutions on industrial development. The Bank, jointly with its member countries, devises a lending program that supports policy reforms and structural change across the whole economy, as well as at the level of the individual enterprise or institution. In recent years the Bank has made several structural adjustment and sector adjustment loans to developing countries in support of changes in their macroeconomic, trade, and industrial policies.

The Bank's lending to industry will continue to evolve in response to the needs of its borrowers. Support for industrialization will continue to emphasize policies at both the economy and the project level. The Bank will need to meet the challenge of providing an integrated package of lending, technical assistance, economic analysis, and policy advice that addresses the needs of individual countries and matches their capacity for reform. At the same time, recognizing the importance of skill and infrastructural development to industry, the Bank will continue with project lending in certain areas.

---

and industrial expansion. But industry was also thought to provide certain spillovers which would benefit other activities: enhancement of skills, training of managers, dispersion of technology, and so on. Moreover, pessimism about the prospects for exports of food and raw materials made the substitution of domestic for imported manufactures seem the most promising route to development.

Subsequent experience showed most of these ideas to be too simple, or even misleading. Many countries have achieved high standards of living based mainly on the production and export of food and raw materials: Australia, Canada, Côte d'Ivoire, Denmark, Kenya, Malaysia, New Zealand, Sweden, and the oil-exporting countries, to name but a few. Industrialization has certainly been associated with growth, but it is not the only cause of growth. At certain stages in a country's

development the highest returns may come from the production of particular types of manufactures, agricultural products, or services. How best to use resources at any time depends on market prospects and costs. So the interesting question is not how fast a country can be industrialized, but how incentives and policies can be designed so that new industries make the maximum contribution to the country's development (see Box 1.1).

Foreign trade preceded industrialization by thousands of years. Early industry relied largely on trade within nations. Yet, as Adam Smith noted, the development of industry is likely to be severely handicapped if it is deprived of the ability to trade widely. The division of labor is limited by the size of the market, and the division of labor is the key to increased productivity.

For small countries—and most developing countries are small in terms of their domestic market for industrial goods—this means that progress depends upon the ability to trade relatively freely with the rest of the world. For large economies domestic trade may provide scope for adequate specialization, economies of scale, and enough competition to keep managers alert. But even large economies, if cut off from international trade, would lack stimuli for efficient industrial development. Competition from abroad forces firms to cut costs, improve quality, and seek new ways of producing and selling their goods. Contacts through trade ease the flow of capital and speed the acquisition of new technology (see Box 1.2).

This is not to deny that throughout history many countries have developed industries behind protective barriers. There are respectable arguments to be made for assisting firms through the difficult learning stages of development. These arguments depend largely on market failures of one sort or another or the existence of external benefits such as the spread of ideas and skills throughout the economy. But history is also full of examples of countries that have given their industries too much protection for too long. Many countries are now struggling to reduce protection in order to improve efficiency and switch resources to more profitable activities.

Much of the bias against trade in developing countries has been unintended. Errors in macroeconomic policy or unexpected changes in the terms of trade have caused balance of payments deficits and shortages of foreign exchange. Domestic inflation, combined with exchange controls, has led to overvalued exchange rates. These damaged

---

Box 1.2   John Stuart Mill on the gains from trade

In his *Principles of Political Economy* (1848), John Stuart Mill discusses the gains that result from "foreign commerce." Although more than a century has passed, his observations are as relevant today as they were in 1848. In referring to David Ricardo, one of the first to analyze formally the benefits of trade, he notes: "From this exposition we perceive in what consists the benefit of international exchange, or in other words, foreign commerce. Setting aside its enabling countries to obtain commodities which they could not produce themselves at all; its advantage consists in a more efficient employment of the productive forces of the world. If two countries which trade together attempted, as far as was physically possible, to produce for themselves what they now import from one another, the labor and capital of the two countries would not be so productive, the two together would not obtain from their industry so great a quantity of commodities, as when each employs itself in producing, both for itself and for the other, the things in which its labor is relatively most efficient. The addition thus made to the produce of the two combined, constitutes the advantage of trade" (p. 96).

Mill goes on to say: "There is much misconception in the common notion of what commerce does for a country. When commerce is spoken of as a source of national wealth, the imagination fixes itself upon the large fortunes acquired by merchants, rather than upon the saving of price to consumers. But the gains of merchants, when they enjoy no exclusive privilege, are no greater than the profits obtained by the employment of capital in the country itself . . . Commerce is virtually a mode of cheapening production and in all such cases the consumer is the person ultimately bene-

fited; the dealer, in the end, is sure to get his profit, whether the buyer obtains much or little for his money" (p. 98).

Mill also discusses the indirect gains from trade. He states: "But there are, besides, indirect effects, which must be counted as benefits of a high order. One is, the tendency of every extension of the market to improve the processes of production. A country which produces for a larger market than its own, can introduce a more extended division of labor, can make greater use of machinery, and is more likely to make inventions and improvements in the processes of production. Whatever causes a greater quantity of anything to be produced in the same place tends to the general increase of the productive powers of the world. There is another consideration, principally applicable to an early stage of industrial advancement. A people may be in the quiescent, indolent, uncultivated state, with all their tastes either fully satisfied or entirely undeveloped, and they may fail to put forth the whole of their productive energies for want of any sufficient object of desire. The opening of a foreign trade, by making them acquainted with new objects, or tempting them by the easier acquisition of things which they had not previously thought attainable, sometimes works a sort of industrial revolution in a country whose resources were previously undeveloped for want of energy and ambition in the people: inducing those who were satisfied with scanty comforts and little work to work harder for the gratification of their new tastes, and even to save and accumulate capital, for the still more complete satisfaction of those tastes at a future time" (p. 99).

exports and fueled a vicious circle of foreign currency shortages, controls, and overvalued exchange rates. The resulting protection of domestic industries was quite inadvertent. And the levels of protection were often far in excess of any that even the most fervent advocate of infant industry protection could support.

For some countries the results of protection have been industries whose contribution to national income was negligible or even negative. Supporting them has burdened other sectors of the economy, in particular the rural community, which contains most of the poorest citizens of the developing countries. The same can be said for many of the industries of the centrally planned economies (CPEs). Lack of exposure to competition from abroad has fostered goods that are expensive and of low quality. The industrialization of the CPEs was impressively rapid, but less efficient than it might have been. Recognizing this, many developing countries and some CPEs are undertaking significant reforms and are trying to reduce their trade barriers, switch more of their efforts into exports, and compete more vigorously in world markets.

From recovery and adjustment to long-term growth (Chapter 2)

Although countries ultimately rise by their own efforts, the world economy conditions their success. The economic recovery that began in 1983 is weakening. For the industrial countries as a group, output growth reached 4.6 percent in 1984, but then dropped to 2.8 percent in 1985 and to an estimated 2.5 percent in 1986. Payments imbalances among the major trading nations persist, as do the debt problems of many developing countries. Real interest rates remain high compared with historical levels, and low commodity prices add to the difficulties of many developing countries. New funds to support the adjustment efforts of the developing countries have been severely limited.

Against this background two positive features stand out. First, inflation is low in most industrial countries and declining in many developing countries. Second, some industrial countries have made steady progress in reducing their fiscal deficits, which leaves more room to expand demand and stimulate growth.

Despite these positive signs, there is the danger that growth may slow further and that payments imbalances will fail to subside. The threat of protectionism might then turn into actual protection on a large scale. Debt difficulties could become intractable, partly because a sluggish world economy will also mean reduced net capital flows to the developing countries. All this will make adjustment much more difficult.

How should governments respond in the short term to avert these risks? The industrial market economies need a reduction in the U.S. current account deficit and in the corresponding surpluses of the major trading partners of the United States. For that to happen there must be both a decline in the U.S. budget deficit and an increase in U.S. exports. But this poses a risk of its own. Expansion in the United States was instrumental in earlier periods of economic growth, and reducing demand in the United States in order to cut its external deficit will slow world growth unless the other industrial countries take steps to offset the decline in global demand. So the policies of the industrial nations need to be carefully coordinated. The task goes beyond replacing the fiscal deficit of one country with a fiscal deficit elsewhere. It requires the careful use of fiscal and monetary policy to smooth the process of adjustment. This adjustment should not be delayed. If the present imbalances persist, they will threaten the stability of the world economy and encourage ''beggar thy neighbor'' protection.

In the longer term, the industrial market economies need to improve their economic flexibility by lowering their trade barriers and tackling rigidities in their markets for labor and goods. Such rigidities, in effect, resist the changes in comparative advantage, technology, and demography that economies must heed if they are to grow and prosper. Reforms such as these may not be feasible unless governments first address the pressing problems of short-term economic adjustment.

The fundamental goals of long-term structural adjustment in developing countries are to enhance efficiency, achieve equity, and expand the stock of physical and human capital. The problems of the highly indebted countries and Sub-Saharan Africa are particularly urgent, and their task would be easier if world growth were to revive. These and many other developing countries would benefit from policy reforms in three areas, although the precise form of appropriate measures will differ from case to case:

• *Trade reform.* Countries should move toward the adoption of an outward-oriented trade strategy. Such a strategy means removing the bias against exports, replacing quantitative restrictions with tariffs, and adopting more realistic exchange rates.

• *Macroeconomic policy.* Many governments need to reduce their budget deficits and to provide incentives for greater savings. Ensuring positive real interest rates, competitive exchange rates, and low inflation will not only increase the supply of domestic financial resources, but also help to support trade reforms.

• *Domestic competitive environment.* In addition to reforming trade and macroeconomic policies, governments need to improve the supply response of the economy, especially by removing price controls, rationalizing investment regulations, and reforming labor market regulations. These policies will complement trade reforms and promote the adoption of cost-minimizing technology.

But reforms alone will not restore growth in most cases. Complementary increases in capital flows are needed.

All told, then, industrial and developing countries alike face formidable tasks of adjustment. Should their policy efforts succeed, the world economy can return to a high-growth path. The alternative is stagnation, even greater instability, increased protection, and a missed opportunity to raise the living standards of the world's poor.

Chapter 2 of this Report tries to be a little more precise about the difference between success and failure. It presents two alternative growth paths. These are not projections but the ranges of outcomes possible under alternative assumptions of policy change. Under the High case, it is assumed that the industrial countries are successful in their adjustment efforts. On this assumption, they grow at a rate of just over 4 percent over the next decade. The prospects for developing countries would also improve. Their growth could reach 6 percent a year if their adjustment efforts are combined with a favorable world environment. But if governments in the industrial and developing countries do not take up the challenge of adjustment, the result will be slow growth, increasing protection, and greater instability in the world economy. So, in the Low case, the developing countries grow at around 4 percent, a rate too slow to enable them to tackle their debt problems. Countries which attempted reforms would do better than those that did not, but in any event the Low case represents a missed opportunity which would have drastic effects on the vast majority of the world's poor.

Industrialization: trends and transformations (Chapter 3)

Industrialization is a part of the open-ended process of economic development that began around the middle of the eighteenth century in Great Britain. New methods of spinning and weaving cotton, together with increasing specialization, sharply increased productivity. These were followed by innovations in iron smelting and by the invention of the steam engine. Continuing innovations led to the production of steel and railways, steamships, and other transport. These boosted trade and spread industrialization, first to the major European nations and then to the United States and Japan.

A second industrial revolution began between 1870 and 1913. During this phase technological advance came to depend on scientific progress. The demands of the new technologies linked industrial growth to supplies from Africa, Asia, and the Caribbean. After World War II a period of unprecedented expansion in output and trade began. The postwar growth in manufacturing was fueled by the widespread use of such prewar innovations as assembly line production, electricity, the automobile, and consumer durables. Entirely new technologies also emerged: synthetic materials, petrochemicals, nuclear energy, jet aircraft, telecommunications, microelectronics, and robotics. Many observers believe that the world is now on the threshold of a third industrial revolution.

From the outset, then, industrialization has involved the interaction of technology, specialization, and trade. This interaction provokes structural change within economies. For example, early industrialization is usually associated with an increase in the share of industry in GDP (see Figure 1.1). Higher agricultural productivity is needed to accommodate that shift. Of course, there are exceptions to the pattern. Some economies have remained agricultural and still achieved high per capita income—Australia and New Zealand, for example. Others have become industrialized without increases in agricultural productivity but through exports of labor-intensive manufactures—Hong Kong, the Republic of Korea, and Singapore, for example.

Within these broad sectoral shifts, early industrialization moved through another series of changes. First it centered on textiles, then iron, steel, and engineering products based on steel. Later the focus shifted to electronics and microelectronics. But today's developing countries need not follow the same sequence. Now that technology is so portable, they can create an engineering industry without producing iron and steel or leap to microelectronics without building large industrial complexes.

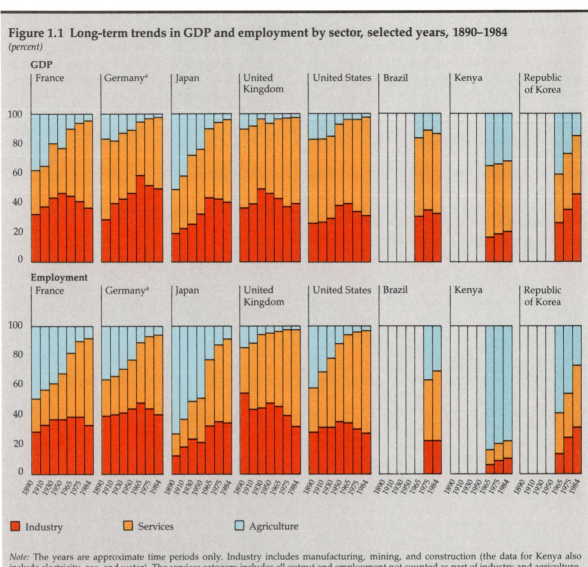

Figure 1.1 Long-term trends in GDP and employment by sector, selected years, 1890–1984
(percent)

Note: The years are approximate time periods only. Industry includes manufacturing, mining, and construction (the data for Kenya also include electricity, gas, and water). The services category includes all output and employment not counted as part of industry and agriculture.
a. Data from 1950 onward refer to the Federal Republic of Germany.
Source: Kuznets 1957, appendix tables 2 and 4; International Labour Organisation 1970, 1980, 1985; and OECD and World Bank data.

The lessons of history, therefore, need to be interpreted with care. There is no unique path to industrialization. That said, some common themes emerge from past experience and point the way for countries that are embarking on industrialization today. For example, countries with large domestic markets are in a better position to establish industrial plants and take advantage of economies of scale. A rich endowment of natural resources provides financial means to support industrialization efforts. But neither size nor natural resources guarantee that a country can industrialize successfully. Indeed, they can lull countries into complacency.

Policy seems to matter more. All countries have protected industry at one time or another, but the successful early industrializers benefited from periods of free trade, and their levels of protection were for the most part low compared with those found today in many developing countries.

Thus far, all of the countries that have industrialized began the process with relatively skilled labor forces. And all except Britain acquired technologies from abroad. The two factors are linked, because technical skills are necessary to make intelligent choices of technologies, and the gains are much greater when those choices are efficiently adapted to each country's special circumstances. Governments have played a key role in this—and in the provision of physical infrastructure. Advances in transport and communications expanded markets, increased specialization, and brought about an integrated industrial world. Except in the United Kingdom, most of the early transport networks were publicly funded. Another key role for government has been the provision of stable yet flexible social and economic institutions: this includes everything from microeconomic "rules of the game" (property rights and so forth) to noninflationary macroeconomic policy.

The role of government (Chapter 4)

Markets and governments have complementary roles in industrialization. Markets are adept at dealing with the growing economic complexity that comes with industrialization, but they are rarely perfect. Government must sometimes intervene to achieve an efficient outcome.

First, governments have to set the rules of the game, which define the use, ownership, and conditions of transfer of physical, financial, and intellectual assets. Irrespective of the type of economy—whether it favors private enterprise or is a command economy—these rules impinge on economic activity. The more they are certain, well defined, and well understood, the more smoothly the economy can work. In many developing countries these rules are often unclear, interpreted in unpredictable ways, and managed by a cumbersome bureaucracy. This tends to raise the costs of doing business and therefore discourages the transactions that are essential for industrial specialization.

Governments must continue to be the main providers of certain services that have facilitated industrialization in the past:

- All governments play a major role in education, especially in providing the basic skills of literacy and numeracy that are vital in a modern industrial labor force. Lack of education, rather than physical assets, is the main bottleneck in industrialization.

- Most governments provide the physical infrastructure of industry: transport, communications, and power systems. Although some parts of such systems can be, and are, profitably operated in the private sector in many countries, government provision of large systems in most developing countries is usually the only feasible option.

- Most governments provide economic information and regulation of standards (weights, measures, safety at work). But there is a limit to the information they can make available in time to be useful, and regulations can often be ineffective or counterproductive.

- Governments in the industrial economies promote scientific and technological research. For developing countries, where it usually makes sense to acquire foreign technology, the arguments for a large government role in industrial research and development are less compelling. But public support may be justified in some cases.

- State-owned enterprises were established to carry out some of these tasks. Some have performed well, but many have disappointed. Efforts are under way to reform them. Such reforms are high on the agenda for structural adjustment in developing countries.

In addition to these forms of direct participation, governments intervene somewhat less directly in the running of their economies. Trade policy, fiscal incentives, price controls, investment regulations, and financial and macroeconomic policies are their instruments. Capital market failures and externalities are the most cited justifications for direct intervention. Both concepts have been used, for example, to defend policies toward infant industries.

Suppose a potentially profitable young firm is unable to find the funds to tide it over the period before it becomes financially viable and can recoup its costs. Without government support such firms would not be able to start production. Or suppose that the firm could generate economic benefits to the rest of the economy—for example, in the form of trained workers who leave and take their skills elsewhere. Again some form of government support is warranted. Import protection is never the best form of intervention in principle, but sometimes there may be no practical alternative.

Different forms of intervention will have different effects on the economy. Indeed, the important question often is not whether to intervene, but how. Quantitative restrictions on imports may be used to protect infant industries, for instance. But they will raise social costs more than a tariff will, because they encourage unproductive activities such as the efforts of producers to avoid or exploit the controls. Tariffs, however, raise prices to consumers. Subsidies to the industry could give the same assistance without raising prices—although not without raising public spending and, possibly, budget deficits.

Trade policy and industrialization (Chapter 5)

Economists and policymakers in developing countries broadly agree that governments need to provide infrastructure, promote market efficiency, and foster a stable macroeconomic environment. Trade policy is a much more contentious issue.

Trade policies can be characterized as outward oriented or inward oriented. An outward-oriented strategy provides incentives which are neutral between production for the domestic market and exports. Because international trade is not positively discouraged, this approach is often, although somewhat misleadingly, referred to as export promotion. In truth, the essence of an outward-oriented strategy is neither discrimination in favor of exports nor bias against import substitution. By contrast, in an inward-oriented strategy trade and industrial incentives are biased in favor of domestic production and against foreign trade. This approach is often referred to as an import substitution strategy. In some countries the bias against trade has been extreme.

An inward-oriented strategy usually means overt protection. What is less obvious is that sheltering domestic industries puts exports at a great disadvantage because it raises the costs of the foreign inputs used in their production. Moreover, an increase in the relative costs of domestic inputs may also occur through inflation—or because of an appreciation of the exchange rate—as the import restrictions are introduced.

In practice, trade policy contains elements of both approaches. Differences arise as much from the choice of instruments as from the absence or presence of intervention. Outward-oriented policies favor tariffs over quantitative restrictions. These tariffs are usually counterbalanced by other measures, including production subsidies and the provision of inputs at "free trade" prices. Governments aim to keep the exchange rate at a level that provides equal incentives to produce exports and import substitutes. Overall protection is lower under an outward-oriented strategy than under inward orientation; equally important, the spread between the highest and lowest rates of protection is narrower.

Inward-oriented strategies typically prefer quantitative restrictions to tariffs, and they involve a higher overall level of protection, together with greater variation across activities. Exchange rates are generally overvalued because of high protection and the use of quantitative restrictions. Indus-trial incentives are administered by an elaborate and expensive bureaucracy.

This Report presents a study of forty-one economies which shows that outward-oriented economies tend to perform better than inward-oriented economies. Their overall output grew faster. They industrialized more smoothly, even though their explicit interventions in support of that goal were far fewer. For the economies that followed more mixed strategies, however, differences in average performance were small; since many factors apart from trade policy influence economic success, this is scarcely surprising. The important lesson is that the strongly inward-oriented economies did badly.

Trade policy reform (Chapter 6)

Like most policy changes, the shift toward outward orientation inevitably involves transitional costs. Major shifts in resources accompany trade liberalization, as some activities contract and others expand in response to the changes in prices that the reforms must entail. If the economy is highly distorted to begin with, larger changes are more likely to be necessary. One visible cost is unemployment, although recent research on trade reform shows that it has caused less unemployment than is generally supposed.

More often than not, trade liberalization comes in the wake of economic crises that are associated with budget and balance of payments deficits and inflation. Such crises may create the political will for change—an important ingredient in undertaking trade liberalization. A government's long-term commitment to reform needs to be credible if economic agents are to respond to the incentives the reform creates. Trade liberalization may therefore be more likely to succeed when the initial shifts in policy are substantial: this adds to the credibility of reform. Moreover, a strong initial shift in policy can quickly boost exports enough to create vested interests in support of further liberalization.

Stable macroeconomic policies—aimed at reducing inflation and preventing the currency from appreciating—are also crucial for the success of trade reforms. Many trade liberalization efforts have foundered owing to poor macroeconomic policies rather than poor trade policies. Once the reforms are undertaken, their fate often rests mainly with the balance of payments—and this is the outcome of macroeconomic policy.

Experience suggests that export performance is closely related to the level and stability of the exchange rate. Conversely, using the exchange rate to stabilize domestic prices is inconsistent with trade reform. In the countries of the Southern Cone of Latin America, capital inflows led to the appreciation of exchange rates, which offset the incentives for increasing the production of exports and import substitutes. Large capital inflows were in some cases the result of liberalization of the financial markets in which domestic interest rates rose very sharply. This provoked heavy borrowing from abroad.

A review of the recent history of trade policy reforms suggests that three elements seem to matter most in their design. The first is the move from quantitative restrictions to tariffs. This links domestic prices to foreign prices. The second is the reduction of the variation in rates of protection alongside reductions in its overall level. Otherwise, protection accorded to value added in some sectors may increase, because as a result of reduced tariffs and quotas the prices of inputs may fall faster than the prices of outputs. The third element is the direct promotion of exports to offset the bias arising from import tariffs. Specific measures to promote exports risk acquiring a permanent status, however, and often lead to the postponement of more fundamental changes relating to the exchange rate. They may also contravene the General Agreement on Tariffs and Trade (GATT), create lobbies that will oppose their removal, and risk countervailing duty actions from importers.

Complementary policies for industrial development (Chapter 7)

Trade policy is only one of the many instruments used by governments to influence the pattern of industrialization. The others fall into four broad categories:

• *Price controls* are used to achieve income distribution goals, to protect consumers from monopoly, to promote industry through their influence on input prices, and to control inflation. They are pervasive in many developing countries. Although they can have some short-run beneficial effects by lowering price expectations in periods of high inflation, their usual long-run effects harm rather than promote efficiency. They restrict supply, encourage the emergence of dual markets, distort cost relationships, entail high administrative costs, and create vested interests in their permanence. Programs targeted to support the poor directly are a better way to attack poverty.

• *Regulations*, of which licensing is the most common, attempt to influence the pattern of private investment in line with government priorities. Investments by foreigners are often subject to more stringent regulations than those of nationals. The result is a distorted pattern of prices and incentives. For example, investments in capital-intensive technology are in many cases the result of the low price of capital and overvalued exchange rates. High domestic protection encourages "tariff jumping" by foreign investors, which in turn leads to investments in activities with low or negative social returns.

• *Financial policies* are another important influence on the pattern of industrialization, through their effects on savings and the cost of capital. Interest rate controls are common in developing countries. They encourage investment at low rates of return and excessively capital-intensive technology. They also discourage financial savings. But dismantling these controls must be done carefully: macroeconomic stability, low public sector deficits, and proper exchange rate management may have to precede attempts to liberalize financial policies.

Because medium- and long-term finance is often found inadequate for industrial investments, governments in developing countries have established medium- and long-term financial institutions such as development banks. They have also tried to promote bond and equity markets. In many cases these institutions have depended heavily on public resources and have been unsuccessful in mobilizing resources for themselves.

• *Labor market policies* involving highly regulated wages, payroll taxes, and rules governing job security are common in developing countries. Minimum wage regulations are particularly prevalent, but they carry certain risks. If minimum wages are set too high, they deter employment by favoring the use of capital over labor, they increase inequalities between the formal and informal sectors, and they reduce returns to education and training by narrowing differentials between skilled and unskilled labor. The other popular forms of intervention—such as payroll taxes, wage policies for the public sector, and rules on job security—all risk, to some extent, distorting the labor market in ways that reduce employment and overall living standards.

The combined effect of trade and domestic policies

Trade and domestic policies jointly influence prices of capital and labor. For example, exchange rate overvaluation increases the demand for capital in relation to the demand for labor. Import licensing systems, which often give priority to capital imports, reinforce this bias. Interest rate controls work in the same direction.

Another aspect of the interaction between trade and domestic policies is their influence on the competitive environment. On the one hand, barriers to entry brought about by import restrictions can create monopolies. On the other hand, stringent laws to limit the size of firms make it harder to achieve economies of scale. Rigid job security regulations, laws against mergers and acquisitions, and the absence of bankruptcy laws can make it difficult for firms to leave an industry. Exit barriers maintain inefficiency and inhibit structural change. And many studies indicate that trade, industrial, and financial policies discriminate against small firms.

Technological development and industrialization

Technological development involves the acquisition and adaptation of technology. Prices strongly influence the process. Governments have attempted to provide public support for technological development in many ways—for example, through systems of patents to protect proprietary rights in technological advances and through subsidized research. Greater contact with producers would increase the impact of the public research institutes. There is little hard evidence on which approaches work best, but a combination of undistorted market signals with targeted public support seems most promising.

The threat of protectionism (Chapter 8)

Since World War II, tariffs in industrial countries on most manufactures have fallen so far that they are no longer significant barriers to trade. But recent years have seen a resurgence of protection in the form of nontariff barriers. The proportion of North American and European Community imports affected by various nontariff restrictions has risen by more than 20 percent from 1981 to 1986. Such restrictions cover large volumes of imports and affect developing countries' exports in particular. Nontariff barriers in clothing and footwear have proved porous, so developing countries have been able to go on increasing their exports to the industrial economies, but at a cost, and with increasing difficulty as leaks in the nontariff barriers are plugged.

Nontariff protection is concentrated on a few industries. Textiles, clothing, footwear, leather goods, steel, and shipbuilding use standard technology and, in many instances, labor-intensive methods. This has made them vulnerable to competition from the newly industrializing countries (NICs—defined here as the economies of Brazil, Hong Kong, Mexico, the Republic of Korea, and Singapore) in recent years. As new entrants, the NICs were able to absorb the existing technology and combine it with labor that was much cheaper and highly productive. Labor in the NICs not only was willing to operate at lower wages than in the industrial countries, and with fewer safeguards for health and safety at work, but also was exempt from the overmanning, job demarcation, and restrictive working practices which were common in the industrial countries.

Management and labor in the industrial countries' traditional industries have a common interest in gaining protection—management to maintain profits, and workers to retain jobs and incomes. Labor unions have the additional motive of retaining members who would be lost to the union if they became unemployed or switched to other industries. Overvalued exchange rates (in some cases) and world recession added to the pressures and led to increased demands for protection. These spread beyond the parties directly involved to others who, in a climate of rapidly rising levels of unemployment, saw protection as a general solution. Yet protection has not, as a rule, saved jobs.

An alternative response to changes in the structure of trade is to ease the movement of resources out of the industries which have lost competitiveness, while providing compensation to workers who need to retrain, move to new forms of work, or opt for early retirement. Protection is justified only if it is necessary to slow the speed of adjustment, and then only if subsidies are not available for the purpose. Even so, the protection could be damaging if it is not designed to be temporary and degressive. Otherwise it will not promote adjustment, but simply delay the shift of resources from dying industries to more productive uses.

Toward a more open trading system (Chapter 9)

A big danger is that industrial countries will act in a negative and defensive way toward increased imports of manufactures from developing countries. This would mean raising trade barriers of the more discriminatory type—that is, more nontariff barriers more effectively administered. This would further undermine the integrity of the GATT system and would restrict the growth of developing countries' exports. Many developing countries are already heavily in debt, so a reduction in their export earnings would aggravate the problems of world debt.

Developing countries—with limited foreign exchange and facing unusually low commodity prices—may soon face even higher barriers against the manufactures which have traditionally been their first industrial exports. Should that happen, there could be widespread disillusion with the outward-oriented trade strategies which have proved so successful for the NICs in recent years. If countries such as the United States or the United Kingdom increase their protection, it would hardly be surprising if many developing countries followed suit. Unfortunately, increased protection will still mean poor economic performance in all countries.

If industrial countries become more protectionist, this would force developing countries to explore a range of second-best options. These would include trying to expand trade with the centrally planned economies, and with other developing countries, on a discriminatory basis. But the prospects of greatly improved trade in either of these directions are not good. Neither could replace trade with the industrial market economies.

The best option for most developing countries is outward orientation, even though the benefits would be reduced in a more protectionist industrial world. But politically it would then be very difficult for them to follow an outward-oriented strategy, even if it were objectively their best bet. In other words, there is a serious risk that increased protection by the industrial nations will set back economic development for many years and inflict unnecessary suffering on some of the poorest people in the world. In any case, the industrial nations themselves stand to gain from open trade.

The risks make it crucial that all countries strive for a successful outcome from the Uruguay Round of multilateral trade negotiations (MTN). For some developing countries that may mean offering to reduce, or at least bind, some of their trade barriers in order to encourage the industrial nations to open markets to them. Most of the ways to achieve greater and more secure access are on the agenda for the MTN. Implementation of the ''standstill and rollback'' provision of the MTN would immediately help developing countries. A reduction in tariff escalation would also aid their exports of manufactures. A more effective safeguard procedure in a reformed Article XIX would contribute to increased security of market access, as would a more liberal Multifibre Arrangement and improved procedures for settling disputes.

*Barriers to Adjustment
and Growth in the World Economy*

From recovery and adjustment to long-term growth

When the world economy is performing well, with rapid growth and low inflation, structural economic change is less difficult. Growth provides a steady increase in the demand for goods and services. This encourages a more liberal trading environment, because it allows countries to adjust more smoothly to the shifts in comparative advantage that follow changes in technology, resources, and tastes. Growth also stimulates investment and eases the absorption of new technology. Low inflation makes for orderly financial markets, greater exchange rate stability, and improved incentives to save. High inflation increases uncertainty, discourages investment and technological change, distorts relative prices, and stands in the way of sustainable growth.

In the two decades between the early 1950s and the early 1970s, the world economy achieved both high growth and low inflation. The developing countries shared in that success. They grew at more than 5 percent a year, probably the best record for any group of countries over such a period.

Without the reduction in trade barriers that was achieved after World War II, economic growth could have been a good deal slower. Only in a liberal trading environment can countries exploit to the full the opportunities provided by change. Successive GATT negotiations kept up the pressure on countries to liberalize trade and to integrate their economies with the world economy. Trade grew at 8 percent a year between the early 1950s and the early 1970s—significantly faster than world output. Some developing countries liberalized their trade regimes in the mid-1960s, became exporters of manufactures, and gained directly

from the expansion in world trade. Most of the others benefited from rising demand for raw materials and foods. So, in one way or another, the developing countries that participated in the expansion of world trade experienced high output growth.

Thanks to this period of growth, some of the elements of a well-functioning world economy have been present since the early 1950s. Yet over the past ten years the system often has not run smoothly, and the developing countries have faced great strain. Output in industrial countries has fluctuated more than in earlier years, causing variations in demand for the products of developing countries. Certain sectors in industrial countries, especially agriculture, have been protected against the exports of developing countries; restrictions on imports of textiles and clothing have been growing since the 1960s. The price of oil went sharply up in the 1970s and sharply down in the 1980s. In the past few years exporters of primary products have suffered a significant deterioration in their terms of trade. Foreign capital has not always been available in the right quantity or on the appropriate terms. Overborrowing by some developing countries resulted in debt difficulties that were compounded by the 1980–82 recession in industrial countries. All the while, concessional financial resources have been too small for the tasks at hand.

Will the developing countries fare better during the next decade? This chapter tries to answer that question. The first part of the chapter reviews the current state of the world economy. The second discusses the response to the immediate problems of sluggish growth and international payments imbalances. The third part takes a longer-term perspective; it presents alternative paths for global output growth and for capital and trade flows over the next decade. These paths are not forecasts or predictions. Their purpose is to illustrate the outcomes that would be consistent with different sets of policies. They do not allow for new shocks to the world economy. The High case shows what is achievable rather than what is likely to be achieved; the Low case shows what may happen if governments fail to act.

The differences between growth rates in the High and Low cases are large. This emphasizes the need for policy changes. The low-growth path would mean economic and social conditions for the developing countries that they and the world must regard as unacceptable. But the rewards for correcting the present imbalances are correspondingly great.

To achieve high growth, governments must change their policies. Concerted action will make adjustment easier for all. Countries need to agree to improve the working of international markets for goods, services, and capital and to improve the efficiency of their own domestic markets. The central theme of this chapter is that such steps, together with adequate financing for investment in the developing countries, would pay off handsomely in higher levels of output, employment, and welfare in industrial and developing countries alike.

The weakening recovery and international payments imbalances

The world economic recovery that started in the United States in 1983 is slowing down. Meanwhile, the international current account imbalances of the past few years persist. The underlying fiscal imbalances have improved only slightly. So far, the bulk of the adjustment to these imbalances has been left to the foreign exchange markets, and the dollar has depreciated sharply against the major currencies. In spite of this, the current account deficit of the United States has been slow to respond. At the same time, progress toward the alleviation of debt problems has also been slow. Real interest rates remain high in relation to historical levels, and external financing is proving inadequate for the restoration of strong and sustained economic growth in the highly indebted countries. Low commodity prices continue to add to the difficulties facing many developing countries.

On the positive side, inflation is low in most in-

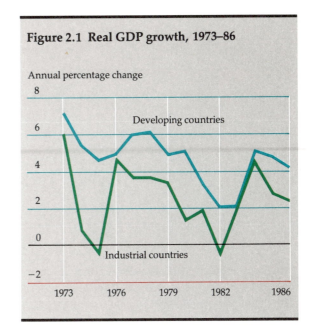

Figure 2.1 Real GDP growth, 1973–86

Annual percentage change

dustrial countries and has been declining in many developing countries. Governments have demonstrated their commitment to restrain monetary growth and keep inflation down. In addition, the governments of many industrial countries have cut their fiscal deficits and thus increased their room for maneuver in the future.

The weakening recovery

The strong expansion in the United States since 1982 paved the way for a moderate world recovery (see Figure 2.1). Real output in the United States fell by 2.5 percent in 1982, then rose by 6.6 percent in 1984. The decline in public sector savings contributed to the high level of the real interest rate—the price of scarce savings. This compounded the effect of tight U.S. monetary policy. High nominal interest rates led to strong demand for dollar-denominated assets and a sharp appreciation of the dollar. After about two years of rapid output growth in the United States and moderate growth in other industrial countries, the pace of recovery slackened in 1985. Real output growth in the industrial countries peaked in 1984 at 4.6 percent, then slowed to 2.8 percent in 1985 and an estimated 2.5 percent in 1986 (see Table 2.1).

Growth slowed in the developing countries too. Their output grew at 4.2 percent in 1986, compared with 4.8 percent in 1985 and an average of 6 percent a year in the two decades prior to 1980 (Table

Table 2.1 Growth of real GDP, 1965–86
(annual percentage change)

Country group	1965–73 average	1973–80 average	1981	1982	1983	1984	1985	1986
Developing countries	6.5	5.4	3.4	2.1	2.1	5.1	4.8	4.2
Low-income countries	5.5	4.6	4.8	5.6	7.7	8.9	9.1	6.5
Middle-income countries	7.0	5.7	2.8	0.8	0.0	3.6	2.8	3.2
Oil exporters	6.9	6.0	4.1	0.4	−1.9	2.3	2.2	−1.1
Exporters of manufactures	7.4	6.0	3.3	4.2	4.9	7.8	7.8	7.0
Highly indebted countries	6.9	5.4	0.9	−0.5	−3.2	2.0	3.1	2.5
Sub-Saharan Africa	6.4	3.2	−1.0	−0.2	−1.5	−1.7	2.2	0.5
High-income oil exporters	8.3	7.9	1.4	−0.5	−6.9	1.2	−3.8	8.2
Industrial market economies	4.7	2.8	1.9	−0.5	2.2	4.6	2.8	2.5

Note: Data for developing countries are based on a sample of ninety countries. Data for 1986 are estimates.

2.1). Output per capita in the developing countries rose by only 2.2 percent in 1986. The slowdown in 1985–86 was largely due to the oil-exporting group, whose output fell by 1.1 percent in 1986. Oil importers gained from the drop in oil prices, but weak prices of their non-oil commodity exports offset this. Non-oil commodity prices rose by only 0.8 percent in dollar terms in 1986.

Cheaper commodities improved the terms of trade of developing countries which export manufactures. The output of exporters of manufactures increased by 7.0 percent in 1986. Some of the more advanced exporters of manufactures experienced very high rates of growth: the Republic of Korea's output, for example, increased by about 11 percent. China and India also achieved strong growth and raised the average growth rate for the low-income countries. Although growth rates rose in Sub-Saharan Africa (excluding the oil producers), high population growth meant that per capita incomes continued to stagnate.

LOWER INFLATION. Average inflation in the industrial countries, as measured by the change in the GDP deflator, declined from 9.3 percent in 1980 to 3.4 percent in 1986. Inflation rates in the developing countries have also fallen since 1980 (see Figure 2.2). The trend was due partly to the drop in oil prices in 1986 and partly to falling commodity prices. Unfortunately, such once-and-for-all changes do not guarantee continued price stability. Governments will therefore need to be cautious. They can afford to permit only brief and minor deviations from a path of monetary growth consistent with low inflation. After a delay, excessive monetary growth tends to produce higher inflation.

REDUCTION OF FISCAL DEFICITS. The governments of the major industrial countries have reduced their budget deficits. The overall deficit has fallen as a percentage of gross national product (GNP) in the seven major industrial countries—from 5.4 percent in 1983 to 4.6 percent in 1986. Allowing for the effects of the economic cycle on revenue and spending, deficits have fallen even further. In the United States the federal budget deficit reached $221 billion, or 5.0 percent of GNP, in 1986. The Gramm-Rudman-Hollings Act may lead to a sig-

Figure 2.2 Inflation, 1973–86

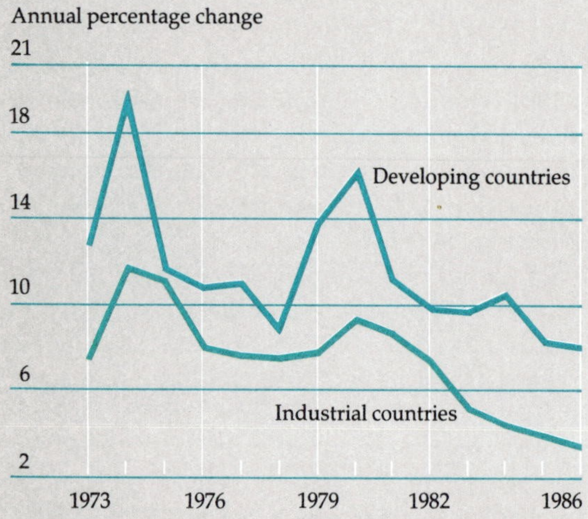

Annual percentage change

Note: Inflation is calculated as the change in the GDP deflator. For developing countries, the data points indicate median values; for industrial countries, average values.

nificant reduction in the future. For 1987 the target deficit is $151 billion.

The international payments imbalances

The recovery was accompanied by large imbalances in international payments (see Table 2.2). By the end of 1986 the U.S. current account deficit reached $126.7 billion, equivalent to about 34 percent of the country's total exports of goods and services, or 3 percent of GNP—despite the sharp depreciation of the dollar since early in 1985. This widening external deficit was mirrored by the surpluses of other industrial countries, especially Japan ($87.5 billion in 1986) and the Federal Republic of Germany ($44.3 billion). The current account deficit of the developing countries dropped from $37.4 billion in 1985 to $35.5 billion in 1986. This can be attributed to the improved current account position of the exporters of manufactures.

These current account imbalances, together with continued high unemployment in industrial countries, have increased the calls for protection, above all in the United States. The Multifibre Arrangement was tightened in the summer of 1986, and the coverage of voluntary export restraints in steel has been extended. One positive sign is that the launching of the Uruguay Round of multilateral trade negotiations in the fall of 1986 produced a commitment to a standstill in protection. It is too early to tell whether this will be honored.

LOWER COMMODITY PRICES. The period between 1984 and 1986 saw real prices for nonfuel primary

Figure 2.3 Real non-oil commodity prices, 1950–86

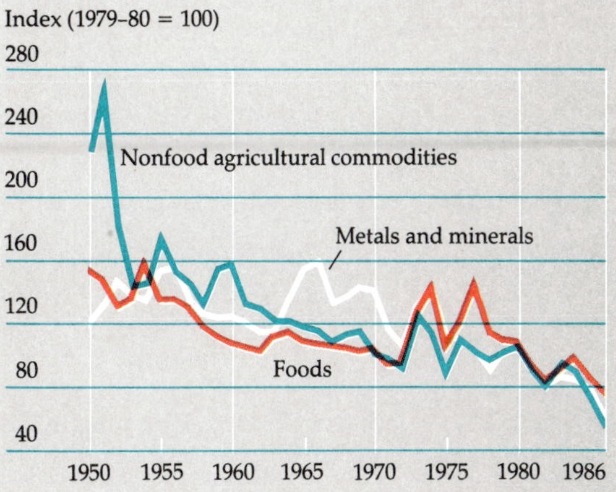

Index (1979–80 = 100)

commodities fall to record lows (see Figure 2.3). In 1985 the World Bank's index of thirty-three nonfuel primary commodity prices, in current dollar terms, fell to its lowest level in nine years: a 4.8 percent decline from the recession low of 1982 and an 11.1 percent fall from the postrecession high reached in the first half of 1984. For the first time in recent history, practically all commodity groups experienced price declines in 1984–86. Between the fourth quarter of 1983 and the second quarter of 1986, the current dollar index for agricultural commodities declined by 13 percent, led by fats and

Table 2.2 Current account balance, 1980–86
(billions of dollars)

Country group	1980	1981	1982	1983	1984	1985	1986
Developing countries	−69.1	−106.7	−103.0	−57.2	−32.1	−37.4	−35.5
Low-income countries	−17.0	−13.9	−8.9	−6.7	−8.1	−25.9	−22.0
Middle-income countries	−52.1	−92.8	−94.1	−50.5	−24.0	−11.5	−13.5
Oil exporters	1.4	−22.7	−30.0	−7.8	1.4	−2.2	−19.0
Exporters of manufactures	−33.9	−27.5	−23.3	−8.4	1.7	−8.8	6.0
Highly indebted countries	−27.9	−50.4	−52.9	−14.7	−0.7	−0.4	−12.0
Sub-Saharan Africa	−4.9	−17.8	−17.9	−12.8	−5.1	−4.0	−8.9
High-income oil exporters	88.5	74.0	26.0	1.2	1.5	12.1	−9.4
Industrial countries	−38.2	2.4	1.4	−2.9	−35.1	−24.7	21.6
United States	8.4	12.8	−1.4	−38.2	−95.8	−104.4	−126.7
Other industrial countries	−46.6	−10.4	2.8	35.3	60.7	79.7	148.3
Total[a]	−18.8	−30.3	−75.6	−58.9	−65.7	−50.0	−23.3

Note: Net official transfers are excluded. Data for developing countries are based on a sample of ninety countries.
a. Reflects errors, omissions, and asymmetries in reported balance of payments statistics on current account, plus balance of listed groups with countries not included.

Table 2.3 Public and private lending to developing countries, 1975 and 1980–86

(billions of dollars)

Country group and item	1975	1980	1981	1982	1983	1984	1985	1986
Low-income countries								
Disbursements	6.2	11.3	10.4	11.0	10.3	10.5	11.4	19.8[a]
From private creditors	1.6	3.4	3.0	3.5	3.0	3.3	3.4	10.0[a]
Principal repayments	1.4	2.5	2.5	2.7	3.1	3.3	4.4	6.8
Net flows	4.8	8.8	7.9	8.3	7.2	7.2	7.0	13.0
Middle-income countries								
Disbursements	38.6	90.2	111.6	105.6	87.6	77.0	67.6	66.4
From private creditors	28.2	71.0	88.8	82.3	63.2	52.6	46.7	43.4
Principal repayments	13.5	40.7	43.8	45.0	40.4	43.4	49.0	53.8
Net flows	25.1	49.5	67.8	60.6	47.2	33.6	18.6	12.6
All developing countries								
Disbursements	44.8	101.5	122.0	116.6	97.9	87.5	79.0	86.2
From private creditors	29.8	74.4	91.8	85.8	66.1	55.9	50.1	53.5
Principal repayments	14.9	43.2	46.3	47.7	43.5	46.7	53.4	60.6
Net flows	29.9	58.3	75.7	68.9	54.4	40.8	25.6	25.6

Note: Data for 1985 and 1986 are provisional estimates of amounts paid, not amounts due. Private nonguaranteed debt has been estimated where not reported by a country. Official grants are excluded. Data are based on a sample of ninety developing countries.

a. Largely reflects increased lending to China.

oils, nonfood agricultural commodities, and cereals. The index for metals and minerals declined by 16 percent over the same period; practically all metals and minerals contributed to this decline. Beverages and timber were the only commodity groups whose prices rose over the period.

The reasons for the depressed state of the commodity markets are complex. First, the demand for commodities in the industrial countries has been weak, especially for agricultural raw materials and metals. Second, the high prices of the mid-1970s led to overexpansion of supply in several important raw materials, especially oil and metals. But, at the same time, those high prices encouraged economy in the use of such materials and the development of alternatives. Third, the markets of some commodities have been disrupted by the ag-

ricultural policies of the industrial countries. Domestic price support programs have caused large surpluses, which have frequently led to the selling of exports at a fraction of domestic prices. Finally, changes in tastes, increased use of synthetic substitutes, and the adoption of production processes that are less intensive in raw materials have all depressed demand.

LENDING FOR DEVELOPING COUNTRIES. In 1986, net lending flows to developing countries remained at about one-third of their level in 1981, just before the outbreak of the debt crisis—although the year did see the first modest increase in net inflows for low-income developing countries since the debt crisis began (see Table 2.3). Borrowing by the highly indebted countries from private

Table 2.4 Debt indicators for developing countries, 1980–86

(percent, unless otherwise noted)

Indicator	1980	1981	1982	1983	1984	1985	1986
Ratio of debt to GNP	20.6	22.4	26.3	31.4	33.0	35.8	35.4
Ratio of debt to exports	90.0	98.0	117.6	134.8	121.2	143.7	144.5
Debt service ratio	16.0	17.5	20.6	19.4	19.5	21.4	22.3
Ratio of debt service to GNP	3.7	4.0	4.6	4.5	4.9	5.3	5.5
Ratio of interest service to exports	6.9	8.3	10.4	10.1	10.3	10.8	10.7
Total debt outstanding and disbursed (billions of dollars)	428.6	490.8	551.1	631.5	673.2	727.7	753.4
Private debt as a percentage of total debt	63.1	64.5	65.0	65.8	65.7	63.9	63.5

Note: Data are based on a sample of ninety developing countries. Data for 1986 are estimates.

sources amounted to $6.8 billion, or about a quarter of the 1980 level. Most of it was "concerted" lending as part of debt restructuring.

The broad debt indicators showed little improvement during 1986 (see Table 2.4). Despite a slight decline in the ratio of debt to GNP, debt service as a proportion of exports of goods and services increased. This largely reflected reduced export earnings. For some of the major oil exporters, the drop in oil prices implied a sharp deterioration of their creditworthiness. That made debt restructuring necessary for Mexico, Nigeria, and other countries (see Box 2.1).

Nominal interest rates continued to decline in 1986. But the deterioration in the export prices of the debtor countries limited the improvement in the "real" terms of their borrowing. The real interest rate for developing countries (the nominal LIBOR deflated by the export price index for developing countries) decreased from 12.1 percent in 1985 to 8.1 percent in 1986 (see Figure 2.4).

The central issue for the highly indebted middle-income countries is their need to finance new investment. The commercial banks have agreed to some debt restructuring packages, but there have been difficulties and delays. As the banks have strengthened their financial position, they have seemed increasingly reluctant to provide new financing. Still, new approaches are emerging. In 1986, schemes for converting debt to equity began to be adopted (see Box 2.2). Chile and Mexico have employed this approach, and others, such as Nigeria and Argentina, are considering similar plans.

For Sub-Saharan Africa, there were welcome increases in concessional flows in 1986. But the debt servicing problems of countries in Africa continue to be severe. Although recent progress with long-term restructuring of official debt is promising, greater and continued coordination of new aid and long-term restructuring of debt is still needed to improve the efficiency of assistance.

The adjustment of the highly indebted developing countries

For several of the highly indebted countries, low commodity prices, high real interest rates, sluggish growth in the industrial countries, and in some cases their own macroeconomic and trade policies mean that present levels of debt cannot be reconciled with present levels of growth. This situation is often referred to as the "debt overhang." Many debtor countries expanded their exports during 1983–84; this helped to stimulate domestic

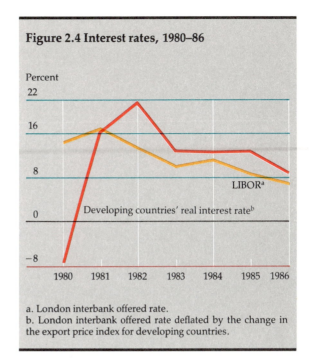

Figure 2.4 Interest rates, 1980–86

Percent

LIBOR[a]

Developing countries' real interest rate[b]

1980 1981 1982 1983 1984 1985 1986

a. London interbank offered rate.
b. London interbank offered rate deflated by the change in the export price index for developing countries.

economic activity and was an important source of income growth through 1986. The achievement of some of the indebted countries in generating trade surpluses to service debt has been remarkable. But the counterpart of that has been lower domestic consumption and investment, with adverse effects on long-run productivity improvements.

Adjustment is needed and must be sustained. Recent difficulties in maintaining the momentum in some countries show the dangers of complacency. Continued improvement requires new investment in the competitive sectors of the economy so as to generate growth and increase the supply of tradables. Trade policy has an important role here. Chapter 5 of this report shows that the countries which provided equal incentives for exports and import substitution have been less affected by external shocks.

The adjustment of Sub-Saharan Africa

For Sub-Saharan Africa as a whole, GDP grew by less than 1 percent in 1986. This reflects, however, the economic decline in the oil-exporting countries, especially Nigeria; 1986 was a much better year than 1984 or 1985 for most other countries. Weather again proved favorable in 1986, and agricultural production continued to expand, rising by almost 4 percent.

Some twenty-five countries in the region, which

Box 2.1 Recent developments in debt restructuring

In 1986, twenty-four countries renegotiated their debts with official creditors or commercial banks in multilateral forums. The total debt so restructured is estimated at $71.1 billion, of which $43.7 billion came from recasting the terms of the 1984 multiyear bank agreement with Mexico (see Box table 2.1). Aside from this, the volume of debt restructuring with commercial banks was about the same in 1986 as in 1985.

Commercial bank consortia continued to improve the terms of relief by offering lower margins and somewhat longer maturities. Four multiyear restructuring agreements (MYRAs) were concluded. The other agreements restructured only those debts falling due in the coming year. Official creditors continued to reschedule debts in a series of short-term agreements, mostly through the Paris Club, at terms and conditions that did not change significantly in 1986.

Commercial bank agreements

Commercial bank debt relief covers (a) restructuring of principal payments falling due during an agreed consolidation period; (b) the related extension of new long-term loans; and (c) understandings to maintain or extend short-term credit lines. Debt relief agreements may contain one or more of these components. During 1986, eight countries negotiated debt relief agreements with commercial bank consortia: Brazil, People's Republic of the Congo, Côte d'Ivoire, Mexico, Nigeria, Poland, Uruguay, and Zaire. The most sweeping agreement was with Mexico. In addition to restructuring previously rescheduled debt of $43.7 billion, it committed new long-term loans of $6.0 billion, provided contingency arrangements for additional long-term loans of $1.7 billion, and reduced the spreads on existing bank debt to 13/16 percent. The agreement with Brazil rescheduled long-term debt falling due in 1985 and deferred payments on 1986 maturities pending further negotiations. Nigeria reached an agreement in principle with the commercial bank steering committee on long-term debt falling due in 1986–87 and arranged for new long-term money. Those negotiations were completed following approval of Nigeria's economic adjustment program by the International Monetary Fund (IMF) and the World Bank. Poland had earlier rescheduled all principal due to banks from March 21, 1981, through December 31, 1987. In June 1986, however, Poland found it necessary to reschedule principal due during 1986 and 1987 under these earlier

Box table 2.1 Amount of debt relief, 1983–86
(billions of dollars)

Item	1983	1984	1985	1986
Debt restructuring[a]				
Banks	33.8	100.5	13.1	57.4[b]
Official creditors	8.4	3.9	16.3[c]	13.7
Total	42.2	104.4	29.4	71.1
New money disbursed[d]	13.0	10.4	5.3	2.6[e]
Short-term credit facilities[d,f]	27.9	36.7	35.0	35.0

Note: Data for 1986 are provisional.
a. Debt restructuring with commercial banks is recorded in the year of agreement in principle; debt restructuring with official creditors is recorded in the year in which the agreement is signed.
b. Includes changed terms of Mexico's 1984 agreement ($43.7 billion).
c. Includes $10.3 billion relief for Poland, covering 1982–84 maturities.
d. Arranged in conjunction with debt restructuring.
e. Does not include $3.5 billion for Mexico scheduled to be disbursed in early 1987, other than $0.8 billion from bridging loans.
f. Agreements to maintain or expand existing trade credit lines or to provide other short-term credits.
Source: International Monetary Fund and World Bank data.

account for a large proportion of Africa's population and output, are implementing major programs of structural reforms or are about to do so. These include policies to keep real effective exchange rates competitive, increase agricultural incentives, maintain budgetary and monetary restraint, reform public enterprises, and improve the allocation of public funds. In some countries such efforts have been under way for several years; in others the adjustment process has barely begun. But resistance to further reform is hardening in the face of stagnating or declining per capita consumption. The fragile political consensus which provided the initial momentum must be strengthened and supported, especially with increased flows of assistance.

agreements. In addition to these reschedulings, Zaire arranged to defer principal due in 1986 on previously rescheduled debt.

The agreements with Congo, Côte d'Ivoire, and Uruguay were MYRAs. Brazil is currently negotiating for one. The global volume of debt restructured by MYRAs in 1986, however, was far below the level for earlier years, excluding the September revision of Mexico's earlier agreement.

An encouraging feature in 1986 was the ability of a few countries, previously dependent on new money arrangements under rescheduling, to obtain new commercial loans: a short-term revolving credit arrangement in the case of Ecuador and long-term loans negotiated under cofinancing agreements with the World Bank in the case of Côte d'Ivoire and Uruguay. In general, however, the failure of commercial bank lending to revive for other countries after the introduction of MYRAs, as had been anticipated, remains a matter of concern.

Agreements with official creditors

In 1986, eighteen countries renegotiated debt with official creditors, mainly through the Paris Club, as compared with twenty-one in 1985. Thirteen of these were Sub-Saharan African countries (Congo, Côte d'Ivoire, The Gambia, Guinea, Madagascar, Mauritania, Niger, Nigeria, Senegal, Sierra Leone, Tanzania, Zaire, and Zambia); two were European (Poland and Yugoslavia); and three were Latin American (Bolivia, Cuba, and Mexico).

The conditions and terms of relief extended in 1986 were little changed from earlier years. Most agreements rescheduled 95 to 100 percent of eligible maturities (principal and interest on loans from governments and on guaranteed export credits). However, the Côte d'Ivoire, Niger, and Yugoslavia agreements excluded interest; the Mexico agreement covered only 60 percent of interest due for a portion of the consolidation period. The Côte d'Ivoire MYRA, like the Ecuador MYRA of 1985, rescheduled a declining proportion of future principal payments due: 80 percent in 1986, 70 percent in 1987, and 60 percent in 1988.

Policies for the short term

The combination of international payments imbalances, sluggish growth, increasing protectionism, and the debt problems of many developing countries is an unpromising base for sustainable growth in the world economy. The more so because policy options have narrowed since the beginning of the 1980s. Adjustment with growth starts with setting the macroeconomic conditions straight. In industrial countries the fiscal imbalances underlying the current account imbalances must be corrected. In developing countries the macroeconomic environment must provide a stable platform for medium-term adjustment with growth.

International payments imbalances

The U.S. fiscal expansion that began in 1981 provided a strong stimulus for growth. But it was an unsustainable one. Unless the United States makes progress in reducing its fiscal deficit, international payments imbalances will be harder to reduce. Increased protectionism and new fears of inflation might then prevent the world economy from returning to a path of long-term growth.

The U.S. current account deficit has been slow to adjust. There are several reasons for this. First, although the dollar fell sharply after the beginning of 1985, its trade-weighted value by December 1986 was still only 6.4 percent lower than its average level in 1982. Over that slightly longer period, therefore, the dollar's fall has done little to change the relative price of U.S. goods. Second, exporters to the United States have not yet raised their dollar prices by the full amount of the depreciation. They accepted lower profits to maintain their share of the market, and their goods remain attractive to buyers in the United States. Third, the ratio of the prices of nontraded goods to traded goods in the United States is still rising. This provides little incentive for resources to switch to the export and import-competing sectors of the economy (see Figure 2.5). Fourth, import and export volumes respond only slowly to any change in relative prices caused by an exchange rate adjustment. Finally, and most important, there remains the underlying fiscal imbalance in the United States. Until that is corrected, or until expenditure falls relative to income for some other reason, the current account deficits will persist.

If the United States does reduce its fiscal deficit, growth in the world economy may slow unless other countries offset the loss of demand. This means that countries which have relied on export demand for output growth may have to shift the emphasis to domestic demand, perhaps through a fiscal expansion. Policies that tackle structural economic rigidities in labor markets and in the markets for goods and services need to accompany these shifts in demand. Such policies not only ease

Box 2.2 Debt-equity swaps

The existing exposure of commercial banks to developing countries is a key constraint to new spontaneous lending. Recently, a secondary market trading developing countries' debt instruments at a discount has emerged. The volume of transactions was initially quite limited, and price quotations on the discounted debt have been regarded as rather artificial in view of the thinness of the market. The market is becoming better organized, participation has widened, and the variety of transactions has increased. In 1986 the volume of trading in such instruments was about $7 billion, or less than 1 percent of the external debt of developing countries. New interpretations of accounting and banking regulations in the United States have contributed to this development. A bank taking a loss on a sale or swap of a loan to a developing country would not be required to reduce the book value of other loans to that country, provided the bank considers the remaining loans collectible.

A few of the debtor countries whose liabilities are being traded at a discount have utilized the existence of the discount market to encourage a flow of private investments and to gain other advantages. The popular term for the conversion of discounted debt into local currency assets is a ''debt-equity swap.'' ''Debt conversion'' would be a more appropriate term, since conversion of external debt instruments into domestic obligations can take place not only for foreign direct investment purposes, but also for more general purposes by residents or nonresidents of the debtor country. In essence, a foreign investor wishing to buy assets in a debtor country can, through a debt-equity swap, obtain local currency at a discount. The foreign investor, in effect, obtains a rebate on the purchase of the currency equivalent to the discount on the loan less the transactions costs of the debt-equity swap.

Chile has a well-developed legal framework for the conversion of external debt into domestic assets. There is a similar procedure for the conversion of debt using foreign currency holdings by domestic investors.

Box figure 2.2 explains the detailed steps involved in the debt conversion. Although they seem complicated, the central steps are conceptually simple.

Debt-equity swaps are open only to nonresidents who intend to invest in fixed assets (equity) in Chile. The first step is to locate and buy at the going discount a Chilean debt instrument denominated in foreign currency. Next, with the intermediation of a Chilean bank, the foreign investor must obtain the consent of the local debtor to exchange the original debt instrument for one denominated in local currency and the permission of the central bank to withdraw the debt. Finally, the foreign investor can sell the new debt instrument in the local financial market and acquire the fixed assets or equity with the cash proceeds of the sale.

The main difference between the debt-equity swap and the straight debt conversion is that the debt conversion is available to resident or nonresident investors with foreign currency holdings abroad. Also, once the conversion has taken place, the investor faces no restriction on the use of the local currency proceeds.

The debt conversion scheme allows the debtor country first to reduce the stock or the rate of growth of external debt. Second, it is a means to attract flight capital as well as foreign direct investment. Third, debt-equity swaps imply a switch from the outflow of interest and principal on debt obligations to the deferred and less certain outflows associated with private direct investment.

For the commercial banks the swaps provide an exit instrument or a means to adjust the risk composition of their portfolio. For banks that wish to continue to be active internationally, losses on the outstanding portfolio can be realized at a time and on a scale of the bank's own choosing and by utilizing a market mechanism.

The emergence of an active market in debt instruments of developing countries offers opportunities to both debtors and lenders. There are, however, obstacles to its development. Debtor countries must ensure that transactions take place at an undistorted exchange rate, otherwise the discounts on the debt may be outweighed by exchange rate considerations. In addition, long-term financial instruments in the domestic markets are needed to ensure that the conversion into domestic monetary assets does not increase monetary growth above established targets. The incentives for foreign investors will be nullified if the broader domestic policy environment is not conducive to inflows of

the short-run adjustment, they also improve the prospects for long-run growth.

International coordination of macroeconomic policies is important too. This is not a matter of altruism. It reflects a shared responsibility for global adjustment. The industrial countries need to assess how their policies will affect world demand in the light of the substantial shifts in trade

flows that adjustment will require.

For the United States to become a net capital exporter again, interest payments on the debt accumulated during the years of large current account deficits will have to be more than offset by substantial surpluses on trade in merchandise and services. Although such an adjustment will not take place abruptly, it still amounts to a profound

foreign investment. Finally, a minimum regulatory framework is required. Documentation for debt restructuring must be adjusted to allow for prepayment for debt conversion purposes. Clear rules will facilitate the transactions. Overregulation, particularly in the form of administrative procedures for investment approval, would be a deterrent.

Box figure 2.2 Debt capitalization

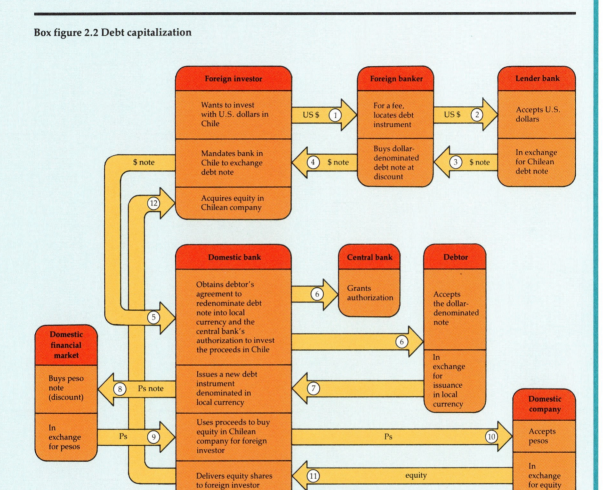

change in recent patterns of international trade—one that cannot easily come about without multilateral trade liberalization.

Sustained stabilization in developing countries

Reduced fiscal imbalances and a more open international trading environment are necessary but not sufficient steps to create the basis for sustained adjustment with growth in developing countries. Progress in two other areas is essential: macroeconomic stabilization and additional external capital. (For an example of a multifaceted stabilization and adjustment program, see Box 2.3 on Indonesia's recent experience.)

A stable macroeconomic environment is a pre-

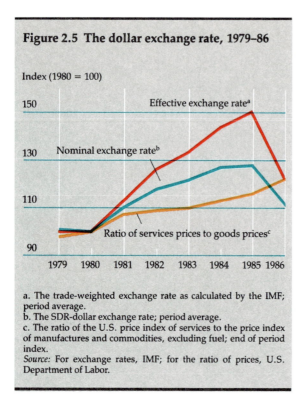

Figure 2.5 The dollar exchange rate, 1979–86

Index (1980 = 100)

a. The trade-weighted exchange rate as calculated by the IMF;
period average.
b. The SDR-dollar exchange rate; period average.
c. The ratio of the U.S. price index of services to the price index
of manufactures and commodities, excluding fuel; end of period
index.
Source: For exchange rates, IMF; for the ratio of prices, U.S.
Department of Labor.

requisite for a successful transition to sustainable economic growth. Maintaining macroeconomic stability typically requires keeping the fiscal deficit to a low fraction of GNP, guarding against rapid monetary expansion, and maintaining a realistic exchange rate. All three elements of this policy mix are necessary for economic growth. Mere reliance on monetary policy in the presence of large budget deficits and overvalued exchange rates, for example, will raise interest rates and deter investment. Similarly, reliance on trade and exchange controls will distort prices. Public sector deficits can be cut by reducing support to inefficient public enterprises or by broadening the tax base. But reducing deficits by curtailing investment reduces the growth on which creditworthiness depends, and an unduly tight rein on maintenance hampers capital efficiency at a time when all efforts should be made to raise it.

Reforms without financial support cannot go far in restoring growth. There are limits to how much consumption can be cut without endangering social and political stability. In addition, adjustment requires new investment to shift resources to the export and import-competing sectors. But, equally important, financial support should be an aid to adjustment—permitting short-term growth and allowing structural reforms to be brought in over time—not an alternative to it.

Box 2.3   Indonesia: adjusting to low oil prices

Appropriate and well-timed stabilization and adjustment policies can help to soften sudden external shocks, such as rapid declines in the terms of trade. The experience of Indonesia during the recent turbulent period in the international oil market is a case in point (see Box figure 2.3A). Despite steadily declining oil revenues since 1982 and a sudden collapse in international oil prices in 1986, Indonesia has managed to maintain macroeconomic stability. How did it do this? The answer lies in its stern adherence to a multifaceted adjustment program that has sought to constrain domestic demand in line with resource availability and that at the same time has attempted to stimulate growth through improvements in efficiency.

Oil and, more recently, liquefied natural gas have played a central role in the Indonesian economy. In 1980–81 these two commodities accounted for almost a quarter of the country's economic output, more than three-quarters of its export earnings, and more than two-thirds of its government revenues (see Box figure

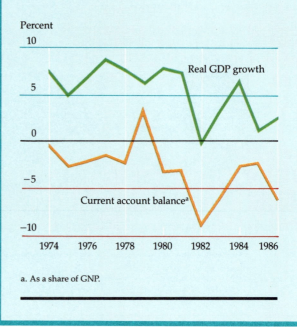

Box figure 2.3A Indonesia's GDP growth and current account balance, 1974–86

a. As a share of GNP.

Policies for medium- and long-term growth

Since the breakdown of the Bretton Woods system of fixed exchange rates in 1971, the volatility of the world economy has revealed structural rigidities in both the industrial and the developing countries.

2.3B). So when the global oil market weakened steadily after 1981, the country's resource position eroded at an alarming rate. The current account deficit jumped upward sharply, and the government's budgetary position, already under strain from several large public investment projects, suddenly began to look untenable. The government quickly took a range of measures aimed at curtailing demand and restoring financial stability. It canceled or postponed several large public investment projects in 1983 and saved about $10 billion of foreign exchange in the process; maintained an austere fiscal stance; devalued the rupiah by 28 percent; reduced domestic subsidies on petroleum products; reformed the financial sector to raise private domestic savings and increase investment efficiency; and reformed the tax system to broaden the tax base and increase public savings.

But no sooner had these measures restored macroeconomic stability—by 1985 the current account deficit was down to 2.1 percent of GNP and inflation was at only 4 percent—than the economy was hit yet again when in 1986 international oil prices collapsed from $28 a barrel in January to $10 a barrel by August. In the face of such a large external shock, and in the absence of any adjustment, the current account deficit was expected to widen to an unsustainable level.

Anticipating its payments difficulties, the government once again responded quickly. It introduced a wide range of measures to curb domestic demand further to stabilize the economy and addressed structural issues to improve the efficiency of resource use. The main elements of this strategy are described below.

• The government introduced an austere budget that kept current expenditures flat in nominal terms and cut capital expenditures by almost 25 percent. In doing so, the government gave priority to current projects, the provision of counterpart funds for foreign-financed projects, the start-up of new projects that focused on equity and employment, and the funding of operations and maintenance expenditures.

• The rupiah was devalued by 31 percent to compensate for the sudden decline in oil revenues and to preempt speculative outflows of capital.

• Trade policy was changed from its previous emphasis on import substitution. For example, "producer-exporters" were given the option of importing their inputs free from licensing restrictions and exempt

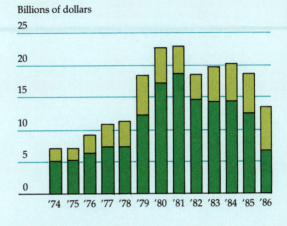

Box figure 2.3B Indonesia's export earnings, 1974–86

Billions of dollars

■ From oil and liquefied natural gas
□ From non-oil commodities

from import duties. More important, the government began to dismantle the cumbersome system of import licensing restrictions and to move toward a system of protection based only on tariffs.

• Finally, the government reformed significantly the regulatory environment for foreign investment. In particular, the requirement for local participation was relaxed, the duration of investment licenses was extended to thirty years, and changes were introduced to treat foreign investors more like local investors.

The combination of demand restraint, devaluation, and trade reform is expected to contain the destabilizing effects of the dramatic deterioration in Indonesia's terms of trade. In addition, the reforms—particularly those of trade and industrial licensing policy—are expected to provide a policy environment conducive to efficient industrial development and a rapid increase in manufactured exports. Finally, by husbanding government resources and stimulating private savings through the financial reform, Indonesia has succeeded in maintaining its credit standing in the international capital markets.

Prospects for the medium term and beyond depend on the willingness of governments to deal with these rigidities. In addition to discussing the reforms that might be necessary, this section sets out alternative paths of future growth (see Tables 2.5 to 2.9).

The High case

The High case assumes that the industrial and developing countries adopt a variety of medium- and long-term adjustment policies. Specifically, it assumes that fiscal and international payments im-

Table 2.5 Economic performance of developing and industrial countries, 1965–95
(average annual percentage change)

Country group and indicator	1965–73	1973–80	1980–86	1986–95 High	1986–95 Low
Developing countries					
Real GDP	6.5	5.4	3.6	5.9	3.9
Low-income countries	5.5	4.6	7.4	6.7	4.6
Middle-income countries	7.0	5.7	2.0	5.4	3.6
Oil exporters	6.9	6.0	0.8	4.4	3.6
Exporters of manufactures	7.4	6.0	6.0	6.9	4.3
Highly indebted countries	6.9	5.4	0.6	5.4	3.5
Sub-Saharan Africa[a]	6.4	3.2	−0.4	4.0	3.2
Merchandise export volumes	4.9	4.7	4.4	7.3	3.6
Manufactures	11.6	13.8	8.4	10.3	5.1
Primary goods	3.7	1.2	1.3	3.6	2.2
Merchandise import volumes	5.7	6.1	0.8	7.8	4.1
Industrial countries					
Real GDP	4.7	2.8	2.3	4.3	2.5
Inflation rate[b]	6.1	10.1	1.7	2.7	3.3
Real interest rate[c,d]	2.3	1.3	5.9	2.5	4.6
Nominal interest rate[d]	6.8	9.3	11.1	6.5	9.4

Note: All growth rates for developing countries are based on a sample of ninety countries.
a. Excluding South Africa.
b. Industrial countries' weighted GDP deflator expressed in dollars.
c. Average six-month dollar-Eurocurrency rate deflated by the GDP deflator for the United States.
d. Average annual rate.

Table 2.6 Growth of GDP per capita, 1965–95
(average annual percentage change)

Country group	1965–73	1973–80	1980–86	1986–95 High	1986–95 Low
Developing countries	3.9	3.2	1.5	3.9	2.0
Low-income countries	2.9	2.5	5.4	4.8	2.8
Middle-income countries	4.4	3.3	−0.3	3.2	1.4
Oil exporters	4.3	3.2	−1.8	1.9	1.1
Exporters of manufactures	4.8	4.1	4.3	5.3	2.7
Highly indebted countries	4.2	2.9	−1.8	3.1	1.2
Sub-Saharan Africa[a]	3.6	0.3	−3.4	0.7	0.0
Industrial countries	3.7	2.1	1.6	3.9	2.0

Note: All growth rates for developing countries are based on a sample of ninety countries.
a. Excluding South Africa.

Table 2.7 Change in the volume of trade in developing countries, 1965–95
(average annual percentage change)

Country group	Exports of goods 1965–73	1973–80	1980–86	1986–95 High	1986–95 Low	Exports of manufactures 1965–73	1973–80	1980–86	1986–95 High	1986–95 Low
Developing countries	4.9	4.7	4.4	7.3	3.6	11.6	13.8	8.4	10.3	5.1
Low-income countries	2.0	4.7	5.4	7.5	3.9	2.4	8.2	8.4	11.3	6.0
Middle-income countries	5.3	4.8	4.2	7.2	3.6	14.9	14.8	8.4	10.2	4.9
Oil exporters	4.1	−0.9	0.2	4.8	2.3	10.1	3.4	20.9	13.4	7.3
Exporters of manufactures	8.4	9.8	8.1	8.7	4.4	11.6	14.0	9.0	10.3	5.1
Highly indebted countries	3.1	1.1	1.3	6.4	3.7	13.4	10.2	5.9	10.9	5.5
Sub-Saharan Africa[a]	15.0	0.1	−1.9	3.9	2.0	7.5	5.6	4.0	9.6	4.4

Note: All growth rates for developing countries are based on a sample of ninety countries.
a. Excluding South Africa.

balances are reduced in a way that maintains growth in the industrial countries. To do this, each government will need to consider the scope for stimulating demand as the pattern of trade shifts. Second, it assumes that unemployment in the industrial countries is reduced substantially by 1995. The European countries are assumed to reduce unemployment by improving the flexibility of their labor markets and by making further efforts to bring the young and long-term unemployed back into the active labor force. Third, it assumes that governments halt the recent advance of protectionism in the industrial countries and thereby increase international trade flows and improve the efficiency of their economies. (Improved efficiency in the steel industry is a case in point; see Box 2.4.) Fourth, it assumes that the developing countries themselves adopt adjustment programs to restructure their economies and spur employment and income growth.

This combination of favorable macroeconomic and structural policies, labor force growth, and improved productivity owing to technological progress implies that industrial countries can grow at an average annual rate of just over 4 percent in the next decade—faster than in 1973–80 and 1980–86, but slower than in 1965–73. The smaller fiscal deficits implicit in this scenario would permit real interest rates to fall to an average of 2.5 percent during the period—close to their historic average and down from 4.1 percent in 1986.

In such circumstances, the developing countries would find it much easier to pursue their own reforms. (These are discussed further in Chapters 6 and 7.) In the High case their output would grow on average by roughly 6 percent a year in 1986–95, compared with 3.6 percent in 1980–86 and 6.5 percent in 1965–73. Exports would grow at an average

rate of about 7 percent a year, compared with 4.4 percent during 1980–86. As a result, the debt service ratio of all developing countries taken together would fall from 22.3 percent in 1986 to roughly 13 percent by 1995 (Table 2.8). Their imports could grow by 7 to 8 percent a year. In sum, a more favorable economic environment resulting from successful adjustment by the industrial countries would facilitate policy reforms in the developing countries and thus lead to faster growth in the world economy.

The Low case

The Low case, by contrast, assumes no major policy changes. The United States fails to cut its budget deficit by much, and European unemployment stays high. That would mean slow growth in the industrial countries, a rising tide of protectionism, and no hope of further trade liberalization. The Low case shows the developing countries growing at an average of close to 4 percent a year. Although a little higher than during the early 1980s, that is more than a percentage point lower than they achieved in 1973–80. And their growth could be considerably lower than this if they undertake no reforms at all, and if the international environment deteriorates.

The long-term adjustment issues

The first of the assumptions underlying the High case is that short-term macroeconomic policies are brought back into balance. This was dealt with in the previous section of this chapter. The rest of the chapter considers the other three assumptions, which are all matters of longer-term economic policy.

Exports of primary goods					Imports of goods					
			1986–95					1986–95		
1965–73	1973–80	1980–86	High	Low	1965–73	1973–80	1980–86	High	Low	Country group
3.7	1.2	1.3	3.6	2.2	5.7	6.1	0.8	7.8	4.1	Developing countries
1.7	2.8	3.1	2.6	1.6	0.9	5.7	7.9	5.7	2.3	Low-income countries
3.9	1.1	1.1	3.7	2.3	6.7	6.1	−0.5	8.2	4.6	Middle-income countries
4.0	−1.0	−1.1	3.3	1.6	4.5	10.3	−6.3	5.8	3.2	Oil exporters
5.5	3.4	6.0	3.6	2.5	9.9	5.9	5.7	8.8	4.6	Exporters of manufactures
2.4	−0.4	0.0	4.4	3.0	6.7	5.5	−6.9	7.5	4.4	Highly indebted countries
15.3	−0.1	−2.2	3.3	1.8	3.8	7.6	−7.9	4.9	2.9	Sub-Saharan Africa[a]

Table 2.8 Current account balance and its financing in developing countries, 1986 and 1995
(billions of dollars)

Item	All developing countries			Low-income countries			Middle-income countries		
		1995			1995			1995	
	1986	High	Low	1986	High	Low	1986	High	Low
Net exports of goods and nonfactor services	3.3	−61	−35	−23.9	−32	−26	27.3	−29	−9
Interest on long-term debt	55.7	60	69	4.1	11	10	51.5	48	59
Official	15.3	25	27	2.7	6	6	12.6	19	21
Private	40.4	35	42	1.4	5	4	38.9	29	38
Current account balance[b]	−35.5	−74	−68	−22.0	−30	−25	−13.5	−44	−43
Net official transfers	15.2	27	25	4.6	10	9	10.6	17	16
Long-term loans, net	25.6	50	34	13.0	28	19	12.6	21	15
Official	12.3	39	34	5.9	15	14	6.4	24	20
Private	13.3	11	0	7.0	13	5	6.2	−3	−5
Debt outstanding and disbursed	753.4	997	958	108.6	273	241	644.7	723	717
As a percentage of GNP	34.4	24	24	17.9	23	21	42.4	24	25
As a percentage of exports	144.5	76	96	159.7	154	180	142.2	64	83
Debt service as a percentage of exports	22.3	13	18	16.2	15	19	23.2	13	18

Note: The table is based on a sample of ninety developing countries. Data for 1986 are estimated. Details may not add to totals because of rounding. Net exports plus interest do not equal the current account balance because of the omission of private transfers and investment income. The current account balance not financed by official transfers and loans is covered by foreign direct investment, other capital (including short-

Structural barriers to growth in industrial countries

Europe's unemployment is at least partly due to the lack of flexibility in its labor markets. This lack of flexibility manifests itself in several ways. One of the most important is that real wage growth has sometimes exceeded productivity growth. This means that employers are unwilling to hire additional workers because the cost would exceed the value of the increase in output. The gap between wages and productivity can arise, in turn, because of wage-setting practices whereby the wage level of the most prosperous regions or sectors applies countrywide. Geographical or occupational immobility prevents workers from closing the gap. High costs of firing and high nonwage costs also keep the real wage (as perceived by employers) high.

Another element of the explanation for persistent unemployment in Europe focuses on the effects of long spells out of work. Employers may regard those who have been unemployed for long periods as unemployable. The unemployed themselves may come to agree. As a result they stop competing for jobs. Because they then cease to apply any downward pressure on real wages, unemployment persists.

More flexible work arrangements are in the interest of employers and employees alike (see Box 2.5). Rules and regulations differ greatly from country to country. Each government needs to review its regulatory instruments and weigh the tradeoff between the protection of existing workers and the risk of stifling new employment. Too many rules protect the employed at the expense of the unemployed.

Education and training are keys to a more flexible work force. Because of their effect on occupational mobility, deficiencies here may be greater obstacles to curing unemployment than rigidities in the labor markets. To meet the challenge of a changing world, education should be a continuing process that starts with broad training and is followed by retraining and updating of skills as necessary.

Another big obstacle to economic efficiency in most industrial countries is agricultural policy. *World Development Report 1986* discussed the issues in detail. It concluded that the policies reduce national income; farmers use inputs inefficiently because artificially high food prices mislead producers into using too many resources. These policies also induce consumers to purchase less food than they would otherwise. The economic losses are substantial. On top of this is the indirect cost of the distortions which high agricultural prices cause in the long term—such as the diversion of fixed investment and research from industry to agriculture.

Oil exporters			Exporters of manufactures			Highly indebted countries[a]			Sub-Saharan Africa[a]		
	1995			1995			1995			1995	
1986	High	Low	1986	High	Low	1986	High	Low	1986	High	Low
−2.5	16	19	13.4	−54	−38	18.8	24	31	−3.0	−6	−4
16.7	12	17	17.8	29	30	31.9	27	37	3.9	4	4
3.3	5	6	4.7	8	9	5.6	8	9	1.9	3	3
13.4	7	11	13.1	21	21	26.3	19	28	2.0	1	1
−19.0	8	5	6.0	−59	−47	−12.0	7	3	−8.9	−10	−9
1.5	2	2	4.7	7	7	0.8	2	2	3.4	7	7
7.8	−10	−6	4.5	53	32	6.8	−7	−5	5.7	2	2
2.8	6	5	2.4	14	11	2.4	9	7	2.5	5	5
5.0	−16	−11	2.1	39	21	4.4	−16	−12	3.3	−3	−3
210.6	173	204	227.5	471	386	374.3	366	400	71.4	83	83
48.7	24	28	21.7	20	19	50.7	25	29	48.4	31	30
251.0	86	123	82.0	64	72	267.8	108	146	221.3	126	145
41.7	20	28	12.7	10	13	37.6	26	37	30.4	17	21

term credit and errors and omissions), and changes in reserves. Ratios are calculated using current price data.
a. Excluding South Africa.
b. Excludes official transfers.

Trade reform

Trade reform means policies that reduce protection. An open trading system is a powerful force for sustained growth and industrial expansion. With trade, enterprises are not bound by narrow domestic markets, but can expand to sell their goods and services in the international market. The economic efficiency gains from trade liberalization in industrial countries are essential if output is to grow as in the High case.

Chapter 8 of this Report describes the increase in protectionism since 1974. International trade has become progressively more discriminatory and managed. The principal tool of this recent protection has been the nontariff barrier, which breaks the link between domestic and foreign prices in several major sectors. Fortunately, protection has increased much less than demands for protection. Many trade barriers have proved surmountable and therefore less costly to exporters in developing countries than they might have been. But existing levels of protection still cause higher prices for consumers, inefficient resource allocation, and a structure of industry and trade which changes in comparative advantage are gradually rendering obsolete.

Improved access for the manufactured exports of developing countries to the markets of industrial countries is a crucial element of the High case. Similarly, the prospects for increased exports by industrial countries depend on expanding markets in the developing countries. In the High case, imports by developing countries could reach $1.3 trillion by 1995. The Low case shows a much slower rise, to less than $1.0 trillion by 1995.

Greater flexibility in the international trading system is desirable on other grounds as well. The increasing internationalization of production, described in Chapter 3, gives rise to patterns of trade and investment that do not always fit traditional notions. Cheaper and better international communications and transportation have transformed the economics of intrafirm trade in intermediate goods. Increasingly, international trade is in processes or components, not in finished products. In addition, the automation of manufacturing has reduced the proportion of low-skilled workers. These developments have widened the scope for specialization among countries and heightened the need for an international trading environment that grants access and flexibility.

Adjustment in developing countries

Three sorts of policies are needed to achieve faster growth. First, outward-oriented trade policies. Second, policies to foster macroeconomic stability.

Box 2.4 Restructuring of the steel industry—a continuing story

In the 1960s, world steel production increased almost without interruption. Expecting continued increases in steel demand, the steel industry planned projects to expand capacity through the late 1960s and the early 1970s. But by the time these projects came on stream in the late 1970s, the growth of world steel demand had ceased almost completely; in fact it had declined substantially in some years. In the latter half of the late 1970s, steel companies canceled or postponed indefinitely many of their investment plans and closed some of the existing capacity. What little expansion has been initiated since the 1970s has taken place mostly in developing countries and has been primarily in the category of scrap- or direct-reduction-based small-scale mills. Although the net increase in steel-making capacity has been minimal, the problem of excess capacity has persisted because of the lack of growth in demand.

Faced with a problem of growing excess capacity, most of the industrial countries took measures to rationalize their steel industries, starting with the closure of inefficient mills. The European Community (EC) has reduced its annual steel production capacity by about 20 million tons since 1977, and a further reduction of 10–15 million tons is planned for the next five years. Around 15 million tons of capacity, or close to 10 percent of capacity, have been eliminated in the United States during the past three to four years, and a further 10 percent reduction can be expected during the next five years. Apart from the closing of obsolete plants, recent activity in the Japanese steel industry has been in investment directed at increasing continuous casting, implementing energy-saving measures, as well as refurbishing existing older facilities.

Labor productivity also improved over the past five years. The European industrial countries, Japan, and the United States employed a total of 1.8 million workers in their iron and steel industries in 1974; in 1984 the total had fallen by 44 percent to close to 1 million.

Box figure 2.4 illustrates the change in the steel industry since 1973. It shows the volume of steel production (plotted cumulatively on the horizontal axis) and the average operating costs per ton (on the vertical axis) of the sixteen leading producers. These two variables allow comparison of a country's competitive position and market share in 1973 and in 1984. Cross-country comparison should be exercised with caution. First, the steel products of the countries in question are not necessarily homogeneous. Second, the data for the operating costs are estimated on the basis of cost information from an average of 65 percent of each country's steel producers. For Brazil, India, and Spain, data are available for between 13 and 30 percent of the firms. These caveats notwithstanding, the bold line in the graph is an approximate long-term cost curve for the world steel industry.

The box figure shows among other things that Brazil and the Republic of Korea, both small, high-cost producers in 1973, have increased their market share and improved their competitive position substantially. Also, steel production in the United States declined from 1973 to 1984, but operating costs there increased more than in the rest of the world, and the country's competitive position was further eroded.

The adjustment of the steel industry has met many barriers in both industrial and developing countries. Preventing a further downward adjustment in capacity and a continued shift in the international division of steel production is costly to individual countries and to the world economy. Calls for protection and overall resistance to adjustment have been the dominant features of this industry despite the progress reported above. If governments prevent markets from determining the future international structure of the steel industry, costs will rise across the board. Governments should thus strive to reduce tariff and nontariff protection of their domestic steel industry. Steel remains an important generic input to much industry and construction. Few countries can afford to subsidize local, inefficient industry simply to prolong an eventually inevitable shift in the structure of production. Being able to compete in the international market for steel remains the best test of the viability of a country's steel industry. In the past ten years the European Community and the United States adopted measures to protect their domestic products from lower-priced imports, while they restructured domestic production. These measures are already costly to domestic consumers and represent a substantial barrier to the exports from developing countries with competitive steel industries.

Box figure 2.4 Costs in the world steel industry, 1973 and 1984

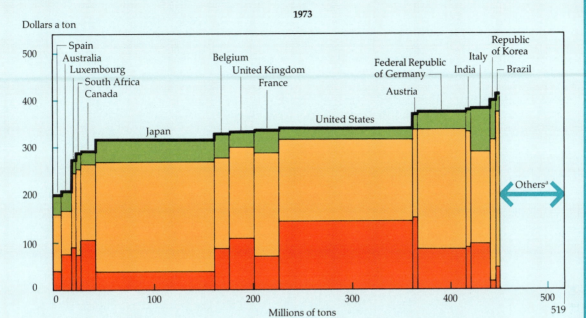

1973

Dollars a ton

Spain
Australia
Luxembourg
South Africa
Canada
Japan
Belgium
United Kingdom
France
United States
Federal Republic of Germany
Austria
India
Italy
Republic of Korea
Brazil
Others[a]

Millions of tons

519

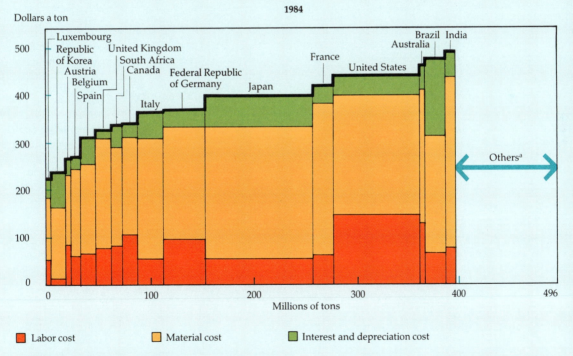

1984

Dollars a ton

Luxembourg
Republic of Korea
Austria
Belgium
Spain
United Kingdom
South Africa
Canada
Italy
Federal Republic of Germany
Japan
France
United States
Brazil
Australia
India
Others[a]

Millions of tons

496

■ Labor cost   ■ Material cost   ■ Interest and depreciation cost

Note: The horizontal axis shows the total output of the world steel industry, with producers ranked in ascending order of unit costs. The bold line therefore represents the long-run cost curve for the world steel industry.
a. Other countries' steel production for which no cost data are available.
Source: Paine Webber and World Bank data.

Third, policies to improve the allocation of resources. (The role of the World Bank in the support of adjustment is discussed in Box 2.6.)

TRADE POLICIES. Since a basic goal of adjustment is to increase international competitiveness, trade policies are an important element in medium-term adjustment. By maintaining realistic exchange rates and replacing quantitative restrictions with tariffs, governments can reduce the bias against exports which faces producers in many developing countries. Removing protection altogether is a desirable long-term goal. Carefully designed trade reforms allow countries to move toward an outward-oriented trade strategy which will not only improve their trade performance but also help them achieve higher rates of economic growth.

MACROECONOMIC POLICIES. Lower fiscal deficits, achieved primarily through the reduction and redirection of public expenditures, are essential to increase savings and improve resource allocation. Fiscal deficits accommodated by monetary expansions have provoked inflation, discouraged savings, and distorted investments. In many cases fis-cal deficits have been allowed to explode in order to finance poorly functioning public enterprises. Often there is scope for higher revenues through improved management of such enterprises or the substitution of tariffs for quantitative trade restrictions. Macroeconomic stability, achieved through lower budget deficits, will also make it easier to reform the financial system. Market-determined interest rates, along with a stable exchange rate, will stem capital outflows and thus increase the supply of finance for domestic investment.

COMPLEMENTARY POLICIES TO IMPROVE RESOURCE ALLOCATION. Fewer price controls would allow prices to reflect the true costs of resources and would encourage the expansion of activities in line with changing incentives. Fewer investment regulations would help to reduce barriers to entry, encourage foreign direct investment, and ease technological progress. Fewer labor market regulations, such as high minimum wages, would promote labor market flexibility and higher employment.

Even if the policy changes needed for the High

case materialize, some groups of developing countries are likely to fare much better than others. Overall, Sub-Saharan Africa has relatively poor prospects compared with other developing countries. Even in the High case, its output growth would be about 4 percent a year, and its per capita income in 1995 would still be below the 1980–86 average. The region's export volumes, dominated by primary commodities, would grow at roughly 4 percent a year up to 1995 because of faster economic growth in the industrial countries.

Exporters of manufactures have the best prospects. Their output growth in the High case is slightly below 7 percent a year up to 1995. Growth in exports of manufactures would reach around 10 percent a year, thanks to the more open trading environment and to strong growth in the indus-trial countries. Per capita incomes would therefore be able to grow by more than 5 percent a year in the group of exporters of manufactures.

Oil exporters face a relatively hard time in the next decade—although they are likely to fare better than they did in the first half of the 1980s, when their output growth fell to 0.8 percent a year. Their pressing need, of course, is to reduce their dependence on fuel exports. In the High case, their manufactured exports increase by about 13 percent a year during 1986–95, and this makes up for part of their decreased earnings from fuel exports.

The scarcity of external finance for the highly indebted countries makes adjustment toward an outward-oriented trade strategy and export growth particularly urgent—and difficult—for them. Their principal source of growth in the High

Table 2.9 External financing, by type of flow, 1973–95
(billions of dollars)

Country group and type of flow	Level					Period average (mean value)			
				1995				1986–95	
	1973	1980	1986	High	Low	1973–80	1980–86	High	Low
All developing countries									
Deficit on goods, services, and private transfers	9.0	69.1	35.5	74	68	42.6	58.9	44	48
Official development assistance, net	8.7	22.8	21.7	45	42	15.7	21.4	35	36
Grants	4.7	11.5	14.1	27	25	8.0	12.7	21	21
Concessional loans	4.0	11.3	7.6	18	17	7.7	8.7	14	15
Direct private investment	4.9	10.0	12.4	22	20	7.2	11.4	17	17
Nonconcessional loans, net	11.6	47.0	18.1	32	17	34.0	39.7	12	8
Official	2.0	9.0	4.8	21	17	5.8	10.2	13	12
Private	9.6	38.0	13.3	11	0	28.2	29.5	−1	−4
Other capital	−5.0	1.6	−0.7	3	−1	−3.7	−11.3	4	2
Sub-Saharan Africa									
Deficit on goods, services, and private transfers	1.7	4.9	8.9	10	9	5.0	10.2	7	7
Official development assistance, net	1.5	5.1	5.2	11	11	3.3	4.9	9	9
Grants	1.0	2.6	3.1	7	7	1.8	2.7	6	6
Concessional loans	0.5	2.5	2.1	4	4	1.5	2.2	3	3
Direct private investment	0.1	0.0	0.0	2	2	0.7	1.0	2	2
Nonconcessional loans, net	0.9	5.2	3.7	−2	−2	3.0	3.5	−2	−2
Official	0.2	1.2	0.4	1	1	0.7	1.0	1	1
Private	0.7	4.0	3.3	−3	−3	2.3	2.5	−3	−3
Other capital	−0.9	−1.2	−2.2	0	0	−1.0	−0.7	0	0
Highly indebted countries									
Deficit on goods, services, and private transfers	2.4	27.9	12.0	−7	−3	18.2	21.8	1	5
Official development assistance, net	0.9	1.6	0.6	3	3	1.2	1.4	2	2
Grants	0.4	0.5	0.7	2	2	0.4	0.8	1	1
Concessional loans	0.5	1.1	−0.1	1	1	0.8	0.6	1	1
Direct private investment	2.7	4.6	3.2	7	7	3.4	4.6	6	6
Nonconcessional loans, net	6.3	27.5	6.9	−9	−6	20.0	20.1	−2	1
Official	1.0	3.6	2.5	7	6	2.2	4.2	5	4
Private	5.3	23.9	4.4	−16	−12	17.8	15.9	−7	−3
Other capital	−1.3	0.5	−7.0	−2	−3	−0.2	−10.9	0	−1

Note: The table is based on a sample of ninety developing countries. Totals for Sub-Saharan Africa exclude South Africa. The deficit on goods, services, and private transfers not financed by ODA, direct investment, long-term loans, and other capital is covered by foreign exchange reserves. Period averages exclude the base year of the corresponding period.

Box 2.6 The role of the World Bank in support of structural adjustment

The World Bank has often stressed the need to identify investment priorities and to undertake only projects with a high rate of return. But the Bank also stresses the importance of the macroeconomic environment. It is increasingly being recognized that it is virtually impossible to have a good project in a bad policy environment. To improve the policy environment the World Bank has supported efforts to adopt appropriate policies in a variety of areas. The Bank emphasizes:

• Mobilizing domestic savings through fiscal and financial sector policies.

• Improving public sector efficiency by rationalizing public investments and improving the efficiency of public enterprises.

• Improving the efficiency of private sector investments by reforming trade and domestic policies.

• Reforming institutional arrangements to support adjustment with growth.

The World Bank's increasing emphasis on macroeconomic policies has been reflected in changes in its lending program. Although project and sector investment activities have continued to absorb the largest portion of World Bank loans and credits, new instruments have been introduced—such as the structural adjustment and the sector adjustment loans and credits—which focus directly on support of developing countries' programs and policies of structural reform. Structural adjustment loans focus on macroeconomic policies and institutional change at the country level—although they frequently emphasize reforms of importance to particular sectors in which adjustment is most urgently needed. The purpose of sector adjustment loans is to promote the introduction and effective implementation of sectoral policies necessary for sustained economic growth.

Most aspects of macroeconomic and sector policy in medium-term adjustment are addressed in Bank nonproject lending. The exception is monetary and exchange rate policy; here the Bank defers to the International Monetary Fund and works along with it to support individual programs that place emphasis on different policy issues which reflect country priorities and objectives.

The main goals of the Bank's sector and structural adjustment loans are to facilitate the adjustment required to achieve sustainable growth and to help mobilize the external financing that can support the country's adjustment efforts. Although the final objective is to achieve sustainable growth compatible with available resources (including foreign financing), achieving this objective is a medium-term target. Thus, adjustment programs focus mostly on the policy framework needed to promote sustainable growth in the medium term. This has also meant that reforms need to be supported with a series of Bank lending operations over a period of several years. In all cases, reform programs have required a firm commitment on the part of governments to sustain the course of the reform effort over time. But reform programs need to be flexible, and the Bank has supported modifications in policy packages in the light of domestic and international developments. Where policy reforms toward desirable structural change give rise to transitional costs that affect the poor, the Bank has worked with governments to develop programs that address this problem.

The size of the World Bank's lending program depends primarily on the adoption and implementation of appropriate adjustment programs. In recent years more countries have embarked on serious policy reform, and lending for adjustment with growth will increase. Discussions among shareholder governments on arrangements to increase the Bank's lending capacity through a general capital increase are continuing. During the past year, negotiations were successfully concluded on the Eighth Replenishment of the International Development Association (IDA8). Donor governments have agreed to provide $12 billion in new resources which will be committed by IDA during fiscal 1988–90. This amount represents, in real terms, about the same level of resources as that available to IDA during the past three years from IDA7 and the temporary Special Facility for Sub-Saharan Africa. About half of the IDA8 funds will be used for operations in Sub-Saharan Africa, and more than a fourth of the total will probably be used to support adjustment programs in African and other IDA recipient countries, partly in conjunction with the IMF's Structural Adjustment Facility.

---

case is exports; long-term lending would be about the same in both the High and the Low case. The lower real interest rates of the High case would also help to reduce the debt service burden. All in all, the highly indebted countries as a group could achieve output growth of about 5 percent. In other words, there will be no quick recovery of the output lost during the first half of the 1980s.

The seventeen highly indebted middle-income countries are in deep trouble if the Low case comes to pass. Higher real interest rates, increased protection, and stagnating exports would make it impossible for them to reduce the debt overhang. Debt service would barely change from its current level of 37.6 percent of exports by 1995. Several of these countries have made remarkable adjustment efforts which have improved their chances of resuming growth. But for this to continue, and for orderly servicing of debt to be maintained, the momentum of reform must not slacken. The industrial countries have a vital part to play—and not just as providers of external finance. The High case depends on their participation. Without many of the elements of that scenario, the highly indebted countries may find it politically intolerable to maintain the servicing of their external debt. Significant interruptions in servicing could damage the financial system and make it harder for the debtor countries to return to normal levels of borrowing from the private capital market.

Conclusion

Nineteen eighty-six was the second successive year of sluggish growth in the world economy. There was little progress in reducing international payments imbalances, and the debt problems of the developing countries persisted. Another year of limited progress has made decisive policy action in the near future all the more important. The low-growth path presented in this chapter illustrates the state of the world economy that would materialize if little or no action is taken. It is a picture of stagnation, if not decline. Domestic policies to achieve economic efficiency and flexibility in the medium and long term, combined with progress during the Uruguay Round in liberalizing international trade, could yield a high return in output and employment growth.

There is no viable alternative to adjustment. The longer governments wait to implement the required policy changes, the harder the task will be. Countries will certainly gain from their own policy reforms, but concerted action would ease and accelerate the process. This does not mean that any country can or should rely on the adjustment of others to improve its own prospects. It is essential that each country improve the conditions for its own interaction with the rest of the world in order to benefit from improved global economic conditions.

Industrialization and Foreign Trade

Industrialization: trends and transformations

Trade and industrialization have reinforced each other. At the international level, trade has allowed countries to specialize between industry and other sectors, between different branches of industry, and increasingly even between different stages in production. Trade has provided access to critical industrial inputs, including technology, for countries incapable of producing them. Expanded demand for exports has spurred technological development and industrial production. In turn, the advent of new industrial technologies has shaped the pattern of specialization and hence the pattern of trade.

At the national level, domestic trade has allowed specialization between economic sectors and within industry. Again, new technologies and industrial progress have altered the internal pattern of specialization and trade. In the other direction, increased domestic trade has provided the demand to stimulate the introduction of new technologies and further industrialization.

The first two parts of this chapter trace some key developments in technology, international specialization, and international trade. Together, these have led to today's integrated system of global trade and industrial production. This historical review highlights the influence of government policies toward trade and ends by discussing the performance of developing countries in this global system since the 1960s. The third part of the chapter discusses the changes in economic structure that have typically resulted from the interaction of technology, specialization, and trade over the course of industrialization. The fourth part discusses the factors that appear to have contributed to the more successful industrialization experi-

ences in the period before World War II. The chapter serves as historical background for the analyses of industrialization since World War II in later chapters. Although industry, broadly defined, includes mining, construction, electricity, gas, and water, in addition to manufacturing, this chapter focuses more on manufacturing—the most dynamic and usually the largest industrial subsector.

Global industrialization in historical perspective

International specialization has evolved beyond the old pattern by which industrialized countries exported manufactures to the developing countries in exchange for primary commodities. Today, some of the world's most successful exporters of manufactures are developing countries; many of their exports go to industrialized countries, from which they in turn import manufactures. Among industrialized countries, this two-way trade in manufactures—intraindustry trade as it is commonly called—has reached the point where comparisons of comparative advantage are meaningful only at the level of finely disaggregated product categories. Much of this intraindustry trade reflects the specialization that has accompanied industrialization. Production of a single good now commonly spans several countries, with each country in this "global factory" performing tasks in which it has a cost advantage (see Figure 3.1).

Some of these changes in international specialization and trade are no doubt responses to government policy. But, on the whole, they reflect the natural economic processes that have shaped industrialization from the start.

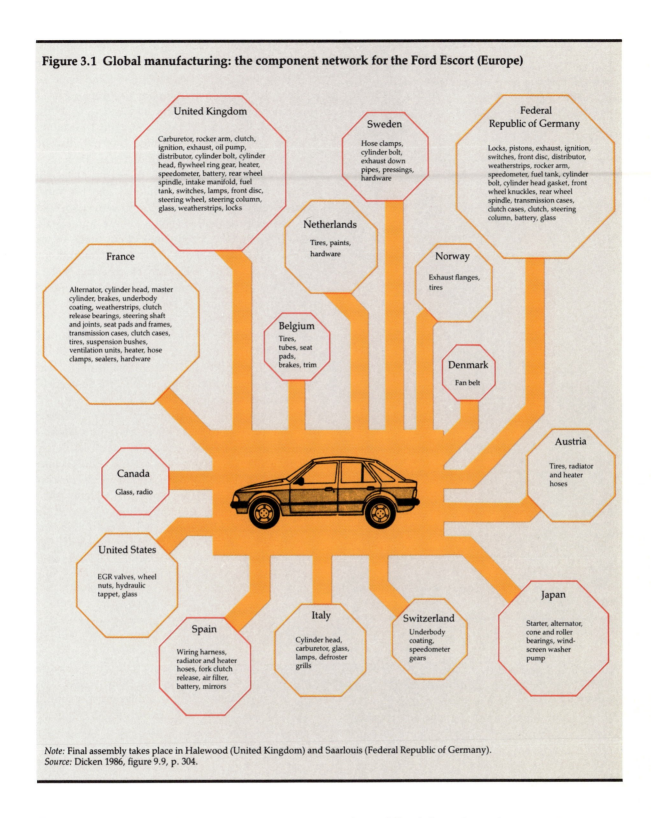

Figure 3.1 Global manufacturing: the component network for the Ford Escort (Europe)

United Kingdom

Carburetor, rocker arm, clutch, ignition, exhaust, oil pump, distributor, cylinder bolt, cylinder head, flywheel ring gear, heater, speedometer, battery, rear wheel spindle, intake manifold, fuel tank, switches, lamps, front disc, steering wheel, steering column, glass, weatherstrips, locks

Sweden

Hose clamps, cylinder bolt, exhaust down pipes, pressings, hardware

Federal Republic of Germany

Locks, pistons, exhaust, ignition, switches, front disc, distributor, weatherstrips, rocker arm, speedometer, fuel tank, cylinder bolt, cylinder head gasket, front wheel knuckles, rear wheel spindle, transmission cases, clutch cases, clutch, steering column, battery, glass

Netherlands

Tires, paints, hardware

France

Alternator, cylinder head, master cylinder, brakes, underbody coating, weatherstrips, clutch release bearings, steering shaft and joints, seat pads and frames, transmission cases, clutch cases, tires, suspension bushes, ventilation units, heater, hose clamps, sealers, hardware

Norway

Exhaust flanges, tires

Belgium

Tires, tubes, seat pads, brakes, trim

Denmark

Fan belt

Canada

Glass, radio

Austria

Tires, radiator and heater hoses

United States

EGR valves, wheel nuts, hydraulic tappet, glass

Spain

Wiring harness, radiator and heater hoses, fork clutch release, air filter, battery, mirrors

Italy

Cylinder head, carburetor, glass, lamps, defroster grills

Switzerland

Underbody coating, speedometer gears

Japan

Starter, alternator, cone and roller bearings, windscreen washer pump

Note: Final assembly takes place in Halewood (United Kingdom) and Saarlouis (Federal Republic of Germany).
Source: Dicken 1986, figure 9.9, p. 304.

The rise of modern industrialization: the mid-1700s to 1820

Although historians differ on details, the consensus is that industrialization began in Britain around the middle of the eighteenth century. Innovations in the spinning and weaving of cotton greatly boosted productivity; cotton output increased a hundredfold from about 1760 to 1827, and cotton textiles overtook wool manufacturing to become

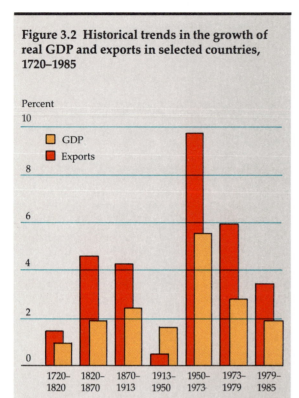

Figure 3.2 Historical trends in the growth of real GDP and exports in selected countries, 1720–1985

Percent

- □ GDP (orange)
- ■ Exports (red)

| Period | 1720–1820 | 1820–1870 | 1870–1913 | 1913–1950 | 1950–1973 | 1973–1979 | 1979–1985 |

Note: Accurate historical data for world exports and GDP are difficult to obtain, so the chart shows average growth rates for six major industrial countries: France, Germany, Italy, Japan, the United Kingdom, and the United States. For exports, the growth rate for 1720–1820 includes only France and the United Kingdom; the average for 1820–70 includes France, Germany, the United Kingdom, and the United States. The GDP growth rates have the same coverage, except that the first period is 1700–1820 instead of 1720–1820, and the United States is excluded from both the first and second periods. More comprehensive world data are provided for the period since World War II in Figure 3.3.
Source: For 1720–1979: Maddison 1982, tables 3.2 and 3.7. For 1979–85: for GDP, World Bank data; for exports, IMF, *International Financial Statistics.*

These innovations are now generally thought to have sparked the Industrial Revolution, but it is unlikely that people at that time would have regarded them as revolutionary. Output in British agriculture and handicrafts had been expanding for about 300 years. In contrast with continental Europe, Britain had eliminated internal customs barriers as well as most guild and state monopoly restrictions on production by the early 1700s. The bill of exchange, deposit banking, and insurance were well developed, and there had also been steady improvements in roads, rivers, and canals. Rising agricultural productivity had increased incomes and expanded the domestic market for other goods. The enclosure of common village lands had pushed labor from the farms and increased the number of people who depended on the market for food.

Throughout the period, domestic trade boomed, and an additional boost in demand came from increasing foreign trade. The expansion of demand gave impetus, within the relatively free enterprise environment that prevailed, to a series of innovations in production. An important pre–Industrial Revolution example was the putting-out system in textiles. Merchant-entrepreneurs supplied materials to textile weavers in the villages, bought back the finished cloth, and sold it to domestic consumers or to export merchants. Ultimately, as the growth of demand for manufactures exceeded the growth of the labor force, the specialization and labor-saving inventions that are generally acknowledged to have constituted the first industrial revolution followed.

The transport revolutions, the spread of industrialization, and the emergence of a global market: 1820 to 1870

After the innovations in cotton textiles, iron smelting, and the steam engine, industrialization centered on steel, railways, and steamships from about 1820 to 1870. Railways integrated national markets and stimulated demand for iron and steel. With steel and steam power, bigger and more reliable ships could be built. Freight costs dropped, which enabled such previously remote areas as the American Midwest to produce bulky agricultural products for distant markets in Europe. Belgium, France, Germany, and the United States began to industrialize in this period. Europe, the United States, Canada, Argentina, and Australia were linked by international trade in agricultural produce, raw materials, and manufactured products.

---

the leading manufacturing product. Most of this growth may be attributed to specialization combined with simple modifications to existing processes. Adam Smith, writing *The Wealth of Nations* in the 1770s, emphasized specialization and the division of labor, not the introduction of machines, as the basis for higher productivity. The innovation that allowed coal to be used in smelting iron and James Watt's improvement of the Newcomen steam engine between 1776 and 1781 were milestones in the development of industrial machinery. But it took several decades for these innovations to be incorporated into production on a wide scale and to make the factory the symbol of manufacturing industry.

The spread of industrialization to the European continent was facilitated by important institutional reforms and the removal of many of the restrictions that had hindered domestic commerce. By 1820, Europe had emerged from the French Revolution and the Napoleonic wars that followed it. In France, tariffs and tolls on domestic trade, as well as guild restrictions on the choice of occupation, were abolished immediately after the Revolution. These reforms were soon followed by a standardized system of weights and measures (the metric system) and new legal codes protecting property rights. The Napoleonic wars helped diffuse this wave of liberalism and reform to other parts of Europe—Belgium, the Netherlands, Switzerland, Italy, and much of Germany. In Germany, after years of effort, barriers to domestic trade were greatly reduced in 1834 by the creation of the Zollverein, a customs union among the different German states.

The United Kingdom, the United States, and many of the European countries also adopted more liberal external trade policies between 1820 and 1870. Initially, the United Kingdom, the leader in industrial technology, prohibited exports of machinery and the emigration of skilled workers. But British entrepreneurs and craftsmen could be found in Belgium, France, and other European countries, often using smuggled machinery to produce textiles and engineering products. Realizing the futility of the prohibition, the United Kingdom removed the legal barriers against emigration of skilled workers (in 1825) and against exports of machinery (in 1842). Thereafter, British entrepreneurs, workers, and financiers helped to develop railways and coal mining in Europe and elsewhere. Subsequently, the United Kingdom abolished the Navigation Acts, which had restricted international shipping; and with the repeal of the restrictions on grain imports (the Corn Laws) in 1846, it moved to free trade. Protective tariffs were replaced with revenue tariffs, which were gradually reduced to an average of 5.8 percent by 1880.

The United States began a series of tariff reductions in 1840, and by 1857 most rates were at or below 24 percent. But an increasing need for government revenue, especially during the Civil War, led to several tariff increases. After the Civil War ended in 1865, tariff increases continued for protection purposes.

France embarked on a policy of reducing tariffs and eliminating import prohibitions around 1852, which culminated in the Cobden-Chevalier free trade treaty of 1860 between France and the United Kingdom. This treaty liberated French industrial development from reliance on expensive domestic coal and iron. French industry and railways, which now had access to cheaper and better coal, iron, and steel—the basic industrial raw materials of that era—were able to develop rapidly. In Germany, the import duties levied by the Zollverein in 1834 were much lower than those in other European countries at the time. Duties on manufactured imports, for example, were about 10 percent in Germany. But these were steadily increased in the 1840s. The Cobden-Chevalier treaty between France and the United Kingdom and agitation by German free traders prompted a series of tariff reductions in Germany in the 1860s. By 1873 all duties levied for protective purposes had been removed in favor of moderate duties levied for revenue purposes.

Economic liberalism between 1820 and 1870, together with the transport revolutions wrought by railways and steamships, boosted world output and international trade (see Figure 3.2). Still, more than three quarters of the world's industrial production in 1870 was accounted for by four countries: the United Kingdom (about 32 percent), the United States (about 23 percent), Germany (about 13 percent), and France (about 10 percent).

*The second industrial revolution
and the waning of liberalism: 1870 to 1913*

The next forty-three years—1870 to 1913—saw major advances in science and technology. The invention of the Gilchrist-Thomas process, which allowed steel to be made from iron ore of high phosphorus content, propelled the industrial development of countries with extensive deposits of phosphoric ores, such as Germany and Sweden. Other innovations in this period—electricity, refrigeration, organic chemicals, the internal combustion engine, the transatlantic telegraph, and the radio—are commonly regarded as the basis of a "second industrial revolution." Some of them reinforced the trend toward greater physical integration of world markets: refrigeration, for example, made it possible to ship frozen meat from Australia to London by the 1880s.

This second revolution differed from the earlier one in two important ways. Technological advances became more dependent on scientific research that was systematically organized in firms and universities for commercial application. Germany, later joined by the United States, led the way. Also, for the first time, industrial growth in the industrialized countries became partly dependent on supplies from elsewhere: raw materials needed by the new technologies (for example, bauxite, petroleum, and rubber) and ingredients for new alloys (for example, tungsten, nickel, and chromium) now had to be supplemented with supplies from outside the group of industrialized countries. As a result, many countries were ushered into global industrialization as suppliers of industrial raw materials. Since many of these products had no economic value until the new technologies created demand for them, people in these areas were now presented with additional income opportunities. But along with these income opportunities came colonization for many of the new suppliers in Africa and Asia. This historical link between participation in international trade and colonization influenced the choice of industrialization and trade strategies in many of the former colonies after World War II.

Despite advances in technology, output in the industrialized countries grew only slightly faster than it had between 1820 and 1870, and the growth rate of exports fell (Figure 3.2). One reason for this was the onset of protectionism in the late 1870s. The United States had increased tariffs to help finance its Civil War. After the war the tariffs were maintained and even increased to protect both agriculture and industry. In Germany, where tariffs on most imports had been abolished by 1877, agricultural producers complaining of ''cheap'' wheat from America and iron and steel producers facing declining prices caused free trade to be abandoned in 1879. Protectionist forces in France quickly followed Germany's example, led again by farmers complaining about imports of cheap American wheat. Other countries did the same, which led to a series of tariff wars in Europe.

A number of countries joined the ''industrial league'' between 1870 and 1913, including Russia and Japan. The state played a more active role in the industrialization of these two countries, particularly in the development of infrastructure, than it did in the countries that had industrialized earlier. Nevertheless, the experience of Russia and Japan paralleled Western Europe's in some respects. Both countries embarked on major reforms that removed restrictions on domestic markets and helped spur domestic commerce. Serfdom was abolished in Russia in 1861, and judicial, administrative, tax, and monetary reforms followed in the late 1860s. In the mid-1880s the domestic market was integrated by the expansion of the railways.

Reforms in Japan were even more far-reaching. After more than 260 years in virtual autarky, Japan was forced in the 1850s to open up to foreign trade. The country was compelled to sign a treaty that for years (1858–98) put a 5 percent ceiling on the tariffs that it could levy on imports. Partly in reaction to this, the old Tokugawa Shogunate that had ruled Japan for centuries was overthrown, the Meiji Emperor was restored in 1868 as head of a centralized state, and a series of reforms was begun. Guilds were eliminated, feudalism was abolished, and private property rights to land were established. People were now free to choose their trade or occupation: they could produce any crop or commodity and could buy and sell land freely. Taxation was reformed and made uniform across the country. Internal tolls on the movement of goods and restrictions on the movement of people were abolished; so too were prohibitions on the exports of rice, wheat, copper, and raw silk. These reforms are generally acknowledged to have been major catalysts in early Japanese industrialization.

The collapse of liberalism and of the global market: 1913 to 1950

Economic liberalism, waxing from 1820 to around 1870, and waning between 1870 and 1913, was practically moribund from 1913 to about 1950. During these years there were two world wars and frequent trade wars, the severest economic depression in history occurred, the socialist approach to industrialization emerged, and several countries that had previously served the world trading system as suppliers of primary products (Argentina and Brazil to name just two) adopted an industrialization strategy that emphasized import substitution behind high protective barriers.

Even within some of the major capitalist industrialized countries, the market lost ground. The cartelization of German industry, which had started around the last quarter of the nineteenth century, greatly intensified in the years between the two world wars. Industrial cartels started in the United States at about the same time as in Germany, but unlike in Germany were promptly outlawed. Nevertheless, a wave of mergers resulted in significant concentration in U.S. industry. International trade also became restricted as the industrialized countries adopted restrictive and predatory commercial policies around the Great Depression years of the 1930s. Tariff wars and quantitative restrictions became common. The United States passed the Smoot-Hawley Tariff Act, which created high protective tariffs. The United Kingdom and France retreated from multilateral trade, each emphasizing trade within its colonial empire at the expense of outside countries. Germany created an elaborate mechanism of bilateral payments and exchange controls for its trade with central and southern Europe and with South America.

Although the period from 1913 to 1950 inherited many technological innovations from the earlier period of industrialization and contributed many of its own, their diffusion was delayed by the political and economic turmoil. The growth of output dropped, and there was an even greater fall in the growth of international trade (Figure 3.2).

Global industrialization after World War II

By the mid–1950s postwar reconstruction was virtually complete, and the world economy entered a period of unprecedented output and trade expansion (Figure 3.2). Manufacturing led the way in both output and export growth (see Figure 3.3). As in the nineteenth century, exports grew faster than output.

Postwar growth in manufacturing was fueled by an explosion of new products, new technologies, liberalization of international trade, and increasing integration of the world economy. Assembly line production, the internal combustion engine and the automobile, electricity and the consumer durables that came with it—all of them predating the war—were given a push by the postwar release of postponed consumer spending. There were entirely new technological advances as well: synthetic materials, petrochemicals, nuclear energy, jet aircraft, and computers and electronic products (notably television). And great strides were made in telecommunications technologies, microelectronics, and robotics. The impact of microelectronics and robots on production processes is potentially so great that many observers believe the world is now on the threshold of a "third industrial revolution."

As before, some of the new technologies assisted the physical integration of world markets. The jet aircraft cut travel time. Telecommunications made it easier for multinational corporations to coordinate subsidiaries in different countries. The associated electronic media helped shape a world market with increasingly similar consumer tastes. Trade liberalization among industrialized market economies under the General Agreement on Tariffs and Trade (see Chapter 8) helped to create a global environment that was conducive to the development and diffusion of the new technologies.

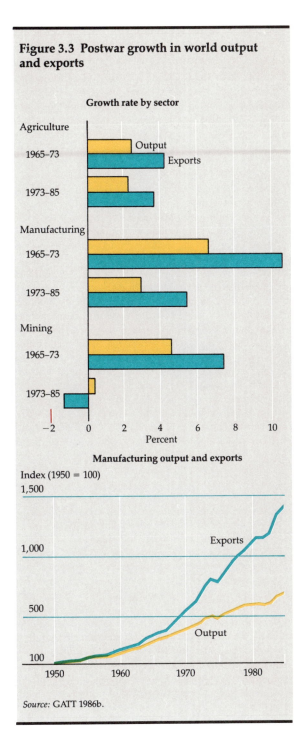

Figure 3.3 Postwar growth in world output and exports

Source: GATT 1986b.

Three other developments marked the pattern of global industrialization in the postwar period. First, the appearance of a nonmarket alternative to industrialization in Eastern Europe and elsewhere (see Box 3.1); second, decolonization in Asia, Africa, and the Caribbean; and third, the rise of the multinational corporation to prominence in world production and trade in manufactures.

Box 3.1 Industrialization and trade in nonmarket economies

Industrialization in the Soviet Union and other non-market economies has evolved differently from the other cases reviewed in this chapter. These countries have suppressed market transactions domestically and have engaged in relatively little foreign trade, even among themselves. Spontaneous responses to economic incentives have contributed little to either technological change or specialization among economic units. The Central Plan prepared by the government has attempted to determine most economic activities. State control of the means of production has been a key feature of this economic system. The Soviet Union pioneered it in 1928, and after World War II the socialist countries of Eastern Europe and elsewhere adopted it.

Statistics on these economies are difficult to obtain. In addition, because relative prices in these economies do not reflect relative scarcities, data on GDP, total investment, domestic consumption, industrial output, and so forth—all of which must rely on relative prices for aggregation—are difficult to interpret. Nevertheless, it is quite clear that the Soviet Union and some of the nonmarket economies have made tremendous progress in industrialization, especially since World War II. According to calculations by Western economists, Soviet GNP grew at an average annual rate of 6.7 percent from 1929 to the mid-1950s; 6.1 percent in 1953–65; 5.3 percent in 1966–70; 3.8 percent in 1971–75; 2.7 percent in 1976–80; and 2.4 percent in 1981–85. In view of the statistical problems, these estimates are debatable. But, if they are reasonably accurate, they suggest that in the two decades following World War II (1950 to 1970), only Japan and Germany, among the industrial market economies, grew faster. Growth in the other nonmarket economies during this period was also rapid, although generally not so rapid as that in the Soviet Union and not sustained over such long periods.

Much of this growth occurred in industry. Government control of the means of production allowed these countries to channel large shares of output to investment in industry. The large investment efforts involved meant that in many of the countries consumption per capita had to be constrained by the state for long periods. Nevertheless, the heavy investments together with the large pools of labor available initially resulted in rapid industrial expansion.

But the industrial sectors that appeared in these economies quickly lost dynamism, owing to the inherent rigidities in central planning. For instance, for most firms the Central Plan specifies what to produce, which inputs to use, where to obtain them, and where to send the outputs. Hence, most firms have had little liberty or incentive to innovate or diversify input sources (in-cluding imports) so as to reduce costs. At the same time, however, each firm is generally assured of a market regardless of quality, since other firms are required by the plan to take its outputs and final consumers have no options. Hence, there is little incentive for most firms, especially those producing nonmilitary products, to improve upon their products, to maintain the goodwill of customers, or to develop new markets (including export markets).

Some Western experts claim that total factor productivity growth (see explanation in Box 3.3) in the Soviet Union has been negative since the mid-1970s. Given the difficulty of getting access to detailed and accurate data on the Soviet economy, however, this assessment of total productivity growth is not beyond dispute. What is beyond dispute is the fact that by the mid-1970s many economists and policymakers within the Soviet Union and other nonmarket economies had openly recognized the inefficiencies in their industrial sectors. Most of the countries then began opening up more to foreign trade with the industrial market economies, with technology acquisition the primary motive. Poland entered into a number of industrial cooperation agreements with Western firms (such as International Harvester). Other East European nonmarket economies, as well as China, entered into similar agreements, although in most cases more conservatively. The Soviet Union eventually also began increasing trade with the industrial market economies. Soviet imports from the industrial market economies expanded at about 17 percent a year in the first half of the 1970s. Some experts estimate that technological imports in the 1970s may have added about 0.5 percent a year to the Soviet industrial growth rate. Recently (1987) the Soviet Union adopted a policy that allows joint ventures with foreign firms inside the Soviet Union.

There are, however, potential problems with a policy of opening up more to foreign trade while still maintaining a rigid system of central planning. Increased imports ultimately require more exports to pay for them, and so domestic firms should have the flexibility to seek and respond quickly to export opportunities. Lack of such flexibility and also of a price system that reflects relative scarcity has already contributed to balance of payments difficulties in some of the nonmarket economies that have opened up their foreign trade, especially Poland. Several countries (for example, Hungary and China) are now trying to relax some of their restrictions on domestic market transactions in order to promote efficiency and innovation. These reforms are complicated and delicate, but the potential economic gains appear to be considerable.

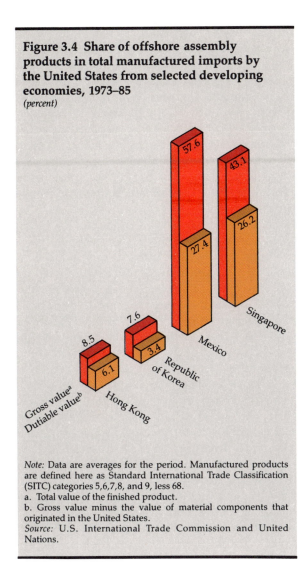

Figure 3.4 Share of offshore assembly products in total manufactured imports by the United States from selected developing economies, 1973–85
(percent)

57.6
43.1
27.4
26.2
7.6
3.4
8.5
6.1

Gross value[a]
Dutiable value[b]

Hong Kong
Republic of Korea
Mexico
Singapore

Note: Data are averages for the period. Manufactured products are defined here as Standard International Trade Classification (SITC) categories 5,6,7,8, and 9, less 68.
a. Total value of the finished product.
b. Gross value minus the value of material components that originated in the United States.
Source: U.S. International Trade Commission and United Nations.

Decolonization

Many of the countries emerging from colonialism in the postwar period chose an industrial development strategy that emphasized import substitution behind high government protection—similar to the strategy adopted by Argentina, Brazil, Turkey, and other independent developing countries in the 1930s. Several factors contributed to the appeal of this approach. First, during the turbulent years spanning the world wars, countries that had specialized as exporters of primary products found their access to export markets and to manufactured imports reduced. Their terms of trade fell drastically. This is what had prompted Argentina and others to take the protective import substitution course in the 1930s. In the first two decades after World War II, predictions of a secular decline in the terms of trade against primary products were common, and many of the newly independent countries thought it sensible to shift quickly to industries. Second, many people in the new countries associated specialization in primary commodities with their previous colonial status. To them, independence called for breaking away from the colonial economic system. Many also believed that protection granted through government restrictions on imports had played a significant role in the early industrialization of Europe, North America, and Japan. In addition, inspired by the Soviet Union's rapid industrialization, several of the newly independent countries combined import substitution with government ownership, planning, and production. In these countries, governments sought to restrict domestic trade, unlike in Europe and Japan where early industrialization had been assisted by the easing of restrictions on domestic trade.

Countries pursuing the import substitution strategy typically started by producing final manufactures to replace imports. Many enjoyed initial bursts in the growth of manufacturing. But since production usually required imported intermediate and capital goods, sustained industrial growth depended on the expansion of exports to provide the necessary foreign exchange. Countries that made an early transition to export expansion, such as the Republic of Korea, sustained their industrial growth. Many others did not make the transition. They stayed in the protective import substitution phase and their industrial development was retarded.

Multinationals

Multinational corporations in manufacturing date back as far as the nineteenth century (Singer, a U.S. firm, established a factory in Glasgow in 1867 to manufacture sewing machines), and those in primary commodities date back even farther. But it is only since the 1960s that multinationals have become major actors in shaping world industrialization. Today, between 25 and 30 percent of the world's stock of foreign direct investment—the channel for multinationals' investments—is in developing countries; about 40 percent of this is in the manufacturing sector. Manufacturing multinationals have been attracted to some of the large developing countries, especially in Latin America, because of trade policies that restricted imports of final manufactures. But in many other countries, especially those in Southeast Asia, the attraction has been the availability of semiskilled industrial labor at low cost. Some developing countries derive a significant part of their manufacturing exports from local subsidiaries of multinationals. Although data for recent years are not available, in the middle and late 1970s the share of multinationals in manufactured exports from Korea and Mexico was around 30 percent. In Brazil the share was more than 40 percent, and in Singapore more than 90 percent.

Multinationals have made it easier for some developing countries to begin exporting manufactures without going through an initial phase of import substitution. Some of these corporations have located in developing countries with the principal aim of producing in order to export to their home and other markets. Typically, this has occurred when the production processes have become routine and thus require large inputs of semiskilled labor. Locating in developing countries then allows the multinational firms to reduce labor costs.

Beginning in the late 1960s several multinationals began rationalizing their global production. Whereas before, most foreign subsidiaries had produced finished products, often with technological and intermediate inputs from the parent company, now all the subsidiaries were increasingly linked into a unified production process. Each performed only those aspects of the manufacturing process in which it had a comparative advantage. New subsidiaries were in some cases set up in developing countries to perform the labor-intensive activities. This system is not always confined to transactions among subsidiaries of the same multinational. Sometimes the arrangements are between locally owned companies and foreign-owned companies. The foreign-owned companies are not always multinationals, and sometimes they may not even be based in the domestic economy. The arrangement is known as international subcontracting. Sometimes the terms ''offshore assembly'' and ''sourcing'' are used. Figure 3.4 shows the share of offshore assembly products in total manufactured imports by the United States from four developing economies. Exemption from duties of the value of U.S. components in the offshore assembly imports has encouraged U.S. firms to use this arrangement. Similar arrangements occur between manufacturing firms in other industrialized countries and producers in developing countries.

An important form of subcontracting, especially in textiles, is an arrangement whereby firms based in the industrialized countries provide design specifications to producers in developing countries, purchase the finished products, then sell them at home and abroad. This is akin to the putting-out system in textiles which was adopted in preindustrial England. With modern transport and communications, it probably is no more difficult for today's merchants to organize a putting-out system between New York and Hong Kong, or between Tokyo and Seoul, than it was for the early English merchants to organize their putting-out system between London and the surrounding villages.

Postwar performance of developing countries

As a group, the developing countries still have only a small share in world manufacturing output, but their output and exports of manufactures have nonetheless grown more rapidly than those of the industrial countries since the 1960s (see Tables 3.1 and 3.2). No developing economy figured among the world's top thirty exporters of manufactured products in 1965. Twenty years later Hong Kong and the Republic of Korea were among the top fifteen, with export shares close to those of Sweden and Switzerland. Singapore and Brazil were among the top twenty, with export shares close to those of Denmark and Finland. Although this performance occurred during a period of unprecedented real growth in world output and trade in manufactured products, it is remarkable that developing countries sustained their progress even when the world economy slowed after 1973. Moreover, manufactured exports from developing countries have become more sophisticated (see Table 3.3). Developing countries have diversified from traditional labor-intensive products (such as textiles) or those based on natural resources (such as crude petrochemicals, cork, and paper) to chemicals and engineering products.

There are now fears that microelectronics and robotics will reduce the labor-cost advantage which the developing countries have exploited to expand their role in world manufacturing. Similar fears about the effects of machinery on employment in earlier times proved unfounded. Increasing mechanization displaced some workers, but it also introduced new opportunities that led in the long run to higher employment. The same could be true of the long-run impact of microelectronics and robotics on industrialization in developing countries. Box 3.2 discusses the effect of technological change in textiles and clothing—two industries that are of special importance to industrialization in developing countries.

Table 3.1 Shares of production and exports of manufactures by country group, 1965, 1973, and 1985
(percent)

Country group	Share in production			Share in exports		
	1965	*1973*	*1985*	*1965*	*1973*	*1985*
Industrial market economies	85.4	83.9	81.6	92.5	90.0	82.3
Developing countries	14.5	16.0	18.1	7.3	9.9	17.4
Low-income	7.5	7.0	6.9	2.3	1.8	2.1
Middle-income	7.0	9.0	11.2	5.0	8.1	15.3
High-income oil exporters	0.1	0.1	0.3	0.2	0.1	0.3
Total	100.0	100.0	100.0	100.0	100.0	100.0

Table 3.2 Growth in production and exports of manufactures by country group, 1965–73, 1973–85, and 1965–85
(percent)

Country group	Growth in production			Growth in exports		
	1965–73	*1973–85*	*1965–85*	*1965–73*	*1973–85*	*1965–85*
Industrial market economies	5.3	3.0	3.8	10.6	4.4	6.8
Developing countries	9.0	6.0	7.2	11.6	12.3	12.2
Low-income	8.9	7.9	7.5	2.4	8.7	6.0
Middle-income	9.1	5.0	6.6	14.9	12.9	13.8
High-income oil exporters	10.6	7.5[a]	8.4[a]	16.2	11.5	16.0
Total	5.8	3.5	4.5	10.7	5.3	7.4

a. End period is 1984 instead of 1985.

Table 3.3 Structure of manufactured exports from developing countries, 1970–84

Description	Share of developing countries' exports[a]		Growth rate[b]
	1970	*1984*	*1970–84*
Traditional manufactured exports			
Labor-intensive			
Textiles and apparel (84 and 65)	31.3	24.8	11.8
Footwear (85)	1.8	2.9	18.2
Other labor-intensive (61 and 83)	2.9	2.3	11.6
Total	36.0	30.0	12.4
Resource-based			
Wood and cork (63)	3.6	1.5	6.9
Paper manufactures (64)	0.8	1.1	17.6
Other resource-based (52 and 56)	0.8	0.9	14.5
Total	5.2	3.5	12.2
Nontraditional manufactured exports[c]			
Electrical machinery (72)	16.1	16.7	14.1
Chemicals (51)	8.3	9.9	15.3
Nonelectrical machinery (71)	4.2	8.7	20.1
Transport equipment (73)	2.6	5.2	20.0
Iron and steel (67)	6.2	6.5	14.2
Other nontraditional[d]	21.4	19.5	12.9
Total	58.8	66.5	15.1
Total	100.0	100.0	14.0

Note: Figures in parentheses are the SITC categories for the respective product group.
a. Developing countries' exports of the listed product as a share of developing countries' total exports of manufactured products defined as SITC categories 5, 6, 7, and 8, less 68.
b. The rate of growth of developing countries' exports of the listed product during 1970–84 in constant dollars.
c. Total manufacturing exports less traditional manufactured exports.
d. Rest of nontraditional exports.
Source: Murray (background paper).

Box 3.2 Technical change and comparative advantage: the case of textiles and clothing

Developing countries that have embarked on a path of efficient industrialization have often done so partly through the export of simple, labor-intensive manufactures, in particular clothing and textiles, to industrial market economies. But rapid technical change in such industries has led to a new form of export pessimism.

Surprisingly, perhaps, the textile industry—not normally considered a leading industry—has consistently registered higher-than-average labor productivity gains in the industrial market economies in recent decades. These gains have been brought about by a series of labor-saving innovations since World War II: the rationalization of production in more specialized factories, dramatically higher speeds in spinning, weaving, and knitting (helped in part by the growing use of synthetic fibers), and the introduction of radical, new techniques (open-end spinning, shuttleless weaving, non-woven fabrics, tufted carpets, and so on). In the 1960s many textile industrialists predicted a sharp reversal of comparative advantage in favor of the advanced industrialized countries.

These predictions turned out to be not entirely right, but not entirely wrong. By and large, innovations in textiles did succeed in halting the further loss of comparative advantage in the high-wage industrialized countries—by means of a substantial reduction in labor content. The textile industries of Germany, Italy, and the United States are, unlike their clothing industries, broadly competitive (although they still cling to protection). The reversal in comparative advantage was incomplete for several reasons. Firms—especially in Europe—found that the market would not allow them to produce standardized textiles on the scale that would justify the most capital-intensive equipment. In addition, the wage gap between the industrial market

economies and the developing economies remained so large that a broad range of techniques could exist side by side.

The clothing industry was never able to make similar strides in productivity because of the inherent obstacles to automating the functions of a machinist manipulating a soft, limp fabric. But thanks to the promise of microelectronics, clothing industrialists are now beginning to echo the textile industrialists of the 1960s.

A recent study sought to assess the likely impact of microelectronics on developing countries' comparative advantage in clothing (Hoffman 1985). This study found signs of an increasing rate of innovations in clothing machinery, most of them based on microelectronics. Recent innovations promised substantial savings in material and labor costs, as well as other advantages (such as time saving) in the preassembly phase of production (when fabrics are cut). In the assembly (or sewing) phase—which accounts for a significantly larger share of total costs than preassembly—productivity gains from microelectronics were also possible, but on a less dramatic scale. The productivity gains in both stages required costly capital investment, a minimum scale of efficient operation larger than that of the normal size of firm in this industry, increasing managerial sophistication, and—in some cases—a loss of flexibility. The study judged that, given the problems in adopting the new technology, its rate of diffusion would be slow in the coming decade, and the new technologies might not reach their maximum impact until the first years of the next century. The study concluded that protection by the industrial countries would remain the more immediate threat to developing countries' exports.

Not all of the developing countries have progressed at the same rate, however. Some have done far better than others. Figure 3.5 compares production and exports of manufactures for forty-three economies before and after 1973. Because of differences in the degree of distortion in exchange rates and in relative sectoral prices, comparisons based on the dollar value of manufactured production mean little. Export shares are more revealing. By 1985, the forty-three economies accounted for two-thirds of manufactured exports from developing countries; the first fifteen alone accounted for about 60 percent. Chapters 4 through 7 attempt to explain why recent performance has varied so widely from country to country. The rest of this chapter discusses the economic processes that

have been common to most industrializations and tries to draw some lessons from the period before World War II.

Industrialization and structural change

Typically, the share of manufacturing in GDP has risen in the early phase of industrialization. After a time, however, it has tended to fall, while the basic underlying forces of industrialization—technological change, specialization, and trade—have continued to propel output per capita upward. Thus, for most countries, the ratio of (a) the share of manufacturing (or of industry) in GDP to (b) GDP per capita follows an inverted U as industrialization proceeds (see Figure 3.6). This same relationship emerges, although not as clearly, when the ratio is compared across different countries at a single point in time (see Figure 3.7). The share of services has also tended to rise over time; its upward trend lasts longer than that of manufacturing. Agriculture's share in output gradually declines to accommodate the increased share of industry and services. Similar trends occur in the sectoral distribution of employment.

Initial discussion of these long-term trends (Colin Clark in 1940 and Simon Kuznets in the 1950s and 1960s) were confined mainly to the industrialized countries. Since then, a number of scholars, notably Hollis Chenery, have studied

Figure 3.5 Indicators of industrial performance of developing economies

1973 Ranking [a]	1966–73 Growth in manufacturing value added	1966–73 Growth in manufactured exports	Share of manufactured exports (1973) [b]	1985 Ranking [a]	1973–85 Growth in manufacturing value added	1973–85 Growth in manufactured exports	Share of manufactured exports (1985) [b]	Change in share of manufactured exports from 1973 to 1985 [c]
1. Hong Kong				1. Hong Kong				−
2. Republic of Korea				2. Republic of Korea				+
3. Yugoslavia				3. Singapore				+
4. Singapore				4. Brazil				+
5. India				5. Yugoslavia				−
6. Brazil				6. India				−
7. Mexico				7. Malaysia				+
8. Argentina				8. Mexico				−
9. Pakistan				9. Turkey				+
10. Greece				10. Philippines				+
11. Malaysia				11. Thailand				+
12. Thailand				12. Indonesia				+
13. Colombia				13. Greece				−
14. Philippines				14. Pakistan				−
15. Egypt				15. Argentina				−
16. Turkey				16. Morocco				+
17. Jamaica				17. Tunisia				+
18. Morocco				18. Colombia				−
19. Zimbabwe				19. Egypt				−
20. Guatemala				20. Peru				+
21. El Salvador				21. Sri Lanka				+
22. Dominican Republic				22. Botswana				+
23. Tunisia				23. Venezuela				−
24. Sierra Leone				24. Zimbabwe				−
25. Costa Rica				25. Jamaica				−
26. Venezuela				26. Trinidad and Tobago				−
27. Zaire				27. Uruguay				−
28. Trinidad and Tobago				28. Costa Rica				−
29. Côte d'Ivoire				29. Chile				+
30. Indonesia				30. Guatemala				−
31. Algeria				31. Cyprus				+
32. Kenya				32. Côte d'Ivoire				−
33. Uruguay				33. Dominican Republic				−
34. Nigeria				34. El Salvador				−
35. Tanzania				35. Kenya				−
36. Sri Lanka				36. Cameroon				−
37. Chile				37. Senegal				−
38. Senegal				38. Zaire				−
39. Ghana				39. Algeria				−
40. Cyprus				40. Sierra Leone				−
41. Cameroon				41. Tanzania				−
42. Peru				42. Nigeria				−
43. Botswana				43. Ghana				−

a. Based on the share in manufactured exports from developing economies.
b. Share of manufactured exports from developing economies.
c. The + sign indicates that the share in 1985 is greater than in 1973, and the − symbol indicates that the share in 1985 is smaller than in 1973.

Growth rates (percent)
- equal to or more than 15.0
- 10.0 to less than 15.0
- 7.5 to less than 10.0
- 5.0 to less than 7.5
- 0.0 to less than 5.0
- less than 0.0

Export share (percent)
- equal to or more than 10.0
- 5.0 to less than 10.0
- 2.5 to less than 5.0
- 0.5 to less than 2.5
- 0.2 to less than 0.5
- less than 0.2

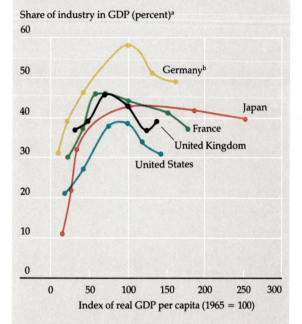

Figure 3.6 Historical relationship between GDP per capita and the share of industry in GDP in selected industrial countries, 1870–1984

Share of industry in GDP (percent)[a]

Germany[b]

Japan

France

United Kingdom

United States

Index of real GDP per capita (1965 = 100)

Note: The six data points shown for each country represent the following approximate time periods: (from left to right) 1870, 1913, 1950, 1965, 1975, and 1984.
a. Industry includes manufacturing, mining, and construction.
b. Data for 1950 onward refer to the Federal Republic of Germany.
Source: Kuznets 1957, appendix table 2; Maddison 1982, tables A4 and B2; and World Bank data.

growth in agricultural employment; in the later phases, high growth of employment in services is made possible by lower growth in industrial and agricultural employment.

Agricultural productivity and industrialization

Agriculture's reduced share in GDP has, in many countries, coincided with higher agricultural output and productivity. Britain experienced large increases in agricultural productivity in the second half of the eighteenth century, before its industrial revolution. Europe and North America went through a similar process later. Japan substantially increased its agricultural yields around the second half of the 1800s.

Increasing agricultural productivity facilitates industrialization in at least four ways:

• Higher rural incomes raise the demand for manufactures along with the demand for other goods. Moreover, because the share of food in total expenditure tends to decline as income rises, rising rural incomes also lead to a larger *proportion* of incomes being spent on manufactures.

• Rising agricultural productivity increases the supply of agricultural raw materials for industry.

• Additional foreign exchange made possible by increased agricultural exports can be used to import inputs for industry. Higher farm incomes from increased agricultural productivity can also generate additional savings, which can then be made available for investment in industry. Japan's success in its transition to rapid industrial growth in the early twentieth century was partly due to its success in mobilizing agricultural savings. Agriculture financed 27 percent of nonagricultural investment from 1888 to 1902, and 23 percent from 1903 to 1922. In the earlier period two-thirds of the investment was channeled through the public sector, courtesy of the land tax. In the later period this share fell to a quarter (the private sector accounted for the rest).

• Rising farm productivity initially allows new entrants to the labor force to be employed outside agriculture. Later, it allows labor to be released from agriculture and to be fed without sharp rises in domestic food prices or recourse to large and unsustainable imports of food.

The service sector and industrialization

Growth in the share of services tends to persist longer than growth in the share of manufacturing as industrialization proceeds. Much of the growth

post–World War II trends in developing countries, extending the analyses to trends within industry (see Box 3.3.). The economic explanations behind the long-term trends rest, on the supply side, on technological change and its differential impacts on economic sectors, the induced specializations, and the resulting trade and flow of resources among and within sectors. On the demand side, the pattern of consumption changes with income growth, and this induces changes in the structure of production.

In the early phases of industrialization, greater use of machinery, especially in manufacturing, increases labor productivity and output. As industrialization continues, further increases in labor productivity reduce the growth of industry's demand for labor. In the early phases, high growth of employment in industry is made possible by low

Figure 3.7 Relationship between GDP per capita and the share of manufacturing value added in GDP in selected economies, 1984

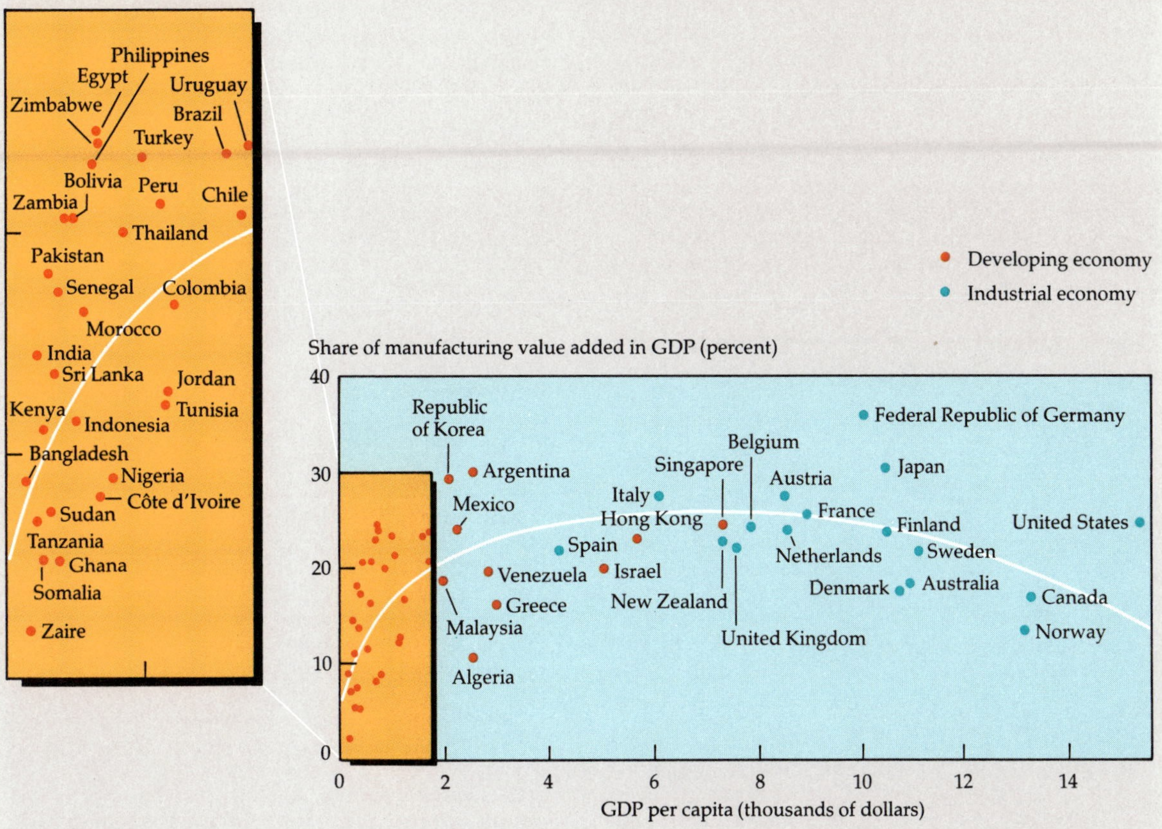

Share of manufacturing value added in GDP (percent)

GDP per capita (thousands of dollars)

- Developing economy
- Industrial economy

in the share of services reflects the increasing specialization and urbanization that come with industrialization. First, the factory—the symbol of industrialization—requires a vast, but less visible service infrastructure to function effectively. Transportation, distribution, communications, finance, and insurance, to name just a few, are all services that have to expand to facilitate industrial growth. Second, some services (for example, cleaning, information processing, advertising, and so forth) that previously were performed in-house by industrial firms have progressively been contracted to firms in the service sector. Third, just as the higher income demand elasticity for manufactures (compared with agricultural products) spurs the rapid growth of manufacturing output in the early phases of industrialization, so the higher income demand elasticity for services (compared with manufactures) encourages the growth of services

in later phases of industrialization. Fourth, increasing labor demand leads to the commercialization of domestic services, as housewives and other domestic workers join the formal labor force. Activities that previously fell outside the statistics thus begin to boost the recorded output of services. Fifth, urbanization, which accompanies industrialization, requires additional services: police, sanitation, city administration, and so forth.

Since service occupations, on the whole, are less amenable to automation, an increase in the value of service output would normally require more labor input than an increase of equal value in the output of industry. This explains why the share of services in employment rises faster than the share of services in GDP.

These factors account for the shift toward services within the individual economy. Growing integration in the world economy has added

Box 3.3   Statistical studies of economic growth and industrialization

Statistical studies of economic growth fall into two broad categories. One category extends the celebrated Clark-Kuznets studies to a large number of industrial and developing countries. The aim is to describe standard patterns of growth in economic sectors and across different branches of manufacturing. Another category tries to account for the different sources of economic growth and to isolate the contribution of rising productivity.

The studies that seek to establish standard patterns focus on income per capita. They postulate that as consumers' incomes increase, their demands shift from

mostly food products, first to industrial products and then to services and leisure. In response to these demand changes, the share of agriculture in production is expected to fall, the share of industry to rise, and later the share of services to rise. In addition to income per capita, many of the studies also examine the role of population size and the endowment of natural resources (or the availability of foreign resources). Strictly speaking, the structural features, such as the share of manufacturing in GDP, and the principal "explanatory" variable, income per capita, are joint outcomes of underlying economic processes that are not explained in the statistical model. Hence, no causality can be inferred. Nevertheless, the standard patterns produced by these studies provide useful statistical benchmarks for inquiries into a very complex process (see Box figure 3.3A).

Some studies attempt to provide similar standard patterns for the various branches of manufacturing. For instance, it is postulated that at low per capita incomes, demand for manufactures is concentrated on food and other light manufactures, but as per capita incomes increase, demand shifts to consumer durables and other heavy manufactures. The demand stimulus thus provided is supposed to be translated into production, in part with the help of higher savings made possible by the higher per capita incomes. While all this may be true in general, rapid change in industrial technology and in international specialization reduces the relevance for policy of statistical patterns at the detailed level of industrial subsectors.

The studies that seek to account for the sources of growth start from the premise that countries can grow either through the accumulation of factor inputs (extensive growth) or through the more productive use of inputs (intensive growth). For fast growth, sustained through time, both are necessary. Rapid growth rates can usually be achieved with expansion in factor inputs at early stages of industrialization, but with time it becomes more difficult to expand factor inputs, especially labor, and efficiency in the use of all economic resources becomes critical to further growth in GDP. Total factor productivity growth is a concept that tries to capture productivity growth in the use of all physical inputs. It is usually derived as a residual, after subtracting the contribution attributable to growth in the use of labor, land, and capital from GDP growth. Since land grows slowly, if at all, in most countries, a good approximation is the residual obtained after subtracting the contributions of labor and capital growth from GDP growth. Box figure 3.3B shows estimates of the growth rates of real GDP, total factor (capital and labor) inputs, and total factor productivity.

The estimates were obtained by examining the growth of countries at different levels of industrialization for the period 1960–75. Changes in the quality of capital and labor that occur over time have been taken into account in deriving the estimates for each country. Differences in the stage of industrialization may account for some of the differences in performance among the countries shown. Nevertheless, the general

Box figure 3.3A Per capita GDP and the share of manufacturing

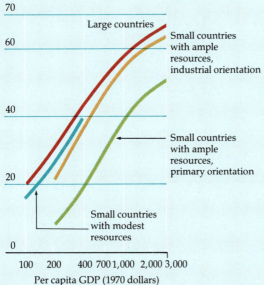

Share of manufacturing in commodity GDP (percent)ᵃ

Per capita GDP (1970 dollars)

Note: A country was classified as large if its population in 1970 was 20 million or more; otherwise, it was classified as small. A small country was classified as having modest resources if its average per capita production of primaries (defined as GDP less services and manufacturing) in 1960–73 was less than $84 (in 1970 prices); otherwise, it was classified as having ample resources. A small country with ample resources was classified as having an industrial orientation if in most years during the period 1969–73 its value added in manufacturing was above the regression plane that predicts manufacturing value added using per capita GDP and population (for small countries with ample resources); if in most years the actual manufacturing value added was below the regression plane, the country was classified as having a primary orientation.

The horizontal axis is in log scale. The curves are plots of a logistic function with the population variable held constant at the average value for each group. The number of observations at higher income levels was insufficient to extend the curve for small countries with modest resources beyond $400 per capita income.

a. Commodity GDP is GDP minus the value of services.

Source: UNIDO 1979, figure VI, p. 47, and Annex I.

picture conveyed by the figure is valid. Japan and the Republic of Korea have achieved high GDP growth rates through higher growth rates in both factor inputs and factor productivity. In contrast, the high GDP growth rates of Brazil and Venezuela have been based mainly on the growth of factor inputs. Furthermore, the figure shows that although factor inputs grew at about the same rate in Argentina and Colombia, the latter's real GDP growth was about 2 percent higher than Argentina's—the result of differences in productivity growth.

Like the patterns-of-growth approach, the sources-of-growth approach does not provide *explanations*; rather it provides a useful way of viewing the outcome of the complex process of economic growth. Some recent studies (Chenery, Robinson, and Syrquin 1986) have attempted to encompass the two methodologies within a single framework.

Box figure 3.3B Total factor productivity and real GDP growth in selected countries, 1960–75

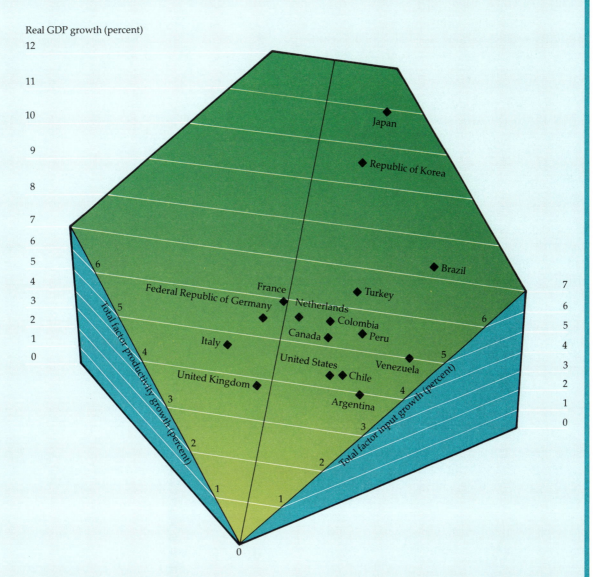

Note: Real GDP growth is the sum of the contributions from total factor input growth and total factor productivity growth. The closer a point is to the total factor productivity growth axis, the greater the relative contribution of productivity to real GDP growth. As one moves horizontally toward the total factor input growth axis, the relative contribution of productivity to real GDP growth falls and that of factor inputs rises.
Source: Adapted from Chenery, Robinson, and Syrquin 1986, figure 2–2.

an international dimension. Several developing countries (for example, Brazil, Mexico, the Republic of Korea, and Singapore) have been able to supply the relatively labor-scarce industrialized countries with labor-intensive manufactures at lower prices. Although the industrialized countries have sometimes tried to resist this trend, they have also adjusted to it, partly by increasing their exports of services such as banking, insurance, engineering, computer software, and marketing.

Structural change within manufacturing

World industrialization initially centered on textiles, later moved to iron, steel, and engineering products based on steel, then to chemicals, electrical products, and, finally, to today's electronic and microelectronic products. Most of the countries that industrialized before World War II followed this product sequence, at least as far as electrical products. Is this pattern of change within the single sector of manufacturing as inevitable as the one by which agriculture first gives way to manufacturing and then manufacturing itself gives way to services?

Textiles are preeminent in the early phase of industrialization mainly because clothing is a good for which there is growing demand in countries with low, but rising, income levels. In addition, most countries have a long history of textile production by artisans. Moreover, until quite recently, textiles technologies have been simple and stable. All in all, then, it was natural for most countries to begin industrializing by producing textiles (Box 3.2). The same factors also explain the early importance of leather goods, food processing, furniture, ceramics, building materials, and household utensils.

By the time most of today's developing countries started to industrialize (in the postwar period), the choice of products and processes in manufacturing was much wider and the world much more integrated. Countries could choose not to follow the product sequence that had occurred in the prewar period. For example, it was possible to create an engineering industry without producing iron and steel and to produce chemicals without refining petroleum. Nonetheless, some developing countries, emulating the previous generation of industrializers, built steel mills, refineries, factories producing consumer durables, and other heavy (or "late") industries. Some of these enterprises survive only with the aid of high protective barriers.

As the industrialized countries moved from textiles to heavier industries, they had to rely on bigger plants to reap economies of scale. This too is changing. It is now profitable to produce steel in mills with a capacity of around half a million tons; in the old integrated steel mills, plants of less than 2 million tons were inefficient. In the microelectronics industry, efficient plants can be much smaller than in the older branches of manufacturing.

Lessons from industrialization experiences before World War II

What are the lessons to be drawn from the experiences of countries which have followed a successful path to industrialization? This section examines five of the most important issues: the initial conditions—country size, population size, and resource endowment; policies toward domestic and foreign trade; education; transportation and communications infrastructure; and the institutional and macroeconomic background.

Initial conditions

A country with a large domestic market is in a better position to establish industrial plants that take advantage of economies of scale. Since distance between countries in many cases confers natural protection to domestic firms, everything else being equal, a country with a larger domestic market can begin industrializing earlier than one with a smaller domestic market. A large geographical size and a large population can, together, produce a large domestic market, unless agricultural productivity is exceptionally low. Hence, a large country with a large population can industrialize earlier. But this has not always been the case.

Although the United Kingdom is a small country, its growing agricultural productivity in the early 1700s supported an increasing population and provided an expanded domestic market that helped spur the Industrial Revolution. Japan, a small country with a relatively large population, went through a similar process. Switzerland has industrialized successfully despite its smallness in size and population. By contrast, Australia and Argentina are both large countries. In the late nineteenth and early twentieth centuries, their populations were expanding. In 1895, the per capita income of Argentina was as high as that of Germany, Holland, and Belgium; Australia's was higher, exceeding that of the United States. Yet neither country industrialized in the nineteenth

century, and neither is among today's major industrial countries.

A rich endowment of natural resources may provide a country with the financial means to import foreign technology and with the high incomes to support a large domestic market for industrial products. But several of the countries that became rich from natural resources were slow to industrialize. In the sixteenth century, Spain was the richest country in Europe, thanks mainly to the mineral resources of South America. But Spain did not initiate the Industrial Revolution, and the great surge in industrialization in eighteenth- and nineteenth-century Europe largely passed it by.

Domestic and foreign trade policies

Many of the countries that industrialized successfully in the nineteenth century first acquired technology through imports, then rapidly moved to producing manufactures for export. Policies that allowed opportunities on foreign markets to be communicated to domestic producers, that allowed domestic resources to move freely in response to the opportunities, and that complemented existing resources through education, training, and infrastructure all contributed to the success.

Unrestricted domestic trade was a precursor of Britain's industrial revolution. Many other European countries and Japan began their industrialization with reforms that liberalized their domestic trade. Foreign trade policies, however, were inconsistent. Episodes of free trade—such as those in the United Kingdom after 1846, in France during the 1860s, in Germany in the 1830s and 1860s, and in the United States during the 1840s and 1850s—were mixed with periods of restrictions on trade. The aims of foreign trade policy varied widely, too. In some cases foreign trade restrictions arose from a desire to protect domestic industry. Examples include British restrictions on machinery exports until 1842 and tariff increases in Germany in the 1840s and in the United States after the Civil War. At other times, import restrictions were prompted by the desire to protect agriculture. This was the motivation behind Britain's Corn Laws, the increases in German and French tariffs in the 1870s, and the Smoot-Hawley tariffs in the United States in 1930. In Germany, France, and the United States, however, the tariffs were also extended to cover manufactured imports. In other cases, import restrictions were adopted with the balance of payments in mind.

It is unclear how these shifts of foreign trade policy—liberal followed by protectionist, and vice versa—shaped industrialization before World War II. Domestic markets were generally competitive, so inefficiencies arising from protectionism may have been reduced, particularly in countries with large internal markets such as Germany and the United States. What is clear is that imports were the main channel of new technology in the initial stages of industrialization in each country except the United Kingdom. Furthermore, exports provided a powerful demand stimulus; the countries whose exports grew rapidly achieved the fastest overall economic growth.

Education, skills formation, and technology adaptation

The transition from a primarily agricultural and trading economy to an industrial economy has required, at least in the initial stages, an increase in the skills of the labor force. To use foreign technology effectively, producers must examine the choices available, make intelligent selections, and adapt them to local conditions (see Box 3.4). All of this calls for education.

More than general education is required, but high achievements at the frontiers of science are not. Science played a minor role in the first industrial revolution in Britain. Scientific excellence played an important role in Germany's rise to industrial prominence in the nineteenth century, but its system of polytechnical institutes, which taught basic industrial skills, probably mattered more. The United States and Japan both rose to world industrial leadership by copying and modifying foreign technologies. (Until the early 1900s the United States trailed behind the United Kingdom, France, and Germany in major scientific discoveries, but not in practical innovations and inventions.)

State support for technical education made significant contributions to French and German industrialization. The United States broadly emulated the German system of technical education. In addition, its government established a system of financial support for research in universities. Private industry also maintained research laboratories that sometimes received public support. Although some of these laboratories conducted original research, one of their main tasks has been to spot innovations elsewhere and provide the expertise that makes rapid imitation possible. Japan has also shown a strong and continuing commitment to education. By 1870 it had achieved a literacy rate that

Box 3.4   Technology acquisition and adaptation: the experiences of Japan and the United States

In a variety of ways the Japanese deliberately adapted Western technology to preserve scarce capital resources and use abundant labor. In textiles, for example, they purchased older, secondhand machines often discarded as obsolete by the Lancashire mills. Once installed, the machines were operated at high speeds and for longer hours than was the prevailing practice in the United Kingdom or the United States. Greater quantities of labor were lavished in servicing the machines and maintaining them in a decent state of repair. When the Japanese eventually reached the point of building their own textile machines, they substituted wood for iron wherever possible. They also introduced cheaper raw materials into production, as in the case of cotton spinning, and added more labor to each spinning machine to handle the increased frequency of broken threads. They also employed ring-spinning technology when virtually every other textile giant, apart from the United States and Brazil, was using mule-spinning machines. When continued improvements in ring-spinning technology and changes in global factor prices made ring spinning the dominant technology in the world, Japan was well positioned to increase its market share (Rosenberg, background paper; Saxonhouse 1985).

It is noteworthy that Japan at first did not understand the need to adapt foreign technology to domestic circumstances. Dutch water control technology, for instance, was introduced without considering that, in addition to tidal forces, mountain runoff was a major source of flooding. Similarly, the Japanese government in 1871 imported a vast mechanized silk-reeling plant from France. Although it was intended as a model factory, private business discovered that it could not profitably operate such capital-intensive plants.

The United States' earlier adaptation of technology in the nineteenth century was very different from that of Japan, but as successful. Endowed with an abundance of natural resources, but with a scarcity of labor, the United States adapted its technology accordingly. Technology imported from Britain was adapted, whenever possible, to the extensive exploitation of natural resources. For example, although the United States had a later industrial start than Britain, it quickly established a worldwide leadership in the design, production, and use of woodworking machinery. It was characteristic of these machines that they were wasteful of wood, which was abundant in the United States.

These examples show that, ultimately, "appropriate" technology is what a country creates for itself, using all the means available to it—including "inappropriate" foreign technology—efficiently.

---

compared favorably with those in Western Europe. Today, industrial research is carried out mostly within private firms, but in the early period of industrialization the government helped to promote technological change, for example by setting up demonstration factories which were later sold to the private sector.

Transportation and communications networks

One of the better known aspects of nineteenth-century industrialization is the importance of railways. Transportation and communications networks integrated and expanded domestic markets and increased their efficiency. They also integrated domestic markets into the global economy, making it easier for exporters to compete. But transportation and communications networks are capital-intensive, and therefore expensive, especially during the early stages of industrialization. Except for Britain, governments of countries industrializing in the nineteenth century helped to finance the construction of transportation and communications networks. In some countries, such as Germany, Italy, and Japan, the financing was often direct. In others, it was indirect—for instance, land grants (as in the United States) and guarantees of debt issues of private companies (as in France).

Stable institutional and macroeconomic environment

Laws and institutions that allow markets to function efficiently—property rights, standardized weights and measures, patent laws and so forth—have helped to promote rapid and efficient industrialization. Laws and institutions should provide a stable environment that promotes long-term investments and risk taking. Yet they should also be flexible enough to allow institutional innovations. For example, faced with the problem of financing the capital-intensive railway system in the early 1800s, Britain lifted its earlier prohibition on the formation of joint-stock companies. Late industrializing countries in Europe, particularly Germany, pioneered such innovations as the joint-stock bank and the investment bank in the second half of the 1800s, and the United States devised the modern corporation in the 1920s. Such flexibility greatly

assisted industrialization.

Industrialization requires large investments in machines and infrastructure, especially in its early stages. Moreover, one of the most important means by which technological innovations have been incorporated in production has been investment in new machines. Macroeconomic policies in the countries industrializing in the nineteenth century encouraged domestic savings and thus provided the funds required for investment. They also made foreigners, especially the British and the French, willing to provide loans and direct investments.

Conclusion

Initial conditions of size, population, and natural resources may influence the timing and pattern of early industrialization, but further progress along the path is greatly influenced by government policy. Provision of infrastructure and education has been important. A stable institutional and macroeconomic environment and domestic and foreign trade policies which allowed producers and factors of production to respond to incentives have been crucial. Much has changed since World War II, but the essence of industrialization is as it was before: the interaction of technological change, specialization, and trade. Some of the policies that proved successful in the years before World War II may not be applicable today. But the key to success is still to choose policies that allow economies to utilize this interaction fully to their advantage. The chapters that follow discuss what this means for today's developing countries.

The role of government

This is the first of four chapters that deal with government policies for industrialization. It considers the conditions under which governments are likely to make their best contribution to industrialization in a market-oriented economy and gives particular emphasis to the services that governments provide *directly*. By way of introduction to the subsequent three chapters, this chapter also takes a preliminary look at government's *indirect* role of intervening to influence the way markets work. Chapter 5 then examines the crucial relationship between trade policies and industrialization; Chapter 6 draws lessons from different countries' experience with trade policy reform; and Chapter 7 analyzes the impact of complementary policies, including financial, labor, regulatory, and technology policies.

Governments and industrialization

Government pervades modern society, and industrialization has to be reconciled with other public objectives—economic, political, social, and cultural. The presence of government varies greatly across countries according to ideology, political structures, administrative capacity, and the level of development. This chapter considers some of the broad principles that govern policy choices for industrialization, but does not aim to judge specific country policies.

Governments have a central role—impinging on, but separate from, their role in industrialization—of providing for a desirable distribution of income and the alleviation of poverty, ill health, and illiteracy. By providing a safety net, governments can fulfill their humanitarian duties and at the same time reinforce a social consensus in favor of economic growth (see Box 4.1 on industrialization and poverty).

Governments have always been central to the industrialization process, whether as economic ringmaster in the laissez-faire Britain of the past century or as central planner and provider in today's Soviet Union. Most developing countries, like the industrial market economies before them, have also relied extensively on the private sector and on markets in their effort to industrialize.

In a market-based system public and private sectors have complementary roles. These roles must be seen in the context of the growing complexity of industrializing economies. While the invisible hand of the market is adept at dealing with this complexity, the visible hand of government needs to provide the rules of the game for markets to work. But even with these rules there are limitations on markets and limitations on governments, the one requiring greater intervention, the other reducing the scope for effective intervention.

In a traditional, preindustrial economy production techniques are primitive, there is relatively little division of labor, markets tend to be local, productive units are small and family-based, and transactions are simple. Industrialization brings greater division of labor and new technology. A cobbler making shoes needs leather, thread, and a few simple tools. A modern shoe factory divides production into many discrete steps. It uses sophisticated machinery, hundreds of material inputs and supplies, financial and commercial services, and many different skills.

Specialization also leads to far more complicated transactions. Separate markets emerge for compo-

Box 4.1 Industrialization and poverty

A fundamental goal of economic development is to improve the welfare of the poor. The evidence suggests that in the long term, in most cases, the benefits of economic growth are dispersed throughout society and reach its poorest members. Yet there is also evidence that the *distribution* of income can worsen during the first decades of development, even if the absolute income of the poorest grows.

Governments seek to raise the incomes of the poorest in several ways, including fiscal redistribution (direct subsidies, for instance), institutional change (land reform, for instance), and policies to affect the structure of the economy. Policies that directly attack poverty or its causes are generally preferable to more indirect approaches which undermine the way markets work.

It is not clear that policies directed at industry can be any better oriented to the alleviation of poverty than policies directed at other sectors. The poorest sections of the population (often landless laborers or small farmers) tend to live in the rural areas, and industry's potential for alleviating poverty is probably a good deal less than agriculture's. Land reform and pricing reforms for farm output can have significant effects on the rural poor.

Nonetheless, many governments have sought to use industry as an instrument of redistribution in the short term. In practice their initiatives have done little for poverty and little for industry. For instance, price controls on such essentials as bread, sugar, and cooking oil subsidize the consumption of rich and poor alike (see Chapter 7). Price controls hardly encourage production sufficient to cover demand, and the informal rationing that ensues may well favor those with more political weight. Legislation that raises the level of wages above the marginal product of labor can have similar perverse effects. In the formal industrial sector it discourages hiring, and those who benefit do so at the expense of the urban poor who do not have factory jobs.

But other aspects of an industrialization strategy may help in the battle against poverty more than is generally realized. First, part of the government's direct—and most useful—role in industrialization is to provide basic education, physical infrastructure, and a set of secure economic rights (to allow, for example, small business to operate legitimately). When governments are effective in this role, they enable the poor to partici-

pate in the more productive activities of the modern sector.

Second, economic reforms (discussed in Chapters 6 and 7) also promise to draw the poor into the development process: they open up employment opportunities in the modern sector by reducing the degree of monopoly in the economy and encouraging the use of labor relative to capital. The demand for labor is likely to be stimulated by the relaxation of controls in the capital market, the removal of minimum wage legislation, and—for economies with abundant labor—a reduction in the protection of capital-intensive activities.

Such improvements for the poor would not be instantaneous. Meanwhile, the transition to a more market-oriented economy might aggravate the situation of some of the poor in the shorter term. In economies with large budget and balance of payments deficits and high inflation, a necessary initial stage of economic reform might involve cuts in government expenditure and employment that hurt the poor directly. At the same time, economic reforms that reduce government intervention in factor and goods markets can be expected to stimulate economic activity. But the net effect could be to make some of the poor (particularly those in towns) worse off in the short term, for example by creating regional pockets of unemployment or through the effect of a devaluation on food prices. The hitherto protected manufacturing sector might bear the brunt of this impact. There is, in fact, surprisingly little evidence that trade liberalization has adversely affected employment even in the short term (see Chapter 6). Of course, some countries—Israel and the Republic of Korea, for example—have liberalized slowly with this very worry in mind.

Economic reform undoubtedly benefits the poor in the long term. It will sometimes hurt them in the short term. Just how large a problem this poses is not yet clear, but governments will need to pay attention to the short-term effects of economic reform, both on humanitarian grounds and to gain broad acceptance for these reforms. Experience suggests that the alleviation of poverty in the short term is best tackled directly through well-targeted programs to provide social services or direct compensation in cash or kind to the poorest, rather than indirectly through interventions in factor or goods markets.

nents, supplies, machinery, differentiated labor skills, and so on. Transactions in these changing markets can be costly. When there is a delay between sale and payment, for instance, contracts have to be drawn up and honored. All this involves commercial risk. If these transactions costs

are too high, they will slow the process of specialization.

Two polar forms of economic organization have emerged to deal with the problem of high transactions costs. Centrally planned economies try to maximize information flows and minimize contractual problems with central ownership and allocation of resources (Box 3.1 in Chapter 3). At the other extreme is the decentralized economy of Hong Kong or nineteenth-century Britain, in which resources are privately owned, a multitude of separate but interconnected markets conveys information and allocates resources, and the government enforces the laws that regulate these markets. In between these poles lie the industrial and developing market economies of the world, which display a variety of forms of economic organization and public and private ownership. All of them try to influence the way markets work, and all at least partially override markets by allocating resources from the center.

The development needs of poor societies are so urgent that tremendous pressures are placed on their governments to stimulate industrialization. Yet the human and physical resources available to developing country governments are so limited that they have great difficulty in attaining their many economic objectives, including physical infrastructure, agricultural development, health, education, or the alleviation of poverty. The governments therefore have to be careful in choosing their priorities for industry. This chapter suggests that the case for government involvement in the industrialization process can be better made in some areas than others.

• There are some economic services that only governments can provide, including certain central economic functions—legal, monetary, and fiscal—and a welfare net for the poor. Particularly vital to modern industrial economies, with their multitude of complex transactions, is an efficient legal and institutional system, which clearly sets out the rules of property and commerce and the respective roles of the public and private sectors.

• Governments have played a major role in providing important parts of the economic infrastructure—transport networks, health and education services, and so forth—on which progress in the rest of the economy so heavily depends. But how this should be done and the point at which the role of government ends and that of the private sector begins will differ from country to country.

• Governments often intervene in markets to improve economic performance, to limit abuses (such as fraud, pollution, and endangerment of health), or to promote the welfare of the poor. But it is here that the government's precise role is most difficult to identify.

Experience suggests that the governments of market economies which have efficiently industrialized have by and large observed the hierarchy of priorities described above. They have established clear rules of the game, contributed judiciously to the construction of an industrial infrastructure, and otherwise intervened sparingly and carefully. Some developing countries, however, have undermined their industrialization efforts by approaching these choices in reverse. In the more extreme cases, public intervention in markets has been heavy, but fragmented and in pursuit of conflicting objectives. The rules of the game have been uncertain. These characteristics—together, in many cases, with an inadequate infrastructure—have resulted in poorly chosen industrial investments, high costs of doing business, and the devotion of substantial private resources to getting around the rules or obtaining special economic privileges.

The next part of this chapter discusses the *direct* role that governments have traditionally played in market-oriented economies, including the provision of economic rules and industrial infrastructure. An analysis then follows of some of the issues that arise in government's *indirect* role of seeking to improve on the working of the market. The discussion focuses, in particular, on the promotion of infant industries. The final part of the chapter examines the costs of doing business that can arise when governments intervene ineffectively in markets.

The direct role of government: public goods and public services

All governments take responsibility for producing a range of goods and services—called public goods—that only they are in a position to supply adequately. These include national defense and internal security, money, and the provision of a legal system. Among the most important public goods is a legal and institutional system which reduces the costs and risks of transactions. Certain other goods and services—for instance, transport, power, education and training, and research—provide a foundation which enables the rest of the economy to work more smoothly. These services of the economic or industrial infrastructure often require the efficient management of large investments, which is difficult to achieve in many developing countries. As a result, costs are higher and markets fail to work as well as they should. The direct presence of government in these areas has been very important to industrialization, although the private sector has also had a significant role in most countries.

The economic rules of the game—"property rights" in the shorthand of economics—provide for the ownership and transfer of factors of production and goods. Every type of economy—market oriented or centrally planned, advanced or developing—can be defined by its economic rules. The question is whether any given set is efficient. In particular, does it provide a climate of stable expectations? Knowing clearly who owns what and how goods and services can be used, bought, and sold reduces uncertainty and provides the basis for the specialization and investment essential to industrialization. Defining a suitable set of rights gives rise to technical problems—how to cope with rights to clean air, with common property that is becoming overexploited (desertification in the Sahel, for instance), with intellectual property such as computer software, with new problems such as theft of computer data, and so on. But the most pressing issue in many developing countries is that, whether these countries embrace the market economy or not, the economic rules may be unclear and the rights that go with them insecure.

ECONOMIC RULES IN MARKET ECONOMIES. In the industrial market economies the economic rules of the game have evolved as a system of laws in which private ownership and freedom to dispose of property are guaranteed, there is some guarantee against arbitrary seizure or punitive taxation by the state, the limits to public ownership are well defined, and private individuals are allowed to associate freely and make contracts which can be upheld in law (see Box 4.2).

Governments need to raise revenues and regulate the economy for a variety of reasons, and they invariably have to make compromises between an ideal set of economic rules for a market economy and their other objectives. For instance, the greater the level of taxation, the more it reduces the real value of assets. The same is true of inflation, which imprudent government policies can provoke. Priv-

---

Box 4.2 The historical evolution of economic rights in England and Spain

Starting in the late Middle Ages, in a number of European countries, commercial interests grew more powerful and sought to force the state to cede to them greater commercial freedom in return for the increasing demands that the state was making on them. Where these commercial interests were successful, the results were momentous. Economic and political decentralization weakened governments' arbitrary powers of confiscation and prompted the evolution of the economic laws and rights that characterize most of today's industrial market economies. The history of these developments from late medieval times in England and Spain is instructive.

The development of expensive new military hardware—the longbow, the crossbow, and gunpowder—meant that medieval rulers needed additional revenue. One way to raise funds was to create representative bodies which could exchange revenue for economic rights. The segment of society capable of supplying this finance was the emerging class of landed gentry and merchants.

For a time the English Crown used its royal prerogative to satisfy the interests of this class and its own financial needs through the sale of offices and the creation of monopoly rights. But the increasing reliance of the English kings on this form of finance pitted them against the landed gentry and merchants who demanded greater commercial freedom in return. The merchants increasingly expressed their power through the parliament. After a long struggle the parliament finally achieved victory over the king in the late seventeenth century. From then on, economic rights became more secure, and capital markets developed rapidly. The subsequent Industrial Revolution reflected these changed institutional conditions. Individuals were free to form enterprises with few political restrictions, enterprises were authorized to acquire and sell goods and switch activities freely, and—although subject to taxation—these enterprises became largely immune from arbitrary seizure.

In Spain, however, the Castilian kings were able to resist demands—expressed through the Cortes—for a better deal for commerce. This was partly because the kings continued to benefit from the riches offered by their colonies in the New World. In turn, the demands of this large overseas empire led to the development of a vast, centralized bureaucracy to administer it.

According to one authority (North 1986), these two different paths of historical development go far to explain the evolution of a set of economic rights compatible with efficient markets in British-colonized North America and Spain's legacy to Latin America of a tradition of bureaucratic centralization. This happened in spite of the similarities of many of the written constitutions in the northern and southern parts of the New World.

ileges granted to certain economic agents—monopolies or subsidies, for instance—reduce the incomes of others. Regulation to protect welfare—to ensure standards of safety and health or to protect minors, for instance—affects private rights. Sudden changes in policy reduce business confidence.

Certain institutional arrangements have helped to shape the system of economic rights that fostered industrialization in the industrial market economies. Legal forms of incorporation promoted the separation of ownership and management of firms. Limited liability and bankruptcy laws—which allow a firm's equity holders to limit their losses to the capital they have subscribed and to spread the remaining losses among the firm's creditors—have helped to spread commercial risk and transfer the assets of failed companies to those who can make better use of them. Various regulatory institutions, public and private alike, have evolved to oversee the functioning of financial markets, partly as a means of preventing abuse. The rules of the game and conventions in business behavior have developed in mutually reinforcing ways: the greater the level of trust in the business community, the more likely it is that contracts will be honored.

ECONOMIC RULES IN DEVELOPING COUNTRIES. Many developing countries have inherited or adapted their legal systems from the Western tradition. This has sometimes meant laws that cannot deal adequately with developing countries' problems. In some countries legal provisions for compensation have taken too little account of inflation. In most developing countries product liability law is weak (particularly in view of the import of hazardous foods, drugs, or pesticides from industrial countries that ban these products at home). In China, in recent years, the government has been seeking to decentralize microeconomic decisions to the individual enterprise. It has, for instance, been seeking ways to modify contract and bankruptcy laws.

For many developing countries the biggest problem is that the nominal rules of the game do not correspond to the real rules, which are unclear and unstable. In the Philippines, for instance, ad hoc decrees in the 1970s—sometimes unpublished—granted favors to certain firms, often at the expense of their domestic competitors. The government granted an import monopoly on black-and-white televisions and a monopoly to produce newsprint. In Brazil, for many years after World War II, a law put a nominal 10 percent ceiling on the rate of return on historic book value for private power utilities. High inflation made this rule useless, so the government permitted the utilities to get around it with various ad hoc regulations which established, for example, surcharges or preferential exchange rates. In the meantime, the ceiling on profits created great uncertainty, which led to a deterioration in the service and encouraged businesses to install their own generating equipment.

The perceived insecurity of economic rights in developing countries has been revealed in several surveys of foreign investors. (In all probability, most of their fears are shared by domestic investors.) According to the surveys, this insecurity derives from the following: internal political pressures (to control prices, for instance); the problems of dealing with the bureaucracy (slow and arbitrary decisionmaking, especially at the base of the bureaucratic hierarchy, and lengthy regulatory procedures); corruption; the risk of expropriation; uncertainty over whether legal and contractual rights would be upheld by the courts; uncertainty about changes in legislation, especially on tax rates; and excessive legalism (a barrage of unclear laws, often flexibly interpreted by governments).

Information and welfare

All governments take steps to increase the information available to producers and to protect consumer welfare. Governments have a comparative advantage in collecting and disseminating certain kinds of information, especially in developing countries, where information is scarce and education often poor. All governments provide basic statistical and other information on their own activities and on the economy in general. Some go further and provide information about likely future developments in domestic or foreign economies. This kind of forecasting can be risky. In some cases, however—notably in Japan and the Republic of Korea—governments have played a useful role as a clearinghouse for information and forecasts on domestic and foreign markets and technologies.

Governments regulate to protect welfare by checking weights and measures, by establishing health standards for foods and drugs and clean water, by requiring product safety standards and product guarantees, and by imposing safety standards in the workplace. Similarly, governments regulate financial markets to prevent abuses such as insider trading, to require companies to disclose more information, and to require financial institutions to insure their smaller depositors.

In all this, regulation is a two-edged sword—even in areas in which the government's role is indisputable, such as welfare protection. Legislation can create barriers to entry, limit consumer choice, and add to production costs. For instance, the licensing procedures for new drugs in industrial economies are a tradeoff between increased safety and the expense and delay to be faced by companies bringing new drugs to the market.

Education

Education spurs the process of industrialization by imparting skills, improving health, and allowing more women to enter the labor force. Education, investment in technological knowledge, and physical investment go hand in hand. Countries that neglect any one of these forms of investment may not be efficient in industrializing. China, Hong Kong, Israel, Japan, Korea, and Singapore have all achieved fast economic growth. All adopted a balanced investment strategy that included education along with increased physical capital and technology transfer. All had achieved universal or almost universal enrollment at the primary school level by 1965. The most successful also achieved high percentages enrolled in secondary schools and near-universal literacy of their labor force—usually just before the economy embarked on rapid and sustained industrial growth. (Figure 4.1 shows a considerably higher level of educational attainment in Korea's labor force than in Sub-Saharan Africa's, with Indonesia's in between.)

Returns to investment have generally been higher in education than in physical assets. Economic rates of return to primary education in developing countries have averaged 26 percent, compared with estimated returns on physical capital of 13 percent. This suggests that lack of education is a greater obstacle to industrialization and development than lack of physical assets.

Economic returns are higher at the lower and more general levels of education (see Table 4.1). General education is profitable because it teaches the skills of basic literacy and numeracy, the ability to think adaptively, and the importance of time-based discipline. Modern industry has little use for illiterates. Some developing country governments have tended to expand higher-level vocational training too fast.

Education can be produced in small units, can be easily charged for, and can be provided privately.

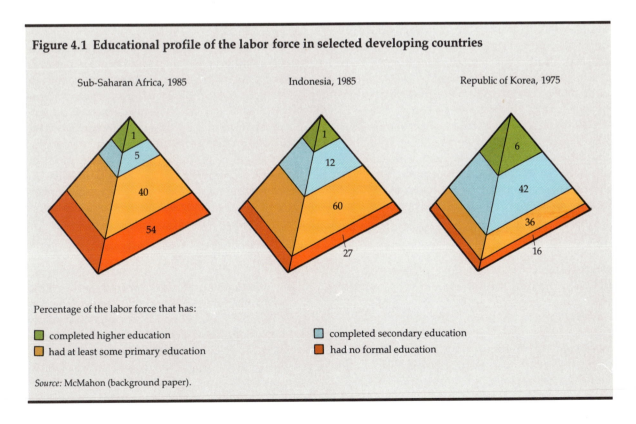

Figure 4.1 Educational profile of the labor force in selected developing countries

Sub-Saharan Africa, 1985

Indonesia, 1985

Republic of Korea, 1975

Percentage of the labor force that has:

- completed higher education
- completed secondary education
- had at least some primary education
- had no formal education

Source: McMahon (background paper).

Table 4.1 Economic rates of return in education
(percent)

Country group	Level of education		
	Primary	*Secondary*	*Higher*
Industrial market economies (ten countries)	15[a]	11	11
Developing country exporters of manufactures[b]	15	13	9
Other developing countries (twenty-six countries)	28	17	14

Note: The economic rates of return (referred to as social rates of return in the literature on the economics of education) on which these averages are based are from studies which for the most part refer to the 1970s and early 1980s. For comparison, economic rates of return to investment in physical capital averaged 13 percent for developing countries and 11 percent for industrial market economies.
a. The lack of a control group of illiterates in the industrial market economies prevents a direct computation; the estimate is based on the return for developing country exporters of manufactures.
b. India, Israel, Singapore, and Yugoslavia.
Source: McMahon (background paper).

Yet the case for a large public effort is strong. The need for national educational standards and for civic responsibility implies elements of a public good. A basic primary and secondary education for those unable to pay for it is both an economic investment and a means of income redistribution.

For vocational and higher education the arguments are different. The more specialized the education or training, the more its beneficiaries will be able to appropriate the return—and the more willing they will be to invest in their own education. Firms will provide training if they can reap the rewards. Individuals will invest in their own education if they can profit from the skills they acquire. (Apprenticeship is one such form of private investment.) Governments could therefore achieve greater cost recovery from students in higher education—or, in poorer developing countries, from students in the higher levels of secondary education. There may be scope, too, for greater decentralization of higher education in order to make it more responsive to market signals.

Technology

Much of the unprecedentedly rapid development of large parts of the world economy in recent decades is due to advances in technology (Chapter 3). These advances can be reproduced for a fraction of the cost borne by the industrial countries that devise them. This explains the emphasis placed on technology in the industrialization process. Often technological knowledge is a commodity that can be traded like many others, but it has some pecu-

liarities which sometimes make trade difficult. These are frequently used to justify public intervention.

Producers of technology often face high risks, since the outcome of innovation is uncertain and technologies can sometimes be easily copied. Purchasers of technology also face risks, because they often cannot know just what they have bought until they have acquired and used it. Technologies often require substantial adaptation to local circumstances; those that come in the form of machines or blueprints require a substantial complementary input of human capital. Although the process of international technology acquisition is complex, the problems are no different from those faced by firms in the normal competitive process in advanced countries. And for the same reasons it is difficult to define the best role for government in developing countries.

In some respects technological knowledge is akin to a public good. Technological knowledge is already produced as a freely available good by universities, publicly subsidized laboratories, or private foundations. This tends to be in areas of purer (less applied, less product- and firm-specific) research, which the more advanced countries are likely to dominate and from which less advanced countries can (eventually) benefit without having to pay the full costs of the research.

The public goods argument can apply to developing countries, particularly the more advanced among them, and thus justify university research, higher education, research and development institutes (such as the Korean Institute of Science and Technology), technological information services (as in Brazil), or even collective research projects (as in Japan). But it may be more advantageous to focus the public sector resources of developing countries on health or agriculture rather than on industry, where the developing countries are clearly technology followers. Thus government regulation of private technology transactions is likely to prove more effective (see Chapter 7).

Transport, communications, and energy

Early in the industrialization process there is rapid growth in the transport and power-generation sectors. In 1980, Rwanda had a per capita income of $223; its transport and communications sectors accounted for 2.2 percent of GDP; gas, electricity, and water had a share of 0.1 percent of GDP. In Malaysia, with a per capita income of $1,787, those sectors had considerably larger shares—5.3 and 1.8

percent, respectively (see Figure 4.2). Once countries are more fully industrialized—at income levels of around $4,000–6,000—these GDP shares start

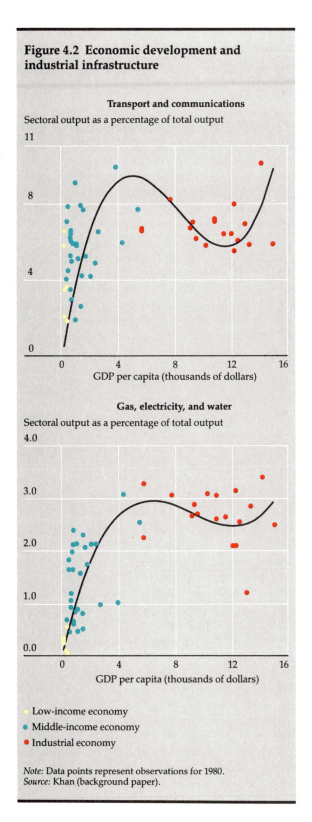

Figure 4.2 Economic development and industrial infrastructure

Transport and communications

Sectoral output as a percentage of total output

GDP per capita (thousands of dollars)

Gas, electricity, and water

Sectoral output as a percentage of total output

GDP per capita (thousands of dollars)

- Low-income economy
- Middle-income economy
- Industrial economy

Note: Data points represent observations for 1980.
Source: Khan (background paper).

to decline. Note that there is also some support for the notion that the share of physical infrastructure in GDP may begin to rise again once per capita GDP is around $12,000. This is reflected in the relationship shown in Figure 4.2. In transport and communications, for instance, this may be explained by rapid growth in telecommunications services in high-income societies.

These sectors provide important services to other parts of the economy as well as to consumers. The phase of rapid growth in transport and communications partly reflects the growth of transactions as more and more firms sell to one another and to households and as interregional trade grows. The increasing demand for power is largely explained by the introduction of mechanized techniques throughout the economy, especially in industry. Both sectors require large investments which, once made, can dramatically reduce costs or open up economic opportunities. In Korea and Yugoslavia, for instance, public decisions to extend the road network led to an increase in traffic, which in turn laid the basis for government decisions to encourage the domestic production of automobiles.

It is difficult to judge whether today's developing countries have invested enough in these infrastructure systems. There is plenty of evidence of unsatisfied demand (at prevailing prices) for power and telecommunications services, as well as of congestion in much of the transport system. In Kenya, for instance, some 55 percent of local phone calls and 87 percent of long-distance calls cannot be completed because of the heavy traffic. Overloaded and undermaintained electricity systems lead to frequent power cuts and encourage many firms to invest in their own power plants. One study estimated the costs of power shortages in India in the mid-1970s to have averaged 2 percent of GDP—most of this representing lost output in the industrial sector.

If such services—now often subsidized—were priced nearer to their costs, their quantity and reliability would be more in line with demand. But the apparently high economic rates of return for infrastructure projects suggest that for many countries the present supply of infrastructural services is still a bottleneck to development. Certainly, infrastructure investment was a priority for the more successful developing economies, whether the burden was on the public sector (as in Korea and Singapore, for instance) or on the private sector (as in Hong Kong).

Government involvement in the provision of

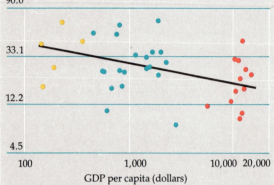

Figure 4.3 Economic development and government expenditure on transport and communications

Ratio of government expenditure to sectoral output (percent)

GDP per capita (dollars)

○ Low-income economy

● Middle-income economy

● Industrial economy

Note: Both axes are in log scale. Data points represent observations for 1982 or the most recent year available. Government expenditure generally includes all transfers to public corporations but excludes the expenditures of the public corporations themselves.
Source: Khan (background paper).

transport, communications, and power occurs for several reasons. There is a public goods argument in cases where user fees are difficult to collect, although governments can sometimes levy indirect user charges—they might finance roads, for example, with gasoline taxes and license fees. Larger projects—telecommunications, railways, and electricity and gas production, for instance—may involve economies of scale. In other words, a single investment—private or public—might be more efficient than a number of competing investments. The preference in most countries for public enterprise may reflect a belief that control is better exercised through ownership than through regulation. For large projects, underdeveloped financial markets or political risks might also deter private investments.

Unlike power, transport services tend to be left more and more to the private sector as development proceeds (see Figure 4.3). This suggests that the scope for competition in some public services may be underestimated. For instance, thanks to

technical progress the market for telecommunications equipment has been liberalized in many industrial countries. In the United Kingdom and the United States a limited amount of competition has even been introduced in the telecommunications network. In some countries cooperatives supply telecommunications services (as in Bolivia, for instance) or electricity. In other countries some public services are subcontracted to the private sector (the telephone system in Botswana, for instance, and road maintenance in Brazil and Costa Rica).

In cases of monopoly, a public authority usually fixes prices, whether the utility is publicly or privately owned. These prices are often set too low, usually for social reasons. The result is that demand at the prevailing price outstrips supply, and the utilities are unable to cover their costs. Experience firmly suggests that the pricing of outputs at their long-run marginal cost (that is, the investment, maintenance, and operational costs of producing an additional unit of output) is the best way to match supply and demand, recover costs, and ensure adequate investment. Often this is easier said than done. Prices may need to be adjusted to account for specific social, fiscal, or financial objectives. Where the level of investment is still inadequate, prices may need to be adjusted to clear the market. Moreover, it is sometimes difficult to measure long-run marginal costs or to meter the use of the services. But analytical techniques to overcome these problems have improved greatly.

State-owned enterprises

State-owned enterprises (SOEs) were extensively discussed in *World Development Report 1983*. Virtually all governments provide at least some commercial goods and services, notably power and telecommunications, through SOEs. SOEs are important producers of a broad range of industrial products such as steel, fertilizers, automobiles, and petrochemicals (see Figure 4.4). Governments have created them for a variety of reasons: to spearhead industrialization in countries with virtually no large-scale industry; to promote industries deemed to be of strategic importance; to save threatened jobs; to reduce the presence, or prevent the entry, of foreign-owned firms; and so on.

The performance of SOEs varies widely within and between countries, but their record has frequently been poor, particularly in developing countries. They have clearly failed to play the strategic role in industrialization that governments had hoped for. Financial rates of return have gen-

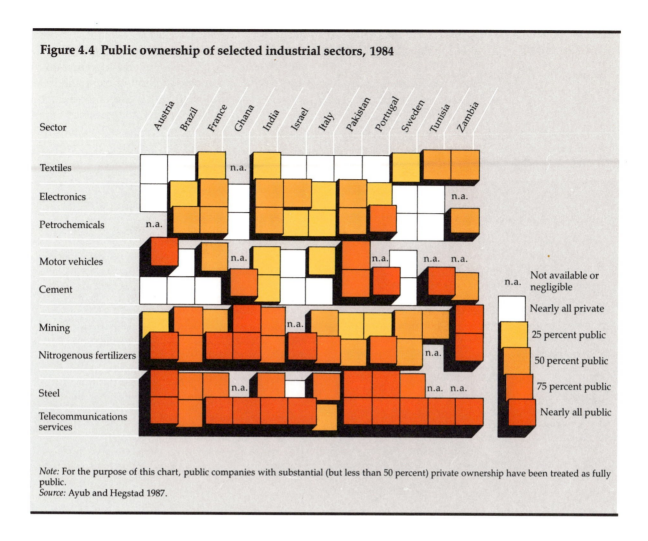

Figure 4.4 Public ownership of selected industrial sectors, 1984

Note: For the purpose of this chart, public companies with substantial (but less than 50 percent) private ownership have been treated as fully public.

Source: Ayub and Hegstad 1987.

erally been lower for SOEs than for the private sector, as recent comparative studies for Brazil, India, and Israel have indicated. Financial profitability has often been compromised by price controls, but the indications are that SOEs have also had a generally poor record of social profitability. They have often put large burdens on public budgets and the external debt. For example, the net deficit of a sample of SOEs accounted for about 4 percent of Niger's GDP in 1982. For the seven largest Latin American economies, the combined deficit of SOEs rose from about 1 percent of GNP in the mid-1970s to about 4 percent in 1980–82. One study has found that countries in which SOEs accounted for higher shares of gross domestic investment generally had lower rates of economic growth.

SOEs perform poorly partly because of the incentives faced by their managements and partly because of the control exercised by governments.

SOEs frequently operate without competition, as a result of protection or barriers to entry. Governments often place little emphasis on efficiency and profitability and are rarely prepared to use the sanction of liquidation. Other objectives set for SOEs—in particular, employment maintenance or price controls on essential goods—weaken any emphasis on profitability. At the same time, SOEs may develop their own momentum and objectives, which often diverge from the public interest. Paradoxically, their public status often gives them greater independence from government control than equivalent private firms.

SOEs have generally improved their performance when competition has been greater, when managers have had more financial autonomy, when poor performers have been removed and good ones have been rewarded, and when government interference with the day-to-day operations has been reduced. Some governments have pursued more radical solutions to the problem of SOEs: liquidation or privatization (see Box 4.3).

The indirect role of government: intervening in markets

Among some 130 developing economies, a broad variety of approaches to industrialization can be observed. These approaches are examined in detail later: trade policies in Chapter 5 and complementary policies in Chapter 7. If a generalization can be made, it is that most developing economies rely extensively on private ownership and markets, but temper this with substantial interventions to influence the way markets work and with at least some

---

Box 4.3 State-owned enterprises and divestiture

Governments in industrial and developing countries alike are divesting their ownership of state-owned enterprises (SOEs) in an effort to improve efficiency and competition. They are doing this in three ways:
- *Liquidation*, which can be either formal or informal. Formal liquidation involves the closure of an enterprise and the sale of its assets. Under informal liquidation, a firm retains its legal status even though some or all of its operations may be suspended.
- *Privatization of ownership* through the sale of assets to the private sector.
- *Privatization of management*, using leases and management contracts. The disposal of inefficient SOEs permits the government to shed an economic and financial burden. Governments hope that it will lead to innovative management. But divestiture also serves other objectives. For example, privatization can increase popular ownership of productive assets. This was an important consideration in the sale of British Telecom and in recent efforts at privatization by Brazil and Chile. In addition, divestiture raises revenues for governments.

Among industrial countries, the United Kingdom has been particularly active in divesting publicly owned manufacturing and service enterprises. Majority control of British Telecom and British Gas was turned over to private shareholders in two of the largest share offerings in history. Among developing countries, Bangladesh, Chile, Kenya, Malaysia, Mexico, the Philippines, Thailand, Togo, and Turkey have shown particular interest in divestiture. But substantial privatization has occurred in only a few countries (Bangladesh and Chile among them) and has mostly involved small manufacturing and service firms that had once been privately owned. Privatization of management has been used less frequently as a form of divestiture. Formal liquidations are rare except in Africa, but informal liquidations are common.

Governments confront several obstacles when they decide to divest SOEs. For example:
- Governments usually want to sell the least profitable enterprises, those that the private sector is least willing to buy at a price acceptable to the government.
- Divestiture tends to arouse political opposition: from employees who may lose their jobs; from politicians who fear the short-term unemployment consequences of liquidation or of cost reductions by private owners; from bureaucrats who stand to lose patronage; and from those sections of the public that fear that national assets are being cornered by foreigners, the rich, or a particular ethnic group.
- Relatively undeveloped capital markets sometimes make it difficult for governments to float shares and for individual buyers to finance large purchases.

The experience of developing countries also highlights some important policy issues. Privatization is meant to introduce a greater emphasis on profitability. Whether or not this leads to greater efficiency depends on the policy framework and, in particular, on the extent to which product markets are subject to competitive forces. Often competition is more important than ownership in inducing efficiency. Thus governments should place priority on lowering entry and exit barriers and removing import barriers that restrict trade. Even where markets are competitive and there is no significant market failure, the efficiency gains from transferring ownership to the private sector can be substantial. For natural monopolies, however, there is a need for a regulatory watchdog irrespective of whether the firm is in private or public hands, and strong measures are needed to deter anticompetitive behavior.

In addition, managing divestiture is a complex task, and a well-prepared strategy is important. The government needs to consider removing price controls and implicit subsidies and amending its pay and employment policies. Some firms can then be divested immediately, so that the search for investors can begin. Inefficient enterprises that are potentially profitable may require physical and financial restructuring before their divestiture. Nonviable enterprises will have to be liquidated; for this to happen, assets must be valued and arrangements made for sale.

Although divestiture of state-owned enterprises is a relatively new and untested instrument, it is a promising avenue for improving the efficiency and dynamism of the industrial sector. It is important to stress, however, that the gains from privatization will be greater if the trade and domestic policy environment encourages competitive markets.

---

measures for the central allocation of resources.

Such interventions can address a number of shortcomings in markets. The smaller the degree of competition, the more limited the information available to buyers and sellers, and the greater the uncertainty in general business conditions, the less effective markets will be. Markets fail to allocate resources efficiently—that is, in a way that equates social marginal costs with social marginal benefits—in two main ways:

• *Monopolized markets.* A single seller (monopoly), or a small number of them (oligopoly), can restrict output and raise prices in the absence of competition. Monopoly, however, is sometimes the most efficient way to allocate resources. Electric power and telecommunications networks, which benefit from economies of scale up to very high levels of output, are often taken to be natural monopolies of this kind. Governments may need to regulate prices in monopolized markets or devise policies to encourage new entrants (see Chapter 7).

• *Externalities.* Externalities occur when economic activities have spillover effects. For example, a polluting factory inflicts a negative externality on those who live downwind. In contrast, a firm which invests in acquiring technical knowledge produces a positive externality when this knowledge passes outside the firm. In both cases, private costs and benefits are different from social costs and benefits. The problem of externalities lies at the core of arguments over policies regarding infant industries, foreign investment, and transfer of technology.

Even if markets allocate resources efficiently, they may still fail to produce a desirable distribution of income.

Designed to compensate for some of these market failures, industrial intervention in developing countries has often been heavy. Many different instruments have been employed, often simultaneously, including tariff and nontariff protection, fiscal incentives, and direct controls on credit allocation, interest rates, and foreign and domestic investment. The nonprice instruments among these policies—nontariff barriers, for instance—have been popular, despite their recognized economic disadvantages, because of the prospects they offer of more immediate public control over the allocation of resources. The typical pattern of intervention has had two other characteristics. First, the level of incentives provided has been high for many activities (see Chapter 5). Second, the objectives pursued have often conflicted (for

instance, price controls imposed on welfare grounds can affect profitability and hence discourage investment).

Intervention along these lines can create distortions elsewhere in the economy, and governments seek to correct these, in turn, through further interventions (see Chapter 7). For instance, import protection can create domestic monopolies; domestic monopolies may be regulated through price controls; price controls may reduce levels of investment; and so on.

The infant industry argument

The most durable argument for intervention is based on the infant industry. This is the main rationale for the discriminatory structure of protection found in most developing countries (see Chapter 5), for policies to acquire foreign technology, and for policies toward foreign investment (see Chapter 7). Although it is plausible to give new industries a "breathing space" through protection, such an argument would apply to most new activities in developing countries. Whatever the merits of this approach in specific cases, many developing countries have offered widespread import protection in the name of support for infant industries in ways likely to frustrate the objectives of the policy.

The governments of many developing countries argue that private investors will not undertake socially desirable investments which take time to come on stream or require a long learning process. The problem of how to finance a project in its initial, loss-making stage—often where a learning process is involved—is a common one. This may indeed be a problem if capital markets do not exist or do not work properly, as is frequently the case in developing countries (although the failure of the capital market to finance a risky project might equally well reflect investors' good judgment).

A different argument is made for cases where entrepreneurs fail to invest in projects that generate benefits for the rest of the economy because the investor would not be able to capture the benefits. One example of this would be investment in technical skills, embodied in individual workers who could then take their skills to a new employer. There would be no market failure if the firm were able to charge the workers for their training, but if this is prevented by laws, trade unions, or social convention, the private value to firms of investment in training will be less than the social value, and there will be underinvestment.

Cases of successful infant industry protection are difficult to prove or disprove. One study (Krueger and Tuncer 1982a) found little support for the notion that infant industry protection had been effective in Turkey: total factor productivity growth was lower in the most protected industries. Japan and some of the newly industrializing countries are often cited in support of infant industry protection. According to a popular view, the Japanese government successfully promoted steel, cars, and cooperative efforts in basic research—especially in electronics (see Box 4.4). Steel, automobiles, and cement have been cited as examples of successful infant industries in Korea, likewise automobiles in Brazil. The debate has gone on for the past century, but there have been surprisingly few attempts to study individual cases or to compare the net costs of infant industry failures with the net benefits of the successes.

It is a sound general principle that interventions should attack the problem of market failure nearest to its source. This may mean policies to make financial markets work better, to provide education, or to establish a patent law, rather than measures directed at particular firms or sectors. Protection may prove counterproductive in several respects. In many developing countries it has become more or less permanent, so that the stimulus for infant industries to mature is removed. Indeed, it has often created a gap between local costs and world prices so wide that it is unlikely ever to be bridged. Protection raises prices and therefore reduces domestic demand for the protected good. By the same token, protection provides no stimulus to exports. This in turn inhibits the achievement of lower costs through greater economies of scale.

Infant industry protection probably works best with a preannounced and credible timetable for withdrawal. In addition, selectivity is vital, for two reasons. First, one activity can be favored, ultimately, only at the expense of others. The more widespread the support, the more the exchange rate becomes overvalued (with a consequent discrimination against exports), and scarce resources are spread thinly through the economy. Second, if support is offered too frequently, firms will divert resources to the task of soliciting favors from government. There is an unresolved debate about whether countries like Korea—which has trade policies that are broadly neutral between import-replacing and export activities, combined with infant industry interventions in specific activities—have succeeded because of, or in spite of, such interventions (Box 4.4). But in addition to maintaining relative neutrality in its trade policies, Korea has kept its interventions limited and its exchange rate competitive. This is not the case in most other developing countries (see Chapter 5).

Externalities and industrialization

With urban and industrial development, pollution has grown alarmingly in many countries. This is an externality problem. For example, the manufacture of bleached paper produces more pollutants than the manufacture of unbleached paper. But if paper mills are not held liable in law for damaging the environment, the price of bleached paper will not reflect the true cost of resources used in its production, and therefore consumers will have no incentive to switch from using bleached to unbleached paper.

Pollution control policies are rare in developing countries. Where pollution control has become an issue, governments have relied heavily on a regulatory approach. But regulations often lead to unintended results, which then require a fresh set of regulations to correct. Alternatively, governments can provide subsidies for purchasing pollution control equipment. But it is very difficult for government officials to determine the most appropriate equipment for a particular process, keep pace with technological change, and make judgments on the tradeoffs between relative costs and effectiveness.

Urban congestion is another example of an externality associated with industrial development. When firms locate in a particular area, they may impose costs on society by adding to congestion, but they may also confer benefits by acting as a magnet for other investments, particularly in underdeveloped regions. Developing country governments, therefore, have adopted a variety of instruments to reduce urban congestion costs or to stimulate economic development in less developed regions. Again, such policies have proved problematic.

The Indian government, for example, has used investment licensing, public investment, and regional incentives to induce new firms to locate away from metropolitan areas. Yet according to a recent study there was no overall improvement in industrial dispersion between 1961 and 1971. And in Northeast Brazil, tax credits alone, among a number of regional incentives, exceeded $15,000 per job created in 1980.

Reducing protection itself may correct a bias in favor of urbanization. For instance, in Brazil dur-

Box 4.4 Industrial targeting: the great debate

A group of economies in East Asia, including Hong Kong, Japan, the Republic of Korea, and Singapore, has had phenomenal success in industrial growth in recent decades. With the exception of free-trading Hong Kong, there is considerable disagreement as to how much of this success is due to governments that have intervened in markets. In fact, the disagreements on the causes of success go a good deal further, covering areas such as foreign aid, regional and cultural factors, and the role of different forms of economic organization.

One school of thought points out that these economies have by and large "got their prices right"—in other words, they have maintained a competitive exchange rate and implemented policies that do not in aggregate discriminate between broad groups of industrial activity. For instance, the net effect of incentives is more neutral between import substitution and exporting activities in Korea than in the great majority of developing countries. And public expenditure on research and development is a considerably smaller fraction of equivalent private expenditures in Japan than in the other large industrial economies.

Other schools point to the evidence that these economies have intervened in the market to promote specific activities or firms, often with considerable success. They may not deny that getting the prices broadly right is a necessary condition of successful industrial growth; indeed, the more that intervention aims at a limited number of targets, the smaller its effect will be on the aggregate level of price distortion. They do, however, stress the importance of strong, capable, and honest government in these countries, close government-industry relations (with a strong national consensus on economic goals), and domestic markets large enough to allow substantial competition. They also cite the selective use of import protection, concessional credit, policies to restructure firms, and in some cases direct public investment to promote specific industrial activities. In some countries interventions appear to have been the outcome of a collective decision-making process in which government acted as an agent for the exchange of information between firms. Of course, the pattern of public intervention has differed from country to country and over time; for instance, in Japan and Korea import protection was more important up to the 1960s than it is now.

The empirical evidence about the success of intervention in these countries is much disputed. The Japanese government is said to have played a role in the development of such industries as steel, automobiles, fertilizers, synthetic fibers, and microelectronics. In automobiles, for instance, nontariff protection was heavy up to the mid-1960s, while the Ministry of International Trade and Industry (MITI) vetted technology transfers (in the 1950s) and inward foreign direct investment (in the 1970s). Yet MITI's role in the industry's phenomenal success has clearly declined since the 1960s. (For instance, it has not always had its way on industrial restructuring.) MITI was also instrumental in establishing the conditions under which foreign firms would be allowed to produce integrated circuits in Japan: only one firm was permitted entry in the late 1960s, and it had to share its knowledge with Japanese firms.

Korea's success in promoting infant industries such as automobiles and steel is also cited. (POSCO, a state-owned enterprise, has emerged as one of the world's lowest-cost steel producers.) But after the mid-1970s the Korean government made a number of expensive mistakes in its promotion of various heavy and chemical industries. The success stories beg a number of questions: Did the benefits of the successes outweigh their initial costs (as well as the costs of infant industry failures)? Did government intervention change decisions, or did it simply put a seal of approval on what the firms would have done anyway?

The flagging fortunes of many other industrial countries in comparison with Japan have revived debates on the role of industrial policy. Western Europe's largest economies have in fact pursued active industrial policies since the 1960s, although with indifferent success. Often these policies have differed from Japan's and put greater emphasis, for instance, on first aid for ailing sectors. In France, indicative planning was accorded some success in modernizing leading industrial sectors for a decade or two after World War II, and the development of civil nuclear energy and the modernization of telecommunications are reckoned to be public sector successes. But intervention has also been conspicuously less successful in such sectors as machine tools and steel.

Whatever the allocative effects of industrial intervention in East Asia, it has been carried out by strong and capable governments. It has also been selective and time-bound, and competition has been maintained in domestic markets. The level of intervention has been reduced over time. Central guidance becomes progressively more demanding as economies become more complex and as the opportunity for imitating more developed economies diminishes. Further research needs to ask many more questions about the East Asian experience, but there is a strong case for suggesting that the government's role as a coordinator and information clearinghouse was important. Finally, if some East Asian governments have intervened successfully, it is not clear whether most developing countries could emulate their administrative capacity, the ability of their firms and governments to cooperate closely in pursuit of agreed economic goals, or the degree of competition in their domestic markets.

ing the 1970s the protection enjoyed by industries in the two largest metropolitan areas was higher than the national average, whereas in the lagging Northeast region it was lower. This suggests that trade policy reforms might have exerted a greater influence on the regional distribution of industry than explicit location policies. Governments can also reduce some of the pressures for urbanization by ensuring that private costs reflect more accurately the broader economic costs of congestion. In particular, governments could enforce the recovery of investment and operating costs in urban services, such as education, transport, waste removal, and disease control, by charging user fees.

Government policies and the high costs of doing business

Analyses of government intervention in developing countries usually concentrate on resource allocation and efficiency in the production of individual products. But extensive intervention also adds to the costs of doing business. This argument starts with the observation that the costs of doing business in many developing countries are generally high—because of regulation and bureaucratic inefficiency. But the evidence is not conclusive, because transactions costs are difficult to measure, and intervention often leads to illegal activities or lobbying efforts which are not publicized, in either industrial or developing countries.

The pattern of intervention which creates these high costs of doing business has its origins in a policymaking capacity that is often weak and fragmented. Intervention sometimes allows two prices to coexist for the same product (because, for instance, one firm enjoys an import duty concession on an input that another does not). Alternatively, intervention creates a barrier to entry (for instance, when an investment license allows one firm to invest where its competitors cannot). These interventions in turn have two consequences. First, they encourage economic dualism—a formal and an informal sector. Second, they create incentives for arbitrage—the practice of buying low in one market and selling high in another.

The policymaking process

Governments have not always made the welfare of the governed their principal aim. Historically, European states sought economic control in order to extract revenues. Then, in some countries, countervailing powers emerged and forced the state to

cede greater commercial freedom in return for the right to tax (Box 4.2). Even today, according to a widely held view, politics remains the battleground in which different groups fight over the distribution of incomes.

For all that, few governments have disclaimed responsibility for achieving growth and equity. Yet, when governments choose an active role in economic development, they may find that their capacity to make and enforce economic policy is weak. In the debate on the role of government it has perhaps been too easy to assume that an ideal policymaking system prevails: namely, that laws are clear, enforcement is effective, and disputes are smoothly resolved. This ideal is never fully attained, any more than markets are ever perfectly competitive.

Economies in transition from traditional to modern forms of organization face special difficulties, because of problems of poor information and because of the way individuals cope with risk. Levels of education are lower than in industrial countries, investment in the machinery of communications is lower, the investigative capacity of the state and of the watchdog professions (lawyers, accountants, journalists, and so on) is lower, and reporting mechanisms are difficult to set up and enforce. Risks arise from the increasing number and complexity of transactions in a modernizing economy, often between people who do not know or may not trust each other and where legal and economic rights are uncertain. So individuals steer clear of impersonal transactions in favor of the more familiar relationships of kinship, friendship, or client and patron. Because of lack of information and risk avoidance, an informal policymaking system often stands behind the formal structure.

In some countries the legislative and judicial branches of government—which would serve as counterweights to the executive in an ideal system—are weak and leave wide discretion for administrative decisionmaking. Tax rates, for instance, often do not correspond to those set by law. Unauthorized and ad hoc concessions are common; noncompliance is rife. In other countries the legal system is well developed. But an abundance of confusing and inflexible regulations has produced a cumbersome bureaucratic process (see Box 4.5). Laws are passed, then not effectively implemented. Litigation is costly, and so few people seek legal redress.

To some extent these features are present in all sorts of countries, industrial and developing, but they are often more pronounced in developing countries. They can have an important effect on economic policymaking. The result is uncertainty for the private sector: the rules of the game are unclear, decisionmaking is fragmented, and many economic decisions are made on a case-by-case basis. Policymaking is subjected to pressure from private interests. This may help to explain why import quotas, which are usually subject to administrative discretion, are more popular than high tariffs, which usually require legislation. In-

---

Box 4.5 Battling the bureaucracy in Brazil

Wherever modern government structures are built on an already highly developed legal and administrative system, bureaucracies are bound to multiply. Brazil is no exception. What is exceptional is the degree to which Brazilians have managed to circumvent the more rigid and obstructive bureaucratic rules. In addition, the government has recently had some success in attacking the rules themselves.

Brazilians have described their federal administrative system as excessively centralized, formal, and distrustful of the public. This view dates back at least to the temporary transfer to Brazil of the Portuguese kingdom and its centralized administration in 1808, and perhaps even further, to 1549, when the first governor-general arrived with a framework of laws and regulations even before there were people to conform to them. The formalism embodied the prejudice that documents are more important than facts. The distrust showed in the controls that required endless lists of certificates, attestations, licenses, and other documents. Not many years ago the case was reported of an export license that required 1,470 separate legal actions and involved thirteen government ministries and fifty agencies.

The *jeito* was employed to overcome such difficulties (Rosenn 1984). This Portuguese term, corresponding roughly to "knack," "way," or "fix" in English, refers to the varied ways that Brazilians, like people in other countries, get around the maze of regulations and legal requirements. The jeito principle has been remarkably effective. It relies significantly on the *despachante* (roughly, an expeditor), who has counterparts in many countries but has been especially active in Brazil, where the lubrication of sticky administrative processes has been essential for social mobility and rapid economic development.

The despachante is an intermediary who, in return for a commission or fee, purchases and fills out the multiplicity of legal forms, delivers them to the proper persons, and extracts the needed permission or document. The system developed when the simplest transactions, such as obtaining a marriage license or identity card, could take ages or days or hours, depending on whether one used despachantes and how much they were paid. The despachantes are thriving, specialized professionals and have their own union and competitive examinations. Some specialize in police work, naturalizations, auto licenses, marriages, or "legalization of real estate." The despachantes who arrange imports and exports have long enjoyed a legal monopoly. Each typically has several employees, and almost all sizable businesses maintain their own despachantes.

Brazil's rapid economic growth and social evolution demonstrate that a complex bureaucracy need not be a barrier to development. The costs are nevertheless substantial. Moreover, such resourceful adaptations of the jeito may have been too effective and undermined attempts to reform public administration.

The most recent efforts to reform the system, rather than live with it, began in 1979. A National Debureaucratization Program was designed to simplify administrative procedures and, more broadly, to reverse what was seen as the relentless trend toward growth in government, excessive centralization, and abundant regulation.

The results in 1979–84 were impressive. On the basis of a citizens' project (which surveyed all the points of contact of individuals, throughout their lives, with bureaucratic requirements) it was possible to eliminate, or simplify, a long list of documents and procedures ranging from notarization requirements and driver's licenses to passport extensions, university enrollment processes, and income tax returns. Evidence of residence, economic dependence, and so on, could be established with simply a written statement by the interested party rather than legal certificates and third-party attestation. Thus a "presumption of truth" displaced the "rule of distrust." Other legal procedures were simplified. In all, more than 600 million documents a year were removed from circulation. The savings have been estimated at close to $3 billion a year, equivalent to about 1.5 percent of Brazil's GDP.

In the economic field the main achievements were to simplify rural credit procedures, to change commercial registration procedures so that forming a company could take three days rather than three to six months, and to bring relief from bureaucracy to 1.5 million small enterprises. For the time being, however, the program has left many areas of regulation untouched, including some that are important to industrialization and trade.

It is significant that, although a minister of debureaucratization was appointed, no new government department was formed. The program was implemented by an executive secretary and just twelve assistants. At the very least—and on a limited front—some progress has been made in simplifying the rules and changing the relationship between citizens and civil servants.

terest groups infiltrate the policymaking process because risk avoidance by government servants and lack of information undermine the capacity of governments to centralize and scrutinize decisions. Finally, policies are often designed with feasibility of implementation an uppermost consideration. Thus, because of the problem of raising public revenues, governments sometimes prefer import protection to direct subsidies in the promotion of selected industries. They may prefer to collect taxes through import duties rather than through direct and indirect taxes (where opportunities for avoidance are much greater). And, rather than regulate private firms, governments may choose to produce through public enterprises, in the hope of gaining easier access to the information on which regulation must be based.

Intervention and the creation of a formal and an informal sector

Privileged firms enjoy access to import quotas, subsidies, investment licenses, subsidized loans, and so on, whereas unprivileged firms have to operate in informal markets. This distinction between privileged and unprivileged sectors, more pronounced in developing countries than in industrial countries, is a simplification. Firms may receive some privileges and not others. Moreover, it is generally the unprivileged firms which more easily evade taxes and ignore minimum wage and social security legislation.

The informal sector has a tacitly tolerated, legally precarious existence in most developing countries. It operates outside the letter of the law and outside the de facto protection that privileged firms receive from governments. In other words, economic rights are insecure in the unprivileged sector. This adds a risk premium to the cost of doing business and can prevent certain transactions altogether. Insecure economic rights are the reason unprivileged firms are likely to remain small and labor-intensive: the larger the firm's tangible assets (building and machinery), the greater the ease with which these assets can be confiscated. Peru, which has a large informal sector, provides an example of the effects of dualism (see Box 4.6).

Intervention and directly unproductive profit seeking

The dual markets created by government intervention, which express themselves in price differentials and scarcities, create opportunities for arbitrage in the form of queuing, illegal operations,

---

Box 4.6   Informality in Peru

Peru has a large informal economy. It comprises small businesses, most of them in Lima, that do not have access to the incentives enjoyed by most larger firms and that operate outside the framework of laws and regulations (although they are not necessarily intrinsically illegal). The informal economy is the outcome of numerous historical factors that have influenced the structure of economic activity—including a chronically overvalued exchange rate, high levels of industrial protection, high taxes (combined with tax reliefs that encourage the use of capital), labor protection laws, powerful labor unions, credit rationing, and the recent recession (see Box 7.6). But the informal economy is also a response to the pervasive regulations that have come to affect economic activity.

The informal economy is perhaps most visible in the explosion of unauthorized housing structures built in and around Lima by the flood of new arrivals from the countryside. Without existing homes to move into, and faced with a multitude of administrative steps to obtain formal land title, these immigrants invade barren state-owned land, typically in large organized groups, and erect *pueblos jovenes* (new minitowns), complete with wooden houses, streets, sewers, and connections to the electric utility grid. The groups organize their own governing councils, which informally settle disputes over property boundaries and other matters. As many as 2 million of greater Lima's total population (more than 5 million) live in these pueblos jovenes.

Informality appears, if anything, to be even more widespread in Lima's transportation system. Only some 10 percent of the city's residents use formal, mu-

---

and lobbying activities to seek or create rents. All of these add further to the costs of doing business in industrial and developing countries alike. Such activities have been christened directly unproductive profit-seeking activities (see Box 4.7). Tax evasion and smuggling are examples of outright lawbreaking to avoid payment of various kinds of taxes; other laws are broken to avoid the cost of meeting standards (on pollution or safety at work, for example). Rent seeking is the devotion of resources to the pursuit of the excess profits that become available when goods, services, and privileges are in short supply. Rent seeking may occur through bribery or lobbying. An example of queuing is the practice of some firms in developing countries of holding a phone line open all day between two offices in order to avoid the interminable wait for a connection.

nicipally owned buses. The rest ride buses operated either by semiformal drivers—those with bus routes granted under a municipal franchise and who charge regulated fares, but who generally do not report their income to the tax authorities—or by informal drivers, who lack a franchise and charge what the traffic will bear.

Informality is also prevalent in the small commercial sector, particularly among an estimated 84,000 street vendors—*ambulantes*—who offer a full menu of goods in direct competition with large formal retail establishments. The ambulantes are well organized. Street vendor organizations assign and enforce informal property rights to slices of sidewalks that have estimated property values averaging $500 to $750. The organizations also collect dues that have enabled Lima's ambulantes to construct more than 270 local markets.

Because informality in Peru's industrial sector is least visible, it has yet to be well documented. Nevertheless, fragmentary evidence suggests that informal industrial enterprises—for instance, textile factories and repair shops—are prevalent in Peru's urban areas.

Since by their nature informal activities tend to be carried out on a cash basis rather than through banks, the size of the informal sector should be positively related to the ratio of cash to broader measures of the money supply. On this basis, informal activity in Peru is estimated to account for roughly one-third of gross domestic product and for about 60 percent of the part- and full-time active population.

In the face of burdensome regulations and incentives that favor a limited number of firms and workers in the formal sector, informality may be an efficient mode of operation. But if regulation could be reformed and the incentive system were to become less discriminatory, the evident dynamism of the population currently engaged in informal activities could, once formalized, lead to greater growth in the economy as a whole.

First, and perhaps most important, excessive regulation and the absence of effective economic rights combine to prevent informal entrepreneurs from realizing scale economies. Informal firms must operate with few workers, often in remote locations, to avoid detection; hence the need to incur other costs simply to remain in business. Moreover, since credit is rationed and informals often operate illegally, they have little access to formal credit and are forced to pay the much higher rates of interest charged by informal lenders. This makes it difficult for informal entrepreneurs to expand, even though their investments may be far more profitable than those of large private and state-owned enterprises which have easier access to credit.

Second, the imperfect protection of property and contract rights for informal citizens diminishes their incentives to save and invest. For example, residents with formal title to their homes in Peru have invested significantly more in housing than have the informal residents of the pueblos jovenes with similar incomes.

Finally, informality undermines the government's own efforts to establish an evenhanded and effective legal system. Such a system could help develop the economic rights and rules often taken for granted in industrial countries.

Since profits are to be made by the firm that succeeds in acquiring a privilege, it is clear that firms will compete with each other and devote real resources to rent seeking. Thus at least part of the rent will be "competed away" with real resources that could otherwise have been put to productive uses. If this were not the case, rent seeking would simply mean transfers of income from one pocket to another. But rent seeking has additional costs: firms come to specialize in rent seeking, to the detriment of production. In consequence, markets operate inefficiently and resources are wasted.

The evidence on directly unproductive activities is patchy. First, there is the evidence of large price differentials in parallel markets—black market premiums on exchange rates, interest rate differentials between formal and informal capital markets, and wage differentials in the labor market. The higher the price differential and the less effective the policing of illegal activities, the stronger the presumption that individuals will engage in directly unproductive activities. Some of the evidence on price distortions was reviewed in *World Development Report 1983*, and other evidence is reviewed in Chapter 7.

The extent of smuggling has been estimated for several countries—cocoa from Ghana, coffee from Uganda, and various commodities from Colombia, for example. There is also evidence—unsystematic and anecdotal for obvious reasons—on the way corruption imposes high costs on doing business. In some countries corruption has been so rife that better evidence has been collected through official inquiries. Rent-seeking activities were estimated to account for 24 percent of Kenyan GDP in 1982 (see also Box 4.7 on estimates of rent seeking in India

Box 4.7   Rent seeking and directly unproductive profit seeking

Economic analysis has traditionally focused on productive activity. But economists are now taking a closer look at unproductive activity. The terms "rent seeking" and "directly unproductive profit seeking" (DUP) have become common parlance in economics. While unproductive activities can certainly arise in the private sector, economists have been particularly interested in those arising from policy interventions of various kinds.

Rent seeking embraces lobbying activities designed to capture the rents—that is, scarcity premiums—that are attached to licenses and quotas. Typical examples include the lobbies that aim to secure import licenses in trade and payments regimes that rely, in many developing countries, on exchange and import controls. Another example is lobbies seeking the lucrative premiums generally associated with industrial licenses. Such rent seeking is common in industrial countries, too—for example, in the allocation of import quotas and in public purchasing.

The concept of directly unproductive profit seeking is more comprehensive. It includes all ways of making a profit by undertaking activities which are directly unproductive. That is, DUP activities yield income or profit but do not produce goods or services directly or indirectly. They are economic activities that produce zero output while using up real resources.

Thus DUP activities include rent seeking. But they also cover activities where resources are devoted to encouraging policy interventions that *create* rents: for ex-ample, lobbying efforts can be directed at creating or sustaining quota or tariff protection against imports. DUP also embraces activities designed to make money by *evading* policies. For instance, tariff evasion yields pecuniary income by exploiting the difference between legal (tariff-paying) imports and illegal (tariff-evading) imports.

In an analysis of the costs and benefits of policy intervention, these activities cannot be ignored. Economists have therefore begun to explore ways of estimating the costs of DUP. The conventional costs of protection are estimated by calculating the loss that arises from distorting the prices faced by consumers and producers (see Box 5.4). These so-called deadweight losses, however, are now supplemented by estimates of significantly larger losses from associated rent seeking and DUP.

For instance, rent-seeking costs have been estimated by assuming that license premiums would lead to equivalent resource costs by lobbyists. For India, the resulting cost estimates for 1964 were roughly 7.3 percent of GNP; for Turkey, they were 15 percent of GNP in 1968. These estimates may be on the high side, because administered allocations may be routine and thus reduce the real resources profitably diverted to seeking the licenses. But the full effects on economies with extensive interventions and associated DUP activities are likely to elude quantification. What is remarkable is that even the quantifiable part of the costs is so large.

and Turkey). Finally, in economies where scarcities and red tape rule, professionals adept at cutting through the knot of bureaucracy are in great demand. These range from the *tolkach* (pusher) of the Soviet Union to the *despachante* (expeditor) of Brazil (Box 4.5).

The priorities for government

At the core of the industrialization process is an ever increasing division of labor which reaps the rewards of specialization, but at the cost of an increasing number of transactions between economic agents. Governments cannot predict the direction or form of this changing division of labor, but they nonetheless have a vital role in facilitating these transactions.

This is not easy for governments. Their capacity for playing this role is limited, particularly in developing countries where the level of information is often deficient and the policymaking process often fragmented and ad hoc. What is more, although economic principles play a useful role in indicating the general conditions under which government action will be most productive, identifying the specific cases in which these principles apply and devising effective measures are often difficult.

Nonetheless, a clear hierarchy of priorities emerges for market-oriented governments seeking to industrialize efficiently. First, developing the web of complex activities and relationships that characterizes a sophisticated industrial sector becomes difficult, if not impossible, in the absence of clear, evenhanded, and predictable rules of the game. These rules must be the primary concern of governments since only governments can provide them. Second, an efficient and adequate supply of infrastructural services such as transport, communications, power, and education is also vital to modern industry. Governments must make sure these needs are effectively met, but this does not always mean the government should be the provider. In some cases it may be more appropriate to regulate private monopolies, in others to allow competition among providers. Finally, governments also intervene to change the way markets work—for instance, to prevent abuses, to improve welfare, and to improve the pattern of investment or output. It is here that the government's task is most difficult: the dividing line between measures that improve and those that worsen the conditions under which the private sector operates is often fine.

In sum, governments must use their scarce resources carefully. The problem is not so much the right or wrong *level* of resources deployed by the government, but rather the particular way these resources are deployed.

Trade policy and industrialization

Which trade strategies have enabled countries to attain high growth and to develop their industrial potential? This chapter attempts to answer the question in two ways. First it examines the thinking that lies behind different strategies, the circumstances under which governments have adopted them, and the economic performance of countries that have pursued them. Then it discusses the economic costs and benefits of alternative trade strategies and suggests some reasons why economic performance has varied so widely under the different strategies.

Economic growth is fundamental to economic development. Without generating greater output and income, a country cannot make a sustained attack on poverty, unemployment, and other social and economic problems. In the first decades following World War II, economists viewed industrialization as an essential stage in reaching the goal of rapid economic growth. But industrialization cannot be a policy objective in its own right. This chapter suggests that the real question is not how fast an economy can industrialize, but how to structure the industrial sector so that it supports sustained economic growth.

Alternative trade strategies

Economists and policymakers in the developing countries have long agreed on the role of government in providing infrastructure, promoting market efficiency, and maintaining stable macroeconomic policies. But they have disagreed on policies toward trade and industry. The form of government intervention in this area is the distinguishing feature of alternative development strategies.

For analytical convenience, trade strategies can be broadly divided into two groups, outward oriented and inward oriented. An outward-oriented strategy is one in which trade and industrial policies do not discriminate between production for the domestic market and exports, nor between purchases of domestic goods and foreign goods (see Box 5.1). Because it does not discourage international trade, this nondiscriminatory strategy is often (somewhat inaptly) referred to as an export promotion strategy. By contrast, an inward-oriented strategy is one in which trade and industrial incentives are biased in favor of production for the domestic over the export market. This approach is well known as the import substitution strategy.

Protection switches demand to products produced domestically. Exporting is then discouraged by both the increased cost of imported inputs and the increased cost of domestic inputs relative to the price received by exporters. This rise in the relative cost of domestic inputs may occur through domestic inflation or an appreciation of the exchange rate following the imposition of barriers to imports. In effect, protection puts a tax on exports (see Box 5.2).

This implicit tax is sometimes offset with export subsidies. As far as the trade account is concerned, a 10 percent tariff on all imports together with a 10 percent subsidy on all exports would be equivalent to a 10 percent depreciated exchange rate with no tariff and no export subsidy. Such a policy does not discriminate between exports and imports, so that it too is an outward-oriented strategy. But combining export subsidies and import tariffs involves administrative cost; in practice, the policy is rarely, if ever, designed to simulate liberal trade.

Box 5.1   Measuring neutrality in trade regimes: nominal and effective rates of protection

The concept of neutrality in trade regimes is straight-forward: it means that the aggregate effect of all trade and industrial policies is to offer equal incentives to the production of all tradables. Measuring departures from neutrality, or bias, is not so simple, however. It involves several different indicators.

One way of measuring bias starts with the *nominal* rate of protection. For any good, this is the difference between the domestic price and the world price, expressed as a percentage of the world price. The overall bias of a trade regime can then be estimated as the ratio of (a) the average nominal rate of protection for importables to (b) the average nominal rate of protection for exportables. If this ratio is greater than one—that is, if importables have a higher nominal rate of protection than exportables—it reveals a bias in favor of import substitution. A ratio of one implies neutrality. (Exactly the same result can be obtained by using the ratio of the effective exchange rate for importables to the effective exchange rate for exportables. The effective exchange rate for importables must take account of any import duties, import premiums resulting from quantitative restrictions, and other incentives. Similarly, the effective exchange rate for exportables must take account of any export subsidies, tax credits, and other export incentives.)

Nominal rates of protection, however, often fail to measure the degree of protection actually received by domestic producers. This is because protection depends not only on the nominal protection given for the product itself, but also on any taxes or subsidies that there may be on inputs. For this reason, a different measure is more widely used to evaluate the orientation of trade regimes.

The *effective* rate of protection is designed to capture the protection accorded to value added in production, rather than to the finished product. It is defined as the difference between value added (per unit of output) in domestic prices and value added in world prices, expressed as a percentage of the latter. The effective rate of protection for importables is therefore equal to $\frac{v'-v}{v} \times 100$, where v' represents value added at domestic prices, and v represents value added at world prices. The result can be positive or negative, depending upon whether v' is greater or less than v. In an extreme case v itself could be negative. This represents the case in which domestic production is so inefficient that it is actually destroying value.

As an example, consider the effects of tariffs on the sweater industry. Suppose a sweater sells for $100 in the absence of import restrictions and that the material inputs—wool and buttons—cost $60 in world prices. The value added at world prices is therefore $40. If a tariff of 20 percent is levied on sweaters, raising their imported price to $120, and inputs remain duty free, the value added in domestic prices is $60. The effective rate of protection is the difference between the value added in domestic prices ($60) and the value added in world prices ($40), as a proportion of the value added in world prices. In other words, the effective rate of protection is 50 percent, as opposed to the 20 percent

Box figure 5.1 Calculating the effective rate of protection

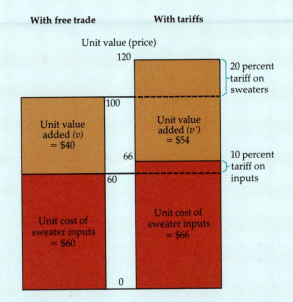

Note: In this example, where the nominal rate of protection is 20 percent on sweaters and 10 percent on inputs, the effective rate of protection is:

$$\frac{v'-v}{v} = \frac{54-40}{40} = 35 \text{ percent.}$$

nominal rate of protection. But if this tariff on sweater production is combined with a tariff of 10 percent on inputs, the domestic cost of inputs rises to $66, which decreases the effective rate of protection to 35 percent (see Box figure 5.1).

The effective rate of protection for export production can be obtained in the same way; now v includes subsidies to exports. As before, the ratio of (a) the average effective rate of protection for importables to (b) the average effective rate of protection for exportables can be used as an indicator of trade orientation. (And again, the same results can be obtained with ratios of effective exchange rates, this time evaluated on the basis of value added.)

The use of any aggregate measure of protection has a serious drawback. It is possible that nominal or effective rates of protection for importables or exportables vary widely across industries, yet have an average value of zero—implying no protection. But the variation in nominal or effective rates of protection across industries is itself an important distortion. Full neutrality of a trade regime therefore requires no variation in nominal or effective rates of protection across the tradable goods industries.

Box 5.2 Protection and the taxation of exports

It is not unusual for a country to pursue policies of import substitution and export promotion at the same time. The objectives may be seen as independent. Thus, instruments designed to encourage import substitution may be introduced in the belief that they have no impact upon the export sector. But this is not so.

The most crucial characteristic of protection is that it is a *relative* concept. When a particular protective instrument is introduced, it is intended to alter relative prices in order to protect the chosen activity relative to other activities. For example, if an import tariff achieves its objective, resources will be induced to move from unprotected activities to the protected activity.

Recent research has shown that the impact of protection depends on the way it influences the prices of nontradable goods. Although the division of an economy into importables, exportables, and nontradables is somewhat artificial, it is also instructive. (Many service industries and industries with high transport costs may be regarded as nontradable: wages are a large component of their costs.) The introduction of a tariff will raise the domestic price of importables relative to the price of exportables, which will generally be determined by world demand and supply. The manner in which the tariff will cause the price of nontradable

goods to change is less clear. If the factors used to produce importables and nontradables are similar, that is, if they are close substitutes in production, the prices of importables and nontradables would tend to be closely linked and their relative price would not be much affected by an import tariff. The tariff would serve to raise the price of *both* importables and nontradables. Since the price of exportables is externally determined, producers in the export sector would find that the price of their output has fallen relative to both imports and nontradables. The effect is akin to a tax on their production. At the same time, domestic demand will tend to switch to the relatively cheaper products—exportables. Both effects will act to tax exports.

By contrast, if nontradables and exportables are close substitutes in production, the price of exports would still fall relative to imports, but there would be little change relative to nontradables. Tariffs discourage exports to a somewhat smaller extent in this case.

Given information on relative prices for exportable output, import substitutes, and nontradables, the relative price effects of protection can be estimated. Box table 5.2 reports the results of several studies which pertain to Latin American and African economies. The "shift parameter" in the table measures the share of any import protection which, because of relative prices, becomes an implicit tax on exports. This ranges from a low of 43 percent in the case of Côte d'Ivoire to a high of 95 percent in the case of Colombia. In almost every case, more than half of the burden of protection is shifted to the export sector.

Several important points arise from this analysis. First, protecting one sector usually makes another worse off. Second, when export incentives are introduced alongside import restraints, the export incentives may do little more than offset the disincentive effects of import protection. This may be one reason why export processing zones (EPZs) have not lived up to expectations—the EPZ incentives may be insufficient to counteract the implicit tax on exports caused by the restrictions on imports. Finally, the analysis implies that if export promotion is a goal of policy, the most direct means of achieving this goal may be import liberalization.

Box table 5.2 Estimates of the shift parameter in selected developing countries

Country and period	Shift parameter
Côte d'Ivoire, 1970–84	0.43
Uruguay, 1959–80	0.53
Chile, 1959–80	0.55
Argentina, 1935–79	0.57
Mauritius, 1976–82	0.59
El Salvador, 1962–77	0.70
Brazil, 1950–78	0.70
Côte d'Ivoire, 1960–84	0.82
Mauritius, 1976–82	0.85
Colombia, 1970–78	0.95

Note: The lower estimates for Mauritius and Côte d'Ivoire refer to nontraditional exportables; the higher estimates, to traditional exportables.
Source: Clements and Sjaastad 1984; Greenaway and Milner 1987.

Export pessimism

In the early postwar years most developing economies were relatively specialized in the production of primary commodities, which they exported in exchange for manufactured products from industrialized countries. But many economists argued that the producers of primary goods faced a secu-

lar decline in their terms of trade. The income elasticity of demand for primary products was low, synthetic substitutes for natural resources were appearing, and technical innovations were cutting the amount of raw materials needed for industrial production. All this suggested that the real prices of primary goods would fall over time. World demand for manufactures, by contrast, would continue to grow. To many this provided a justification for encouraging industrial production.

The prediction of declining terms of trade for primary products has been much debated. Critics say it ignored supply conditions: with diminishing returns to limited natural resources, slow growth in demand for primary products will not necessarily cause their terms of trade to decline. The prediction also overlooked the growth of developing countries and their demand for primary products as well as the early industrial transformation of developing economies with poor natural resource endowments, such as Hong Kong, Singapore, and, to a lesser extent, the Republic of Korea. The data in Chapter 2 do show a long-term decline in the terms of trade for exports of primary goods. But they should be interpreted with caution because they take no account of quality improvements in manufactures. And some of the recent surplus in primary commodities arose from investments encouraged by past high prices.

In spite of these uncertainties, it may well be true that the relative price of primary commodities is in long-term decline. The question, however, is whether an inward-oriented strategy is the right response to this prospect. The overriding need is for flexibility in shifting the economy's resources to take account of the changing pattern of comparative advantage. Inward-oriented strategies are unlikely to promote this kind of flexibility.

New arguments against nondiscriminatory trade policies and their implicit encouragement of manufactured exports have recently appeared. One is known as the fallacy of composition; it holds that if all developing countries followed an export-promoting strategy modeled on the example of the newly industrializing countries (NICs) of East Asia, industrial countries would refuse to absorb the resulting volume of imports.

This has been challenged on at least four grounds. First, the capacity of industrial nations to absorb new imports may be greater than supposed. Developing country exports currently account for only a tiny share—2.3 percent as of 1983—of the markets for manufactures in the industrial economies. (Of course, the proportion is much higher for certain products and in certain countries.) Second, the idea that a large number of economies might suddenly achieve export-to-GDP ratios for manufactures like those of Hong Kong, Korea, or Singapore is highly implausible. The resource endowments of the East Asian NICs are quite different from those of countries such as Argentina, Brazil, Indonesia, Côte d'Ivoire, Malay-

sia, and Thailand, which are among the next tier of industrializing countries. Third, export-oriented countries would produce different products, and intraindustry trade (as occurred with the lowering of trade barriers within Europe) is likely to be important. Finally, the first wave of newly industrializing countries is already providing markets for the labor-intensive products of the countries that are following.

Policy instruments

Commercial policy, industrial policy, and exchange rate policy can all be instruments of an inward-oriented strategy. Policymakers often prefer direct controls, such as import licensing and quantitative restrictions, to tariffs. In addition, hidden import duties such as stamp taxes, port duties, and advance deposit requirements are common, as are a number of other quasi-tariff measures. Finally, domestic content requirements for certain industrial products have become increasingly common.

Publicly owned firms or industries have expanded rapidly in many developing countries, particularly in industrial sectors such as steel, fertilizers, cement, or petrochemicals (Chapter 4). These give the policymaker administrative control over investments and purchasing, for example. Governments can also use fiscal policy to provide production subsidies, credit subsidies, wage subsidies, and tax holidays of various kinds. In general, these incentives are offered in a discretionary, and hence discriminatory, way. Administrative allocation of foreign exchange is also common in inward-oriented regimes—sometimes to defend the overvalued exchange rates that are partly due to the import barriers themselves. Certain sectors are given preferential access to foreign exchange.

Thus, inward-oriented regimes are generally characterized by high levels of protection for manufacturing, direct controls on imports and investments, and overvalued exchange rates. By contrast, outward orientation links the domestic economy to the world economy. The discriminatory use of tariffs, quotas, investment licensing, tax and credit subsidies, and so on, would be incompatible with the purest sort of outward-oriented strategy. In practice, however, outward orientation does not necessarily mean less government intervention. Some countries have pursued outward orientation by offsetting some of the anti-export bias of import barriers: they have promoted exports while dismantling import barriers only slowly.

Some governments have tried to promote exports by creating free trade zones. For individual firms, bonded warehouses often offer subsidized facilities. But such zones have had little aggregate effect, since they have applied to only a small segment of the economy. In many countries free trade status has also been provided to the export sector in general, through duty exemptions or other administrative measures to allow exporters access to imported inputs at world prices. But this is usually too little to offset the incentives to produce for domestic markets when import protection is significant.

Positive export incentives fall into three groups: rebates in excess of actual import charges on imported intermediate inputs, or excessive "wastage" allowances on imported inputs; access to loans at below-market rates; and other explicit and implicit subsidies. Such policies require institutional sophistication and budgetary resources. They can be discriminatory and are open to abuse. Even relatively nondiscriminatory schemes have proved difficult to administer. Furthermore, they are increasingly threatened by countervailing measures imposed by some importing countries.

Defining trade strategy

Trade strategy has a great influence on industrial performance and economic development. To illustrate this, it is first necessary to classify countries according to their trade policies. In principle, the distinction between an inward-oriented and an outward-oriented strategy is straightforward, a matter of the effective protection provided to production for domestic markets as compared with export markets (Box 5.1). In practice, however, it is rather more difficult, because a trade strategy contains many policies at work simultaneously and because the data are very limited.

An attempt is made here to classify the orientation of a country's trade strategy by combining the following quantitative and qualitative indicators:
• *Effective rate of protection*. The higher the effective protection for domestic markets, the greater the bias toward import substitution (Box 5.1).
• *Use of direct controls such as quotas and import-licensing schemes*. The greater the reliance on direct controls on imports, the more inward oriented the economy.
• *Use of export incentives*.
• *Degree of exchange rate overvaluation*. Inward orientation generally leads to an overvaluation of the exchange rate.

Information for the period 1963 to 1985 has been collected for forty-one countries. (The availability of data limited the choice of countries, but the countries selected nonetheless accounted for 66.5 percent of the total output of developing countries in 1985.) This information was then used to divide the countries into "strongly outward-oriented," "moderately outward-oriented," "strongly inward-oriented," and "moderately inward-oriented" economies. Policies change, and world trade has been unsettled since 1973, so each group was examined for two periods, 1963–73 and 1973–85. The criteria for the four categories follow.

STRONGLY OUTWARD ORIENTED. Trade controls are either nonexistent or very low in the sense that any disincentives to export resulting from import barriers are more or less counterbalanced by export incentives. There is little or no use of direct controls and licensing arrangements, and the exchange rate is maintained so that the effective exchange rates for importables and exportables are roughly equal.

MODERATELY OUTWARD ORIENTED. The overall incentive structure is biased toward production for domestic rather than export markets. But the average rate of effective protection for the home markets is relatively low and the range of effective protection rates relatively narrow. The use of direct controls and licensing arrangements is limited, and although some direct incentives to export may be provided, these do not offset protection against imports. The effective exchange rate is higher for imports than for exports, but only slightly.

MODERATELY INWARD ORIENTED. The overall incentive structure distinctly favors production for the domestic market. The average rate of effective protection for home markets is relatively high and the range of effective protection rates relatively wide. The use of direct import controls and licensing is extensive, and although some direct incentives to export may be provided, there is a distinct bias against exports, and the exchange rate is clearly overvalued.

STRONGLY INWARD ORIENTED. The overall incentive structure strongly favors production for the domestic market. The average rate of effective protection for home markets is high and the range of effective protection rates relatively wide. Direct controls and licensing disincentives to the traditional export sector are pervasive, positive incentives to nontraditional exportables are few or non-

Figure 5.1 Classification of forty-one developing economies by trade orientation, 1963–73 and 1973–85

Period	Outward oriented		Inward oriented	
	Strongly outward oriented	Moderately outward oriented	Moderately inward oriented	Strongly inward oriented
1963–73	Hong Kong Korea, Republic of Singapore	Brazil Cameroon Colombia Costa Rica Côte d'Ivoire Guatemala Indonesia Israel Malaysia Thailand	Bolivia El Salvador Honduras Kenya Madagascar Mexico Nicaragua Nigeria Philippines Senegal Tunisia Yugoslavia	Argentina Bangladesh Burundi Chile Dominican Republic Ethiopia Ghana India Pakistan Peru Sri Lanka Sudan Tanzania Turkey Uruguay Zambia
1973–85	Hong Kong Korea, Republic of Singapore	Brazil Chile Israel Malaysia Thailand Tunisia Turkey Uruguay	Cameroon Colombia Costa Rica Côte d'Ivoire El Salvador Guatemala Honduras Indonesia Kenya Mexico Nicaragua Pakistan Philippines Senegal Sri Lanka Yugoslavia	Argentina Bangladesh Bolivia Burundi Dominican Republic Ethiopia Ghana India Madagascar Nigeria Peru Sudan Tanzania Zambia

Source: Based on Greenaway (background paper) and World Bank data.

existent, and the exchange rate is significantly overvalued.

Figure 5.1 sets out the forty-one developing economies, classified according to the orientation of their trade strategy in two periods, 1963–73 and 1973–85. Although there may be scope for disagreement over the two intermediate subgroups, the countries which are scored as extreme cases are not likely to be ambiguous.

Figure 5.1 is the basis for the analysis in the rest of this section. It shows that, over the period studied, several countries underwent policy shifts toward more outward orientation—Chile, Turkey, and Uruguay, along with Pakistan, Sri Lanka, and

Tunisia. Others moved in the opposite direction, toward more inward orientation—Bolivia, Cameroon, Colombia, Costa Rica, Côte d'Ivoire, Guatemala, Indonesia, Madagascar, and Nigeria.

Trade strategy and economic performance

The links between trade strategy and macroeconomic performance are not entirely clear. Does outward orientation lead to better economic performance, or does superior economic performance pave the way for outward orientation? Nevertheless, Figure 5.2 provides indicators of the macroeconomic performance of the forty-one countries, grouped by the strategies defined above. The spe-

Figure 5.2 Macroeconomic performance of forty-one developing economies grouped by trade orientation

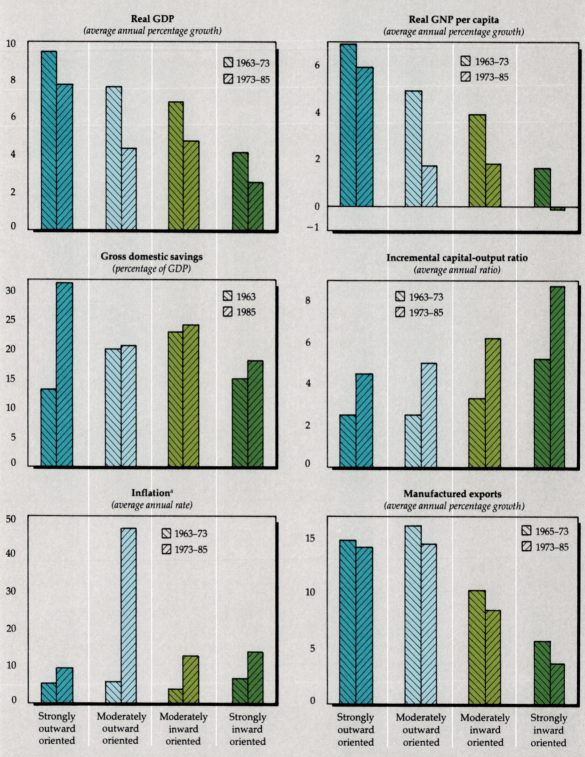

Note: Averages are weighted by each country's share in the group total for each indicator. See Figure 5.1 for a listing of the economies in each of the trade groups.
a. Inflation rates are measured by the implicit GDP deflator. Values are group medians.

cific indicators, given for weighted group averages, are the average annual growth rates of real GDP and per capita income, the gross domestic savings ratio, the average incremental capital-output ratio, the average annual growth rate of real manufactured exports, and the group median of average annual rates of inflation.

The figures suggest that the economic performance of the outward-oriented economies has been broadly superior to that of the inward-oriented economies in almost all respects. First of all, growth rates of GDP show a clear descending pattern from the strongly outward-oriented to the strongly inward-oriented economies. For the 1963–73 period the annual average was 9.5 percent for the strongly outward-oriented group, more than double the 4.1 percent attained by the strongly inward-oriented group. The respective rates for 1973–85 (7.7 percent and 2.5 percent) show that the gap has widened.

As a result of these trends in GDP, the average annual growth rate in real per capita income for 1963–73 was highest in the strongly outward-oriented economies (6.9 percent) and lowest in the strongly inward-oriented economies (1.6 percent). Despite the economic slowdown during 1973–85, per capita income in the strongly outward-oriented economies grew by an annual average of 5.9 percent, whereas in the strongly inward-oriented countries it fell on average by 0.1 percent a year. Performance differences are less marked between the moderately outward-oriented and the moderately inward-oriented economies; this reflects the relatively modest differences in their policy environments. (Figure 5.3 shows the per capita growth performance of each of the forty-one economies.)

GDP growth is influenced by the level of savings as well as by the efficiency of investment. The average ratio of gross domestic savings to GDP of the strongly outward-oriented economies was exceeded by all other groups in 1963, registering only 13.0 percent. By 1985, however, the strongly outward-oriented economies had more than doubled their savings ratio to 31.4 percent, whereas the savings ratios of the other three groups grew only slightly, or stagnated.

Given the gross savings rate, efficiency in the use of additional capital resources in an economy can be reflected in the economy's incremental capital-output ratio—the ratio of gross investment to the increase in GDP. Lower values suggest more productive investment. For both periods, there is a clear association between lower incremental capital-output ratios and increased outward orien-

tation. The average for both strongly and moderately outward-oriented groups for 1963–73 is 2.5, while the moderately and strongly inward-oriented groups averaged 3.3 and 5.2, respectively. In the 1973–85 period, the data register a substantial deterioration for all groups—incremental capital-output ratios are 4.5 and 5.0 for the outward-oriented groups and 6.2 and 8.7 for the inward-oriented groups.

By removing barriers, outward-oriented economies tend to tie themselves to the inflation rates of the international economy. This may restrain their own inflation rates; however, at times of rapid inflation in the world economy, it can result in imported inflation, unless the exchange rate appreciates. In 1963–73, median inflation rates differed little between any of the groups; moderately inward-oriented economies had the lowest rate. In 1973–85, the median inflation rate reached double digits in all groups. The highest median inflation rate is that of the moderately outward-oriented group; four of the eight economies experienced high or hyperinflation in the 1980s—Brazil, Israel, Turkey, and Uruguay. The other economies in the sample with particularly high inflation—Argentina, Bolivia, and Peru—are in the strongly inward-oriented group. In the higher inflation environment of the 1970s and early 1980s, however, the strongly outward-oriented economies were able to maintain relatively low and stable rates of inflation.

The last graph in Figure 5.2 shows the average annual growth of manufactured exports from 1965 to 1973 and from 1973 to 1985. Again, the strongly outward-oriented economies performed best. Between 1965 and 1973 the manufactured exports of the two outward-oriented groups grew by 14.8 and 16.1 percent, compared with 10.3 and 5.7 percent for the inward-oriented groups. Between 1973 and 1985 the growth rates were 14.2 and 14.5 percent versus 8.5 and 3.7 percent. This growth of manufactured exports was probably an important factor in producing rapid overall economic growth.

Finally, a good case can be made for suggesting that outward orientation leads to a more equitable distribution of income. First, the expansion of labor-intensive exports means higher employment. Second, reinforcing this, outward orientation removes the bias in favor of capital-intensive industries which is often implicit under inward-oriented policies. Third, the direct controls of an inward-oriented strategy generate rents that channel income to those with access to import licenses or subsidized credits.

Figure 5.3 Economic and industrial performance by trade orientation

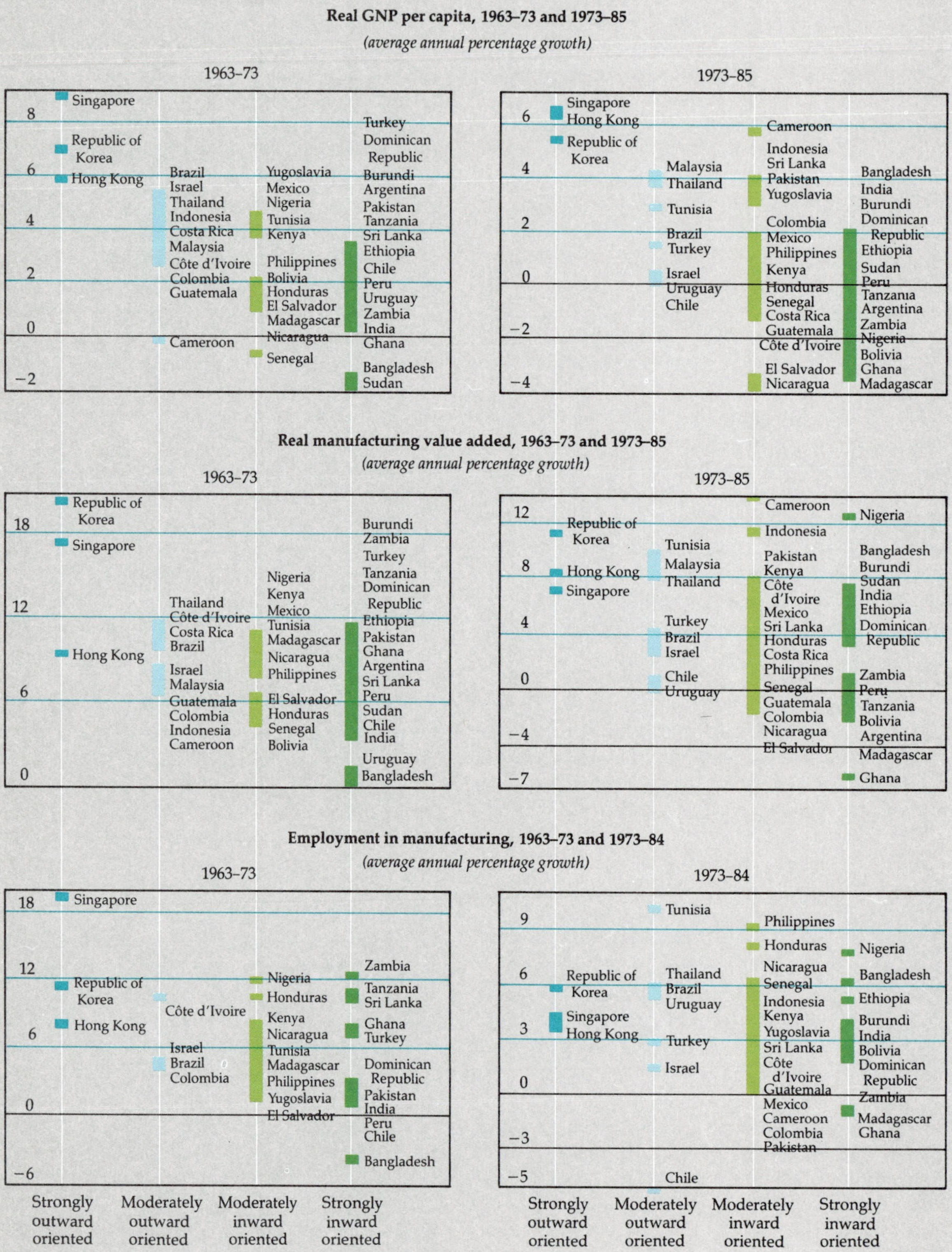

Real GNP per capita, 1963–73 and 1973–85

(average annual percentage growth)

1963–73

8 — Singapore			
			Turkey
6 — Republic of Korea			Dominican Republic
— Hong Kong	Brazil	Yugoslavia	Burundi
	Israel	Mexico	Argentina
	Thailand	Nigeria	Pakistan
4 — Indonesia	Tunisia	Tanzania	
	Costa Rica	Kenya	Sri Lanka
	Malaysia		Ethiopia
	Côte d'Ivoire	Philippines	Chile
2 — Colombia	Bolivia	Peru	
	Guatemala	Honduras	Uruguay
		El Salvador	Zambia
		Madagascar	India
0 —		Nicaragua	Ghana
— Cameroon		Senegal	
			Bangladesh
−2			Sudan

1973–85

6 — Singapore			
— Hong Kong		Cameroon	
— Republic of Korea		Indonesia	
4 —	Malaysia	Sri Lanka	Bangladesh
	Thailand	Pakistan	India
		Yugoslavia	Burundi
2 —	Tunisia	Colombia	Dominican Republic
	Brazil	Mexico	Ethiopia
	Turkey	Philippines	Sudan
0 —	Israel	Kenya	Peru
	Uruguay	Honduras	Tanzania
	Chile	Senegal	Argentina
−2 —		Costa Rica	Zambia
		Guatemala	Nigeria
		Côte d'Ivoire	Bolivia
		El Salvador	Ghana
−4 —		Nicaragua	Madagascar

Real manufacturing value added, 1963–73 and 1973–85

(average annual percentage growth)

1963–73

18 — Republic of Korea			Burundi
			Zambia
— Singapore			Turkey
		Nigeria	Tanzania
		Kenya	Dominican Republic
12 —	Thailand	Mexico	
	Côte d'Ivoire	Tunisia	Ethiopia
	Costa Rica	Madagascar	Pakistan
— Hong Kong	Brazil	Nicaragua	Ghana
	Israel	Philippines	Argentina
	Malaysia		Sri Lanka
6 — Guatemala	El Salvador	Peru
	Colombia	Honduras	Sudan
	Indonesia	Senegal	Chile
	Cameroon	Bolivia	India
			Uruguay
0 —			Bangladesh

1973–85

12 —		Cameroon	Nigeria
— Republic of Korea		Indonesia	
	Tunisia		Bangladesh
8 — Hong Kong	Malaysia	Pakistan	Burundi
— Singapore	Thailand	Kenya	Sudan
		Côte d'Ivoire	India
4 —	Turkey	Mexico	Ethiopia
	Brazil	Sri Lanka	Dominican
	Israel	Honduras	Republic
		Costa Rica	
0 —	Chile	Philippines	Zambia
	Uruguay	Senegal	Peru
		Guatemala	Tanzania
		Colombia	Bolivia
−4 —		Nicaragua	Argentina
		El Salvador	Madagascar
−7 —			Ghana

Employment in manufacturing, 1963–73 and 1973–84

(average annual percentage growth)

1963–73

18 — Singapore			
12 —			Zambia
— Republic of Korea		Nigeria	Tanzania
	Côte d'Ivoire	Honduras	Sri Lanka
6 — Hong Kong		Kenya	Ghana
	Israel	Nicaragua	Turkey
	Brazil	Tunisia	
	Colombia	Madagascar	Dominican Republic
		Philippines	Pakistan
0 —		Yugoslavia	India
		El Salvador	Peru
			Chile
−6 —			Bangladesh

1973–84

9 — Tunisia			
		Philippines	
		Honduras	Nigeria
6 —		Nicaragua	
— Republic of Korea	Thailand	Senegal	Bangladesh
	Brazil	Indonesia	Ethiopia
3 —	Uruguay	Kenya	Burundi
— Singapore		Yugoslavia	India
— Hong Kong	Turkey	Sri Lanka	Bolivia
		Côte d'Ivoire	Dominican
0 —	Israel	Guatemala	Republic
		Mexico	Zambia
		Cameroon	
−3 —		Colombia	Madagascar
		Pakistan	Ghana
−5 —		Chile	

Strongly outward oriented	Moderately outward oriented	Moderately inward oriented	Strongly inward oriented

Empirical evidence also indicates that an outward-oriented strategy can improve the distribution of income. For example, the Gini coefficient (a measure of income inequality) declined in Hong Kong from 0.49 in 1966 to 0.45 in 1981 and in Singapore from 0.50 in 1966 to 0.46 in 1980. The Gini coefficient declined in Korea from 0.34 in 1964 to 0.33 in 1970, but it increased to 0.38 in 1976, partly because of credit subsidies to promote certain priority investments during the 1970s (Fields 1984).

Trade strategy and industrialization performance

Governments often adopt an inward-oriented strategy in order to promote industrialization through import substitution. But it seems that countries have industrialized faster under outward orientation. Table 5.1 sets several indicators of industrialization against the four categories of trade strategy. The indicators are the growth of manufacturing and agricultural value added, the share of manufacturing value added in GDP, the share of the active labor force employed in industry (defined to include mining, construction, and utilities, in addition to manufacturing activity), and the growth of employment in manufacturing.

During both periods, average annual growth of manufacturing value added was highest in the strongly outward-oriented group and lowest in the strongly inward-oriented group—15.6 percent versus 5.3 percent during 1963–73 and 10.0 versus 3.1 percent during 1973–85. Although both the moderately outward-oriented and the moderately inward-oriented economies achieved fairly high rates for 1963–73 (9.4 and 9.6 percent respectively), both saw a strong decline in the following period.

The smallest decline was in the strongly inward-oriented economies—but this group's manufactures had grown at a substantially slower rate than all other groups in the 1963–73 period. Even with a one-third fall in the growth of manufacturing in 1973–85, growth in the strongly outward-oriented economies remained higher than in any of the other groups during the more favorable economic climate of the previous period. The strongly outward-oriented economies have clearly coped better than the others with the economic shocks since 1973. (Again, Figure 5.3 shows the growth of manufacturing value added in the individual economies.)

The outward-oriented economies also achieved a higher share of manufacturing value added in GDP in 1963 (20.1 percent compared with 15.2 percent for the inward-oriented economies) and in 1985 (23.0 percent compared with 15.8 percent). The strongly outward-oriented and moderately inward-oriented groups both increased the share of manufacturing value added in their GDP by more than half from 1963 to 1985. The increase in the moderately inward-oriented economies, however, merely brought their share of manufacturing to a level achieved by all other groups two decades before. The share of manufacturing declined by 1.7 percent in the strongly inward-oriented group. The gap between the outward-oriented economies taken together and the inward-oriented economies taken together increased slightly.

Industry provides more of the jobs in the outward-oriented economies than it does in the inward-oriented ones. The share of labor in industry reached 30.0 percent in the strongly outward-oriented economies in 1980, considerably more

Table 5.1 Characteristics of industrialization for forty-one developing economies grouped by trade orientation

Trade strategy[a]	Average annual growth of real manufacturing value added[b]		Average annual growth of real agricultural value added		Average share of manufacturing value added in GDP[b]		Average share of labor force in industry		Average annual growth of employment in manufacturing[c]	
	1963–73	1973–85	1963–73	1973–85	1963	1985	1963	1980	1963–73	1973–84
Strongly outward oriented	15.6	10.0	3.0	1.6	17.1	26.3	17.5	30.0	10.6	5.1
Moderately outward oriented	9.4	4.0	3.8	3.6	20.5	21.9	12.7	21.7	4.6	4.9
Outward oriented (average)	10.3	5.2	3.7	3.3	20.1	23.0	13.2	23.0	6.1	4.9
Moderately inward oriented	9.6	5.1	3.0	3.2	10.4	15.8	15.2	23.0	4.4	4.4
Strongly inward oriented	5.3	3.1	2.4	1.4	17.6	15.9	12.1	12.6	3.0	4.0
Inward oriented (average)	6.8	4.3	2.6	2.1	15.2	15.8	12.7	14.1	3.3	4.2

Note: Averages are weighted by each country's share in the group total for each indicator.
a. See Figure 5.1 for a listing of the economies in each of the trade groups.
b. Data not available for Yugoslavia.
c. Data not available for Costa Rica and Malaysia (1963–73, 1973–84); nor for Thailand and Mexico (1963–73).

than in the moderately inward-oriented (23.0 percent) and the moderately outward-oriented (21.7 percent). In the strongly inward-oriented economies, manufacturing was a source of employment for only 12.6 percent of the work force.

Moreover, employment has grown faster in the outward-oriented economies. Manufacturing employment grew by 6.1 percent a year in 1963–73 (compared with 3.3 percent in the inward-oriented economies) and by 4.9 percent in 1973–84 (compared with 4.2 percent). In the first period, manufacturing employment grew three times faster in the strongly outward-oriented economies than in the strongly inward-oriented economies, 10.6 percent a year versus 3.0 percent. Growth slowed in the strongly outward-oriented group in 1973–84, narrowing the gap between the two extreme groups. But manufacturing in the strongly outward-oriented economies still increased employment at a faster rate (5.1 percent) than the strongly inward-oriented group (4.0 percent) and at a slightly faster rate than the moderately outward- and moderately inward-oriented economies (4.9 percent and 4.4 percent, respectively).

The outward-oriented countries fared better not only in industrialization and manufactured export growth, but also in agriculture. Their agricultural value added grew by 3.7 percent in 1963–73, compared with 2.6 percent in the inward-oriented economies, and by 3.3 percent in 1973–85, compared with 2.1 percent.

Why outward orientation works

The evidence of the previous section strongly suggests that outward-oriented trade policies have been more successful than inward-oriented trade policies. It is a harder task to explain precisely why. The two regimes confront economic decisionmakers with radically different signals and incentives. A full answer would call for an analysis of the effect of each of these elements. The best that can be achieved in practice is to consider the broad economic themes that seem to be at work.

It is well known that the protection associated with inward-oriented policies imposes economic costs, not least on the country that puts the policy into effect. Some of this economic burden, which is part of the reason inward-oriented policies have failed, can be seen from the structure of incentives that have resulted from tariffs and other protective measures (see Box 5.3). These incentives are bound to have important influences on the efficiency of resource allocation.

Box 5.3 Trade orientation and the structure of protection

Although estimates of effective rates of protection are widely available for many developing countries, they are not strictly comparable for various reasons. For instance, estimates available for different economies pertain to different years; some are based on tariffs only, whereas others include the effects of other policies that encourage or discourage production; and in some cases the protection-induced exchange rate effects are netted out, but in other cases they are not. These shortcomings notwithstanding, estimates may be suggestive of the relationship between the structure of protection and the trade strategies they followed.

Box table 5.3 provides a glimpse of typical structures of effective protection by sector and by sales destination. Several features are noteworthy. First of all, the structure of protection clearly shows that there was, on average, bias against exports in all countries for which data are available—with the possible exception of Singapore and the Republic of Korea, where the bias was so small that it could easily have been offset by assistance (although the data are insufficient to say whether this was the case). For the rest of the sample countries, the extent of such bias, measured by the difference of effective protection between domestic and export sales, ranges from 9 percentage points for Colombia (1969) to 229 percentage points for Chile (1967).

The data also reveal that there was a clear bias against the primary or agricultural sector and favoring the manufacturing sector in every country considered except Korea, where the opposite was true because of the rising price support for rice production. In the case of Colombia, the negative rate of protection for agriculture in 1969 was largely due to the export tax applied to coffee. Such a negative rate of protection for primary exports may be justifiable when import demand is inelastic so that disincentives to export sales can provide larger export revenues. But such cases are probably exceptional. The extent of bias against the primary sector in relation to the manufacturing sector is more conspicuous in the inward-oriented sample of countries. These figures indicate the negative incentives provided to export sales in countries in which primary goods constituted major exports.

Finally, the range of effective protection rates measures the scale of discrimination between different industries. As indicated in the table, the ranges for the countries are based on different numbers of sectors and are therefore not strictly comparable. Nonetheless, they reveal that ranges tend to be greater in countries where the overall level of protection is higher.

Box table 5.3 Structure of effective protection in selected economies by sector and sales destination
(percent)

Economy and year	Trade orientation	Effective protection rates by sector			Range and number of sectors	Effective protection rates by sales destination	
		Primary	Manufacturing	Overall		Domestic market	Export market
Singapore 1967[a]	■	5	0	0	−7 to 21 (9)	2	−5[b]
Korea, Republic of 1968[a]	■	11[c]	−17	−1	31 to 119 (11)	−1	−3[b]
1978	■	77[c]	5	31	−38 to 135 (11)	31	18[b]
Brazil 1967[a]	□	−4[c]	45	19	−4 to 123 (12)	..	..
1980–81[a]	□	−21[c]	23	..	−48 to −17 (3 primary) −85 to 219 (67 manufacturing)	..	..
Colombia 1969[a]	□	−23[c]	4	−15	−23 to 161 (10)	−14	−23[b]
1979[d]	■	39	55	44	22 to 88 (5 primary) 25 to 127 (29 manufacturing)	..	..
Philippines 1965[a]	■	−13[c]	99	0	−34 to 238[e] (10)	..	..
1980	■	9	44	36	..	..	..
Chile 1967	■	−7[c]	217	168	−23 to 1,140 (22)	233	4
Nigeria[a] 1980	■	−12	82[f]	..	−4 to 31 (7 primary) −62 to 1,119 (107 manufacturing)	..	..

■ Strongly outward oriented
□ Moderately outward oriented
■ Moderately inward oriented
■ Strongly inward oriented

a. Estimates are net of exchange rate overvaluation (compared with a hypothetical free trade situation) owing to import protection.
b. Estimates are adjusted for subsidies through credit and tax preferences.
c. Includes agriculture, forestry, and fishing only.
d. These estimates are based on tariff observations only, whereas all other estimates are based on direct price comparisons between domestic and world prices at the border.
e. An extreme case with negative value added in world prices is excluded.
f. Estimate is for 1979–80.
Source: For Brazil 1967 and Philippines 1965: Balassa and others 1971; for Korea 1968, Singapore 1967, and Colombia 1969: Balassa and Associates 1982; for Colombia 1979: Echeverri 1979; for Chile 1967: Krueger and others 1981; for Korea 1978: Nam 1981; and for others: World Bank data.

It may well be, however, that other policies not necessarily part of the inward- or outward-oriented strategies as they have been defined here account for some of the differences in performance. Chapter 4 has already examined the appropriate role of government. Chapter 7 will examine the ways in which other policies affect the allocation of resources and hence the prospects for growth. The rest of this chapter focuses on the links between trade policy and economic growth.

Trade policies and growth

The advantage of an outward-oriented strategy over an inward-oriented strategy is that it promotes the efficient use of resources. The gains from this go well beyond the ones which are re-

vealed by conventional analyses of the costs of protection (see Box 5.4). The rationing of import licenses, credit, and foreign exchange has invariably generated premiums and, in turn, rent seeking. By dismantling these administrative systems entrepreneurs could direct their energies away from unproductive activities, such as lobbying for changes in regulations. Further gains derive when firms achieve economies of scale: in an outward-oriented regime, the size of the domestic market does not limit the output of exporting firms.

Foreign investment is often attracted to the protected domestic markets of an inward-oriented economy—in the form of so-called tariff-jumping investments. But this kind of investment may actually reduce rather than improve the recipient's welfare. An outward-oriented policy will not at-

Box 5.4 Measuring the costs of protection

The objective of import tariffs and quotas is generally to raise the domestic price of a product above its world price and thereby stimulate increased domestic production. The attainment of this objective will not be costless, however. Protection generally imposes costs on the citizens of the protecting economy. Moreover, the magnitude of these costs differs between one instrument of protection and another. For example, quantitative restrictions are likely to impose substantially greater costs on society than tariffs that restrain imports to an equal extent.

Protection imposes a variety of costs on society. Economists frequently divide the efficiency costs into consumption losses and production losses. Consumption losses refer to the losses in real income of consumers of the protected product that occur because protection generally induces consumers to buy less of the protected product while paying a higher price. Producers benefit from the higher price and will often respond by increasing their output. A production loss is involved here to the extent that resources have to be drawn from other activities (including production for export), where they can be more efficiently used. Many studies on the cost of protection have attempted to estimate the magnitude of these production and consumption losses: estimates of less than 1 percent of GDP are common. It should be noted that these are annually recurring costs which apply for as long as protection is in force.

These production and consumption losses are not, however, the sole costs of protection. In addition, there can be losses associated with so-called X inefficiency when protection leads to domestic monopoly. For example, monopoly can permit the entrepreneur to relax

and not undertake the necessary effort to minimize costs. Moreover, monopoly can also cause conventional inefficiencies by restricting output.

The cost of protection is also underestimated if the costs of rent seeking and directly unproductive profit seeking are ignored (Box 4.7 in Chapter 4). Lobbies spend resources enacting protection. Similarly, once protection is enacted, it may lead to further resource-wasting lobbying—for example, in pursuit of import quotas carrying scarcity premiums.

Most of the earlier studies which measured the costs of protection have been conducted using "partial equilibrium" methods. In other words, the analysts focused attention only on the industry or sector being protected. But protection has effects which reverberate beyond the sector or sectors in which the initial restraint is imposed. Some analysts have attempted to estimate the costs of protection in models where such secondary effects are allowed for, that is, using "general equilibrium" methods. In principle, such models incorporate *all* the repercussions of protection on production and consumption, including effects on X inefficiency, the terms of trade and income, and employment beyond the industry under consideration. These studies generally provide substantially greater estimates of the cost of protection than do the partial equilibrium studies. For example, recent studies show that removing quotas alone in Turkey in 1978 would have increased its GDP by as much as 5.4 percent (Grais, de Melo, and Urata 1986) and that eliminating tariffs, quotas, and export taxes in the Philippines in 1978 would have increased its GNP by as much as 5.2 percent (Clarete and Whalley 1985).

tract investment projects which depend on the retention of import barriers.

While protected firms are sheltered, often within monopolistic markets, firms under outward orientation face greater competition—and hence incentives to increase their production efforts. So-called X inefficiency—the economic cost of a quiet life—is likely to be greater under inward orientation than under outward orientation.

All of these factors are important, but the scale and persistence of the growth rate differentials between the strongly outward-oriented economies and the others suggest that more subtle economic forces might also have been at work.

INNOVATIONS. It is tempting to argue that a more competitive environment for firms could lead to more incentives for increased productivity through technological innovations. Equally, it can be argued that ''uncompetitive'' profits might be needed before firms will engage in the efforts of technological innovations. Little is known about technological innovation in relation to trade policy. Nonetheless, there is increasing evidence that adoption of new technology has been faster in outward-oriented than in inward-oriented developing economies (see the section below on productivity growth). It is worth noting that exporting firms often benefit from a considerable transfer of technology from abroad, including advice on production engineering and aid in product design and marketing. Exposure to foreign know-how may help to speed innovations.

SELF-CORRECTING POLICIES. Arguably, outward-oriented regimes provide self-correcting mechanisms to align the macroeconomic variables that affect growth. For instance, if the exchange rate is permitted to become overvalued, the misalignment is quickly obvious under outward orientation because the balance of trade goes into deficit. In an inward-oriented regime the effect of the misalignment would take the subtler form of rising premiums on import licenses.

Savings, investment, and productivity

Growth performance can be looked at in another way: what has happened to the stock of capital and to its level of productivity? Much work remains to be done on this question, but there are a few indications that outward orientation might have encouraged higher savings rates and productivity growth.

SAVINGS RATES AND TRADE STRATEGY. As noted earlier, some outward-oriented economies have achieved spectacular growth in savings rates (Figure 5.2). Lack of empirical work makes it difficult to establish the relationship between savings rates and trade strategies, but several links seem plausible. First, a policy shift from inward to outward orientation should generate additional real income, partly by reducing the misallocation of resources and partly by raising income through multiplier effects as rising exports bring spare capacity into use. In developing countries the marginal propensity to save tends to exceed the average propensity to save, so that the increase in real income would help to raise the average propensity to save.

Another possibility is that domestic savings rise further under outward orientation because a higher-than-average share of income generated by exports is saved. Several studies found a strong positive correlation between export growth and domestic savings, but the issue remains unresolved.

A third link between trade policy and savings may be that high real interest rates are an important incentive for personal (and especially small-scale) savers. Capital markets are often highly distorted and underdeveloped in developing countries, and they tend to be more so in inward-oriented than in outward-oriented economies, even to the point of offering negative real interest rates in some instances. This could discourage savings in some inward-oriented countries (see Chapter 7).

Investment may be financed by foreign savings as well as by domestic savings. Under inward orientation, tariff-jumping foreign investment is common. In contrast, foreign investment is often attracted to exporting industries in outward-oriented economies. Foreign capital is more likely to generate the income (and exports) for its own servicing in export-oriented countries. Overvalued exchange rates maintained by exchange control systems, which are so common in inward-oriented economies, also deter foreign capital inflow.

PRODUCTIVITY GROWTH. Proponents of import substitution base their policies partly on the infant industry argument. They argue for temporary protection while firms raise their technical efficiency by creating industrial skills and mastering modern technology. But high protection may have the opposite effect. By limiting competition in sheltered domestic markets, it may inhibit specialization and promote risk aversion among managers (see Box

Box 5.5 Productive inefficiency under import protection: an example at the plant level

An intensive examination of the cotton spinning and weaving sector in Kenya and the Philippines illustrates some of the productivity losses that can occur in countries in which import substitution is the dominant strategy. Productivity of individual plants in these countries was calculated in relation to productivity in textile mills using identical equipment in industrial countries. Total factor productivity in the two sets of developing country plants ranged from 55 to 73 percent of that in the industrial country factories. On the basis of both engineering and economic analyses, the source of the difference in productivity was decomposed into three factors: the absence of horizontal specialization; technical expertise in management; and task-level productivity in the work force. The results of this decomposition are shown in Box table 5.5. Each number in the table shows the percentage of best-practice productivity in industrial countries realized in each activity. The sources of deviation from best practice are multiplicative, so that the product of the bottom three rows yields the relative total factor productivity shown in the top row.

The main cause of low total factor productivity was the inability of firms to obtain the benefits that specializing in a narrow range of products brings. Inadequate managerial skills reduce total factor productivity by 9 to 25 percent. Surprisingly, once the other productivity-reducing factors are taken into account, labor produc-

Box table 5.5 Total factor productivity relative to best practice in Kenyan and Philippine textile plants, 1980

Relative productivity and sources of deviation	Spinning		Weaving	
	Kenya	Philippines	Kenya	Philippines
Relative total factor productivity	0.70	0.73	0.68	0.55
Sources of deviation from best practice				
Horizontal specialization	0.85	0.79	0.63	0.70
Technical expertise in management	0.93	0.91	0.99	0.75
Task-level productivity	0.85	1.03	1.11	1.03

Note: The values are a productivity index of developing country plants relative to best practice in industrial countries.
Source: Pack 1987.

tivity is close to industrial country levels. Productivity losses from excessive product variety and from inadequate incentives to obtain technical competence have been a standard criticism of import-substituting industrialization. Although it is not correct to attribute all of the shortcomings shown in Box table 5.5 to this strategy, it was undoubtedly an important factor.

5.5). To maintain or improve their market position, however, exporting firms need to keep up with modern technology and bring managerial skills up to international standards.

The empirical evidence is far from conclusive, but postwar experience of productivity growth in developing countries suggests that trade policy is important. Table 5.2 presents data on factor productivity and factor growth in selected developing economies. It shows that total factor productivity increased much faster in the strongly outward-oriented economies than in the strongly inward-oriented economies. The annual growth rate was more than 4.0 percent in Hong Kong and Korea during the 1960s and early 1970s, compared with 1.5 percent or less in Argentina, Chile, and Peru. In India, total factor productivity declined in 1960–79. Singapore is an exception: its total factor productivity declined between 1972 and 1980. But this was a period when the government put an increasing emphasis on industries that required high levels of skill, capital, and technology. The productiv-

ity growth rates of the moderately inward- and outward-oriented groups were similar.

Recent World Bank studies of Turkey and Mexico show that total factor productivity growth was low or declined during periods when foreign exchange control and protection increased. At the level of the individual industry, another World Bank study (covering Korea, Turkey, and Yugoslavia) found that total factor productivity grew faster in most exporting industries than it did in most import-substituting industries.

Trade strategy in perspective

The evidence discussed in this chapter suggests that rapid economic growth and efficient industrialization are usually associated with outward-oriented policies on trade. Outward orientation encourages efficient firms and discourages inefficient ones. And by creating a more competitive environment for both the private and public sectors, it also promotes higher productivity and

Table 5.2 Growth of GDP, inputs, and total factor productivity
(percent)

Trade strategy and period		Average growth of GDP	Total factor productivity		Factor inputs		
			Growth rate	Share in GDP growth	Growth of capital	Growth of labor	Share of total inputs in GDP growth
Strongly outward oriented							
Hong Kong	1960–70	9.10	4.28	47.0	7.60	2.97	53.0
Korea, Republic of	1960–73	9.70	4.10	42.3	6.60	5.00	57.7
Singapore	1972–80	8.00	−0.01	−0.1	9.48	5.52	100.1
Moderately outward oriented							
Brazil	1960–74	7.30	1.60	21.9	7.50	3.30	78.1
Colombia	1960–74	5.60	2.10	37.5	3.90	2.80	62.5
Israel	1960–65	11.00	3.40	30.9	13.10	5.00	69.1
Moderately inward oriented							
Mexico	1960–74	5.60	2.10	37.5	3.90	2.80	62.5
Strongly inward oriented							
Argentina	1960–74	4.10	0.70	17.1	3.80	2.20	82.9
Chile	1960–74	4.40	1.20	27.3	4.20	1.90	72.7
India	1959/60–1978/79	6.24	−0.18	−2.9	4.77	1.65	102.9
Peru	1960–70	5.30	1.50	28.3	4.40	2.70	71.7
Turkey	1963–75	6.40	2.23	34.8	6.82	1.02	65.2

Note: Total factor productivity measures the growth of GDP above and beyond the growth in the use of both labor and capital inputs.
Source: Adapted from Chenery, Robinson, and Syrquin 1986, pp. 20–22.

Box 5.6 Alternative outward-oriented policies

Ideally, the shift to an outward-oriented strategy from an inward-oriented one can best be accomplished by removing existing trade barriers, devaluing the exchange rate, and relying on the price mechanism to allocate productive resources. In practice, many developing countries—including, for example, the Republic of Korea, Brazil, and Mexico—have used export incentives to offset bias against exports without dismantling all of their import barriers and without devaluing their currencies.

There are several ways to justify this approach. First, devaluations are feared because they may be inflationary. Compared with import restrictions, however, it is unclear whether this is so. Import prices under protection already reflect scarcity premiums, which the devaluation could simply cut into. Second, where import tariffs rather than quantitative restrictions are used, the loss of fiscal revenue in shifting to outward orientation may be a problem for some governments. Third, import tariffs and quantitative restrictions can be used selectively, which stimulates focused resistance to their removal.

Empirical studies, however, underscore the folly of resorting to export subsidies to offset antiexport bias. The selectivity of import barriers is economically damaging. Often governments are not aware of this. A study of the incentive system in Korea shows, for ex-

ample, that effective rates of protection ranged from −38 to 135 percent for eleven sectors in 1978, although average effective rates of protection did not significantly differ between domestic and export sales (Nam 1981). Second, when export subsidies are used to offset the antiexport bias, they have sometimes been captured by selective interests. Third, if import subsidies are used through preferential loans at below-market rates, the choice of production technique may also be distorted in favor of capital, which adversely affects employment. Finally, using import tariffs and export subsidies puts a heavy strain on the government's administrative machinery and encourages evasion, rent seeking, and other directly unproductive profit-seeking activities (Box 4.7 in Chapter 4).

In any event, the alternative route to outward orientation in trade—subsidizing exports—faces two problems. First, where the overvaluation of exchange rate caused by high import protection is large, as in Brazil and Mexico, the export subsidies required to offset the antiexport bias are simply too great. Second, subsidies by developing countries have increasingly become subject to countervailing duties in some industrial countries. The developing countries most frequently subject to countervailing measures by the United States include Brazil, Korea, and Mexico—although export subsidies had been removed in Korea by the early 1980s.

hence faster economic growth. Economies that have followed inward-oriented trade policies have performed poorly.

Many arguments for industrialization through import substitution have been advanced at various times. They are questionable, however, for several reasons. For example, suppose that export pessimism were justified, in the sense that when a country expanded its exports of a primary commodity, the price fell in world markets. The appropriate policy response would then be to levy an export tax on that commodity, not provide blanket import protection for the industrial sector as a whole. Or suppose that the infant industry argument applies and that some sort of government assistance is therefore in order. A policy of restricting imports is unlikely to be the best answer. Subsidies directed at the source of any external benefits avoid the costs of protecting an entire industry from import competition.

The new protectionism in some industrial countries (see Chapter 8) raises an important question for developing countries: can an outward-oriented strategy be successfully adopted in these adverse circumstances? Protection by industrial countries reduces the gains from trade both for themselves and for the developing countries, but developing countries may only make matters worse by turning inward. In other words, however protectionist the industrial countries, from an economic standpoint the best choice for developing countries is an outward-oriented strategy. But as protection increases, such an orientation becomes much more difficult politically. Note that outward-oriented policies involving export subsidies are increasingly threatened by countervailing actions by some industrial countries. This tilts the balance even more in favor of the policy which, on economic grounds, is in any case the better one: import liberalization combined with currency devaluation, rather than protection offset by export subsidies. Often countries such as Korea have adopted the second approach for their transition from inward- to outward-oriented policies, and it is still in use in such countries as Brazil and Mexico (see Box 5.6).

The evidence in favor of outward-oriented over inward-oriented policies may be convincing, but the issue of *how* an economy may be successfully moved from one to the other is a separate question. Recent experience in Argentina, Chile, and Uruguay suggests that the transition to outward-oriented policies should be carefully phased. Chapters 6 and 7 examine this in greater detail.

Trade policy reform

Chapter 5, in reviewing the experience of today's developing countries, concluded that rapid economic growth and efficient industrialization are more likely to be achieved by outward-oriented trade strategies than inward-oriented ones. In the light of that evidence, it is not surprising to find increasing disenchantment with the inward-oriented approach and greater interest in trade policy reforms that increase the degree of neutrality in trade regimes and lead to competitive exchange rates. Yet the number of countries which have experimented seriously with trade reform is limited, and—until recently, at least—relatively little attention has been paid to the lessons to be drawn from their experience (see Box 6.1).

Few of the developing economies which adopted such reforms sustained them for any length of time. Greece, Spain, Israel, and the Republic of Korea were among the first to embark on trade policy reform; today, they all have relatively outward-oriented regimes. Singapore and Hong Kong have, of course, inherited open trading regimes from their status as trading ports. Chile (in the mid-1970s) and Turkey (in 1980) adopted reforms more recently—they were particularly ambitious in Chile's case—but they have not yet stood the test of time.

Elsewhere, trade reform has been spasmodic. For instance, Pakistan undertook halting and limited reforms starting in the early 1960s. Somewhat more ambitious attempts by Yugoslavia (also starting in the early 1960s), Brazil (in the later 1960s), and Argentina (from the mid-1970s) have since been reversed.

This limited progress reflects a number of problems—real or perceived—in the transition from inward to outward orientation. The transition means that some activities become more profitable and others less so. Often it is protected manufacturing activities whose profitability is most threatened. The more inward-oriented the original policies, the greater these shifts—and the costs associated with them—will be. The pattern of transition may need to be designed to suit specific national situations.

• The more rapid and fundamental the policy changes, the greater the immediate benefits to the economy. But there is also a greater likelihood that more people will face transitional costs as workers are displaced from old jobs and firms abandon old activities.

• As some activities or occupations become less remunerative, resistance to policy change will emerge. Those who are threatened will use political means to obstruct reform.

• Trade policy reform is closely related to reform of other economic policies. In particular, the exchange rate and the way domestic inflation affects it in real terms are crucial to competitiveness in import-replacing and export activities. In turn these are influenced by domestic fiscal, monetary, and credit policies and by policies affecting capital flows.

All these problems of transition make the design of policy reform important. How can policies best be selected, phased, and sequenced to gain the benefits of reform as quickly as possible while minimizing transitional costs and political resistance? The second half of this chapter tries to answer this question. First, to put the issues in perspective, the chapter reviews the experience of trade liberalization around the world.

Box 6.1   Studying the process of trade liberalization

There is an extensive literature comparing policies and performance in outward- and inward-oriented economies, but until recently less attention has been paid to the transition from the one to the other. One multi-country study of foreign trade regimes and economic development looked at the relationship between liberalization and economic stabilization (Krueger 1978). In recent years several multicountry research projects have tried to deal with trade liberalization more directly. One of these is a World Bank project that looks at the experience of liberalization with stabilization in the Southern Cone—Argentina, Chile, and Uruguay (*World Development* 1985).

Another project is under way at the World Bank on

the timing and sequencing of trade liberalization policies (Papageorgiou, Michaely, and Choksi 1986). Thirty-seven episodes of liberalization in nineteen countries have been studied. The research is asking such questions as: Should the switch from quantitative restrictions to tariffs, say, or the direct promotion of exports be undertaken as separate stages of trade liberalization? What national and international conditions affect the chances of success? How do other policies affect trade liberalization?

In this study trade liberalization has two meanings: first, a reduction in the levels and dispersion of rates of protection and, second, a change in the *form* of protection from quantitative restrictions to tariffs. In any

Box figure 6.1 Trade liberalization indexes for selected countries, 1946–86

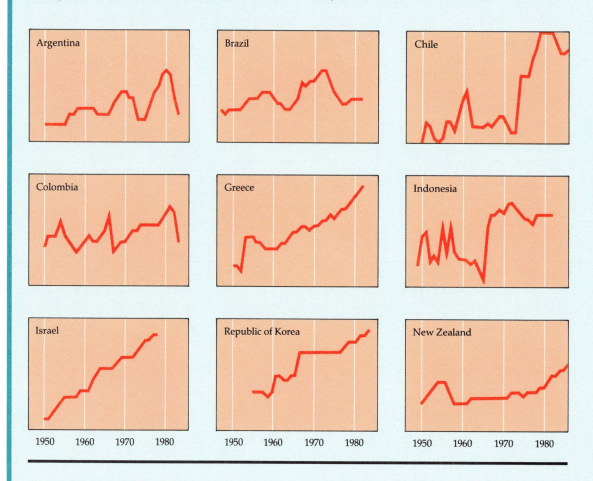

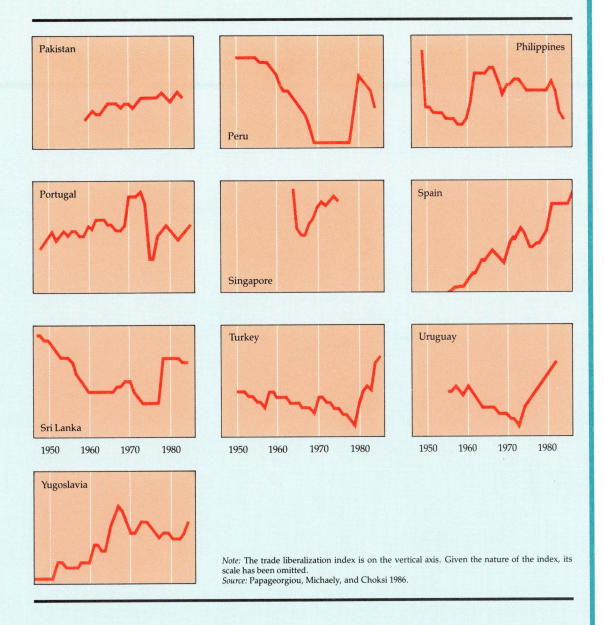

Pakistan

Peru

Philippines

Portugal

Singapore

Spain

Sri Lanka

Turkey

Uruguay

1950   1960   1970   1980

1950   1960   1970   1980

1950   1960   1970   1980

Yugoslavia

Note: The trade liberalization index is on the vertical axis. Given the nature of the index, its scale has been omitted.
Source: Papageorgiou, Michaely, and Choksi 1986.

given episode of liberalization, these two elements often appear together; occasionally, they may be in conflict.

As part of the research, a synthetic measure of changes in trade policy over time—the trade liberalization index—was established for each of the countries studied. In the indexes reported in Box figure 6.1 the vertical axis represents a synthetic measure of increasing trade liberalization: the more the curve rises, the fewer the trade restrictions. The indexes reflect judgments by different authors, based on quantitative indicators, such as the degree of antiexport bias and nontariff protection, and qualitative information about the trade regimes. Thus, the index is strictly ordinal, meaningful only in a comparison within one country over time; it cannot be used to compare the degree of trade liberalization across countries.

The diversity of country experience

The modern trend toward trade liberalization got under way in Western Europe in the late 1940s. It was encouraged by treaty obligations under the General Agreement on Tariffs and Trade (GATT) as well as by such arrangements as the European Payments Union of 1949—underwritten by U.S. aid under the Marshall Plan—and the European Economic Community established in 1958. A series of GATT-sponsored tariff-cutting rounds, as well as the expansion of various preferential trading arrangements within Western Europe, continued the process of trade liberalization. In spite of increasing protection in agriculture and in spite of the new protectionism against exports from developing countries (see Chapter 8), the economies of the industrial countries were probably as open by 1980 as they had been at the height of the free trade era before World War I.

Southern Europe and the Mediterranean

Some of the then-developing countries of Southern Europe and the Mediterranean began to liberalize on the coattails of other European countries—Greece, Israel, and Portugal in the 1950s and Spain in the 1960s. The process is not yet complete. It has suffered a number of temporary reversals, although the entry of some of these countries into the European Community (EC)—Greece in 1981 and Spain and Portugal in 1986—makes it likely that the liberalization will continue, even if their entry may complicate EC trade policy.

A broad pattern emerges for these liberalizing countries. The reforms started when a macroeconomic crisis led the government to stabilize the economy over a relatively short period; the exchange rate was devalued (and the impact of multiple exchange rates reduced); and nontariff barriers were replaced by substantial tariff protection. (See Box 6.2 for a discussion of the relationship between liberalization and stabilization.) The later moves toward neutrality in trade policy—mainly through tariff reduction, but also through export subsidy in some cases—happened over a far longer period. Within that period, each country sequenced its trade reforms differently. Greece took the boldest initial steps, devaluing and abolishing import controls in one go in 1953. Israel, by contrast, started with a series of devaluations in 1952–55, but did not take the step of replacing quantitative restrictions with tariffs until it had enacted a further series of devaluations in 1962–65.

Trade liberalization in these countries was put under great pressure with the onset of interna-

---

Box 6.2   Trade liberalization and economic stabilization

Economies often follow a certain pattern when controls are used to try to suppress inflation and trade deficits. This has been particularly true of some economies in Latin America. The cycle may start with inflation, which is provoked, as a rule, by government deficits that are financed by the creation of money. Typically, governments then seek to offset this inflation by maintaining the nominal exchange rate—the price of foreign currency in units of domestic currency. Their aim is to hold down the domestic price of imports to dampen inflation. But, as a result, the exchange rate becomes progressively overvalued. At the same time governments may also use price controls or subsidies to hold down prices.

This approach may work in the short term, but it creates other distortions which then require new controls. For instance, the overvaluation of the exchange rate will reduce the supply of exports, while the aggregate excess demand created by inflation will increase the demand for imports. Together these may result in a balance of payments crisis, followed by the introduc-

tion of tighter direct controls on imports. The external deficit will have to be financed by extra borrowing, and so debt builds up. Price controls, meanwhile, will either increase the budget deficit (if they are sustained through subsidies) or simply reduce the incentive to produce.

In these extreme circumstances governments are faced with the need to act on several fronts. For the short term they need to stabilize the economy, usually through a combination of devaluation and deflation. To improve resource allocation they also need to ease the various controls. The reform of trade policy is, like the liberalization of labor and financial markets, part of this broader economic program.

It is virtually impossible to sustain trade reform in an economy facing a stabilization crisis. On the one hand, inflation leads to a progressive overvaluation of the exchange rate, which increases the bias against exporting; on the other, inflation distorts relative prices and makes them unpredictable. Yet an atmosphere of crisis has sometimes been the political stimulus for reform.

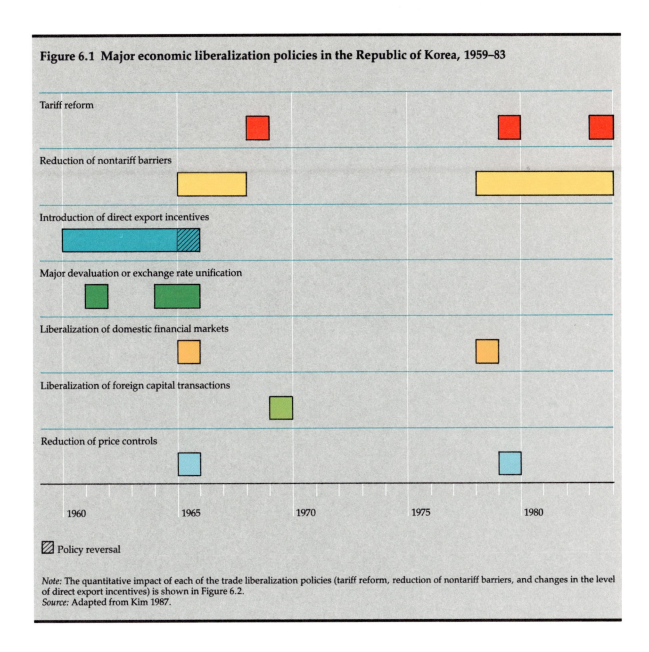

Figure 6.1 Major economic liberalization policies in the Republic of Korea, 1959–83

Tariff reform

Reduction of nontariff barriers

Introduction of direct export incentives

Major devaluation or exchange rate unification

Liberalization of domestic financial markets

Liberalization of foreign capital transactions

Reduction of price controls

1960   1965   1970   1975   1980

Policy reversal

Note: The quantitative impact of each of the trade liberalization policies (tariff reform, reduction of nontariff barriers, and changes in the level of direct export incentives) is shown in Figure 6.2.
Source: Adapted from Kim 1987.

tional recession in the 1970s. Recession and shocks in the terms of trade led to expanding public sector deficits, inflation, and growing balance of payments problems. At first governments were unwilling to consider devaluation. Trade liberalization may have survived, in some cases, only because of commitments to the European Community. Another Mediterranean country, Turkey, followed a more inward-oriented strategy for a long time even though, like Greece, it had an association agreement with the EC. In recent years Turkey has embarked on ambitious economic reforms, including trade policy reform, with positive results.

East Asia

In the 1960s a few East Asian economies responded to the market opportunities offered by economic growth in the industrial countries (and in some cases to the opportunities for foreign direct investment from these countries) by embarking on an aggressive export-oriented strategy. Hong Kong had been following such a strategy since the 1950s. Singapore—another city-state that had grown up on trading activities—had initially taken a different direction, protecting its domestic market in a short-lived arrangement with Malaysia

99

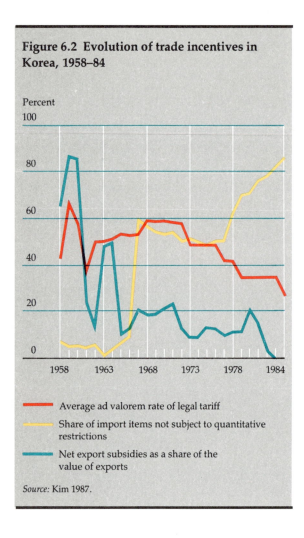

Figure 6.2 Evolution of trade incentives in Korea, 1958–84

Percent

Legend:
- Average ad valorem rate of legal tariff
- Share of import items not subject to quantitative restrictions
- Net export subsidies as a share of the value of exports

Source: Kim 1987.

switched its import control system from a list of goods that could be imported to the more liberal device of a list of goods that could not be. Starting in 1978 it made further cuts in quantitative restrictions and tariffs.

From early on, incentives were more neutral—between import substitution and exports—in Korea than in most other developing countries. On the import side, Korea's liberalization has been slow. Another feature was the stability of the real exchange rate. (The real exchange rate is the nominal rate corrected for inflation in domestic prices relative to inflation in world prices; see Box 6.3.) This reflected the government's emphasis on maintaining export competitiveness in spite of persistent inflation. There has been almost no visible cost of adjustment in this rapidly growing economy. This in turn has helped to make further trade liberalization feasible.

Korea's trade liberalization remains limited in several respects: selective import controls are still significant (although they are being phased out), controls on the domestic financial market remain, and there has been little liberalization of the capital account.

Several other countries in the region have successfully promoted manufactured exports, but in some cases this success has been limited by incentives that continue to encourage import substitution. In the Philippines, for instance, a substantial volume of nontraditional exports developed in the 1970s. That would have been much harder to achieve if not for a large initial devaluation of the currency and the maintenance of a stable exchange rate thereafter. In addition, bonded warehouses and free trade zones partially offset the continuing high levels of import protection. Nontraditional exporting has remained an enclave activity with little impact on the rest of the economy. Most of this activity involves the assembly of imported precut garments and electronic components. As a result, the net foreign exchange earnings of nontraditional exports are far lower than their gross value.

Latin America

For decades many of the Latin American economies suffered large fiscal deficits, balance of payments problems, runaway inflation, and distorted financial systems. The depression of the 1930s and the enforced self-reliance of World War II gave an impetus to import substitution. This became the region's dominant industrial strategy in the 1950s.

Several limited experiments in stabilization and

in 1963–65. But by the early 1970s it had returned to a strategy of low protection.

The Republic of Korea has pursued an export-promoting strategy that combines trade liberalization with considerable intervention (see Figures 6.1 and 6.2). Introduced in the late 1950s, export incentives were ineffective at first because of import protection and the overvaluation of the exchange rate. In the early 1960s the government abandoned multiple exchange rates, and in 1964 it devalued the currency substantially. This enabled it to cut its direct export subsidies. The government stabilized the economy and liberalized the domestic financial markets in 1965 and then reduced price controls. The reforms that started in 1964 led to strong growth in exports—but this was also partly due to the fact that import protection was at the outset not as heavy as in many other developing countries. In 1967 the government

Box 6.3 The real exchange rate

When domestic inflation is higher than world inflation, a country must devalue its currency if it wishes its prices to remain competitive abroad. When the devaluation exactly offsets the inflation differential, the *real exchange rate* is said to remain constant.

The real exchange rate is an index of relative domestic and world prices expressed in terms of a common currency (that is, the index of the number of units of domestic currency per unit of foreign currency multiplied by the ratio of a domestic price index to a foreign price index). Thus, when the real exchange rate is rising over time it is said to *appreciate*, and when it is falling it is said to *depreciate*. (Many analysts calculate the index inversely, with the foreign price series in the numerator and the domestic in the denominator. The coexistence of the two conventions can be confusing. The convention adopted here has the merit of consistency—appreciations go up, and depreciations go down.)

There are two main variants of the real exchange rate. The older variant is the "purchasing power parity" real exchange rate. This compares the domestic price of a representative basket of goods and services with the price of the same basket at world prices converted into local currency. It is, in effect, a measure of overall competitiveness. It can be approximated by comparing changes in consumer prices or changes in labor costs. It does not distinguish between traded and nontraded goods, because it implicitly assumes that their prices move together.

The other variant, which has recently come to be emphasized, compares the price of *nontradables* in the national economy (typically services and labor, whose prices can be proxied by the GDP deflator) with world prices for *tradables* (foreign wholesale price indexes, for instance, or the import and export price indexes for the national economy). For a small country that cannot affect the world price of traded goods, this variant provides a measure of the changing incentives to move in and out of production and consumption of nontradable and tradable goods. For instance, a depreciating real exchange rate raises the relative price of tradables, encouraging more production and less consumption of import substitutes and exports. This is the interpretation that is most useful to bear in mind when looking at the effect of changing trade and macroeconomic policies on the structure of incentives and on the current account of the balance of payments.

The two variants do not necessarily move together. This may be important, particularly for economies with quantitative restrictions, which break the link between changes in the foreign prices and domestic prices of traded goods. Goods subject to quantitative restrictions become nontraded goods, whose domestic price is set by domestic supply and demand.

In practice, there are problems of measurement. Few published indexes of domestic prices correspond to baskets of either tradable or nontradable goods. There are also weighting problems in constructing an index of foreign prices. So real exchange rates calculated using different statistical series fail to move in tandem.

Excessive variability in the real exchange rate increases risk and therefore discourages investment and production. Frequent adjustments in the nominal exchange rate (if inflation persists), stable macroeconomic policy (implying a stable rate of domestic inflation), and few quantitative restrictions on imports all promote stability in the real exchange rate.

---

liberalization were carried out in the 1960s, notably in Brazil and Chile from 1964 and in Colombia from 1967. These countries adopted more realistic exchange rate policies—partly through domestic stabilization efforts—and tried to reduce the bias against manufactured exports. They made less progress, however, in reducing import protection. Brazil and Colombia—whose reforms were more extensive than Chile's—saw much improved export performance.

The most significant experiments in trade liberalization in the 1970s took place in the countries of the Southern Cone of Latin America: Argentina, Chile, and Uruguay. These countries tried to stabilize and liberalize their highly controlled economies against an international background of recession, inflation, declining terms of trade, and the volatile capital flows which helped to provoke the international debt crisis of the 1980s. New governments came to power in the mid-1970s in all three countries and designed far-reaching liberalization programs. These radical reforms were undertaken in the face of entrenched political opposition to economic reform, which had grown out of the failure of several earlier attempts.

All three countries carried out an initial stabilization program of reduced public expenditure and devaluation, together with a program of economic liberalization measures which included removing quantitative restrictions, cutting the highest tariffs, reducing price controls, and reforming the financial system. But important differences in the em-

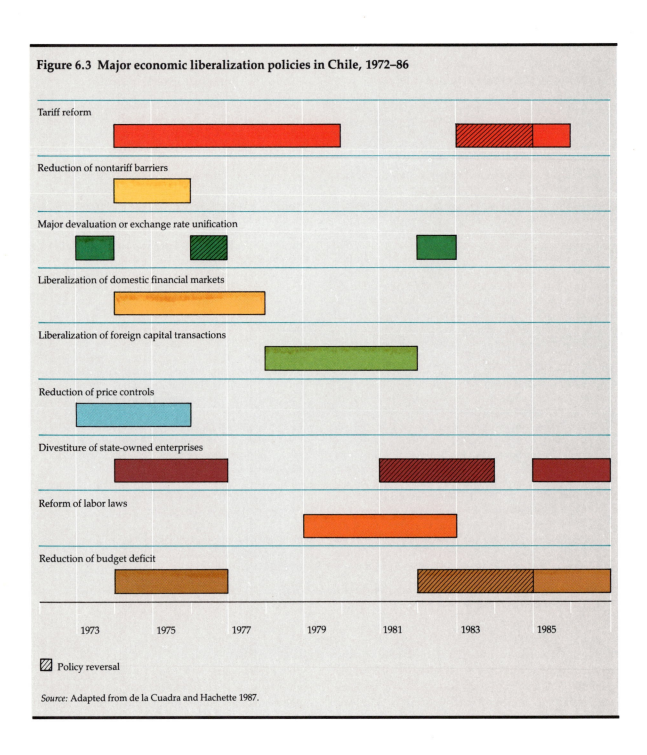

Figure 6.3 Major economic liberalization policies in Chile, 1972–86

Tariff reform

Reduction of nontariff barriers

Major devaluation or exchange rate unification

Liberalization of domestic financial markets

Liberalization of foreign capital transactions

Reduction of price controls

Divestiture of state-owned enterprises

Reform of labor laws

Reduction of budget deficit

1973   1975   1977   1979   1981   1983   1985

▨ Policy reversal

Source: Adapted from de la Cuadra and Hachette 1987.

phasis and sequencing of policies in the three countries contributed to different outcomes for the three experiments. Chile attached great importance to a radical reform of trade policy, and this reform was achieved before the liberalization of capital account transactions. Argentina and Uruguay liberalized the capital account comparatively early and made less progress in reducing protec-

tion. In the early 1980s all three countries faced severe economic crises that were the result partly of international conditions but largely of their own mistakes, particularly in pursuing policies that encouraged a real appreciation of the exchange rate. Chile, whose trade reforms survived the crisis, and Argentina, whose reforms did not, provide an instructive contrast.

Chile's trade liberalization was unprecedented for its speed and breadth. Trade reforms followed in the immediate wake of other major reforms (see Figure 6.3). These included the virtual elimination of a large budget deficit (starting in 1974); the elimination of multiple exchange rates (between 1973 and 1976); a large real devaluation (in 1973), followed by the adoption of a crawling peg exchange rate; the removal of price controls (from 1973); divestiture of public enterprises (from 1974); and liberalization of domestic financial markets (from 1974). In 1974–75 the government removed quantitative restrictions on imports. It had already started to introduce a series of progressively more liberal tariff reforms, and by 1979 it had achieved a uniform tariff of 10 percent. Exports were neither taxed nor subsidized (although an import duty without a corresponding export subsidy is equivalent to a tax on exports).

Inflation, although much reduced, still persisted after the stabilization, and the government began in 1976 to use the exchange rate in its fight against inflation. Its use of the exchange rate became more systematic from 1978 on when it adopted a crawling peg exchange rate that entailed a series of preannounced nominal devaluations at less than the differential between domestic and international rates of inflation. This system, intended to fight inflation expectations, in fact contributed, with the continued indexation of wages and the lifting of controls on capital inflows, to a gradual *appreciation* of the real exchange rate. This eroded much of the substantial real depreciation that had occurred since 1973 (see Figure 6.4). Nonetheless, the real exchange rate in the years following 1974 was on average far more favorable to the production of tradables than that for the decade preceding 1973.

After a recession in 1975—the result of stabilization measures adopted since 1973 and an adverse movement in the terms of trade from 1974—the economy responded clearly to liberalization. From 1976 to 1981 GDP grew by 8 percent a year. Trade grew even faster—exports after 1973 and imports after 1976—until the beginning of the 1980s, by which time the effects of the real appreciation of the peso were being felt in earnest (Figure 6.4). In the 1970s Chile began to send new products abroad—for example, fruits, vegetables, and forestry products. Its share in world exports grew, although this was also helped by favorable international markets for its nontraditional products until the beginning of the 1980s.

Chile's unemployment rate increased to 10 percent in 1974. The 1975 recession helped make the

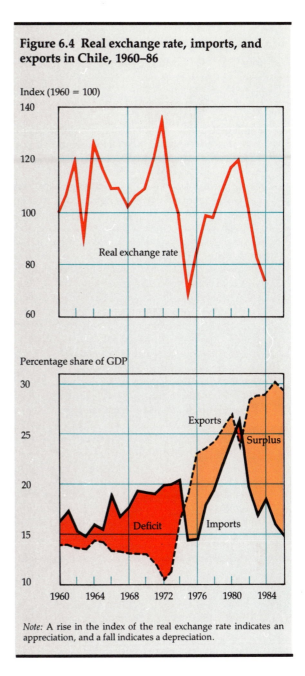

Figure 6.4 Real exchange rate, imports, and exports in Chile, 1960–86

Index (1960 = 100)

Real exchange rate

Percentage share of GDP

Exports

Surplus

Deficit

Imports

Note: A rise in the index of the real exchange rate indicates an appreciation, and a fall indicates a depreciation.

rate higher, and it remained high (between 13 and 17 percent) for the rest of the decade. Effective import barriers came down significantly only after 1976. According to one estimate, trade liberalization in isolation did not lead to net job displacement: lower import protection cut employment in manufacturing, but this was offset by employment gains caused by trade liberalization elsewhere in the economy, particularly agriculture. Jobs were lost as firms went out of business or were taken

Box 6.4 Sri Lanka: the 1977 trade liberalization

Sri Lanka's United National Party came to power in 1977 with a large majority and a commitment to reintegrate Sri Lanka with the world economy after more than a decade and a half of heavy protectionism. The government saw trade reform as the only way out of the country's economic trouble. It hoped that liberalization would quickly raise employment and improve the supply of goods to meet the widespread shortages. It also hoped that trade reform would help the country attract external assistance.

The government replaced most of the quantitative restrictions with tariffs. The new tariff structure had six bands, with rates varying between zero on essential consumer goods (rice, flour, and drugs) and 500 percent on luxuries. The exchange rate was devalued by 46 percent against the dollar, and the prevailing dual exchange rates were unified at the new rate. The reforms removed a wide range of domestic price controls. Food subsidies were reduced and targeted at the poor. Licensing requirements were relaxed, and repatriation of profits was allowed in order to encourage direct investment from private foreign sources.

By most standards the two years following the liberalization were successful. The economy rebounded with GDP growth rates of 5.7 and 6.4 percent in 1978 and 1979, respectively, and continued to grow at 5.8 percent in 1980 (see Box figure 6.4). GDP growth averaged 5.2 percent a year from 1978 to 1985, against 3.8 percent from 1970 to 1977. Growth was spread across nearly all sectors of the economy. By 1983 the unemployment rate had fallen by half, to 12 percent of the labor force.

Merchandise exports (excluding petroleum products)

increased from $0.7 billion (constant 1960 prices) in 1977 to $1.1 billion in 1984. Manufacturing output grew quickly (by 7.8 percent in 1978), and capacity utilization in manufacturing increased from 54 percent in 1974 to 74 percent in 1981. During the initial stage of reform, the economy's capital-output ratio declined and its output-labor ratio increased: this points to an improvement in the allocation of resources. Labor also began to replace capital in the medium term.

These early successes stemmed from, first, the shift from quotas to tariffs (which increased the availability of raw material inputs); second, capacity increases that led to higher employment; and third, an expansion in the production of tradable goods (compared with nontradables) brought on by the depreciation of the real exchange rate.

By 1980 the program's initial successes were beginning to wane because of poor macroeconomic management and deteriorating external conditions. Liberalization was partly reversed by a massive increase in domestic aggregate demand, thanks to a rapid expansion of public investment. Financed by foreign borrowing, this increased the demand for domestic goods, which caused the inflation rate to rise and the real exchange rate to appreciate.

Abroad, the hike in oil prices in 1979 triggered a world recession. This reduced the demand for Sri Lanka's exports and worsened the terms of trade. External events and the appreciation of the real exchange rate combined to squeeze the export sector. Only in late 1984 did the government make efforts to get back onto the path of trade policy reform.

over; other firms survived by achieving large gains in productivity. This rationalization was achieved with little additional investment.

An exchange rate policy that led to real appreciation, post-1977 measures to liberalize exchange controls, and high domestic interest rates all contributed to heavy borrowing from abroad. The peso's appreciation was particularly marked from 1979 to 1981. Exports became uncompetitive, and the trade deficit soared. By late 1981 a domestic recession was setting in, and in 1982 the peso was substantially devalued. The recession was so deep that unemployment reached 25 percent (in June 1982), and the financial sector was virtually bankrupted. The uniform import tariff was raised to 35 percent in 1984, but came down to 20 percent in 1985. Thus trade reform survived the crisis, and

the rationalization it had fostered left Chile's industrial sector in a far stronger position to withstand the shocks of the 1980s. In recent years the economy has grown strongly, and unemployment has come down to under 10 percent. Economic liberalization clearly contributed to this recovery.

Argentina acted with as much speed as Chile in an initial phase of macroeconomic stabilization in 1976. The new government devalued the currency and dismantled its multiple exchange rates. The government also attacked the budget deficit, but was never able to reduce it below 6 percent of GDP. From 1976 the government began to liberalize the capital account, and from 1977 it embarked on a series of domestic financial reforms. Its trade policy reforms were, however, far more limited than Chile's. In 1976–78 export taxes were substan-

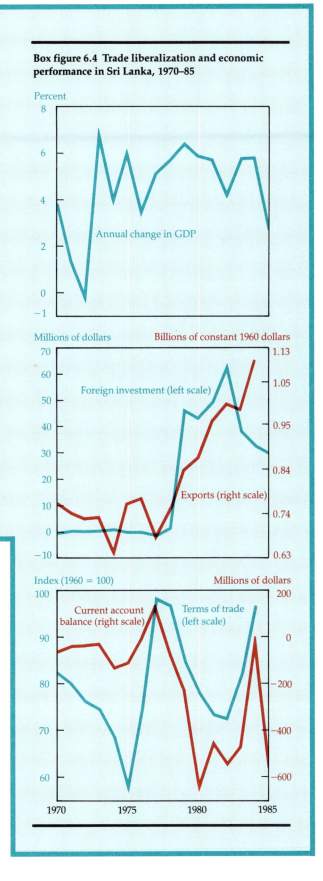

Box figure 6.4 Trade liberalization and economic performance in Sri Lanka, 1970–85

Percent

Annual change in GDP

Millions of dollars   Billions of constant 1960 dollars

Foreign investment (left scale)

Exports (right scale)

Index (1960 = 100)   Millions of dollars

Current account balance (right scale)

Terms of trade (left scale)

tially reduced from their average level of 50 percent. Quantitative restrictions on imports were replaced with tariffs, and some of the highest tariffs were cut. But, on average, tariffs remained high and protective. A program of further reductions was announced in 1978.

Argentina compromised its trade liberalization from the beginning in the way it phased its reforms. The exchange rate was used right from the start as a tool for curbing inflation. By contrast with Chile, the ordering of reforms encouraged an appreciation of the real exchange rate. Traditional exporters responded to the removal of large export taxes, and—since exports were liberalized *before* imports—this helped to fuel expectations of currency appreciation. At the same time, internal financial liberalization resulted in higher interest rates, and external financial liberalization thus attracted foreign capital. The stubbornly high public sector deficit helped push up the interest rate and sucked in more foreign loans.

Around 1979 the situation became critical. The terms of trade deteriorated severely in 1979–80. By 1980 the currency was highly overvalued. This led to an outflow of dollars (in the form of capital and foreign tourist expenditure), which culminated in the inevitable balance of payments crisis, a huge devaluation, an explosion of the budget deficit, raging inflation, and a virtual closing of the economy. Economic liberalization was dead, and trade liberalization was stillborn.

South Asia

South Asian countries have made little attempt to liberalize trade. The region has followed a strategy of import substitution similar to Latin America's. This has created industrial sectors with vested interests in continued protection. The governments of India, Pakistan, and Sri Lanka have also emphasized macroeconomic stability, and the success of their stabilization policies has done much to avoid the economic crises that have been the spur to major trade liberalizations elsewhere. Perhaps the most important attempt at liberalization in South Asia was Sri Lanka's package of reforms in 1977 (see Box 6.4).

Sub-Saharan Africa

It was not until the 1960s that countries in Sub-Saharan Africa began to adopt inward-oriented industrialization strategies. Several countries have recently undertaken adjustment programs which

Box 6.5 Trade policy reform in Sub-Saharan Africa

With independence, many countries in Sub-Saharan Africa saw industrialization as the main route to economic development. Indeed, from 1965 to 1973 the region's industry grew at 14 percent a year and played a leading role in economic progress. But this changed dramatically in the 1970s. Industrial growth slowed to 5 percent a year between 1973 and 1980 and was negative between 1980 and 1985. Industries were plagued by massive excess capacity, and exports remained a small part of output. The sector had consumed a great deal of foreign exchange for little benefit in jobs or output. This rapid decline was part of an overall deterioration of African economies, which included the stagnation of agriculture.

The disappointing performance of manufacturing in Sub-Saharan Africa was the result of several complex factors. Formidable resource constraints, which included a critical shortage of local skills and inadequate infrastructure, combined with inappropriate policies to create high-cost and inefficient manufacturing industries. Among the policies that contributed to this were:

• *Exchange rate policies.* Most African countries maintained overvalued exchange rates. The weighted index of the real effective exchange rate for all Sub-Saharan countries appreciated by 75 percent between 1974 and 1984. (In comparison, the index for Asia depreciated by 26 percent over the same period.) This hurt export profitability and discouraged investment in export industries.

• *Tariffs and quantitative restrictions on imports.* Shortages of foreign exchange, caused by the overvaluation of exchange rates, led governments to restrict imports through tariffs and quantitative restrictions. This protected domestic manufacturers from foreign competition and fostered inefficient local production. Smuggling flourished, aided by a booming black market for foreign exchange. For some industries, smuggling and overvalued exchange rates have in fact led to negative or uncertain protection.

• *Price controls.* Governments controlled the prices of products subject to import controls in order to prevent local manufacturers from making excessively high profits. Where they were effective, price controls merely discouraged domestic production; but often they were ineffective, and black markets emerged for several controlled items (see Chapter 7).

• *Nationalization.* Several countries nationalized foreign or joint ventures, discouraged investment from abroad, and became less hospitable to private domestic investors.

The combination of these policies proved extremely damaging to industrial growth and efficiency. High protection and precious little domestic competition often permitted large profits in protected industries. Technological development languished. With time, industries became less competitive internationally. When oil prices rose in 1979 and the international recession followed, Sub-Saharan countries were plunged into a foreign exchange crisis. Policies intended to cope with this only made matters worse. In recent years firms have been starved of inputs, profits have plummeted, and real wages have fallen in the formal manufacturing sector.

Reforming the exchange rate and trade regimes may not produce an immediate increase in export growth, but such measures will at least improve the efficiency of investment and production.

Since the early 1980s there has been a fundamental shift in the policies of some Sub-Saharan countries. The success of these changes is difficult to judge, since most are recent and several are incomplete. Several countries have substantially devalued their currencies (see Box figure 6.5).

Nigeria made radical policy changes in 1986. It abolished the compulsory surrender of export proceeds and the licensing of imports and introduced a more moderate tariff structure. (Further tariff reforms and the removal of some import bans are yet to come.) The

include elements of trade liberalization—for example, the auctions of foreign exchange in Ghana and Nigeria, the elimination of quantitative restrictions in Mauritius, and tariff reforms in Côte d'Ivoire, Senegal, and Zaire. It is too early to judge the success of these experiments (see Box 6.5).

The transition to more outward-oriented policies

Liberalization means abandoning old activities and adopting new ones. Perhaps the most important and politically sensitive cost in this process is unemployment. Protected sectors may contract as protection is lowered, which can cause temporary unemployment, especially if certain skills are specific to certain sectors. Other sectors will take time to expand, and workers will need to prepare for and seek out the new jobs. Note that trade liberalization cannot cause *permanent* increases in unemployment. In the long run the level of unemployment depends on macroeconomic policies and the efficiency of the labor market. In the short run, however, resistance to trade policy reform is likely to arise, both from displaced workers and from

demand for foreign exchange is now largely met by authorized dealers (mainly commercial banks). They purchase the auctioned proceeds of oil exports and foreign loans and buy other foreign exchange earnings directly from their customers. In *Ghana* reform is proceeding almost as rapidly. The government devalued the cedi several times before it began to auction foreign exchange, a practice that is being steadily extended to all merchandise imports. To complement this, the government has taken measures to liberalize imports and promote exports.

Mauritius dismantled its quantitative restrictions on imports within the space of fifteen months. It has since enjoyed an export boom and an economic upsurge. Contributing factors were the recovery in international markets, the promotion of export processing zones, and the country's improved competitiveness after a devaluation and a period of wage restraint. *Zaire's* devaluation in 1983 and its subsequent move to a market-determined exchange rate have already provided a stimulus to exports. These reforms are to be followed by lower import tariffs and the abolition of all export duties and other taxes on manufactured exports. Finally, *Côte d'Ivoire, Senegal*, and *Togo* are rationalizing their tariff structures, *Malawi* is promoting exports through better duty rebate systems and improved export credit and insurance facilities, and *Burundi* is eliminating all export taxes on locally manufactured products.

There is ample scope in the rest of Sub-Saharan Africa for trade and exchange rate reform. Such reforms would need to be supported both by other policy changes that allow a greater role for domestic competition and by the provision of adequate infrastructure, skills, and institutional support. With a policy environment conducive to efficient industrial development, there is no reason why the Sub-Saharan countries cannot compete in international markets and benefit from the advantages of international trade.

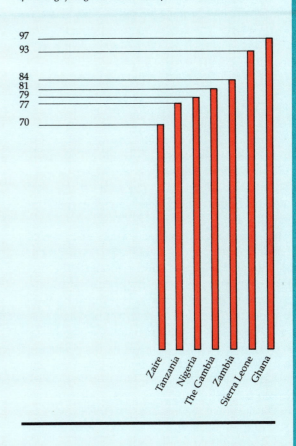

Box figure 6.5 Currency devaluation in selected Sub-Saharan African countries
(percentage fall against the dollar, September 1983—March 1987)

producers in those sectors which suffer the biggest loss of protection.

Short-term costs

In fact, there is evidence that the unemployment cost of more liberal trade policies may be smaller than commonly supposed. Employment losses are often more concentrated, and hence more visible, than the employment gains which liberalization may spread over the rest of the economy. Gross unemployment—that is, unemployment caused by

discharging labor from the activities which contract because of trade liberalization—has sometimes been substantial. But, as a rule, timely absorption of labor into other activities has helped to prevent large rises in aggregate unemployment. Often there have been relatively few layoffs, even in the sectors which lost their protection. Shifts of labor within sectors—possibly even within individual firms—have been common and have dampened the effect on aggregate unemployment.

After Brazil cut its tariffs in 1967, for instance, there was no apparent increase in unemployment or business failures. The dramatic dismantling of Indonesia's restrictive import-licensing regime in 1966–67 led to a much improved performance in an economy that had been on the verge of collapse—and there was no rise in unemployment. Sri Lanka's experience in 1977 was similar. A broad dismantling of its highly protective barriers was followed by higher employment, even in the sectors which had seemed to depend most on the trade barriers.

The big exception to this pattern is Chile in the second half of the 1970s. The country's shift from a highly restrictive trade regime to virtually free trade was implemented within five and a half years. One estimate places the manufacturing jobs lost by 1979 owing to trade liberalization at 11–12 percent of the 1974 manufacturing labor force. These losses, however, were offset by liberalization-induced employment gains elsewhere. (The study does not try to account for the rise in unemployment caused by factors other than trade liberalization.)

These generally low transitional costs support the view that even partial liberalizations can open up enough new opportunities to allow the economy to adjust rapidly. Replacing quotas with tariffs is a case in point. In many developing countries controls on foreign exchange transactions are a particularly important form of quota. When access to foreign exchange is controlled, some firms will find it hard to obtain imported supplies; once these controls are removed, efficient firms will be free to buy the inputs they need and new firms may enter. Such effects help to explain why this form of trade liberalization seems to have been especially fruitful.

Popular perceptions of the unemployment problem can be mistaken. Sometimes trade liberalization really has led to unemployment, but the rise was disguised by other developments, and so the public did not connect the rise in unemployment with trade policy. Occasionally, however, unemployment caused in other ways has been blamed on liberalization (as it was in Chile, for instance). In any case, when trade liberalization has been aborted, the reversal has rarely had anything to do with unemployment.

Political sustainability

Historically, the single most important factor providing the spur to trade liberalization has been crisis—either of the country's own making or imposed from outside. Its most common form has been an economic stabilization crisis springing from excessive budgetary and balance of payments deficits and rising inflation. But history should not be taken as prescription: countries that do not face such crises should grasp the opportunity for reform that stability offers.

To sustain trade liberalization beyond its initial stage, economic and political stability has proved essential. Few governments have been willing to commit themselves to liberal trade policies. One way to make the commitment and to make it credible is to participate in a treaty. In Greece, Israel, Portugal, and Spain the long-term commitment to an economic alliance with the European Community has helped keep the trade regime relatively open compared with other developing countries.

Another way to boost credibility is to act decisively. Hesitant policy which leads to gradual liberalization is much more likely to run out of steam. This is particularly true of countries with a long history of trade restrictions.

In Chile, for instance, a liberalization in 1956–61 had a weak initial impact. It left high import protection in place, provided little incentive to exports, and failed to prevent a real appreciation of the currency. These reforms were quickly reversed. But a second set of reforms, in 1974–81, is still in place thirteen years after its implementation, in spite of minor reversals in 1983–85. The experience of Indonesia is similar. The initial impact of the first episode (1950–51) was weaker than that of the second (1966–72). The first liberalization was short-lived and largely reversed; the second has, with some reversals in the mid-1970s, remained in effect. So even when a first liberalization attempt collapses, a second has a good chance of success if it is boldly done.

A clear shift in policy is important in two ways. First, without it producers may expect the reform to be quickly reversed. This, in turn, can be a self-fulfilling prophecy because, unless the pattern of production changes to take advantage of the new pattern of incentives, the reform may prove unsustainable. Pressure to reverse it will rise as soon as lower protection allows imports to come in without any offsetting rise in exports. Second, a major reform should spur exports appreciably. It will thus create vested interests in support of the new trade regime.

Macroeconomic policy and trade liberalization

One of the clearest lessons from previous trade reforms is the link between trade liberalization and macroeconomic policy. Many trade reforms have started with a program of stabilization in which inflation has been reduced through the control of public spending and the application of tighter monetary control and the trade deficit has been reduced both by domestic deflation and a substantial devaluation. The devaluation, improving the incentive for both import substitution and exporting, is a vital step in trade policy reform. Indeed, it is probably more important than the way vested interests or the economic costs of transition are handled.

The more ambitious and long-lasting liberalizations—in Portugal, Greece, Spain, Israel, Chile, and Turkey—all started with macroeconomic stabilization. The countries which have tried to liberalize trade in the midst of macroeconomic crisis have failed. The Philippines, for example, embarked on trade policy reform in the early 1980s as inflation, the trade deficit, and foreign debt were all rising rapidly. Attempts at reform were abandoned after a severe balance of payments crisis in 1983. But there was a subsequent stabilization, and the trade liberalization process has now been resumed.

The evidence also stresses the importance of balance of payments equilibrium once trade liberalization is under way. A large deficit involving a substantial loss of foreign exchange reserves is almost sure to undermine trade reform. This happened in the Philippines after the liberalization of the early 1960s, in Argentina and Uruguay after the liberalizations of the 1970s, and elsewhere. By the same token, Pakistan has been cautious in liberalizing trade for fear of its effect on the balance of payments.

The balance of payments can be affected by changes in capital flows or in foreign remittances of labor income and by other factors over which governments have little control. But what seems to matter most for successful liberalization is export performance. Exports too can change exogenously, because of shifts in the terms of trade or fluctuations in crop output because of the weather. The crucial determinant of export performance, however, has been the real exchange rate for exports. Good performance usually goes hand in hand with a depreciation of the real exchange rate and—possibly even more important—with a real exchange rate which is stable in the long run. The real exchange rate, in turn, depends on changes in the nominal exchange rate and in local prices—and hence on fiscal and monetary policy. The experience of the Southern Cone countries has shown that appreciating the real exchange rate to reduce inflation expectations is inconsistent with maintaining it at a level appropriate for trade liberalization.

FINANCIAL LIBERALIZATION. Efficient capital markets ought to improve economic flexibility and thus facilitate trade liberalization (see Chapter 7). But, again, the real exchange rate complicates the picture. The trade reforms of Argentina and Uruguay were derailed in the early 1980s after abnormally high capital inflows appreciated the real exchange rate. To guard against excessive appreciation, governments may need to monitor capital flows and, where necessary, influence their timing or sterilize them. (See Box 7.4 for a discussion of the role of financial sector reforms in Chile's macroeconomic problems.)

LIBERALIZATION IN OTHER DOMESTIC MARKETS. Governments often maintain substantial controls on labor markets, industrial prices, and industrial investment (through investment licensing or state-owned enterprises, for instance). Maintaining these controls will, as in the case of financial controls, hamper the effects of trade policy reform on resource reallocation. Fortunately, easing these controls is unlikely to influence the real exchange rate as directly as capital market liberalization (see Chapter 7).

The design of trade policy reform

Reform in the conventional instruments of trade policy can be discussed under three headings: replacing quantitative restrictions with tariffs, reforming tariff protection, and the direct promotion of exports.

Replacing quantitative restrictions with tariffs

It is broadly accepted that moving from nontariff barriers to tariffs is a move toward a more open trade policy. This is so for two reasons. First, tariffs are generally less protective than quantitative restrictions (although it is possible to have tariffs set so high that they prohibit imports). Second, a tariff is a price instrument, not a quantity instrument. As a result, tariffs are more "transparent"—changes in foreign prices feed through more readily to the domestic economy. Quotas, by contrast, uncouple national economies from the world economy. For example, in India cotton is protected by quantitative restrictions, and textile producers are required to use Indian cotton. As a result, movements in the price of this crucial raw material are not always related to those of world cotton prices, which determine the cost of this input to competitors. It is therefore difficult for Indian producers to commit themselves to production for export: the conditions under which they have to compete are unpredictable.

In many cases a shift from quotas to tariffs has been a key element in the early stages of trade policy reform. Sometimes it has been the only element. For example, Israel's first and second phases of reform focused on imports and consisted of the gradual removal of quotas and their replacement with tariffs. Greece's first reforms removed almost all quotas and replaced them with tariffs which were for the most part lower than the tariff equivalent of the quotas.

The evidence of similar episodes strongly suggests that this shift in the form of protection was highly beneficial (Box 6.4). Often, not only did the economy's growth speed up following such shifts, but even in the sectors whose protection had been lowered, production increased as firms began to operate in a less restrictive and more transparent regime. This suggests that in an economy in which trade is regulated largely by quantitative restrictions—and this is true for most economies in which trade is severely restricted—a liberalization policy should start with a shift from the use of quotas to the use of tariffs, even if it means very high tariffs.

What level of tariffs is needed to replace any given quantitative restriction? In practice it is difficult to measure the protection from quantitative restrictions. And, even if this could be done with confidence, the switch to tariffs brings about such large changes in the way protection works that the exercise is likely to be pointless. Some countries have sought to replace quantitative restrictions with more or less equivalent tariffs. For example, Sri Lanka replaced quantitative restrictions with high tariffs in 1977, and the Philippines did this in an ad hoc process from 1957 to the mid-1960s (and ended up unintentionally reducing average protection). In Argentina, however, the tariffs used to replace most of the quantitative restrictions in 1976–78 were on average so high that they shut out imports just as effectively.

Reforming tariffs

The movement toward greater neutrality has two dimensions: the lowering of the average level of protection and the reduction in the average disper-

sion, or variance, of protection. If the dispersion of tariffs is not reduced as the tariff average is reduced, the tariff structure may not become more neutral. Indeed, a reform that reduces tariffs on intermediate and capital goods but leaves intact those on final outputs could *increase* effective protection—the level of protection afforded to domestic value added—even though it *reduced* the average level of tariffs.

Of course, it is possible to reduce at the same time both the average level of tariffs and their dispersion. Governments have approached the task in several ways: an equiproportional cut in all tariffs, an equiproportional reduction of the excess of each tariff over some target level, higher proportional reductions of higher tariffs, or some combination of these and other methods. As a rule, simple schemes widely applied work better than case-by-case and fine-tuning methods. Some tariff reforms have attempted to target the effective, rather than the nominal, rate of protection (the Philippine reforms of 1981–85 are one example). This is unnecessarily complicated and may misfire anyway because of measurement problems.

Many economists favor the so-called concertina approach to tariff cutting. First, all tariffs above a certain ceiling are lowered to that ceiling; next, all tariffs above a new, lower ceiling are lowered to that ceiling; and so on. This should yield the lowest adjustment costs without leading to inadvertent increases in effective protection. Chile's tariff reductions in the 1970s more or less followed this scheme.

Lessons about the amount of time necessary to eliminate quantitative restrictions and tariffs are difficult to draw. Some reforms have taken a long time—Korea and the countries of southern Europe, for instance, have still not completed their reforms after at least two decades. Fewer have been completed within the medium term—the process lasted five years in Chile, for example. But none have been fully implemented over the short term. There is no obvious relationship between the length of the period of policy reform and its chances of success. But the apparently low adjustment costs in most trade reforms, together with the danger that lengthier reforms will be less credible, are arguments for faster reform.

Some tariff reforms have used institutions, typically tariff commissions, either to set tariffs on a case-by-case basis or to hear appeals for exceptions to the reforms that have been scheduled. Tariff commissions such as those in Australia, New Zealand, the Philippines, and Sri Lanka have often approached their task with too many objectives. Their work has probably not contributed to increasing neutrality (see Box 6.6).

Direct promotion of exports

The logic of trade liberalization is that the tariffs should be as low as possible. As long as the average tariff is not zero, an element of discrimination against exports remains (unless they are equivalently subsidized). Chile's reforms achieved a uniform tariff of 10 percent with no exceptions. Later, this was revised, and Chile ended up with a uniform tariff of 20 percent, which left a mild discrimination against exports, but not enough to prevent export growth. The experience of Brazil and the

---

Box 6.6 Can governments ease the trade reform process?

Governments are seldom able to bring about economic reform at the stroke of a pen. They first have to overcome the opposition of groups which fear they may be adversely affected.

Transparency and persuasion

There is sometimes a bias in government decisionmaking: pressure groups can noisily voice their narrow interests, but when benefits are spread widely across the community no single group sees that it has much to gain. For example, it is easier to grasp the costs of closing down an inefficient car manufacturing plant than to see the benefits of cheaper cars and employment opportunities spread across the rest of the economy.

Another bias can arise when governments, to accommodate tensions between a sectional interest and the public interest, pass laws so vague that they appear to satisfy both. The law must then be implemented by administrative decision, and the special interest groups will attempt to influence the relevant administrators.

One way to promote public understanding of the public interest is to set up a "transparency" agency whose job would be to provide an overview of government intervention. The aim would be to help the government and the public see sectoral proposals in an economywide framework. Tariff commissions, established in such countries as Australia, Canada, New Zealand, the Philippines, Sri Lanka, and the United States, are intended to carry out this role, but the results have been mixed. The commissions have often spent much of their time working on highly technical questions such as whether an industry has suffered "damage" or "injury," whether it can be attributed to imports, and whether these imports are unfair in some sense.

Transparency agencies can, in fact, claim some real successes, but the problems they face should not be underestimated. On top of the sheer difficulty of predicting the future, governments are always under pressure to mute their role by diluting their terms of reference.

A possible defense against this kind of pressure would be to make full review a legislative requirement.

With sufficient independence and investigative powers a transparency agency could influence other branches of the bureaucracy. A bipartisan agreement that such review would be mandatory could serve as a kind of legislative constraint on government.

Safeguards and compensation

A government trying to convince the public that a certain reform will proceed smoothly might tip the scales by offering guarantees against disruption. These might include strengthened antidumping provisions (a safeguard measure) or additional income support for those who stand to lose (a compensation measure).

Unfortunately, the experience with safeguard measures is not encouraging. In practice, the search for safeguards has become a complicated process which is carried along by its own momentum and has precious little to do with economic efficiency. For example, a recent antidumping case in Australia dealt with cherries in brine from Italy. It turned on the appropriate valuation to be attached to the drums in which these cherries were packed for shipment. It seems that "dumping" could be "proved" if the drums were valued at their price when new—but if, as turned out to be the case, some drums were secondhand, then dumping could be not proved.

Compensation measures are an alternative approach, but they too have had many defects. The costs of identifying winners and losers are very large. This is because of the practical difficulties of sorting out policy changes and their impacts—people win and lose for all sorts of economic reasons, and it is seldom possible to be sure of the cost inflicted on a particular group by any given policy. Compensation measures also create "moral hazard," in which people are given incentives to behave inefficiently to qualify for compensation.

Buying off pressure groups differs from straightforward compensation—at least in principle. It is a way of overcoming obstacles to change in an overtly political way. Even with this more limited objective, however, the record is discouraging. Far from softening resistance to change, this approach merely channels protest into pressure on governments about who should get the most compensation.

Philippines shows that export growth can be achieved in the presence of significant import protection, as long as governments can prevent the real exchange rate from appreciating.

Where significant import protection remains, governments might consider offsetting the discrimination against exports with administrative measures to provide imported inputs at world prices or with subsidies. Directly promoting exports in this way may also help to form a constituency for continued protection. But it may come to be seen as a long-term alternative to further import liberalization. This appears to have been the case in Pakistan and, in the 1970s at least, in the Philippines.

Direct export promotion is a difficult alternative to cuts in import protection. It raises administrative problems and often requires significant budgetary resources. Like any other selective intervention, it will also encourage rent seeking. Above all, the risk of GATT disputes and of countervailing duties in importing countries has made direct export promotion increasingly unattractive.

The lessons of trade liberalization

Trade policy reform is complicated. It is closely linked to liberalization in capital, labor, and domestic product markets and to macroeconomic policy. It is partly a political process, in which credibility and expectations play an important role. Feasible policy choices may differ from country to country, and reform may be vulnerable to changes in the international environment. Because of this complexity, there is no single optimal path to reform. But there are, nonetheless, lessons to be drawn from previous attempts.

• Trade liberalization must involve large shifts of resources, but it has not always raised unemployment by as much as is commonly supposed.

• Strong and decisive reforms have carried greater credibility and have been better sustained than more timid reforms.

• Replacing quantitative restrictions with tariffs is a useful first stage of trade liberalization.

• Providing a realistic real exchange rate is vital to the successful introduction of trade reform. Keeping it stable is essential if the reform is to be sustained. All this requires a macroeconomic policy that manages inflation and the nominal exchange rate so as to keep domestic costs in line with world prices.

• The scope for successful trade liberalization depends on complementary reforms in the domestic economy—especially in financial and labor markets. (These issues are explored further in Chapter 7.)

Trade liberalization—like any major economic reform—is not easy. Above all, it requires a strong political commitment, most likely in the face of resistance from those who, in the short term at least, stand to lose. It is to be hoped that this commitment will come more easily as the evidence mounts that trade policy reform will quickly bring benefits at a lower cost than policymakers have sometimes feared.

Complementary policies for industrial development

The previous chapters noted the benefits of international trade for efficient industrialization and discussed the problems in shifting from an inward- to an outward-oriented trade strategy. But governments also use other policies to promote industrial development. This chapter describes these policies and examines their effects. It also shows how they interact with trade policies to influence, first, the markets for capital and labor; second, the pattern of domestic competition; and, third, the acquisition and mastery of technology.

The policy choices

Governments often complement their trade strategy with a variety of policies. The most important among these involve regulating product prices, directing private investment, controlling interest rates and credit allocation, and intervening in labor markets.

Regulating product prices

Prices play a powerful role in directing industrialization. High prices reflect scarcity; they raise profitability and attract resources for increased production. Low prices reflect abundance and keep resources away. Prices best fulfill this role in competitive markets. Market imperfections—such as monopoly or poor information—distort these signals. But governments sometimes regulate prices deliberately, either to correct such distortions or to pursue other objectives. These objectives might include the redistribution of income, the promotion of high-priority industries, or the control of inflation.

In pursuit of these goals many countries have adopted price controls. Often they have found that such controls are difficult to enforce because black markets mushroom and drive large sections of the economy underground. In addition, multiproduct firms, such as those in the textile industry, tend to compensate for price controls on one product by expanding production of uncontrolled products. As a result, fewer "essential goods" are produced in favor of more "nonessential goods."

As a rule, the wider the controls, the harder they are to enforce. In 1970 the Ghanaian government attempted to control 6,000 prices for 700 groups of products. Yet its Prices and Incomes Board had only 400 personnel. The scale of such a task is beyond even the most competent agencies. Prices in such a system are often set by adding a fixed margin to costs. This removes any incentive for firms to reduce costs. Furthermore, controlled prices discourage new investments; therefore, as demand expands, shortages begin to appear. Often the poorest consumers, the supposed beneficiaries of price controls, suffer the consequences along with others.

Attempts to remove price controls have been most successful in countries where stable macroeconomic policies provided a low inflation environment and governments introduced the reforms gradually by reducing the number of controlled items in manageable steps. Producers and consumers are responsive to price incentives. When cement prices were freed in India in 1982, the increase in supply was so strong that market prices fell rapidly. (See Box 7.1 for a discussion of Ghana's experience with removing price controls.)

Apart from controlling prices directly, govern-

Box 7.1 Removing price controls: lessons from Ghana

Ghana has used assorted price controls since 1962 for several purposes: to limit rents accruing to sellers in times of scarcity, to combat inflation, and to keep down prices of key items in the cost of living. But price controls have proved ineffective in times of extreme scarcity and rapid inflation and have often exacerbated the problems brought about by currency overvaluation and expansionary fiscal and monetary policies.

By 1970 nearly 6,000 prices relating to more than 700 product groups were controlled. Efforts to liberalize the system were reversed following a change of government, and the Prices and Incomes Board was given authority over all price and wage changes. But with inflation reaching 100 percent a year during the 1970s, frequent requests for price adjustments greatly exceeded its administrative capacity. Delays of up to six months forced firms to choose between accumulating stocks, losing money by selling at the old price, or evading the controls altogether.

Rapid inflation increased the gap between market prices and official prices. Failure to adjust the exchange rate meant that imports through official channels cost as little as a tenth of their market value. Price controls prevented producers from realizing this scarcity rent, which would have given them extra incentive to produce more. But the inability to enforce controls at the retail level made trading an increasingly lucrative activity. Obtaining access to goods at the official price for resale—a practice known as *kalabule*—became an important source of income. By the early 1980s the market value of civil servants' monthly allocation of rice, milk, soap, and so forth (although not received regularly) could equal their monthly take-home pay.

Controls over the distribution of scarce goods became increasingly important. During the 1970s, military trucks transported canned milk to the north for sale at the same price as in the southern cities of origin. But this greatly increased the profits from smuggling it to neighboring countries. Similarly, northern rice was smuggled out because price controls made it impossible to cover transport costs to the south. The tighter the controls on a commodity, the scarcer it became. The markets of Togo became well stocked with soap, milk,

textiles, and other products that were made in Ghana and then smuggled out, while liquor and other luxuries with high scarcity premiums and less stringent controls were brought in. During the 1980s, land borders were closed for some time in an effort to stem smuggling, and storekeepers were forced to sell their stocks at controlled prices (often below what they had paid). But this worsened the scarcity of goods on the market and drove up prices further.

Price and distribution controls became interwoven with political power in 1982, as the new government attempted to broaden and decentralize political participation. Many of those who joined village and workers' committees were more concerned with obtaining access to goods at controlled prices than with the government's difficulty in subsequently moving away from controls.

As the economy worsened, the government recognized that price controls were not working and that economic recovery required shifting profits from black marketeers to producers. It reduced underlying distortions and inflationary pressures through a reform program introduced in April 1983 that featured devaluation and restrained fiscal and monetary management. The government also wished to lessen its direct responsibility for prices and distribution, which entailed high administrative costs as well as political pressures. Yet it could not totally abandon such controls while monopolies and excess profits were seen to exist and while it was also trying to restrain wage increases. It therefore adopted a strategy of gradually softening the enforcement of controls.

The first step was to shift most commodities to a system whereby producers simply notified the Prices and Incomes Board of price changes; the board retained its right to intervene. The list of goods requiring prior approval was reduced first to twenty-three and gradually (over sixteen months) to eight, which greatly reduced the board's workload and turnaround time. Firms were permitted to charge a provisional price approved quickly by the board, and the review of its recommendations was shifted from the Ministry of Finance and Economic Planning to a tripartite com-

---

ments have also subsidized the consumption of essential industrial products. Well-targeted subsidies are preferable to price controls: although such subsidies reduce prices for consumers, they do not lower incentives to producers. But subsidies have often led to budgetary deficits and, in turn, to high inflation. Furthermore, once installed, subsidies can be hard to remove. In Egypt in 1977 the gov-

ernment's attempt to reduce subsidies on a range of basic commodities led to riots.

Directing domestic investment

Regulations, coupled with fiscal incentives, have been used to guide private investment in industry at one time or another in many countries, includ-

mission with representatives from government, labor, and business. This public review process maintained the principle of intervening whenever changes were out of line, while eliminating the need to publish official prices.

The consumer price index rose by only 10 percent in 1985, the year after price controls were eased; inflation had fallen from 122 percent in 1983 to 40 percent in 1984 following the introduction of the reform program. The inflationary impact of massive devaluations and price liberalization during 1983–85 was limited, because market prices already reflected scarcities and because various measures operated to reduce the gap between supply and demand. On the supply side, the incentive effects of price liberalization helped in four ways: hoarded consumer goods were released, scarcity rents were shifted from distributors to producers, agricultural producers responded to favorable rainfalls by greatly increasing food availability, and industrial producers sought additional foreign exchange through a newly opened auction window for foreign exchange. On the demand side, the ability of consumers to absorb price increases was limited through fiscal and monetary restraint.

These policies generally improved the market situation. Increased local supplies of some commodities such as milk, bread, soap, and beer brought market prices down, sometimes below the previous official prices, while increased imports eliminated scarcity rents for other goods (for example, tires and vegetable oil).

Three main factors contributed to the success of Ghana's liberalization of price controls. First, market prices already reflected scarcities, so that liberalization mainly shifted scarcity rents from distributors to producers. Second, complementary policies helped raise marketed supplies and restrain inflationary pressures, so that consumer resistance was minimized. Third, price control enforcement was depoliticized by permitting provisional price changes while retaining the right of review and by including representatives of interested groups in the review process.

ing Benin, Brazil, Ethiopia, India, Indonesia, Liberia, Malaysia, Mauritius, Mexico, Pakistan, Sri Lanka, Tanzania, Togo, and Zambia. They reflect the view that markets fail to allocate resources according to national priorities. These priorities are often embodied in development plans, and the regulatory and tax systems are used to ensure that plan priorities are reflected in the pattern of private investment. Other objectives include the prevention of industrial concentration, the promotion of regionally balanced industrial development, and, finally, public sector control over key industries.

Perhaps the most common tool of investment regulation is the industrial license. Under such systems governments grant licenses for the creation of new industrial capacity according to their projections of future demand. Studies of Brazil, Egypt, India, Indonesia, Mexico, Pakistan, and Spain indicate that in these countries licensing involved unexpected costs, but delivered few of the expected benefits. The systems are often too complex and implemented ad hoc. For example, in Spain, government agencies developed economic criteria for the granting of licenses, but were unable to implement them on a systematic basis. This creates uncertainty among investors. In some countries the licensing process can take six months or longer, and even then the applicant may fail. Investment is discouraged, and research suffers because there is little assurance that firms will receive licenses to turn plans for new products into reality.

Licensing usually favors large firms over small. (Although very small firms often lie outside the licensing system altogether.) Large firms tend to be better informed and can allocate more resources to deal with the licensing system. Where multiple applications are permitted, large firms have been known to preempt the entire capacity available through licensing. In some countries the authorities have attempted to promote competition by licensing several small firms. But in industries where economies of scale are important, investment in firms of less than optimal size has merely fostered inefficiency.

Another drawback is that countries need to commit manpower to administer their licensing systems. This carries a high price, particularly in African economies where skilled manpower is scarce. Furthermore, industrial licensing can engender corruption, especially when the interpretation of rules is left to the discretion of a few officials.

Some developing countries, notably in East Asia and Latin America, have avoided using rigid systems to influence the pattern of investment. Their resources have been better able to respond to changes in incentives following trade liberalization and to flow to industries offering the highest financial returns. Firms in these countries are motivated to be more competitive since there are few legal restrictions to entry by new firms (see Box 7.2). Such benefits have prompted some countries to

Box 7.2 Capacity licensing in India

Capacity licensing is perhaps the most important of India's regulatory policies for the industrial sector. The government has used this instrument to influence total domestic industrial capacity and its allocation among sectors, firms, and locations. In all but a few industries, investors must have a license to establish or relocate a plant, manufacture a new product, or expand output beyond 5 percent a year or 25 percent in five years. Only firms with assets of less than Rs50 million (about $4 million) and located at least thirty miles outside urban areas are exempt.

The aim of capacity licensing has been to ensure that industrial activities are consistent with industrial and social policy objectives. These objectives include the promotion of priority industries, the decentralization of plant location to "backward" regions, and the conservation of scarce resources by striking a physical balance between domestic supply and demand.

But India's capacity licensing system has constrained competition between domestic firms. High rejection rates, long delays, and changing subsector priorities have made it a significant barrier to entry and growth. It has contributed to the high concentration of Indian industry, suboptimal scales of production, and slow technical progress.

As the scale of India's markets has increased and the adverse effects of capacity licensing have become more apparent, the government has relaxed or modified some of its licensing requirements to promote growth and productivity in a few industries. In cases where capacity licensing has been relaxed, competition and efficiency have tended to improve rapidly. For example:

• Until recently, attempts by large, relatively efficient producers of two-wheeled motor vehicles to expand production and meet the rapidly growing demand for low-cost transport were thwarted by capacity licensing requirements. As a result, large firms capable of capturing economies of scale existed side by side with small firms of limited capacity. For example, in 1984 the largest scooter manufacturer produced

250,000 vehicles, while the two smallest produced fewer than 5,500 vehicles each. Not only did the rigidities in the licensing system lead to an inefficient structure of the scooter industry, it also led to substantial unmet demand in the domestic market. By 1985 the government had relaxed its capacity licensing requirements for two-wheeled motor vehicles and had eased its restrictions on technical collaboration with foreign firms. The result was a rapid expansion of capacity. The largest scooter manufacturer in India is now expanding its capacity to 750,000 vehicles a year and will eventually become the fourth largest in the world. And competition between companies has stimulated the production of technically superior products at international standards of price and quality.

• The first three nylon filament plants in India were licensed and established in 1962, when total domestic demand was less than the capacity of one plant of minimum economic scale. Eight others were added by 1985, which raised the total number of firms to eleven. Each firm had a single plant, and capacities ranged from 500 to 5,000 tons a year. The average capacity of nylon plants in other countries is usually much higher; for example, in the Republic of Korea the average capacity is 33,800 tons a year. Smaller plants, although inefficient, were financially profitable in India because they were sheltered by import barriers and the capacity licensing system. In an effort to redress the inefficient structure of the nylon industry, the Indian government announced in 1986 a minimum scale for new nylon plants of 12,000 tons a year.

• The removal of licensing restrictions in the professional instruments industry prompted a challenge by new entrants and forced a major producer to shed outdated lines and offer improved products. Similarly, when licensing requirements were relaxed selectively for the manufacture of telecommunications equipment, several private sector firms drew up plans to enter and thus put pressure on the largest producer to improve efficiency.

streamline their licensing systems. Others have tried to dismantle their systems gradually. One approach is to relax restrictions and raise the lower limit for investments that require licenses.

Directing foreign investment

Foreign investors in developing countries are often subject to regulations and requirements that are more stringent than those faced by domestic inves-

tors. These regulations may require exclusion from some sectors, limits on foreign equity participation, domestic content minima, export obligations, employment quotas, establishment of research and development facilities, appointment of host-country nationals to senior managerial positions, ceilings on repatriation of profits and royalties, and limits to the duration of technology licensing agreements. At the same time, governments offer foreign investors a wide variety of incentives such as tax holidays, tax concessions, accelerated depreciation allowances, duty-free imports of capital goods, investment subsidies, and guarantees against expropriation.

This mixture of restrictions and incentives reflects an ambivalence on the part of some developing countries. On the one hand, they fear that foreign direct investment may undermine their sovereignty, limit their tax revenues, displace domestic firms, blunt local initiative, introduce inappropriate technology, pollute the environment, and squander exhaustible resources. On the other hand, they recognize that foreign direct investment augments domestic investment, transfers new technologies, and avoids some of the risks of external borrowing.

Many of the concerns about foreign direct investment arise when countries use protection to stimulate local output. Foreign (as well as domestic) investors can then earn financial returns that are often much higher than the economic returns to the country. Thus, protection attracts foreign direct investment. But this can mean a net loss of foreign exchange for the developing country if the sum of repatriated profits and imported inputs exceeds the foreign exchange saved through local production. In such circumstances, foreign direct investment can even reduce a country's real income.

Many controls on foreign investors therefore take the rents from protection that accrue to foreign firms and channel them to groups within the country, such as organized labor, shareholders, or domestic entrepreneurs. But this may deter foreign firms from investing in the first place. Controls seem to matter more than incentives to foreign investors. Most regard incentives as volatile and transitory. Empirical studies suggest that a country's natural resources, its recent growth performance, and its political and economic stability are the factors that attract foreign investment. This may help explain why eight countries account for more than half the stock of foreign investment in developing countries (see Figure 7.1). Many of these countries do offer tax concessions, but it is unlikely that in the absence of a favorable economic and political climate for investment, tax concessions alone would be enough.

Countries that follow outward-oriented strategies tend to have fewer problems with foreign direct investment. Since a country following an outward-oriented strategy does not discriminate between import substitution and exports, it tends to attract foreign firms wishing to take advantage

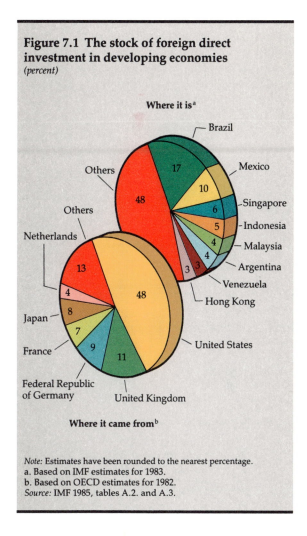

Figure 7.1 The stock of foreign direct investment in developing economies
(percent)

Where it is[a]

Brazil 17
Mexico 10
Singapore 6
Indonesia 5
Malaysia 4
Argentina 4
Venezuela 3
Hong Kong 3
Others 48

Where it came from[b]

Others 48
Netherlands 13
Japan 4
France 8
Federal Republic of Germany 7
United Kingdom 9
United States 11

Note: Estimates have been rounded to the nearest percentage.
a. Based on IMF estimates for 1983.
b. Based on OECD estimates for 1982.
Source: IMF 1985, tables A.2. and A.3.

of its resources. Foreign investments, therefore, are more likely to align themselves with the country's comparative advantage and to augment domestic resources in fostering efficient industrial development.

Controlling interest rates

Firms need finance to exploit investment opportunities. Not surprisingly, therefore, governments have often made the financial sector an instrument of industrial policy. For example, in a majority of developing countries, governments control at least some interest rates to encourage investment in some sectors. Interest rate controls also help governments finance their budget deficits: many state-owned enterprises (SOEs) rely on low-interest loans from the banking system, and many governments require banks to buy low-yielding government bonds or place some of their assets in low-interest reserves with the central bank.

Although interest rate controls and selective credit policies may serve specific purposes, they tend to have broad and, on the whole, unfavorable effects on the behavior of savers, lenders, and borrowers.

• *They reduce the efficiency of investment.* This is particularly true when controls on interest rates

Table 7.1 Real interest rates and selected growth indicators, 1971–85
(average annual percentage)

Range of real interest rates	Average real interest rate	Average GDP growth rate	Average growth rate of industry
−60 and −10	−21.1	2.3	1.1
−10 and −5	−7.8	3.0	3.3
−5 and 5	−1.4	5.5	7.2

Note: Data are unweighted group averages based on a sample of thirty-one developing countries.
Source: IMF, *International Financial Statistics*, various years; World Bank data.

make them negative in real terms (see Table 7.1). As well as promoting investment in low-return projects, interest rate controls encourage firms to build up their inventories. Furthermore, faced with the need to ration credit, banks lend to the borrowers they know well—large-scale enterprises and parastatals—or even to the industrial groups that own them (see Box 7.3). In Colombia, interest rate controls reduced the funds available for smaller-scale industrial enterprises; the efficiency of investment fell as a result. Interest rate controls also keep credit cheap in relation to labor for those firms with unrestricted access to loans from the formal financial sector and thus encourage capital-intensive investments in some parts of industry. These distortions ultimately affect growth. A study of seven Asian developing countries found that interest rate controls reduced economic growth by roughly half a percentage point for every percentage point by which the real interest rate was below its market-determined rate.

• *They inhibit savings.* In countries where inflation is high, controls on deposit rates can make

---

Box 7.3   The "iron law of interest rate restrictions"

The "iron law of interest rate restrictions," as formulated by Claudio González-Vega (1976), states that as government-regulated interest rate ceilings become more restrictive, the share of credit granted to large borrowers increases while that to small borrowers decreases. Although the iron law was originally put forward and tested in the context of subsidized lending to small farmers, it applies with equal force to any financial system in which interest rates are subsidized.

The starting point of the iron law is that interest rates are the price of loanable funds. In an unregulated market, therefore, interest rates move to balance the demand for funds and the supply of funds. But when interest rates are suppressed by government regulations at below market-clearing levels, the demand for funds will exceed the supply, and some would-be borrowers will be denied credit.

The iron law says that under these circumstances banks tend to deny credit to small borrowers first. The reason is that for each loan the share of overhead costs in the total costs of lending tends to be higher for small borrowers than for large borrowers. In the absence of interest rate restrictions, banks can accommodate higher costs and maintain the profitability of lending to small borrowers by increasing the rate of interest. But with interest rate controls, the only option that banks possess for maintaining profitability is to concentrate

increasingly on lending to large borrowers.

The iron law also has implications for the distribution of income. Subsidized credit is often recommended as the only politically and administratively feasible way of redistributing income to low-income earners. But the iron law implies that subsidized interest rates tend to be inefficient instruments for income redistribution. Subsidized interest rates influence income distribution through their effect on the access to credit afforded to different classes of borrowers. Since the size of the loan tends to rise with the wealth of the borrower, the large subsidies that go with large loans accrue to wealthy borrowers. Nonborrowers—usually the poorest—receive no subsidy at all. So the subsidies make the distribution of income even less equitable.

Ultimately, it is access to credit that is important. Low interest rate ceilings cannot create the missing physical inputs, the missing markets, or the missing technologies that affect the performance of entrepreneurs. Instead, below-market interest rates create distortions in the price of capital and contribute to inequalities. By contrast, if financial intermediaries are free to set their own interest rates in competition with others in the financial market, small borrowers will stand a better chance of gaining access to credit, and investments will tend to be financed on the basis of their financial profitability.

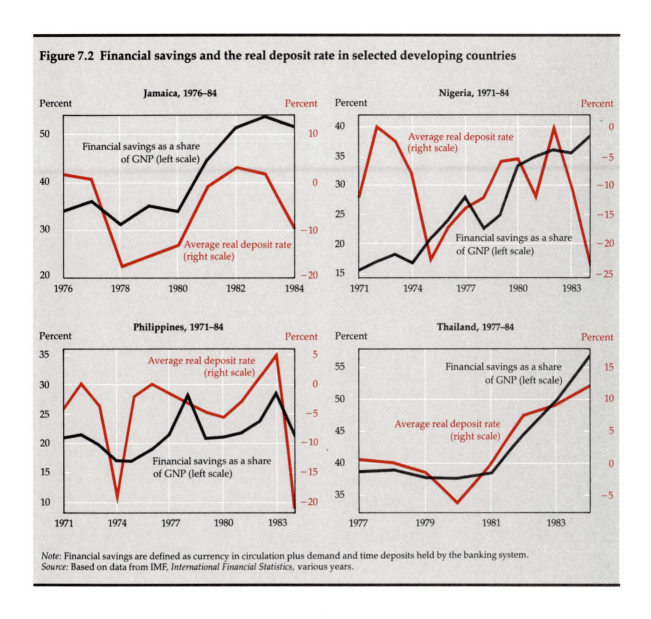

Figure 7.2 Financial savings and the real deposit rate in selected developing countries

Jamaica, 1976–84

Financial savings as a share of GNP (left scale)

Average real deposit rate (right scale)

Nigeria, 1971–84

Average real deposit rate (right scale)

Financial savings as a share of GNP (left scale)

Philippines, 1971–84

Average real deposit rate (right scale)

Financial savings as a share of GNP (left scale)

Thailand, 1977–84

Financial savings as a share of GNP (left scale)

Average real deposit rate (right scale)

Note: Financial savings are defined as currency in circulation plus demand and time deposits held by the banking system.
Source: Based on data from IMF, *International Financial Statistics,* various years.

them negative in real terms. Even where interest rate ceilings apply only to loans, they control deposit rates indirectly by acting as a constraint on the yield and liquidity that banks can offer savers. In a sample of eight developing countries between 1970 and 1985, average real deposit rates ranged from about −11 percent in Peru to 2 percent in Thailand (see Table 7.2). The sensitivity of financial savings to real interest rates is illustrated in Figure 7.2 for Jamaica, Nigeria, the Philippines, and Thailand.

When interest rates are kept low and the demand for credit outstrips its supply, the banking system must ration credit according to other criteria. Often the government directs the banks to lend to certain sectors. Such sectors typically include farmers, small firms, export industries, and SOEs. In a recent study of interest rate policies in ten developing countries, the share of credit subject to government control ranged from nearly 100 percent in Nigeria to 33 percent in Thailand.

Directed credit has usually failed to promote efficient and competitive industries. Often it goes not to its intended use, but to finance other low-productivity investments—largely because credit is fungible and also because of favoritism and abuse. Where directed credit does reach its intended beneficiaries, many high-return activities are starved of finance because they are not deemed "high priority." The result is a stock of capital that is less efficient than it could be.

Several developing countries adopted financial

Table 7.2 Real interest rates and inflation
(average annual percentage)

Country	Period	Deposit rate	Lending rate	Inflation rate
Bangladesh	1971–85	−7.4	−5.1	18.5
Kenya	1970–85	−4.3	−1.2	12.0
Korea, Republic of	1971–85	−1.1	2.6	13.1
Morocco	1978–83	−4.2	−2.8	10.1
Nigeria	1970–85	−9.7	−7.0	16.5
Pakistan	1970–84	−1.7	0.2	10.7
Peru	1970–82	−10.6	−0.2	38.2
Thailand	1970–85	1.7	7.9	7.8

Source: World Bank estimates based on IMF, International Financial Statistics, various years.

sector reforms during the 1970s and early 1980s. These ranged from major reforms, as in Uruguay, to more limited realignments of the structure of nominal interest rates, as in Nigeria. Yet regulations continue to hamper market forces in most developing countries. Many governments are convinced of the need for reform, but are concerned about the transition to market-determined interest rates.

The experience of financial reform in countries such as Argentina, Chile, Indonesia, the Republic of Korea, and Uruguay provides some guidelines on this.

• The transition to a more competitive financial sector is easier to manage when inflation is low and real exchange rates are stable. In economies with high inflation and appreciating real exchange

Table 7.3 Pre- and postreform nominal deposit rates
(average annual percentage)

Country	Reform period	Preform interest rate[a]	Postreform interest rate[b]
Bangladesh	1980	7.5	13.0
Indonesia	1983	9.0[c]	17.5[c]
Kenya	1980–82	5.4	13.2
Morocco	1978–82	4.5	8.5
Nigeria	1982	6.0	8.5
Pakistan	1973–75	5.6	8.9
Peru	1978–82	14.0	71.2
Thailand	1980	7.0	10.0
Turkey	1980–82	12.0	50.0
Uruguay	1974–79	18.0	50.6

Note: Each increase in nominal deposit rates is usually accompanied by similar increases in lending rates.
a. Refers to the rate prevailing at the end of the year preceding the reform period.
b. Refers to the rate prevailing at the end of the last year of the reform period.
c. Nominal deposit rate for state banks only.
Source: Hanson and Neal 1986; World Bank data.

rates, stabilization policies should precede financial reforms. If financial reforms are undertaken at the same time as stabilization policies, the result may be insolvencies in both firms and financial intermediaries.

• Controls on international movements of capital should remain until the financial sector reforms are complete. If the capital account is liberalized when domestic interest rates are still fixed, the resulting outflow of capital may destabilize the economy. Similarly, the rise in interest rates immediately after reform might induce a sudden capital inflow and an appreciation of the exchange rate.

• The speed of reform is often an important consideration. Interest rates need to rise slowly to re-

loans and spurred by a growing recognition that a devaluation was becoming necessary, the financial sector began to charge real rates of 40 percent by early 1981. The crisis peaked with the international recession in 1982: foreign lending fell sharply, capital fled the country, aggregate demand collapsed, and the government was forced to devalue the peso. Several conglomerates and banks failed and had to be rescued by the government, and unemployment climbed to 30 percent by 1983.

Ironically, the most serious defect in Chile's financial reforms was that they went too far. There was a lack of effective supervision of the financial sector and virtually no monitoring of bank portfolios. As a result, most of the financial intermediaries were acquired by one of several large conglomerates. These industrial-financial conglomerates, or *grupos*, used the financial resources obtained through a newly acquired bank either to buy firms that were being privatized or to expand their own operations. Many newly privatized firms had to spend fresh resources to operate, modernize, and expand. A large number turned unprofitable as the real exchange rate appreciated and had to resort to additional borrowing to stay afloat. As a result, when the international debt crisis broke in 1982, Chile was already in a deep financial crisis.

Other countries contemplating financial sector reforms can draw three important lessons from Chile's experience:

• Financial reforms need to be accompanied by strict supervision of the banking and financial sectors to avoid undue financial concentration and prevent unsound banking practices. Governments need to be particularly alert in countries where conglomerates form an important segment of the industrial sector.

• Opening the capital account before financial sector reforms are complete provokes destabilizing capital flows.

• A realistic exchange rate policy is important. Using the nominal exchange rate to stabilize domestic inflation could lead to an appreciation of the real exchange rate and create incentives to hedge against devaluation.

Box figure 7.4 Net capital inflows and interest rate differentials in Chile, 1979–81

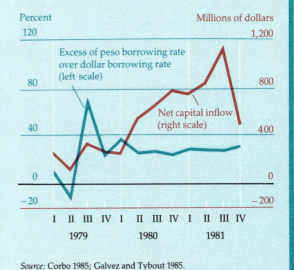

Source: Corbo 1985; Galvez and Tybout 1985.

duce disruption to investors. A precipitous rise in the cost of borrowing would only push many firms into insolvency and threaten, in turn, the solvency of the banking system itself. At the same time, interest rate controls need to be lifted fast enough so that loans based on expected postreform rates are not postponed indefinitely.

• Once interest rate controls are relaxed, nominal and real interest rates in the formal sector are likely to rise (see Table 7.3). In some instances, postreform real lending rates may exceed the real rate of return on industrial investment. This may threaten growth and jeopardize the trade reforms that seek to change the structure of industry. The problem arises in two ways. First, high budget deficits may fuel expectations of exchange rate devaluations and push nominal interest rates well above the rate of inflation. In such circumstances, lower budget deficits are a precondition for financial sector reform. Second, high taxes on financial intermediation and lack of competition between banks may mean large spreads between lending rates and deposit rates. Smaller budget deficits help here too, by reducing the need for taxes on financial intermediaries. And central banks need to monitor competition between financial institutions. Otherwise, financial concentration may lead to noncompetitive practices, particularly in those banking systems where industry-bank conglomerates play an important role (see Box 7.4).

• Better supervision of the banking system is an important element of financial reform. All well-established banking systems are governed by regulations that temper competition with prudence. One of these requires that banks possess a minimum amount of capital in relation to their assets. A second requires that banks maintain a prudent deposits-to-capital (or gearing) ratio. Furthermore, central banks usually urge banks to adopt an accurate system for evaluating the quality of their assets and potential loan losses. Prudence also suggests that limits be placed on loan concentration. Finally, central banks often act as lenders of last resort and sometimes offer deposit insurance schemes to protect small depositors.

Establishing development banks and equity markets

Financial reform may do little by itself to increase the supply of medium- and long-term finance. Commercial banks usually concentrate on trade finance and short-term lending. This reduces their risks and matches the maturity structure of their liabilities. As a result, many governments have intervened to increase the supply of medium- and long-term finance for industrial development.

DEVELOPMENT BANKS. In the 1950s and 1960s many governments established development banks. The banks were given long-term financial resources, which they would then lend, in accordance with accepted economic criteria, mainly to industrial projects with high returns. Then, during the 1970s, development banks were encouraged (with the support of multilateral and bilateral lending institutions) to pursue development objectives. Sometimes this was at the expense of portfolio quality. Their financial frailty became clear when the world economy entered a recession in the early 1980s. For a sample of development banks at the end of 1983, almost half had 25 percent of their loans in arrears and almost a quarter had more than 50 percent in arrears. Some have since been bailed out by the government or the central bank, but many remain under heavy financial pressure, and some under threat of insolvency.

Well-functioning equity markets would have eased these difficulties. Firms did not have sufficient equity to absorb financial shocks; instead, they relied on borrowed funds. Some development banks performed badly because their managements were forced to finance unviable government projects. In addition, interest rate controls together with excessively high interest rate mar-

gins inhibited development banks from mobilizing deposits. As a result, most of these institutions remained small and narrowly focused and depended on official or semiofficial sources for funding.

EQUITY MARKETS. Thirty-five developing countries have active equity markets. These widen the options to savers by offering high-return, high-risk financial assets. By competing for funds with the rest of the financial sector, they may increase the total supply of savings. In addition, they improve the allocative efficiency of the financial sector by giving firms greater access to risk finance, they bring a new element of competition to the financial sector and thus provide firms with an alternative to long-term borrowing, and they improve the flow of financial information.

Capital markets depend on the health of the economy. A well-developed banking system and macroeconomic stability are preconditions for their growth. In addition, by taxing dividends and capital gains on equity at the same rate as the returns on other financial investments, governments can avoid discriminating against the development of an equity market. Above all, for equity markets to work properly, rules on trading, intermediation, information disclosure, and takeovers need to be clear. The investing public needs to be protected from stock market manipulation, and brokers and underwriters need to follow professional codes of conduct.

Intervening in labor markets

Just as financial and capital markets play a crucial role in industrialization, so too do labor markets. Labor and capital join as factors in the transformation of raw materials into final products. One of the aims of economic policy is to ensure that these two factors are combined efficiently. But in addition to this, governments in developing countries are also anxious to expand employment opportunities for those entering the labor force in ever increasing numbers. In the next few decades, industrial employment will be a key element in meeting the challenge of creating jobs, reducing poverty, and raising standards of living.

As noted in Chapter 5, industry's demand for labor depends partly on the country's strategy for trade and development. An overvalued exchange rate, when combined with industrial protection and tariff exemptions on imported capital goods, tends to encourage a pattern of industrial development that limits employment growth. In addition, protecting industry discourages the farm sector, a sector that tends to be significantly more labor-intensive than manufacturing. Outward-oriented strategies that provide equal incentives to the agricultural and manufacturing sectors are better able to blend the twin objectives of employment growth and efficiency in the allocation of resources.

Urban labor markets also play an important role in the employment performance of industry, especially in the modern manufacturing sector. Urban labor markets in developing countries often have formal and informal sectors. The informal sector comprises small family-owned enterprises that usually lie outside the purview of government labor regulations. The formal sector usually comprises the government itself and the modern manufacturing sector.

In some countries, labor markets are reasonably efficient, and wage differentials are determined largely by differences in education and experience. But in others there are large wage differentials for unskilled labor between the formal and informal sectors; and high rates of urban unemployment, especially for educated labor, are common. Some wage differentials can arise as a result of sex, ethnic, or race discrimination and can be corrected only through education and social and cultural change. Other differentials may be due to minimum wage laws, payroll taxes, and the hiring practices of the public sector.

WAGE REGULATION. Achieving greater equity and promoting social justice have been important goals in many developing countries. To achieve these objectives, governments have intervened in labor markets to protect the real wages of particular groups of workers. The most common method, minimum wage legislation, has been an important influence on real wages in manufacturing, but its significance has declined gradually over the past three decades. In the 1950s and 1960s several African governments raised wages in regulated sectors temporarily faster than the growth of labor productivity. In East Asia, market forces played a more important role. During the early 1980s, minimum wage policies began to recede, and real wages declined substantially as a result. But in a few Latin American countries with high inflation, wage indexation is a well-entrenched government policy. In these countries, minimum wages, in conjunction with the indexation mechanism, continue to exert an influence on the level and structure of wages in manufacturing.

Although minimum wages in Africa and parts of Asia are now of less importance than they were thirty years ago, governments will come under increasing pressure to reactivate them once their economies adjust and expansion resumes. The reintroduction of such policies can reduce employment in the formal sector. The magnitude will obviously tend to vary by country and by sector, but recent research shows that on average a 1 percent increase in the real wage will tend to reduce employment by about 0.03 to 0.04 percent. Minimum wage laws also increase inequalities between the formal and informal sectors. Moreover, they reduce wage differentials between skilled and unskilled workers and thereby reduce incentives for education and training.

PAYROLL TAXES. Many governments, especially in Latin America, tax employers on the number of their employees. Studies show that industries with relatively high payroll taxes tend to pay lower wages, which pushes nearly all the tax onto the workers. But when a binding minimum wage law or strong workers' unions prevent wages from falling, the effect of a payroll tax on employment is identical to an increase in the legal minimum wage.

PUBLIC SECTOR WAGE POLICIES. The public sector's leading role as employer (see Figure 7.3) makes it an important force in the determination of wages. Because governments usually wish to be model employers, pay scales for unskilled workers in the public sector are generally higher than in the private sector, and they are usually unresponsive to labor market conditions. These pay scales often extend to public industrial enterprises, where managers usually do not have the same discretion as their private sector counterparts in dealing with their staff (see Box 7.5). The consequent loss in competitiveness can be transmitted to the rest of the industrial sector, particularly if the output of public industrial enterprises is used as inputs by the rest of the industrial sector.

JOB SECURITY. Sometimes governments limit the freedom of employers to lay off workers. Even where reductions in the work force are allowed, employers are sometimes required by law to provide severance payments based on wage and length of service. These legal provisions can make it difficult to respond to changes in demand and production requirements. They raise the effective cost of labor and lead managers to substitute capi-

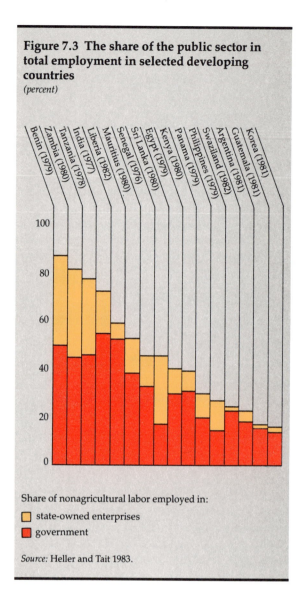

Figure 7.3 The share of the public sector in total employment in selected developing countries
(percent)

Benin (1979)
Zambia (1980)
Tanzania (1980)
India (1978)
Liberia (1977)
Mauritius (1982)
Senegal (1980)
Sri Lanka (1980)
Egypt (1979)
Kenya (1980)
Panama (1980)
Philippines (1979)
Swaziland (1979)
Argentina (1982)
Guatemala (1981)
Korea (1981)

Share of nonagricultural labor employed in:

▨ state-owned enterprises
▨ government

Source: Heller and Tait 1983.

---

force to stagnant incomes. Average wages should rise as workers shift from low-wage, low-productivity jobs to higher paying jobs in high-productivity industries. In the Republic of Korea, for example, five to seven years after the shift from an import substitution strategy to an export-oriented one in the early 1960s, wages rose rapidly despite the absence of government intervention.

The functioning of labor markets also has important implications for trade liberalization. As Chapter 6 noted, trade liberalization involves a reallocation of resources from the nontradables sector to the tradables sector. Efficient labor markets help in two ways. First, a devaluation of the exchange rate can shift incentives in favor of tradables only if real wage rates are flexible downward. And, second, the production of tradables can expand only if labor moves out of the nontradables sector as real wages fall.

Factor prices

Virtually all the policies discussed in this Report influence the relative price of labor and capital. What is the net effect? As Chapter 5 showed, inward-oriented trade strategies tend to protect capital-intensive industries at the expense of labor-intensive industries; this increases the demand for capital relative to labor and raises the rental on capital relative to the price of labor. But, at the same time, inward-oriented trade strategies may have effects that work in the opposite direction. Overvaluation of the exchange rate, common in inward-oriented economies, reduces the cost of imported capital goods and therefore raises wages in relation to the rental on capital (see Box 7.6). (Import tariffs may offset some of the effects of exchange rate overvaluation on the domestic price of capital goods, but since many imported capital goods are either subject to low tariffs or exempted from tariffs altogether, this offsetting factor is probably insignificant.)

Interest rate controls cut the cost of capital to some firms; so do tax holidays, tax discounts, and accelerated depreciation. Minimum wage legislation, payroll taxation, and high public sector pay scales raise the cost of labor. Thus, policies on finance, labor, and taxes tend to work in the same direction: they raise wages relative to the cost of capital and therefore depress employment. A study based on a seventy-country sample showed that if the level of wages increased by, say, 10 percent relative to the rental rate of capital, the proportion of labor employed would fall on average by 10 percent relative to the amount of capital em-

---

tal for labor. And legally guaranteed job security reduces the incentives of workers and managers to increase their productivity.

Panama introduced a labor code in 1972 that restricted layoffs of workers with more than two years of employment. A decline in private sector investment followed, and over the next few years employment fell much faster than output. Eventually, firms began to discharge workers before they had two years of seniority.

The evidence suggests that if governments reduced their labor market interventions, their economies would grow faster. Repealing minimum wage laws would not condemn the urban labor

Box 7.5 Performance of state-owned enterprises and wage and employment policies in Egypt

State-owned enterprises (SOEs) occupy a central position in the Egyptian economy. They absorb about 45 percent of total fixed investment, account for 40 percent of GDP, and generate about 83 percent of total exports of goods and services. Egypt's development prospects, therefore, depend in large part on the performance of its SOEs. But taken as a group, SOEs have not been efficient in their use of resources. Most suffer a large and growing overall deficit, a low rate of capacity utilization, and an inadequate and weakening financial rate of return. As a result, they impose a heavy burden on the budget. About a third of the national fiscal deficit can be attributed to SOEs, and more than three-quarters of this can be found in the industrial sector.

The poor financial performance of SOEs stems from many factors, of which wage and employment policies can be regarded as important. Following large-scale nationalization in 1961–62, Egypt embarked on a deliberate policy to increase employment in the public sector. This policy included a reduction of work hours from forty-eight a week to forty-two a week, the hiring of new employees beyond the immediate needs of individual enterprises, and employment guarantees for graduates and military conscripts. Subsequently, between 1974 and 1982, other laws were enacted that restricted the ability of the management to hire and lay off workers. In addition, prior to the Public Sector Reform Law of 1983, transferring labor from one company to another was rarely possible.

Managers of SOEs also had little discretion over wages and salaries. Basic wages were determined by the central government and required cabinet approval. The chief criterion used in fixing the basic wage was the level of formal education. Promotions and annual salary increments were based on seniority. Apart from the basic wage, there were provisions for bonuses, overtime pay, and special merit awards. These were, in principle, designed to reward outstanding performance but, in practice, were applied uniformly. Furthermore, public sector wages for skilled workers were well below the pay for equivalent labor in the private sector.

The absence of a link between performance and reward, lower wages for skilled workers in the public sector than in the private sector, and the guarantee of job security—all these combined to reduce productivity and lower morale. Most specialized skilled workers left the public sector for either the private sector or other Arab countries. Those who stayed were not sufficiently motivated to raise productivity because of the uniformity of bonuses and allowances. At the same time, low-skilled workers were encouraged to remain in public employment because of the guarantees of job security. Consequently, state-owned industries had fewer specialized and skilled workers (engineers, technicians, and so forth) and an abundance of underemployed workers with few skills.

Mandatory employment policies are no longer enforced in Egypt, but public sector wage policies continue to impede management flexibility in SOEs. In particular, wages continue to be tied to education, not job content; promotion and incentives are not linked to performance and productivity improvements; and management still has little flexibility in dealing with labor-related issues. The government is beginning to focus on the problem and is preparing a reform program to improve public sector performance.

ployed. Other studies of twenty-five individual countries indicate that the fall in the proportion of labor would range between 6 percent and 20 percent.

Systematic studies of the effects of government policy on the choice of technology and the employment of labor and capital are rare. One such study indicates that distortions in the relative cost of labor and capital can be large, particularly in countries following inward-oriented trade strategies (see Table 7.4).

Trade and domestic policies in the outward-oriented economies—Brazil, Côte d'Ivoire, Hong Kong, and the Republic of Korea—did not influence the level of wages relative to the rental rate of capital by as much as they did in two of the inward-oriented economies—Pakistan and Tunisia. But no single pattern emerges of the contribution of different policies to factor price distortion. Among the inward-oriented economies in the sample of countries studied, trade policies were more important than financial market policies in reducing capital costs in Tunisia, but the reverse was true in Argentina and Pakistan. Similarly, in Argentina, Brazil, Côte d'Ivoire, and Tunisia, distortions arising from labor market policies have been more important than distortions from financial market policies, whereas the opposite was true in Korea and Pakistan.

The study also examined the potential effects on

employment of liberalizing trade and domestic policies. Most of the increase in employment per unit of output came from removing factor market interventions, except in Tunisia (see Table 7.5). Reducing trade distortions had a smaller effect, and in Argentina it actually lowered the labor coefficient. Nevertheless, to the extent that export industries are more labor-intensive than import-

---

Box 7.6 Peru's factor market distortions

During the government of Velasco Alvarado (1968–75), Peru introduced several policies that significantly distorted the price of productive factors. Despite efforts to reverse them, many were still in force during the early 1980s. They have had a pervasive effect on the Peruvian industrial sector in at least two important ways:

• *Increased capital intensity and reduced employment.* The measures included taxes on wages, interest rate subsidies, fiscal incentives for investment, exemptions from import duties, and, at times, currency overvaluation. All tended to increase wage costs and reduce the price of capital goods, so that firms had an incentive to invest in relatively capital-intensive techniques and to reduce their demand for labor.

Capital goods were exempted from payment of import duties. This, plus an overvalued exchange rate, lowered the relative price of imported capital goods by 42 percent. All told, the price of labor rose by 102 percent relative to the price of capital.

Estimates indicate that if factor prices had been undistorted, employment in the formal sector could have been 39 percent higher. This is probably an underestimate. Other policies—such as minimum wages, tax concessions to investors, and concessionary credit policies—increased distortions in the price of labor relative to capital and further reduced employment in the formal sector. Furthermore, the effect of these distortions on employment should also take into account lost opportunities for exports of labor-intensive products. High labor costs reduced Peru's natural comparative advantage in these commodities. The government tried to alleviate the problem by providing export subsidies. But international rules of trade forbid the rebate of direct taxes, so Peru's exports have faced high countervailing duties on several occasions.

• *Reduced factor mobility.* The policies also reduced factor mobility. Government-supervised land reform enterprises eliminated markets for the most productive land. The government also allocated credit directly and introduced a stringent job security law. These interventions reduced Peru's ability to adapt to structural change—one reason, arguably, why Peru's attempt at trade liberalization failed in the early 1980s. Trade liberalization exposed Peru's protected manufacturing sector to foreign competition, but labor market rigidities prevented firms from shedding labor to increase efficiency and improve cost competitiveness. Import penetration was increased by an overvalued exchange rate and expansionary fiscal policies. Meanwhile, protected entrepreneurs mounted a campaign against trade liberalization. Eventually, trade liberalization was reversed.

Table 7.4 Policy effects on labor and capital costs in selected developing economies
(percent)

Economy and development strategy	Period	Increase in labor costs as a result of labor market policies (1)	Reduction in capital costs as a result of trade, fiscal, and financial policies (2)	Source of reduction in capital costs			Increase in the wage-rental ratio as a result of trade, fiscal, and financial policies (6)
				Trade policies (3)	Fiscal policies (4)	Financial sector policies (5)	
Outward oriented							
Brazil	1968	27	4	0	. .	4	31
Côte d'Ivoire	1971	23	15	0	12	3	45
Hong Kong	1973	0	0	0	0	0	0
Korea, Republic of	1969	0	10	0	2	8	11
Inward oriented							
Argentina	1973	15	17	8	. .	9	38
Chile	1966–68	. .	. .	37	. .	. .	. .
Pakistan	1961–64	0	76	38	10	53	316
Tunisia	1972	20	36	30	. .	6	87

Note: Column 6 is derived from columns 1 and 2.
Source: Krueger 1983, table 7.1.

substituting industries, liberal trade policies should boost employment.

The competitive environment

Trade and other policies affect industrial efficiency in another way—they help define the rules of competition. This, in turn, affects industrial flexibility in the face of changing economic conditions.

Entry barriers and competition

In developing countries, regulatory barriers to trade are often a cause of high industrial concentration. For example, when quantitative restrictions are used in conjunction with import licensing, the flow of imports is controlled by a restricted group of importers. This gives them considerable market power. In Bangladesh, for instance, the government, until recently, granted sole importing rights to public enterprises and "recognized industrial units." The market power that this bestowed

allowed them to raise prices well above international levels.

The barriers to entry caused by trade restrictions are sometimes reinforced by domestic policies. Industrial licensing, fiscal and financial incentives, interest rate controls, and credit rationing can all help deter new entrants and allow monopolies and collusive oligopolies to earn excess profits.

Many governments have used antitrust laws to discourage monopolies and collusive oligopolies. In such cases, the evolution of the market structure hinges on the interpretation of these laws. In the United States, for example, the focus on price-fixing arrangements after the first round of antitrust legislation led to a wave of mergers. Indian antitrust laws, however, have restricted changes in the industrial structure by blocking the entry of large firms that could challenge the dominance of existing firms.

Properly designed antitrust laws can encourage competitive behavior, but they are less appropriate when efficiency calls for large plants with scale

Table 7.5 Sources of potential increases in labor coefficients of production

Country and development strategy	Period	Observed direct labor coefficient (1)	Potential percentage increase in the direct labor coefficient under different scenarios			Potential direct labor coefficient (5)
			No intervention in factor markets (2)	No trade policy distortions (3)	Equal effective protection across industries (4)	
Import-competing industries						
Outward oriented						
Brazil	1970	100	15	. .	. .	115
Côte d'Ivoire	1972	100	25	0	12	140
Korea, Republic of	1968	100	8	0	0	108
Inward oriented						
Argentina	1973	100	16	−6	0	110
Chile	1966–68	100	. .	7	. .	107
Pakistan	1969–70	100	271	0	. .	371
Tunisia	1972	100	17	38	51	243
Export industries						
Outward oriented						
Brazil	1970	207	15	. .	. .	238
Côte d'Ivoire	1972	135	25	0	0	169
Korea, Republic of	1968	100	8	0	0	108
Inward oriented						
Argentina	1973	130	25	−6	0	149
Chile	1966–68	80	. .	7	68	144
Pakistan	1969–70	142	271	0	. .	384
Tunisia	1972	128	17	38	0	198

Note: Column 1 gives an index expressing the actual labor required per unit of domestic value added in the countries listed for import-competing and export industries. The index for import-competing industries in each country is set at 100. Columns 2, 3, and 4 show the potential increases in labor coefficients attainable by eliminating: factor market distortions induced by domestic policies (column 2), the factor price effects of trade policies (column 3), and the factor price effects of different levels of protection afforded to import substitution and export industries (column 4). Column (5) indicates the potential labor coefficient obtainable by removing all distortions.
Source: Krueger 1983, table 8.10, p. 177.

Box 7.7 Exit barriers and industrial adjustment in Portugal

Portugal's industrial sector faces considerable uncertainty now that the country has entered the European Community. The abolition of quantitative restrictions and the harmonization of tariffs on third-country imports may lead to the closure of many of Portugal's low-productivity firms and to reorganization and rationalization of many others. The costs and difficulties of these adjustments are likely to be considerable because of rigidities in the capital and labor markets that hinder the exit of firms.

The failure of bankruptcy mechanisms

The low rate of corporate bankruptcies in Portugal may suggest a healthy industrial sector. But this is deceptive. In fact, financial weakness is endemic in many parts of Portuguese industry. Regardless of the source of their financial difficulties, Portuguese firms with more than 100 employees rarely go out of business. Troubled firms receive public assistance, which may mean a direct subsidy, concessional refinancing of overdue loans by public sector banks, or special purchase programs by the public sector. Moreover, the financial position of many banks has been weakened owing to a high share of nonperforming corporate loans. But banks have little incentive to resort to the bankruptcy mechanism for three reasons. First, recoverable assets are usually low, especially after preferential creditors, employees, and tax and pension liabilities have been paid off. Second, the legal requirements of the Portuguese bankruptcy mechanism are invariably expensive to fulfill. Third, public sector nationalized banks, which account for more than 90 percent of the banking system, can count on an eventual government bailout. Thus the banks tend to collude with their financially troubled clients and continue to lend with little hope of restoring their borrowers' financial health.

The limited use of bankruptcy to provide an orderly method of writing down debt leaves the book value of net assets at levels that do not reflect their market value. An active capital market is only just starting to operate. Meanwhile, the high book value inhibits buyers and sellers from transacting at realistic prices. The resulting immobility of capital and management increases the costs of adjustment.

Labor market rigidities

The relatively high degree of labor market rigidity may also impair the industrial sector's ability to adjust to the new incentive structure that has accompanied EC membership. Until the early 1970s, Portugal relied heavily on emigration to keep real wages growing in the domestic economy. Waning emigration to OECD countries and decolonization in the post-1974 period changed this age-old custom; and decolonization also led to a large inflow of returnees that needed to be absorbed in the domestic economy.

In response to these conditions, as well as to political commitments following the 1974 revolution, the government introduced a comprehensive set of measures designed to protect the interests of labor. These measures have greatly restricted the mobility of labor both within and between firms. Firms have little, if any, flexibility in reducing their labor force or indeed in changing the tasks or workplace assigned to each individual. By institutionalizing the overmanning of Portuguese industry, these laws have succeeded in slowing industrial progress and are even less justifiable now that Portugal has gained entry into the EC. Although a decade has gone by since the passage of these labor laws, Portugal has yet to fashion a set of labor policies that is conducive to industrial growth and adjustment while addressing the legitimate concerns of the labor force.

economies. In such situations, lower entry barriers at least discourage large firms from exercising their market power for fear that this may stimulate new firms to enter the industry. But lower entry barriers alone cannot curtail monopoly behavior, particularly when a single firm capturing scale economies can satisfy the entire domestic market. Foreign competition may then be the best answer.

As well as limiting monopoly power in domestic markets, foreign competition promotes competitive behavior through rivalry in export markets. The opportunity to export makes room for larger and more efficient producers in the domestic market. If the economies of scale are substantial, export activities may raise industry's profits.

Exit barriers and resource mobility

In some countries the costs of shutting down a firm can be prohibitive. In many ways exit barriers are barriers to entry as well, because they reduce the return on investment. They also tend to reduce any improvements in efficiency stimulated by liberalization or technological change (see Box 7.7).

Perhaps the most forbidding exit barriers are restrictions on labor retrenchment. (In one country with particularly rigid rules on job security, producers had to adopt ingenious methods for closing plants—for example, by paying bribes to ensure electricity blackouts or arranging strikes to bring about de facto closure.) Laws against mergers and acquisitions also hinder the exit of firms. Through mergers and acquisitions an industry may move toward a more efficient structure. Governments in developing countries tend to oppose them because of their effect on industrial concentration. But the need for restrictive policies toward mergers diminishes when markets have low entry barriers or are open to foreign competition. Finally, complex or nonexistent bankruptcy procedures may make exit difficult.

Small-scale industries

Many studies suggest that trade, industrial, and financial policies can interact to discriminate against small firms. For example, trade policies in some countries protect large firms more than they do small firms. In Sierra Leone, large garment producers are granted fifteen times as much protection as small garment producers. Similarly, small firms are often excluded from lucrative investment incentives. In fact, many of the capital goods used by small firms, such as sewing machines or outboard motors, are often classified as luxury goods and taxed accordingly. Moreover, surveys indicate that less than 1 percent of small firms in developing countries obtain credit at controlled rates from formal financial institutions; the remainder rely on the informal sector. The combined net effect is to raise their capital costs and reduce their ability to compete against large firms (see Table 7.6).

But some developing countries adopt special programs to support small-scale industries. For example, they might provide working capital and investment finance at preferential rates of interest through development banks or selected commercial banks. In a few countries, governments have attempted to introduce management and vocational training, provide infrastructural services and industrial estates, and promote subcontracting.

Except perhaps in the notable case of India (see Box 7.8), such measures compensate only partially for the discrimination against small firms in economies with import substitution strategies and interest rate controls. Policies that are neutral between industry and agriculture and between firms of different size probably do more to help small firms than direct intervention. Agricultural growth, for example, raises rural incomes and expands the markets for small industries. This is especially true when the agricultural sector is made up primarily of smallholdings that use labor-intensive techniques of production. Agricultural growth also increases the supply of raw materials for small-scale industries such as food processing and basket weaving. Movement toward more open trade policies and foreign exchange markets would also help reduce some of the bias against small firms. And greater freedom for financial institutions would give small firms better access to credit.

Economic policy and technological development

In the course of economic growth, gains in efficiency arising from changes in the allocation of resources are complemented by productivity improvements as a result of technological development. As Chapter 3 has noted, technological development is central to industrialization.

Technological development means more than creating new technological knowledge or even acquiring existing technological knowledge. It also involves developing the ability to assess, choose, and adapt such knowledge. Studies have found that the economic benefit from a new innovation is generally less than the cumulative benefits from gradual improvements made after its introduction.

Table 7.6 The relative cost of capital in large and small firms
(percentage difference in capital costs of large firms relative to small firms)

		Source of difference in capital costs			
Economy	*Period*	*Trade policy*	*Interest rate policy*	*Fiscal policy*	*Total*
Brazil	1968	0	−33	. .	. .
Ghana	1972	−25	−42	26	−41
Hong Kong	1973	0	0	0	0
Korea, Republic of	1973	−5	−35	10	−30
Sierra Leone	1976	−25	−60	20	−65
Tunisia	1972	−30	−33	. .	. .

Note: A negative number implies that the capital costs of large firms are lower than the capital costs of small firms.
Source: Haggblade, Liedholm, and Mead 1986.

Box 7.8 Is small always beautiful?

Many developing countries promote small firms in the belief that they use more labor per unit of capital than large firms, use capital more productively, and thus combine abundant labor with scarce capital more efficiently. Recent studies, however, indicate that this may not always be the case. First of all, small firms do not always produce the same products or serve the same markets as large firms. Making a direct comparison between small and large is therefore fraught with difficulty. But where careful comparisons have been made, size does not emerge as a good indicator of efficiency. The efficiency of small firms appears to be influenced by the same factors that influence efficiency in large firms—the nature of the industry, the array of available technologies, the framework of prices and incentives, and the competitive environment. In most developing economies, the overall trade and industrial policy framework tends to discriminate in favor of large firms. In such an environment, if small firms survive, they tend to do so on account of their higher efficiency or their superior ability in servicing a particular market. But where government policies are biased heavily in favor of small firms, there is a substantial risk that this may lead to the establishment of small firms that use resources inefficiently.

India is a case in point. It has encouraged small firms probably more than any other country. The government has encouraged village industries that use traditional techniques in the production of soap, cloth, and other items. In addition, more than 800 products, mainly chemicals and light engineering goods, are allowed to be produced by small firms only. These firms also get additional incentives, such as cheap credit, tax breaks, and preferential treatment in government tenders.

Have the economic benefits of these measures exceeded their economic costs? Recent evidence suggests not (Little 1987). In the textile industry, for example, the ban on new looms in mills encouraged the use of economically less profitable power looms. Although power looms are more labor-intensive than mills, economic benefit-cost analysis indicates that these extra jobs have been "bought" too dearly. Similarly, in the sugar industry, the government has restricted the expansion of sugar-refining mills to encourage the production of semirefined sugar. But the production of semirefined sugar is not only economically less profitable than the production of refined sugar, it is less labor-intensive as well. Finally, government restrictions on the expansion of large engineering firms have fostered the rapid growth of small engineering firms that lack the technical capacity for producing high-quality goods or adopting new technology. As a result, exports of light engineering goods, such as bicycles and diesel engines, have suffered.

Evidence from other countries also suggests that small may not always be beautiful. Small firms tend to be economically more efficient than large firms only in those industries in which the nature of the technology or the characteristics of the market put small firms at an advantage over their larger competitors. In the Republic of Korea, for example, small firms employing fewer than 50 workers were the most efficient in only 32 of 139 industries. In a study of the Colombian metalworking industry, the economic benefit-cost ratio was highest for the largest firms. In sharp contrast, a study of large- and small-scale manufacturing enterprises in Sierra Leone revealed that in all six of the industrial subsectors studied, small firms were consistently more efficient than large firms. The Sierra Leone study also revealed that industrial and trade policies were biased consistently against small firms. The firms that continued to operate and compete against large firms tended to be economically more efficient and had higher economic benefit-cost ratios.

The mastery of technology cannot be bought; it must be learned.

The history of a Brazilian steel producer shows how technological capabilities can develop. The steel producer's first plant was set up by Japanese steelmakers. Subsequently, through a series of capacity-stretching technological improvements over seven years, the plant's capacity was more than doubled. This involved very little new investment and no addition to the work force. As a result of the experience gained through these technological efforts, the firm was able to make further additions to its capacity without outside technical help and was even able to sell technical assistance to other steel producers in Brazil and neighboring Latin American countries.

Once acquired through production experience, technological capabilities can be extended gradually to investment appraisal, design, and construction. For example, efforts to extend capacity or remove bottlenecks may increase knowledge of plant design. But firms need not wait for production experience before acquiring these new capabilities. Many countries begin production in a new sector by contracting for a turnkey plant. If domestic firms involve local technical personnel in design and implementation from the beginning, they can absorb a substantial transfer of know-how.

As firms acquire a greater command over the technologies they use, modifications and improvements require more applied research. These efforts often lead to minor innovations that can have a cumulative effect on productivity greater than the initial innovation. In its quest to increase productivity, a Mexican firm producing tableware with U.S. technology succeeded in developing an innovation that doubled the speed of glass making. The same technology was later sold to a Brazilian firm; with further minor innovations the energy requirements of the process were cut by half.

Firms starting up in new areas of production usually find it cheaper to acquire technology from abroad. The transfer of technology from abroad can come in a variety of forms. Sometimes it is embodied in equipment, as in turnkey projects or imported capital goods. In other instances it is packaged along with equipment, finance, and management, as in foreign direct investment. And in others, technology comes ''unbundled,'' through technical assistance or technology licenses.

The benefits to be gained from foreign technology derive less from the method of its transfer than from the details of implementation. The technological benefits from a turnkey contract are likely to be much greater if local personnel participate at every stage. Moreover, except for a few processes, there are always several sources of technology available, and firms may benefit by negotiating for the best terms. Some inexpensive modes of technology transfer are growing in importance. In particular, the newly industrializing countries have found that exporting firms receive valuable technical assistance from foreign buyers. Concerned with the quality and competitiveness of the products they purchase, foreign buyers are keen to assist their suppliers in improving efficiency and quality control. They are also important sources of information on market trends in tastes and fashions and on legal product standards and market requirements in the purchasing country.

Successful technological development ultimately depends upon the desire of firms to improve efficiency. To encourage this behavior, the policy environment needs to reward firms that lower their costs and to penalize those that do not. Given also that technological change in developing countries is mainly adaptive and incremental, small firms can display just as much technological dynamism as large firms. Therefore, policies that promote competition and freedom of entry and exit will tend to foster technological development. In addition, technological effort needs to be guided by price signals that reflect scarcity; so it is important that domestic prices reflect international prices and that factor markets are competitive. Policies that encourage trade and create a conducive environment for foreign direct investment will also facilitate the inflow of new technologies from other countries. Finally, the better educated the labor force, the more rapid its mastery of new technology.

Chapter 4 noted that firms may expend less technological effort than desirable if they are unable to reap the benefits for themselves. Governments have attempted to deal with this externality problem in several ways. One is to allow firms to register patents. Another is to subsidize technological effort. And a third approach is to promote specialized agents for technological development, usually publicly supported research and development institutes. Experience suggests that in most cases these institutes tend to have little contact with producing firms and are not of much help in developing the kinds of technologies needed by producers.

Technology information centers are another approach. Brazil and Mexico have such centers, which charge private users a small fee for access to their data banks. Finally, governments of many developing countries intervene in the transfer of technology from abroad partly to protect local suppliers and partly to check the market power of foreign suppliers. Carried to extremes, such measures may prevent the inflow of new technology. One study concluded that specific interventions mattered less for technological development than the general policy environment for industrial development.

Conclusion

The experience of developing countries over the past three decades suggests that when direct controls replace market mechanisms, economies work less efficiently. An economy that imposes few barriers to trade and encourages domestic competition is likely to develop an industrial sector that is more efficient in its use of resources and more competitive in international markets. Many governments in developing countries, however, continue to control a wide range of economic activities. Policy reform is therefore a vital step in improving economic and industrial growth.

Domestic policy also interacts with trade policy. The success of trade reforms hinges on the ability of firms to expand export production and meet the challenge of increased import competition. The speed of that adjustment depends on the flexibility of domestic product and factor markets. Government policies can aid flexibility by removing barriers to resource reallocation and by encouraging competition in the domestic economy. Outward-oriented trade strategies and government policies encouraging domestic competition are therefore complementary.

The threat of protectionism

More than twenty-five years of progressive liberalization of trade, from 1947 to 1974, saw unprecedented growth in world prosperity. Then the economic climate changed for the worse. Currency crises, oil crises, debt crises, world recession, and high unemployment produced an atmosphere in which demands for protection increased dramatically. The success of Japanese exports, and then of exports from the newly industrializing countries (NICs), produced pressure for changes in the older industrial nations. Such changes are painful when unemployment is high. Attempts to avoid the pain are the main cause of today's protectionism in the industrial countries. Trade in textiles was the first victim, followed closely by trade in footwear, leather goods, steel, shipbuilding, cars, and consumer electronics.

Instead of tariffs, which are now very low, the main instrument of recent protection has been the nontariff barrier (NTB). It contravenes widely accepted principles of nondiscrimination and transparency in measures to restrict trade—principles which remain sound. NTBs usually discriminate against the lowest-cost sources of imports, so they raise prices to consumers and keep inefficient industries in business. The costs to the country imposing the NTB, and to the world as a whole, are higher than under an equivalent tariff. Moreover, NTBs are unfair, because they do not treat exporters equally. Often it is the exporters with the least bargaining power whose exports are most reduced.

Although demands for protection have proliferated and the quantity of trade covered by nontariff barriers has increased, the effects on trade are not easy to quantify. Many trade barriers have proved porous: businessmen in the Republic of Korea and Hong Kong, for example, have to some extent overcome the restrictive effects of NTBs, and their exports of manufactures have continued to grow. But the latest Multifibre Arrangement (MFA) has broader coverage and tighter restrictions than its predecessors. New exporters will find its barriers harder to penetrate. If protection in the industrial nations increases still further, it will be hard for the developing countries to expand their exports.

Although the developing countries have been able to avoid some of the effects of industrial countries' protection, the industrial countries themselves have not. Clearly the main costs of protection fall on the importing country. NTBs cause higher prices for consumers, lost tariff revenue for governments, inefficient resource allocation, and diminished competition.

The pattern of trade cannot remain static. Since the early 1960s developing countries have been increasing their exports not only to industrial countries but also to other developing countries. Today their exports account for nearly one-third of world exports to developing countries. They have also expanded trade with the centrally planned economies (CPEs), although these exports have stagnated in the past few years. But it remains unlikely that exports to these other countries will expand enough to lessen the importance of industrial country markets or the significance of the threat of industrial country protectionism (see Boxes 8.1 and 8.2).

The international trading system since World War II has, at least in principle, been guided by the rules and procedures agreed to by the signatories to the General Agreement on Tariffs and Trade

Box 8.1   Trade options for the developing countries: trade with centrally planned economies

If developing countries had to face increased protectionism in the industrial market economies, could they expand their exports of manufactured products to European centrally planned economies? At present, the CPEs (defined here as Bulgaria, Czechoslovakia, German Democratic Republic, Hungary, Poland, Romania, and the U.S.S.R.) import only 5 percent of developing countries' exports, compared with 66 percent imported by the industrial countries. But if increased protectionism in the industrial countries were to hinder developing countries' exports, the CPEs would become much more important.

The external trade contacts of the CPEs have always been limited. While imports from the developing countries have increased from 3.4 to 5.0 percent in the 1980s, they still lag far behind both developing and industrial country trade. In addition, these imports consist almost entirely of primary goods and fuels. Primary goods and fuels account for 85 percent of Eastern Europe's and 81 percent of the U.S.S.R.'s imports from developing countries. In contrast to a shift in favor of manufactures in their exports to the EC, the share of manufactures in developing countries' exports to the CPEs fell during the period 1980–84.

Several factors restrict trade between the CPEs and the rest of the world. First, the U.S.S.R. is the CPEs' main supplier of raw materials (with the exception of food) and mineral fuels. Only when the U.S.S.R. is unable to supply the other CPEs' needs do they turn to developing country sources. Romania, the only country not dependent on Soviet fuel supplies, has expanded its trade with the developing countries. Its imports from developing countries form a larger share of its total imports than is the case for any other CPE.

Second, most CPEs borrowed heavily in the 1970s and now have sizable foreign debts. A study by Kaminski (background paper) shows that the CPEs with the highest debt have the lowest level of trade with the developing countries. Kaminski estimates that exports from the developing countries would have been 34 percent higher between 1982 and 1985 if the indebted CPEs had not deliberately run surpluses by cutting imports from developing countries. Of course, the CPEs with large foreign debts had to find some way of generating trade surpluses to repay these debts. It is just an unfortunate result of these policies that this significantly reduced their imports from developing countries and seems likely to continue to do so.

Third, among the CPEs, geographic and political considerations are important in determining trading partners. Cuba, for example, accounts for one-third of all Soviet trade with developing countries. About one-fourth of U.S.S.R. trade is with neighboring developing countries.

Fourth, with a few recent exceptions, particularly Hungary, CPEs have generally followed economic policies which insulate domestic producers from both internal and external competition. Their inconvertible and overvalued exchange rates and other import substitution policies are far more restrictive than any barriers to trade erected in the industrial countries.

The lure of advanced Western technology is a motive for increased trade between the CPEs and the industrial countries. But the continued lack of emphasis on comparative advantage in most CPEs means that they have no incentive to increase their imports of manufactures from developing countries. An appropriate emphasis on comparative advantage could generate an increase in exports to developing countries as easily as it could an increase in imports.

(GATT). The GATT is simply an agreement signed by member nations which are admitted on the basis of their willingness to accept the GATT disciplines; it provides rules governing trade between the signatories, a forum for negotiations, and mechanisms for resolving disputes. As a legal document it is detailed, complex, and in various areas open to differing interpretations. But the main objectives are the reduction of trade barriers and the prevention of discrimination in trade. The means by which these objectives have been pursued in the GATT include: first, successive rounds of trade negotiations about tariffs, other barriers to trade, and specific disputes; second, the GATT rule of most favored nation (MFN) treatment, which says that the lowest tariff (or other trade barrier) applied by a signatory to the GATT on a product must be applied to all signatories; third, the principle of reciprocity, whereby trade barriers are lowered in return for changes of rough equivalence by trading partners. (Box 9.1 in Chapter 9 gives the origins, objectives, and rules of the GATT.)

The rise and fall of trade liberalization

From the end of World War II until 1974, protectionism seemed to be in decline. Successive rounds of negotiations in the GATT had cut tariffs on trade in manufactures—from an average level of 40 percent in 1947 to between 6 and 8 percent for most of the industrial countries—even before the

Trade among developing countries represents another possible direction for expansion of trade. The share of total developing country manufactured exports going to other developing countries grew from the early 1960s to 1981 but fell slightly thereafter (see Box figure 8.2).

While the volume of trade in manufactures has been increasing, developing countries still trade more heavily in commodities and raw materials. This is partially a result of trade among countries with different resource endowments as well as trade between primary goods exporters and resource-poor NICs. It is also a result of protective policies in the developing countries. The high incidence of tariff escalation restricts trade in manufactures and processed agricultural goods. But it is the web of nontariff barriers—including foreign exchange licensing, special taxes on imports, import licensing and quotas, and health and safety regulations—which is the main constraint on intradeveloping country trade. While protection costs of NTBs cannot be measured precisely, their effect on limiting trade is substantial and bears heavily on the types of manufactures exported by other developing countries.

Proponents of increased intradeveloping country trade have suggested a system of special trade barrier reductions among developing countries called the Global System of Trade Preferences (GSTP). In addition to expanded total exports, supporters of the GSTP cite such benefits as increased efficiency from economies of scale, more rapid industrialization through efficient use of resources, and stimulation of services connected with trade, including shipping, finance, and communications.

A recent study has attempted an evaluation of the likely trade gains to developing countries from various levels of tariff reductions (Erzan, Laird, and Yeats 1986). With a 100 percent cut in tariffs the increase in intradeveloping country trade could be as much as $14 billion a year. But this would require that all significant NTBs also be abolished, that the elasticity of supply of exports be perfect, that bottlenecks in transport between developing countries be overcome, and that equitable solutions be found for the asymmetric distribution of the increases in trade (most would go to the NICs in Asia, whereas Africa would be likely to suffer a terms of trade loss).

Even though expanded trade among developing countries certainly is beneficial, there is no conflict in

their exporting to both industrial and developing countries. Such a policy would be preferable because it would enable them to find markets for both high- and low-skill products, attain "frontier" technology from the industrial countries, and discourage those infant industries which would never grow up to be internationally competitive. Given the importance of industrial country markets and the threat of protectionism in them, for developing countries to liberalize within a broader global context might serve both to reduce the distortions of domestic trade policies which limit intradeveloping country trade and to gain more secure access to industrial country markets.

Box figure 8.2   Developing countries' exports of manufactures by destination, selected years, 1963–85

Percentage of world exports of manufactures

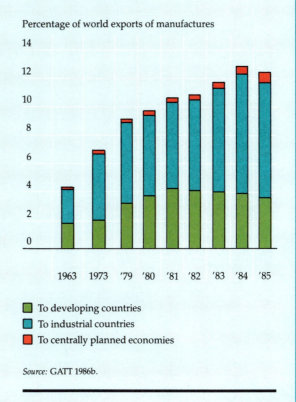

☐ To developing countries
☐ To industrial countries
☐ To centrally planned economies

Source: GATT 1986b.

last round of multilateral trade negotiations (the Tokyo Round, 1974–79) had taken place. Full implementation of the Tokyo Round cuts would mean that tariffs on manufactures would average

6.0 percent in the European Community, 5.4 percent in Japan, and 4.9 percent in the United States (see Table 8.1). In fact, Japan's recent tariff cuts have gone further than this.

Table 8.1 Tariff averages before and after the implementation of the Tokyo Round and percentage changes in tariffs in the major industrial countries

Country or country group	Tariffs on total imports of finished and semifinished manufactures			Tariffs on imports from developing countries of finished and semifinished manufactures		
	Pre-Tokyo	Post-Tokyo	Percentage change	Pre-Tokyo	Post-Tokyo	Percentage change
European Community						
Weighted	8.3	6.0	28	8.9	6.7	25
Simple	9.4	6.6	30	8.5	5.8	32
Japan						
Weighted	10.0	5.4	46	10.0	6.8	32
Simple	10.8	6.4	41	11.0	6.7	39
United States						
Weighted	7.0	4.9	30	11.4	8.7	24
Simple	11.6	6.6	43	12.0	6.7	44

Source: GATT 1980, p. 37.

Box 8.3 The history of the Arrangement Regarding International Trade in Textiles, or the Multifibre Arrangement

In 1935 the United States negotiated the first voluntary export quota on Japanese textile exports. This was despite the fact that the U.S. textile industry was already highly protected by tariffs of 40 to 60 percent. Although these tariff levels have been substantially reduced, the single voluntary export quota has been replaced by the Multifibre Arrangement (MFA), a worldwide system of managed trade in textiles and clothing.

Managed trade in cotton textiles, 1961–73

The precursor of the MFA, the Short Term Cotton Textile Arrangement, negotiated in 1961 under GATT auspices at the request of the United States, was replaced in October 1962 by the Long Term Arrangement Regarding International Trade in Cotton Textiles (LTA), which controlled cotton textile exports for the next ten years. Although the LTA was a multilateral document, it essentially functioned as a set of bilateral agreements which allowed importing countries to negotiate quotas on a country-by-country basis and in some cases to impose unilateral quotas without penalty.

MFA I, 1974–77

The LTA remained in place until 1974, when the MFA took its place. Supporters deemed the new textile agreement necessary for several reasons. First, the use of synthetic fibers which were not restricted under the LTA had increased tremendously. Second, overall productivity in the textile industry had grown substantially during this period, which led to a decline in textile employment in the industrial countries. Third,

because the LTA placed quota restrictions on large exporters such as Japan, smaller developing countries had gained a progressively larger market share. Among the most rapidly growing were the Asian NICs.

The United States was willing to accept a fairly liberal MFA because it wished to broaden the agreement to include synthetic fibers. As a result, the United States made concessions on quantitative restrictions. The MFA specified a minimum of 6 percent annual growth in imports, more flexibility in negotiating the bilateral agreements in which quotas for each country were set, and the right of an exporting country to transfer quotas among categories of goods and between years. The Textile Surveillance Body was established by the GATT to supervise the implementation of the agreement and to arbitrate disputes arising from it.

MFA II, 1978–81

The United Kingdom and France, which experienced a 21 percent increase in textile imports from 1973 to 1977, supported a more restrictive MFA in 1977. The failure of the EC to negotiate quickly with its major suppliers, the worldwide recession, and increased productivity in the EC textile industry led to a 16 percent decrease in textile employment from 1973 to 1977.

MFA II reflected the strong protectionist sentiments of the EC. It allowed more restrictive quotas than did MFA I. The EC negotiated bilateral agreements with all

This picture of a progressive liberalization of trade has to be qualified in several respects:

• *Agriculture.* Agricultural trade is a clear exception. Far from becoming freer, trade in agriculture became progressively more distorted by the support given to farmers in the industrial nations. Support took the form of severe barriers to imports, subsidized inputs, and subsidies to exports. The policies and their costs were analyzed in *World Development Report 1986.*

• *Economic integration.* A second qualification stems from the trend toward economic integration, which culminated in the enlarged European Community. The formation of free trade areas and customs unions has an ambiguous effect upon world trade and welfare. On the one hand, a customs union abolishes barriers to trade among its mem-

bers. This creates new trade flows between them. But, on the other hand, the union now has a common tariff which discriminates against external suppliers. Goods which were formerly bought from nonmembers would be replaced by more expensively produced substitutes from other members of the union.

• *Textiles.* A third important exception to the general decline in trade barriers is textiles. The first international cotton textiles agreement was set up in 1961. The Long Term Arrangement Regarding International Trade in Cotton Textiles followed in October 1962. Its claimed purpose was to control disruption in industrial countries' markets stemming from imports from low-wage developing countries. At the same time it was supposed to provide developing countries with growing access

its major suppliers which reduced and in some cases completely stopped the growth of imports. Although the EC initiated measures to restrict import quotas severely, other industrial countries were quick to follow suit. For the first time, global ceilings were placed on certain categories of "sensitive products" and thereby put an absolute limit on some types of imports.

MFA III, 1982–86

MFA III maintained the restrictions of earlier arrangements and added some additional constraints on large exporters and a "surge mechanism" which limited growth of medium-size exporters. Under MFA III, the United States negotiated forty-one bilateral agreements with its major suppliers, which covered the growth rate of specific types of clothing and textile exports. The United States also initiated a "call" system, which allows the restriction of exports not covered by any specific bilateral agreement.

The call system attempts to add a greater degree of restrictiveness by limiting the export potential of new entrants and is therefore particularly harmful to countries which are starting at a very low export base. It maintains the status quo in both the industrial and newly industrialized countries at the expense of the newer, and possibly more efficient, textile-exporting countries.

Under MFA II the EC had developed a similar device for restricting imports which are not directly covered by any bilateral agreement. This device, known as the

"basket extractor," allows the EC to limit any textile or clothing import when it reaches a designated percentage of the preceding year's total.

MFA IV, 1986–91

Despite the severe limitations, textile and clothing exports to the industrial countries have continued to grow. In response to this the latest agreement, signed in July 1986, specifically adds silk, linen, ramie, and jute to the existing fibers in an attempt to finally control trade in all products. In effect, the new agreement will restrict additional trade—including (using 1985 figures) $813 million of Hong Kong's exports, $368 million of the Republic of Korea's exports, and $203 million of China's exports (Pelzman, background paper).

MFA IV continues the historic tradition of including all conceivable fibers in the MFA and of plugging all the "leaks" which allowed imports of clothing and textiles to grow under the previous arrangements. With the inclusion of these natural fibers, the industrial countries have at least temporarily eliminated the possibility of having trade diverted into non-MFA fibers. Despite its elaborate new extension, MFA IV still cannot preclude the possibility of increased uncontrolled industrial country exports. It will be through extending increasingly restrictive bilateral agreements to every textile producer, as well as the call and basket extractor systems, that the industrial countries will continue to exert protectionist pressures on developing country exporters.

to these markets. In due course, the agreement evolved into the MFA (see Box 8.3). Far from proving temporary, the MFA's successively tougher versions have acquired an air of permanence.

• *The trade of developing countries.* Against the broad trend of trade liberalization, many developing countries have retained or increased their own import barriers; these remain considerably higher than those of industrial countries. But developing countries' exports gained significantly less from tariff reductions in the GATT rounds than did exports from the industrial nations. This was mainly because relatively few of the MFN tariff cuts af-

fected the types of products which developing countries traditionally exported. As shown in Table 8.1, even after the Tokyo Round reductions, the average tariffs facing developing countries' exports remained higher than those facing the exports of industrial countries.

• *Tariff escalation.* A particular problem facing developing countries that would like to expand their manufacturing base by exporting processed versions of their raw materials is tariff escalation. Most countries levy higher tariffs on manufactures than on the raw materials used to make them. As explained in Chapter 5, this means that the effec-

Table 8.2 Pre- and post-Tokyo Round tariffs for twelve processing chains

Stage of processing	Product description	Tariff rate	
		Pre-Tokyo	Post-Tokyo
1	Fish, crustaceans, and mollusks	4.3	3.5
2	Fish, crustaceans, and mollusks, prepared	6.1	5.5
1	Vegetables, fresh or dried	13.3	8.9
2	Vegetables, prepared	18.8	12.4
1	Fruit, fresh or dried	6.0	4.8
2	Fruit, provisionally preserved	14.5	12.2
3	Fruit, prepared	19.5	16.6
1	Coffee	10.0	6.8
2	Processed coffee	13.3	9.4
1	Cocoa beans	4.2	2.6
2	Processed cocoa	6.7	4.3
3	Chocolate products	15.0	11.8
1	Oilseeds and flour	2.7	2.7
2	Fixed vegetable oils	8.5	8.1
1	Unmanufactured tobacco	56.1	55.8
2	Manufactured tobacco	82.2	81.8
1	Natural rubber	2.8	2.3
2	Semimanufactured rubber (unvulcanized)	4.6	2.9
3	Rubber articles	7.9	6.7
1	Rawhides and skins	1.4	0.0
2	Semimanufactured leather	4.2	4.2
3	Travel goods, handbags, and so on	8.5	8.5
4	Manufactured articles of leather	9.3	8.2
1	Vegetable textiles and yarns (excluding hemp)	4.0	2.9
2	Twine, rope, and articles; sacks and bags	5.6	4.7
3	Jute fabrics	9.1	8.3
1	Silk yarn, but not for retail sale	2.6	2.6
2	Silk fabric	5.6	5.3
1	Semimanufactured wood	2.6	1.8
2	Wood panels	10.8	9.2
3	Wood articles	6.9	4.1
4	Furniture	8.1	6.6

Note: Rates are the unweighted average of the tariffs actually facing developing country exports (under the Generalized System of Preferences, the most favored nation rule, other special preferential arrangements, and so forth) in the EC; Austria, Finland, Norway, Sweden, Switzerland; Australia, New Zealand, and Japan; and Canada and the United States.
Source: Balassa and Michalopoulos 1985.

tive protection, or protection given to domestic value added, is much higher than the nominal tariff. This discriminates against processing in developing countries. The Tokyo Round did little or nothing to reduce tariff escalation. As can be seen from Table 8.2, it remains a distinctive feature of protection for products in the twelve processing chains displayed there.

Despite these exceptions, the general trend up to the early 1970s was one of liberalization of the more rapidly growing areas of international trade, particularly manufactures. Trade did not just grow quickly, it grew more quickly than world output. Liberal trade policies were not the only reason for this. There were other factors: buoyant demand, postwar reconstruction, a catching-up process in Europe and Japan on American industrial know-how, and favorable demographics. (But several of these factors were also present in the period after World War I without any similar expansion of trade and growth.) During this great liberalization of trade, unemployment was not a serious problem in the industrial market economies. For the industrial nations as a group it never exceeded 3.3 percent up until the 1973 oil crisis. Indeed, one motive for creating the GATT was the view that the protectionism of the 1930s had hastened the spread of unemployment from one nation to another and had deepened the recession (see Box 8.4).

The increase in protectionist measures

From the end of World War II until 1974 the United States was a force for trade liberalization. It adopted special measures of protection for manu-

---

Box 8.4   "Beggar thy neighbor" policies in the 1930s

Inappropriate monetary policies in the United States and Europe and the subsequent boom and crash of the U.S. stock market are commonly held responsible for the Great Depression of the 1930s. Other factors, most notably the U.S. Smoot-Hawley tariff of 1930 and the retaliation which followed, also contributed to the worldwide depression.

Some policymakers in the late 1920s understood the threat to world and national welfare posed by the use of high retaliatory tariffs. In 1927 and again in 1930 the World Economic Conference met to consider a tariff truce. But it was already too late. The Smoot-Hawley tariff was signed into law on June 17, 1930. It raised the effective rate of tariffs in the United States by almost 50 percent between 1929 and 1932 and triggered retaliatory tariffs. Spain passed the Wais tariff in July in reaction to tariffs on grapes, oranges, cork, and onions. Switzerland, objecting to new tariffs on watches, embroideries, and shoes, boycotted U.S. exports. Italy retaliated against tariffs on hats and olive oil with high tariffs on U.S. and French automobiles in June 1930. Canada reacted to high duties on many food products, logs, and timber by raising tariffs threefold in August 1932. Australia, Cuba, France, Mexico, and New Zealand also joined in the tariff wars (Kindleberger 1973).

Other "beggar thy neighbor" policies, including currency depreciations and foreign exchange controls, were used in attempts to improve domestic economies at the expense of foreign countries. The attempt by all countries to run a trade surplus by cutting imports led to a breakdown of the entire system of trade.

As a result of these policies, all countries suffered from idle productive capacity and low prices. The increased domestic demand for U.S. farm products protected by high tariffs, for example, was more than offset by the loss of export markets. Exports of U.S. agricultural products dropped 66 percent from 1929 to 1932 (Brunner 1981). This aggravated the decline in farm prices, which in turn contributed to rural bank failures.

Some economists disagree with this assessment of retaliatory tariffs during the 1930s. They argue that, although tariff levels were substantially raised, they made little difference to the volume or direction of trade. They argue that the reason for the drop in the volume of trade in manufactures during the Depression was not beggar thy neighbor policies, but the fall in the demand for primary commodities. The failure of international financial markets and the lack of credit, rather than tariffs, crippled trade.

While a consensus on the causes of the Depression is yet to be reached, it is probable that the beggar thy neighbor trade policies at least added to the severity of the Depression and contributed to the breakdown of international trade. It was the intention of the framers of the postwar economic order to disallow a repetition of 1930s-style trade policies. Thus the General Agreement on Tariffs and Trade supports tariff liberalization and specifies the use of nondiscriminatory, bound tariffs as the only acceptable form of protection except in extraordinary circumstances. Despite the rise of the new protectionism, it is likely that the memories of the Depression have played a role in checking the increasing calls for protection.

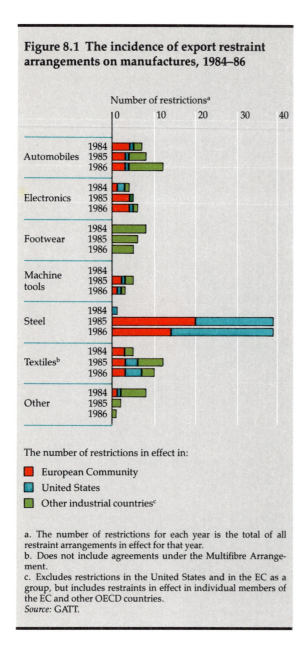

Figure 8.1 The incidence of export restraint arrangements on manufactures, 1984–86

Number of restrictions[a]

The number of restrictions in effect in:

- 🟥 European Community
- 🟦 United States
- 🟩 Other industrial countries[c]

a. The number of restrictions for each year is the total of all restraint arrangements in effect for that year.
b. Does not include agreements under the Multifibre Arrangement.
c. Excludes restrictions in the United States and in the EC as a group, but includes restraints in effect in individual members of the EC and other OECD countries.
Source: GATT.

facturing in only two instances, apart from the cotton textiles arrangement. These, for canned tuna in 1951 and carbon steel in 1969, involved only a tiny fraction of total U.S. imports. Since 1974, however, there have been many more such measures. Most of them are concentrated on textiles and clothing, steel, cars, motorcycles, nonrubber footwear, color televisions, and citizens band radios. As Figure 8.1 shows, this is generally true of all industrial countries' restrictions on imports of manufactures. Agricultural and fuel imports are also subject to NTBs in most industrial countries. Barriers against goods such as these mainly affect

the exports of other industrial countries. Only Brazil and Korea are significant exporters of steel and automobiles; several other developing countries are affected by NTBs on consumer electronics.

The barriers which most affect many developing countries are the NTBs against textiles and clothing. The manufacture of these products seemed suitable for many developing countries because, at least until quite recently, the technologies were simple and relatively labor-intensive. Textiles and clothing represent approximately 25 percent of developing countries' manufactured exports. Each successive version of the MFA has been more restrictive and has covered more products and exporters (Box 8.3).

A detailed analysis of the extent of NTBs has been carried out by staff of the World Bank using the UNCTAD/World Bank data base on trade measures. It showed that about 17 percent of industrial countries' imports in 1986 were subject to "hardcore" NTBs. Table 8.3 shows the extent of these NTBs for the main industrial regions. It gives no indication of the restrictiveness of the measures; the data simply show the presence or absence of some measures which may restrain trade.

In addition to the formal restrictions shown in the table, many countries make use of other devices to protect domestic interests. France, for example, used an administrative measure to restrict the imports of videocassette recorders (see Box 8.5).

The study also showed that NTBs bear more heavily on the major exports of developing countries than on similar exports from industrial market economies, mainly because of the much greater importance of textiles and clothing in the exports of developing countries (see Table 8.4). Nontariff measures increased significantly between 1981 and 1986, particularly in Canada, the EC, and the United States (see Table 8.5). Some $230 billion of 1981 imports would have been covered by one or more of the selected NTBs as they applied in 1983. Post-Tokyo Round tariffs are now so low on most goods that they represent relatively minor barriers to trade. Even where they remain high, as on textiles and garments, the binding constraint on trade is normally bilateral quotas and voluntary export restraints (VERs) under the MFA.

Explanations for the growth of protectionism

Why has the movement toward a more liberal trading environment stalled? Is the new protectionism a temporary response to the current crisis or the

The "new protectionism" usually refers to the use of nontariff barriers such as VERs and orderly marketing arrangements. But it only takes a little ingenuity to introduce an administrative regulation which can be an effective barrier to trade.

In October 1982, citing a "Japanese invasion" in consumer electronics, the French government decreed that all imports of videocassette recorders (VCRs) would have to pass through Poitiers. Although not the most obvious point of entry, Poitiers could hardly be better suited to the purpose. It is a town hundreds of miles inland from France's northern ports where the VCRs are landed. It has a tiny customs crew that is obviously inadequate to the task of clearing hundreds of thousands of VCR imports. As the town where the French repelled an earlier invader, the Moors, Poitiers seemed an apt choice.

Moreover, a particularly long and tedious set of customs regulations were strictly enforced at Poitiers. All the accompanying documents were thoroughly examined and each container opened. A large number of VCRs were taken out of their boxes by the customs inspectors, who carefully checked their serial numbers and made sure that instructions were written in French. Finally, a number of VCRs were dismantled to make sure that they were actually built in their reported country of origin. The regional customs director responsible for Poitiers said of the new regulations: "Before the new policy, it took a morning to clear a lorry-load of video recorders. Now it takes two to three months. We are still clearing consignments that arrived here [three months ago] when the policy went into effect" (Lewis 1982).

As planned, the "Poitiers effect" severely limited VCR imports into France. Before the use of Poitiers, more than 64,000 VCRs, mostly from Japan, entered France each month for the first ten months of 1981. Afterward, less than 10,000 VCRs cleared the customs point at Poitiers each month, while the rest of the supply waited in bonded warehouses throughout the town. Exporters did not passively concede to the French barriers. Denmark, the Federal Republic of Germany, and the Netherlands, which also export VCRs to France, filed a complaint with the EC Executive Committee in Brussels, which in turn brought charges against France at the European Court of Justice for breach of EC free trade rules. Japan brought its complaint to the GATT and then suspended or curbed VCR shipments to France.

It is not clear what the French hoped to gain from the use of the Poitiers weapon. The French electronics firm Thomas-Brandt did not make its own VCRs, but sold Japanese VCRs under its own label. It experienced a shortage of these when the government required all the imports to go through Poitiers. Shortly after the establishment of Poitiers, the EC Commission negotiated a VER limiting Japan's exports to the entire European Community. This was followed by an agreement between Thomas-Brandt and Japan's JVC to manufacture component parts in France and later the lifting of the Poitiers restrictions. It is likely that several complex issues concerning intragovernment and government-industry relations played a role in the Poitiers scheme. Yet, although the motives remain somewhat obscure, the protective effect of it is clear.

---

beginning of a new trend brought about by a lack of faith in an open trading system? If the former, the tide of protectionism may ebb with economic recovery. But if major countries no longer feel that their interests are served by the GATT rules, then an open trading system is indeed in peril.

The demand for protection

Protection is demanded by groups who see their interests damaged by imports and is supplied by governments that see their interests served by giving way to these demands. Economic arguments play a role, but probably a minor one. The demand for protection has usually involved an alliance of owners and workers (although the internationalization of production through multinational corporations and international subcontracting may be undermining such alliances to some extent). Three factors seem likely to have stimulated such domestic interest groups to demand protection in recent years:

• *Structural changes in trade.* Japan's dependence on imports of energy and raw materials forced it to become an even more aggressive exporter of manufactures in response to the oil crises and a slowdown in growth. Since 1978 it has consistently had a trade surplus. The rise in Japan's share of imports of manufactures from other members of the Organisation for Economic Co-operation and Development (OECD) coincided with an increase in the NICs' share from 1980 onward; the pressure on some OECD countries' import-competing industries was great (see Figure 8.2).

The growth in intra-OECD trade in the 1960s and 1970s was largely in intraindustry trade. This meant there was less need to adjust. No industries needed to shrink to accommodate imports because they were able to expand exports. But the exports of the NICs tend to be labor-intensive and concentrated on a few products: textiles, clothing, footwear, leather, and sporting goods. They import machinery and sophisticated manufactures. Even

though the overall balance of trade with the NICs is positive, certain OECD industries are under intense pressure from the NICs' highly competitive exports; the labor displaced may not be easily reabsorbed by exports. As Table 8.6 shows, the OECD countries' imports from developing countries have a higher direct labor content than their imports from other OECD countries. The ratios imply that a billion dollar increase in OECD exports would not create enough jobs to absorb the labor displaced by a billion dollar increase in developing country imports. (But, if such a matched expansion of trade did occur, real incomes would rise, demand would increase, and jobs would be created in other OECD industries.)

The new markets created in the NICs for OECD exports are intensely competitive. There are no brand loyalties, and costs of entry are low. This has led OECD exporters to demand help from their governments. The help could be subsidized loans, measures to tie trade to aid projects, or other forms of concealed assistance to exporters.

• *Reduced flexibility.* As pointed out in Chapter 2, labor markets in Britain and some other European nations have changed in ways which have made labor less mobile between occupations and regions. Because the impact of NIC exports is mainly on industries which tend to be labor-intensive and concentrated in regions of high unemployment (textiles, clothing, and leather goods), labor market rigidities cause demands for protection.

Table 8.3 Industrial country imports subject to "hard-core" NTBs, 1981 and 1986
(percent)

| | Source of imports | | | |
| | Industrial countries | | Developing countries | |
Importer	1981	1986	1981	1986
EC	10	13	22	23
Japan	29	29	22	22
United States	9	15	14	17
All industrial countries	13	16	19	21

Note: "Hard-core" NTBs represent a subgroup of all possible NTBs. They are the ones most likely to have significant restrictive effects. Hard-core NTBs include import prohibitions, quantitative restrictions, voluntary export restraints, variable levies, MFA restrictions, and nonautomatic licensing. Examples of other NTBs which are excluded include technical barriers (including health and safety restrictions and standards), minimum pricing regulations, and the use of price investigations (for example, for countervailing and antidumping purposes) and price surveillance. Percentage of imports subject to NTBs measures the sum of the value of a country's import group affected by NTBs, divided by the total value of its imports of that group. Data on imports affected in 1986 are based on 1981 trade weights. Variations between 1981 and 1986 can therefore occur only if NTBs affect a different set of products or trading partners.

Table 8.4 Import coverage ratios of a subgroup of NTBs applied by selected industrial market economies, 1981 and 1986

| | Source of imports | | | | | | | |
| | World | | Industrial countries | | Developing countries | | CPEs | |
Product coverage	1981	1986	1981	1986	1981	1986	1981	1986
Ore and metals (27, 28, 67, and 68)	12.7	24.7	13.1	29.4	8.6	12.8	26.2	30.0
Iron and steel (67)	29.0	64.2	26.8	65.2	24.8	54.6	58.1	68.2
Nonferrous metals (68)	3.8	6.4	1.9	6.0	6.1	6.4	7.9	8.0
Chemicals (5)	13.2	12.7	13.8	12.9	11.4	12.6	10.5	13.5
Manufactures, not chemicals (6 and 8, less 67 and 68)	18.6	20.5	15.4	17.8	31.3	31.0	41.3	43.0
Leather (61)	8.2	13.9	5.5	17.9	9.9	9.9	3.9	8.5
Textile yarn and fabrics (65)	37.3	39.6	18.6	21.2	57.6	61.4	74.3	75.6
Clothing (84)	67.3	67.4	40.2	38.9	77.1	77.9	74.8	74.9
Footwear (85)	71.3	32.5	65.1	24.1	71.0	27.0	81.5	62.4

Note: The figures in the table are to be regarded as preliminary and subject to revision. Numbers in parentheses refer to SITC codes. The import coverage ratios (the sum of the value of a country's import groups affected by NTBs divided by the total value of its imports of these groups) have been computed using 1981 import trade weights. Computations have been made at the tariff-line level and results aggregated to relevant product group levels. The data cover a broad range of NTBs, including para-tariff measures (for example, variable levies, seasonal tariffs, and countervailing and antidumping duties), quantitative restrictions (including prohibitions, quotas, nonautomatic licensing, state monopolies, voluntary export restraints, and restraints under MFA and similar textile arrangements), import surveillance (including automatic licensing), and price control measures. Standards to comply with health and technical regulations as well as excise taxes are not included because the data base information coverage is not even for all countries. The industrial market economies covered are Austria, Canada, EC (excluding Portugal and Spain), Finland, Japan, New Zealand, Norway, Switzerland, and the United States.
Source: UNCTAD 1987.

• *Effects of recession and instability in the international economy.* Slowly growing economies find adjustment more difficult and painful than economies which are growing rapidly. They lack the expansion of new activities to absorb the labor displaced from their "twilight" industries. High average levels of unemployment increase the net costs of losing a job and make governments more sensitive to unemployment caused by imports. All this reinforces demands for protection.

• *Misaligned exchange rates.* In the 1980s, in both Britain and the United States, appreciating exchange rates meant that import-competing and export industries suffered a severe loss of competitiveness. Producers and politicians responded with louder demands for protection. Unfortunately, the recent depreciation of the dollar has failed to stifle these demands.

Recent arguments used to justify special protection

Those who demand protection offer several economic arguments in support. For the most part, these are merely variants on the traditional case for protection (Chapter 5). But as advanced by the industrial countries, some take on a different slant.

MAINTAINING EMPLOYMENT. If a rise in imports causes the sales of an industry to contract, protecting that industry can, at least in the short run, help to maintain jobs. But this neglects the effect of the resulting price increase on demand, focuses too narrowly on the directly affected industry, and

Table 8.5 Import coverage index of a subgroup of NTBs applied by selected industrial market economies, 1981–86
(1981 = 100)

Importer	NTBs[a]				
	1982	1983	1984	1985	1986
Austria	100.0	100.0	100.0	100.0	99.3
Canada	108.6	106.0	108.4	112.1	121.3
EC[b]	105.7	110.9	113.9	120.8	118.3
Finland	102.5	102.5	102.5	101.0	101.0
Japan	99.2	99.2	99.2	99.2	98.6
New Zealand	100.0	100.0	100.0	92.6	86.1
Norway	101.1	96.4	94.4	86.6	85.3
Switzerland	100.4	100.4	100.8	100.8	100.8
United States	105.5	105.6	112.1	119.2	123.0
All	104.6	107.1	110.2	115.3	115.8

Note: The figures in the table are to be regarded as preliminary and subject to revision. The data cover all products other than fuels.
a. See note to Table 8.4.
b. Excluding Portugal and Spain.
Source: UNCTAD 1987.

Table 8.6 Ratio of labor content of manufactured imports to labor content of manufactured exports for selected OECD countries, 1980

Country	Trade with OECD countries	Trade with developing countries
Belgium	1.06	1.28
France	1.02	1.32
Germany, Federal Republic of	1.06	1.31
Italy	0.88	1.15
Japan	1.08	1.38
Netherlands	1.05	1.16
United Kingdom	0.98	1.19
United States	0.94	1.41

Note: Imports and exports are valued at 1977 prices.
Source: OECD 1985, p. 189.

pays no attention to the unintended effects of the protection on other industries. If the protected industry is a source of inputs to other industries, then tariffs or controls on imports will raise costs and reduce employment in the industries which use the protected materials. Their job losses may exceed those temporarily saved in the protected industries.

Moreover, if the exchange rate is flexible, an increase in protection which reduces expenditure on imports will, if nothing else changes, cause the exchange rate to appreciate. This will reduce profits in both exporting and import-substituting

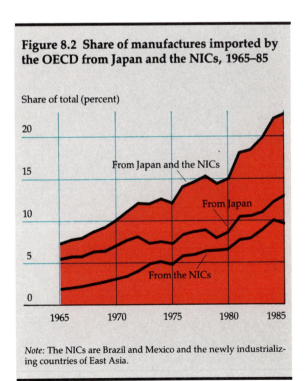

Figure 8.2 Share of manufactures imported by the OECD from Japan and the NICs, 1965–85

Share of total (percent)

From Japan and the NICs

From Japan

From the NICs

Note: The NICs are Brazil and Mexico and the newly industrializing countries of East Asia.

industries, which would cause employment to fall in all tradable goods industries apart from those given the increased protection. If, in addition, trading partners react to the protection by increasing their own trade barriers, the protection to save jobs would be not only self-defeating but potentially disastrous.

What at first seems self-evident—that protecting an industry against a surge in imports will save jobs—turns out to be a risky proposition.

SLOWING THE PACE OF ADJUSTMENT. A modification of the employment argument carries more weight. The idea is to use temporary controls to allow a slower pace of adjustment on the grounds that resources may not be very mobile and that time may be required to retrain labor and allow new investment to take place. The need to slow down adjustment is acknowledged by the inclusion of safeguard provisions in most trade treaties such as the GATT and the Treaty of Rome. The argument is valid, but it can be used to justify protection which is far from temporary and in situations where no effort is made to shift resources from the area in which comparative advantage has been lost.

PRESERVING THE INCOMES OF CERTAIN GROUPS. This is one of the main arguments used for the protection of agriculture in industrial nations. As *World Development Report 1986* showed, the main effect of such a policy is to push up the price of land, which benefits only landowners. Direct income support would be more successful in preserving wages in farming at a much lower real cost to the community. In other industries, where there is no factor of production in fixed supply, such as land, there is no reason in principle why incomes could not be supported by protecting the industry, but direct income transfers would still be far less costly.

PRESERVING KEY INDUSTRIES. Protection for agriculture, steel, and automobiles is frequently buttressed with the idea that these industries have strategic importance. One industrial country has argued that its clothing industry is essential for defense because it produces uniforms for the army. This shows the lengths to which the argument has been pushed. For many products stockpiling is a cheaper way to preserve supplies for emergencies than protecting the industry. If an industry really is essential, the question is how best to preserve it. The orthodox economic answer is

through subsidies, not tariffs or import controls. Subsidies do not raise prices, hurt consumers, or raise costs to users. But the precedents are ominous. Subsidies often get out of hand and play havoc with budgets.

Some industries are claimed to be essential for economic reasons. It is not clear why a country should need its own aircraft industry or computer industry if it can buy more cheaply from foreign suppliers. But one extension of this argument may be defensible. If allowing these domestic producers to collapse meant the creation of a worldwide monopoly, which could then raise prices to very high levels, a case for subsidies to preserve some competition could be made. But this would be a special and somewhat speculative case.

SUPPORTING NEW (HIGH TECHNOLOGY) INDUSTRIES. One variant of the infant industry argument (Chapter 4) cites the need to assist new industries through the learning period (when the local industry cannot compete with already established foreign firms). Another variant relies on external benefits such as technical spin-offs as a justification for protection. The learning period argument is subject to the standard criticism that it implies a failure in the capital market. Otherwise, if an industry cannot attract adequate capital to see it through this learning period, investors evidently cannot be convinced that it offers a competitive rate of return. It is implausible that the capital markets of the industrial nations suffer from such weaknesses. True, because of misinformation or inadequate information investors can make mistakes, but why should that be any less true of governments, whose economic vision may be clouded by political requirements?

External economies are another matter. In this case governments, provided they are well informed and pursue the public well-being in a disinterested way, are necessarily superior to markets because market prices cannot capture genuine externalities (Chapter 4).

USING PROTECTION AS A LEVER TO OPEN MARKETS. Recently, some industrial countries have used the threat of protection as a lever to open other countries' markets. At first glance this seems an almost benign strategy, opening markets to trade rather than closing markets by protection. But it is yet another step down the road to managed trade. Each individual bilateral trade deal may seem insignificant, but it invites further political action of the same kind and undermines the system of rules

Box 8.6 Reciprocity and fair trade

The GATT incorporates the principle of *first-difference* reciprocity: mutual and balanced concessions characterize tariff negotiations among contracting parties other than developing countries. First-difference reciprocity is thus reciprocity at the margin, reciprocity of changes in trade restrictiveness. First-difference reciprocity has been the principal technique for liberalizing trade under successive GATT rounds since World War II.

By contrast, full reciprocity implies mutuality and balance of total market access and of overall tariff and nontariff restrictions between trading partners. This is what is commonly meant by "a level playing field," or fair trade.

Interestingly, the terms reciprocity and free trade, each arrogating to its advocates the benefit of unassailable virtue, were in vogue also in nineteenth-century Britain. Organizations such as the National Fair Trade League and the Reciprocity Free Trade Association had arisen in the 1870s and 1880s (Bhagwati and Irwin 1987). At the time, they were a response to the erosion of economic leadership as Britain confronted the rise of Germany and the United States. Now there has been a similar response as the United States and the EC face the rise of the Far Eastern economies.

Full reciprocity, however, poses a threat to the maintenance of an open trading system. Thus full reciprocity has recently been demanded within individual sectors (cars, construction, computer chips). This would deny the flexibility of tradeoffs between sectors that is politically necessary in negotiating reductions in trade barriers.

Again, in recent attempts at trade legislation, reciprocity has been taken to imply bilateral trade balances. The simple fact that a rival enjoys a trade surplus is taken to be adequate evidence that it is not granting equal reciprocal market access.

Such demands violate the canons of good economics. They lead to unwarranted inferences of unfair trade by rivals and strengthen protectionist forces in consequence.

For export markets, the result has been a tendency to judge openness of markets not by rules, but by quantity outcomes for one's exports. Pressures are brought to show "results" and to sign trade pacts to ensure a specific market share for one's exports in the other's domestic market. Voluntary export restrictions are then matched by voluntary import expansions (VIEs), creating a new form of "export protectionism" (Bhagwati 1987).

For imports, the deleterious effect of the focus on fair trade lies in the contribution it makes toward turning the twin measures of countervailing and antidumping duties, designed to maintain fair competition, into de facto protection. When protectionist statements are allied with notions of fair trade, there is a strong likelihood that these means will be used by protectionists to harass successful foreign rivals. In fact, in both the United States, where countervailing duties are more fashionable, and the EC, where antidumping duties are favored, a trend toward rapid escalation of such actions, often as a prelude to VERs and VIEs, has been observed.

Given procedures where these actions are often decided upon by national bodies rather than impartial arbitrators and no costs are levied against unsuccessful petitioners, the possibility of petitions designed to harass foreign rivals is always a real one. The probability of this perverse outcome increases as fair trade sentiments gather strength, as in recent years.

governing trade in the GATT. Such arrangements may in any case backfire, as happened with the U.S.-Japan accord on trade in semiconductors. U.S. firms suffered rather than gained from the protection. The failures of the accord seem to have sown the seeds of further conflict.

COMBATING UNFAIR TRADE. There have been increasing demands in industrial countries for "fair trade" rather than free trade (see Box 8.6). Normally, unfair trade practices mean such things as nontariff barriers, covert means to restrict imports, government subsidies (direct or indirect) to exports, and dumping (selling to export markets below the price in domestic markets). Demands that trade should take place on "a level playing field" sometimes go beyond the question of unfair practices and attack the very basis of trade—differences in comparative advantage. For example, in pleading for stiffer protection of the garment industry, a labor union representative in the United States put forward a common view: "Apparel produced in countries with abysmally low living standards and virtually no workers' rights threatens living standards in this country and destroys badly needed employment opportunities for our low-skilled workers" (U.S. Congress, House Committee on Energy and Commerce 1985, p. 81). But protecting U.S. garment production will, at best, preserve jobs and incomes for garment workers only at the cost of jobs and incomes elsewhere in the economy and will make it more difficult for workers in developing countries to raise their "abysmally low" living standards.

The supply of protection

A combination of domestic and international factors seems likely to influence the readiness of governments to be persuaded by such arguments and to accede to demands for protection. Policymakers are influenced by the relative power and persuasiveness of different interest groups in the economy. On the side of protection are the injured import-competing industries. On the other side are users of imported products: consumers; retailers; industries, including multinational corporations which use the products as inputs; and exporting firms. In the past, opponents of protection have found it hard to organize effective lobbying against it. The costs of protection seem too small and too diffuse to arouse public opinion, whereas the benefits, such as jobs saved directly in the threatened industries, have appealed to public sentiment.

DOMESTIC FACTORS. The willingness of policymakers to respond to demands for trade barriers depends partly on the alternatives at their disposal. For most of the postwar era, governments have responded to rising unemployment with expansionary policies to create new jobs or with regional policies to switch investment to new activities in the area where unemployment had risen. In France, Italy, and the United Kingdom, regional policies were used vigorously in the 1950s and 1960s. By creating new jobs in the electrical goods and other light manufacturing industries, they probably helped to cope with some of the labor displaced by competition from textile imports and the loss of shipbuilding orders to Japan and Sweden. (Whether regional policies brought net gains to these economies is a subject of considerable controversy.) The much tighter fiscal restraints imposed upon governments by the need to control inflation and reduce tax burdens in the 1970s and 1980s have reduced their ability to use fiscal policies to expand demand and to increase subsidies.

In the United States, the policies to assist adjustment which were introduced in the trade act that preceded the Kennedy Round have provoked considerable disillusionment, although the United States still favors the principle. Other countries, such as the Netherlands, have experimented with

Table 8.7 Value and destination of exports of manufactures by developing and industrial countries, 1963, 1973, 1979, and 1980–85
(billions of dollars)

	Importer			
Exporter	Industrial countries	Developing countries	CPEs	World
Developing countries				
1963	2	1	0	3
1973	16	7	1	24
1979	53	31	2	86
1980	63	40	3	106
1981	67	45	4	116
1982	67	43	4	114
1983	77	42	4	123
1984	96	45	6	147
1985	97	43	9	149
Industrial countries				
1963	48	17	2	67
1973	222	54	13	289
1979	552	187	38	777
1980	624	230	42	896
1981	592	251	38	881
1982	572	235	36	843
1983	585	211	37	833
1984	648	206	39	893
1985	696	197	50	943

Note: Industrial countries include Australia, Japan, New Zealand, North America, South Africa, and Western Europe. Developing countries include Africa (excluding South Africa), Asia (excluding China and other centrally planned economies), Latin America, and the Middle East. CPEs include China and other Asian centrally planned economies, Eastern Europe, and the U.S.S.R.
Source: GATT 1986b.

Table 8.8 Shares of domestic consumption: North Atlantic industrial countries combined
(percent)

	Shares of home demand		
Commodity and source	1975	1983	Change 1975–83
Textiles			
Domestic	83.9	80.6	−3.3
NAICs	14.8	16.0	1.2
Rest of world	1.3	3.4	2.1
Clothing			
Domestic	78.6	69.3	−9.3
NAICs	12.0	13.0	1.0
Rest of world	9.4	17.7	8.3
Footwear			
Domestic	73.1	56.1	−17.0
NAICs	18.5	23.9	5.4
Rest of world	8.4	20.0	11.6
Steel			
Domestic	85.0	84.5	−0.5
NAICs	13.8	14.4	0.6
Rest of world	1.2	1.1	−0.1

Note: North Atlantic industrial countries (NAICs) include Canada, European OECD members, and the United States.
Source: Hamilton (background paper).

146

special assistance for import-displaced workers; they too have been less than satisfied. As their policy options have narrowed, governments have been more willing to concede to demands for protection.

INTERNATIONAL FACTORS. Risk of retaliation also influences governments. The United States and the EC are important customers for each other's exports. Both sides have used retaliation, or the threat of it, to attack barriers against their exports. Most of the developing countries import relatively few manufactures for consumption. The goods they import from OECD nations tend to be necessary inputs into their own production. This makes it difficult for them to produce a credible retaliatory threat. The inability to retaliate may be one reason the developing countries now face the tough bilateral constraints of the MFA in textiles and other NTBs in agriculture, footwear, and leather goods.

The combination of increasing demands for protection and governments' diminishing will to resist accounts for the rise of the new protectionism in the 1970s and 1980s. The current multilateral negotiations in the Uruguay Round are an opportunity to check this trend, but that can happen only if governments make a determined effort.

Has protectionism retarded trade?

Some analysts maintain that recent protectionism has been more talk than action. The rate of growth of world exports of manufactures has slowed, but this is adequately explained by recession. If anything, the exports of developing countries, which have often been the target of protectionist talk and actions, have grown faster than the industrial countries' exports (see Table 8.7 and Figure 8.3).

If the increase in protection were in the form of tariffs, it would be simple to show that they had retarded trade. But it is nearly impossible to estimate the combined effect of NTBs on the quantity or value of a country's imports. Many studies have been able, however, to make reasonable estimates of the costs of NTBs for individual commodities (or groups) for particular areas.

NTBs should, it seems, reduce the share of controlled imports in domestic consumption. But the barriers may be porous. Enterprising exporters can increase the value of their exports by improving their quality, and hence their value, or by switching from restrained categories of goods to ones not yet subject to NTBs. For example, an exporter can avoid an NTB on cotton blouses by producing silk

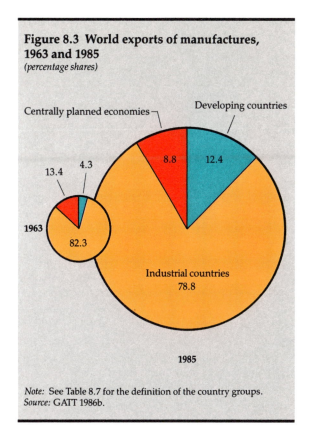

Figure 8.3 World exports of manufactures, 1963 and 1985
(percentage shares)

Note: See Table 8.7 for the definition of the country groups.
Source: GATT 1986b.

ones instead. The developing countries' share of domestic consumption could, therefore, continue to increase. (Of course, the share could grow still faster in the absence of NTBs.)

Table 8.8 shows the share of domestic consumption in North Atlantic industrial countries (NAICs) which is supplied by domestic producers, producers in other NAICs, and the rest of the world. It shows that in spite of NTBs on textiles, clothing, footwear, and steel, home producers' shares of their domestic markets fell in all four categories between 1975 and 1983. This implies that the NTBs have been porous, which has allowed imports from developing countries to rise. But intra-NAIC trade also increased as a result of trade diversion.

Trade in textiles, tightly controlled by the MFA, and trade in footwear, also subject to many NTBs, provide good examples of the ways in which developing countries have mitigated the effects of NTBs on their exports.

TEXTILES AND CLOTHING. There was a rapid increase in U.S. imports of textiles and clothing from industrial countries in the 1980s (see Table 8.9). In spite of the MFA, imports from developing countries also grew substantially, albeit less rapidly. A

Table 8.9 U.S. textile and clothing imports, 1980 and 1985
(billions of standard yard equivalents)

Source of imports	1980	1985	Increase 1980–85	Percentage increase 1980–85
OECD countries (excluding Japan)	546	2,014	1,468	269
Restricted suppliers	4,339	8,831	4,492	104
China	325	977	652	201
East Asian NICs	2,210	3,784	1,574	71
Japan	461	716	255	55
"New starters"	279	470	191	68
Others	1,064	2,886	1,822	171
All exporters (total)	4,884	10,845	5,961	122

Source: Hamilton (background paper).

U.S. government study concluded that these imports were in categories of products and fibers not covered by existing quotas and from countries not covered by quotas under the MFA. Also, when MFA III was negotiated, aggregate ceilings on wider product groups were removed in exchange for cutbacks in quotas. These allowed countries to diversify rapidly into nonrestricted products.

FOOTWEAR. The effect of the U.S. voluntary export restraint (1977–81) on the Republic of Korea's exports of nonrubber footwear provides another example of the tactic of switching to unrestricted product categories and unrestricted suppliers. By switching to rubber-sole shoes, Korea was able to increase the volume of footwear exports to the United States by 115 percent during the first year of restrictions. Meanwhile, exporters from nonrestricted countries increased their share of U.S. consumption from 4 to 15 percent from 1977 to 1981. When the restrictions were lifted in 1981, Korea and other previously restrained exporters increased their share to more than 40 percent of U.S. consumption. But this was at the expense of domestic suppliers (whose share fell from 49 percent in 1981 to 29 percent in 1983), not the other developing country exporters.

Net costs to developing countries of industrial countries' protection

The fact that the industrial countries' NTBs have been porous does not mean that they have done no economic harm. Clearly, they have forced developing country exporters to adopt stratagems which they would not choose in either a free trade environment or one in which trade restrictions are nondiscriminatory. Protection frustrates comparative advantage. It shores up dying industries and slows the development of new ones. It diverts energies to rent seeking (Chapter 4).

Estimating the effects

Few studies exist of the costs of protection to developing countries. And they measure only one aspect of the costs: the increase in export earnings which would arise from reduced tariffs and NTBs. Studies by the World Bank, the IMF, and the Commonwealth Secretariat show that the result would be substantial export gains—worth several billion dollars a year.

There have been more detailed studies for individual countries such as Korea. Restrictions on Korean exports of carbon steel cut sales to the United States by $207 million, or 24 percent; but Korea had offsetting gains in the form of higher prices and increased sales to other markets, and the end result may have been a small net gain.

Hong Kong faces quantitative restrictions on many of its exports. It seems unique in permitting firms to trade their quota rights. The prices offered for these are a good indicator of the rent which firms expect to earn from the right to export their permitted share. This, together with information on import and export unit values, enables estimates to be made of both the quota rents and the import tariff equivalents of the restrictions. The rents are shown in Table 8.10. They show gains—of $724.6 million over the two years 1982–83—equivalent to 1.4 percent of Hong Kong's GDP.

Such large gains are unusual. Hong Kong is a small economy with a high ratio of manufactured exports to income. For other economies the rents would be much less significant. And the quota rents are not pure gain. They arise from restrictions on exports, so although profits may rise, jobs and wages in these labor-intensive industries are likely to contract.

Losses from voluntary export restraints

Even if VERs brought quota rents sufficient to compensate for lower export volumes, these gains could be small in relation to the growth in exports which trade restrictions may have frustrated. Firms which could have expanded output face a shriveled market. For many industries that means lost economies of scale. If quota shares are allocated on the basis of historic shares of exports (the usual method), the pattern of production would be frozen and entry by new firms prevented. If governments use more discretionary means to allocate quotas, they immediately create uncertainty and powerful incentives for lobbying and corruption. Entrepreneurs' energies are diverted from management to rent seeking.

Other responses to quotas involve economic costs. Upgrading quality to increase the profit per unit exported is common. The evidence is clear from sales of Japanese cars in the United States and Britain and from developing countries' exports of clothing and footwear. Diversification into new markets and new products is another frequent response. But, on the face of it, both product upgrading and diversification seem likely to be costly; otherwise the firms would have adopted these procedures without the spur of the VER. In other words, VERs seem likely to push countries up the ladder of comparative advantage faster than market forces would take them into products which are too capital- and technology-intensive for their present resource endowments.

VERs also divert sales to other exporters. A switch from Korean- to Italian-made clothes does nothing for developing countries, but a switch to clothes made in Bangladesh, Malaysia, or Thailand would. Together with Mauritius and Macao, these countries have benefited from Hong Kong firms that have set up factories overseas to evade the restrictions on their exports. These countries gain increased exports and some transfers of investment and technology. But where trade is managed through an institution such as the MFA, with its patchwork of increasingly restrictive bilateral deals, the gains to these new countries could be short-lived.

The desire of industrial countries to block loopholes in their barriers to textile and clothing imports is likely to limit newcomers to minimal quotas (despite a special provision for new suppliers) in MFA IV. Evading restrictions by upgrading or by product diversification is likely to become harder. This may deter newcomers from their first, and most natural, step up the ladder of comparative advantage: exporting textiles and clothing. What does this imply for the future? Should developing countries be more wary of following outward-oriented strategies in a world of slower growth and perhaps continually rising protection?

Such a response would be unfortunate. As Chapter 5 pointed out, recent revival of export pes-

Table 8.10 Estimates of rent income to Hong Kong from voluntary export restraints on clothing, 1981–83
(millions of 1984 dollars)

Country	1981	1982	1983	Total 1982–83
European Community				
Denmark	4.3	3.2	3.1	6.3
France	3.3	2.3	1.4	3.7
Germany	86.9	19.9	39.0	58.9
Italy	. .	0.4	. .	. .
United Kingdom	71.9	36.4	26.2	62.6
Belgium-Luxembourg[a]	2.1	0.6	0.6	1.2
Netherlands[a]	10.1	4.4	4.7	9.7
European Free Trade Association				
Austria	. .	0.9	. .	. .
Finland	. .	0.1	0.2	0.3
Sweden	24.3	24.7	21.8	46.5
Switzerland	0.0	0.0	0.0	0.0
Total Europe	202.9	92.9	97.6	190.5
United States	. .	124.9	409.2	534.1
Total Europe and United States	. .	217.8	506.8	724.6

a. Derived from the weighted average tariff equivalent of the other EC countries.
Source: Hamilton 1986.

simism has been an exaggerated response to the threat of protectionism. But if the worst were to happen and the industrial nations were to increase protection, how should developing countries react? The best response is flexibility—that is, the ability to shift resources rapidly from an export where sales are proving difficult to an export or import substitute where profit opportunities are now superior. This seems more likely to be done successfully where managers in developing countries are faced with international prices and the requirement to make profits than where they are sheltered by protection. Their decisions should take account of different levels of risk in different activities in exporting or replacing imports. But, of course, this is politically a difficult line of action to follow. The instinctive reaction to increased protection, encouraged by the idea of reciprocity, is to respond with increased protection of one's own.

Retaliation is an easier policy to understand than liberalization—especially when resources are stretched.

Net costs to industrial countries of their own protection

OECD governments seem to recognize the merits of free trade. Every act of special protection tends to be accompanied by a claim that its advocates are against protectionism. Each proposal for protection has a specific objective, and specific arguments are advanced for it. These are based on the view that benefits from achieving the objective will exceed the costs of the protective measures. But the governments may be wrong in that assessment, or the objectives may be attainable at lower cost. For example, the injury to workers whose jobs are lost as a result of import penetration may

Table 8.11 Some estimates of the costs to consumers of protection in selected sectors
(millions of dollars)

Sector and country	Year and source	Cost
Clothing		
United States	1984 (Hickok 1985)	8,500–12,000
United States	1984 (Hufbauer, Berliner, and Elliott 1986)	18,000
Textiles		
United States	1980 (Munger 1984)	3,160[a]
United States	1981 (Wolf 1982)	2,000–4,000[b]
Textiles and clothing		
United States	1980 (Consumers for World Trade 1984)	18,400
Steel		
United States	1980 (Consumers for World Trade 1984)	7,250
United States	1984 (Hickok 1985)	2,000
Specialty steel		
United States	1984 (Hufbauer, Berliner, and Elliott 1986)	520
Automobiles		
United States	1983 (Tarr and Morkre 1984)	1,109
United Kingdom	1983 (Greenaway and Hindley 1985)	265
Videocassette recorders		
United Kingdom	1983 (Greenaway and Hindley 1985)	121
EC	1984 (Kalantzopoulos 1986)	459

Note: Values in dollars for costs in the United Kingdom are based on average market exchange rates for the period as reported in IMF, *International Financial Statistics*. Sources are referenced in full in the Selected bibliography.
a. Tariffs only.
b. Quotas only.

Table 8.12 Some estimates of the welfare costs of protection in selected sectors
(millions of dollars)

Sector and country	Year and source	Cost
Clothing		
Canada	1979	92
	(Jenkins 1980)	
EC	1980	1,409
	(Kalantzopoulos 1986)	
United States	1980	1,509
	(Kalantzopoulos 1986)	
Textiles and clothing		
United States	1984	6,650
	(Hufbauer, Berliner, and Elliott 1986)	
Steel		
United States	1985	1,992
	(Kalantzopoulos 1986)	
Specialty steel		
United States	1984	80
	(Hufbauer, Berliner, and Elliott 1986)	
Automobiles		
United States	1981	327
	(Feenstra 1984)	
United States	1983	2,192
	(Kalantzopoulos 1986)	
United States	1983	994
	(Tarr and Morkre 1984)	
Videocassette recorders		
EC	1984	422
	(Kalantzopoulos 1986)	

Note: Values in dollars for costs in Canada are based on average market exchange rates for the period as reported in IMF, *International Financial Statistics.* Sources are referenced in full in the Selected bibliography.

be compensated more cheaply by a combination of financial compensation, retraining, and new job creation than by protection of the contracting industry. Often, normal retirements and reduced recruitment are sufficient to reduce employment, without the need for dismissals. Protection, for reasons argued below, may not even succeed in preserving threatened jobs. Textiles, clothing, and steel have been the most heavily protected industries, but between 1973 and 1984 the numbers of workers employed in North America and the EC declined inexorably, by 54 percent for U.S. iron and steel and by 46 percent for EC textiles.

Evidence on the costs of protection

The costs of protection are complex. Most analysts have contented themselves with measuring only the simplest ones, and these are difficult enough. Estimates generally ignore the effects of competition on managerial efficiency, or of trade on the acquisition of new techniques, on economies of scale, on saving, and on investment. As a result, most estimates are probably too low. Most, however, also omit the adjustment costs incurred when

protection is removed. But these are normally short-run, once-and-for-all costs whereas the gains from trade go on indefinitely.

COSTS TO CONSUMERS. Table 8.11 sets out estimates of the costs to consumers of protection in various industries in the European Community, the United Kingdom, and the United States. For textiles and clothing, all of the estimates for the United States amounted to many billions of dollars. The same is true for standard grades of steel. For cars the estimates are just over $1 billion for the United States and $265 million for the United Kingdom. For the EC the cost of protecting videocassette recorders is estimated at nearly half a billion dollars.

WELFARE COSTS. Table 8.12 shows estimates of the broader welfare costs. This concept recognizes that what matters is the extra cost to the economy as a whole of producing more of the goods domestically rather than importing them. It is a net cost, because the extra price paid by consumers goes partly to local producers whose production expands to replace imports and partly to the govern-

Figure 8.4 The cost to consumers of preserving a job in selected industries, 1983

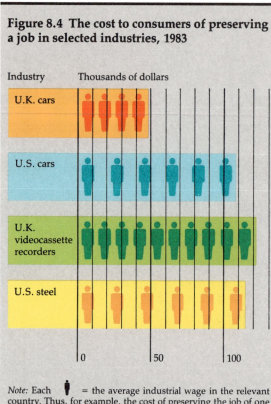

Industry   Thousands of dollars

U.K. cars

U.S. cars

U.K. videocassette recorders

U.S. steel

0   50   100

Note: Each 👤 = the average industrial wage in the relevant country. Thus, for example, the cost of preserving the job of one British carworker is equivalent to the wages of four British industrial workers. Average industrial wages are based on the earnings of male manual workers in the United Kingdom and the earnings of nonsupervisory industrial workers in the United States.
Source: For U.K. cars and VCRs: Greenaway and Hindley 1985; for U.S. steel: Tarr and Morkre 1984; for U.S. cars: Kalantzopoulos 1986.

ment in revenue from the tariff. (Where protection is by quotas, importers will usually gain at the expense of consumers. Where it is by VERs, foreign suppliers will normally capture the benefit of the increased price.) Normally, the welfare cost will be considerably less than the consumer cost—particularly for tariffs or quotas (Chapter 5). Even so, the estimates for textiles and clothing range from $1.4 billion to $6.6 billion in the EC and the United States, and for steel in the United States the estimate is approximately $2 billion.

THE COST OF PRESERVING A JOB. The striking fact about protection to preserve jobs is that each job often ends up costing consumers more than the worker's salary. For example, each job preserved in the car industry in Britain is estimated to have cost consumers between $19,000 and $48,000 a year. In the United States the cost was between $40,000 and $108,500 a year. Looked at another way, in the United Kingdom the cost to consumers of preserving one worker in car production was equivalent to four workers earning the average industrial wage in other industries. In the U.S. car industry, the equivalent cost would be the wages of six ordinary industrial workers (see Figure 8.4). VERs in the U.S. steel industry cost consumers $114,000 per protected job each year. For every dollar paid to steelworkers who would have lost their jobs, consumers lost $35 and the U.S. economy as a whole lost $25.

ARE JOBS REALLY SAVED? It is of course questionable whether protection can do any more than temporarily preserve some jobs in the protected industry at the expense of jobs in other industries in the economy. The extra cash spent on steel and VCRs implies less cash to spend on other goods and services and therefore fewer jobs in production of these other goods and services. Even in the protected sector the effects of protection on saving jobs are usually small.

British and American VERs on Japanese car exports stimulated imports of similar cars from the rest of Europe. Much of the effect of the MFA was to divert trade from some developing country suppliers to others and to other OECD suppliers. The textile industry has invested heavily in capital-intensive production methods, because of controls on imports which yielded economic rents to domestic producers and (in many countries) because of subsidies for new capital equipment. The industry's new technology has displaced workers at a much higher rate than imports. In the United States, the new jobs in textiles have been located in the South rather than in New England and are for a type of labor different from before. Geographic and skill barriers have meant that protecting textiles did little to save jobs or reduce costs of adjustment. Even when protection has a positive effect on output in the domestic industry, it tends to be small in relation to macroeconomic change. For example, the 1982 United States–Japan VER on cars is estimated to have increased demand for domestic production by 100,000 units, less than 1 percent of industry sales. By contrast, stagnation and high interest rates in the U.S. economy reduced demand by about 4 million units in 1982 compared with 1978.

Protection has not been particularly successful in maintaining jobs or reducing adjustment costs even in the protected industry. For the economy as a whole, because of the intersectoral and macroeconomic effects, it probably lowered employment. Few jobs have been saved, and the costs have been inordinate.

Conclusion

Protectionism has been growing since the mid-1970s. Measures such as VERs and orderly marketing arrangements have been porous. The NICs and some other developing countries have been ingenious in finding ways to penetrate these measures or to turn them to their advantage. Nevertheless, the measures have had adverse effects. The increased coverage and tighter administration of the MFA and increased vigilance in administering NTBs may mean worse to come. As it is, protection has diverted trade from developing country exporters to OECD suppliers. The response of the developing countries has not been costless.

The industrial countries bear the main costs of their own protection. Estimates of the costs seem small in relation to GNP, but they are probably underestimates. Moreover, the appropriate test is not to compare the costs with GNP. As with any economic policy, protection should be evaluated on the balance of costs and benefits. On that basis protection should win few friends.

Traditionally, pressure for protection eases when a new round of trade negotiations is in the offing. This reinforces the need to make a success of the new multilateral trade negotiations. The best way to overcome protectionism is to renew the momentum of progress toward multilateral liberalization of trade. This is the subject of Chapter 9.

Toward a more open trading system

An open trading system is a key to sustained industrial expansion. With trade, enterprises are not limited to narrow domestic markets, but can expand to sell their goods and services around the world. Open trade, in turn, requires a framework of rules. Since 1948 such a system has existed in the articles and codes of the General Agreement on Tariffs and Trade. Ninety-three countries are full signatories; in all, about 122 countries follow the GATT rules in principle and receive GATT treatment from the signatories. About 80 percent of the world's trade is affected by, although not necessarily in conformity with, the GATT rules.

As Chapter 8 showed, the share of trade that is transparent and nondiscriminatory is shrinking. The international economic order has shown signs of weakening under the strains of stagnating growth and the need to adjust to international indebtedness and structural change. The symptoms of growing disorder show in the increased demands for protection, the shift from tariffs to discriminatory restrictions on trade, and the movement from transparent to opaque protective measures such as quotas, voluntary export restraints, and subsidies. The dangers in these trends are that protection will increase and that the fundamental principles of the GATT—nondiscrimination in trade and transparency in methods of protection—will be abandoned.

Such a breakdown in the "rule of law" is against the interests of all trading nations, but the developing countries would stand to lose most. In a world where bilateral arrangements became the norm, developing countries' lack of bargaining chips would place them in a weak position. Fear of losing access to adequate markets could under-

mine the drive toward outward-looking policies and turn many developing countries back toward autarky, which would damage their prospects of improved efficiency and growth.

Further erosion of the GATT rules would deprive governments of a useful appeal to external authority. Although the GATT has no direct sanctions to use against nations that break its rules, it provides a forum for dispute settlement. It also derives moral authority from its contractual nature. Governments can cite their obligations to GATT rules when resisting pressures for protection. This makes strengthening and, where necessary, reforming the GATT vital to all nations, especially the weaker ones.

Developing countries have powerful reasons for taking a more active part in the latest round of multilateral trade negotiations (MTN) than they have in the past. In previous rounds, few offered to reduce their trade barriers. They relied upon the most favored nation rule to bring tariff cuts as a byproduct of negotiations among the industrial nations, and they also relied on "special and differential" treatment accorded them in the GATT to gain additional tariff concessions. This may not have been the best strategy—witness their relatively small gains from the Generalized System of Preferences (GSP) and other preferential schemes for developing countries, the fact that tariffs on manufactures have fallen less on products of special interest to developing countries, and the increase in the breadth and severity of the nontariff barriers that discriminate against them.

The new MTN, the Uruguay Round (so named because the meeting of ministers which initiated the negotiations was held in Punta del Este), offers developing countries the chance to take a more active approach. That may involve identifying interests which they share with other developing or industrial countries, forming coalitions, and pursuing a common objective. Recently such coalitions have formed: one coalition of agricultural exporters, both industrial and developing countries, did so and showed it had the ability to bargain. Another group had an impact on the way in which the services issue is being handled in the Uruguay Round.

In the GATT the process of negotiating reductions in trade barriers is based on the principle of reciprocity. Nations reduce their tariffs in the knowledge that other countries are making equivalent cuts in theirs. This has clear political advantages: it seems fair and attracts the support of exporting industries. But the developing countries which sought and obtained special and differential treatment within the GATT are exempt from making reciprocal tariff cuts.

The combination of reciprocity for industrial countries and special and differential treatment for developing countries has meant that negotiations have focused mainly on items of interest to the industrial countries. When developing countries' markets for imports were small they had, in any case, little to offer. Now some developing countries' domestic markets are big and getting bigger. For them at least, some reduction and binding of their tariffs or other trade barriers could gain reciprocal concessions from the industrial countries. If they do not deal multilaterally through the GATT negotiations, some developing countries will find that industrial nations will press less advantageous bilateral deals upon them. Instances of this have already occurred.

Most developing countries would benefit by reducing their own levels of protection. But the costs of adjustment would be less, and the benefits even greater, if they could gain greater access for their exports to the markets of industrial countries. Indeed, to achieve faster growth they need access. This requires that trade barriers not increase and, preferably, that they decline. For developing countries, significant gains from the Uruguay Round will require their full and active participation.

Problems with the trading system

The main success of the GATT since 1948 has been the dramatic reduction in tariffs on trade in manufactures. Quantitative restrictions, however, have returned in new forms since the 1970s. Under GATT rules quantitative restrictions are permissible, but only on a strictly temporary basis, to deal with a balance of payments deficit or as an emergency safeguard action under GATT Article XIX. Another requirement is that they be nondiscriminatory. Most of the quantitative restrictions introduced in recent years have breached this principle. They have generally taken the form of selective restraints which have discriminated between imports from different countries.

For the developing countries this is sanctioned by the GATT on the grounds that their circumstances are special and that most developing countries tend to have chronic balance of trade deficits. But the industrial nations are either in breach of the GATT (for example, when they pay subsidies) or outside the GATT (for example, when they set voluntary export restraints or orderly marketing arrangements). The Multifibre Arrangement has an ambiguous position. Legally it is a separate instrument, but it was negotiated under GATT auspices and is administered by the GATT. Despite this, it is clearly inconsistent with the GATT principles (see Box 9.1).

A major failure of the GATT negotiations has been lack of progress toward liberalizing trade in agriculture. The industrial nations, for reasons discussed at length in *World Development Report 1986*, have kept and even increased their restrictions on imports and their subsidies to production and exports of agricultural products.

From the start, the GATT rules exempted customs unions and free trade areas from the MFN rule. Members of these groups are permitted to reduce or eliminate trade barriers against each other's exports, so long as they meet certain criteria (for example, they must not increase trade barriers against the rest of the world and should progress fairly rapidly toward substantially free trade within the group). Since 1979 the GATT has also allowed developing countries to receive special preferences or to extend them to each other. The degree to which customs unions, free trade areas, and other exceptions to the MFN rule have been exploited may not have been envisaged by the founders. Trade in services and trade between the subsidiaries of multinational corporations are also outside the GATT rules. The rapid growth of multinational corporations means that intrafirm transactions are now a large and expanding share of world trade. The trend has implications for taxation and foreign exchange control which are causing concern to many members of the GATT. Another development which has allowed a large

The foundation of today's international economic system was laid in 1944 at the Bretton Woods Conference when the World Bank, the IMF, and the International Trade Organization (ITO) were initiated. Together these institutions were intended to ensure a reconstructed Europe, stable international monetary relations, and an open and orderly trading system.

Because of objections that its enforcement provisions would interfere with the autonomy of domestic policymaking, the ITO charter was never ratified. Instead, the GATT, which had been drawn up only as an interim agreement to fill the gap until the ITO was ratified, became the framework for the international trading system in 1948. Today there is a small GATT secretariat, which is responsible for overseeing the settlement of trade disputes, serving committees on special trade issues, and monitoring compliance with GATT regulations. The GATT's membership has grown from twenty-three nations in 1948 to ninety-three full signatories today.

The main objectives of the GATT reflect the desire of the founding members to prevent a recurrence of the protectionism of the 1930s, which they believed deepened the Great Depression and helped give rise to World War II. First, the GATT embraced nondiscrimination or most favored nation (MFN) treatment to prevent the cycle of selective retaliations and countermeasures fostered by discriminatory trade. This means, for example, that footwear from Canada and footwear from Brazil or from any other signatory should face an identical tariff when imported into France. Because MFN rules prevent an importing country from using tariffs selectively, the country is less likely to raise its protective barriers and risk retaliation.

Second, uncertainty and lack of transparency in trade policies in the prewar period created tension between countries. Foreign producers could not be sure what kind of barriers they would face at the border and so were discouraged from exporting. Consequently, the GATT emphasized the use of bound tariffs over less transparent forms of protection such as quotas.

Third, the GATT adopted reciprocal reductions in tariff barriers as a means of mobilizing political support for reducing the worldwide level of protection. Countries could have some assurance that their exports as well as their imports would increase without causing a worsening of their terms of trade. The tariff cuts in turn were applied to all GATT signatories because of MFN treatment.

GATT regulations allow countries to use protective measures in case of balance of payments difficulties or as a safeguard against a sudden surge of imports which threatens a domestic industry (see Box 9.4). These measures, however, are supposed to be temporary, to conform to GATT provisions on nondiscrimination, and to be subject to compensation or retaliation by injured exporters. The GATT also permits the use of selective duties in cases where exporters are found to be subsidizing exports or dumping. In these cases the importer can raise the tariff on the individual exporter's product by an amount equivalent to the subsidy or to the difference between the exporter's home- and foreign-market prices (see Box 9.5).

Because the international economic environment is no longer the same as it was in the 1940s and countries have adopted new protectionist instruments, the GATT often seems inadequate for the task of promoting an open trading system. The GATT explicitly disallows many of the discriminatory quota restrictions and other trade barriers in common use by its signatories today. As with all organizations, especially those with no enforcement power, the GATT can only be as effective as its members allow it to be.

---

volume of trade to bypass the GATT rules is the growth of countertrade, in which goods are bartered for goods in bilateral arrangements. Long normal in the trading relationships of the centrally planned economies, the practice has now spread to many other countries.

The effect of these developments—continued protection in agriculture; the management of trade in textiles, clothing, and steel and similar tendencies in footwear, cars, and electronics; the spread of special trading relationships, the growing importance of multinational corporations; and the growth of barter—is that the share of trade which conforms to GATT rules is shrinking steadily. A set of laws which is more breached than obeyed is likely to lose all capacity to command respect.

Since the GATT was founded the players on the international scene have changed. In 1948 only the Western industrial countries were important in international trade. Since then Japan has become a major trading nation. Developing countries' share of world trade has increased. New trading blocs have appeared, of which the European Community is by far the most important. Most of these blocs conform to the GATT articles, but they do mean that a large volume of trade is not subject to the most favored nation rule. The Generalized System of Preferences, which grants developing countries some tariff preferences in industrial countries, and other preferential arrangements for developing countries, such as the Lomé Convention, also conform to the GATT. But they too involve discrimination in trade (see Box 9.2).

One cause of increased strain in trade relations has been the growth of government involvement in the management of the national economy. Governments have accepted responsibility for maintaining full employment and regional equity and for meeting other social objectives. Various industries were nationalized in many of the European nations. The growth of the public sector has increased the importance of government procurement. Such activities have been the breeding ground of nontariff barriers. Government procurement typically favors local suppliers. Nationalized industries attract subsidies and protection. Regional subsidies intended to attract new industries to areas of high unemployment can also affect the relative costs of exports or import substitutes and thus risk running afoul of GATT rules. A good deal of trade friction among the European nations, Japan, and the United States has arisen over such matters. Some developing countries have also attracted attention for their alleged subsidies to exports.

On top of these mounting tensions has come the shock of recessions, monetary instability, international debt, slow growth, and extremely high levels of unemployment in many industrial nations. In these circumstances, adjustment to surges of imports or to a rapid decline in certain industries' comparative advantage is difficult. The difficulties are particularly great in economies which may have ossified as a result of past protection, government assistance, and lack of labor mobility.

The attraction of nontariff barriers

Countries can restrict imports in many ways apart from tariffs—for example, by using quotas, voluntary export restraints, and orderly marketing arrangements. Antidumping or countervailing duty actions, surveillance, and health and safety standards can be used to create uncertainty and harass foreign exporters. In GATT parlance most of these are ''gray area'' measures, meaning that they are ''either inconsistent with countries' obligations to the GATT or are of uncertain consistency with the GATT.'' Of these, the most frequently used today is the voluntary export restraint.

At first sight this is surprising. VERs are particularly costly to the country that uses them to restrict imports. Not only does a VER inflict the same costs as a quota, by raising prices to consumers and switching resources from more efficient to less efficient uses, it also transfers rents to foreigners by allowing them to raise their prices (Chapter 5). Often it has the additional effect of reducing the volume of cheap, lower-quality imports as exporters raise the quality of their products and their profits per unit in the restricted market.

Despite these disadvantages governments clearly prefer VERs to legitimate GATT instruments. Indeed, GATT statistics show that since 1978 VERs have outnumbered Article XIX safeguard actions by more than 3 to 1. (By value of trade affected, this actually understates the growth of VERs.) The reasons are largely political. Consider the pros and cons, as perceived by governments, of invoking Article XIX compared with negotiating a VER if a domestic industry demands protection.

Under Article XIX the importing country's government has to claim that the increase in imports is causing or threatening serious injury to its domestic industry (see Box 9.3). If the government is satisfied on this count, it can apply a tariff or quota to this type of import. But it must apply the restriction to all the nations which export to its market, not merely the offending country. This is a deterrent to the use of Article XIX not only because the restriction could harm the export interests of powerful nations, but also because nations which see their interests harmed can demand compensation in the form of the removal of restrictions on an equivalent amount of other imports. If they are not compensated, they are entitled to retaliate in a reciprocal manner for the injury done to them. Clearly, there will be many cases in which a government will hesitate before embarking on this dangerous route. How much better to call in the representatives of the ''offending'' exporter for a quiet discussion of the need for restraint on their ''overenthusiastic'' penetration of the domestic market.

Targets for reform

The weaknesses in the original GATT framework and major changes in the postwar international environment have undermined the liberal international trading system. The GATT faces a barrage of disputes. Without a new commitment to the principles of the GATT, the trading system will see an

Box 9.2 The Lomé Convention

The most important regional agreement providing special and differential treatment is the Lomé Convention. Signed in 1975 and renewed in 1979 and 1984, it gives a group of sixty-six African, Caribbean, and Pacific (ACP) countries preferential access to EC markets. The Lomé accord differs from the Generalized System of Preferences in that it encompasses more than simple tariff reductions. It includes the relaxation of some nontariff barriers, less stringent enforcement of some trade regulations, and exemptions from certain multilateral trade agreements such as the MFA. Like the GSP, however, the Lomé accord is subject to regulations which severely limit "free access" for beneficiaries' exports, including a safeguard clause which allows the EC to suspend any concession unilaterally.

One problem with all such preferential trade schemes is that they amount to a "zero-sum game": preferential treatment for one country or group of countries is gained at the expense of others. Christopher Stevens describes special and differential treatment as a "pyramid of privilege" where "those at the top receive more favorable treatment than those at the base" and where all those in the pyramid do better than other countries (see Box table 9.2A). The pyramid is in fact a shifting one. As one country or group advances toward the top, it necessarily pushes others down. Portugal, for instance, was once near the base. After joining the EC it moved to the top, above all non-EC members.

One would assume that the Lomé Convention, in granting preferential tariff rates and exemption from the MFA, would have to be beneficial to the ACP countries. On the contrary, empirical evidence shows that

Box table 9.2A EC trade arrangements with the developing countries in order of preferential treatment

	Country	Trade agreement
More favorable treatment ↑	ACP: African, Caribbean, and Pacific countries	Lomé Convention
	Maghreb countries: Algeria, Morocco, Tunisia	Preferential trade and cooperation agreements
	Mashreq countries: Egypt, Jordan, Lebanon, Syria	Preferential trade and cooperation agreements
	Israel, Yugoslavia	Preferential trade and cooperation agreements with each country
	Cyprus, Malta, Turkey	Association agreements
	Other developing countries	Generalized System of Preferences
	Bangladesh, India, Pakistan, Sri Lanka	Nonpreferential commercial cooperation agreements with each country
Less favorable treatment ↓	Association of South East Asian Nations (ASEAN): Indonesia, Malaysia, Philippines, Singapore, Thailand	Regional framework agreement
	Argentina, Brazil, Mexico, Uruguay	Nonpreferential commercial cooperation agreements with each country
	Central America	Regional framework agreement 1986
	China, Romania	Nonpreferential trade agreements with each country

Source: Stevens (background paper) 1986.

Box 9.3 Reform of the emergency safeguard code: GATT Article XIX

The existing provisions

Unforeseen emergencies can always arise, so most trade treaties make some provision for releasing a country from its obligations if damage to an industry may result from a surge in imports. The GATT is no exception, and Article XIX is its emergency safeguard code. A country may impose a tariff or a quota to restrain imports which "cause or threaten serious injury" to domestic producers, provided that:

• The development was unforeseen at the time of the tariff cuts.

• The country warns major suppliers and notifies the GATT.

• The country maintains the import restraint for only as long as "necessary to prevent or remedy the injury."

• The country seeks agreement from suppliers who

may be injured, and if they are not satisfied (for example, by compensation such as cuts in tariffs on other products which they export to the country), they can retaliate with the withdrawal of an equivalent concession.

Proposed reforms

Two extreme positions can be held on reform of Article XIX. First there is the view that it is too easily abused. It does not define "serious injury," and including "threat of injury" makes it much too easy to claim an emergency. It allows either a tariff or a quota to be placed on the injurious imports. There is no time limit on the duration of the restriction. Supposedly temporary protection too often seems to become permanent. Finally, nations may find it difficult to make compensatory cuts in protection on other imports from the coun-

there has actually been a decrease in trade between ACP countries and the EC. In the pre-Lomé period 1970–75, the ACP share of EC imports from the developing countries was 20.5 percent. In 1975–84 the ACP share dropped to 16.6 percent. When oil exports are discounted, no significant change is found in the growth of trade between the ACP countries and the EC (see Box table 9.2B).

Although the ACP countries as a group have not done better under the Lomé, there have been gains at the margin. Among those countries which were "nonassociated" with EC members before the convention, there was an increase in ACP imports.

Analysis of the ACP exports by commodity shows some trade-creating effects. From 1975 to 1980, eleven ACP countries increased exports of manufactures and processed agricultural and temperate agricultural goods. These exports covered seventy-five product categories. Up until 1984, this process of diversification had continued: ACP exports were recorded in 128 categories. It is important to note that these diversifying countries included both middle- and low-income members of the ACP, for example, Benin, Central African Republic, Ethiopia, Mali, Tanzania, and Zaire. Just over half of the sixty-six countries diversified into at least four new products. Yet, one cannot be certain if this diversification was due to preferential treatment of certain goods or to developing countries' attempts to skirt trade barriers by diversifying into "free" products.

What then has been the net effect of the special and differential treatment of the ACP countries? It is difficult to state categorically where they would be without special and differential treatment. Perhaps, in the face of rising protectionism in the industrial countries, the very existence of an accord which promotes trade provides policymakers with a lever against future protectionist demands in the EC.

Box table 9.2B Trade shares: the EC and the ACP countries
(percent)

| | Time period | | | |
Share	Pre-Lomé, 1970–75	Lomé I, 1975–79	Lomé II, 1979–84	Average
EC share of ACP exports	45.6	38.7	36.7	37.7
EC share of non-oil ACP exports	46.3	47.1	41.9	44.5
ACP share of total EC imports from developing countries	20.5	16.4	16.9	16.6
ACP share of total EC imports from non-oil-exporting developing countries	27.3	22.8	20.1	21.5

Source: Stevens (background paper).

tries whose export is restrained by the Article XIX restriction.

On this view, recommendations for reform are as follows:

• There should be a time limit on the application of the import restraint.

• The restraint should be progressively relaxed (made degressive over time).

• The restraint should be a tariff; a quota should be permissible only in urgent cases.

• The restraint should be nondiscriminatory to conform with the general MFN rule of the GATT.

• Compensation, certainly in its current form, should be abandoned, although other forms of compensation could be considered.

• Retaliation by exporters should not be permitted so long as the country which invokes the safeguard conforms to the rules.

The second view is represented by those (mainly the European Community) who argue against applying the MFN requirement. They see no reason to injure exporters who are causing them no problems when there is a need to deal with one country whose exports are disrupting their domestic industry. They want to be free to take selective safeguard action against the disrupter. They buttress their argument with the point that the MFN requirement is the main reason for the drift to VERs. If the MFN requirement were abolished, the VERs would largely disappear, nations' safeguard actions would be brought back within the GATT, and the "rule of law" would be restored. This is rather like solving the drug problem by legalizing cocaine.

Box 9.4   The Multifibre Arrangement and a new exporter: Bangladesh

Article 13 of MFA IV reads in part: "The participating countries (are) conscious of the problems posed by restraints on exports of new entrants and small suppliers . . . They agree that restraints shall not normally be imposed on exports from small suppliers, new entrants and the least industrial countries."

There can be no question that Bangladesh fits this description. With a 1984 per capita income of $140, it is one of the poorest countries in the world. In 1978, when it began building a textile and clothing industry with the help of the Republic of Korea, there were less than a dozen textile manufacturers in Bangladesh. By 1985 the number had grown to about 450 operational companies; these employed a total of 140,000 people and produced more than 300 million pieces a year. With 300 more companies ready to start up, Bangladesh has the potential to produce and export much more, although it will remain a tiny supplier compared with such textile giants as China, Hong Kong, and Korea.

Despite the agreement not to restrain exports from countries like Bangladesh, France and the United Kingdom imposed quotas as early as 1984. The United States initiated an arrangement in February 1986 which restricted Bangladesh's textile exports through January 31, 1988. Although the industrial countries are allowed under the MFA to limit imports in the case of a sudden surge of imports and market disruption, there is no apparent justification for such limits on Bangladesh. In 1984, even after achieving spectacular growth, Bangladesh still held only 0.25 percent of the developing country share of clothing exports to the industrial countries. The four biggest Asian NIC exporters held 60 percent. In the United States, Bangladesh's market share was 0.32 percent while the "superexporters" held 66.7 percent. Bangladesh hardly posed a serious threat to the U.S. industry.

The bilateral agreement signed between Bangladesh and the United States allowed a mere 6 percent yearly growth rate in MFA imports. Between 1981 and 1983–84 Bangladesh had an unrestrained growth rate of 386 percent. Moreover, the agreement was extremely detailed: it restricted exports down to seven-digit SITC categories. This meant, for example, that Bangladesh had a quota not only on shirts but also on shirts made from dyed yarn in particular sizes. So detailed an arrangement would make diversification into uncontrolled goods well nigh impossible. Because of it, Bangladesh stopped expanding its textile industry and for a time had operational facilities standing idle. Since the most recent bilateral arrangement, the situation has eased somewhat. But quotas are still detailed, and Bangladesh has already (in May 1987) reached the ceiling on quotas for major categories. It is possible for Bangladesh to borrow, within limits, from other categories underused quotas from the previous year or the succeeding year's quota. But these complications create uncertainty, and the administration of the quotas absorbs scarce managerial ability and discourages investment in a subsector in which Bangladesh clearly has a comparative advantage.

---

increase in bilateralism, a further spread of non-tariff barriers, more trade managed on the MFA model, and greater use of domestic trade laws to obstruct imports.

Agriculture

From its inception, the GATT has imposed little discipline on trade in agricultural products—reflecting the sensitivity of agricultural issues in domestic politics. The costs of protection in agriculture fall most heavily on the industrial countries themselves, but they also fall on some of the developing countries. Despite an increase in their manufactured exports, most developing countries still export mainly raw materials and agricultural products. They get some relief from preferential trade agreements, but still face severe problems. Access to the industrial countries is limited by import restrictions; in other markets the developing countries have to compete with subsidized exports from industrial countries. Sugar, for example, is highly protected in the domestic markets of the EC and the United States; these countries then sell their surpluses at subsidized prices.

Reduced barriers to trade in agriculture would also bring benefits to manufacturing in developing countries. As pointed out in *World Development Report 1986,* a prosperous agricultural sector fosters success in manufacturing. It creates demand for manufactures, generates savings, and earns foreign exchange.

GATT signatories have recognized that trade in agriculture is a primary concern and needs to be incorporated properly into the GATT. The GATT Committee on Agricultural Trade was established with that aim in 1982. In 1984 and 1985 it proposed reducing export subsidies and requiring a level of minimum access for exports to highly protected markets. This may be a modest start, but there are some other encouraging signs. The recent coalition between several major developing and industrial country exporters, such as Argentina and Australia, and the high and rising budgetary costs of agricultural support in industrial countries point to the possibility of a better outcome for agriculture in the new GATT round.

The Multifibre Arrangement

Trade in textiles and clothing has become the paradigm of managed trade. Its use of discriminatory quota restrictions, negotiated bilaterally, violates the most basic rule of the GATT. The history of the MFA has shown increasing coverage and stringency, and it has recently been renegotiated (in July 1986).

The importing nations and most developing countries have much to gain from dismantling the MFA. The past success of the newly industrializing countries in beating this system has been based mainly on their ability to diversify into new fibers and products which were not covered by the MFA. As each successive MFA plugs the leaks in the earlier version, however, it will become increasingly difficult to diversify into non-MFA products and to maintain export growth (Chapter 8). Under these conditions, it is likely that all developing country exporters will feel the effect of textile and clothing restrictions. The major Asian exporters will find all their exports bound by quotas, and relative newcomers may be held to tiny market shares despite the special provision for small suppliers in the new MFA (see Box 9.4).

Moreover, a system of managed trade in textiles and clothing bodes ill for free trade in other industries where industrial country producers are threatened by the exports of developing countries. The legitimacy of MFA protection for textiles sets a precedent. And, once established, such systems tend to become permanent. Protected industries use the help they receive not to move to other

sectors but to introduce new technology and more capital-intensive methods to try to regain market share. Higher prices give some exporters a reason to support the scheme. The MFA was intended as a temporary measure, but instead has increased in scope and magnitude and become institutionalized. The expanding system of managed trade in steel seems to be following the same path. Eventually, the members of the GATT must grasp this nettle if the spread of managed trade is to be halted.

Safeguards

Safeguard actions under GATT Article XIX permit the use of either a tariff or a quota for temporary protection. The quota has been the instrument of choice (see Table 9.1). The trouble with safeguard actions, however, is that most of them are taken outside the GATT.

Developing countries are particularly vulnerable to industrial country safeguards. Their most successful exports are likely to be those that are produced by labor-intensive industries such as footwear and other low-skill manufactures. These are sensitive industries because of the social problems which their collapse can cause.

Developing countries are also quite unable to pose a realistic retaliatory threat, because of the relatively small size of their markets and their reliance on capital goods imports. Only a few of the larger developing countries—Brazil, China, India, and Indonesia—may be able to threaten to cut some import and thereby inflict damage on an industrial nation.

Changes in comparative advantage mean the decline of older industries in the industrial countries. Safeguard actions against the developing countries will continue. The GATT needs a new and strengthened safeguard code which allows temporary protection in the industrial countries, but encourages adjustment and stops the use of "illegal" and discriminatory barriers against exporters (Box 9.3). The Tokyo Round failed to achieve an acceptable solution. Assuring access for developing country exports to industrial countries' markets will depend on the ability of the participants to amend and strengthen Article XIX in the Uruguay Round.

Countervailing and antidumping measures

The countervailing and antidumping policies of the industrial countries are closely linked to the

Table 9.1 Frequency of use of tariffs and quotas under Article XIX

Period	Tariff measures	Quantitative restrictions	Total	Ratio of quantitative restrictions to total
1949–58	13	3	16	19
1959–68	20	16	36	44
1969–78	15	28	43	65
1979–86	17	25	42	60

Source: Frank 1981; Anjaria, Kirmani, and Peterson 1985; GATT.

Box 9.5 Antidumping and countervailing duties and subsidies in the GATT

The existing provisions

The provisions on antidumping and countervailing duties (CVDs) are contained in GATT Articles VI and XVI and a subsidies code added in the Tokyo Round.

"Dumping" is defined as exporting a product at a price below its normal value or below the comparable price of a similar product sold in the exporting country. An importing country can offset or prevent dumping by levying an antidumping duty not greater than the difference between the price of the exported good and the price of a similar good in the exporter's domestic market.

A government subsidy on the manufacture, production, or export of any merchandise which operates directly or indirectly to increase exports or to reduce imports may be subject to CVDs. A countervailing duty is levied by the importing country to offset the exporter's subsidy and cannot exceed the amount of this subsidy. The use of antidumping and countervailing duties is limited to situations in which the import is causing or threatens to cause material injury to a domestic industry.

The code on subsidies and CVDs was negotiated during the Tokyo Round with the aim of ensuring that subsidies would not harm the interests of trading partners and that countervailing duty procedures would not unjustifiably impede international trade. The signatories made a renewed agreement not to subsidize

agricultural exports so as to gain "more than an equitable share of world export trade." They also agreed not to use domestic production subsidies which would seriously harm the trade of other countries. Finally, they pledged to abide by GATT Article VI, which states that CVDs are to be used only when the imported goods are causing or threaten to cause material injury to a domestic industry. A GATT committee was established under the code to deal with the settlement of disputes arising from the use of subsidies and CVDs as well as to monitor the application of the code by the signatories.

Proposed reforms

The subsidies code negotiated in the Tokyo Round proved little better than the original articles. The number of disputes continues to rise. Indeed, the record shows a strong upward trend in countervailing actions against developing countries. Recently, most of the CVD and antidumping actions have been initiated by the United States and the European Community against developing country exporters (see Box tables 9.5A and 9.5B).

Two approaches to the reform of countervailing duty and subsidy practices have emerged. The first views developing countries which subsidize exports as simply damaging their long-run development. Subsidies then become the target for reform, not the countervail-

Box table 9.5A The frequency of U.S. countervailing actions, 1970–85

| | | Number of | Final outcome of action | | | Average |
Year	Exporter	initiations	Affirmative	Negative	Pending	CVD rate
1970–74	Industrial countries	9	8	1	—	..
	Developing countries	2	2	—	—	..
1975–79	Industrial countries	59	20	39	—	..
	Developing countries	45	18	27	—	..
1980–85	Industrial countries	63	30 (19)	25	8	10.5
	Developing countries	108	69 (26)	30	9	11.5

Note: Numbers in parentheses represent cases considered affirmative although they were withdrawn from CVD actions and settled through alternative arrangements between the exporting and importing countries.
Source: Nam 1986a.

issue of safeguards. An importing country imposes countervailing duties if the exporting country's government is subsidizing its exports. It takes antidumping measures when an exporter sells a product abroad at less than its domestic price or cost of production. Whereas safeguard actions taken under Article XIX can be imposed by the importing country regardless of the exporting

countries' policies, countervailing duties and antidumping actions can be taken only if the exporter is engaging in one of these two forms of "unfair" trade (see Box 9.5).

As indicated in Chapter 8, countervailing duties and antidumping policies may be abused so as to become just another form of protection. They can inflict additional costs on exporters through the

ing duty. From this viewpoint, CVDs are a means to induce developing countries to abandon subsidies and to adopt other means, such as exchange rate devaluations, to promote exports.

A related solution is for the GATT to approach the problem not through an international code, but through direct negotiations among participants on dismantling subsidies. This is likely to be the approach for dealing with agricultural subsidies.

The second approach is based on the belief that CVD actions are simply a way to protect declining industries in the industrial countries against developing country exporters. CVD procedures deter exports because of the direct costs to exporters of the investigations. If that is their purpose, the requirements for starting CVD actions could be tightened so as to reduce their use as substitutes for safeguard actions. The signatories could also be required to have a greater regard for the situation of developing countries when applying CVD measures. Another suggestion is that there should be a program of technical assistance to help developing countries defend their interests in CVD cases.

Box table 9.5B Frequency of antidumping cases, 1980–85

Initiated by	Number of cases	Against	Number of cases
Australia	393	EC	276
United States	280	United States	105
EC	254	Japan	96
Canada	219	Korea, Republic of	71
Sweden	4	China	58
Finland	3	Spain	43
Austria	1	Brazil	39
Spain	1	Czechoslovakia	34
		Canada	32
		Sweden	16
		Austria	11
		Finland	9
		Others (44)	398

Source: Finger and Nogues 1986.

use of investigations, legal proceedings, and complicated tariff formulas. These procedures can slow down exports or convince an exporter that a negotiated VER is better than "unfair" trade proceedings.

"UNFAIR" TRADE AND THE DEVELOPING COUNTRIES. Countervailing and antidumping policies impose a disproportionate cost on developing country exporters. This is due, in part, to the administrative procedures involved. Firms and governments in the developing countries often lack the trained staff to deal with these procedures. They often have to hire foreign specialists, and the expense can be great. UNCTAD estimates that the cost of a fairly routine antidumping proceeding in the United States can easily exceed $100,000. This may have to be borne by a single exporting firm.

Many new producers are willing to forgo some export profit (by selling the export at a lower price than they would domestically) to gain market share. This standard business practice makes them liable to be charged with dumping. Moreover, the methods used to justify subsidies and dumping tend to ignore the differences between developing and industrial country markets. Often the high trade barriers which prevail in developing countries will raise the domestic price of exportable goods. But the protection will also cause the exchange rate to be overvalued. The overvalued exchange rate reduces the price in local currency of goods exported, which lowers the incentive to export (Chapter 6). A developing country may feel it is quite legitimate to offset this by an export subsidy of some type. But the price will now be lower than the protection-induced price in the home market and may be treated as subsidized or dumped in the industrial country, even though it is a result of distortions in the exporter's domestic economy.

"UNFAIR" TRADE AND THE CENTRALLY PLANNED ECONOMIES. Distinctions between fair and unfair trade are often difficult to establish even in market economies. In centrally planned economies, where the government plays the central role in production, the distinction is even more obscure. How can a country determine if exports from a CPE are subsidized if all prices are set without regard to supply and demand? Dumping can be hard to identify for the same reason. If the CPE is producing only for export, it is impossible even to try to compare the export price and the domestic selling price; the importing country must try to determine the cost of production in the CPE. This is done (at least for legal purposes) by examining the cost of production of a similar product in a market economy—a cumbersome and dubious procedure (see Box 9.6).

The Uruguay Round should examine whether countervailing and antidumping procedures can

Box 9.6 Antidumping actions: the golf cart case

Imports from centrally planned economies which are sold at less than the full market price are often targets of antidumping actions in industrial countries. Yet it is extremely difficult to determine if a CPE supplier has dumped, because official exchange rates, domestic prices, and production costs often bear little resemblance to market-determined ones. A case involving golf carts imported from Poland is a vivid example of the extraordinarily complex techniques the United States and the EC have had to adopt in investigating antidumping actions against CPEs.

Since 1972, Poland has been exporting several thousand golf carts to the United States each year. In 1975, antidumping charges were brought against Pezetel, the Polish foreign trade organization, for selling golf carts at less than "fair value." Because Poland made golf carts for export only and sold them only to the United States, fair value could not be determined by the domestic market price or the price of the export to a third country. The United States used the "constructed value" approach to approximate the fair value of Polish golf carts. Using a value based on the costs to a Canadian golf cart manufacturer, the United States charged Pezetel with dumping. Duties were assessed until 1976, when the sole Canadian producer went out of business. Because no third country produced similar golf carts at that time, fair value could not be obtained by looking at another producer's prices. The United States therefore determined the constructed value by choosing a market economy, Spain, with a level of development similar to Poland's and estimating what it would have cost a Spanish producer to make golf carts. When the cost was converted into dollars, it was determined that the Polish golf carts were not being sold at less than fair value, and in 1980 the earlier dumping finding was revoked.

This method can hardly be considered foolproof. Even if a "surrogate" country had identical factor proportions and prices, there is still no reason to assume its products would be equally competitive. Moreover, studies have shown that there is little correlation between the level of development as measured by GDP and relative prices. Although this investigation ended happily for the Polish golf cart industry, it could easily have turned out otherwise.

---

be further refined and whether the industrial countries are using these procedures legitimately or as yet another means of safeguarding domestic industry from import competition.

Escalation of trade barriers

Tariff escalation has long been a grievance of the developing countries. Recent research, as reported in Chapter 8, has shown a similar trend in the use of nontariff barriers. A much higher level of effective protection for copper wire than for crude copper or for instant coffee than for coffee beans handicaps processing in developing countries. Possession of a raw material, such as bauxite, does not necessarily give a comparative advantage in producing an intermediate good, such as aluminum, where cheap energy and capital are more

---

Box 9.7 Barriers to trade in services

The GATT does not cover services, which in many countries are highly protected. For example, Colombian imports can be insured only by Colombian companies, no foreign insurance firms are allowed to operate in India, and those applying for licenses in Turkey are told to wait until a new insurance law is passed. Belgium, Italy, and the Netherlands effectively bar foreign communications firms from providing enhanced communications services by prohibiting their use of government-owned lines. Foreign construction firms are restricted in their ability to provide technical services in Brazil and are excluded from designing and constructing oil-drilling platforms in the United Kingdom. Movie and television exporters, especially those from the United States, are hampered by a variety of barriers. In Indonesia they must use local dubbing facilities; in Venezuela they must process 60 percent of all 35-millimeter prints in local laboratories. Pakistani theaters are required to devote 15 percent of playing time to local films. Britain limits foreign productions to 14 percent of air time on independent television stations. In short, few countries seem prepared to allow foreigners to compete on an equal footing with locals in the provision of services.

important costs—but it can be crucial for some products. The Tokyo Round of the MTN was supposed to deal with this problem, but in fact tariff escalation slightly increased (Chapter 8). This source of trade distortion will have to be taken up again in the current MTN.

Trade in services

The United States and the EC, on the one side, and a group of developing countries led by Brazil and India, on the other, disagreed over whether to include services in the Uruguay Round. Important issues are at stake in this. Trade in services might be considered the same as trade in goods. After all, to buy a good is simply to buy something which yields services. From that point of view it makes obvious sense to include rules on trade in services within the GATT, perhaps merely by adding "and services" wherever goods are mentioned in the agreement. The problem is not so simple.

THE NEED FOR PHYSICAL PRESENCE. Some services can be provided without physical proximity between provider and user. These "long-distance" services include, for instance, wireless transmission of concerts. But more services are "embodied"; they need a physical presence for their delivery. For example, a construction engineer needs to be on site to provide engineering services; a doctor or a dentist has to visit or be visited. A bank or a legal firm may not need to be on the spot to provide many of its services, but efficiency is likely to be much higher if clients have easy access. What this implies for trade in many types of services is that staff and possibly full branches of the business need to be established in the importing country. (Such services are somewhat inelegantly known as "temporary-factor-relocation-requiring" services, as distinct from long-distance services.)

The right of establishment is crucial for multinational service companies such as American Express and Morgan Grenfell; construction companies need permits to bring in engineers, managers, and essential workers. So service transactions are qualitatively different from trade in goods. This suggests that careful analysis is needed before deciding how to amend the GATT rules.

PROTECTION IN SERVICES. Countries have several devices for protecting domestic suppliers of services from foreign competition. These include visa requirements, investment regulations, restrictions on the ability to repatriate earnings, and so on.

Italy requires the hiring of local actors and film crews for commercials. Argentina, Mexico, Peru, and Venezuela insist that local accountants supervise foreign auditors (see Box 9.7).

Developing countries fear that many of their own service industries are insufficiently developed to withstand foreign competition. They have also felt that the reforms hinted at so far, in return for opening their markets to service transactions, are unsatisfactory. The services in which developing countries have a comparative advantage seem to be excluded by being labeled "immigration." Developing countries think it unfair that access to their service markets should be made a condition for reductions in illegal, or at least gray area, protection. So the developing countries have insisted upon separate negotiations on services.

DEVELOPING COUNTRY INTERESTS. Now that services have been brought within the Uruguay Round, albeit on "a parallel track," developing countries have to consider where the balance of advantage lies for them in the negotiations. Some developing countries already have considerable exports of services such as tourism, shipping, and construction services. There may be a case for infant industry assistance to some sectors of services. But if developing countries protect more expensive or lower quality services produced by local firms, they run the risk of handicapping their exports of goods: many services are upstream or downstream services to producers. In the industrial countries large companies often internalize many services—research, marketing, financial analysis, and so forth. Small to medium companies usually have easy access to specialist firms which supply such services. In developing countries this is seldom the case.

Access at reasonable cost to quality services can make the difference between success or failure in exporting. In many developing countries, the need for such services argues for at least selective liberalization. If this encouraged the multinational corporations of the industrial countries to provide these services to developing countries, it would help developing countries' exports of manufactures in three ways. First, it would lower their costs and help them to develop markets. Second, it would encourage the multinational corporations to move away from goods in favor of producing more services. Third, if industrial nations can sell more services, they may be more willing to lower protective barriers elsewhere.

Developing countries are likely to have comparative advantage in labor-intensive services such as tourism and construction. Countries in the Caribbean, Latin America, and the Mediterranean have successfully developed tourist industries; India and the Republic of Korea have successfully exported construction services. Activities like keypunching for the computer software industry are also moving to some developing countries.

Those developing countries which have invested heavily in education may earn returns in such areas as computer software and research and development services. Other developing countries have the capacity to export legal and accounting services. For the most part, however, the industrial countries will have a comparative advantage in skill- and capital-intensive services, such as banking, insurance, and passenger and freight transport, for some time to come.

India, Korea, and probably several other developing countries are likely to have a keen interest in how the issue of "the right to establish" is settled. The industrial countries have suggested rules which provide not merely for a branch office but also for the right to employ foreign personnel in it. The construction industry may need to go further. It may wish to bring in not only managers and technicians but also supervisors, skilled workers, and even laborers. For countries where comparative advantage in constructing a road or a bridge may rest mainly on disciplined, and relatively low-paid, teams of construction workers—Korea, for example—it would be important to be able to bring in whole work crews on temporary permits. Once the right to bring in foreign employees is established, it is difficult to see how the right of the construction firm to bring in its whole team can be excluded.

A final reason for developing countries to pursue negotiations on a multilateral basis is that the alternative is likely to be bilateral or regional negotiations. That would result in inefficient and discriminatory freeing of some service transactions, in ways that would not necessarily be in the interests of the developing countries.

The stake of the developing countries in the Uruguay Round

The argument of the preceding chapters is that the gains from trade for developing countries are substantial. Both economic theory and the empirical evidence show that fuller participation in world trade should increase their efficiency and growth. This suggests that developing countries ought to

gain if they reduce their trade barriers and liberalize their own economies. But they would find such policies much easier in an environment of more liberal and expanding world trade. This gives developing countries a keen interest in a successful outcome from the MTN.

What, more precisely, do they hope to get out of it? Developing countries want greater access to the markets of the industrial nations. Most want an end to VERs and selective quotas, and they want a safeguard code which ensures that restrictions imposed under Article XIX are limited, temporary, degressive, and nondiscriminatory. But they also want to retain their special and differential status. Several of them are opposed to negotiations in the GATT on services and trade-related investment and would prefer that any discussions on these matters be handled in UNCTAD.

In fact the agenda for the Uruguay Round broadly meet their wishes. The subjects for negotiation include tariffs, nontariff measures, safeguards, tropical products, and products based on natural resources. Negotiations on textiles and clothing (the MFA) are included, but in language which is so hedged as to provide few grounds for hope of significant improvement. The developing countries' desire to retain special and differential treatment seems to be fully met in sections B(IV) and (V) of the General Principles Governing Negotiations. These preserve "differential and more favorable treatment" and state that industrial countries will not expect "reciprocity" for concessions to developing countries. Section B(VI) repeats the GATT's usual formula for recognizing the graduation principle: the "less developed contracting parties expect that their capacity to make contributions or negotiated concessions . . . would improve with the progressive development of their economies . . . and they would accordingly expect to participate more fully in the framework of rights and obligations under the General Agreement."

Developing countries clearly have to consider whether their interests lie in preserving or in negotiating away some of their special and differential status. The industrial countries have long argued that the more successful economies should graduate from the Generalized System of Preferences and take on most of the responsibilities of full GATT membership. Unable to incorporate "graduation" officially into the GSP itself, the industrial countries have unilaterally incorporated aspects of it into their own trade laws.

As a result of the limitations adopted by most industrial countries, the developing countries have gained little from the GSP. In 1981, for example, the United States imported $120.3 billion of goods from the developing countries. From GSP beneficiaries the total was $68.5 billion, and of this only a meager $8.4 billion, or 12.3 percent, actually entered duty free. Studies of the GSP in the European Community show that imports from non-beneficiaries were growing at a faster rate than those from countries covered by the GSP. Yet the developing countries continue their strong support for special and differential treatment and reject graduation. They may have underestimated both the potential benefits of negotiating for reciprocal reduction of trade barriers in the multilateral trade negotiations and the costs associated with continued dependence on the GSP.

In most countries the GSP excludes such crucial items as textiles, clothing, steel, and footwear. Normally the highest protection is on the products most likely to be exported by the developing countries. GSP treatment carries no long-term guarantee. Because preferences are unilaterally granted to the developing countries by the industrial country ''benefactors,'' tariff and quota levels are not bound: they can be withdrawn or altered. The uncertainty this creates leads the larger exporters to restrain exports for fear of triggering import restrictions in the industrial countries. The uncertainty can also adversely affect firms' plans to invest in export industries. Bound MFN tariffs in the GATT are much more secure than unbound GSP preferences.

Part IV of the GATT allows developing countries access to MFN or GSP tariffs without the need to make reciprocal cuts in their own trade barriers. As a result, few developing countries have lowered their trade barriers significantly. High barriers in the developing countries, whose exports are of growing importance in world trade, are an increasing source of irritation in many industrial countries. Some of the more advanced developing countries run the risk of having reciprocal restrictions placed on their exports—or of being forced by such a threat into making concessions bilaterally.

It has been suggested that by accepting special and differential treatment the developing countries have struck a Faustian bargain. In exchange for preferences, which brought them limited and risky gains, they have given up a voice in reciprocal trade negotiations and left themselves open to attack by protectionists in the industrial countries, who accuse them of unfair trade. The most mature developing countries, at least, should ask themselves whether this bargain still makes sense.

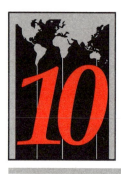

Industrialization and the world economy: a policy agenda

Industrialization results from the interaction of technological change, specialization, and trade. Good transport, efficient communications, and an educated labor force help to promote the rapid development of industries. Well-defined rules reduce the costs of transactions as specialization increases and economies become more complex. When governments seek to improve the working of markets rather than replace them, the economy generally works better.

This Report has stressed policies that facilitate change, overcome constraints imposed by initial conditions, and use natural resources and infrastructure efficiently. Policies that increase international competitiveness and mobilize domestic and foreign resources are crucial for successful industrialization.

A policy agenda for industrial countries

Because of the weight of the industrial countries' share in world output, trade, and capital flows, sustained growth in the world economy as a whole depends on their policies.

Payments imbalances

Sustainable growth in the world economy calls for policies to reduce the growing payments imbalances between the major industrial countries. If these imbalances continue, the threat of protectionism might become a reality. That would cripple world markets, aggravate the debt problem, and thwart the developing countries in their efforts to adjust.

The current account deficit of the United States and the current account surpluses of Japan and the Federal Republic of Germany are the main source of international imbalance. They reflect the fiscal deficit of the United States and an excess of savings over investment in the other two countries. Because of the large role of the United States in the world economy, any slowing down of its growth without compensating policies of expansion in the surplus countries would act as a drag on the growth of the world economy. The required adjustment means that the countries which previously relied on export demand for output growth may need to remove some of their restraints on domestic demand and ease access to their domestic markets. Adjustment will be less painful if the countries on both sides of the imbalance make a contribution to the process.

Structural rigidities

Macroeconomic policies can be the first step back to international equilibrium, but microeconomic policies are essential to reinforce them. Industrial countries need to remove their structural economic rigidities. Resistance to changes in comparative advantage, technology, and demography has inhibited the movement of labor and capital from old to new activities. These rigidities have limited growth, caused higher unemployment, and retarded industrial development.

Three areas of policy are particularly important. First, the reduction of trade barriers in protected sectors such as agriculture, steel, textiles, clothing, footwear, leather, and shipbuilding would go a long way to increase competition and promote flexibility. Simply shifting the form of protection from quantitative restrictions—such as VERs and orderly market arrangements—toward tariffs would help to restore the influence of prices. Moreover, a reciprocal reduction of trade barriers in the context of the Uruguay Round will ease political resistance by expanding the exports of industrial countries.

The second area of policy concerns labor markets—particularly those in Europe. The lack of flexibility in these markets has significantly added to Europe's unemployment problems. The tendency to set wages at the level of the most prosperous regions, geographical and occupational immobility, the high costs of dismissing labor, and high payroll taxes have all inhibited the efficient working of labor markets. High unemployment is, in turn, an obstacle to the removal of trade restrictions, because it fuels anxiety over job losses. Partial remedies include abolishing unnecessary labor market regulations and providing financial help for education, training, and job-related relocations.

Third, industrial regulation and subsidies in agriculture distort goods markets. A gradual withdrawal of agricultural subsidies, together with assistance for industries that need to restructure, would improve flexibility. Alongside reduced protection and more efficient labor markets, these measures would provide more room for expansion without inflation.

A policy agenda for developing countries

Growth in the world economy will help the developing countries to industrialize, but for *efficient* industrialization their own domestic policies are much more important.

Trade policies

Trade policy reform is a top priority. The fundamental goal should be to increase competitiveness in world markets. This Report has shown that the countries which adopted outward-oriented trade strategies have outperformed those that followed inward-oriented trade strategies—in income growth, export growth, employment, and savings. An outward-oriented trade strategy means lowering trade barriers, replacing quantitative restrictions with tariffs, and adopting realistic exchange rates. The objectives are to improve resource allocation, to force domestic firms to become more efficient by having to compete with foreign firms, and to open the economy to new opportunities.

Replacing quantitative restrictions with tariffs is a useful first step. It lets firms operate in a less restrictive environment, allows them to buy imported inputs more easily, and removes the incentives for unproductive activities. The next step is to lower the level and variation of rates of protection. The simpler the scheme, the better. Getting off to a bold start seems to strengthen the credibility of reform.

Macroeconomic policies

In many developing countries, expansionary fiscal policies have led to inflation, which in turn has distorted relative prices, raised nominal interest rates and the real exchange rate, discouraged savings, and stimulated capital flight. All too often in such circumstances, trade barriers are quickly reintroduced. Experience suggests that macroeconomic stability is a precondition for successful liberalization of financial markets. But seeking macroeconomic stability by cutting government expenditure requires care to protect essential spending on health, education, and the maintenance of infrastructure. Improving the efficiency of public enterprises so as to reduce the need to subsidize them should also help to cut the budget deficit and aid stability.

Complementary policies

For efficiency in resource allocation, prices should reflect the true costs of production. So price controls should be reduced as quickly as possible and eliminated altogether over the medium term. In many developing countries private investment is channeled to specific activities. Direct investment by foreigners is usually controlled even more stringently. If, as far as possible, governments offer similar incentives to *all* investors, they will increase competition, promote efficiency, and help businesses select technology that fits the country's resource endowments. Minimum wage regulations have been introduced in many developing countries to protect the wages of particular groups of workers. Reforming these regulations so that they act as a safety net for only the lowest-paid workers will meet equity objectives while reducing the distortionary effects.

The international environment for trade and finance

Steady growth in the world economy would make it much easier for the industrial countries to tackle their economic rigidities and for the developing countries to adjust their trade policies while pursuing complementary reforms. At the same time, such reforms would help the world economy to grow faster. The aim must be to prevent a vicious circle of stagnation and growing protection and establish instead a virtuous circle of lower trade barriers and faster growth.

The Uruguay Round

The agenda for the Uruguay Round negotiations cover areas of great interest to developing countries: trade in agriculture, tropical products, and textiles and clothing are all included. The developing countries would also benefit from an end to VERs and from the introduction of an effective safeguard code that would ensure that restrictions are limited, temporary, degressive, and nondiscriminatory. The "standstill and rollback" provisions of the Uruguay Round could increase developing countries' access to markets in industrial countries and to the markets of other developing countries.

The Uruguay Round provides a valuable opportunity to prevent domestic protectionist forces from gaining further ground. The timing is opportune. If trade can be liberalized, that will support increased growth in the world economy, reduce payments imbalances, allow countries to address debt repayment difficulties through increased exports, and provide an environment which makes long-term adjustment easier.

Availability of new funds

If developing countries are to adopt the reforms proposed, most will need increased external finance to sustain their adjustment efforts. Trade policy alone cannot achieve much without infrastructure, new investment, and finance for education, health, and human resources. Reforms take time to bring about increased output and exports. Besides, there are limits to how much consumption can be cut in order to free the resources for increased investment. Additional funds will be imperative for the highly indebted countries and for Sub-Saharan Africa. The highly indebted countries need to grow and to service debt at the same time, and without drastic cuts in consumption. They have already made substantial adjustments; without fresh funds to sustain growth their efforts will be in danger. A slowing down of their demand would retard world trade, and their debt problems could become intractable. This would put financial stability in both debtor and creditor countries at risk. Additional finance to support their adjustment efforts should be a high priority for the international community.

The need for concessional assistance for Sub-Saharan African countries is clear. The need to recover from a famine and restore income levels poses a formidable challenge for these countries. Many have undertaken substantial policy reforms despite the handicaps of low commodity prices, inadequate domestic savings, poor infrastructure, and insufficient social expenditures. Policy reforms in these countries need the backing of external finance for education, health, and institution building.

In sum, to improve the world economic outlook and promote efficient industrialization in developing countries, major policy reforms will be needed. Their success will depend to a substantial degree on the commitment of all nations to make the Uruguay Round a success and on the provision of financial support for the adjustment efforts of the developing countries.

Statistical appendix

The tables in this statistical appendix present data for a sample panel of ninety developing countries, along with information for industrial countries and high-income oil exporters where available. The tables show data on population, national accounts, trade, and external debt. Readers should refer to the technical notes to the World Development Indicators for definitions and concepts used in these tables.

Table A.1 Population growth, 1965–85 and projected to 2000

Country group	1985 population (millions)	Average annual growth (percent)				
		1965–73	1973–80	1980–85	1985–90	1990–2000
Developing countries	3,451	2.5	2.1	2.0	2.0	1.8
Low-income countries	2,323	2.6	2.0	1.9	1.9	1.7
Middle-income countries	1,128	2.4	2.4	2.3	2.3	2.0
Oil exporters	461	2.5	2.6	2.6	2.7	2.8
Exporters of manufactures	2,048	2.5	1.9	1.7	1.6	1.4
Highly indebted countries	555	2.6	2.4	2.4	2.5	2.4
Sub-Saharan Africa[a]	385	2.7	2.8	3.1	3.1	2.9
High-income oil exporters	19	4.6	5.5	4.4	4.2	3.2
Industrial countries	737	1.0	0.7	0.6	0.5	0.4
World[b]	4,207	2.2	1.9	1.8	1.8	1.6

a. Excludes South Africa.
b. Excludes nonmarket industrial economies.

Table A.2 Population and GNP per capita, 1980, and growth rates, 1965–86

Country group	1980 GNP (billions of dollars)	1980 population (millions)	1980 GNP per capita (dollars)	Average annual growth of GNP per capita (percent)						
				1965–73	1973–80	1982	1983	1984	1985[a]	1986[a]
Developing countries	2,078	3,123	670	4.0	3.1	−0.7	0.1	3.1	2.7	2.5
Low-income countries	565	2,118	270	2.9	2.6	3.5	5.9	6.9	7.0	4.3
Middle-income countries	1,513	1,005	1,500	4.6	3.1	−2.4	−2.5	1.1	0.5	1.4
Oil exporters	506	405	1,250	4.7	3.1	−3.6	−4.5	0.0	−0.2	−3.2
Exporters of manufactures	946	1,886	500	4.8	4.0	2.1	3.3	6.2	6.1	5.4
Highly indebted countries	868	492	1,770	4.4	2.8	−4.6	−5.9	−0.3	0.6	0.5
Sub-Saharan Africa[b]	182	331	550	3.4	0.5	−4.3	−4.9	−4.8	−0.2	−2.3
High-income oil exporters	223	16	14,400	3.9	5.7	−6.7	−14.3	−2.4	−8.6	−1.0
Industrial market economies	7,613	716	10,630	3.7	2.1	−1.3	1.6	4.1	2.4	1.9

a. Preliminary.
b. Excludes South Africa.

Table A.3 GDP, 1980, and growth rates, 1965–86

Country group	1980 GDP (billions of dollars)	Average annual growth of GDP (percent)						
		1965–73	1973–80	1982	1983	1984	1985[a]	1986[a]
Developing countries	2,116	6.5	5.4	2.1	2.1	5.1	4.8	4.2
Low-income countries	564	5.5	4.6	5.6	7.7	8.9	9.1	6.5
Middle-income countries	1,552	7.0	5.7	0.8	0.0	3.6	2.8	3.2
Oil exporters	522	6.9	6.0	0.4	−1.9	2.3	2.2	−1.1
Exporters of manufactures	958	7.4	6.0	4.2	4.9	7.8	7.8	7.0
Highly indebted countries	890	6.9	5.4	−0.5	−3.2	2.0	3.1	2.5
Sub-Saharan Africa[b]	187	6.4	3.2	−0.2	−1.5	−1.7	2.2	0.5
High-income oil exporters	216	8.3	7.9	−0.5	−6.9	1.2	−3.8	. .
Industrial market economies	7,570	4.7	2.8	−0.5	2.2	4.6	2.8	2.5

a. Preliminary.
b. Excludes South Africa.

Table A.4 Population and composition of GDP, selected years, 1965–86
(billions of dollars, unless otherwise specified)

Country group and indicator	1965	1973	1980	1982	1983	1984	1985[a]	1986[a]
Developing countries								
GDP	338	755	2,116	2,160	2,073	2,107	2,098	2,186
Domestic absorption[b]	342	759	2,165	2,209	2,089	2,092	2,089	2,176
Net exports[c]	−3	−5	−48	−50	−15	14	11	11
Population (millions)	2,207	2,691	3,123	3,255	3,320	3,385	3,451	3,519
Low-income countries								
GDP	147	259	564	556	584	582	587	609
Domestic absorption[b]	150	258	589	570	600	599	618	651
Net exports[c]	−2	0	−21	−14	−16	−17	−30	−42
Population (millions)	1,504	1,839	2,118	2,203	2,243	2,283	2,323	2,366
Middle-income countries								
GDP	190	496	1,552	1,604	1,490	1,525	1,511	1,578
Domestic absorption[b]	192	500	1,576	1,639	1,489	1,493	1,471	1,525
Net exports[c]	−1	−5	−23	−36	−1	31	41	53
Population (millions)	703	852	1,005	1,053	1,077	1,102	1,128	1,153
Oil exporters								
GDP	50	135	522	529	493	517	531	451
Domestic absorption[b]	49	134	505	531	481	495	513	454
Net exports[c]	0	1	16	−2	9	22	18	−2
Population (millions)	276	337	405	426	437	449	461	473
Exporters of manufactures								
GDP	166	368	958	990	940	951	969	1,094
Domestic absorption[b]	169	372	993	1,001	943	941	965	1,075
Net exports[c]	−2	−5	−34	−11	−2	11	4	20
Population (millions)	1,363	1,657	1,886	1,954	1,985	2,016	2,048	2,080
Highly indebted countries								
GDP	116	288	890	893	770	786	779	775
Domestic absorption[b]	115	287	898	900	748	750	745	734
Net exports[c]	2	1	−7	−7	22	36	35	40
Population (millions)	339	415	492	516	529	542	555	568
Sub-Saharan Africa[d]								
GDP	25	56	187	176	173	168	164	152
Domestic absorption[b]	24	55	188	189	181	169	164	156
Net exports[c]	0	1	−2	−14	−8	−1	0	−4
Population (millions)	219	272	331	352	363	375	385	398

(continued)

Table A.4 *(continued)*

Country group and indicator	1965	1973	1980	1982	1983	1984	1985[a]	1986[a]
High-income oil exporters								
GDP	8	28	224	255	217	203	185	..
Domestic absorption[b]	4	14	161	200	199	..	..	..
Net exports[c]	3	14	63	55	18	..	..	..
Population (millions)	7	11	16	17	18	18	19	20
Industrial market economies								
GDP	1,368	3,225	7,570	7,580	7,831	8,173	8,575	9,900
Domestic absorption[b]	1,363	3,212	7,623	7,581	7,832	8,201	8,595	9,950
Net exports[c]	5	12	−52	−1	−1	−28	−20	−50
Population (millions)	632	681	716	725	730	734	737	741

Note: Components may not add to totals due to rounding.
a. Preliminary.
b. Private consumption plus government consumption plus gross domestic investment.
c. Includes goods and nonfactor services.
d. Excludes South Africa.

Table A.5 GDP structure of production, selected years, 1965–86
(percent of GDP)

Country group	1965 Agriculture	1965 Industry	1973 Agriculture	1973 Industry	1980 Agriculture	1980 Industry	1983 Agriculture	1983 Industry	1984 Agriculture	1984 Industry	1985[a] Agriculture	1985[a] Industry	1986[a] Agriculture	1986[a] Industry
Developing countries	29	29	24	32	19	37	20	35	19	35	19	34	18	34
Low-income countries	41	27	38	32	33	35	35	32	34	33	32	33	32	33
Middle-income countries	20	30	16	33	13	37	13	36	14	36	14	35	13	34
Oil exporters	22	29	18	33	14	42	15	39	16	39	17	36	17	35
Exporters of manufactures	34	31	27	35	21	37	22	36	21	36	20	36	19	36
Highly indebted countries	18	32	14	34	12	37	14	35	14	35	15	33	14	32
Sub-Saharan Africa[b]	39	19	31	26	27	35	32	27	34	27	33	27	35	24
High-income oil exporters	4	54	2	62	1	64	2	54	2	49	2	58	2	56
Industrial market economies	5	40	5	38	3	36	3	35	3	35	3	36	3	36

a. Preliminary.
b. Excludes South Africa.

Table A.6 Sector growth rates, 1965–85

Country group	Agriculture 1965–73	Agriculture 1973–80	Agriculture 1980–85	Industry 1965–73	Industry 1973–80	Industry 1980–85	Services 1965–73	Services 1973–80	Services 1980–85
Developing countries	3.2	2.7	4.0	8.9	6.5	3.6	6.8	5.8	2.9
Low-income countries	3.0	2.4	6.0	8.7	7.2	9.3	6.3	4.4	6.3
Middle-income countries	3.4	3.0	2.1	8.9	6.3	1.4	7.0	6.1	2.0
Oil exporters	3.3	2.3	1.9	9.9	6.4	0.2	6.1	6.9	1.4
Exporters of manufactures	3.2	2.8	6.0	10.0	8.1	6.6	8.8	6.1	4.4
Highly indebted countries	3.2	2.7	1.9	8.3	5.7	−0.9	7.2	6.0	0.3
Sub-Saharan Africa[a]	2.7	0.4	0.9	13.8	4.5	−2.3	5.1	4.3	−0.4
High-income oil exporters	..	..	..	13.3	4.1	−9.1	..	..	..
Industrial market economies	1.7	0.9	1.5	5.0	2.4	2.5	4.7	3.2	2.0

a. Excludes South Africa.

Table A.7 Consumption, savings, and investment indicators, selected years, 1965–86
(percent of GDP)

Country group and indicator	1965	1973	1980	1983	1984	1985[a]	1986[a]
Developing countries							
Consumption	80.0	76.4	75.4	77.7	76.4	76.2	76.0
Investment	21.2	24.1	26.9	23.1	22.8	23.4	23.5
Savings	20.2	24.2	25.1	22.9	24.2	24.5	24.6
Low-income countries							
Consumption	81.1	75.9	78.4	78.3	77.8	76.3	78.5
Investment	20.5	23.9	26.0	24.4	25.0	28.9	28.5
Savings	19.8	24.6	22.3	22.5	22.9	24.4	22.2
Middle-income countries							
Consumption	79.2	76.6	74.3	77.4	75.9	76.1	75.1
Investment	21.7	24.3	27.2	22.6	22.0	21.3	21.6
Savings	20.6	24.0	26.1	23.1	24.7	24.6	25.6
Oil exporters							
Consumption	79.8	76.0	69.4	74.9	73.3	74.0	76.6
Investment	19.7	23.1	27.4	22.4	22.4	22.6	24.0
Savings	20.1	24.8	31.0	25.4	27.0	26.4	23.7
Exporters of manufactures							
Consumption	78.6	74.4	75.2	75.0	73.5	72.3	71.7
Investment	23.1	26.9	28.4	25.3	25.5	27.3	26.6
Savings	21.2	25.9	25.0	25.3	26.9	28.2	28.8
Highly indebted countries							
Consumption	77.2	76.4	75.2	78.6	77.4	78.2	76.9
Investment	22.3	23.2	25.7	18.5	18.0	17.5	17.8
Savings	20.8	23.7	24.9	21.5	22.7	21.9	23.2
Sub-Saharan Africa[b]							
Consumption	81.6	77.0	78.3	88.2	86.8	86.6	88.4
Investment	15.7	20.1	22.2	16.0	13.5	13.1	14.2
Savings	12.5	24.7	23.0	13.6	14.9	15.2	13.8
Industrial market economies							
Consumption	76.8	74.9	77.9	80.3	79.2	79.4	83.0
Investment	22.9	24.7	22.8	19.8	21.1	20.8	22.0
Savings	23.3	24.8	21.4	19.2	20.3	20.6	17.0

a. Preliminary.
b. Excludes South Africa.

Table A.8 Growth of exports, 1965–86

Country group and commodity	Average annual change in export volume (percent)						
	1965–73	1973–80	1982	1983	1984	1985[a]	1986[b]
Export volume, by commodity							
Developing countries	4.9	4.7	0.2	5.1	11.5	1.4	3.6
Manufactures	11.6	13.8	0.0	11.3	20.3	1.1	6.3
Food	2.9	4.3	−2.5	−1.1	4.6	3.5	−2.6
Nonfood	2.7	1.2	−2.0	0.9	5.9	4.4	0.1
Metals and minerals	4.8	7.0	−0.9	−1.0	1.6	6.1	7.9
Fuels	4.0	−0.8	3.1	2.4	5.2	−1.2	2.4
World[c]	8.8	4.4	−3.2	0.7	9.5	3.5	3.2
Manufactures	10.7	6.1	−2.7	4.2	12.6	5.2	3.2
Food	5.0	6.6	0.1	−5.1	6.8	0.7	−4.7
Nonfood	3.1	1.0	−3.0	−0.5	7.3	7.8	0.0
Metals and minerals	6.8	8.7	−0.6	−1.5	7.7	3.9	2.4
Fuels	8.6	0.0	−7.0	−6.5	1.2	−2.3	10.2
Export volume, by country group							
Developing countries	4.9	4.7	0.2	5.1	11.5	1.4	3.6
Manufactures	11.6	13.8	0.0	11.3	20.3	1.1	6.3
Primary goods	3.7	1.2	0.4	0.8	4.7	1.6	1.2
Low-income countries	2.0	4.7	5.3	4.1	7.3	2.9	9.5
Manufactures	2.4	8.2	0.8	12.8	9.0	2.0	16.2
Primary goods	1.7	2.8	8.8	−2.1	6.0	3.6	3.9
Middle-income countries	5.3	4.8	−0.4	5.3	12.1	1.2	2.9
Manufactures	14.9	14.8	−0.1	11.1	22.0	1.0	5.0
Primary goods	3.9	1.1	−0.7	1.2	4.5	1.3	0.9
Oil exporters	4.1	−0.9	−3.5	4.6	4.8	−2.2	2.7
Manufactures	10.1	3.4	−9.9	57.5	46.1	0.5	11.8
Primary goods	4.0	−1.0	−3.2	2.1	1.8	−2.5	1.8
Exporters of manufactures	8.4	9.8	0.9	8.1	18.5	2.7	5.6
Manufactures	11.6	14.0	−1.2	10.4	21.8	1.8	7.5
Primary goods	5.5	3.4	5.6	3.1	10.9	5.0	0.9
Highly indebted countries	3.1	1.1	−5.6	0.9	10.4	0.4	0.8
Manufactures	13.4	10.2	−10.7	6.8	29.7	−3.3	2.5
Primary goods	2.4	−0.4	−4.1	−0.7	4.7	1.8	0.0
Sub-Saharan Africa[d]	15.0	0.1	−11.0	−4.1	10.3	6.9	3.8
Manufactures	7.5	5.6	−1.8	8.4	1.8	8.6	7.1
Primary goods	15.3	−0.1	−12.0	−5.0	11.0	6.7	3.4
High-income oil exporters	12.8	−0.6	−21.3	−23.5	−7.0	−11.6	29.5
Industrial market economies	9.4	5.4	−1.8	1.9	10.2	5.3	1.7

a. Estimated.
b. Projected.
c. Excludes nonmarket industrial countries.
d. Excludes South Africa.

Table A.9 Change in export prices and in terms of trade, 1965–86
(average annual percentage change)

Country group	1965–73	1973–80	1981	1982	1983	1984	1985[a]	1986[b]
Change in export prices								
Developing countries	6.4	14.0	0.5	−6.7	−2.4	−1.0	−3.1	−1.2
Manufactures	7.2	8.1	0.3	−3.3	−2.6	−1.3	0.7	19.3
Food	5.3	9.1	−8.1	−8.5	5.3	1.9	−9.5	8.2
Nonfood	4.5	10.3	−13.5	−8.6	5.5	−1.0	−14.5	0.7
Metals and minerals	2.5	4.7	−10.1	−10.4	2.1	−3.0	−5.5	−4.6
Fuels	8.0	27.1	12.5	−9.7	−9.0	−2.5	−3.0	−49.4
High-income oil exporters	7.6	26.9	12.0	−9.2	−8.8	−3.1	−3.1	−49.5
Industrial market economies								
Total	4.8	10.4	−4.9	−3.4	−3.0	−3.1	−1.6	15.3
Manufactures	4.6	10.8	−5.7	−1.5	−4.1	−3.3	−0.3	19.3
Change in terms of trade								
Developing countries	0.7	1.6	−0.9	−1.8	−0.0	0.7	−0.8	−4.3
Low-income countries	1.7	−2.5	−1.5	0.0	0.9	1.3	−0.6	0.6
Middle-income countries	0.6	2.2	−0.8	−2.0	−0.1	0.6	−1.0	−5.0
Oil exporters	0.0	10.0	8.1	−4.8	−5.2	0.1	−2.1	−41.5
Exporters of manufactures	1.8	−2.7	−1.1	3.1	0.3	0.4	1.2	9.6
Highly indebted countries	1.4	3.5	−0.1	−2.1	−0.1	1.0	−2.4	−13.6
Sub-Saharan Africa[c]	−8.4	4.8	−1.4	−4.8	−0.1	1.8	−3.3	−26.3
High-income oil exporters	0.3	13.4	19.5	−5.4	−6.6	1.3	−1.3	−56.2
Industrial market economies	−1.0	−3.0	−1.8	3.0	0.1	0.3	1.0	8.3

a. Estimated.   b. Projected.   c. Excludes South Africa.

Table A.10 Growth of long-term debt of developing countries, 1970–86
(average annual percentage change, nominal)

Country group	1970–73	1973–80	1982	1983	1984	1985[a,b]	1986[a,c]
Developing countries							
Debt outstanding and disbursed	18.0	21.6	12.3	14.6	6.6	8.1	5.2
Official	15.4	17.4	10.6	12.0	7.0	13.7	5.5
Private	20.6	24.6	13.2	16.0	6.4	5.2	5.0
Low-income countries							
Debt outstanding and disbursed	12.4	14.9	10.5	9.5	5.6	16.6	8.8
Official	12.4	14.5	10.4	10.9	4.7	16.3	8.7
Private	12.2	17.0	10.7	3.4	9.6	18.0	9.0
Middle-income countries							
Debt outstanding and disbursed	19.6	22.9	12.6	15.3	6.8	6.9	4.6
Official	17.2	18.9	10.7	12.5	7.9	12.6	4.2
Private	21.2	25.0	13.3	16.5	6.3	4.7	4.8
Oil exporters							
Debt outstanding and disbursed	21.7	25.9	9.5	20.1	7.2	4.5	6.5
Official	15.3	20.0	9.6	5.0	6.3	11.6	6.2
Private	26.8	29.0	9.5	25.7	7.5	2.4	6.7
Exporters of manufactures							
Debt outstanding and disbursed	22.4	19.5	11.3	10.5	6.8	7.8	1.5
Official	15.1	13.4	9.0	10.5	6.5	10.3	3.7
Private	31.3	23.7	12.3	10.4	6.9	6.7	0.4
Highly indebted countries							
Debt outstanding and disbursed	17.5	22.3	13.1	19.1	7.5	3.8	4.7
Official	13.3	14.8	11.8	19.4	11.0	14.4	4.8
Private	19.3	24.5	13.4	19.0	6.8	1.6	4.7
Sub-Saharan Africa[d]							
Debt outstanding and disbursed	19.5	24.7	13.0	11.2	1.0	9.4	8.9
Official	17.8	23.2	12.4	16.0	7.1	13.1	9.1
Private	22.0	26.6	13.7	5.7	−6.7	3.9	8.5

a. The increase in debt outstanding and disbursed and the shift from private to official sources are due in part to the impact of rescheduling.
b. Preliminary.   c. Estimated.   d. Excludes South Africa.

Table A.11 Savings, investment, and the current account balance, 1965–85
(percent)

Country	Gross domestic investment/GNP			Gross national savings/GNP			Current account balance/GNP[a]		
	1965–73	1973–80	1980–85	1965–73	1973–80	1980–85	1965–73	1973–80	1980–85
Latin America and Caribbean									
*Argentina	19.8	21.8	16.3	19.7	21.2	11.3	0.0	−0.6	−5.0
*Bolivia	25.4	24.9	16.0	25.2	18.2	6.9	−0.2	−6.7	−9.1
*Brazil	26.1	26.2	20.4	24.3	21.7	16.9	−1.7	−4.5	−3.5
*Chile	14.4	17.4	17.5	12.9	12.2	6.9	−1.4	−5.2	−10.6
*Colombia	18.9	18.8	20.0	17.2	19.2	15.0	−1.8	0.4	−5.0
*Costa Rica	21.8	25.5	28.0	16.8	13.8	16.1	−5.0	−11.7	−11.8
*Ecuador	19.0	26.7	23.2	16.3	21.2	18.3	−2.7	−5.5	−4.9
Guatemala	13.3	18.7	13.5	12.9	16.4	9.9	−0.4	−2.3	−3.6
*Jamaica	32.1	20.3	21.6	25.4	12.6	9.6	−6.7	−7.7	−12.1
*Mexico	21.4	25.2	25.4	19.9	21.3	23.5	−1.5	−3.9	−1.9
*Peru	27.7	28.9	28.0	27.2	24.9	23.7	−0.5	−4.1	−4.3
*Uruguay	12.0	15.7	13.9	11.7	11.3	10.0	−0.3	−4.4	−3.9
*Venezuela	29.3	32.6	19.9	30.0	34.5	24.9	0.7	1.9	5.0
Africa									
Cameroon	16.8	22.3	26.3	..	17.4	24.6	..	−4.9	−1.7
*Côte d'Ivoire	22.8	29.2	22.2	..	16.6	10.0	..	−12.6	−12.2
Ethiopia	12.8	9.5	10.7	12.6	6.6	3.6	−0.3	−2.9	−7.1
Ghana	12.3	8.7	5.7	12.1	6.9	−0.2	−0.2	−1.8	−5.8
Kenya	22.6	26.2	24.9	18.7	16.4	15.6	−4.0	−9.8	−9.3
Liberia	19.1	28.7	15.8	..	27.5	9.6	..	−1.2	−6.2
Malawi	20.0	29.7	20.7	..	13.3	9.2	..	−16.5	−11.5
Niger	9.7	23.8	20.2	..	9.1	5.2	..	−14.7	−15.0
*Nigeria	21.0	26.5	18.7	19.4	28.3	16.4	−1.7	1.8	−2.3
Senegal	14.7	17.5	16.3	..	4.1	−3.5	..	−13.4	−19.7
Sierra Leone	13.8	13.9	13.3	11.2	−1.2	1.0	−2.7	−15.1	−12.3
Sudan	11.9	16.4	13.7	11.2	12.7	5.3	−0.7	−3.6	−8.4
Tanzania	19.9	23.9	17.7	16.9	13.0	8.3	−3.1	10.9	−9.4
Zaire	13.7	15.0	14.6	9.8	8.8	7.2	−3.9	−6.2	−7.4
Zambia	31.9	28.5	18.3	30.2	19.9	4.6	1.7	−8.6	−13.7
South Asia									
India	18.4	22.6	24.4	17.9	22.3	22.6	−0.5	−0.3	−1.8
Pakistan	16.0	16.5	16.2	..	10.9	12.5	..	−5.6	−3.7
Sri Lanka	15.8	20.6	28.9	14.6	13.5	17.1	−1.2	−7.2	−11.8
East Asia									
Indonesia	15.8	24.5	29.4	13.7	24.6	26.6	−2.2	0.1	−2.8
Korea, Republic of	25.1	31.8	30.7	21.5	26.4	26.9	−3.6	−5.3	−3.8
Malaysia	22.3	28.7	35.1	21.6	29.3	27.5	−0.7	0.6	−7.6
Papua New Guinea	27.8	22.1	28.6	..	11.5	1.6	..	−10.5	−27.1
*Philippines	20.6	29.1	25.8	20.6	24.3	20.0	0.0	−4.8	−5.9
Thailand	23.8	26.6	24.4	22.6	21.5	18.5	−1.1	−5.1	−5.9
Europe and North Africa									
Algeria	32.1	44.5	38.2	29.9	38.9	38.6	−2.2	−5.6	0.4
Egypt	14.0	29.8	31.4	10.9	19.6	20.0	−3.1	−10.3	−11.4
*Morocco	15.0	25.6	23.3	14.5	16.4	12.6	−0.5	−9.1	−10.6
Portugal	26.6	29.7	32.1	..	25.9	25.7	..	−3.8	−6.4
Tunisia	23.3	29.9	31.3	21.5	23.2	22.6	−1.8	−6.7	−8.7
Turkey	18.5	21.8	20.9	19.1	18.1	17.2	0.6	−3.7	−3.7
*Yugoslavia	29.9	35.6	38.5	30.0	32.9	37.9	0.1	−2.7	−0.6

Note: Asterisk indicates a highly indebted country.
a. Excludes net unrequited transfers.

Table A.12 Composition of debt outstanding, 1970–85
(percentage of total long-term debt)

Country	Debt from official sources			Debt from private sources			Debt at floating rates[a]		
	1970–72	1980–82	1985	1970–72	1980–82	1985	1973–75	1980–82	1985
Latin America and Caribbean									
*Argentina	12.6	9.0	10.3	87.4	91.0	89.7	13.9	53.2	60.2
*Bolivia	58.4	52.7	65.7	41.6	47.3	34.3	7.5	35.6	26.4
*Brazil	30.6	11.8	15.4	69.4	88.2	84.6	44.1	65.8	71.5
*Chile	47.1	10.9	12.6	52.9	89.1	87.4	9.3	58.1	81.5
*Colombia	68.2	46.0	47.2	31.8	54.0	52.8	6.2	39.4	40.7
*Costa Rica	39.8	37.5	44.1	60.2	62.5	55.9	24.6	50.2	56.8
*Ecuador	51.8	29.3	27.3	48.2	70.7	72.7	12.7	50.9	71.7
Guatemala	47.5	71.0	60.1	52.5	29.0	39.9	5.2	6.8	36.9
*Jamaica	7.4	68.8	81.4	92.6	31.2	18.6	12.5	16.7	18.8
*Mexico	19.5	10.8	9.4	80.5	89.2	90.6	46.8	74.5	80.1
*Peru	15.6	40.6	40.3	84.4	59.4	59.7	31.0	28.3	40.3
*Uruguay	48.5	21.1	15.9	51.5	78.9	84.1	11.6	33.5	64.3
*Venezuela	29.8	2.4	0.6	70.2	97.6	99.4	20.6	81.4	93.4
Africa									
Cameroon	82.2	57.0	66.6	17.8	43.0	33.4	2.0	12.5	5.3
*Côte d'Ivoire	51.6	23.4	36.9	48.4	76.6	63.1	20.5	43.6	47.6
Ethiopia	87.4	92.7	83.9	12.6	7.3	16.1	1.5	2.1	5.4
Ghana	57.6	82.7	87.7	42.4	17.3	12.3	0.0	0.0	0.0
Kenya	59.1	52.8	74.7	40.9	47.2	25.3	3.3	11.7	4.3
Liberia	81.1	75.1	80.5	18.9	24.9	19.5	0.0	15.7	13.5
Malawi	77.1	67.5	87.3	22.9	32.5	12.7	2.3	21.3	9.4
Niger	97.0	42.2	62.6	3.0	57.8	37.4	0.0	20.2	13.3
*Nigeria	68.7	14.9	17.1	31.3	85.1	82.9	0.8	58.8	41.7
Senegal	59.1	69.3	86.8	40.9	30.7	13.2	26.5	8.6	7.3
Sierra Leone	60.8	67.3	73.3	39.2	32.7	26.7	3.8	0.1	0.6
Sudan	86.2	74.6	82.0	13.8	25.4	18.0	2.2	10.2	2.0
Tanzania	60.3	76.2	80.7	39.7	23.8	19.3	0.4	0.2	0.1
Zaire	25.5	65.8	84.2	74.5	34.2	15.8	32.8	11.5	7.7
Zambia	21.9	70.6	78.4	78.1	29.4	21.6	22.9	10.0	17.9
South Asia									
India	95.2	91.8	78.0	4.8	8.2	22.0	0.0	3.0	8.4
Pakistan	90.8	92.4	92.9	9.2	7.6	7.1	0.0	3.4	4.9
Sri Lanka	81.6	80.6	74.4	18.4	19.4	25.6	0.0	11.9	11.4
East Asia									
Indonesia	72.1	51.8	49.1	27.9	48.2	50.9	6.3	18.0	21.7
Korea, Republic of	36.1	34.3	26.1	63.9	65.7	73.9	13.0	35.0	54.3
Malaysia	50.8	23.1	18.1	49.2	76.9	81.9	23.0	47.4	54.8
Papua New Guinea	6.2	25.6	23.8	93.8	74.4	76.2	0.0	37.4	37.7
*Philippines	21.0	32.2	41.6	79.0	67.8	58.4	15.6	32.3	35.2
Thailand	40.1	40.1	43.3	59.9	59.9	56.7	0.9	30.7	32.6
Europe and North Africa									
Algeria	45.9	16.8	19.6	54.1	83.2	80.4	34.0	24.2	30.0
Egypt	66.5	82.9	80.0	33.5	17.1	20.0	3.1	3.2	2.3
*Morocco	79.3	52.0	62.8	20.7	48.0	37.2	2.7	31.7	36.3
Portugal	72.0	62.3	66.5	28.0	37.7	33.5	0.0	13.9	16.7
Tunisia	39.1	26.3	22.5	60.9	73.7	77.5	0.0	23.6	36.5
Turkey	92.4	65.1	69.0	7.6	34.9	31.0	0.8	23.1	29.1
*Yugoslavia	38.1	24.1	27.4	61.9	75.9	72.6	7.6	31.8	61.0

Note: Asterisk indicates a highly indebted country.
a. Percentage of public long-term debt.

Bibliographical note

This Report has drawn on a wide range of World Bank reports and numerous outside sources. World Bank sources include ongoing economic analysis and research, as well as project and sector work on individual countries. Outside sources include research publications and reports, published and unpublished, of other organizations working on global economic and development issues. The principal sources used in each chapter are briefly noted below. These and other sources are then listed alphabetically by author or organization in two groups: background papers and notes commissioned for this Report and a selected bibliography. The background papers, some of which will be made available through future publications, synthesize relevant literature and Bank work. The views they express are not necessarily those of the World Bank or this Report.

In addition to the sources listed, many persons in and outside the World Bank helped prepare this Report by writing informal notes or providing extensive comments. Among these were Bela Balassa, Jagdish Bhagwati, Max Corden, Sebastian Edwards, Isaiah Frank, Anne O. Krueger, Jacques J. Polak, Richard Snape, Paul Streeten, and Martin Wolf.

Chapter 2

The data used in this chapter come from GATT, IMF, and OECD publications as well as World Bank sources. The discussion of recent macroeconomic issues relies on Feldstein 1986. The discussion of debt and capital market issues relies in particular on World Bank 1987 (*World Debt Tables*) and Ardalan and Handjinicolaou 1986. The discussion of unemployment in industrial countries relies on OECD 1986b. The discussion of adjustment programs in developing countries is based on Michalopoulos 1987. Box 2.6 draws on the Commission of the European Communities 1986.

Chapter 3

The discussion of industrialization and trade from the eighteenth century up to World War II is drawn from Ashley 1970; Cipolla 1973; Dawson 1904; Foreman-Peck 1983; Freeman, Clark, and Soete 1982; Gerschenkron 1962; Heckscher 1935; Henderson 1954; Kemp 1978; Kindleberger 1973; Kuznets 1957; Lewis 1978; Maddison 1982; Maizels 1963; Rosenberg and Birdzell 1985; Takahashi 1969; Taussig 1967; and the background paper by Rosenberg. The discussion of the post–World War II period relies heavily on data from the Bank, GATT, ILO, IMF, OECD, United Nations, and U.S. International Trade Commission, as well as the background papers by Balasubramanyam and Murray. In addition, Chenery, Robinson, and Syrquin 1986, Chenery and Syrquin 1975, and Dicken 1986 were consulted. Box 3.1 is based on the background paper by Campbell; Box 3.3 on the background paper by Nixson, UNIDO 1979, and Chenery, Robinson, and Syrquin 1986; and Box 3.4 on the background paper by Rosenberg. Figure 3.1 is reprinted with permission of Harper & Row, London: Dicken, P. (1986) *Global Shift: Industrial Change in a Turbulent World*, Figure 9.9, p. 304, Harper & Row, London. Taken from U.S. Department of Transportation (1981) *The U.S. Automobile Industry, 1980*, Washington, D.C.: U.S. Government Printing Office, p. 57.

Chapter 4

This chapter covers a broad range of economic topics, including microeconomics, institutional economics, and the new political economy. On transactions costs and property rights it draws on North 1985; on the problems of public administration, the background paper by Gray; and on the new political economy, Srinivasan 1985. The discussion of the direct and indirect role of government in industrialization relies on World Bank country and sector work, as well as on the background paper by McMahon on education, by Khan on infrastructure, and by Smith on infant industry. Evidence on the high costs of doing business comes from a variety of sources, some of them collected together in the background paper by Kimenyi. The principal source for Box 4.2 is North 1986. Box 4.5 was prepared by Graeme Thompson (partly on the basis of

Rosenn 1984), Box 4.6 by Robert Litan, and Box 4.7 by Jagdish Bhagwati.

Chapter 5

The data used in this chapter are largely drawn from World Bank data files and country economic reports, contributions from the Bank's operational staff, and the background paper by Greenaway. The discussion of the relationship of trade strategies and economic growth and industrialization is based largely on the following publications: Balassa and Associates 1982; Bhagwati 1986a; Chenery, Robinson, and Syrquin 1986; and Krueger 1983. Box 5.2 is based on Clements and Sjaastad 1984 and Greenaway and Milner 1987. Box 5.4 draws on Pack 1987.

Chapter 6

A principal source for this chapter is a current World Bank research project on "The Timing and Sequencing of a Trade Liberalization Policy" which compares the liberalization experiences of nineteen countries (see Box 6.1 for the countries covered). The interim findings of this project are in Papageorgiou, Michaely, and Choksi 1986. The chapter also draws on two further cross-country studies of liberalization: a World Bank research project on "Liberalization with Stabilization in the Southern Cone" (see *World Development* 1985 and Corbo and de Melo 1986) and some of the reports from a Trade Policy Research Centre (London) study program on "The Participation of Developing Countries in the International Trading System" (see Congdon 1985). Box 6.6 is based on the background paper by Cuthbertson.

Chapter 7

Chapter 7 is based on several background papers, a wide range of books and articles, and World Bank reports and memorandums. The discussion of regulatory policies is based on the background papers by Spiller and Balasubramanyam, and on numerous World Bank reports. The section on financial markets relies partially on the background paper by Burkett. The analysis of labor markets uses the background paper by Gregory as well as Squire 1981. The discussion of small-scale industries benefited from the background paper by Elkan and from Haggblade, Liedholm, and Meade 1986. The presentation of technology issues is based largely on Dahlman and Westphal 1982 and

Dahlman, Ross-Larson, and Westphal 1985. The material for two boxes came from individual contributors: Box 7.1 from William Steel and Box 7.6 from Julio Nogues. Box 7.4 on the Chilean financial reforms draws on the analysis in Galvez and Tybout 1985. Boxes 7.2, 7.5, and 7.7 on India, Egypt, and Portugal, respectively, use material from World Bank studies. Box 7.8 is drawn from Little 1987.

Chapters 8 and 9

The data used in these chapters come from GATT, IMF, OECD, UNCTAD, and World Bank sources. The discussion of trade policies draws on three sources in particular: Balassa and Michalopoulos 1985, GATT 1985, and OECD 1985. The background paper by Hindley provides information on the Generalized System of Preferences and the graduation issue. The discussion of the Multifibre Arrangement draws on the background paper by Pelzman, and the discussion of the effect of nontariff barriers on the growth of trade draws on information and data provided in the background paper by Hamilton. The costs of protection come from many sources, including Feenstra 1984; Greenaway and Hindley 1985; Hufbauer, Berliner, and Elliott 1986; Kalantzopoulos 1986; Tarr and Morkre 1984. Box 8.1 is based on the background paper by Kaminski. Box 8.6 was written by Jagdish Bhagwati. Box 9.2 is based on the background paper by Stevens, Box 9.6 on Holzman 1983 and U.S. International Trade Commission 1980a, and Box 9.7 on U.S. Trade Representative 1986.

Background papers

Balassa, Bela. "The Interaction of Domestic Distortions with Development Strategies."

Balasubramanyam, V. N. "Direct Foreign Investment and Industrialization in Developing Countries."

Burkett, Paul. "Financial Sector Intermediation Policies and Industrial Development: Some Lessons from Developing Country Experiences."

Campbell, Robert. "International Economic Relations in the Soviet-Type Growth Model."

Cuthbertson, A. G. "Reducing Trade Distortions: Transitional Measures."

Donges, Juergen B., and Hans-Hinrich Glismann. "Industrial Adjustment in Western Europe—A Survey of Successes and Failures."

Elkan, Walter. "Policy for Small-Scale Industry: A Critique."

Fransman, Martin. "Science and Technology Policy in Developing Countries."

Gersovitz, Mark. "Export Credit Insurance Agencies for Developing Countries."

Gray, Cheryl Williamson. "The Legal Process and Public Administration in Developing Countries."

Greenaway, David. "Characteristics of Industrialization and Economic Performance under Alternative Strategies."

Gregory, Peter. "Urban Employment and the Functioning of Labor Markets: Issues and Policies."

Guisinger, Stephen, and Gerald Scully. "Public and Private Approaches to Industrialization: Theory and Evidence."

Hamilton, Carl. "The New Protectionism with Special Reference to Europe."

Havrylyshyn, Oli. "Penetrating the Fallacy of Export Composition: or Hobson's 'Second Falsehood' Revisited."

Hindley, Brian. "The Graduation Issue."

Holmes, Peter. "Market Failure, Information, and the Role of Governments."

Hughes, Helen. "Post-War Industrialization: Patterns and Performance."

Kaminski, Bartlomiej. "Impact of Central Planning on East-South Trade."

Khan, M. Shahbaz. "Infrastructure and the Development Process."

Kimenyi, Mwangi S. "Intervention, Dualism, and the High Costs of Doing Business."

Lawrence, Robert Z. "The Global Environment over the Next Decade."

Lucas, Robert E. B. "Industrial Regulation and Trade Liberalization: Illustrations from India."

McMahon, Walter W. "Education and Industrialization."

Murray, Tracy. "Post-War Industrialization: Patterns and Performance."

Nixson, Frederick I. "Development, Structural Change, and Industrialization."

Pack, Howard. "The Links between Development Strategies and Industrial Growth."

Pelzman, Joseph. "The Multifibre Arrangement: A Further Refinement or the Cartelization Drive Continues."

Pitt, Mark M., and Joanico Ketterer. "The Structure and Costs of Protection in Developing Countries."

Rosenberg, Nathan. "A Historical Look at Technological Change in the Industrialized Countries."

Smith, Alasdair. "The Infant Industry Argument and the Reform of Trade Policy."

Spiller, Pablo T. "Industrial Regulations in Developing Countries: Causes and Consequences."

Srinivasan, T. N. "Recent Theories of Imperfect Competition and International Trade: Any Implications for Development Strategy?"

Stevens, Christopher. "The Impact of EEC Preferential Trade Policies."

Selected bibliography

Aho, C. Michael, and Jonathan Aronson. 1985. *Trade Talks: America Better Listen!* New York: Council on Foreign Relations.

Anderson, Dennis. 1982. "Small Industry in Developing Countries: A Discussion of Issues." *World Development* 10.

Anderson, Dennis, and Farida Khambata. 1985. "Financing Small-Scale Industry and Agriculture in Developing Countries: The Merits and Limitations of Commercial Policies." *Economic Development and Cultural Change* 33: 349–71.

Anjaria, Shailendra, Naheed Kirmani, and Arne Peterson. 1985. *Trade Policy Issues and Developments.* IMF Occasional Paper 38. Washington, D.C.: International Monetary Fund.

Ardalan, Cyrus, and George Handjinicolaou. 1986. "Developments in Financial Markets and the LDCs: New Ways to Tackle Old Problems." Washington, D.C.: Financial Operations Department, World Bank. Processed.

Ashley, Percy. 1970. *Modern Tariff History.* New York: Howard Fertig.

Ayub, Mahmood A., and Sven O. Hegstad. 1987. "Management of Public Industrial Enterprises." *World Bank Research Observer* 2, 1 (January): 79–101.

Balassa, Bela. 1980. *The Process of Industrial Development and Alternative Development Strategies.* World Bank Staff Working Paper 438. Washington, D.C.

Balassa, Bela, and Associates. 1982. *Development Strategies in Semi-Industrial Economies.* Baltimore, Md.: Johns Hopkins University Press.

Balassa, Bela, and Constantine Michalopoulos. 1985. *Liberalizing World Trade.* Development Policy Issues Series Report VPERS4. Washington, D.C.: Office of the Vice President, Economics and Research, World Bank.

Balassa, Bela, and others. 1971. *The Structure of Protection in Developing Countries.* Baltimore, Md.: Johns Hopkins University Press.

Baldwin, Robert. 1969. "The Case against Infant Industry Protection." *Journal of Political Economy* 77, 3 (May/June): 295–305.

———. 1986. *The New Protectionism: Response to Shifts in National Economic Power.* NBER Working Paper 1823. Cambridge, Mass.: National Bureau of Economic Research.

Baldwin, Robert, and Anne O. Krueger, eds. 1984. *The Structure and Evolution of Recent U.S. Trade Policy.* Chicago, Ill.: University of Chicago Press.

Baum, Warren C., and Stokes M. Tolbert. 1985. *Investing in Development: Lessons of World Bank Experience.* New York: Oxford University Press.

Betts, Paul. 1986. "France Removes Tax on VCRs." *Financial Times*, May 15, p. 6.

Bhagwati, Jagdish. 1978. *Anatomy and Consequences of Exchange Control Regimes.* Cambridge, Mass.: Ballinger.

———. 1982. "Directly-Unproductive, Profit-seeking (DUP) Activities." *Journal of Political Economy* 90, 5 (October): 988–1,002.

———. 1986a. *Export Promoting Trade Strategy: Issues and Evidence.* Development Policy Issues Series Report VPERS7. Washington, D.C.: Office of the Vice President, Economics and Research, World Bank.

———. 1986b. "Trade in Services and the Multilateral Negotiations." Paper prepared for the Conference on the Role and Interests of the Developing Countries in Multilateral Trade Negotiations, sponsored by the World Bank and the Thailand Development Research Institute, Bangkok, October 30—November 1. Processed.

———. 1987. "VERs, Quid Pro Quo Foreign Investment & VIEs: Political-Economy Theoretic Analyses." *International Economic Journal* 1, 1 (Spring): 1–14.

Bhagwati, Jagdish, and Douglas Irwin. 1987. "The Return to the Reciprocitarians: U.S. Trade Policy Today." *World Economy* 10, 2 (June): 109–30.

Bitros, G. C. 1981. "The Fungibility Factor in Credit and the Question of the Efficacy of Selective Credit Controls." *Oxford Economic Papers* 33: 459–77.

Blackhurst, Richard. 1986. "The Economic Effects of Different Types of Trade Measures and Their Impact on Consumers." In OECD. *International Trade and the Consumer.* Paris: Organisation for Economic Co-operation and Development.

Brittain, J. A. 1971. "The Incidence of Social Security Taxes." *American Economic Review* 61, 1: 110–25.

Brunner, Karl, ed. 1981. *The Great Depression Revisited.* Boston, Mass.: Martinus Nijhoff.

Cable, Vincent. 1983. *Economics and the Politics of Protection: Some Case Studies of Industries.* World

Bank Staff Working Paper 569. Washington, D.C.

Cairncross, Alec, and others. 1982. *Protectionism: Threat to International Order.* London: Commonwealth Secretariat.

Chenery, Hollis, Sherman Robinson, and Moshe Syrquin. 1986. *Industrialization and Growth: A Comparative Study.* New York: Oxford University Press.

Chenery, Hollis, and Moises Syrquin. 1975. *Patterns of Development, 1950–1970.* New York: Oxford University Press.

Cho, Y. J. 1986. "Inefficiencies from Financial Liberalization in the Absence of Well-Functioning Equity Markets." *Journal of Money, Credit, and Banking* 18: 191–99.

Choksi, Armeane M. 1979. *State Intervention in the Industrialization of Developing Countries.* World Bank Staff Working Paper 341. Washington, D.C.

Choksi, Armeane M., and Demetris Papageorgiou, eds. 1986. *Economic Liberalization in Developing Countries.* Oxford: Basil Blackwell.

Cipolla, Carlo M. 1973. *The Fontana Economic History of Europe.* Vol. 3, *The Industrial Revolution,* and vol. 4, *The Emergence of Industrial Societies,* part 1. Glasgow: Collins/Fontana.

Clarete, Ramon L., and John Whalley. 1985. *Interactions between the Trade Policies and Domestic Distortions.* Centre for the Study of International Economic Relations Working Paper 8522C. London, Ontario: University of Western Ontario.

Clements, Kenneth, and Larry A. Sjaastad. 1984. *How Protection Taxes Exporters.* Thames Essays 39. London: Trade Policy Research Centre.

Cline, William. 1982. *"Reciprocity": A New Approach to World Trade Policy?* Washington, D.C.: Institute for International Economics.

Cline, William, ed. 1983. *Trade Policy in the 1980s.* Washington, D.C.: Institute for International Economics.

Commission of the European Communities. 1986. "Employment Problems: Views of the Businessmen and the Workforce." *European Economy* 27 (March).

Congdon, T. G. 1985. *Economic Liberalism in the Cone of Latin America.* London: Trade Policy Research Centre.

Consumers for World Trade. 1984. "How Much Do Consumers Pay for U.S. Trade Barriers?" CWT Information Paper. Washington, D.C.

Corbo, Vittorio. 1985. "Reforms and Macroeconomic Adjustments in Chile during 1974–84." *World Development* 13, 8: 893–916.

Corbo, Vittorio, and Jaime de Melo. 1986. *Lessons from the Southern Cone Policy Reforms.* Discussion Paper DRD251. Washington, D.C.: Development Research Department, World Bank.

Corbo, Vittorio, Jaime de Melo, and James Tybout. 1986. "What Went Wrong with the Recent Reforms in the Southern Cone." *Economic Development and Cultural Change* 34: 607–40.

Corden, Max. 1985. *Protection, Growth and Trade.* Oxford: Basil Blackwell.

Corden, W. M. 1984. *The Revival of Protectionism.* Occasional Paper 14. New York: Group of Thirty.

Dahlman, Carl, Bruce Ross-Larson, and Larry Westphal. 1985. *Managing Technological Development: Lessons from the Newly Industrializing Countries.* World Bank Staff Working Paper 717. Washington, D.C.

Dahlman, Carl, and Larry Westphal. 1982. "Technological Effort in Industrial Development: An Interpretative Survey of Recent Research." In Frances Stewart and Jeffrey James, eds. *The Economics of New Technology in Developing Countries.* Boulder, Colo.: Westview Press.

Dale, Richard. 1982. *Bank Supervision around the World.* New York: Group of Thirty.

Dawson, W. H. 1904. *Protection in Germany.* London: P. S. King & Son.

de la Cuadra, Sergio, and Dominique Hachette. 1987. "The Timing and Sequencing of a Trade Liberalization Policy: The Case of Chile." Washington, D.C.: Country Policy Department, World Bank. Processed.

de Soto, Hernando. 1986. *El otro sendero: La revolucion informal* [The other path: the informal revolution]. Lima: Editorial Barranco.

Dicken, Peter. 1986. *Global Shift: Industrial Change in a Turbulent World.* London: Harper & Row.

Donges, Juergen B. 1971. "From an Autarkic towards a Continuously Outward-Looking Industrialization Policy: The Case of Spain." *Weltwirtschaftliches Archiv* [Review of world economics] 107: 33–72.

Doublet, Jean-Michel, Sujin Hur, Orsalia Kalantzopoulos, Mehdi Khoshand, and Peter A. Petri. "Indicators of Industrial Performance." Washington, D.C.: Industry Department, Industrial Strategy and Policy Division, World Bank.

Drake, P. J. 1977. "Securities Markets in Less Developed Countries." *Journal of Development Studies* 13: 73–91.

Duchêne, François, and Geoffrey Shepherd, eds. 1987. *Managing Industrial Change in Western Europe.* London: Frances Pinter.

Echeverri, Gonzalo G. 1979. "Estructura de la protección arancelaria y para-arancelaria en Colombia despuès de las reformas de 1979" (The structure of tariff and para-tariff protection in Colombia after the reforms of 1979). *Revista de Planeacion y Desarrollo* (Journal of Planning and Development) 11, 2: 7–47.

Edwards, Sebastian, and Mohsin S. Khan. 1985. "Interest Rate Determination in Developing Countries: A Conceptual Framework." *IMF Staff Papers* 32: 377–403.

Edwards, Sebastian, and Simon Teitel, eds. 1986. "Growth, Reform, and Adjustment: Latin America's Trade and Macroeconomic Policies in the 1970s and 1980s." *Economic Development and Cultural Change* 34, 3. Special issue.

Eichengreen, Barry. 1984. *The Smoot-Hawley Tariff and the Start of the Great Depression.* Discussion Paper 1115. Cambridge, Mass.: Harvard Institute of Economic Research.

Erzan, Refrik, Samuel Laird, and Alexander Yeats. 1986. *On the Potential for Expanding South-South Trade through the Extension of Mutual Preferences among Developing Countries.* UNCTAD Discussion Paper 16. Geneva: United Nations Conference on Trade and Development.

Fallon, P. R., and L. A. Riveros. 1986. "Labor Market Institutions: An Across Country Analysis of Wage and Non-Wage Regulations." Paper presented at the World Bank Conference on Adjustment of Labor Markets in LDCs to External Changes, 1970–85, Washington, D.C., June.

Feenstra, Robert. 1984. "Voluntary Export Restraint in US Autos, 1980–81: Quality, Employment and Welfare Effects." In Baldwin and Krueger, eds.

Feldstein, Martin 1986. *The Budget Deficit and the Dollar.* NBER Working Paper 1898. Cambridge, Mass.: National Bureau of Economic Research.

Fields, Gary S. 1980. *How Segmented Is the Bogota Labor Market?* World Bank Staff Working Paper 434. Washington, D.C.

———. 1984. "Employment, Income Distribution and Economic Growth in Seven Small Open Economies." *Economic Journal* 94: 74–83.

Finger, Michael, and Julio Nogues. 1986. "International Control of Subsidies and Countervailing Duties." Paper prepared for the Conference on the Role and Interests of the Developing Countries in Multilateral Trade Negotiations, sponsored by the World Bank and the Thailand Development Research Institute, Bangkok, October 30—November 1. Processed.

Foreman-Peck, James. 1983. *A History of the World Economy: International Economic Relations since 1850*. Brighton, Sussex: Harvester Press.

Frank, Isaiah. 1981. *Trade Policy Issues for the Developing Countries in the 1980s*. World Bank Staff Working Paper 478. Washington, D.C.

Freeman, Christopher, John Clark, and Luc Soete. 1982. *Unemployment and Technical Innovation: A Study of Long Waves and Economic Development*. London: Frances Pinter.

Fry, Maxwell. 1980. "Savings, Investment, Growth, and the Cost of Financial Repression." *World Development* 8: 317–27.

GATT. General Agreement on Tariffs and Trade. 1952. *Basic Instruments and Selected Documents*. Vol. 1. Geneva.

———. 1979. *The Tokyo Round of Multilateral Trade Negotiations*. Vol. 1. Geneva

———. 1980. *The Tokyo Round of Multilateral Trade Negotiations*. Vol. 2, *Supplementary Report*. Geneva.

———. 1984. *Textiles and Clothing in the World Economy: Background Study*. Geneva.

———. 1985. *Trade Policies for a Better Future*. Geneva.

———. 1986a. "Draft Ministerial Declaration on the Uruguay Round." Geneva.

———. 1986b. *International Trade 1985/6*. Geneva.

———. 1986c. "Prospects for International Trade." Press communiqué, September 1. Geneva.

Galvez, J., and James Tybout. 1985. "Microeconomic Adjustments in Chile during 1977–81: The Importance of Being a 'Grupo'." *World Development* 13, 8 (August).

Geroski, P. A., and Alexis Jacquemin. 1985. "Industrial Change, Barriers to Mobility, and European Industrial Policy." *Economic Policy* 1 (November): 169–218.

Gerschenkron, Alexander, ed. 1962. *Economic Backwardness in Historical Perspective: A Book of Essays*. Cambridge, Mass.: Harvard University Press.

Giesen, Hans-Michael. 1985. "Upstream Subsidies: Policy and Enforcement Questions after the Trade and Tariff Act of 1984." *Law and Policy in International Business* 17, 2.

González-Vega, Claudio. 1976. "On the Iron Law of Interest Rate Restrictions: Agricultural Credit Policies in Costa Rica and in Other Less Developed Countries." Ph.D. thesis, Stanford University.

Grais, Wafik, Jaime de Melo, and Shujiro Urata. 1986. "A General Equilibrium Estimation of the Effects of Reduction in Tariffs and Quantitative Restrictions in Turkey in 1978." In T. N. Srinivasan and John Whalley, eds. *General Equilibrium Trade Policy Modelling*. Cambridge, Mass.: MIT Press.

Greenaway, David. 1983. *Trade Policy and the New Protectionism*. New York: St. Martins Press.

Greenaway, David, and Brian Hindley. 1985. *What Britain Pays for Voluntary Export Restraints*. London: Trade Policy Research Centre.

Greenaway, David, and Chris R. Milner. 1987. "'True Protection' Concepts and Their Role in Evaluating Trade Policies in LDCs." *Journal of Development Studies* 23 (January): 200–19.

Gregory, Peter. 1986. *The Myth of Market Failure: Employment and the Labor Market in Mexico*. Baltimore, Md.: Johns Hopkins University Press.

Haggblade, Steve, Carl Liedholm, and D. C. Mead. 1986. *The Effect of Policy and Policy Reforms on Non-Agricultural Enterprises and Employment in Developing Countries: A Review of Past Experiences*. MSU International Development Papers, Working Paper 27. East Lansing, Mich.: Michigan State University.

Hamilton, Carl. 1986. "An Assessment of Voluntary Restraints on Hong Kong's Exports to Europe and the United States." *Economica* 53 (August).

Hanson, J. A., and C. R. Neal. 1986. "Interest Rate Policies in Selected Developing Countries, 1970–1982." Industry and Finance Paper 14. Washington, D.C.: World Bank.

Havrylyshyn, Oli, and Martin Wolf. 1981. *Trade among Developing Countries: Theory, Policy Issues, and Principal Trends*. World Bank Staff Working Paper 479. Washington, D.C.

Heckscher, Eli F. 1935. *Mercantilism*. London: George Allen & Unwin.

Heller, Peter S., and Alan A. Tait. 1983. *Government Employment and Pay: Some International Comparisons*. IMF Occasional Paper 24. Washington, D.C.: International Monetary Fund.

Henderson, W. O. 1954. *Britain and Industrial Europe 1750–1870: Studies in British Influence on the Industrial Revolution in Western Europe*. Liverpool: University Press.

Hickok, Susan. 1985. "Consumer Cost of U.S. Trade Restraints." *Federal Reserve Bank of New York Quarterly Review* (Summer).

Hindley, Brian. 1986. "The VER System and GATT Safeguards." Paper prepared for the Conference on the Role and Interests of the Developing Countries in Multilateral Trade Negotiations, sponsored by the World Bank and the Thailand Development Research Institute, Bangkok, October 30—November 1. Processed.

Hoffman, Kurt. 1985. "Clothing, Chips, and Competitive Advantage: The Impact of Microelectronics on Trade and Protection in the Garment Industry." *World Development* 13, 3 (March): 371–92.

Holzman, Franklyn. 1983. "Dumping in the Centrally Planned Economies: The Polish Golf Cart Case 133." In Padma Desai, ed. *Marxism, Central Planning, and the Soviet Economy: Economic Essays in Honor of Alexander Erlich.* Cambridge, Mass.: MIT Press.

Hufbauer, Gary, Diane Berliner, and Kimberly Elliott. 1986. *Trade Protection in the U.S.: 31 Case Studies.* Washington, D.C.: Institute for International Economics.

ILO. International Labour Organisation. 1970, 1980, 1985. *Year Book of Labour Statistics.* Geneva.

IMF. International Monetary Fund. Various years. *International Financial Statistics.* Yearbook. Washington, D.C.

———. 1985. *Foreign Investment in Developing Countries.* Washington, D.C.

———. 1986. *World Economic Outlook* (April and October).

Jenkins, Glenn. 1980. *Costs and Consequences of the New Protectionism.* Cambridge, Mass.: Harvard Institute for International Development.

Julius, DeAnne, and Adelaida P. Alicbusan. 1986. "Public Sector Pricing Policies: A Review of Bank Policy and Practice." Washington, D.C.: Projects Policy Department, World Bank. Processed.

Kalantzopoulos, Orsalia. 1986. "The Cost of Voluntary Export Restraints for Selected Industries." Washington, D.C.: Industry Department, Industrial Policy and Strategy Division, World Bank.

Karsentry, Guy, and Sam Laird. 1986. *The Generalized System of Preferences: A Quantitative Assessment of the Direct Trade Effects and of Policy Options.* UNCTAD Discussion Paper 18. Geneva: United Nations Conference on Trade and Development.

Kay, J. A., and D. J. Thompson. 1986. "Privatization: A Policy in Search of a Rationale." *Economic Journal* 96: 18–32.

Kemp, Tom. 1978. *Historical Patterns of Industrialization.* New York: Longman.

Kessing, Donald, and Martin Wolf. 1980. *Textile Quotas against Developing Countries.* London: Trade Policy Research Centre.

Kim, Chungsoo. 1986. *Effects of Neo-Protectionism on Korean Exports.* Seoul: Korea Institute for Economics and Technology.

Kim, Kwang Suk. 1987. "The Timing and Sequencing of a Trade Liberalization Policy: The Case of Korea." Washington, D.C.: Country Policy Department, World Bank. Processed.

Kindleberger, Charles. 1973. *The World in Depression: 1929–1939.* Berkeley, Calif.: University of California Press.

———. 1983. "Standards as Public, Collective and Private Goods." *Kyklos* 36, 3: 377–96.

———. 1984. *A Financial History of Western Europe.* London: George Allen & Unwin.

Kirmani, Naheed, Pierluigi Molajoni, and Thomas Mayer. 1984. "Effects of Increased Market Access on Exports of Developing Countries." *IMF Staff Papers* 31, 4.

Krueger, Anne O. 1974. "The Political Economy of the Rent-Seeking Society." *American Economic Review* 64, 3 (June): 291–303.

———. 1978. *Liberalization Attempts and Consequences.* Cambridge, Mass.: Ballinger.

———. 1980. "Trade Policy as an Input to Development." *American Economic Review* 70: 2.

———. 1983. *Trade and Employment in Developing Countries,* vol. 3, *Synthesis and Conclusions.* Chicago, Ill.: University of Chicago Press.

———. 1985. "Importance of General Policies to Promote Economic Growth." *World Economy* 8, 2: 93–108.

Krueger, Anne O., Hal B. Lary, Terry Monson, and Narongchai Akrasanee, eds. 1981. *Trade and Employment in Developing Countries,* vol. 1, *Individual Studies.* Chicago, Ill.: University of Chicago Press.

Krueger, Anne O., and Baran Tuncer. 1982a. "Empirical Test of the Infant Industry Argument." *American Economic Review* 72 (December): 142–52.

———. 1982b. "Growth of Factor Productivity in Turkish Manufacturing Industries." *Journal of Development Economics* 11 (December): 307–25.

Kuznets, Simon. 1957. "Quantitative Aspects of the Economic Growth of Nations: Industrial Distribution of National Product and Labor Force." *Economic Development and Cultural Change* 5, 4 (July). Supplement.

Laird, Sam, and J. Michael Finger. 1986. "Protection in Developed and Developing Countries." Paper prepared for the Conference on the Role and Interests of the Developing Countries in Multilateral Trade Negotiations, sponsored by the World Bank and the Thailand Development Research Institute, Bangkok, October 30—November 1. Processed.

Lal, Deepak, and Sarath Rajapatirana. 1986. "Foreign Trade Regimes and Economic Growth in

Developing Countries." Paper prepared for the Conference on Free Trade in the World Economy: Towards an Opening of Markets, sponsored by the Institute for World Economics, Kiel, June 24–26. Processed.

Lall, Sanjaya. 1980. "Exports of Manufactures by Newly Industrialising Countries: A Survey of Recent Trends." *Economic and Political Weekly* 15, 50 (December): 2,103–112.

———. 1984. "South-South Economic Cooperation and Global Negotiations." In Jagdish Bhagwati and John Ruggie, eds. *Power, Passion and Purpose.* Cambridge, Mass.: MIT Press.

Langhammer, Rolf. 1983. "Problems and Effects of a Developing Countries' Tariff Concession Round on South-South Trade." Working Paper 167. Kiel: Institute for World Economics.

Leff, Nathaniel. 1979. "Entrepreneurship and Economic Development: The Problem Revisited." *Journal of Economic Literature* 17: 46–64.

Levitsky, Jacob. 1986. *World Bank Lending to Small Enterprises.* Industry and Finance Paper 16. Washington, D.C.: World Bank.

Lewis, Paul. 1982. "The Latest Battle of Poitiers." *New York Times,* January 13, p. D1.

Lewis, W. Arthur. 1978. *Growth and Fluctuations, 1870-1913.* London: George Allen & Unwin.

Liedholm, Carl, and Donald Meade. 1986. "Industries in Developing Countries: Empirical Evidence and Policy Implications." Draft paper prepared for the Employment and Enterprise Division, Office of Rural and Institutional Development, Bureau for Science and Technology, USAID. Washington, D.C.: U.S. Agency for International Development.

Lindbeck, Assar. 1987. *Public Finance for Market-Oriented Developing Countries.* Discussion Paper DRD214. Washington, D.C.: Development Research Department, World Bank.

Little, Ian M. D. 1987. "Small Manufacturing Enterprises in Developing Countries." *World Bank Economic Review* 1, 2: 203–35.

Little, Ian M. D., Tibor Scitovsky, and Maurice F. Scott. 1970. *Industry and Trade in Some Developing Countries: A Comparative Study.* New York: Oxford University Press.

MacBean, Alasdair, and P. N. Snowden. 1981. *International Institutions in Trade and Finance.* London: George Allen & Unwin.

Maddison, Angus. 1969. *Economic Growth in Japan and the USSR.* London: George Allen & Unwin.

———. 1982. *Phases of Capitalist Development.* New York: Oxford University Press.

Maizels, Alfred. 1963. *Industrial Growth and World Trade.* Cambridge: Cambridge University Press.

Marsden, Keith, and Thérèse Bélot. 1987. "Creating a Better Environment for Private Enterprise in Africa." Washington, D.C.: Industry Department, World Bank. Processed.

Marsh, David. 1982. "Alarm at French Curbs on Japanese Video Imports." *Financial Times,* November 10, p.6.

Mazumdar, Dipak. 1979. *Paradigms in the Study of Urban Labor Markets in LDCs: A Reassessment in the Light of an Empirical Survey in Bombay City.* World Bank Staff Working Paper 366. Washington, D.C.

McKinnon, R. I. 1973. *Money and Capital in Economic Development.* Washington, D.C.: Brookings Institution.

Meier, G. M., ed. 1983. *Pricing Policy for Development Management.* Baltimore, Md.: Johns Hopkins University Press.

Michalopoulos, Constantine. 1987. "World Bank Programs for Adjustment and Growth." Paper prepared for the Symposium on Growth-Oriented Adjustment Programs, sponsored by the World Bank and the International Monetary Fund, Washington, D.C., February 25–27. Processed.

Mill, John Stuart. [1848] 1900. *Principles of Political Economy.* Vol. 2. New York: P. F. Collier and Son.

Morkre, Morris, and David Tarr. 1980. *Effects of Restrictions on U.S. Imports: Five Case Studies and Theories.* Bureau of Economics, Federal Trade Commission. Washington D.C.: General Printing Office.

Munger, Michael. 1984. *The Costs of Protectionism: Estimates of the Hidden Tax of Trade Restraint.* Working Paper 80. St. Louis, Mo.: Center for the Study of American Business, Washington University.

Nam, Chong-Hyun. 1981. "Trade and Industrial Policies and the Structure of Protection in Korea." In Wontack Hong and Lawrence B. Krause, eds. *Trade and Growth of the Advanced Developing Countries in the Pacific Basin.* Seoul: Korean Development Institute.

———. 1986a. *Export Promoting Policies under Countervailing Threats: GATT Rules and Practice.* Development Policies Issues Series Report VPERS9. Washington, D.C.: Office of the Vice President, Economics and Research, World Bank.

———. 1986b. "Política comercial y desarrollo económico en Corea" (Trade policy and economic development in Korea). *Comercio Exterior* 36, 1 (January): 13–22.

Nayyar, Deepak. 1978. "Transnational Corporations and Manufactured Exports from Poor Countries." *Economic Journal* 88, 3 (March): 59–84.

Nellis, John R. 1986. *Public Enterprises in Sub-Saharan Africa.* World Bank Discussion Paper 1. Washington, D.C.

Nishimizu, Mieko, and Sherman Robinson. 1984. "Trade Policies and Productivity Change in Semi-Industrialized Countries." *Journal of Development Economics* 16 (September/October): 177–206.

Nogues, Julio, Andrzej Olechowski, and L. Alan Winters. 1986. *The Extent of Nontariff Barriers to Imports of Industrial Countries.* World Bank Staff Working Paper 789. Washington, D.C.

North, Douglass C. 1985. *Institutions, Transactions Costs and Economic Growth.* Political Economy Working Paper 103. St. Louis, Mo.: School of Business and Center in Political Economy, Washington University.

———. 1986. *Institutions, Economic Growth and Freedom: An Historical Introduction.* Political Economy Working Paper 110. St. Louis, Mo.: School of Business and Center in Political Economy, Washington University.

OECD. Organisation for Economic Co-operation and Development. 1985. *Costs and Benefits of Protection.* Paris.

———. 1986a. *Economic Outlook* (May and December). Paris.

———. 1986b. *Employment Outlook* (September). Paris.

———. 1986c. *Labour Force Statistics, 1964–1984.* Paris.

———. 1986d. *National Accounts, 1960–1984.* Paris.

Pack, Howard. 1980. *Macroeconomic Implications of Factor Substitution in Industrial Processes.* World Bank Staff Working Paper 377. Washington, D.C.

———. 1987. *Productivity, Technology, and Industrial Development.* New York: Oxford University Press.

Pack, Howard, and Larry E. Westphal. 1986. "Industrial Strategy and Technological Change: Theory versus Reality." *Journal of Development Economics* 22 (June): 87–128.

Papageorgiou, Demetris, Michael Michaely, and Armeane Choksi. 1986. "The Phasing of a Trade Liberalization Policy: Preliminary Evidence." Paper prepared for the annual meeting of the American Economic Association, New Orleans, December 28–30.

Prebisch, Raul. 1950. *The Economic Development of Latin America and Its Principal Problems.* New York: United Nations Economic Commission on Latin America.

Rajapatirana, Sarath. 1986 "Foreign Trade and Economic Development: Sri Lanka's Experience." Paper prepared for the World Bank's Executive Directors Colloquium on Trade and Development, Fredericksburg, Virginia, April 10—May 2. Processed.

Rhee, Yung Whee. 1984. *A Framework for Export Policy Administration: Lessons from the East Asian Experience.* Industry and Finance Paper 10. Washington, D.C.: World Bank.

Rhee, Yung Whee, Bruce Ross-Larson, and Garry Pursell. 1984. *Korea's Competitive Edge: Managing the Entry into World Markets.* Baltimore, Md.: Johns Hopkins University Press.

Riedel, James. 1986. "United States Trade Policy: From Multilateralism to Bilateralism?" Paper prepared for the Conference on Free Trade in the World Economy: Towards an Opening of Markets, sponsored by the Institute for World Economics, Kiel, June 24–26. Processed.

Rosenberg, Nathan, and L. E. Birdzell Jr. 1985. *How the West Grew Rich: The Economic Transformation of the Industrial World.* New York: Basic Books.

Rosenn, Keith S. 1984. "Brazil's Legal Culture: The Jeito Revisited." *Florida International Law Journal* 1, 1 (Fall).

Roth, Gabriel. 1987. *The Private Provision of Public Services in Developing Countries.* New York: Oxford University Press.

Sapir, André, and Lars Lundberg. 1984. "The U.S. Generalized System of Preferences and Its Impact." In Baldwin and Krueger, eds.

Sato, Akihiro. 1982. "Japanese Makers of VTRs Cut Shipments to France as Customs Barriers Take Hold." *Wall Street Journal,* December 2.

Saxonhouse, Gary. 1985. "Technology Choice in Cotton Textile Manufacturing." In Kazushi Ohkawa and Gustav Ranis, eds. *Japan and the Developing Countries: A Comparative Analysis.* New York: Basil Blackwell.

Schlender, Brenton, and Stephen Yoder. 1987. "Semi-Conductor Accord with Japan Fails to Aid U.S. Firms, as Intended." *Wall Street Journal,* February 12, p. 1.

Schuck, Peter H., and Robert Litan. 1986. "Regulatory Reform in the Third World: The Case of Peru." *Yale Journal on Regulation* 4, 51: 51–78.

Shaw, Edward. 1973. *Financial Deepening in Economic Development.* New York: Oxford University Press.

Spinanger, Dean. 1986. "How the MFA Keeps Bangladesh Humble." Kiel: Institute for World Economics. Processed.

Squire, Lyn. 1981. *Employment Policy in Developing Countries: A Survey of Issues and Evidence.* New York: Oxford University Press.

Srinivasan, T. N. 1985. "Neoclassical Political Economy, the State and Economic Development." *Asian Development Review* 3, 2.

Strange, Susan. 1985. "Protectionism and World Politics." *International Organization* 39, 2.

Takahashi, Kamekichi. 1969. *The Rise and Development of Japan's Modern Economy.* Tokyo: Jiji Press.

Tarr, David. 1986. "Effects of Restraining a Nation's Exports: The Case of Restraints on Korean Steel Exports by the U.S. and the European Community." Washington, D.C.: Development Research Department, Economic Research Division, World Bank. Processed.

Tarr, David, and Morris Morkre. 1984. *Aggregate Costs to the United States of Tariffs and Quotas on Imports: General Tariff Cuts and Removal of Quotas on Automobiles, Steel, Sugar, and Textiles.* Washington, D.C.: Bureau of Economics, Federal Trade Commission.

Taussig, F. W. 1967. *The Tariff History of the United States.* New York: Augustus M. Kelley.

Time. 1982. "The Second Battle of Poitiers." December 6, p.31.

Tybout, James. 1983. "Credit Rationing and Investment Behavior in a Developing Country." *Review of Economics and Statistics* 65: 598–607.

UNCTAD. United Nations Conference on Trade and Development. 1976, 1983. *Handbook of International Trade and Development Statistics.* Geneva.

———. 1984a. "Protectionism and Structural Adjustment: An Improved and More Efficient Safeguard System." TD/B/978. Note by the UNCTAD Secretariat. Geneva.

———. 1984b. "Protectionism and Structural Adjustment: Anti-Dumping and Countervailing Duty Practices." TD/B/979/Corr. 1. Note by the UNCTAD Secretariat. Geneva.

———. 1987. *Problems of Protectionism and Structural Adjustment: Restrictions on Trade.* TD/B/1126. Part 1. Report by the UNCTAD Secretariat. Geneva.

UNIDO. United Nations Industrial Development Organization. 1979. *World Industry since 1960: Progress and Prospects.* New York: United Nations.

United Nations. 1986. *Monthly Bulletin of Statistics* 40, 5 (May). New York.

United Nations Centre on Transnational Corporations. 1983. *Transnational Corporations in World Development: Third Survey.* New York: United Nations.

U.S. Congress. House Committee on Energy and Commerce. Subcommittee on Oversight and Investigations. 1985. *Unfair Foreign Trade Practices.* Part 1. 99th Cong., 1st sess. Serial 99–11.

U.S. Department of Transportation. 1981. *The U.S. Automobile Industry, 1980.* Washington, D.C.: Government Printing Office.

U.S. International Trade Commission. 1977. *U.S. Imports for Consumption, Tariff Items 807.00 and 806.30, Specified Years 1966–67.* Washington, D.C.: Data Development Division, USITC.

———. 1980a. *Electric Golf Cars from Poland.* USITC Publication 1069. Washington, D.C.

———. 1980b. *Import Trends in TSUS Items 806.30 and 807.00.* USITC Publication 1029. Washington, D.C.

———. 1984. *Imports under Items 806.30 and 807.00 of the Tariff Schedules of the United States, 1979–82.* USITC Publication 1467. Washington, D.C.

———. 1986a. *Imports under Items 806.30 and 807.00 of the Tariff Schedules of the United States, 1981–84.* USITC Publication 1867. Washington, D.C.

———. 1986b. *Imports under Items 806.30 and 807.00 of the Tariff Schedules of the United States, 1982-85: Report on Investigation No. 332-237, under Section 332(b) of the Tariff Act of 1930.* USITC Publication 1920. Washington, D.C.

U.S. Trade Representative, Office of. 1986. *Foreign Trade Barriers.* Washington, D.C.: Government Printing Office.

van Agtmael, A. W. 1984. *Emerging Securities Markets: Investment Banking Opportunities in the Developing World.* London: Euromoney Publications.

Wade, Robert. 1987. "The Role of Government in Overcoming Market Failure: Taiwan, South Korea, and Japan." In Helen Hughes and Thomas Parry, eds. *Explaining the Success of Industrialization in East Asia.* Sydney: Cambridge University Press.

Watson, Maxwell, Donald Mathieson, Russell Kincaid, and Eliot Kalter. 1986. *International Capital Markets: Developments and Prospects.* IMF Occasional Paper 43. Washington, D.C.: International Monetary Fund.

Wayne, Leslie. 1986. "Services: The Star of U.S. Trade." *New York Times*, September 14.

Whalley, John, and Randall Wigle. 1982. *Are Developed Country Multilateral Tariff Reductions Beneficial?* Center for the Study of International Economics Paper 8216C. London, Ontario: University of Western Ontario.

Wolf, Martin. 1982. "Textile Pact: The Outlook." *New York Times*, January 12.

———. 1986a. "Differential and More Favourable Treatment of Developing Countries and the International Trading System." Paper prepared for the Conference on the Role and Interests of the Developing Countries in Multilateral Trade Negotiations, sponsored by the World Bank and the Thailand Development Research Institute, Bangkok, October 30—November 1. Processed.

———. 1986b. "Timing and Sequencing of Trade Liberalization in Developing Countries." *Asian Development Review* 4, 2: 1–24.

Wolf, Martin, Hans Glismann, Joseph Pelzman, and Dean Spinanger. 1984. *Costs of Protecting Jobs in Textiles and Clothing.* London: Trade Policy Research Centre.

World Bank. 1983a. *World Development Report 1983.* New York: Oxford University Press.

———. 1983b. *World Tables: The Third Edition.* Vols. 1 and 2. Washington, D.C.

———. 1985. *Colombia: The Investment Banking System and Related Issues in the Financial Sector.* Washington D.C.

———. 1986a. *Financing Adjustment with Growth in Sub-Saharan Africa, 1986–90.* Washington, D.C.

———. 1986b. *World Development Report 1986.* New York: Oxford University Press.

———. 1987. *World Debt Tables: External Debt of Developing Countries.* 1986–87 ed. Washington, D.C.

World Development. 1985. "Liberalization with Stabilization in the Southern Cone of Latin America." 13, 8, (August). Special issue.

Yarrow, George. 1986. "Privatization in Theory and Practice." *Economic Policy* (April): 323–77.

World Development Indicators

Contents

Key

In each table, economies are listed in their group in ascending order of GNP per capita except for those for which no GNP per capita can be calculated. These are listed in alphabetical order, in italics, at the end of their group. The reference numbers below reflect the order in the tables.

Figures in the colored bands are summary measures for groups of economies. The letter w after a summary measure indicates that it is a weighted average; m, a median value; t, a total.

All growth rates are in real terms.

.. Not available.

(.) Less than half the unit shown.

Blank means not applicable.

Figures in italics are for years or periods other than those specified.

Afghanistan	32	Haiti	24	Panama	83
Albania	120	Honduras	51	Papua New Guinea	49
Algeria	86	Hong Kong	91	Paraguay	59
Angola	121	Hungary	76	Peru	61
Argentina	84	India	17	Philippines	46
Australia	110	Indonesia	42	Poland	80
Austria	107	*Iran, Islamic Republic of*	94	Portugal	77
Bangladesh	2	*Iraq*	95	*Romania*	96
Belgium	105	Ireland	102	Rwanda	18
Benin	15	Israel	89	Saudi Arabia	98
Bhutan	5	Italy	103	Senegal	27
Bolivia	39	Jamaica	60	Sierra Leone	26
Botswana	58	Japan	114	Singapore	93
Brazil	74	Jordan	71	Somalia	19
Bulgaria	122	*Kampuchea, Democratic*	34	South Africa	79
Burkina Faso	3	Kenya	20	Spain	101
Burma	10	*Korea, Democratic People's*		Sri Lanka	30
Burundi	11	*Republic of*	126	Sudan	22
Cameroon	56	Korea, Republic of	85	Sweden	115
Canada	116	Kuwait	99	Switzerland	118
Central African Republic	16	*Lao People's Democratic Republic*	35	Syrian Arab Republic	72
Chad	33	*Lebanon*	73	Tanzania	21
Chile	70	Lesotho	40	Thailand	55
China	23	Liberia	41	Togo	12
Colombia	69	Libya	97	Trinidad and Tobago	90
Congo, People's Republic of the	64	Madagascar	13	Tunisia	66
Costa Rica	68	Malawi	8	Turkey	62
Côte d'Ivoire	48	Malaysia	78	*Uganda*	36
Cuba	123	Mali	4	*Union of Soviet Socialist*	
Czechoslovakia	124	Mauritania	38	*Republics*	128
Denmark	113	Mauritius	63	United Arab Emirates	100
Dominican Republic	53	Mexico	82	United Kingdom	106
Ecuador	65	*Mongolia*	127	United States	119
Egypt, Arab Republic of	47	Morocco	45	Uruguay	75
El Salvador	57	Mozambique	6	Venezuela	87
Ethiopia	1	Nepal	7	*Viet Nam*	37
Finland	111	Netherlands	108	Yemen Arab Republic	44
France	109	New Zealand	104	Yemen, People's Democratic	
German Democratic Republic	125	Nicaragua	52	*Republic of*	43
Germany, Federal Republic of	112	Niger	14	Yugoslavia	81
Ghana	28	Nigeria	54	Zaire	9
Greece	88	Norway	117	Zambia	31
Guatemala	67	Oman	92	Zimbabwe	50
Guinea	25	Pakistan	29		

Note: For U.N. and World Bank member countries with populations of less than 1 million, see Box A.1.

Introduction

The World Development Indicators provide information on the main features of social and economic development. Most of the data collected by the World Bank are on its developing member countries. Because comparable data for developed market economies are readily available, these are also included in the indicators. National accounts data for economies that are not members of the World Bank are not included, because they are either not available or not in a comparable form.

Every effort has been made to standardize the data. However, full comparability cannot be ensured, and care must be taken in interpreting the indicators. The statistics are drawn from sources thought to be most authoritative, but many of them are subject to considerable margins of error. Variations in national statistical practices also reduce the comparability of data which should thus be construed only as indicating trends and characterizing major differences among economies, rather than taken as precise quantitative indications of those differences.

The indicators in Table 1 give a summary profile of economies. Data in the other tables fall into the following broad areas: national accounts, industry, agriculture, energy, external trade, external debt, aid flows, other external transactions, central government finances and income distribution, and population, health, education, labor force, and urbanization indicators. Two new tables have been added this year—one providing data on industrial output and earnings and the other introducing a number of monetary indicators—making a total of 33 main tables.

Countries with populations of less than 1 million are not included in the main tables, but basic indicators for those that are members of the World Bank or the U.N. are in a separate table on page 269.

The national accounts data are obtained from member governments by World Bank economic missions and are, in some instances, adjusted to conform with international definitions and concepts to provide better consistency. Data on external debt are reported to the Bank by member countries through the Debtor Reporting System. Other data sets are drawn from the International Monetary Fund, the United Nations, and specialized agencies.

For ease of reference, ratios and rates of growth are shown; absolute values are reported in only a few instances. Most growth rates are calculated for two periods, which have been changed this year to 1965–80 and 1980–85. All growth rates related to national accounts are in constant prices and are computed, unless noted otherwise, by using the least-squares method. Because this method takes all observations in a period into account, the resulting growth rates reflect general trends that are not unduly influenced by exceptional values, particularly at the end points. Table entries in italics indicate that they are for years or periods other than those specified—up to two years earlier for economic indicators and up to three years on either side for social indicators. All dollar figures are U.S. dollars. The various methods used for converting from national currency figures are described, where appropriate, in the technical notes.

Some of the differences between figures shown in this year's and those in last year's edition reflect not only updating but also revisions to historical series.

As in the *World Development Report* itself, the economies included in the World Development Indicators are grouped into several major categories. These groupings are analytically useful for distinguishing economies at different stages of development. Many of the economies are further classified by dominant characteristics; to distinguish exporters, for instance. The major classifications used in the tables this year are 37 low-income developing economies with a per capita income of $400 or less in 1985, 59 middle-income developing economies with a per capita income of $401 or more, 4 high-income oil exporters, 19 industrial market economies, and 9 nonreporting nonmember economies. This last is a new classification for a revised group of countries; because of the paucity of data, the differences in method for computing national income, and difficulties of conversion, estimates of GNP per capita for these economies are not included.

The format of this edition follows that used in previous years. In each group, economies are listed in ascending order of income per capita except for those for which no GNP per capita figure can be calculated. These are listed in italics in al-phabetical order at the end of each appropriate group. This order is used in all tables. The alphabetical list in the key shows the reference number for each economy; italics indicate economies with no GNP per capita figures.

In the colored bands are *summary measures*—totals or weighted averages—that are calculated for economy groups if data are adequate. Because China and India heavily influence the overall summary measures for the low-income economies, summary measures are shown for two subgroups: *China and India* and *other low-income economies.* This year, for analytical purposes, data for all developing economies have also been summarized in the following overlapping groupings: oil exporters, exporters of manufactures, highly indebted countries, and Sub-Saharan Africa. Sub-Saharan Africa

Groups of economies

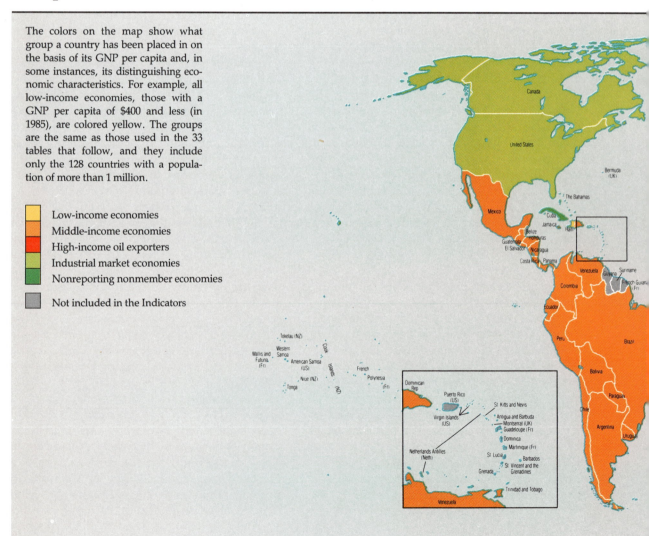

The colors on the map show what group a country has been placed in on the basis of its GNP per capita and, in some instances, its distinguishing economic characteristics. For example, all low-income economies, those with a GNP per capita of $400 and less (in 1985), are colored yellow. The groups are the same as those used in the 33 tables that follow, and they include only the 128 countries with a population of more than 1 million.

Low-income economies
Middle-income economies
High-income oil exporters
Industrial market economies
Nonreporting nonmember economies

Not included in the Indicators

includes all countries south of the Sahara, except South Africa. For definitions and lists of countries in the other groups, see pages xi and xii.

The methodology used for computing the summary measures is described in the technical notes. For these numbers, *w* indicates that the summary measures are weighted averages, *m*, median values, and *t*, totals. The coverage of economies is not uniform for all indicators, and the variation from measures of central tendency can be large; therefore readers should exercise caution in comparing the summary measures for different indicators, groups, and years or periods.

The technical notes should be referred to in any use of the data. These notes outline the methods, concepts, definitions, and data sources used in compiling the tables. The bibliography gives details of the data sources, which contain comprehensive definitions and descriptions of concepts used.

The report includes three world maps. The first map, below, shows country names and the main groups in which economies have been placed. The maps on the following pages show population and the share of agriculture in gross domestic product (GDP). The Eckert IV projection has been used for these maps because it maintains correct areas for all countries, although it slightly distorts shape, distance, and direction. The maps have been prepared exclusively for the convenience of the readers of this report; the denominations used and the boundaries shown do not imply on the part of the World Bank and its affiliates any judgment on the legal status of any territory or any endorsement or acceptance of such boundaries.

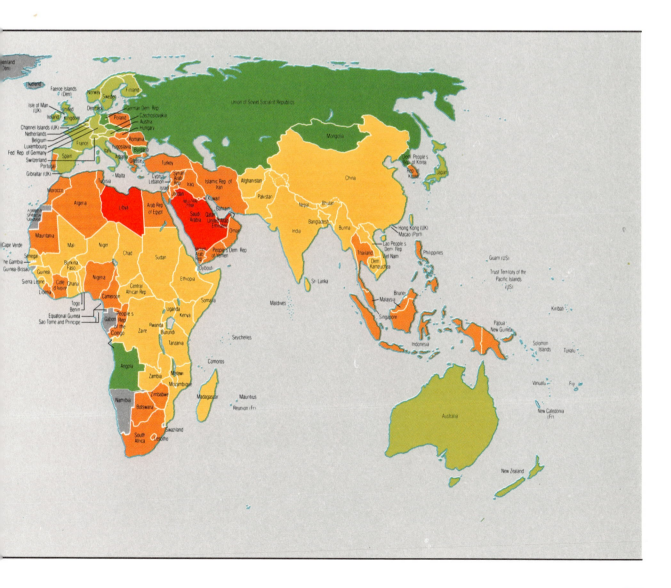

Population

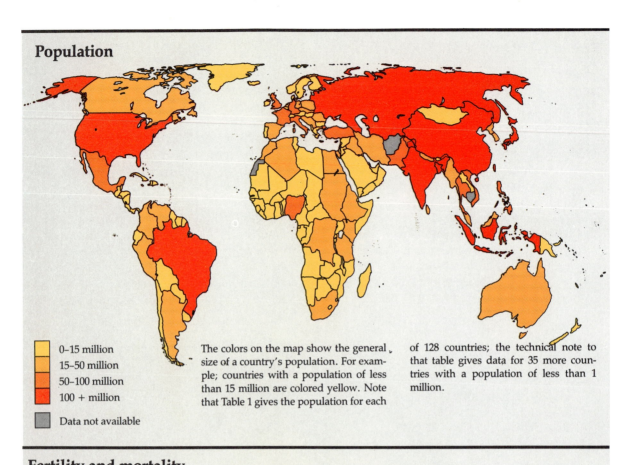

0–15 million
15–50 million
50–100 million
100 + million

Data not available

The colors on the map show the general size of a country's population. For example; countries with a population of less than 15 million are colored yellow. Note that Table 1 gives the population for each of 128 countries; the technical note to that table gives data for 35 more countries with a population of less than 1 million.

Fertility and mortality

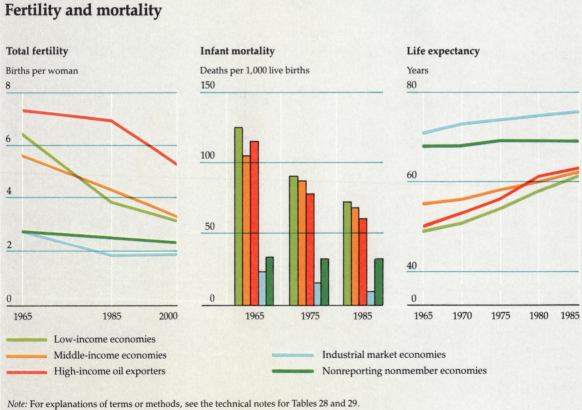

Total fertility

Births per woman

Infant mortality

Deaths per 1,000 live births

Life expectancy

Years

Low-income economies
Middle-income economies
High-income oil exporters
Industrial market economies
Nonreporting nonmember economies

Note: For explanations of terms or methods, see the technical notes for Tables 28 and 29.

Size of GDP and sectoral shares

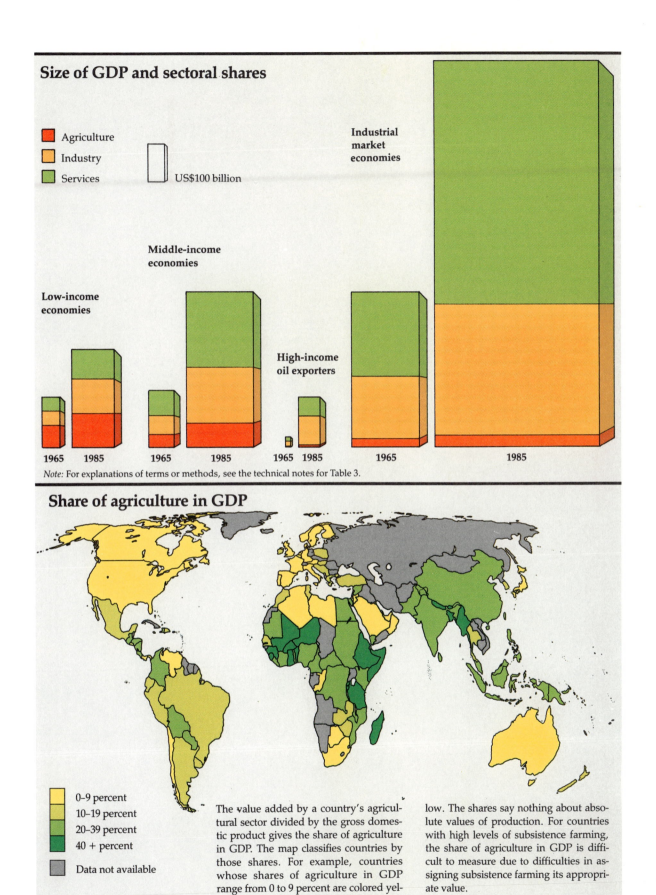

- 🟥 Agriculture
- 🟧 Industry
- 🟩 Services
- ▢ US$100 billion

Industrial market economies

Middle-income economies

Low-income economies

High-income oil exporters

| 1965 | 1985 | 1965 | 1985 | 1965 | 1985 | 1965 | 1985 |

Note: For explanations of terms or methods, see the technical notes for Table 3.

Share of agriculture in GDP

- 🟨 0–9 percent
- 🟩 10–19 percent
- 🟩 20–39 percent
- 🟩 40 + percent
- ⬜ Data not available

The value added by a country's agricultural sector divided by the gross domestic product gives the share of agriculture in GDP. The map classifies countries by those shares. For example, countries whose shares of agriculture in GDP range from 0 to 9 percent are colored yellow. The shares say nothing about absolute values of production. For countries with high levels of subsistence farming, the share of agriculture in GDP is difficult to measure due to difficulties in assigning subsistence farming its appropriate value.

Table 1. Basic indicators

	Population (millions) mid-1985	Area (thousands of square kilometers)	GNP per capita[a] Dollars 1985	GNP per capita[a] Average annual growth rate (percent) 1965-85	Average annual rate of inflation[a] (percent) 1965-80	Average annual rate of inflation[a] (percent) 1980-85	Life expectancy at birth (years) 1985
Low-income economies	**2,439.4** *t*	**32,547** *t*	**270** *w*	**2.9** *w*	**4.5** *w*	**7.5** *w*	**60** *w*
China and India	**1,805.5** *t*	**12,849** *t*	**290** *w*	**3.5** *w*	**2.7** *w*	**4.4** *w*	**63** *w*
Other low-income	**633.9** *t*	**19,698** *t*	**200** *w*	**0.4** *w*	**11.4** *w*	**18.9** *w*	**52** *w*
1 Ethiopia	42.3	1,222	110	0.2	3.3	2.6	45
2 Bangladesh	100.6	144	150	0.4	14.9	11.5	51
3 Burkina Faso	7.9	274	150	1.3	6.5	7.2	45
4 Mali	7.5	1,240	150	1.4	..	7.4	46
5 Bhutan	1.2	47	160	..	..	..	44
6 Mozambique	13.8	802	160	..	..	25.8	47
7 Nepal	16.5	141	160	0.1	7.8	8.4	47
8 Malawi	7.0	118	170	1.5	7.3	11.4	45
9 Zaire	30.6	2,345	170	−2.1	24.5	55.3	51
10 Burma	36.9	677	190	2.4	8.7	2.6	59
11 Burundi	4.7	28	230	1.9	8.4	6.6	48
12 Togo	3.0	57	230	0.3	7.1	6.9	51
13 Madagascar	10.2	587	240	−1.9	7.7	19.4	52
14 Niger	6.4	1,267	250	−2.1	7.5	8.5	44
15 Benin	4.0	113	260	0.2	7.4	9.7	49
16 Central African Rep.	2.6	623	260	−0.2	8.4	10.8	49
17 India	765.1	3,288	270	1.7	7.4	7.8	56
18 Rwanda	6.0	26	280	1.8	12.5	7.6	48
19 Somalia	5.4	638	280	−0.7	10.1	45.4	46
20 Kenya	20.4	583	290	1.9	7.3	10.0	54
21 Tanzania	22.2	945	290	(.)	9.6	19.6	52
22 Sudan	21.9	2,506	300	(.)	11.5	31.7	48
23 China	1,040.3	9,561	310	4.8	(.)	2.4	69
24 Haiti	5.9	28	310	0.7	7.3	7.0	54
25 Guinea	6.2	246	320	0.8	2.8	8.3	40
26 Sierra Leone	3.7	72	350	1.1	7.8	25.0	40
27 Senegal	6.6	196	370	−0.6	6.5	9.7	47
28 Ghana	12.7	239	380	−2.2	22.8	57.0	53
29 Pakistan	96.2	804	380	2.6	10.2	8.1	51
30 Sri Lanka	15.8	66	380	2.9	9.5	14.7	70
31 Zambia	6.7	753	390	−1.6	6.4	14.7	52
32 *Afghanistan*	..	648	..	..	4.9	..	..
33 *Chad*	5.0	1,284	..	−2.3	6.2	..	45
34 *Kampuchea, Dem.*	..	181	..	..	..	..	..
35 *Lao PDR*	3.6	237	..	..	..	..	45
36 *Uganda*	14.7	236	..	−2.6	23.8	..	49
37 *Viet Nam*	61.7	330	..	..	..	..	65
Middle-income economies	**1,242.1** *t*	**38,071** *t*	**1,290** *w*	**3.0** *w*	**21.1** *w*	**57.4** *w*	**62** *w*
Lower middle-income	**674.6** *t*	**16,090** *t*	**820** *w*	**2.6** *w*	**22.2** *w*	**22.3** *w*	**58** *w*
38 Mauritania	1.7	1,031	420	0.1	7.5	8.1	47
39 Bolivia	6.4	1,099	470	−0.2	15.7	569.1	53
40 Lesotho	1.5	30	470	6.5	8.6	11.4	54
41 Liberia	2.2	111	470	−1.4	6.5	1.6	50
42 Indonesia	162.2	1,919	530	4.8	34.3	10.7	55
43 Yemen, PDR	2.1	333	530	..	..	5.7	46
44 Yemen, Arab Rep.	8.0	195	550	*5.3*	..	9.7	45
45 Morocco	21.9	447	560	2.2	5.8	7.8	59
46 Philippines	54.7	300	580	2.3	11.8	19.3	63
47 Egypt, Arab Rep.	48.5	1,001	610	3.1	7.5	11.0	61
48 Côte d'Ivoire	10.1	322	660	0.9	9.2	10.0	53
49 Papua New Guinea	3.5	462	680	0.4	8.1	5.5	52
50 Zimbabwe	8.4	391	680	1.6	5.7	13.2	57
51 Honduras	4.4	112	720	0.4	6.3	5.4	62
52 Nicaragua	3.3	130	770	−2.1	8.9	33.8	59
53 Dominican Rep.	6.4	49	790	2.9	6.6	14.6	64
54 Nigeria	99.7	924	800	2.2	14.5	11.4	50
55 Thailand	51.7	514	800	4.0	6.8	3.2	64
56 Cameroon	10.2	475	810	3.6	9.0	11.8	55
57 El Salvador	4.8	21	820	−0.2	7.0	11.6	64
58 Botswana	1.1	600	840	8.3	8.0	5.2	57
59 Paraguay	3.7	407	860	3.9	9.2	15.8	66
60 Jamaica	2.2	11	940	−0.7	12.6	18.3	73
61 Peru	18.6	1,285	1,010	0.2	20.5	98.6	59
62 Turkey	50.2	781	1,080	2.6	20.8	37.1	64
63 Mauritius	1.0	2	1,090	2.7	11.8	8.5	66
64 Congo, People's Rep.	1.9	342	1,110	3.8	7.1	12.6	58
65 Ecuador	9.4	284	1,160	3.5	11.3	29.7	66
66 Tunisia	7.1	164	1,190	4.0	6.7	10.0	63
67 Guatemala	8.0	109	1,250	1.7	7.1	7.4	60

Note: For comparability and coverage, see the technical notes.   Figures in italics are for years other than those specified.   For U.N. and World Bank member countries with populations of less than 1 million, see Box A.1.

	Population (millions) mid-1985	Area (thousands of square kilometers)	GNP per capita[a] Dollars 1985	GNP per capita[a] Average annual growth rate (percent) 1965–85	Average annual rate of inflation[a] (percent) 1965–80	Average annual rate of inflation[a] (percent) 1980–85	Life expectancy at birth (years) 1985
68 Costa Rica	2.6	51	1,300	1.4	11.2	36.4	74
69 Colombia	28.4	1,139	1,320	2.9	17.5	22.5	65
70 Chile	12.1	757	1,430	−0.2	129.9	19.3	70
71 Jordan	3.5	98	1,560	5.8	. .	3.9	65
72 Syrian Arab Rep.	10.5	185	1,570	4.0	8.4	6.1	64
73 *Lebanon*	. .	10	. .	. .	9.3	. .	. .
Upper middle-income	**567.4 t**	**21,981 t**	**1,850 w**	**3.3 w**	**20.5 w**	**74.7 w**	**66 w**
74 Brazil	135.6	8,512	1,640	4.3	31.6	147.7	65
75 Uruguay	3.0	176	1,650	1.4	57.7	44.6	72
76 Hungary	10.6	93	1,950	5.8	2.7	5.6	71
77 Portugal	10.2	92	1,970	3.3	11.7	22.7	74
78 Malaysia	15.6	330	2,000	4.4	4.9	3.1	68
79 South Africa	32.4	1,221	2,010	1.1	9.9	13.0	55
80 Poland	37.2	313	2,050	. .	. .	35.2	72
81 Yugoslavia	23.1	256	2,070	4.1	15.2	45.1	72
82 Mexico	78.8	1,973	2,080	2.7	13.2	62.2	67
83 Panama	2.2	77	2,100	2.5	5.5	3.7	72
84 Argentina	30.5	2,767	2,130	0.2	78.5	342.8	70
85 Korea, Rep. of	41.1	98	2,150	6.6	18.7	6.0	69
86 Algeria	21.9	2,382	2,550	3.6	9.9	6.9	61
87 Venezuela	17.3	912	3,080	0.5	8.7	9.2	70
88 Greece	9.9	132	3,550	3.6	10.3	20.6	68
89 Israel	4.2	21	4,990	2.5	25.2	196.3	75
90 Trinidad and Tobago	1.2	5	6,020	2.3	14.2	7.6	69
91 Hong Kong	5.4	1	6,230	6.1	8.1	7.9	76
92 Oman	1.2	300	6,730	5.7	20.5	*4.9*	54
93 Singapore	2.6	1	7,420	7.6	4.8	3.1	73
94 *Iran, Islamic Rep.*	44.6	1,648	. .	. .	15.2	. .	60
95 *Iraq*	15.9	435	. .	. .	. .	. .	61
96 *Romania*	22.7	238	. .	. .	. .	. .	72
Developing economies	**3,681.5 t**	**70,618 t**	**610 w**	**3.0 w**	**16.8 w**	**44.2 w**	**61 w**
Oil exporters	523.3 t	12,785 t	1,060 w	3.1 w	15.3 w	28.9 w	58 w
Exporters of manufactures	2,098.3 t	22,473 t	520 w	4.0 w	13.3 w	47.7 w	64 w
Highly indebted countries	554.5 t	21,213 t	1,410 w	2.5 w	26.6 w	89.0 w	62 w
Sub-Saharan Africa	418.0 t	21,874 t	400 w	1.0 w	12.7 w	16.7 w	50 w
High-income oil exporters	**18.4 t**	**4,012 t**	**9,800 w**	**2.7 w**	**16.6 w**	**−2.5 w**	**63 w**
97 Libya	3.8	1,760	7,170	−1.3	15.4	−0.3	60
98 Saudi Arabia	11.5	2,150	8,850	5.3	17.6	−3.2	62
99 Kuwait	1.7	18	14,480	−0.3	14.1	−3.6	72
100 United Arab Emirates	1.4	84	19,270	. .	. .	−1.4	70
Industrial market economies	**737.3 t**	**30,935 t**	**11,810 w**	**2.4 w**	**7.6 w**	**5.8 w**	**76 w**
101 Spain	38.6	505	4,290	2.6	12.2	12.6	77
102 Ireland	3.6	70	4,850	2.2	11.9	10.8	74
103 Italy	57.1	301	6,520	2.6	11.2	14.2	77
104 New Zealand	3.3	269	7,010	1.4	10.1	9.8	74
105 Belgium	9.9	31	8,280	2.8	6.5	5.9	75
106 United Kingdom	56.5	245	8,460	1.6	11.2	6.4	75
107 Austria	7.6	84	9,120	3.5	5.7	4.9	74
108 Netherlands	14.5	41	9,290	2.0	7.5	3.5	77
109 France	55.2	547	9,540	2.8	8.0	9.5	78
110 Australia	15.8	7,687	10,830	2.0	8.8	9.1	78
111 Finland	4.9	337	10,890	3.3	10.5	8.6	76
112 Germany, Fed. Rep.	61.0	249	10,940	2.7	5.1	3.2	75
113 Denmark	5.1	43	11,200	1.8	9.2	8.1	75
114 Japan	120.8	372	11,300	4.7	7.5	1.2	77
115 Sweden	8.4	450	11,890	1.8	8.0	8.6	77
116 Canada	25.4	9,976	13,680	2.4	7.4	6.3	76
117 Norway	4.2	324	14,370	3.3	7.7	8.5	77
118 Switzerland	6.5	41	16,370	1.4	5.3	4.5	77
119 United States	239.3	9,363	16,690	1.7	6.1	5.3	76
Nonreporting nonmember economies	**362.6 t**	**25,826 t**	**. .**	**. .**	**. .**	**. .**	**69 w**
120 *Albania*	3.0	29	. .	. .	. .	. .	70
121 *Angola*	8.8	1,247	. .	. .	. .	. .	44
122 *Bulgaria*	9.0	111	. .	. .	. .	. .	71
123 *Cuba*	10.1	115	. .	. .	. .	. .	77
124 *Czechoslovakia*	15.5	128	. .	. .	. .	. .	70
125 *German Dem. Rep.*	16.6	108	. .	. .	. .	. .	59
126 *Korea, Dem. Rep.*	20.4	121	. .	. .	. .	. .	68
127 *Mongolia*	1.9	1,565	. .	. .	. .	. .	63
128 *USSR*	277.4	22,402	. .	. .	. .	. .	70

a. See the technical notes.

Table 2. Growth of production

	GDP		Agriculture		Industry		(Manufacturing)[a]		Services	
	1965–80	1980–85	1965–80	1980–85	1965–80	1980–85	1965–80	1980–85	1965–80	1980–85
Low-income economies	4.8 w	7.3 w	2.7 w	6.0 w	7.6 w	9.3 w	7.8 w	10.8 w	5.0 w	6.3 w
China and India	5.3 w	8.3 w	2.9 w	7.1 w	8.2 w	10.0 w	8.1 w	11.2 w	5.5 w	7.5 w
Other low-income	3.2 w	2.8 w	2.0 w	1.9 w	4.4 w	3.7 w	5.3 w	5.5 w	4.0 w	3.0 w
1 Ethiopia	2.8	0.3	1.2	−3.4	3.2	2.8	5.0	..	5.3	3.2
2 Bangladesh	2.4	3.6	1.5	2.8	3.8	4.7	6.8	2.0	3.4	4.3
3 Burkina Faso	3.2	2.4	..	2.7	..	2.1	..	..	..	2.4
4 Mali	4.1	−0.5	2.8	−4.1	4.2	3.8	..	..	7.0	4.0
5 Bhutan	..	..	..	..	..	..	..	..	..	..
6 Mozambique	..	−9.6	..	−16.5	..	−13.9	..	..	..	0.1
7 Nepal	2.3	3.4	..	..	..	..	..	..	..	..
8 Malawi	5.8	2.0	..	2.7	..	1.3	..	..	..	1.8
9 Zaire	1.4	1.0	..	2.5	..	2.0	..	−1.4	..	−0.8
10 Burma	3.9	5.5	3.7	5.4	4.4	7.0	3.9	6.0	4.0	5.1
11 Burundi	3.6	1.9	3.3	0.8	7.8	4.8	5.9	6.8	2.7	3.3
12 Togo	4.4	−1.8	1.9	0.9	6.8	−2.8	..	−3.4	5.4	−3.2
13 Madagascar	1.8	−0.8	..	2.4	..	−6.8	..	..	..	−0.6
14 Niger	0.3	−3.6	−3.4	(.)	11.4	−3.6	..	..	3.4	−7.4
15 Benin	2.3	3.4	..	0.9	..	13.5	..	7.2	..	2.4
16 Central African Rep.	2.6	0.6	2.1	2.2	5.3	1.0	..	−1.8	2.0	−1.4
17 India	3.8	5.2	2.8	2.7	4.1	5.4	4.4	5.6	4.8	7.5
18 Rwanda	4.9	1.8	..	2.6	..	4.9	..	4.8	..	−0.4
19 Somalia	2.8	4.9	..	7.9	..	−5.1	..	−3.4	..	3.6
20 Kenya	6.4	3.1	4.9	2.8	9.8	2.0	10.5	3.8	6.4	3.9
21 Tanzania	3.9	0.8	1.7	0.7	4.2	−4.5	5.6	−4.6	6.7	2.8
22 Sudan	3.8	−0.7	2.9	−5.5	3.1	4.3	..	..	4.9	0.6
23 China	6.4	9.8	3.0	9.4	10.0	11.1	9.5[b]	12.4[b]	7.0	7.5
24 Haiti	2.9	−0.8	1.0	−1.3	7.1	−2.4	6.2	−2.6	2.7	0.5
25 Guinea	3.9	0.9	..	0.3	..	0.1	..	1.5	..	2.1
26 Sierra Leone	2.8	2.1	2.3	1.1	−1.1	−2.5	4.0	5.2	5.8	4.3
27 Senegal	2.0	3.3	1.4	1.8	4.8	4.5	3.4	4.9	1.3	3.3
28 Ghana	1.4	−0.7	1.6	−1.3	1.4	−5.5	2.5	−5.6	1.1	2.2
29 Pakistan	5.2	6.0	3.3	2.1	6.2	8.8	5.3	10.1	6.1	6.8
30 Sri Lanka	4.0	5.1	2.7	4.0	5.1	4.2	3.2	5.5	4.3	6.1
31 Zambia	1.8	0.1	2.2	2.9	2.1	−0.5	5.3	0.4	1.5	−0.4
32 *Afghanistan*	3.0	..	..	..	..	..	..	..	..	..
33 *Chad*	0.1	..	..	..	..	..	..	..	..	..
34 *Kampuchea, Dem.*	..	..	..	..	..	..	..	..	..	..
35 *Lao PDR*	..	..	..	..	..	..	..	..	..	..
36 *Uganda*	0.6	4.9	1.2	6.5	−4.1	1.8	−3.7	2.3	1.1	3.0
37 *Viet Nam*	..	..	..	..	..	..	..	..	..	..
Middle-income economies	6.5 w	1.7 w	3.5 w	2.1 w	7.6 w	1.2 w	..	..	6.7 w	1.9 w
Lower middle-income	6.3 w	1.6 w	3.3 w	1.9 w	8.5 w	0.6 w	7.3 w	3.2 w	6.4 w	2.3 w
38 Mauritania	2.1	0.2	−2.0	1.6	2.2	4.2	..	..	6.5	−3.2
39 Bolivia	4.5	−4.5	3.8	−3.7	3.7	−7.3	5.4	−10.6	5.6	−2.9
40 Lesotho	6.7	0.5	..	..	..	..	..	..	..	..
41 Liberia	3.2	−1.9	5.5	1.1	2.2	−6.7	10.0	−5.1	2.4	−0.2
42 Indonesia	7.9	3.5	4.3	3.1	11.9	1.0	12.0	6.4	7.3	6.3
43 Yemen, PDR	..	1.6	..	..	..	..	..	..	..	..
44 Yemen, Arab Rep.	..	4.5	..	0.2	..	8.3	..	16.5	..	5.2
45 Morocco	5.7	3.0	2.2	1.0	6.1	1.3	5.9	0.7	6.5	4.3
46 Philippines	5.9	−0.5	4.6	1.7	8.0	−2.8	7.5	−1.2	5.2	0.1
47 Egypt, Arab Rep.	6.7	5.2	2.8	1.9	7.0	7.0	..	..	9.5	5.1
48 Côte d'Ivoire	6.8	−1.7	3.3	−1.1	10.4	−1.5	9.1	..	9.4	−2.5
49 Papua New Guinea	4.1	1.3	..	..	..	..	..	..	..	..
50 Zimbabwe	4.9	2.5	..	3.7	..	0.4	..	0.9	..	3.8
51 Honduras	4.1	0.6	1.6	2.2	5.7	−0.8	6.0	−2.1	5.4	0.3
52 Nicaragua	2.6	0.2	3.3	1.4	4.2	0.3	5.2	0.8	1.4	−0.4
53 Dominican Rep.	7.3	2.2	3.8	*3.3*	10.9	*2.1*	8.9	*2.0*	7.0	*2.0*
54 Nigeria	7.9	−3.4	1.7	1.0	13.4	−5.8	14.6	3.0	8.8	−3.5
55 Thailand	7.4	5.1	4.9	3.4	9.5	5.1	10.9	5.3	8.0	6.0
56 Cameroon	4.9	8.6	4.2	1.3	8.1	17.8	7.0	18.4	4.4	7.1
57 El Salvador	4.4	−1.8	3.6	−2.9	5.3	−1.7	4.6	−2.1	4.3	−1.3
58 Botswana	14.3	12.1	9.3	−8.1	23.2	21.1	12.5	5.8	12.2	6.0
59 Paraguay	7.0	1.4	4.9	2.8	8.8	0.4	7.0	0.3	7.5	1.2
60 Jamaica	1.5	0.5	0.5	1.9	−0.1	−1.6	0.4	0.8	2.7	1.3
61 Peru	3.9	−1.6	1.0	1.9	4.4	−3.0	3.8	−3.8	4.3	−1.2
62 Turkey	6.3	4.5	3.2	2.6	7.2	6.0	7.5	7.9	7.6	4.5
63 Mauritius	4.9	3.9	..	5.2	..	4.3	..	6.1	..	3.5
64 Congo, People's Rep.	5.9	7.8	3.1	−1.5	10.3	11.3	..	6.2	4.7	7.0
65 Ecuador	8.4	1.5	3.4	0.2	13.7	4.0	11.5	0.5	7.6	0.2
66 Tunisia	6.6	4.1	5.5	4.2	7.4	3.8	9.9	6.7	6.5	4.3
67 Guatemala	5.9	−1.4	5.1	−0.6	7.3	−3.8	6.5	−2.2	5.7	−0.8

Note: For data comparability and coverage, see the technical notes.   Figures in italics are for years other than those specified.

	Average annual growth rate (percent)									
	GDP		Agriculture		Industry		(Manufacturing)[a]		Services	
	1965–80	1980–85	1965–80	1980–85	1965–80	1980–85	1965–80	1980–85	1965–80	1980–85
68 Costa Rica	6.3	0.5	4.2	2.1	8.7	−0.1	..	..	6.0	0.2
69 Colombia	5.6	1.9	4.3	1.8	5.5	2.9	6.2	..	6.4	1.6
70 Chile	1.9	−1.1	1.6	2.1	0.8	−0.5	0.6	−1.9	2.7	−2.1
71 Jordan	..	4.1	..	6.4	..	4.0	..	5.6	..	3.8
72 Syrian Arab Rep.	8.7	1.5	4.8	−1.4	12.2	0.6	..	..	9.0	2.9
73 *Lebanon*	−1.2	..	..	..	..	..	..	..	..	..
Upper middle-income	**6.6** *w*	**1.7** *w*	**3.7** *w*	**2.3** *w*	**7.2** *w*	**1.4** *w*	**..**	**..**	**6.9** *w*	**1.7** *w*
74 Brazil	9.0	1.3	4.7	3.0	10.0	0.3	9.8	..	9.4	1.8
75 Uruguay	2.4	−3.9	1.0	−1.3	3.1	−7.2	..	..	2.3	−2.9
76 Hungary	5.5	1.8	2.7	3.5	6.4	2.0	..	..	6.2	0.9
77 Portugal	5.3	0.9	..	−0.7	..	0.9	..	..	..	1.3
78 Malaysia	7.3	5.5	..	3.0	..	6.7	..	6.1	..	5.9
79 South Africa	4.0	0.8	..	..	..	..	..	..	..	..
80 Poland	..	0.5	..	..	..	..	..	..	..	..
81 Yugoslavia	6.1	0.8	3.1	1.3	7.8	0.6	..	..	5.5	0.9
82 Mexico	6.5	0.8	3.2	2.3	7.6	0.3	7.4	..	6.6	0.8
83 Panama	5.5	2.4	2.4	2.7	5.9	−2.2	4.7	−0.3	6.0	3.6
84 Argentina	3.3	−1.4	1.4	2.8	3.3	−2.5	2.7	−1.6	3.9	−1.8
85 Korea, Rep. of	9.5	7.9	3.0	6.3	16.6	9.6	18.8	9.0	9.4	6.7
86 Algeria	7.5	4.9	5.8	2.1	8.1	5.3	9.5	9.0	7.1	4.9
87 Venezuela	5.2	−1.6	4.0	1.5	3.5	−1.8	5.9	1.4	6.6	−1.9
88 Greece	5.8	1.0	2.3	−0.7	7.1	−0.6	8.4	−0.9	6.2	2.4
89 Israel	6.7	1.7	..	..	..	..	..	..	..	..
90 Trinidad and Tobago	*4.8*	−4.1	*0.1*	1.4	*3.8*	−4.0	..	−4.8	*5.7*	−4.5
91 Hong Kong	8.5	5.9	..	..	..	..	..	..	..	..
92 Oman	12.5	*4.0*	..	..	..	..	..	..	..	..
93 Singapore	10.2	6.5	3.1	−1.8	12.2	5.9	13.3	2.1	9.7	6.9
94 *Iran, Islamic Rep.*	6.2	..	4.5	..	2.4	..	10.0	..	13.3	..
95 *Iraq*	..	..	..	..	..	..	..	..	..	..
96 *Romania*	..	..	..	..	..	..	..	..	..	..
Developing economies	**6.0** *w*	**3.3** *w*	**3.1** *w*	**4.0** *w*	**7.6** *w*	**3.5** *w*	**..**	**..**	**6.4** *w*	**2.8** *w*
Oil exporters	**6.8** *w*	**1.0** *w*	**3.2** *w*	**1.9** *w*	**8.3** *w*	**0.2** *w*	**8.5** *w*	**1.8** *w*	**6.9** *w*	**1.4** *w*
Exporters of manufactures	**6.7** *w*	**5.5** *w*	**3.2** *w*	**6.1** *w*	**8.8** *w*	**6.6** *w*	**..**	**..**	**7.4** *w*	**4.3** *w*
Highly indebted countries	**6.4** *w*	**0.1** *w*	**3.2** *w*	**1.9** *w*	**7.3** *w*	**−0.9** *w*	**7.3** *w*	**−0.3** *w*	**6.8** *w*	**0.3** *w*
Sub-Saharan Africa	**5.3** *w*	**−0.7** *w*	**1.9** *w*	**0.9** *w*	**9.7** *w*	**−2.4** *w*	**9.8** *w*	**3.5** *w*	**5.4** *w*	**−0.4** *w*
High-income oil exporters	**7.5** *w*	**−2.2** *w*	**..**	**7.8** *w*	**..**	**−8.3** *w*	**..**	**9.2** *w*	**..**	**5.1** *w*
97 Libya	4.2	−6.1	10.7	7.3	1.2	−8.8	13.7	*11.5*	15.5	−3.7
98 Saudi Arabia	10.9	−2.1	4.1	8.0	11.6	−9.7	8.1	7.7	10.5	7.3
99 Kuwait	3.1	*0.3*	..	..	..	..	..	..	..	..
100 United Arab Emirates	..	−2.8	..	*13.3*	..	−6.1	..	20.2	..	*5.9*
Industrial market economies	**3.7** *w*	**2.3** *w*	**1.2** *w*	**1.5** *w*	**3.6** *w*	**2.5** *w*	**4.0** *w*	**3.0** *w*	**3.9** *w*	**2.0** *w*
101 Spain	4.8	1.6	2.7	2.5	5.8	0.6	6.7	0.3	4.6	2.2
102 Ireland	4.7	1.5	..	..	..	..	..	..	..	..
103 Italy	3.8	0.8	0.9	0.5	4.2	−0.3	..	..	4.1	1.8
104 New Zealand	3.0	3.1	..	..	..	..	..	..	..	..
105 Belgium	3.8	0.7	1.1	3.4	4.5	0.6	4.8	1.6	3.4	0.6
106 United Kingdom	2.2	2.0	1.7	3.2	1.2	0.6	1.1	*0.1*	2.9	*2.1*
107 Austria	4.4	1.7	1.9	1.5	4.6	1.4	4.8	2.1	4.6	2.1
108 Netherlands	3.9	0.7	*4.3*	7.8	*3.6*	0.4	*4.3*	1.4	*4.0*	0.2
109 France	4.3	1.1	0.8	*3.1*	4.6	*0.3*	5.3	*0.4*	4.6	*1.4*
110 Australia	4.2	2.5	2.6	3.9	2.9	1.0	1.2	−0.4	5.4	3.3
111 Finland	4.1	2.7	0.4	(.)	4.8	2.7	5.2	3.0	4.4	3.2
112 Germany, Fed. Rep.	3.4	1.3	1.6	*4.0*	3.1	−0.5	3.4	−0.2	3.8	*2.0*
113 Denmark	2.8	2.4	0.3	5.1	2.2	2.2	3.4	2.9	3.3	2.2
114 Japan	6.3	3.8	0.8	1.6	8.5	5.9	9.4	7.8	5.2	1.6
115 Sweden	2.7	2.0	−0.2	3.1	2.2	2.8	2.3	2.9	3.3	1.4
116 Canada	4.8	2.4	1.6	*0.5*	4.0	−0.6	4.2	−0.2	5.4	2.7
117 Norway	4.4	3.3	1.1	−1.3	5.0	2.4	2.8	−0.1	4.4	4.1
118 Switzerland	2.0	1.2	..	..	..	..	..	..	..	..
119 United States	2.9	2.5	1.3	1.8	2.3	2.4	2.7	3.3	3.4	2.6
Nonreporting nonmember economies	**..**	**..**	**..**	**..**	**..**	**..**	**..**	**..**	**..**	**..**
120 *Albania*	..	..	..	..	..	..	..	..	..	..
121 *Angola*	..	..	..	..	..	..	..	..	..	..
122 *Bulgaria*	..	..	..	..	..	..	..	..	..	..
123 *Cuba*	..	..	..	..	..	..	..	..	..	..
124 *Czechoslovakia*	..	..	..	..	..	..	..	..	..	..
125 *German Dem. Rep.*	..	..	..	..	..	..	..	..	..	..
126 *Korea, Dem. Rep.*	..	..	..	..	..	..	..	..	..	..
127 *Mongolia*	..	..	..	..	..	..	..	..	..	..
128 *USSR*	..	..	..	..	..	..	..	..	..	..

a. Because manufacturing is generally the most dynamic part of the industrial sector, its growth rate is shown separately.   b. World Bank estimate.

Table 3. Structure of production

	GDP[a] (millions of dollars)		Distribution of gross domestic product (percent)							
			Agriculture		Industry		(Manufacturing)[b]		Services	
	1965	1985	1965	1985	1965	1985	1965	1985	1965	1985
Low-income economies	147,330 t	587,020 t	41 w	32 w	28 w	33 w	21 w	26 w	32 w	35 w
China and India	111,850 t	441,240 t	41 w	31 w	30 w	37 w	24 w	29 w	29 w	32 w
Other low-income	35,480 t	145,780 t	41 w	36 w	17 w	19 w	10 w	12 w	42 w	45 w
1 Ethiopia	1,180	4,230	58	44	14	16	7	..	28	39
2 Bangladesh	4,380	16,110	53	50	11	14	5	8	36	36
3 Burkina Faso	260	930	53	45	20	22	..	..	27	33
4 Mali	..	1,100	..	50	..	13	..	7	..	37
5 Bhutan	..	180	..	50	..	18	..	4	..	32
6 Mozambique	..	3,230	..	35	..	11	..	..	..	53
7 Nepal	730	2,340	65	62	11	12	3	5	23	26
8 Malawi	220	970	50	38	13	19	..	..	37	44
9 Zaire	3,140	4,810	21	31	26	34	16	1	53	36
10 Burma	1,600	7,070	35	48	13	13	9	10	52	39
11 Burundi	160	970	..	61	..	15	..	9	..	24
12 Togo	190	700	45	30	21	24	10	7	34	47
13 Madagascar	730	2,340	31	42	16	16	11	..	53	42
14 Niger	670	1,580	68	47	3	16	2	4	29	37
15 Benin	220	960	59	48	8	16	..	4	33	36
16 Central African Rep.	140	610	46	39	16	20	4	8	38	41
17 India	46,260	175,710	47	31	22	27	15	17	31	41
18 Rwanda	150	1,710	75	45	7	21	2	16	18	34
19 Somalia	220	2,320	71	58	6	9	3	6	24	34
20 Kenya	920	5,020	35	31	18	20	11	13	47	49
21 Tanzania	790	5,600	46	58	14	8	8	5	40	33
22 Sudan	1,330	6,930	54	26	9	18	4	9	37	57
23 China	65,590	265,530	39	33	38	47	30[c]	37[c]	23	20
24 Haiti	350	1,930	..	..	..	..	..	..	..	..
25 Guinea	520	1,980	..	40	..	22	..	2	..	38
26 Sierra Leone	320	1,190	34	44	28	14	6	6	38	42
27 Senegal	810	2,560	25	19	18	29	14	18	56	52
28 Ghana	2,050	4,860	44	41	19	15	10	11	38	43
29 Pakistan	5,450	28,240	40	25	20	28	14	20	40	47
30 Sri Lanka	1,770	5,500	28	27	21	26	17	15	51	46
31 Zambia	1,060	2,330	14	14	54	39	6	22	32	46
32 Afghanistan	620	..	..	..	..	..	..	..	..	..
33 Chad	290	..	42	..	15	..	12	..	43	..
34 Kampuchea, Dem.	870	..	..	..	..	..	..	..	..	..
35 Lao PDR	..	..	..	..	..	..	..	..	..	..
36 Uganda	1,100	..	52	..	13	..	8	..	35	..
37 Viet Nam	..	..	..	..	..	..	..	..	..	..
Middle-income economies	186,300 t	1,439,960 t	20 w	14 w	30 w	34 w	..	..	50 w	52 w
Lower middle-income	66,800 t	509,630 t	29 w	22 w	24 w	32 w	16 w	17 w	47 w	47 w
38 Mauritania	160	600	32	29	36	25	4	..	32	47
39 Bolivia	730	2,980	23	27	31	30	15	19	46	42
40 Lesotho	50	260	65	..	5	..	1	..	30	..
41 Liberia	270	1,000	27	37	40	28	3	5	34	36
42 Indonesia	3,830	86,470	56	24	13	36	8	14	31	41
43 Yemen, PDR	..	900	..	..	..	..	..	..	..	..
44 Yemen, Arab Rep.	..	3,700	..	34	..	16	..	7	..	50
45 Morocco	2,950	11,850	23	18	28	32	16	17	49	50
46 Philippines	6,010	32,590	26	27	28	32	20	25	46	41
47 Egypt, Arab Rep.	4,550	30,550	29	20	27	31	..	..	44	49
48 Côte d'Ivoire	760	5,220	47	36	19	26	11	17	33	38
49 Papua New Guinea	340	2,270	42	..	18	..	..	..	41	..
50 Zimbabwe	960	4,530	18	13	35	43	20	29	47	44
51 Honduras	460	2,960	40	27	19	25	12	14	41	48
52 Nicaragua	570	2,860	25	23	24	33	18	27	51	44
53 Dominican Rep.	960	4,910	26	15	20	31	14	19	53	53
54 Nigeria	4,190	75,300	53	36	19	32	7	9	29	32
55 Thailand	4,050	38,240	35	17	23	30	14	20	42	53
56 Cameroon	750	7,940	32	21	17	37	10	12	50	42
57 El Salvador	800	3,820	29	19	22	22	18	16	49	60
58 Botswana	50	830	34	6	19	49	12	8	47	46
59 Paraguay	440	5,810	37	29	19	25	16	16	45	46
60 Jamaica	870	1,980	10	6	37	36	17	20	53	58
61 Peru	5,030	16,850	18	11	29	38	17	20	53	51
62 Turkey	7,660	48,820	34	19	25	35	16	25	41	46
63 Mauritius	190	890	16	15	23	29	14	20	61	56
64 Congo, People's Rep.	200	2,160	19	8	19	54	..	6	62	38
65 Ecuador	1,150	12,550	27	14	22	42	18	19	50	45
66 Tunisia	880	7,240	22	17	24	34	9	14	54	49
67 Guatemala	1,330	11,020	..	..	..	..	..	..	..	..

Note: For data comparability and coverage, see the technical notes. Figures in italics are for years other than those specified.

| | GDP[a] (millions of dollars) | | Distribution of gross domestic product (percent) | | | | | | | |
| | | | Agriculture | | Industry | | (Manufacturing)[b] | | Services | |
	1965	1985	1965	1985	1965	1985	1965	1985	1965	1985
68 Costa Rica	590	3,810	24	20	23	29	..	..	53	51
69 Colombia	5,570	*34,400*	30	*20*	25	*30*	18	*18*	46	*50*
70 Chile	5,940	16,000	9	..	40	..	24	..	52	..
71 Jordan	..	3,450	..	8	..	28	..	12	..	64
72 Syrian Arab Rep.	1,470	16,370	29	22	22	21	..	..	49	57
73 *Lebanon*	1,150	..	12	..	21	..	..	..	67	..
Upper middle-income	**119,500 t**	**930,330 t**	**15 w**	**10 w**	**34 w**	**35 w**	**..**	**..**	**51 w**	**54 w**
74 Brazil	19,260	*188,250*	19	*13*	33	*33*	26	..	48	*54*
75 Uruguay	930	4,380	15	11	32	33	..	..	53	56
76 Hungary[d]	..	20,560	..	16	..	41	..	..	..	43
77 Portugal	3,740	20,430	..	9	..	40	..	..	..	51
78 Malaysia	3,130	31,270	28	..	25	..	9	..	47	..
79 South Africa	10,540	*67,710*	10	*5*	42	*45*	23	*23*	48	*50*
80 Poland	..	70,439	..	..	..	..	..	..	..	..
81 Yugoslavia	11,190	44,370	23	12	42	46	..	..	35	42
82 Mexico	20,160	177,360	14	11	31	35	21	..	54	54
83 Panama	660	4,880	18	9	19	18	12	9	63	73
84 Argentina	16,500	65,920	17	..	42	..	33	..	42	..
85 Korea, Rep. of	3,000	86,180	39	14	26	41	19	28	35	45
86 Algeria	3,170	58,180	15	8	34	48	11	11	51	43
87 Venezuela	8,290	49,600	7	8	41	42	..	21	52	50
88 Greece	5,270	29,150	24	17	26	29	16	18	50	54
89 Israel	3,590	20,270	..	..	..	..	..	..	..	..
90 Trinidad and Tobago	660	7,770	5	3	38	44	19	7	57	53
91 Hong Kong	2,150	*30,730*	2	*1*	40	*31*	24	24	58	68
92 Oman	60	*8,820*	61	*3*	23	59	(.)	*3*	16	*38*
93 Singapore	970	17,470	3	1	24	37	15	24	73	62
94 *Iran, Islamic Rep.*	6,170	..	26	..	36	..	12	..	38	..
95 *Iraq*	2,430	..	18	..	46	..	8	..	36	..
96 *Romania*	..	..	..	..	..	..	..	..	..	..
Developing economies	**333,630 t**	**2,026,970 t**	**29 w**	**20 w**	**29 w**	**34 w**	**..**	**..**	**42 w**	**47 w**
Oil exporters	**57,090 t**	**533,070 t**	**22 w**	**17 w**	**29 w**	**36 w**	**15 w**	**13 w**	**50 w**	**47 w**
Exporters of manufactures	**163,420 t**	**907,600 t**	**34 w**	**21 w**	**31 w**	**35 w**	**..**	**..**	**36 w**	**44 w**
Highly indebted countries	**115,530 t**	**779,100 t**	**18 w**	**15 w**	**32 w**	**33 w**	**23 w**	**17 w**	**49 w**	**52 w**
Sub-Saharan Africa	**24,620 t**	**160,660 t**	**39 w**	**34 w**	**19 w**	**27 w**	**10 w**	**10 w**	**42 w**	**40 w**
High-income oil exporters	**6,960 t**	**170,300 t**	**5 w**	**2 w**	**65 w**	**58 w**	**5 w**	**8 w**	**30 w**	**39 w**
97 Libya	1,500	25,420	5	4	63	57	3	5	32	39
98 Saudi Arabia	2,300	95,050	8	3	60	56	9	8	32	41
99 Kuwait	2,100	*21,710*	(.)	*1*	73	*58*	3	*8*	27	*41*
100 United Arab Emirates	..	*28,120*	..	*1*	..	67	..	*10*	..	*32*
Industrial market economies	**1,367,050 t**	**8,568,920 t**	**5 w**	**3 w**	**40 w**	**36 w**	**30 w**	**23 w**	**55 w**	**61 w**
101 Spain	23,320	164,250	15	..	36	..	25	..	49	..
102 Ireland	2,690	18,430	..	..	..	..	..	..	..	..
103 Italy	62,600	358,670	11	5	41	39	..	..	48	56
104 New Zealand	5,580	22,140	..	*11*	..	*33*	..	24	..	*56*
105 Belgium	16,840	79,080	5	2	41	33	30	23	53	64
106 United Kingdom	99,530	454,300	3	*2*	41	*36*	30	22	56	62
107 Austria	9,470	66,050	9	3	46	38	33	28	45	59
108 Netherlands	19,700	124,970	..	4	..	34	..	..	..	62
109 France	97,930	510,320	8	*4*	39	*34*	29	*25*	52	62
110 Australia	22,140	162,490	11	4	40	33	28	17	48	63
111 Finland	8,190	54,030	15	7	33	33	21	23	52	60
112 Germany, Fed. Rep.	114,800	624,970	4	*2*	53	*40*	40	*31*	43	*58*
113 Denmark	10,180	57,840	8	5	32	24	20	17	60	71
114 Japan	90,970	1,327,900	9	3	43	41	32	30	48	56
115 Sweden	21,670	100,250	6	3	40	31	28	21	53	66
116 Canada	51,840	346,030	5	*3*	34	*30*	23	*16*	61	67
117 Norway	7,080	57,910	8	4	33	43	21	14	59	54
118 Switzerland	13,920	92,690	..	..	..	..	..	..	..	..
119 United States	688,600	3,946,600	3	2	38	31	29	20	59	67
Nonreporting nonmember economies	**..**	**..**	**..**	**..**	**..**	**..**	**..**	**..**	**..**	**..**
120 *Albania*	..	..	..	..	..	..	..	..	..	..
121 *Angola*	..	..	..	..	..	..	..	..	..	..
122 *Bulgaria*	..	..	..	..	..	..	..	..	..	..
123 *Cuba*	..	..	..	..	..	..	..	..	..	..
124 *Czechoslovakia*	..	..	..	..	..	..	..	..	..	..
125 *German Dem. Rep.*	..	..	..	..	..	..	..	..	..	..
126 *Korea, Dem. Rep.*	..	..	..	..	..	..	..	..	..	..
127 *Mongolia*	..	..	..	..	..	..	..	..	..	..
128 *USSR*	..	..	..	..	..	..	..	..	..	..

a. See the technical notes.   b. Because manufacturing is generally the most dynamic part of the industrial sector, its share of GDP is shown separately.   c. World Bank estimate.   d. Services include the unallocated share of GDP.

Table 4. Growth of consumption and investment

	General government consumption		Private consumption		Gross domestic investment	
	1965–80	1980–85	1965–80	1980–85	1965–80	1980–85
Low-income economies	5.4 w	6.6 w	3.9 w	5.6 w	7.2 w	11.4 w
China and India	6.1 w	7.6 w	4.3 w	6.4 w	8.2 w	13.2 w
Other low-income	3.2 w	2.3 w	3.0 w	3.1 w	3.2 w	−2.1 w
1 Ethiopia	6.4	5.8	3.6	1.0	−0.6	1.6
2 Bangladesh	a	a	2.7	3.7	0.0	0.5
3 Burkina Faso	8.7	3.2	2.1	0.8	8.8	−3.2
4 Mali	5.1	9.0	5.0	2.5	1.8	−7.9
5 Bhutan	. .	. .	. .	. .	. .	. .
6 Mozambique	. .	−9.4	. .	−7.4	. .	−22.1
7 Nepal	. .	. .	. .	. .	. .	. .
8 Malawi	5.7	1.5	3.9	1.9	9.0	−7.5
9 Zaire	0.7	−15.5	−0.2	0.6	6.7	−4.4
10 Burma	a	5.9	3.7	3.6	5.6	−1.8
11 Burundi	7.3	1.9	3.9	1.4	9.0	5.6
12 Togo	9.5	−3.9	5.4	−1.9	9.0	−6.8
13 Madagascar	2.0	−1.5	1.5	−0.2	1.5	−8.2
14 Niger	2.9	2.5	−0.6	−1.3	6.3	−26.5
15 Benin	0.7	4.8	1.7	3.3	10.4	−17.9
16 Central African Rep.	−1.1	−4.6	4.2	−0.7	−5.4	14.3
17 India	6.3	10.7	3.1	4.4	4.8	4.6
18 Rwanda	6.2	0.8	4.0	0.6	9.0	7.4
19 Somalia	12.7	−9.1	3.1	2.7	0.4	21.5
20 Kenya	10.4	−0.3	5.3	2.2	7.1	−8.9
21 Tanzania	a	a	4.6	1.9	6.2	−3.4
22 Sudan	0.2	−8.9	4.5	2.7	6.5	−12.9
23 China	6.0	6.3	5.3	7.7	10.5	16.5
24 Haiti	1.9	2.9	2.4	−2.7	14.8	0.0
25 Guinea	. .	−5.2	. .	5.4	. .	−7.6
26 Sierra Leone	−0.2	5.3	4.0	−2.9	−0.6	−11.7
27 Senegal	2.9	4.3	1.8	1.7	3.9	0.7
28 Ghana	3.8	0.1	1.2	−0.9	−1.3	−1.6
29 Pakistan	4.7	10.5	5.5	5.1	2.4	6.1
30 Sri Lanka	1.1	6.8	3.2	9.2	11.5	−4.4
31 Zambia	5.1	−6.4	0.1	2.2	−3.6	−14.0
32 Afghanistan	. .	. .	. .	. .	. .	. .
33 Chad	. .	. .	. .	. .	. .	. .
34 Kampuchea, Dem.	. .	. .	. .	. .	. .	. .
35 Lao PDR	. .	. .	. .	. .	. .	. .
36 Uganda	a	. .	1.1	. .	−5.7	. .
37 Viet Nam	. .	. .	. .	. .	. .	. .
Middle-income economies	7.2 w	2.9 w	6.3 w	1.5 w	8.6 w	−3.9 w
Lower middle-income	8.6 w	3.1 w	5.5 w	1.9 w	9.1 w	−3.5 w
38 Mauritania	10.0	−7.2	1.8	6.3	19.2	−8.1
39 Bolivia	8.0	−2.6	4.0	−4.4	4.4	−9.5
40 Lesotho	12.3	. .	8.5	. .	17.5	. .
41 Liberia	3.4	4.2	3.1	1.9	6.4	−20.0
42 Indonesia	11.4	5.2	6.3	5.9	16.1	5.6
43 Yemen, PDR	. .	. .	. .	. .	. .	. .
44 Yemen, Arab Rep.	. .	9.9	. .	2.3	. .	−12.5
45 Morocco	11.0	3.0	4.6	2.6	11.1	−3.1
46 Philippines	7.7	−0.6	4.5	2.3	8.5	−14.4
47 Egypt, Arab Rep.	a	8.5	5.7	3.0	11.5	0.7
48 Côte d'Ivoire	12.7	−5.1	7.9	−0.1	10.4	−22.0
49 Papua New Guinea	0.1	−2.2	3.7	1.4	1.4	−2.0
50 Zimbabwe	10.6	9.6	5.4	1.7	0.9	−2.4
51 Honduras	7.3	−0.1	4.3	−1.3	6.6	−2.7
52 Nicaragua	6.6	20.6	2.0	−9.0	1.5	0.2
53 Dominican Rep.	0.3	−0.1	7.3	0.5	13.5	−2.7
54 Nigeria	13.5	1.3	7.0	−1.5	14.7	−18.0
55 Thailand	9.3	4.3	6.8	4.7	7.6	1.7
56 Cameroon	5.0	8.7	3.8	3.0	9.9	10.8
57 El Salvador	7.0	0.6	4.1	−2.3	6.6	−2.1
58 Botswana	12.0	12.0	9.2	5.5	21.0	−14.8
59 Paraguay	5.1	7.1	6.3	3.1	13.5	−8.8
60 Jamaica	9.8	1.0	1.5	0.1	−3.3	2.1
61 Peru	5.6	−1.4	4.2	−1.0	0.2	−16.5
62 Turkey	6.1	3.0	5.4	3.6	8.8	3.6
63 Mauritius	7.1	1.9	6.2	1.5	8.3	5.5
64 Congo, People's Rep.	5.5	6.4	2.8	8.4	4.5	0.8
65 Ecuador	12.2	−1.7	6.8	1.3	9.5	−7.2
66 Tunisia	7.2	6.2	7.9	4.7	4.6	1.2
67 Guatemala	6.2	0.3	5.3	−0.9	7.4	−9.0

Note: For data comparability and coverage, see the technical notes.   Figures in italics are for years other than those specified.

	General government consumption		Private consumption		Gross domestic investment	
	1965–80	1980–85	1965–80	1980–85	1965–80	1980–85
68 Costa Rica	6.8	−1.4	5.1	0.2	9.4	−1.9
69 Colombia	6.7	1.4	5.9	2.6	5.8	0.6
70 Chile	4.0	−0.6	1.0	−2.2	0.5	−13.5
71 Jordan	..	4.9	..	4.5	..	−2.0
72 Syrian Arab Rep.	15.0	4.8	10.1	0.2	14.3	3.1
73 *Lebanon*	..	..	..	..	..	..
Upper middle-income	**6.5 w**	**2.8 w**	**6.8 w**	**1.2 w**	**8.4 w**	**−4.1 w**
74 Brazil	6.5	0.2	9.1	2.2	10.2	−5.5
75 Uruguay	3.2	−0.3	2.4	−5.7	8.0	−19.1
76 Hungary	..	−0.8	..	1.6	..	−4.0
77 Portugal	8.1	3.4	6.0	0.1	4.7	−10.1
78 Malaysia	8.5	3.6	6.0	3.8	10.4	5.3
79 South Africa	5.7	..	4.3	..	4.2	..
80 Poland	..	2.2	..	−2.3	..	−3.2
81 Yugoslavia	3.6	−0.8	7.7	−0.8	6.5	−0.3
82 Mexico	8.5	3.3	5.9	0.1	8.5	−9.1
83 Panama	7.4	3.3	4.7	6.2	5.9	−9.4
84 Argentina	3.2	−3.0	2.7	−1.2	4.4	−13.8
85 Korea, Rep. of	6.7	3.4	7.9	5.5	16.5	9.6
86 Algeria	8.6	5.3	9.0	5.4	15.9	3.8
87 Venezuela	7.4	..	8.5	..	8.5	..
88 Greece	6.6	3.4	5.5	1.8	5.3	−4.6
89 Israel	8.4	−0.7	6.1	3.5	5.9	−1.0
90 Trinidad and Tobago	a	1.2	7.5	−3.0	7.3	−10.1
91 Hong Kong	7.7	6.2	9.0	6.6	8.6	−1.7
92 Oman	..	..	..	..	..	..
93 Singapore	10.1	9.4	7.8	4.5	13.9	7.4
94 *Iran, Islamic Rep.*	14.9	..	8.4	..	10.6	..
95 *Iraq*	..	..	..	..	..	..
96 *Romania*	..	..	..	..	..	..
Developing economies	**6.6 w**	**4.1 w**	**5.6 w**	**2.7 w**	**8.2 w**	**0.8 w**
Oil exporters	**9.4 w**	**2.8 w**	**6.6 w**	**0.6 w**	**11.2 w**	**−4.8 w**
Exporters of manufactures	**6.2 w**	**5.9 w**	**6.2 w**	**4.4 w**	**8.7 w**	**6.2 w**
Highly indebted countries	**6.9 w**	**1.6 w**	**6.4 w**	**0.2 w**	**8.2 w**	**−9.4 w**
Sub-Saharan Africa	**8.0 w**	**0.7 w**	**4.4 w**	**0.3 w**	**9.0 w**	**−11.4 w**
High-income oil exporters	**..**	**..**	**..**	**..**	**..**	**..**
97 Libya	*19.2*	..	*17.5*	..	7.2	..
98 Saudi Arabia	a	..	15.4	..	27.5	..
99 Kuwait	a	..	8.4	..	11.7	..
100 United Arab Emirates	..	6.5	..	6.4	..	0.2
Industrial market economies	**3.0 w**	**2.7 w**	**4.0 w**	**2.2 w**	**2.9 w**	**2.7 w**
101 Spain	5.0	4.0	4.9	0.3	4.0	−2.6
102 Ireland	6.1	1.0	4.0	−1.9	6.8	−1.0
103 Italy	3.3	4.3	3.9	0.3	2.8	−2.3
104 New Zealand	2.9	0.3	3.2	1.1	2.6	8.5
105 Belgium	4.3	0.2	4.1	0.2	2.9	−4.2
106 United Kingdom	2.2	1.0	2.1	2.4	1.1	5.3
107 Austria	4.0	1.6	4.2	2.4	4.6	0.2
108 Netherlands	3.0	0.6	4.3	−0.2	2.3	0.9
109 France	3.5	1.7	4.7	1.8	3.7	−1.2
110 Australia	5.4	3.8	4.1	2.8	2.4	0.8
111 Finland	5.4	3.7	3.8	2.9	2.8	0.8
112 Germany, Fed. Rep.	3.5	1.0	4.0	0.6	1.8	−0.8
113 Denmark	4.8	0.9	2.4	1.7	1.3	4.9
114 Japan	5.1	2.8	6.1	3.0	6.7	2.4
115 Sweden	4.0	1.5	2.5	0.5	1.1	0.5
116 Canada	4.8	1.9	5.1	2.2	4.9	0.4
117 Norway	4.7	3.0	4.5	3.4	2.7	2.9
118 Switzerland	2.7	2.3	2.6	1.1	0.8	0.9
119 United States	1.9	4.2	3.5	3.0	1.8	5.2
Nonreporting nonmember economies	**..**	**..**	**..**	**..**	**..**	**..**
120 *Albania*	..	..	..	..	..	..
121 *Angola*	..	..	..	..	..	..
122 *Bulgaria*	..	..	..	..	..	..
123 *Cuba*	..	..	..	..	..	..
124 *Czechoslovakia*	..	..	..	..	..	..
125 *German Dem. Rep.*	..	..	..	..	..	..
126 *Korea, Dem. Rep.*	..	..	..	..	..	..
127 *Mongolia*	..	..	..	..	..	..
128 *USSR*	..	..	..	..	..	..

Average annual growth rate (percent)

a. General government consumption figures are not available separately; they are included in private consumption.

Table 5. Structure of demand

Distribution of gross domestic product (percent)

	General government consumption		Private consumption		Gross domestic investment		Gross domestic savings		Exports of goods and nonfactor services		Resource balance	
	1965	1985	1965	1985	1965	1985	1965	1985	1965	1985	1965	1985
Low-income economies	**13** w	**13** w	**69** w	**64** w	**21** w	**29** w	**19** w	**24** w	**7** w	**10** w	**−1** w	**−5** w
China and India	**13** w	**13** w	**67** w	**59** w	**22** w	**33** w	**20** w	**28** w	**4** w	**9** w	**−1** w	**−4** w
Other low-income	**11** w	**12** w	**74** w	**82** w	**15** w	**15** w	**15** w	**6** w	**19** w	**14** w	**−1** w	**−9** w
1 Ethiopia	11	20	77	86	13	10	12	−6	12	12	−1	−16
2 Bangladesh	9	8	83	89	11	13	8	3	10	6	−4	−10
3 Burkina Faso	9	15	87	91	12	20	4	−7	9	16	−8	−26
4 Mali	..	23	..	81	..	19	..	−5	..	21	..	−24
5 Bhutan	..	..	..	..	..	..	..	..	..	..	..	..
6 Mozambique	..	16	..	87	..	7	..	−3	..	4	..	−10
7 Nepal	a	8	100	80	6	21	(.)	12	8	13	−6	−9
8 Malawi	16	15	84	73	14	16	(.)	11	19	25	−14	−4
9 Zaire	10	6	61	78	14	13	29	16	36	39	15	2
10 Burma	a	14	87	73	19	17	13	14	14	6	−6	−3
11 Burundi	7	11	90	84	6	15	4	5	10	11	−2	−10
12 Togo	8	14	76	71	22	26	17	15	20	41	−6	−11
13 Madagascar	23	13	74	78	10	14	4	9	16	14	−6	−5
14 Niger	6	12	90	83	8	14	3	5	9	17	−5	−9
15 Benin	11	9	87	92	11	14	3	−1	13	24	−8	−15
16 Central African Rep.	22	12	67	86	21	16	11	2	27	25	−11	−14
17 India	10	12	77	67	18	25	14	21	4	6	−2	−3
18 Rwanda	14	17	81	75	10	17	5	8	12	9	−5	−9
19 Somalia	8	12	84	93	11	15	8	−5	17	7	−3	−21
20 Kenya	15	18	70	66	14	19	15	16	31	25	1	−2
21 Tanzania	10	9	73	87	15	13	17	4	26	7	1	−10
22 Sudan	12	11	79	92	10	7	9	−3	15	10	−1	−10
23 China	15	14	59	52	25	38	25	34	4	11	1	−5
24 Haiti	8	13	90	81	7	15	2	6	13	16	−5	−8
25 Guinea	..	14	..	73	..	9	..	13	..	25	..	4
26 Sierra Leone	8	12	83	80	12	9	9	8	30	11	−3	−1
27 Senegal	17	18	75	80	12	14	8	1	24	31	−4	−13
28 Ghana	14	9	77	84	18	9	8	7	17	13	−10	−2
29 Pakistan	11	12	76	83	21	17	13	5	8	11	−8	−12
30 Sri Lanka	13	9	74	78	12	25	13	13	38	26	1	−12
31 Zambia	15	15	45	67	25	12	40	13	49	39	15	1
32 Afghanistan	a	..	99	..	11	..	1	..	11	..	−10	..
33 Chad	20	..	74	..	12	..	6	..	19	..	−6	..
34 Kampuchea, Dem.	16	..	71	..	13	..	12	..	12	..	−1	..
35 Lao PDR	..	..	..	..	..	..	..	..	..	..	..	..
36 Uganda	10	..	78	..	11	..	12	..	26	..	1	..
37 Viet Nam	..	..	..	..	..	..	..	..	..	..	..	..
Middle-income economies	**11** w	**12** w	**68** w	**65** w	**22** w	**21** w	**21** w	**23** w	**17** w	**26** w	**(.)** w	**2** w
Lower middle-income	**11** w	**13** w	**74** w	**68** w	**18** w	**20** w	**15** w	**19** w	**16** w	**23** w	**−2** w	**−1** w
38 Mauritania	19	15	54	76	14	25	27	8	42	60	13	−17
39 Bolivia	9	9	78	71	22	17	13	20	21	18	−6	3
40 Lesotho	18	..	109	..	11	..	−26	..	16	..	−38	..
41 Liberia	12	21	61	65	17	9	27	14	50	43	10	6
42 Indonesia	5	12	87	56	8	30	8	32	5	23	(.)	2
43 Yemen, PDR	..	..	..	..	..	..	..	..	..	..	..	..
44 Yemen, Arab Rep.	..	22	..	93	..	21	..	−15	..	5	..	−36
45 Morocco	12	16	77	72	10	22	12	12	18	27	1	−10
46 Philippines	9	7	76	80	21	16	15	13	17	22	(.)	3
47 Egypt, Arab Rep.	19	23	67	61	18	25	14	16	18	27	−4	−9
48 Côte d'Ivoire	11	14	61	60	22	13	29	26	37	46	7	13
49 Papua New Guinea	34	23	64	63	22	22	2	13	18	44	−20	−10
50 Zimbabwe	12	19	65	58	15	23	23	23	..	26	..	(.)
51 Honduras	10	17	75	70	15	17	15	13	27	27	(.)	−4
52 Nicaragua	8	45	74	57	21	19	18	−2	29	14	−3	−21
53 Dominican Rep.	18	8	75	74	9	21	7	18	15	28	−2	−3
54 Nigeria	7	9	76	77	19	10	17	14	18	17	−2	4
55 Thailand	10	13	70	65	20	23	21	21	18	27	−1	−1
56 Cameroon	14	9	73	53	13	26	13	38	25	35	−1	13
57 El Salvador	9	13	79	81	15	13	12	6	27	23	−2	−7
58 Botswana	24	23	89	49	6	21	−13	27	32	63	−19	7
59 Paraguay	7	8	79	83	15	17	14	9	15	21	−1	−9
60 Jamaica	8	16	69	72	27	23	23	12	33	55	−4	−11
61 Peru	10	11	63	64	34	20	27	25	16	22	−4	6
62 Turkey	12	9	74	75	15	20	13	16	6	19	−1	−4
63 Mauritius	13	12	74	67	17	22	13	21	36	54	−4	−1
64 Congo, People's Rep.	14	16	80	51	22	30	5	33	36	56	−17	3
65 Ecuador	9	12	80	65	14	18	11	24	16	27	−3	6
66 Tunisia	15	16	71	63	28	27	14	20	19	33	−14	−6
67 Guatemala	7	7	82	84	13	12	10	9	17	19	−3	−2

Note: For data comparability and coverage, see the technical notes. Figures in italics are for years others than those specified.

	Distribution of gross domestic product (percent)											
	General government consumption		Private consumption		Gross domestic investment		Gross domestic savings		Exports of goods and nonfactor services		Resource balance	
	1965	1985	1965	1985	1965	1985	1965	1985	1965	1985	1965	1985
68 Costa Rica	13	16	78	62	20	23	9	22	23	32	−10	−2
69 Colombia	8	10	75	73	16	18	17	17	11	15	1	−1
70 Chile	11	14	73	69	15	14	16	16	14	29	1	3
71 Jordan	..	26	..	87	..	31	..	−13	..	49	..	−44
72 Syrian Arab Rep.	14	25	76	62	10	24	10	14	17	11	(.)	−11
73 *Lebanon*	10	..	81	..	22	..	9	..	36	..	−13	..
Upper middle-income	**11 *w***	**12 *w***	**65 *w***	**62 *w***	**24 *w***	**22 *w***	**24 *w***	**26 *w***	**18 *w***	**28 *w***	**(.) *w***	**4 *w***
74 Brazil	11	*9*	62	*69*	25	*16*	27	*22*	8	*14*	2	*6*
75 Uruguay	15	*12*	68	*75*	11	*8*	18	*12*	19	*25*	7	*4*
76 Hungary	a	*10*	75	*63*	26	*25*	25	*27*	..	*42*	−1	*2*
77 Portugal	12	*15*	68	*66*	25	*21*	20	*20*	27	*39*	−5	*−2*
78 Malaysia	15	*15*	61	*52*	20	*28*	24	*33*	42	*55*	4	*5*
79 South Africa	11	17	60	52	28	21	30	28	26	34	(.)	10
80 Poland	..	9	..	62	..	28	..	29	..	18	..	1
81 Yugoslavia	18	13	52	46	30	39	30	41	22	30	(.)	2
82 Mexico	7	10	72	64	22	21	21	26	9	16	−1	5
83 Panama	11	21	73	63	18	15	16	15	36	36	−2	1
84 Argentina	8	10	69	74	19	9	23	16	8	15	2	6
85 Korea, Rep. of	9	10	84	59	15	30	7	31	9	36	−8	1
86 Algeria	15	15	66	46	22	36	19	38	22	24	−3	3
87 Venezuela	12	13	54	62	24	15	34	24	31	27	10	10
88 Greece	12	20	73	71	26	21	15	9	9	22	−11	−12
89 Israel	20	31	64	61	29	16	15	9	19	42	−13	−8
90 Trinidad and Tobago	11	*20*	66	*52*	23	*26*	23	*28*	39	*31*	(.)	*3*
91 Hong Kong	7	7	64	65	36	21	29	27	71	106	−7	6
92 Oman	..	a	..	*57*	..	*30*	..	*43*	..	*50*	..	*13*
93 Singapore	10	13	79	45	22	43	10	42	123	..	−12	−2
94 *Iran, Islamic Rep.*	13	..	63	..	17	..	24	..	20	..	6	..
95 *Iraq*	20	..	49	..	16	..	31	..	38	..	15	..
96 *Romania*	..	..	..	..	..	..	..	..	..	..	..	..
Developing economies	**12 *w***	**12 *w***	**68 *w***	**64 *w***	**21 *w***	**23 *w***	**20 *w***	**23 *w***	**13 *w***	**21 *w***	**−1 *w***	**(.) *w***
Oil exporters	**10 *w***	**12 *w***	**70 *w***	**62 *w***	**20 *w***	**23 *w***	**20 *w***	**26 *w***	**16 *w***	**21 *w***	**(.) *w***	**3 *w***
Exporters of manufactures	**13 *w***	**12 *w***	**66 *w***	**61 *w***	**23 *w***	**28 *w***	**22 *w***	**27 *w***	**8 *w***	**21 *w***	**−1 *w***	**−1 *w***
Highly indebted countries	**10 *w***	**10 *w***	**67 *w***	**68 *w***	**22 *w***	**18 *w***	**23 *w***	**22 *w***	**14 *w***	**17 *w***	**2 *w***	**5 *w***
Sub-Saharan Africa	**11 *w***	**12 *w***	**70 *w***	**76 *w***	**16 *w***	**13 *w***	**18 *w***	**13 *w***	**25 *w***	**21 *w***	**1 *w***	**(.) *w***
High-income oil exporters	**15 *w***	**31 *w***	**32 *w***	**40 *w***	**19 *w***	**29 *w***	**53 *w***	**30 *w***	**61 *w***	**47 *w***	**34 *w***	**(.) *w***
97 Libya	14	..	36	..	29	..	50	..	53	..	21	..
98 Saudi Arabia	18	37	34	41	14	31	48	21	60	40	34	−9
99 Kuwait	13	*20*	26	*50*	16	*21*	60	*30*	68	*60*	45	*9*
100 United Arab Emirates	..	17	..	24	..	31	..	59	..	60	..	28
Industrial market economies	**15 *w***	**17 *w***	**61 *w***	**62 *w***	**23 *w***	**21 *w***	**23 *w***	**21 *w***	**12 *w***	**18 *w***	**(.) *w***	**(.) *w***
101 Spain	7	14	71	64	25	19	21	22	11	23	−3	2
102 Ireland	14	19	72	57	24	22	15	24	35	62	−9	2
103 Italy	15	19	62	62	20	19	23	18	16	28	3	−1
104 New Zealand	12	16	63	60	27	28	25	24	22	31	−2	−3
105 Belgium	13	17	64	65	23	15	23	18	36	78	(.)	2
106 United Kingdom	17	21	64	60	20	17	19	18	20	29	−1	1
107 Austria	13	19	59	57	28	24	27	25	26	40	−1	(.)
108 Netherlands	15	16	59	59	27	20	26	25	43	64	−1	5
109 France	13	16	61	65	25	19	26	19	14	25	1	(.)
110 Australia	10	17	63	60	29	24	27	23	15	16	−2	−2
111 Finland	14	20	60	54	28	24	26	26	21	30	−2	1
112 Germany, Fed. Rep.	15	20	56	57	28	20	29	24	18	33	(.)	4
113 Denmark	16	25	59	55	26	20	25	20	29	37	−2	(.)
114 Japan	8	10	58	58	32	28	33	32	11	15	1	4
115 Sweden	18	27	56	51	27	19	26	21	22	35	−1	2
116 Canada	15	20	60	57	26	20	25	23	19	29	(.)	3
117 Norway	15	19	56	49	30	25	29	33	41	47	−1	8
118 Switzerland	10	13	60	62	30	24	30	25	29	39	−1	(.)
119 United States	17	18	62	65	20	19	21	16	5	7	1	−3
Nonreporting nonmember economies	**..**	**..**	**..**	**..**	**..**	**..**	**..**	**..**	**..**	**..**	**..**	**..**
120 *Albania*	..	..	..	..	..	..	..	..	..	..	..	..
121 *Angola*	..	..	..	..	..	..	..	..	..	..	..	..
122 *Bulgaria*	..	..	..	..	..	..	..	..	..	..	..	..
123 *Cuba*	..	..	..	..	..	..	..	..	..	..	..	..
124 *Czechoslovakia*	..	..	..	..	..	..	..	..	..	..	..	..
125 *German Dem. Rep.*	..	..	..	..	..	..	..	..	..	..	..	..
126 *Korea, Dem. Rep.*	..	..	..	..	..	..	..	..	..	..	..	..
127 *Mongolia*	..	..	..	..	..	..	..	..	..	..	..	..
128 *USSR*	..	..	..	..	..	..	..	..	..	..	..	..

a. General government consumption figures are not available separately; they are included in private consumption.

Table 6. Agriculture and food

	Value added in agriculture (millions of 1980 dollars)		Cereal imports (thousands of metric tons)		Food aid in cereals (thousands of metric tons)		Fertilizer consumption (hundreds of grams of plant nutrient per hectare of arable land)		Average index of food production per capita (1979–81=100)
	1970	1985	1974	1985	1974/75	1984/85	1970[a]	1984	1983–85
Low-income economies			**24,110 t**	**21,674 t**	**5,656 t**	**7,282 t**	**177 w**	**657 w**	**120 w**
China and India			**15,101 t**	**10,403 t**	**1,582 t**	**566 t**	**230 w**	**923 w**	**123 w**
Other low-income			**9,009 t**	**11,271 t**	**4,074 t**	**6,716 t**	**78 w**	**197 w**	**112 w**
1 Ethiopia	1,663	1,511	118	986	54	869	4	35	97
2 Bangladesh	5,922	7,393	1,866	2,102	2,076	1,500	142	611	110
3 Burkina Faso	461	607	99	113	28	124	3	50	114
4 Mali	717	816	281	281	107	266	29	75	114
5 Bhutan	. .	. .	3	16	0	5	0	25	110
6 Mozambique	. .	477	62	426	34	366	27	48	98
7 Nepal	1,102	1,456	18	18	0	9	30	198	116
8 Malawi	258	426	17	23	(.)	5	52	183	105
9 Zaire	2,518	3,362	343	331	1	138	8	14	113
10 Burma	1,705	3,519	26	0	9	0	34	158	129
11 Burundi	468	598	7	20	6	17	5	21	106
12 Togo	238	325	6	79	11	23	3	21	103
13 Madagascar	1,111	1,293	114	205	7	98	56	46	112
14 Niger	1,466	1,070	155	247	73	218	1	5	96
15 Benin	410	515	8	54	9	21	33	30	121
16 Central African Rep.	256	333	7	17	1	12	11	2	105
17 India	46,456	61,710	5,261	9	1,582	304	114	394	120
18 Rwanda	295	614	3	24	19	36	3	7	106
19 Somalia	589	911	42	344	111	248	31	23	102
20 Kenya	1,198	2,263	15	365	2	340	224	376	99
21 Tanzania	1,834	2,088	431	231	148	127	30	44	108
22 Sudan	1,754	1,511	125	1,082	46	812	31	30	103
23 China	69,147	139,482	9,840	10,394	0	262	418	1,806	125
24 Haiti	. .	. .	83	227	25	101	4	36	104
25 Guinea	. .	805	63	140	49	47	18	1	102
26 Sierra Leone	259	358	72	81	10	21	13	7	108
27 Senegal	603	615	341	510	27	130	20	51	105
28 Ghana	2,320	2,398	177	292	33	94	9	77	118
29 Pakistan	5,007	7,231	1,274	982	584	411	168	594	114
30 Sri Lanka	812	1,294	951	1,071	271	276	496	767	98
31 Zambia	473	659	93	247	5	112	71	130	107
32 *Afghanistan*	. .	. .	5	50	10	50	24	70	104
33 *Chad*	416	. .	37	134	20	163	7	18	106
34 *Kampuchea, Dem.*	. .	. .	223	60	226	22	13	16	153
35 *Lao PDR*	. .	. .	53	38	8	5	4	6	129
36 *Uganda*	2,558	3,031	37	20	0	30	13	2	125
37 *Viet Nam*	. .	. .	1,854	455	64	21	512	627	122
Middle-income economies			**44,161 t**	**73,509 t**	**2,325 t**	**4,881 t**	**291 w**	**558 w**	**110 w**
Lower middle-income			**15,865 t**	**28,415 t**	**1,942 t**	**4,787 t**	**149 w**	**395 w**	**111 w**
38 Mauritania	200	222	115	240	48	135	6	23	94
39 Bolivia	380	496	209	459	22	111	13	25	101
40 Lesotho	88	. .	49	118	14	72	17	151	93
41 Liberia	235	373	42	116	3	20	55	75	114
42 Indonesia	12,037	22,011	1,919	1,444	301	270	119	746	117
43 Yemen, PDR	. .	. .	149	357	(.)	25	0	130	100
44 Yemen, Arab Rep.	452	825	158	654	33	34	1	118	112
45 Morocco	2,784	3,214	891	2,270	75	518	130	295	113
46 Philippines	5,115	9,104	817	1,524	89	68	214	319	103
47 Egypt, Arab Rep.	3,283	4,885	3,877	8,904	610	1,951	1,282	3,639	115
48 Côte d'Ivoire	1,999	2,853	172	272	4	0	71	95	115
49 Papua New Guinea	662	*958*	71	144	. .	. .	76	182	109
50 Zimbabwe	556	955	56	106	0	131	466	579	100
51 Honduras	477	702	52	99	31	118	160	159	104
52 Nicaragua	400	533	44	114	3	43	184	557	90
53 Dominican Rep.	953	*1,235*	252	492	16	107	354	288	113
54 Nigeria	17,943	18,858	389	2,199	7	0	3	87	109
55 Thailand	5,631	10,132	97	174	0	4	76	250	119
56 Cameroon	1,233	2,245	81	139	4	12	28	63	107
57 El Salvador	740	847	75	224	4	194	1,048	1,132	100
58 Botswana	20	72	21	112	5	39	14	10	96
59 Paraguay	733	*1,565*	71	83	10	4	58	46	111
60 Jamaica	213	236	340	454	1	225	886	473	109
61 Peru	2,245	2,432	637	1,187	37	216	297	224	111
62 Turkey	8,701	13,776	1,276	1,022	16	0	166	625	108
63 Mauritius	178	169	160	184	22	9	2,081	2,538	105
64 Congo, People's Rep.	147	184	34	90	2	1	112	24	104
65 Ecuador	1,054	1,523	152	293	13	18	123	297	104
66 Tunisia	712	1,602	307	732	59	192	82	157	114
67 Guatemala	. .	. .	138	164	9	23	224	375	108

Note: For data comparability and coverage, see the technical notes. Figures in italics are for years other than those specified.

	Value added in agriculture (millions of 1980 dollars)		Cereal imports (thousands of metric tons)		Food aid in cereals (thousands of metric tons)		Fertilizer consumption (hundreds of grams of plant nutrient per hectare of arable land)		Average index of food production per capita (1979–81 = 100)
	1970	1985	1974	1985	1974/75	1984/85	1970[a]	1984	1983–85
68 Costa Rica	666	949	110	146	1	164	1,086	1,391	100
69 Colombia	4,248	7,106	503	1,021	28	4	310	558	103
70 Chile	1,597	2,262	1,737	486	323	10	317	249	103
71 Jordan	187	327	171	720	79	28	20	394	121
72 Syrian Arab Rep.	1,057	2,572	339	1,081	47	31	67	319	108
73 Lebanon	. .	. .	354	590	26	15	1,279	1,191	112
Upper middle-income			28,296 t	45,094 t	383 t	94 t	402 w	684 w	108 w
74 Brazil	18,425	37,540	2,485	4,857	31	10	169	304	115
75 Uruguay	913	953	70	31	6	. .	392	292	107
76 Hungary	2,816	4,385	408	134	. .	. .	1,485	2,998	111
77 Portugal	. .	2,380	1,860	2,204	(.)	(.)	411	634	100
78 Malaysia	3,391	6,274	1,017	2,218	1	. .	436	1,304	116
79 South Africa	3,571	. .	127	821			425	644	88
80 Poland	. .	. .	4,185	2,396	. .	68	1,715	2,314	106
81 Yugoslavia	5,849	8,346	992	136	. .	. .	766	1,178	102
82 Mexico	11,125	17,669	2,881	4,507	. .	6	246	602	110
83 Panama	275	375	63	115	3	1	391	411	109
84 Argentina	3,254	4,452	(.)	1			24	37	106
85 Korea, Rep. of	8,408	12,995	2,679	6,826	234	0	2,466	3,311	109
86 Algeria	1,731	4,054	1,816	5,271	54	2	174	221	108
87 Venezuela	2,477	3,620	1,270	2,793			165	411	101
88 Greece	4,929	6,164	1,341	453			858	1,611	104
89 Israel	. .	. .	1,176	1,705	53	8	1,394	1,915	117
90 Trinidad and Tobago	153	168	208	195	0	. .	640	494	95
91 Hong Kong	. .	. .	657	861	0	. .	0	0	108
92 Oman	. .	. .	52	203			0	322	. .
93 Singapore	119	132	682	907	(.)	. .	2,667	7,833	98
94 Iran, Islamic Rep.	10,314	. .	2,076	4,479	0	. .	76	699	109
95 Iraq	. .	. .	870	3,385	(.)	(.)	35	165	114
96 Romania	. .	. .	1,381	596	. .	. .	559	1,559	110
Developing economies			68,271 t	95,183 t	7,981 t	12,163 t	232 w	608 w	116 w
Oil exporters			15,964 t	34,983 t	1,038 t	2,288 t	131 w	472 w	112 w
Exporters of manufactures			31,606 t	31,025 t	1,900 t	652 t	341 w	919 w	121 w
Highly indebted countries			13,655 t	22,636 t	637 t	1,348 t	165 w	296 w	109 w
Sub-Saharan Africa			3,921 t	10,205 t	910 t	4,812 t	32 w	70 w	107 w
High-income oil exporters			1,327 t	7,180 t			58 w	959 w	. .
97 Libya	168	723	612	1,024			64	430	. .
98 Saudi Arabia	833	2,045	482	5,036			44	1,896	. .
99 Kuwait	42	. .	101	683			0	4,200	. .
100 United Arab Emirates	. .	378	132	437			0	2,991	. .
Industrial market economies			65,494 t	63,940 t			986 w	1,228 w	103 w
101 Spain	10,929	15,999	4,675	4,183			595	710	104
102 Ireland	. .	. .	631	500			3,573	6,973	108
103 Italy	22,099	25,215	8,100	7,052			962	1,684	103
104 New Zealand	. .	. .	92	78			8,875	11,468	110
105 Belgium[b]	2,370	3,220	4,585	5,322			5,686	5,382	98
106 United Kingdom	7,907	11,476	7,541	3,521			2,521	3,746	109
107 Austria	2,939	3,565	165	107			2,517	2,522	108
108 Netherlands	3,949	8,492	7,199	5,252			7,165	7,879	107
109 France	24,070	30,219	654	1,216			2,424	3,115	107
110 Australia	7,009	10,377	2	25			246	262	110
111 Finland	4,096	4,265	222	130			1,931	2,220	114
112 Germany, Fed. Rep.	14,859	19,040	7,164	6,482			4,208	4,211	110
113 Denmark	2,490	4,020	462	404			2,254	2,660	118
114 Japan	39,216	41,435	19,557	26,720			3,849	4,365	106
115 Sweden	4,067	4,477	301	111			1,639	1,603	108
116 Canada	8,501	10,634	1,513	692			192	484	110
117 Norway	2,035	2,455	713	227			2,471	2,970	109
118 Switzerland	. .	. .	1,458	926			3,842	4,296	108
119 United States	61,880	85,063	460	992			800	1,041	100
Nonreporting nonmember economies			15,476 t	49,800 t			561 w	1,111 w	110 w
120 Albania	. .	. .	48	3			745	1,446	109
121 Angola	. .	. .	149	377	0	78	45	25	102
122 Bulgaria	. .	. .	649	1,140			1,446	2,437	101
123 Cuba	. .	. .	1,622	2,073			1,539	1,642	110
124 Czechoslovakia	. .	. .	1,296	598			2,402	3,435	118
125 German Dem. Rep.	. .	. .	2,821	2,083			3,202	2,901	105
126 Korea, Dem. Rep.	. .	. .	1,108	200			1,484	3,452	116
127 Mongolia	. .	. .	28	75			18	122	111
128 USSR	. .	. .	7,755	43,251			437	988	110

a. Average for 1969–71. b. Includes Luxembourg.

Table 7. Structure of manufacturing

	Value added in manufacturing (millions of 1980 dollars)		Distribution of manufacturing value added (percent; 1980 prices)									
			Food and agriculture		Textiles and clothing		Machinery and transport equipment		Chemicals		Other[a]	
	1970	1984	1970	1984	1970	1984	1970	1984	1970	1984	1970	1984
Low-income economies												
China and India												
Other low-income												
1 Ethiopia	282	*453*	30	*38*	34	*28*	1	..	2	2	33	*32*
2 Bangladesh	659	1,381	18	15	51	39	3	6	13	24	15	16
3 Burkina Faso	..	..	72	*63*	10	*16*	2	*1*	(.)	..	16	*19*
4 Mali	..	..	22	*25*	54	*57*	5	*6*	2	*2*	17	*10*
5 Bhutan	..	..	..	..	..	..	..	..	..	..	..	..
6 Mozambique	..	*178*	40	..	16	..	5	..	5	..	33	..
7 Nepal	..	..	..	*69*	..	*13*	..	..	..	*2*	..	*17*
8 Malawi	..	..	33	46	23	16	3	..	..	..	42	38
9 Zaire	356	288	40	*44*	15	*11*	7	*9*	5	*7*	33	*29*
10 Burma	373	692	30	*37*	6	*12*	2	*2*	4	*6*	57	*44*
11 Burundi	52	101	..	*78*	..	..	..	..	..	*5*	..	*17*
12 Togo	..	67	51	*43*	38	*38*	..	..	..	..	12	*19*
13 Madagascar	..	..	22	*23*	31	*42*	10	..	4	*5*	32	*31*
14 Niger	..	..	..	*33*	..	*27*	..	..	..	*11*	..	*28*
15 Benin	69	74	..	..	..	..	..	..	..	..	..	..
16 Central African Rep.	..	47	14	*41*	72	*38*	(.)	*1*	3	*4*	11	*17*
17 India	16,281	30,035	11	12	37	26	14	19	8	11	30	32
18 Rwanda	99	210	75	*72*	..	..	..	..	2	*3*	23	*25*
19 Somalia	85	86	69	..	4	..	(.)	..	1	..	27	..
20 Kenya	263	919	39	38	10	11	11	13	10	8	29	29
21 Tanzania	353	407	23	*26*	27	*26*	7	*9*	9	*9*	34	*31*
22 Sudan	325	..	30	*38*	24	..	2	*3*	2	*4*	42	*56*
23 China	46,484[b]	143,822[b]	..	..	..	..	..	..	..	..	..	..
24 Haiti	..	..	19	..	42	..	15	..	2	..	22	..
25 Guinea	..	41	..	..	..	..	..	..	..	..	..	..
26 Sierra Leone	41	75	35	*42*	..	..	..	..	3	*6*	61	*52*
27 Senegal	366	574	55	*49*	23	*22*	..	*7*	6	*5*	15	*17*
28 Ghana	410	223	14	*27*	42	*19*	3	*1*	5	*5*	36	*49*
29 Pakistan	2,359	5,624	19	*28*	57	*23*	7	*10*	7	*21*	11	*18*
30 Sri Lanka	548	834	45	*44*	8	*15*	7	*4*	6	*7*	34	*31*
31 Zambia	524	729	49	42	8	11	10	10	8	9	26	29
32 *Afghanistan*	..	..	..	..	..	..	..	..	..	..	..	..
33 *Chad*	..	..	46	*48*	37	*34*	..	..	(.)	*(.)*	17	*18*
34 *Kampuchea, Dem.*	..	..	..	..	..	..	..	..	..	..	..	..
35 *Lao PDR*	..	..	..	..	..	..	..	..	..	..	..	..
36 *Uganda*	285	120	59	59	8	*17*	(.)	..	8	*2*	26	*22*
37 *Viet Nam*	..	..	..	..	..	..	..	..	..	..	..	..
Middle-income economies												
Lower middle-income												
38 Mauritania	..	..	91	*91*	..	..	..	..	..	..	9	*9*
39 Bolivia	331	360	24	*36*	43	*16*	1	*2*	4	*4*	28	*42*
40 Lesotho	4	22	..	..	..	..	..	..	..	..	..	..
41 Liberia	47	63	16	*24*	..	..	..	..	..	..	84	*75*
42 Indonesia	2,723	13,165	18	*20*	7	*7*	5	*7*	7	*6*	62	*60*
43 Yemen, PDR	..	..	..	..	..	..	..	..	..	..	..	..
44 Yemen Arab Rep.	43	273	..	..	..	..	..	..	..	..	..	..
45 Morocco	1,772	3,117	28	35	27	21	9	4	6	10	30	30
46 Philippines	4,383	8,644	42	*44*	11	*14*	9	*8*	6	*7*	32	*28*
47 Egypt, Arab Rep.	..	..	22	24	35	29	5	13	7	8	32	26
48 Côte d'Ivoire	376	1,229	24	*38*	24	*27*	18	*8*	6	*8*	29	*19*
49 Papua New Guinea	..	..	..	..	..	..	..	..	..	..	..	..
50 Zimbabwe	798	1,259	22	25	18	19	10	9	8	9	42	38
51 Honduras	196	316	43	*48*	13	*11*	(.)	*1*	2	*5*	41	*35*
52 Nicaragua	408	580	60	*62*	10	*14*	2	*1*	11	*7*	17	*16*
53 Dominican Rep.	527	1,082	83	*70*	5	*6*	(.)	..	3	*5*	8	*20*
54 Nigeria	2,012	8,039	32	*30*	11	*9*	10	*20*	9	*14*	39	*27*
55 Thailand	2,526	8,325	32	*23*	21	..	6	*12*	6	*8*	36	*56*
56 Cameroon	295	1,289	37	*41*	..	..	4	*2*	5	*5*	54	*52*
57 El Salvador	401	454	46	40	24	22	4	6	3	10	24	21
58 Botswana	11	52	..	..	..	..	..	..	..	..	..	..
59 Paraguay	330	737	57	*41*	17	*19*	1	*2*	3	*4*	23	*34*
60 Jamaica	533	446	41	*43*	9	*6*	7	..	11	*16*	32	*35*
61 Peru	3,020	3,549	29	*26*	17	*13*	11	*12*	5	*11*	38	*38*
62 Turkey	6,993	15,692	16	*21*	27	*16*	12	*16*	8	*11*	38	*37*
63 Mauritius	81	181	61	..	5	..	7	..	4	..	23	..
64 Congo, People's Rep.	..	177	70	*52*	2	*4*	3	..	3	*6*	21	*38*
65 Ecuador	835	2,214	51	39	19	17	(.)	*1*	3	*4*	27	*39*
66 Tunisia	353	1,375	26	*24*	28	*21*	3	*8*	10	*10*	33	*37*
67 Guatemala	..	..	39	..	16	..	4	..	17	..	24	..

Note: For data comparability and coverage, see the technical notes.   Figures in italics are for years other than those specified.

		Value added in manufacturing (millions of 1980 dollars)		Distribution of manufacturing value added (percent; 1980 prices)									
				Food and agriculture		Textiles and clothing		Machinery and transport equipment		Chemicals		Other[a]	
		1970	1984	1970	1984	1970	1984	1970	1984	1970	1984	1970	1984
68	Costa Rica	..	..	55	..	8	..	6	..	8	..	23	..
69	Colombia	3,297	5,787	37	45	18	13	5	5	6	8	34	29
70	Chile	5,275	5,422	23	27	17	10	6	3	7	8	48	52
71	Jordan	102	585	26	26	..	..	..	..	2	4	72	71
72	Syrian Arab Rep.	..	..	27	33	38	31	1	2	6	7	28	27
73	Lebanon	..	..	..	..	..	..	..	..	..	..	..	..
Upper middle-income													
74	Brazil	26,963	56,878	21	19	15	10	16	18	4	11	44	41
75	Uruguay	..	..	30	28	17	25	9	7	9	9	35	30
76	Hungary	..	..	11	11	15	10	25	29	8	12	41	38
77	Portugal	..	..	16	16	32	28	12	11	5	7	35	37
78	Malaysia	1,681	6,770	27	18	4	6	16	28	4	4	49	42
79	South Africa	9,747	..	12	14	9	8	26	20	7	9	46	50
80	Poland	..	..	22	17	19	15	23	30	7	8	29	30
81	Yugoslavia	..	..	13	11	18	15	21	24	5	7	44	42
82	Mexico	21,533	43,331	29	28	16	12	11	13	9	13	35	34
83	Panama	249	344	30	42	10	11	1	1	4	8	55	37
84	Argentina	10,192	11,044	22	24	13	9	17	15	8	12	39	40
85	Korea, Rep. of	4,239	26,650	13	9	16	17	9	29	16	11	46	35
86	Algeria	1,578	5,195	33	18	29	26	5	7	4	3	29	47
87	Venezuela	5,790	9,981	22	28	10	6	6	6	8	6	55	54
88	Greece	3,852	6,635	21	20	21	21	14	11	6	8	39	39
89	Israel	..	..	10	13	12	10	20	25	7	8	51	44
90	Trinidad and Tobago	395	308	15	27	6	7	5	15	5	8	69	43
91	Hong Kong	..	..	4	..	50	..	16	..	1	..	28	..
92	Oman	..	..	..	..	..	..	..	..	..	..	..	..
93	Singapore	1,174	3,854	8	3	8	4	20	52	3	6	61	35
94	Iran, Islamic Rep.	4,711	..	25	11	18	19	8	18	7	5	42	48
95	Iraq	..	..	19	..	24	..	18	..	4	..	35	..
96	Romania	..	..	25	16	8	9	21	34	9	11	36	30

Developing economies
Oil exporters
Exporters of manufactures
Highly indebted countries
Sub-Saharan Africa

		1970	1984	1970	1984	1970	1984	1970	1984	1970	1984	1970	1984
High-income oil exporters													
97	Libya	197	1,066	..	..	..	..	..	..	..	..	..	..
98	Saudi Arabia	2,987	8,179	7	10	..	..	..	..	..	..	93	90
99	Kuwait	696	1,790	3	8	..	..	..	..	3	7	94	85
100	United Arab Emirates	..	2,657	..	..	..	..	..	..	..	..	..	..
Industrial market economies													
101	Spain	38,119	59,816	8	13	22	15	24	20	8	8	39	44
102	Ireland	..	..	34	32	19	10	12	18	5	15	30	25
103	Italy	..	..	10	11	18	18	24	25	8	8	40	38
104	New Zealand	..	..	26	24	12	12	17	17	5	5	41	41
105	Belgium	21,791	31,497	16	19	13	9	24	24	10	12	37	35
106	United Kingdom	130,154	124,809	11	13	8	7	34	33	7	11	39	36
107	Austria	14,555	22,642	15	15	12	8	21	24	5	7	47	46
108	Netherlands	..	..	16	19	8	4	27	28	11	13	38	37
109	France	119,708	175,519	16	17	10	7	29	35	10	9	36	32
110	Australia	21,725	25,026	19	19	7	8	23	19	5	8	46	46
111	Finland	8,370	14,488	13	11	9	7	18	22	5	6	55	54
112	Germany, Fed. Rep.	215,818	265,225	10	10	8	5	37	41	8	9	38	34
113	Denmark	8,485	12,430	21	22	7	6	23	23	6	8	43	40
114	Japan	157,344	412,667	12	9	8	5	27	41	6	6	47	38
115	Sweden	23,355	29,213	9	9	6	3	28	32	5	7	52	50
116	Canada	34,285	50,007	15	13	8	7	19	24	6	7	52	48
117	Norway	7,715	9,071	15	11	6	3	27	27	5	8	47	51
118	Switzerland	..	..	12	15	9	8	26	24	8	12	45	40
119	United States	439,097	651,315	9	9	7	6	30	35	7	9	46	41
Nonreporting nonmember economies													
120	Albania	..	..	..	..	..	..	..	..	..	..	..	..
121	Angola	..	..	..	..	..	..	..	..	..	..	..	..
122	Bulgaria	..	..	30	19	17	14	11	21	6	7	36	39
123	Cuba	..	..	73	53	6	6	2	10	5	6	15	25
124	Czechoslovakia	..	..	11	8	12	9	30	40	7	8	40	34
125	German Dem. Rep.	..	..	12	9	15	12	27	34	12	13	35	32
126	Korea, Dem. Rep.	..	..	..	..	..	..	..	..	..	..	..	..
127	Mongolia	..	..	29	21	35	31	..	..	2	4	34	43
128	USSR	..	..	27	21	19	15	19	30	5	6	29	28

a. Includes unallocable data; see the technical notes. b. World Bank estimate.

Table 8. Manufacturing earnings and output

	Earnings per employee					Total earnings as percentage of value added				Gross output per employee (1980=100)			
	Growth rates		Index (1980=100)										
	1970–80	1980–85	1983	1984	1985	1970	1983	1984	1985	1970	1983	1984	1985
Low-income economies													
China and India													
Other low-income													
1 Ethiopia	−6.0	−2.7	93	89	..	24	19	18	17	63	103	128	142
2 Bangladesh	−2.9	−5.2	84	81	78	26	32	32	32	116	90	90	89
3 Burkina Faso	..	1.5	94	109	106	..	18	20	20	..	91	101	104
4 Mali	−8.4	..	..	..	..	46	..	..	..	97	..	..	..
5 Bhutan	..	..	..	..	..	..	..	..	..	..	..	..	..
6 Mozambique	..	..	..	..	..	29	41	41	41	..	..	..	..
7 Nepal	..	..	..	..	..	..	..	..	..	..	..	..	..
8 Malawi	..	..	105	..	..	36	59	..	..	121	92	..	..
9 Zaire	..	..	..	..	..	..	..	..	..	..	..	..	..
10 Burma	..	..	..	..	..	..	..	..	..	..	..	..	..
11 Burundi	−6.1	..	133	..	..	..	18	..	..	..	135	..	..
12 Togo	..	..	..	..	..	..	..	..	..	..	..	..	..
13 Madagascar	−0.8	..	..	..	..	36	..	..	..	89	..	..	..
14 Niger	..	..	..	..	..	..	..	..	..	..	..	..	..
15 Benin	..	..	..	..	..	..	25	25	25	..	..	..	..
16 Central African Rep.	..	−0.6	87	97	103	..	46	46	46	..	75	81	87
17 India	−0.2	1.6	103	106	..	47	49	49	49	84	120	123	128
18 Rwanda	..	..	..	..	..	22	..	19	..	..	..	..	..
19 Somalia	−6.4	..	68	40	..	28	31	31	32	..	67	39	31
20 Kenya	−3.4	−6.1	80	79	..	53	46	46	47	38	90	90	92
21 Tanzania	..	..	..	..	..	42	35	35	35	122	81	81	86
22 Sudan	..	..	..	..	..	31	..	..	..	..	..	..	..
23 China	..	..	..	..	..	..	..	..	..	..	..	..	..
24 Haiti	−3.1	0.2	107	106	107	..	..	..	..	..	..	..	..
25 Guinea	..	..	..	..	..	..	..	..	..	..	..	..	..
26 Sierra Leone	..	..	..	..	..	..	..	..	..	..	..	..	..
27 Senegal	..	..	..	..	..	..	42	46	46	..	..	..	..
28 Ghana	..	..	64	..	..	23	23	..	..	193	77	..	..
29 Pakistan	3.4	9.6	128	144	149	21	21	21	21	60	134	145	158
30 Sri Lanka	..	−2.0	82	89	89	..	27	27	27	70	87	94	95
31 Zambia	−3.2	−3.6	96	89	..	33	26	25	25	110	98	91	81
32 *Afghanistan*	..	..	..	..	..	..	..	..	..	..	..	..	..
33 *Chad*	..	..	..	..	..	..	..	..	..	..	..	..	..
34 *Kampuchea, Dem.*	..	..	..	..	..	..	..	..	..	..	..	..	..
35 *Lao PDR*	..	..	..	..	..	..	..	..	..	..	..	..	..
36 *Uganda*	..	..	..	..	..	..	..	..	..	..	..	..	..
37 *Viet Nam*	..	..	..	..	..	..	..	..	..	..	..	..	..
Middle-income economies													
Lower middle-income													
38 Mauritania	..	..	..	..	..	..	..	..	..	68	..	..	..
39 Bolivia	2.5	..	..	..	..	44	..	..	..	68	..	..	..
40 Lesotho	..	2.8	112	114	118	..	48	48	48	..	115	..	..
41 Liberia	..	*5.4*	102	118	..	..	..	..	..	..	..	..	..
42 Indonesia	4.7	7.3	128	128	147	26	27	24	23	42	129	126	140
43 Yemen, PDR	..	..	..	..	..	..	..	..	..	..	..	..	..
44 Yemen Arab Rep.	..	..	..	..	..	..	..	..	..	..	..	..	..
45 Morocco	..	−4.2	88	82	82	..	51	51	51	..	89	83	79
46 Philippines	−1.8	−11.5	78	67	54	21	25	25	25	107	79	67	56
47 Egypt, Arab Rep.	4.0	..	..	..	..	54	..	..	..	91	..	..	..
48 Côte d'Ivoire	−0.9	..	138	..	..	27	..	..	..	52	..	..	..
49 Papua New Guinea	3.0	−4.3	83	82	..	42	36	36	37	..	..	..	..
50 Zimbabwe	1.6	−1.9	102	92	99	43	45	45	45	98	93	85	80
51 Honduras	..	..	..	..	..	..	38	38	38	..	..	..	..
52 Nicaragua	..	−9.0	76	71	..	16	22	20	..	206	122	107	..
53 Dominican Rep.	−1.0	−0.2	98	100	..	35	22	24	23	53	88	86	..
54 Nigeria	−0.4	..	..	..	..	18	22	22	22	97	106	82	83
55 Thailand	1.1	10.5	135	151	159	25	24	24	24	70	146	160	166
56 Cameroon	..	..	..	..	..	29	37	37	37	..	..	..	..
57 El Salvador	2.4	..	90	..	..	28	28	..	..	71	92	..	..
58 Botswana	*10.4*	..	80	..	..	..	39	..	..	..	70	68	62
59 Paraguay	..	..	..	..	..	..	..	..	..	..	..	..	..
60 Jamaica	−0.2	..	..	..	..	43	..	..	..	..	..	..	..
61 Peru	..	−11.8	78	80	52	..	15	15	15	83	80	78	51
62 Turkey	3.4	−0.5	98	99	101	26	26	25	23	108	127	122	137
63 Mauritius	1.0	..	97	..	..	34	50	..	..	139	107	..	..
64 Congo, People's Rep.	..	..	..	..	..	34	..	57	..	..	..	..	..
65 Ecuador	3.2	3.7	110	121	126	27	36	36	36	87	..	..	..
66 Tunisia	4.2	−5.1	83	83	79	44	47	47	47	95	93	90	88
67 Guatemala	..	0.5	101	104	..	..	..	..	..	..	..	..	..

Note: For data comparability and coverage, see the technical notes.   Figures in italics are for years other than those specified.

	Earnings per employee					Total earnings as percentage of value added				Gross output per employee (1980=100)			
	Growth rates		Index (1980=100)										
	1970–80	1980–85	1983	1984	1985	1970	1983	1984	1985	1970	1983	1984	1985
68 Costa Rica	..	..	..	..	..	42	..	..	..	..	..	..	..
69 Colombia	−0.2	3.2	109	115	114	25	21	20	20	84	102	103	..
70 Chile	..	5.5	112	131	141	19	17	17	18	60	123	..	..
71 Jordan	..	1.9	109	104	115	37	30	29	31	..	172	204	250
72 Syrian Arab Rep.	..	4.3	109	114	..	36	42	33	..	73	138	188	..
73 Lebanon	..	..	..	..	..	..	..	..	..	..	..	..	..
Upper middle-income													
74 Brazil	3.8	..	85	..	..	22	20	19	19	71	74	..	..
75 Uruguay	..	1.1	102	78	136	..	29	20	27	..	114	113	125
76 Hungary	4.0	1.2	101	106	108	28	32	33	32	41	114	116	118
77 Portugal	2.5	1.1	105	103	106	34	45	45	44	..	106	107	112
78 Malaysia	..	..	..	..	..	..	..	..	..	..	..	..	..
79 South Africa	..	..	108	..	..	46	53	50	51	55	..	..	..
80 Poland	..	..	..	..	..	24	25	24	..	..	..	..	..
81 Yugoslavia	1.3	−4.3	91	86	..	39	33	30	29	59	105	109	77
82 Mexico	2.9	−4.1	87	90	82	39	29	27	25	80	105	113	110
83 Panama	0.2	1.8	117	106	..	32	32	30	30	67	92	87	92
84 Argentina	1.4	5.4	103	126	113	30	19	21	19	100	129	131	123
85 Korea, Rep. of	10.0	5.6	109	124	126	25	26	27	27	39	126	146	149
86 Algeria	0.2	−0.1	95	98	..	45	53	53	53	101	98	100	102
87 Venezuela	3.8	8.1	119	147	154	31	32	32	33	118	115	122	122
88 Greece	5.0	−2.3	89	90	90	32	39	39	39	57	91	91	93
89 Israel	8.8	..	55	52	..	36	43	42	..	..	..	..	..
90 Trinidad and Tobago	..	1.3	119	103	94	..	41	41	41	..	107	97	85
91 Hong Kong	..	2.2	103	110	..	..	47	49	48	..	..	..	..
92 Oman	..	..	..	..	..	..	61	61	61	..	..	..	..
93 Singapore	3.0	8.9	130	140	..	36	37	36	..	70	102	110	..
94 Iran, Islamic Rep.	..	..	..	..	..	25	..	..	..	85	..	..	..
95 Iraq	..	..	..	..	..	36	..	..	..	..	..	..	..
96 Romania	..	..	..	..	..	..	..	..	..	..	..	..	..

	Earnings per employee					Total earnings as percentage of value added				Gross output per employee (1980=100)			
	1970–80	1980–85	1983	1984	1985	1970	1983	1984	1985	1970	1983	1984	1985
High-income oil exporters													
97 Libya	..	..	..	..	..	37	..	..	..	46	..	..	..
98 Saudi Arabia	..	..	..	..	..	..	..	..	..	..	..	..	..
99 Kuwait	..	−1.5	92	98	..	12	27	27	29	96	117	..	..
100 United Arab Emirates	..	..	..	..	..	..	40	40	40	..	..	..	..
Industrial market economies													
101 Spain	4.5	3.1	108	110	116	52	45	43	41	72	114	120	128
102 Ireland	4.1	0.2	86	94	105	49	42	42	42	..	..	..	..
103 Italy	4.3	4.1	105	113	124	41	38	38	..	59	108	119	134
104 New Zealand	1.2	−2.4	94	92	90	62	62	56	54	..	..	..	..
105 Belgium	4.6	3.0	105	110	115	46	50	50	50	50	118	124	135
106 United Kingdom	1.7	5.9	106	123	132	52	44	46	46	83	119	132	..
107 Austria	3.4	2.5	103	110	114	47	55	57	57	63	111	117	124
108 Netherlands	2.5	2.1	106	108	108	52	58	58	58	69	107	114	113
109 France	..	..	..	..	..	..	..	..	..	64	105	111	..
110 Australia	2.9	1.9	106	107	111	53	56	51	51	66	99	100	110
111 Finland	2.6	2.5	105	107	115	47	44	42	42	70	109	113	128
112 Germany, Fed. Rep.	3.5	0.1	99	101	100	46	48	47	47	55	108	114	115
113 Denmark	2.5	0.5	100	98	103	56	53	52	51	64	112	113	121
114 Japan	3.1	2.5	105	109	113	32	36	36	35	40	110	121	132
115 Sweden	0.5	−0.6	96	97	96	52	37	37	35	73	121	125	134
116 Canada	1.8	−0.1	90	98	102	53	49	49	49	70	100	109	..
117 Norway	2.6	0.3	98	101	..	50	58	55	..	71	104	108	..
118 Switzerland	..	..	..	..	..	..	..	..	..	..	..	..	..
119 United States	0.1	0.1	102	98	101	47	40	40	40	63	104	..	..
Nonreporting nonmember economies													
120 Albania	..	..	..	..	..	..	..	..	..	..	..	..	..
121 Angola	..	..	..	..	..	..	..	..	..	..	..	..	..
122 Bulgaria	..	..	..	..	..	..	..	..	..	..	..	..	..
123 Cuba	..	..	..	..	..	..	..	..	..	..	..	..	..
124 Czechoslovakia	..	..	..	..	..	..	..	..	..	..	..	..	..
125 German Dem. Rep.	..	..	..	..	..	..	..	..	..	..	..	..	..
126 Korea, Dem. Rep.	..	..	..	..	..	..	..	..	..	..	..	..	..
127 Mongolia	..	..	..	..	..	..	..	..	..	..	..	..	..
128 USSR	..	..	..	..	..	..	..	..	..	..	..	..	..

Table 9. Commercial energy

	Average annual energy growth rate (percent)				Energy consumption per capita (kilograms of oil equivalent)		Energy imports as a percentage of merchandise exports	
	Energy production		Energy consumption					
	1965-80	1980-85	1965-80	1980-85	1965	1985	1965	1985
Low-income economies	**9.0** w	**6.7** w	**8.2** w	**5.7** w	**131** w	**306** w	**7** w	**32** w
China and India	**9.1** w	**6.8** w	**8.8** w	**5.9** w	**147** w	**382** w	..	..
Other low-income	**8.9** w	**3.8** w	**2.9** w	**3.9** w	**72** w	**86** w	**7** w	**33** w
1 Ethiopia	7.5	5.5	4.1	−1.8	10	17	8	43
2 Bangladesh	..	18.8	..	7.6	..	43	..	41
3 Burkina Faso	..	..	10.4	−0.4	8	20	11	..
4 Mali	37.0	25.0	7.0	4.1	15	25	16	55
5 Bhutan	..	..	..	..	..	..	..	..
6 Mozambique	19.3	−22.1	2.3	1.4	81	86	13	37
7 Nepal	18.3	16.7	5.7	8.6	6	17	..	49
8 Malawi	18.3	5.1	8.0	−2.6	25	39	7	23
9 Zaire	9.4	3.8	3.6	0.7	74	73	6	12
10 Burma	8.4	6.7	4.8	6.3	39	74	4	3
11 Burundi	..	23.7	5.4	14.8	5	26	11	18
12 Togo	7.1	−2.1	11.2	−5.4	27	47	6	..
13 Madagascar	3.9	12.5	4.7	−10.5	34	33	8	34
14 Niger	..	21.0	12.5	7.0	8	48	9	3
15 Benin	..	..	9.9	−0.7	21	35	14	23
16 Central African Rep.	6.6	1.9	2.9	2.1	22	33	7	1
17 India	5.5	9.6	5.8	6.4	100	201	8	30
18 Rwanda	8.8	9.0	15.2	6.1	8	43	10	25
19 Somalia	..	..	16.7	2.0	15	82	9	43
20 Kenya	13.1	12.2	5.0	−5.7	114	103	..	..
21 Tanzania	7.3	2.9	3.7	2.8	37	39	..	..
22 Sudan	17.8	0.8	2.0	0.3	67	61	5	51
23 China	10.0	6.2	9.8	5.7	178	515	..	..
24 Haiti	..	4.1	8.4	1.9	25	55	..	..
25 Guinea	14.9	0.2	2.0	0.7	56	53	..	..
26 Sierra Leone	..	..	0.8	−1.3	104	82	11	63
27 Senegal	..	..	7.2	−2.3	79	110	8	17
28 Ghana	17.7	−15.6	7.7	−7.4	76	131	6	9
29 Pakistan	6.5	8.8	3.3	9.4	136	218	7	52
30 Sri Lanka	10.4	9.2	2.2	3.4	107	139	6	33
31 Zambia	25.7	1.4	4.1	(.)	464	412	5	29
32 Afghanistan	15.7	2.3	5.7	11.7	30	73	8	2
33 Chad	..	..	..	..	..	..	..	1
34 Kampuchea, Dem.	..	−2.1	7.6	1.6	19	58	7	..
35 Lao PDR	..	3.5	4.2	8.0	22	58	..	..
36 Uganda	−0.5	3.3	−0.6	5.2	36	24	..	..
37 Viet Nam	5.3	−1.2	−2.6	(.)	106	76	..	..
Middle-income economies	**4.9** w	**2.9** w	**6.7** w	**2.7** w	**483** w	**886** w	**9** w	**16** w
Lower middle-income	**10.6** w	**2.0** w	**7.3** w	**4.4** w	**171** w	**358** w	**8** w	**21** w
38 Mauritania	..	..	9.4	0.4	48	127	2	23
39 Bolivia	9.4	−0.7	7.7	−1.5	156	263	1	1
40 Lesotho	..	..	..	..	..	..	..	..
41 Liberia	14.6	1.2	7.8	0.7	182	345	6	16
42 Indonesia	9.9	0.2	8.4	4.4	91	219	3	12
43 Yemen, PDR	..	..	−4.6	17.7	982	750	63	..
44 Yemen, Arab Rep.	..	..	21.0	20.0	7	117	..	..
45 Morocco	2.4	−4.5	8.3	(.)	124	237	5	50
46 Philippines	9.0	19.6	6.0	1.8	160	255	12	44
47 Egypt, Arab Rep.	10.7	9.3	6.2	7.9	313	588	11	10
48 Côte d'Ivoire	11.1	28.9	8.6	0.6	109	166	5	14
49 Papua New Guinea	13.7	7.7	13.0	3.2	56	235	7	25
50 Zimbabwe	−0.9	−4.4	5.1	−2.4	441	427	(.)	1
51 Honduras	14.0	2.5	7.6	1.7	111	201	5	28
52 Nicaragua	2.6	1.0	6.5	0.3	172	259	6	21
53 Dominican Rep.	10.9	−5.0	11.5	3.3	130	372	7	71
54 Nigeria	17.3	−4.6	12.9	9.0	34	165	7	3
55 Thailand	9.0	56.1	10.5	6.6	80	343	11	33
56 Cameroon	13.0	17.2	6.3	7.7	67	145	6	1
57 El Salvador	9.0	3.1	7.0	0.9	140	186	5	..
58 Botswana	8.8	0.1	9.4	1.2	211	380	..	..
59 Paraguay	..	15.1	9.9	6.1	86	281	14	57
60 Jamaica	−0.9	5.4	6.1	−5.0	707	954	12	59
61 Peru	6.7	−0.3	5.1	0.7	403	543	3	4
62 Turkey	4.3	7.2	8.6	6.8	258	712	12	53
63 Mauritius	2.1	2.8	7.2	−0.1	163	311	6	23
64 Congo, People's Rep.	41.1	12.4	7.8	5.7	90	232	8	1
65 Ecuador	35.0	7.8	11.6	11.1	162	720	11	1
66 Tunisia	20.4	−0.1	9.0	4.4	170	546	12	19
67 Guatemala	12.5	7.2	6.8	−2.7	150	176	9	17

Note: For data comparability and coverage, see the technical notes. Figures in italics are for years other than those specified.

	Average annual energy growth rate (percent)				Energy consumption per capita (kilograms of oil equivalent)		Energy imports as a percentage of merchandise exports	
	Energy production		Energy consumption					
	1965-80	1980-85	1965-80	1980-85	1965	1985	1965	1985
68 Costa Rica	8.2	7.1	8.8	0.6	269	534	8	*14*
69 Colombia	1.0	5.4	6.1	2.4	413	755	1	*14*
70 Chile	1.8	3.0	3.1	−1.2	657	726	5	*16*
71 Jordan	. .	. .	9.5	9.8	226	771	33	73
72 Syrian Arab Rep.	56.0	2.9	12.0	4.0	212	838	13	76
73 *Lebanon*	2.0	−8.4	2.0	−2.1	713	777	50	*33*
Upper middle-income	**3.7 w**	**3.2 w**	**6.5 w**	**2.2 w**	**826 w**	**1,510 w**	**9 w**	**14 w**
74 Brazil	8.6	12.6	10.0	3.2	286	781	14	37
75 Uruguay	3.7	20.8	1.3	−3.1	765	745	13	*30*
76 Hungary	0.9	2.7	3.9	0.7	1,825	2,974	12	21
77 Portugal	3.5	9.3	6.3	4.3	506	1,312	13	36
78 Malaysia	36.9	21.0	6.9	7.7	312	826	10	*9*
79 South Africa	5.1	3.3	4.4	0.8	1,702	2,184	10	*1*
80 Poland	4.0	1.9	4.8	0.8	2,027	3,438	. .	. .
81 Yugoslavia	3.5	3.9	5.9	2.6	898	1,926	7	31
82 Mexico	9.7	4.8	7.9	1.2	622	1,290	4	*1*
83 Panama	6.9	11.1	5.9	0.5	576	634	. .	. .
84 Argentina	4.5	3.6	4.3	2.2	975	1,468	8	*6*
85 Korea, Rep. of	4.1	9.3	12.1	5.0	237	1,241	18	24
86 Algeria	5.3	5.7	11.9	11.8	226	1,123	(.)	*2*
87 Venezuela	−3.1	−3.6	4.7	1.7	2,319	2,409	(.)	*1*
88 Greece	10.5	12.2	8.5	2.3	615	1,841	29	66
89 Israel	−15.2	−21.5	4.4	2.4	1,574	1,949	13	21
90 Trinidad and Tobago	3.8	−3.8	6.4	−5.3	2,776	3,641	. .	*4*
91 Hong Kong	. .	. .	8.4	6.6	424	1,264	4	5
92 Oman	*16.0*	14.3	30.3	14.3	14	2,683	. .	. .
93 Singapore	. .	. .	11.3	−1.1	670	2,165	17	34
94 *Iran, Islamic Rep.*	3.6	9.3	9.0	3.8	537	1,026	(.)	*4*
95 *Iraq*	6.2	−6.1	7.5	2.1	399	662	(.)	*1*
96 *Romania*	4.3	1.5	6.6	1.2	1,536	3,453	. .	
Developing economies	**5.8 w**	**4.1 w**	**7.2 w**	**3.8 w**	**251 w**	**502 w**	**8 w**	**17 w**
Oil exporters	**5.0 w**	**1.6 w**	**7.8 w**	**3.7 w**	**300 w**	**629 w**	**5 w**	**5 w**
Exporters of manufactures	**7.0 w**	**6.0 w**	**7.8 w**	**4.3 w**	**246 w**	**555 w**	**11 w**	**22 w**
Highly indebted countries	**3.6 w**	**2.1 w**	**6.9 w**	**2.3 w**	**422 w**	**776 w**	**6 w**	**10 w**
Sub-Saharan Africa	**15.7 w**	**−2.6 w**	**6.3 w**	**2.3 w**	**62 w**	**107 w**	**6 w**	**10 w**
High-income oil exporters	**6.4 w**	**−14.5 w**	**7.5 w**	**8.4 w**	**1,861 w**	**3,699 w**	**(.) w**	**2 w**
97 Libya	0.6	−7.9	17.2	11.1	222	3,042	2	6
98 Saudi Arabia	11.5	−19.6	7.2	8.1	1,759	3,653	(.)	*1*
99 Kuwait	−1.6	−4.8	1.7	7.7	. .	4,569	(.)	*4*
100 United Arab Emirates	14.7	−5.5	36.6	7.4	108	5,102	. .	. .
Industrial market economies	**2.1 w**	**1.8 w**	**3.0 w**	**0.1 w**	**3,745 w**	**4,958 w**	**11 w**	**21 w**
101 Spain	3.6	8.2	6.6	0.2	901	1,932	31	45
102 Ireland	(.)	14.2	3.9	1.8	1,504	2,627	14	11
103 Italy	1.3	1.5	3.7	0.4	1,568	2,606	16	30
104 New Zealand	4.7	9.2	3.6	3.5	2,622	3,823	7	13
105 Belgium	−3.9	14.5	2.9	−1.3	3,402	4,666	9	17
106 United Kingdom	3.6	2.6	0.8	(.)	3,481	3,603	13	14
107 Austria	0.8	−1.0	4.1	−0.7	2,060	3,217	10	18
108 Netherlands	15.2	−0.3	4.9	−0.1	3,134	5,138	12	21
109 France	−0.9	9.8	3.7	−0.4	2,468	3,673	16	25
110 Australia	10.5	5.9	5.1	0.9	3,287	5,116	10	7
111 Finland	3.9	11.4	5.4	−0.6	2,233	4,589	11	24
112 Germany, Fed. Rep.	−0.1	0.9	2.9	−0.1	3,197	4,451	8	17
113 Denmark	2.6	63.1	2.4	0.3	2,911	4,001	13	19
114 Japan	−0.4	5.0	6.0	1.4	1,474	3,116	19	32
115 Sweden	4.9	8.6	2.6	2.2	4,162	6,482	12	18
116 Canada	5.7	3.4	4.6	0.4	6,007	9,224	7	5
117 Norway	12.4	5.9	4.1	2.8	4,650	8,920	11	7
118 Switzerland	3.7	1.8	3.1	1.7	2,501	3,952	8	11
119 United States	1.1	0.2	2.3	−0.4	6,535	7,278	8	26
Nonreporting nonmember economies	**4.6 w**	**2.9 w**	**4.4 w**	**2.9 w**	**2,509 w**	**4,487 w**	**. .**	**. .**
120 *Albania*	8.7	8.2	6.8	7.5	415	1,267	. .	. .
121 *Angola*	19.9	10.3	5.3	2.4	114	207	2	*1*
122 *Bulgaria*	1.2	3.3	6.1	1.5	1,788	4,332	. .	. .
123 *Cuba*	8.1	28.1	5.8	0.9	604	1,075	12	*13*
124 *Czechoslovakia*	1.0	1.0	3.2	0.6	3,374	4,853	. .	. .
125 *German Dem. Rep.*	0.7	3.9	2.4	1.2	3,762	5,680	. .	. .
126 *Korea, Dem. Rep.*	6.4	2.7	6.6	2.9	1,196	2,118	. .	. .
127 *Mongolia*	10.3	7.4	9.5	5.5	471	1,313	. .	. .
128 *USSR*	4.9	2.9	4.5	3.3	2,603	4,885	. .	. .

Table 10. Growth of merchandise trade

	Merchandise trade (millions of dollars)		Average annual growth rate[a] (percent)				Terms of trade (1980=100)	
	Exports 1985	Imports 1985	Exports 1965-80	Exports 1980-85	Imports 1965-80	Imports 1980-85	1983	1985
Low-income economies	**52,704** t	**82,554** t	**2.7** w	**5.0** w	**2.4** w	**7.3** w	**93** m	**94** m
China and India	**37,587** t	**57,134** t	**4.8** w	**7.6** w	**4.5** w	**12.1** w	**105** m	**107** m
Other low-income	**15,117** t	**25,420** t	**0.2** w	**0.1** w	**0.3** w	**−0.5** w	**93** m	**94** m
1 Ethiopia	338	989	−0.5	−0.8	−0.9	6.8	92	100
2 Bangladesh	999	2,772	..	7.1	..	3.1	102	113
3 Burkina Faso	68	261	4.0	0.8	5.7	−5.2	95	81
4 Mali	172	363	10.2	4.2	5.3	−1.0	93	82
5 Bhutan	..	..	..	..	..	..	..	..
6 Mozambique	174	547	..	..	..	..	..	..
7 Nepal	161	459	−2.3	8.4	3.0	7.8	89	94
8 Malawi	251	287	4.3	2.9	3.3	−6.4	113	101
9 Zaire	1,568	1,178	4.4	−2.9	−1.9	−0.2	84	83
10 Burma	303	283	−2.1	0.2	−5.8	−6.7	77	70
11 Burundi	110	194	3.0	12.5	2.1	5.1	90	99
12 Togo	242	321	5.4	−4.2	8.4	−12.5	90	86
13 Madagascar	311	323	0.7	−2.8	−0.4	−11.6	.95	103
14 Niger	250	353	12.8	−17.4	6.6	−8.1	107	107
15 Benin	152	437	−2.3	−1.3	9.4	−2.3	93	89
16 Central African Rep.	115	140	−1.4	6.5	−4.8	3.7	90	95
17 India	10,260[b]	14,608	3.7	4.6	1.6	2.2	111	115
18 Rwanda	75	235	5.9	−0.9	7.3	2.1	91	102
19 Somalia	91	380	4.4	−7.4	4.4	9.2	97	90
20 Kenya	976	1,436	(.)	−3.9	1.7	−9.0	94	94
21 Tanzania	255	1,017	−4.0	−11.1	1.6	−3.9	91	90
22 Sudan	374	771	−0.3	6.1	2.4	−8.9	99	87
23 China	27,327	42,526	5.5	8.8	8.0	17.6	100	100
24 Haiti	455	512	2.5	1.3	5.5	1.9	93	95
25 Guinea	465	370	..	..	..	..	..	..
26 Sierra Leone	137	166	−3.9	−3.5	−2.7	−16.7	95	96
27 Senegal	526	862	2.4	5.2	4.1	−0.1	99	98
28 Ghana	617	727	−1.8	−7.9	−1.4	−8.6	88	91
29 Pakistan	2,740	5,890	4.3	2.4	0.5	3.9	96	95
30 Sri Lanka	1,333	1,832	0.5	7.3	−1.1	1.5	101	97
31 Zambia	829[b]	654	1.7	−0.3	−5.5	−7.7	78	72
32 Afghanistan	566	999	..	..	..	..	..	..
33 Chad	113	218	..	..	..	..	..	..
34 Kampuchea, Dem.	..	..	..	..	..	..	..	..
35 Lao PDR	19	64	..	..	..	..	..	..
36 Uganda	332	380	−3.9	4.7	−5.3	6.0	89	96
37 Viet Nam	..	..	..	..	..	..	..	..
Middle-income economies	**379,877** t	**360,816** t	**3.2** w	**3.7** w	**6.0** w	**−1.0** w	**96** m	**94** m
Lower middle-income	**91,343** t	**101,265** t	**6.8** w	**1.1** w	**5.9** w	**−1.3** w	**95** m	**93** m
38 Mauritania	374	234	2.7	14.9	6.6	−3.6	99	96
39 Bolivia	662	550	2.5	−2.4	5.0	−4.3	90	86
40 Lesotho[c]	..	..	..	..	..	..	..	..
41 Liberia	452	293	4.5	−1.4	1.5	−7.1	95	91
42 Indonesia	18,590	12,069	9.7	1.1	13.0	4.9	97	97
43 Yemen, PDR	645	1,543	−13.6	1.3	−7.3	3.7	96	100
44 Yemen, Arab Rep.	10	1,360	−0.3	1.8	25.2	−3.0	95	96
45 Morocco	2,156	3,885	3.6	3.5	6.6	0.3	86	86
46 Philippines	4,629	5,459	4.7	−2.1	2.9	−5.9	99	96
47 Egypt, Arab Rep.	4,150[b]	11,200[b]	2.0	3.9	6.0	8.0	99	93
48 Côte d'Ivoire	2,972	1,749	5.6	1.8	8.0	−10.7	92	94
49 Papua New Guinea	920	1,077	12.8	1.5	1.7	0.3	95	94
50 Zimbabwe	1,061	854	3.4	−2.7	−2.0	−7.7	95	89
51 Honduras	406	585	3.1	−7.2	2.6	−5.2	99	95
52 Nicaragua	303	849	2.4	−2.9	1.3	−0.1	95	89
53 Dominican Rep.	735	1,276	3.7	−1.5	5.0	−0.3	87	83
54 Nigeria	12,567	8,877	11.5	−9.9	15.1	−11.5	97	95
55 Thailand	7,100	9,231	8.5	8.4	4.1	2.8	84	77
56 Cameroon	2,322[b]	1,132[b]	5.2	12.2	5.6	−4.6	94	93
57 El Salvador	705	999	2.4	−5.3	2.7	1.8	92	98
58 Botswana[c]	..	..	..	..	..	..	..	..
59 Paraguay	304	502	6.5	4.0	3.6	−1.7	96	83
60 Jamaica	538	1,124	−0.2	−7.3	−1.8	(.)	95	95
61 Peru	2,966	1,835	2.3	1.4	−0.2	−10.3	84	81
62 Turkey	8,255	11,035	5.5	25.3	7.8	10.1	94	92
63 Mauritius	414	522	3.4	7.4	6.4	−1.1	86	78
64 Congo, People's Rep.	1,097	716	12.5	6.5	1.0	6.3	97	95
65 Ecuador	2,905	1,606	15.2	6.3	6.9	−4.3	97	94
66 Tunisia	1,738	2,757	8.5	−1.8	10.4	−2.8	91	91
67 Guatemala	1,060	1,175	4.9	−1.3	4.6	−6.1	93	91

Note: For data comparability and coverage, see the technical notes. Figures in italics are for years other than those specified.

	Merchandise trade (millions of dollars)		Average annual growth rate[a] (percent)				Terms of trade (1980 = 100)	
	Exports 1985	Imports 1985	Exports 1965–80	Exports 1980–85	Imports 1965–80	Imports 1980–85	1983	1985
68 Costa Rica	957	1,108	7.1	0.4	5.8	−4.4	98	97
69 Colombia	3,696	4,113	1.5	1.6	5.3	−1.4	92	97
70 Chile	3,743	2,743	7.9	2.3	1.5	−12.5	84	79
71 Jordan	789	2,733	13.5	8.3	9.8	3.1	92	93
72 Syrian Arab Rep.	1,640	3,844	11.4	0.4	8.6	−0.9	99	94
73 *Lebanon*	482	2,230	. .	. .	. .	. .	. .	. .
Upper middle-income	288,534 *t*	259,551 *t*	1.6 *w*	5.0 *w*	6.0 *w*	−0.8 *w*	97 *m*	94 *m*
74 Brazil	25,637	14,346	9.4	6.6	8.3	−9.1	87	87
75 Uruguay	855	666	4.6	(.)	1.2	−16.5	88	85
76 Hungary	8,513	8,224	. .	. .	. .	. .	. .	. .
77 Portugal	5,680	7,652	3.4	10.0	3.8	−2.4	87	90
78 Malaysia	15,282	12,302	4.4	10.7	2.2	6.4	88	85
79 South Africa[c]	16,523	11,469	7.9	−3.0	0.1	−8.8	86	85
80 Poland	11,447	10,761	. .	. .	. .	. .	. .	. .
81 Yugoslavia	10,700	12,207	5.6	2.1	6.6	−3.3	110	111
82 Mexico	21,866	13,459	7.7	10.1	5.7	−11.3	98	98
83 Panama	1,949	2,603	. .	−3.6	. .	−1.5	105	94
84 Argentina	8,396	3,814	4.7	3.2	1.8	−17.2	96	88
85 Korea, Rep. of	30,283	31,129	27.3	13.0	15.2	9.8	101	105
86 Algeria	13,034	9,061	1.6	0.9	13.1	−0.2	97	94
87 Venezuela	12,272	8,178	−9.4	−5.8	8.7	−9.1	96	94
88 Greece	4,539	10,134	12.0	2.5	5.3	1.8	96	91
89 Israel	6,601	10,163	8.9	5.0	6.2	3.8	94	95
90 Trinidad and Tobago	2,196	1,586	−5.5	−9.9	−5.7	−11.8	97	97
91 Hong Kong	30,184	29,705	9.5	9.4	8.3	7.7	109	110
92 Oman	4,962	3,153	. .	. .	. .	. .	. .	. .
93 Singapore	22,812	26,285	4.8	5.9	7.0	4.2	101	101
94 *Iran, Islamic Rep.*	13,186	11,658	. .	. .	. .	. .	. .	. .
95 *Iraq*	9,050	9,780	. .	. .	. .	. .	. .	. .
96 *Romania*	12,167	10,969	. .	. .	. .	. .	. .	. .
Developing economies	432,581 *t*	443,370 *t*	3.1 *w*	3.9 *w*	5.3 *w*	0.4 *w*	95 *m*	94 *m*
Oil exporters	119,837 *t*	96,319 *t*	−0.2 *w*	−0.3 *w*	7.9 *w*	−4.2 *w*	97 *m*	94 *m*
Exporters of manufactures	202,011 *t*	218,822 *t*	7.9 *w*	7.9 *w*	7.5 *w*	5.3 *w*	102 *m*	103 *m*
Highly indebted countries	117,517 *t*	85,719 *t*	0.5 *w*	1.1 *w*	6.3 *w*	−8.6 *w*	96 *m*	94 *m*
Sub-Saharan Africa	31,861 *t*	28,004 *t*	9.6 *w*	−5.0 *w*	9.8 *w*	−9.4 *w*	95 *m*	94 *m*
High-income oil exporters	63,573 *t*	44,087 *t*	4.4 *w*	−17.1 *w*	19.3 *w*	−1.1 *w*	105 *m*	107 *m*
97 Libya	10,841	6,186	−2.1	−9.1	15.0	−8.9	96	97
98 Saudi Arabia	27,403	23,697	8.8	−24.0	25.9	−0.1	106	107
99 Kuwait	10,992	6,614	−1.9	−9.2	11.8	3.8	110	108
100 United Arab Emirates	14,337	7,590	10.9	−3.9	20.2	−0.1	104	103
Industrial market economies	1,089,810 *t*	1,227,022 *t*	7.5 *w*	3.7 *w*	6.7 *w*	3.9 *w*	100 *m*	100 *m*
101 Spain	24,307	30,066	18.6	8.3	11.3	0.6	88	93
102 Ireland	10,399	10,049	9.2	9.7	7.5	3.2	105	104
103 Italy	78,943	91,123	8.1	4.7	6.3	3.2	98	97
104 New Zealand	5,731	5,982	4.5	4.8	3.3	4.8	107	94
105 Belgium[d]	53,316	56,147	7.6	3.4	7.7	1.1	95	95
106 United Kingdom	101,096	109,110	5.5	2.6	4.2	4.3	100	100
107 Austria	17,102	20,803	8.4	5.7	8.7	3.4	101	99
108 Netherlands	68,283	65,212	8.3	3.4	6.3	2.6	101	104
109 France	97,457	107,588	8.9	2.2	8.9	1.1	99	103
110 Australia	22,760	25,890	6.1	5.7	2.1	4.2	97	90
111 Finland	13,609	13,226	5.6	3.2	5.0	1.0	101	102
112 Germany, Fed. Rep.	25,684	25,268	7.9	4.6	7.2	2.6	99	98
113 Denmark	17,082	18,246	5.3	6.0	4.4	3.8	99	100
114 Japan	175,858	130,488	11.5	7.3	8.7	2.4	106	113
115 Sweden	30,403	28,538	5.0	6.4	4.5	3.8	100	104
116 Canada	87,502	81,477	6.0	8.8	7.0	5.4	97	92
117 Norway	19,853	15,556	7.2	5.8	5.5	4.2	109	115
118 Switzerland	27,281	30,626	5.9	3.5	5.4	3.6	112	107
119 United States	213,144	361,627	6.7	−2.8	6.6	8.4	112	114
Nonreporting nonmember economies	. .	. .	. .	. .	. .	. .	. .	. .
120 *Albania*	. .	. .	. .	. .	. .	. .	. .	. .
121 *Angola*	*2,061*	*1,018*	. .	. .	. .	. .	. .	. .
122 *Bulgaria*	13,341	13,647	. .	. .	. .	. .	. .	. .
123 *Cuba*	. .	. .	. .	. .	. .	. .	. .	. .
124 *Czechoslovakia*	17,554	17,548	. .	. .	. .	. .	. .	. .
125 *German Dem. Rep.*	25,684	25,268	. .	. .	. .	. .	. .	. .
126 *Korea, Dem. Rep.*	. .	. .	. .	. .	. .	. .	. .	. .
127 *Mongolia*	. .	. .	. .	. .	. .	. .	. .	. .
128 *USSR*	87,201	82,596	. .	. .	. .	. .	. .	. .

a. See the technical notes.   b. World Bank estimate.   c. Figures are for the South African Customs Union comprising South Africa, Namibia, Botswana, and Swaziland; trade between the component territories is excluded.   d. Includes Luxembourg.

Table 11. Structure of merchandise exports

Percentage share of merchandise exports

	Fuels, minerals, and metals		Other primary commodities		Machinery and transport equipment		Other manufactures		(Textiles and clothing)[a]	
	1965	1985	1965	1985	1965	1985	1965	1985	1965	1985
Low-income economies	..	25 w	..	31 w	..	4 w	..	41 w	..	20 w
China and India	..	25 w	..	22 w	..	5 w	..	47 w	..	23 w
Other low-income	24 w	23 w	67 w	53 w	1 w	1 w	9 w	23 w	4 w	13 w
1 Ethiopia	(.)	10	100	89	0	(.)	(.)	1	(.)	(.)
2 Bangladesh	..	3	..	32	..	(.)	..	65	..	55
3 Burkina Faso	1	(.)	94	89	1	4	4	6	2	2
4 Mali	1	2	96	81	1	1	2	16	1	3
5 Bhutan	..	..	..	..	..	..	..	..	..	..
6 Mozambique	14	12	84	64	(.)	1	2	24	1	(.)
7 Nepal	..	(.)	..	56	..	1	..	43	..	34
8 Malawi	(.)	(.)	99	94	(.)	1	1	4	(.)	3
9 Zaire	72	74	20	17	(.)	(.)	8	10	(.)	(.)
10 Burma	5	15	94	79	(.)	1	(.)	5	(.)	(.)
11 Burundi	(.)	2	94	82	(.)	(.)	6	16	1	(.)
12 Togo	33	52	62	35	1	(.)	4	13	(.)	(.)
13 Madagascar	4	5	90	86	1	1	4	8	1	4
14 Niger	(.)	..	95	..	1	..	4	..	1	..
15 Benin	1	45	94	39	2	13	3	3	(.)	1
16 Central African Rep.	1	3	45	64	(.)	(.)	54	33	(.)	(.)
17 India	10	25	41	26	1	4	48	45	36	18
18 Rwanda	40	5	60	94	0	(.)	1	1	..	..
19 Somalia	(.)	(.)	86	98	4	1	10	1	..	..
20 Kenya	13	22	77	65	(.)	2	10	11	(.)	(.)
21 Tanzania	1	17	86	76	0	(.)	13	7	(.)	4
22 Sudan	1	2	98	94	1	1	(.)	3	(.)	1
23 China	..	25	..	21	..	6	..	48	..	24
24 Haiti	..	..	..	..	..	..	..	..	..	..
25 Guinea	..	..	..	..	..	..	..	..	..	..
26 Sierra Leone	25	34	14	33	(.)	(.)	60	32	(.)	(.)
27 Senegal	9	18	88	72	1	1	2	9	1	2
28 Ghana	13	30	85	65	1	(.)	2	5	(.)	(.)
29 Pakistan	2	2	62	35	1	2	35	61	29	45
30 Sri Lanka	2	10	97	63	(.)	1	1	26	(.)	21
31 Zambia	97	94	3	4	(.)	(.)	(.)	2	(.)	(.)
32 *Afghanistan*	(.)	..	87	..	..	..	13	..	13	..
33 *Chad*	5	..	92	..	..	..	..	..	..	..
34 *Kampuchea, Dem.*	(.)	..	99	..	(.)	..	(.)	..	(.)	..
35 *Lao PDR*	62	..	32	..	(.)	..	6	..	(.)	..
36 *Uganda*	13	(.)	86	99	(.)	(.)	1	(.)	(.)	(.)
37 *Viet Nam*	..	..	..	..	..	..	..	..	..	..
Middle-income economies	34 w	40 w	46 w	19 w	4 w	14 w	15 w	27 w	5 w	9 w
Lower middle-income	28 w	51 w	63 w	29 w	1 w	3 w	7 w	17 w	2 w	7 w
38 Mauritania	94	58	5	41	1	(.)	(.)	1	(.)	(.)
39 Bolivia	93	82	3	12	0	1	4	6	(.)	1
40 Lesotho[b]	..	..	..	..	..	..	..	..	..	..
41 Liberia	72	65	25	34	1	(.)	3	1	(.)	0
42 Indonesia	43	75	53	14	3	1	1	10	(.)	2
43 Yemen, PDR	79	94	15	4	2	1	4	1	2	(.)
44 Yemen, Arab Rep.	..	..	..	..	..	..	..	..	..	..
45 Morocco	40	32	55	28	(.)	1	5	39	1	14
46 Philippines	11	13	84	36	(.)	5	6	46	1	7
47 Egypt, Arab Rep.	8	72	71	18	(.)	(.)	20	10	15	8
48 Côte d'Ivoire	2	10	93	80	1	2	4	8	1	2
49 Papua New Guinea	(.)	51	90	46	0	(.)	10	2	0	(.)
50 Zimbabwe	24	25	47	51	6	1	23	24	6	1
51 Honduras	6	7	90	84	(.)	(.)	4	9	1	1
52 Nicaragua	4	2	90	85	(.)	(.)	6	13	(.)	1
53 Dominican Rep.	10	(.)	88	76	(.)	4	2	19	(.)	(.)
54 Nigeria	32	96	65	3	0	(.)	2	(.)	(.)	(.)
55 Thailand	11	5	84	60	(.)	7	4	28	(.)	13
56 Cameroon	17	63	77	34	3	(.)	2	2	(.)	(.)
57 El Salvador	2	2	81	70	1	10	16	17	6	7
58 Botswana[b]	..	..	..	..	..	..	..	..	..	..
59 Paraguay	(.)	(.)	92	93	(.)	(.)	8	7	(.)	(.)
60 Jamaica	28	67	41	21	(.)	2	31	10	4	2
61 Peru	45	70	54	18	(.)	1	1	10	(.)	6
62 Turkey	9	10	89	36	(.)	5	2	49	1	32
63 Mauritius	0	(.)	100	69	(.)	1	(.)	30	(.)	23
64 Congo, People's Rep.	4	89	45	6	2	(.)	49	5	(.)	(.)
65 Ecuador	2	74	96	25	(.)	(.)	2	1	1	(.)
66 Tunisia	31	47	51	11	(.)	5	19	37	2	18
67 Guatemala	(.)	6	86	69	1	1	13	24	4	4

Note: For data comparability and coverage, see the technical notes.   Figures in italics are for years other than those specified.

	Percentage share of merchandise exports									
	Fuels, minerals, and metals		Other primary commodities		Machinery and transport equipment		Other manufactures		(Textiles and clothing)[a]	
	1965	1985	1965	1985	1965	1985	1965	1985	1965	1985
68 Costa Rica	(.)	(.)	84	70	1	5	15	25	2	8
69 Colombia	18	15	75	67	(.)	1	6	17	2	3
70 Chile	89	64	7	29	1	1	4	6	(.)	(.)
71 Jordan	27	32	54	16	11	14	7	38	1	7
72 Syrian Arab Rep.	1	65	89	22	1	1	9	12	7	8
73 *Lebanon*	14	..	52	..	14	..	19	..	2	..
Upper middle-income	**37 w**	**37 w**	**38 w**	**16 w**	**6 w**	**18 w**	**20 w**	**30 w**	**6 w**	**9 w**
74 Brazil	9	15	83	44	2	14	7	27	1	3
75 Uruguay	(.)	(.)	95	62	0	1	5	36	2	16
76 Hungary	5	8	25	24	32	33	37	35	9	6
77 Portugal	4	5	34	17	3	16	58	62	24	29
78 Malaysia	35	34	59	39	2	19	4	8	(.)	3
79 South Africa[b]	24	39	44	20	3	2	29	39	1	2
80 Poland	..	..	..	..	..	..	..	..	..	..
81 Yugoslavia	10	8	33	12	24	33	33	46	8	9
82 Mexico	22	64	62	9	1	16	15	12	3	1
83 Panama	35	3	63	83	(.)	(.)	2	13	1	4
84 Argentina	1	5	93	77	1	5	5	13	(.)	1
85 Korea, Rep. of	15	4	25	5	3	36	56	55	27	23
86 Algeria	57	98	39	(.)	2	(.)	2	2	(.)	(.)
87 Venezuela	97	94	1	1	(.)	(.)	2	5	(.)	(.)
88 Greece	8	19	78	31	2	3	11	46	3	23
89 Israel	6	3	28	14	2	21	63	63	9	6
90 Trinidad and Tobago	84	84	9	2	(.)	3	7	11	(.)	(.)
91 Hong Kong	2	2	11	6	6	24	81	68	43	32
92 Oman	..	92	..	1	..	5	..	2	..	(.)
93 Singapore	21	29	44	12	10	32	24	26	6	4
94 *Iran, Islamic Rep.*	88	98	8	1	(.)	(.)	4	1	4	1
95 *Iraq*	95	99	4	1	(.)	(.)	1	(.)	(.)	(.)
96 *Romania*	..	..	..	..	..	..	..	..	..	..
Developing economies	**32 w**	**39 w**	**48 w**	**21 w**	**4 w**	**13 w**	**16 w**	**28 w**	**6 w**	**10 w**
Oil exporters	**66 w**	**84 w**	**29 w**	**7 w**	**1 w**	**4 w**	**5 w**	**6 w**	**2 w**	**1 w**
Exporters of manufactures	**9 w**	**13 w**	**40 w**	**17 w**	**11 w**	**23 w**	**40 w**	**47 w**	**18 w**	**17 w**
Highly indebted countries	**38 w**	**46 w**	**51 w**	**26 w**	**3 w**	**11 w**	**8 w**	**18 w**	**1 w**	**3 w**
Sub-Saharan Africa	**32 w**	**63 w**	**60 w**	**31 w**	**1 w**	**1 w**	**7 w**	**5 w**	**1 w**	**1 w**
High-income oil exporters	**98 w**	**98 w**	**1 w**	**(.) w**	**1 w**	**1 w**	**(.) w**	**1 w**	**(.) w**	**(.) w**
97 Libya	99	98	1	(.)	1	1	(.)	1	(.)	(.)
98 Saudi Arabia	98	98	1	(.)	1	1	1	1	(.)	(.)
99 Kuwait	98	95	1	(.)	1	1	(.)	3	(.)	(.)
100 United Arab Emirates	99	95	1	1	0	1	0	(.)	0	(.)
Industrial market economies	**9 w**	**11 w**	**21 w**	**13 w**	**31 w**	**40 w**	**38 w**	**37 w**	**7 w**	**4 w**
101 Spain	9	12	51	17	10	27	29	44	6	4
102 Ireland	3	3	63	27	5	30	29	39	7	5
103 Italy	8	6	14	9	30	32	47	53	15	13
104 New Zealand	1	7	94	67	(.)	5	5	21	(.)	3
105 Belgium[c]	13	11	11	12	20	23	55	53	12	7
106 United Kingdom	7	24	10	8	41	32	41	35	7	4
107 Austria	8	6	17	9	20	31	55	55	12	9
108 Netherlands	12	25	32	23	21	16	35	35	9	4
109 France	8	7	21	19	26	34	45	41	10	5
110 Australia	13	44	73	36	5	5	10	15	1	1
111 Finland	3	8	40	15	12	26	45	51	2	5
112 Germany, Fed. Rep.	7	5	5	7	46	47	42	41	5	5
113 Denmark	2	7	55	35	22	25	21	33	4	5
114 Japan	2	1	7	1	31	62	60	36	17	3
115 Sweden	9	9	23	11	35	42	33	38	2	2
116 Canada	28	22	35	17	15	40	22	21	1	1
117 Norway	21	62	28	7	17	14	34	16	2	1
118 Switzerland	3	3	7	4	30	33	60	59	10	6
119 United States	8	8	27	17	37	48	28	27	3	2
Nonreporting nonmember economies	..	..	..	..	..	..	..	..	..	..
120 *Albania*	..	..	..	..	..	..	..	..	..	..
121 *Angola*	6	97	76	3	1	(.)	17	(.)	(.)	(.)
122 *Bulgaria*	..	..	..	..	..	..	..	..	..	..
123 *Cuba*	4	..	92	..	(.)	..	4	..	(.)	..
124 *Czechoslovakia*	..	..	..	..	..	..	..	..	..	..
125 *German Dem. Rep.*	..	..	..	..	..	..	..	..	..	..
126 *Korea, Dem. Rep.*	..	..	..	..	..	..	..	..	..	..
127 *Mongolia*	..	..	..	..	..	..	..	..	..	..
128 *USSR*	..	..	..	..	..	..	..	..	..	..

a. *Textiles and clothing* is a subgroup of *other manufactures*.   b. Figures are for the South African Customs Union comprising South Africa, Namibia, Lesotho, Botswana, and Swaziland; trade between the component territories is excluded.   c. Includes Luxembourg.

Table 12. Structure of merchandise imports

Percentage share of merchandise imports

	Food		Fuels		Other primary commodities		Machinery and transport equipment		Other manufactures	
	1965	1985	1965	1985	1965	1985	1965	1985	1965	1985
Low-income economies	**20 w**	**10 w**	**5 w**	**11 w**	**8 w**	**9 w**	**31 w**	**27 w**	**35 w**	**40 w**
China and India	**..**	**11 w**	**..**	**7 w**	**..**	**11 w**	**..**	**27 w**	**..**	**45 w**
Other low-income	**19 w**	**17 w**	**6 w**	**21 w**	**4 w**	**4 w**	**28 w**	**28 w**	**43 w**	**30 w**
1 Ethiopia	6	29	6	15	6	4	37	29	44	23
2 Bangladesh	..	24	..	17	..	8	..	18	..	33
3 Burkina Faso	23	23	4	17	14	6	19	24	40	30
4 Mali	20	14	6	18	5	3	23	26	47	40
5 Bhutan	..	..	..	..	..	..	..	..	..	..
6 Mozambique	17	20	8	18	7	4	24	33	45	26
7 Nepal	..	13	..	11	..	5	..	20	..	51
8 Malawi	15	8	5	18	3	3	21	25	57	47
9 Zaire	18	11	7	20	5	2	33	36	37	31
10 Burma	15	5	4	3	5	3	18	53	58	37
11 Burundi	16	9	6	15	8	6	15	37	55	33
12 Togo	14	15	4	44	5	3	32	11	45	27
13 Madagascar	19	12	5	28	2	4	25	27	48	30
14 Niger	12	15	6	4	6	7	21	25	55	49
15 Benin	18	12	6	5	7	5	17	17	53	60
16 Central African Rep.	13	17	7	2	2	4	29	36	49	41
17 India	22	13	5	21	14	6	37	25	22	34
18 Rwanda	12	9	7	16	5	6	28	35	50	35
19 Somalia	31	22	5	18	8	4	24	32	33	24
20 Kenya	..	9	..	36	..	4	..	23	..	28
21 Tanzania	..	..	..	..	..	..	..	..	..	..
22 Sudan	23	11	5	21	4	3	21	31	47	33
23 China	..	10	..	(.)	..	13	..	27	..	50
24 Haiti	..	..	..	..	..	..	..	..	..	..
25 Guinea	..	..	..	..	..	..	..	..	..	..
26 Sierra Leone	17	27	9	35	3	2	29	15	41	21
27 Senegal	36	26	6	10	4	4	15	28	38	32
28 Ghana	12	15	4	8	3	9	33	40	48	28
29 Pakistan	20	19	3	24	5	6	38	27	34	24
30 Sri Lanka	41	15	8	26	4	3	12	24	34	32
31 Zambia	9	5	10	43	3	1	33	29	45	22
32 Afghanistan	17	..	4	..	1	..	8	..	69	..
33 Chad	13	..	20	..	4	..	21	..	42	..
34 Kampuchea, Dem.	6	..	7	..	2	..	26	..	58	..
35 Lao PDR	27	..	14	..	6	..	19	..	34	..
36 Uganda	..	..	..	..	..	..	..	..	..	..
37 Viet Nam	..	..	..	..	..	..	..	..	..	..
Middle-income economies	**15 w**	**11 w**	**8 w**	**18 w**	**11 w**	**7 w**	**30 w**	**31 w**	**37 w**	**33 w**
Lower middle-income	**16 w**	**13 w**	**7 w**	**19 w**	**6 w**	**6 w**	**31 w**	**28 w**	**40 w**	**34 w**
38 Mauritania	9	25	4	19	1	2	56	35	30	20
39 Bolivia	19	23	1	2	3	3	34	25	42	48
40 Lesotho[a]	..	..	..	..	..	..	..	..	..	..
41 Liberia	17	24	8	20	3	3	33	27	39	27
42 Indonesia	6	6	3	20	2	7	39	36	50	31
43 Yemen, PDR	19	23	39	37	5	3	10	19	26	17
44 Yemen, Arab Rep.	..	..	..	..	..	..	..	..	..	..
45 Morocco	36	17	5	28	10	13	18	18	31	24
46 Philippines	20	8	10	27	7	5	33	21	30	39
47 Egypt, Arab Rep.	26	25	7	4	12	10	23	25	31	36
48 Côte d'Ivoire	18	16	6	22	3	4	28	22	46	36
49 Papua New Guinea	23	15	4	21	3	2	25	29	45	33
50 Zimbabwe	7	5	(.)	1	4	3	41	65	47	26
51 Honduras	11	10	6	22	1	2	26	18	56	47
52 Nicaragua	12	13	5	19	2	1	30	21	51	46
53 Dominican Rep.	24	14	10	36	4	3	23	17	40	29
54 Nigeria	9	21	6	5	3	3	34	35	48	37
55 Thailand	6	5	9	23	6	8	31	29	49	34
56 Cameroon	11	17	5	2	4	2	28	38	51	41
57 El Salvador	15	20	5	9	4	4	28	21	48	46
58 Botswana[a]	..	..	..	..	..	..	..	..	..	..
59 Paraguay	14	8	14	27	2	3	37	33	33	29
60 Jamaica	21	19	9	23	5	3	23	22	42	32
61 Peru	17	25	3	3	5	3	41	38	34	31
62 Turkey	6	5	10	36	10	7	37	25	37	26
63 Mauritius	35	25	5	19	3	5	15	12	42	39
64 Congo, People's Rep.	15	12	6	2	1	2	34	48	44	36
65 Ecuador	10	10	9	2	4	5	33	36	44	47
66 Tunisia	16	15	6	11	7	10	31	31	41	33
67 Guatemala	11	9	7	17	2	4	29	18	50	53

Note: For data comparability and coverage, see the technical notes. Figures in italics are for years other than those specified.

	Food		Fuels		Other primary commodities		Machinery and transport equipment		Other manufactures	
	1965	1985	1965	1985	1965	1985	1965	1985	1965	1985
68 Costa Rica	9	10	5	17	2	3	29	18	54	52
69 Colombia	8	10	1	11	10	7	45	35	35	37
70 Chile	20	18	6	21	10	5	35	22	30	33
71 Jordan	28	19	6	22	6	4	18	20	42	35
72 Syrian Arab Rep.	22	18	10	34	9	4	16	19	43	24
73 *Lebanon*	28	..	9	..	9	..	17	..	36	..
Upper middle-income	**15** *w*	**10** *w*	**8** *w*	**17** *w*	**13** *w*	**7** *w*	**29** *w*	**32** *w*	**35** *w*	**33** *w*
74 Brazil	20	9	21	53	9	5	22	15	28	17
75 Uruguay	7	8	17	36	16	8	24	19	36	30
76 Hungary	12	7	11	22	22	10	27	27	28	34
77 Portugal	16	15	8	26	19	11	27	22	30	26
78 Malaysia	25	11	12	10	10	5	22	46	32	28
79 South Africa[a]	5	6	5	1	11	5	42	55	37	34
80 Poland	..	..	..	..	..	..	..	..	..	..
81 Yugoslavia	16	5	6	27	19	14	28	25	32	30
82 Mexico	5	17	2	3	10	6	50	45	33	29
83 Panama	11	10	21	26	2	1	21	22	45	40
84 Argentina	6	4	10	10	21	11	25	32	38	43
85 Korea, Rep. of	15	6	7	24	26	13	13	34	38	23
86 Algeria	27	19	(.)	2	6	6	15	32	52	41
87 Venezuela	12	19	1	1	5	6	44	43	39	31
88 Greece	15	13	8	30	11	7	35	23	30	28
89 Israel	16	9	6	16	12	6	28	27	38	42
90 Trinidad and Tobago	12	17	49	3	2	5	16	37	21	38
91 Hong Kong	25	10	3	5	13	7	13	24	46	55
92 Oman	..	14	..	2	..	2	..	41	..	41
93 Singapore	23	9	13	29	19	5	14	31	30	26
94 *Iran, Islamic Rep.*	16	12	(.)	5	6	6	36	39	42	38
95 *Iraq*	24	15	(.)	1	7	2	25	45	44	37
96 *Romania*	..	..	..	..	..	..	..	..	..	..
Developing economies	**16** *w*	**11** *w*	**7** *w*	**17** *w*	**10** *w*	**7** *w*	**30** *w*	**30** *w*	**36** *w*	**34** *w*
Oil exporters	**14** *w*	**16** *w*	**6** *w*	**7** *w*	**6** *w*	**6** *w*	**34** *w*	**37** *w*	**40** *w*	**35** *w*
Exporters of manufactures	**19** *w*	**9** *w*	**8** *w*	**20** *w*	**16** *w*	**9** *w*	**25** *w*	**27** *w*	**31** *w*	**35** *w*
Highly indebted countries	**14** *w*	**12** *w*	**7** *w*	**21** *w*	**10** *w*	**7** *w*	**34** *w*	**29** *w*	**35** *w*	**31** *w*
Sub-Saharan Africa	**15** *w*	**18** *w*	**6** *w*	**13** *w*	**4** *w*	**3** *w*	**30** *w*	**32** *w*	**45** *w*	**34** *w*
High-income oil exporters	**22** *w*	**10** *w*	**2** *w*	**3** *w*	**5** *w*	**3** *w*	**32** *w*	**44** *w*	**40** *w*	**40** *w*
97 Libya	13	10	4	10	3	3	36	36	43	40
98 Saudi Arabia	30	10	1	1	5	3	27	45	37	41
99 Kuwait	22	10	1	5	7	3	32	44	39	38
100 United Arab Emirates	..	..	..	..	..	..	..	..	..	..
Industrial market economies	**19** *w*	**10** *w*	**11** *w*	**20** *w*	**20** *w*	**8** *w*	**19** *w*	**29** *w*	**31** *w*	**33** *w*
101 Spain	19	10	10	36	16	12	27	22	28	21
102 Ireland	18	12	8	12	10	5	25	31	39	40
103 Italy	24	14	16	27	24	12	15	21	21	27
104 New Zealand	7	6	7	13	10	5	33	36	43	41
105 Belgium[b]	14	11	9	17	21	10	24	23	32	39
106 United Kingdom	30	11	11	13	25	8	11	32	23	36
107 Austria	14	6	7	15	13	9	31	30	35	40
108 Netherlands	15	14	10	22	13	6	25	23	37	35
109 France	19	10	15	22	18	8	20	25	27	35
110 Australia	5	5	8	7	10	4	37	42	41	42
111 Finland	10	5	10	24	12	8	35	30	34	33
112 Germany, Fed. Rep.	22	12	8	20	21	9	13	23	35	37
113 Denmark	14	11	11	17	11	6	25	26	39	40
114 Japan	22	14	20	44	38	16	9	9	11	18
115 Sweden	12	6	11	19	12	7	30	33	36	35
116 Canada	10	6	7	6	9	5	40	56	34	28
117 Norway	10	6	7	9	12	7	38	38	32	40
118 Switzerland	16	8	6	10	11	6	24	26	43	50
119 United States	19	7	10	16	20	5	14	38	36	35
Nonreporting nonmember economies	**..**	**..**	**..**	**..**	**..**	**..**	**..**	**..**	**..**	**..**
120 *Albania*	..	..	..	..	..	..	..	..	..	..
121 *Angola*	17	26	2	3	3	2	24	36	54	33
122 *Bulgaria*	..	..	..	..	..	..	..	..	..	..
123 *Cuba*	29	..	10	..	3	..	15	..	43	..
124 *Czechoslovakia*	..	..	..	..	..	..	..	..	..	..
125 *German Dem. Rep.*	..	..	..	..	..	..	..	..	..	..
126 *Korea, Dem. Rep.*	..	..	..	..	..	..	..	..	..	..
127 *Mongolia*	..	..	..	..	..	..	..	..	..	..
128 *USSR*	..	..	..	..	..	..	..	..	..	..

a. Figures are for the South African Customs Union comprising South Africa, Namibia, Lesotho, Botswana, and Swaziland; trade between the component territories is excluded.   b. Includes Luxembourg.

Table 13. Origin and destination of merchandise exports

	Destination of merchandise exports (percentage of total)							
	Industrial market economies		Nonreporting nonmember economies		High-income oil exporters		Developing economies[a]	
Origin	1965	1985	1965	1985	1965	1985	1965	1985
Low-income economies	..	**52** w	..	**4** w	..	**4** w	..	**41** w
China and India	..	**45** w	..	**8** w	..	**2** w	..	**45** w
Other low-income	**65** w	**60** w	**4** w	**3** w	**2** w	**6** w	**29** w	**32** w
1 Ethiopia	78	71	3	8	6	4	14	17
2 Bangladesh	..	48	..	4	..	2	..	46
3 Burkina Faso	17	35	..	..	..	..	83	65
4 Mali	7	54	4	..	..	(.)	89	45
5 Bhutan	..	15	..	..	..	..	..	85
6 Mozambique	24	44	4	..	(.)	4	72	52
7 Nepal	..	39	..	4	..	(.)	..	57
8 Malawi	69	61	(.)	..	(.)	..	31	39
9 Zaire	93	66	(.)	..	(.)	(.)	7	34
10 Burma	29	28	7	4	1	3	63	66
11 Burundi	24	81	..	(.)	..	(.)	76	19
12 Togo	92	54	2	(.)	..	..	6	46
13 Madagascar	85	90	(.)	1	(.)	1	15	8
14 Niger	61	..	(.)	..	(.)	..	39	..
15 Benin	88	92	..	..	..	..	12	8
16 Central African Rep.	71	66	..	..	..	(.)	29	33
17 India	58	57	15	17	2	6	25	20
18 Rwanda	96	81	..	..	..	(.)	4	19
19 Somalia	40	18	(.)	..	3	67	57	15
20 Kenya	69	51	1	1	1	1	29	48
21 Tanzania	66	63	(.)	4	1	1	33	32
22 Sudan	56	29	9	(.)	4	36	31	34
23 China	..	41	..	5	..	1	..	53
24 Haiti	..	95	..	..	..	(.)	..	5
25 Guinea	..	89	..	..	..	(.)	..	11
26 Sierra Leone	92	97	(.)	..	(.)	..	8	3
27 Senegal	92	..	(.)	..	..	..	7	..
28 Ghana	74	86	14	(.)	(.)	(.)	12	14
29 Pakistan	48	49	4	5	3	13	46	32
30 Sri Lanka	56	45	6	5	3	6	35	44
31 Zambia	87	71	2	..	..	(.)	12	29
32 *Afghanistan*	47	..	27	..	..	..	26	..
33 *Chad*	64	78	..	..	2	..	34	22
34 *Kampuchea, Dem.*	36	..	6	..	..	..	58	..
35 *Lao PDR*	9	..	..	..	..	..	91	..
36 *Uganda*	69	88	(.)	..	1	2	30	9
37 *Viet Nam*	..	..	..	..	..	..	..	..
Middle-income economies	**68** w	**64** w	**8** w	**7** w	**1** w	**2** w	**24** w	**28** w
Lower middle-income	**74** w	**71** w	**5** w	**2** w	**1** w	**2** w	**20** w	**25** w
38 Mauritania	96	76	(.)	..	..	(.)	4	24
39 Bolivia	97	37	..	2	..	(.)	3	61
40 Lesotho[b]	..	..	..	..	..	..	..	..
41 Liberia	98	92	..	(.)	..	(.)	2	8
42 Indonesia	72	76	4	(.)	(.)	(.)	24	24
43 Yemen, PDR	38	..	(.)	..	1	..	61	..
44 Yemen, Arab Rep.	..	23	..	..	..	13	..	64
45 Morocco	80	65	6	5	(.)	3	14	27
46 Philippines	95	78	(.)	2	(.)	1	5	18
47 Egypt, Arab Rep.	28	53	38	7	1	2	33	38
48 Côte d'Ivoire	84	71	1	5	1	(.)	15	24
49 Papua New Guinea	98	82	..	(.)	..	(.)	2	18
50 Zimbabwe	50	82	1	..	(.)	1	48	17
51 Honduras	80	81	..	1	..	2	20	17
52 Nicaragua	81	75	..	(.)	..	(.)	19	25
53 Dominican Rep.	99	84	..	7	..	(.)	1	9
54 Nigeria	91	89	1	(.)	(.)	(.)	7	11
55 Thailand	44	56	(.)	1	2	4	54	39
56 Cameroon	93	92	(.)	(.)	(.)	(.)	7	8
57 El Salvador	73	79	(.)	(.)	..	(.)	27	21
58 Botswana[b]	..	..	..	..	..	..	42	..
59 Paraguay	58	46	..	..	..	(.)	42	53
60 Jamaica	93	80	(.)	(.)	(.)	(.)	6	20
61 Peru	86	77	2	1	(.)	(.)	12	22
62 Turkey	71	51	10	3	(.)	9	19	37
63 Mauritius	94	95	..	(.)	..	(.)	6	5
64 Congo, People's Rep.	86	94	1	(.)	..	(.)	13	6
65 Ecuador	89	63	(.)	(.)	..	(.)	11	37
66 Tunisia	61	81	3	1	3	4	32	15
67 Guatemala	75	57	..	2	(.)	2	25	39

Note: For data comparability and coverage, see the technical notes.   Figures in italics are for years other than those specified.

	Destination of merchandise exports (percentage of total)							
	Industrial market economies		Nonreporting nonmember economies		High-income oil exporters		Developing economies[a]	
Origin	1965	1985	1965	1985	1965	1985	1965	1985
68 Costa Rica	79	76	(.)	(.)	0	1	20	24
69 Colombia	86	81	1	1	(.)	(.)	13	18
70 Chile	90	74	(.)	1	0	2	10	23
71 Jordan	20	9	4	1	22	19	54	70
72 Syrian Arab Rep.	26	40	14	15	8	4	53	42
73 Lebanon	43	14	3	(.)	35	66	19	20
Upper middle-income	**64 w**	**62 w**	**10 w**	**6 w**	**(.) w**	**2 w**	**26 w**	**30 w**
74 Brazil	77	62	4	5	(.)	2	19	31
75 Uruguay	76	40	4	8	(.)	3	20	49
76 Hungary	22	27	58	48	(.)	2	20	23
77 Portugal	65	85	15	4	(.)	(.)	20	11
78 Malaysia	56	52	6	2	(.)	2	37	45
79 South Africa[b]	96	84	(.)	(.)	(.)	1	4	15
80 Poland	..	32	..	36	..	1	..	31
81 Yugoslavia	40	33	33	42	(.)	2	26	23
82 Mexico	82	86	(.)	1	(.)	(.)	18	13
83 Panama	87	82	(.)	1	(.)	2	13	15
84 Argentina	67	43	7	19	(.)	(.)	27	38
85 Korea, Rep. of	75	69	(.)	(.)	(.)	6	25	25
86 Algeria	90	92	2	1	(.)	(.)	8	8
87 Venezuela	63	75	(.)	(.)	(.)	(.)	37	25
88 Greece	64	68	16	6	2	6	19	20
89 Israel	72	74	1	(.)	..	..	27	26
90 Trinidad and Tobago	92	74	(.)	(.)	(.)	(.)	8	26
91 Hong Kong	67	54	(.)	(.)	1	2	32	43
92 Oman	..	..	..	..	..	..	..	..
93 Singapore	28	47	5	1	2	4	65	48
94 Iran, Islamic Rep.	67	74	2	(.)	1	(.)	30	26
95 Iraq	83	33	1	(.)	(.)	(.)	16	67
96 Romania	..	..	..	..	..	..	..	..
Developing economies	**67 w**	**63 w**	**8 w**	**7 w**	**1 w**	**2 w**	**25 w**	**30 w**
Oil exporters	**71 w**	**77 w**	**4 w**	**2 w**	**(.) w**	**(.) w**	**25 w**	**22 w**
Exporters of manufactures	**52 w**	**53 w**	**19 w**	**9 w**	**1 w**	**3 w**	**28 w**	**35 w**
Highly indebted countries	**74 w**	**71 w**	**5 w**	**6 w**	**(.) w**	**1 w**	**21 w**	**22 w**
Sub-Saharan Africa	**78 w**	**81 w**	**2 w**	**2 w**	**1 w**	**1 w**	**19 w**	**17 w**
High-income oil exporters	**70 w**	**59 w**	**(.) w**	**(.) w**	**3 w**	**1 w**	**27 w**	**40 w**
97 Libya	97	43	(.)	(.)	(.)	(.)	3	57
98 Saudi Arabia	71	60	0	0	8	(.)	21	40
99 Kuwait	56	49	0	(.)	1	4	44	47
100 United Arab Emirates	69	75	0	(.)	2	1	30	24
Industrial market economies	**70 w**	**71 w**	**2 w**	**2 w**	**1 w**	**3 w**	**27 w**	**24 w**
101 Spain	73	66	5	4	(.)	3	21	26
102 Ireland	91	89	1	(.)	(.)	1	8	9
103 Italy	71	70	3	3	2	5	25	22
104 New Zealand	88	66	1	2	(.)	2	11	30
105 Belgium[c]	86	84	1	2	(.)	2	12	13
106 United Kingdom	63	77	2	1	1	4	33	18
107 Austria	71	73	9	7	(.)	2	19	18
108 Netherlands	83	85	1	1	1	1	15	12
109 France	68	71	2	3	(.)	2	29	24
110 Australia	69	51	4	3	1	3	27	42
111 Finland	71	65	17	23	(.)	1	12	12
112 Germany, Fed. Rep.	77	78	2	3	1	2	21	18
113 Denmark	85	81	3	1	(.)	2	12	16
114 Japan	49	58	3	2	2	4	47	36
115 Sweden	85	83	3	2	(.)	2	12	13
116 Canada	87	89	4	2	(.)	(.)	10	9
117 Norway	82	88	3	1	(.)	(.)	14	11
118 Switzerland	76	75	2	2	1	4	21	20
119 United States	61	60	(.)	1	1	3	38	36
Nonreporting nonmember economies	**..**	**..**	**..**	**..**	**..**	**..**	**..**	**..**
120 Albania	..	..	..	..	..	..	..	..
121 Angola	55	..	(.)	..	(.)	..	45	..
122 Bulgaria	..	..	..	..	..	..	..	..
123 Cuba	14	..	61	..	(.)	..	24	..
124 Czechoslovakia	..	15	..	57	..	1	..	27
125 German Dem. Rep.	..	..	..	..	..	..	..	..
126 Korea, Dem. Rep.	..	..	..	..	..	..	..	..
127 Mongolia	..	..	..	..	..	..	..	..
128 USSR	..	..	..	..	..	..	..	..

a. Includes unallocable data.   b. Figures are for the South African Customs Union comprising South Aftrica, Namibia, Lesotho, Botswana, and Swaziland; trade between the component territories is excluded.   c. Includes Luxembourg.

Table 14. Origin and destination of manufactured exports

	Manufactured exports (millions of dollars)		Destination of manufactured exports (percentage of total)							
			Industrial market economies		Nonreporting nonmember economies		High-income oil exporters		Developing economies[a]	
Origin	1965	1985	1965	1985	1965	1985	1965	1985	1965	1985
Low-income economies			**56** *w*	**45** *w*	**9** *w*	**3** *w*	**2** *w*	**4** *w*	**33** *w*	**49** *w*
China and India			..	**39** *w*	..	**5** *w*	..	**3** *w*	..	**53** *w*
Other low-income			**58** *w*	**64** *w*	**4** *w*	**4** *w*	**2** *w*	**6** *w*	**37** *w*	**27** *w*
1 Ethiopia	(.)	4	67	63	(.)	21	20	3	13	13
2 Bangladesh	..	645	..	53	..	3	..	(.)	..	43
3 Burkina Faso	1	6	2	34	..	..	..	..	98	66
4 Mali	(.)	30	14	11	8	(.)	..	..	78	89
5 Bhutan	..	(.)	..	..	..	..	..	..	..	..
6 Mozambique	3	59	27	2	5	(.)	(.)	9	68	89
7 Nepal	..	76	..	65	..	7	..	(.)	..	28
8 Malawi	(.)	14	3	39	..	..	..	..	97	61
9 Zaire	28	138	93	22	(.)	(.)	(.)	(.)	7	78
10 Burma	1	26	73	43	1	(.)	(.)	7	26	51
11 Burundi	1	16	(.)	28	..	..	..	..	99	72
12 Togo	1	30	37	11	(.)	1	..	..	63	89
13 Madagascar	5	32	80	77	..	(.)	..	6	20	17
14 Niger	1	..	43	..	..	..	..	..	57	..
15 Benin	1	13	15	82	..	..	..	..	85	18
16 Central African Rep.	14	36	60	7	..	0	..	(.)	40	93
17 India	828	5,890	55	59	11	10	2	7	32	24
18 Rwanda	(.)	1	95	93	..	..	..	..	4	7
19 Somalia	4	3	21	65	(.)	..	2	1	77	33
20 Kenya	13	128	23	8	(.)	(.)	2	1	75	91
21 Tanzania	23	31	93	86	(.)	2	(.)	1	7	12
22 Sudan	2	..	79	..	(.)	..	2	..	20	..
23 China	..	13,380	..	32	..	3	..	2	..	63
24 Haiti	..	337	..	99	..	..	..	(.)	..	1
25 Guinea	..	5	..	44	..	..	..	3	..	53
26 Sierra Leone	53	29	99	99	(.)	..	..	..	1	1
27 Senegal	4	..	48	..	(.)	..	..	..	52	..
28 Ghana	7	26	60	40	10	..	..	1	29	60
29 Pakistan	190	1,731	40	59	7	5	2	12	52	24
30 Sri Lanka	5	398	59	89	5	(.)	(.)	(.)	36	10
31 Zambia	1	21	14	67	(.)	..	..	1	86	32
32 *Afghanistan*	11	..	98	..	(.)	..	..	..	2	..
33 *Chad*	1	11	6	11	..	..	25	..	69	89
34 *Kampuchea, Dem.*	1	..	28	..	1	..	..	..	71	..
35 *Lao PDR*	(.)	..	14	..	..	..	..	..	88	..
36 *Uganda*	1	3	7	81	(.)	..	..	1	93	18
37 *Viet Nam*	..	..	..	..	..	..	..	..	..	..
Middle-income economies			**45** *w*	**57** *w*	**22** *w*	**9** *w*	**1** *w*	**4** *w*	**33** *w*	**31** *w*
Lower middle-income			**38** *w*	**55** *w*	**11** *w*	**2** *w*	**6** *w*	**6** *w*	**46** *w*	**37** *w*
38 Mauritania	1	2	61	34	..	..	..	(.)	39	66
39 Bolivia	6	54	86	71	..	..	..	(.)	14	29
40 Lesotho[b]	..	..	..	..	..	..	..	..	..	..
41 Liberia	4	5	77	60	..	..	..	(.)	23	39
42 Indonesia	27	2,365	25	50	2	(.)	..	4	73	46
43 Yemen, PDR	11	5	32	33	..	4	6	2	62	61
44 Yemen, Arab Rep.	..	7	..	70	..	..	..	23	..	7
45 Morocco	23	876	63	52	5	7	(.)	6	32	36
46 Philippines	43	2,534	93	77	..	(.)	(.)	2	7	21
47 Egypt, Arab Rep.	126	375	20	37	44	36	4	5	32	21
48 Côte d'Ivoire	15	273	50	32	(.)	(.)	(.)	(.)	50	68
49 Papua New Guinea	5	27	100	85	..	0	..	(.)	(.)	15
50 Zimbabwe	116	167	12	78	2	..	(.)	..	86	22
51 Honduras	6	58	2	28	..	..	..	..	98	72
52 Nicaragua	8	56	4	38	..	..	..	(.)	96	62
53 Dominican Rep.	3	155	95	87	..	..	..	(.)	5	13
54 Nigeria	17	78	85	64	(.)	(.)	(.)	(.)	15	36
55 Thailand	30	2,583	39	63	(.)	(.)	(.)	6	61	31
56 Cameroon	6	47	46	47	..	(.)	(.)	(.)	54	52
57 El Salvador	32	231	1	46	..	..	..	(.)	99	53
58 Botswana[b]	..	..	..	..	..	..	..	..	..	..
59 Paraguay	5	50	93	49	..	..	..	..	7	51
60 Jamaica	64	89	93	38	(.)	..	..	(.)	7	62
61 Peru	5	236	51	72	(.)	(.)	..	(.)	49	27
62 Turkey	11	3,849	83	56	1	1	(.)	7	15	36
63 Mauritius	(.)	115	16	89	..	..	..	(.)	84	11
64 Congo, People's Rep.	24	59	88	39	1	..	..	..	11	61
65 Ecuador	3	21	25	19	..	(.)	..	..	75	81
66 Tunisia	23	756	19	70	3	1	5	4	73	25
67 Guatemala	26	278	9	3	..	..	..	..	91	97

Note: For data comparability and coverage, see the technical notes.   Figures in italics are for years other than those specified.

Origin	Manufactured exports (millions of dollars)		Destination of manufactured exports (percentage of total)							
			Industrial market economies		Nonreporting nonmember economies		High-income oil exporters		Developing economies[a]	
	1965	1985	1965	1985	1965	1985	1965	1985	1965	1985
68 Costa Rica	18	*320*	6	*41*	..	..	..	*(.)*	94	*59*
69 Colombia	35	*611*	43	*58*	(.)	*1*	(.)	*(.)*	57	*41*
70 Chile	28	*255*	38	*35*	(.)	..	..	*(.)*	62	*65*
71 Jordan	5	*408*	49	8	(.)	*(.)*	23	19	28	73
72 Syrian Arab Rep.	16	*246*	5	6	12	66	25	7	59	20
73 *Lebanon*	29	*457*	19	*15*	1	..	61	70	19	15
Upper middle-income			**46 w**	**57 w**	**23 w**	**9 w**	**1 w**	**3 w**	**31 w**	**31 w**
74 Brazil	134	*8,911*	40	52	1	*1*	(.)	*3*	59	*43*
75 Uruguay	10	*346*	71	*51*	5	6	..	*(.)*	24	*43*
76 Hungary	1,053	*5,866*	11	21	65	53	(.)	2	24	24
77 Portugal	355	*4,412*	59	87	18	4	(.)	*(.)*	23	8
78 Malaysia	75	*4,404*	17	69	(.)	*(.)*	2	2	81	29
79 South Africa[b]	443	*4,111*	94	*84*	..	..	(.)	*(.)*	6	*16*
80 Poland	..	7,403	..	17	..	46	..	2	..	36
81 Yugoslavia	617	*8,421*	24	28	41	46	1	2	35	24
82 Mexico	165	*7,129*	71	90	(.)	..	(.)	*(.)*	29	*9*
83 Panama	1	*35*	7	39	..	5	..	*(.)*	93	56
84 Argentina	84	*1,423*	45	45	1	5	(.)	*(.)*	54	*50*
85 Korea, Rep. of	104	27,669	68	68	..	*(.)*	(.)	6	32	26
86 Algeria	24	*184*	50	77	2	4	1	1	48	*19*
87 Venezuela	51	*647*	59	66	(.)	..	(.)	*(.)*	41	*34*
88 Greece	44	2,241	56	67	6	3	9	8	29	23
89 Israel	281	5,212	67	71	1	*(.)*	..	..	31	29
90 Trinidad and Tobago	28	*330*	78	79	..	*(.)*	..	*(.)*	22	*21*
91 Hong Kong	995	27,540	71	56	(.)	*(.)*	1	2	28	41
92 Oman	..	262	..	30	..	..	..	43	..	27
93 Singapore	338	13,317	9	52	(.)	1	3	4	88	42
94 *Iran, Islamic Rep.*	58	*281*	61	*81*	(.)	..	10	*11*	28	*8*
95 *Iraq*	8	*45*	24	*83*	1	..	13	*4*	63	*13*
96 *Romania*	..	..	..	..	..	..	..	..	..	..
Developing economies			**47 w**	**56 w**	**19 w**	**8 w**	**2 w**	**4 w**	**32 w**	**32 w**
Oil exporters			**52 w**	**75 w**	**12 w**	**8 w**	**4 w**	**2 w**	**34 w**	**16 w**
Exporters of manufactures			**42 w**	**52 w**	**24 w**	**9 w**	**1 w**	**3 w**	**34 w**	**36 w**
Highly indebted countries			**43 w**	**56 w**	**20 w**	**16 w**	**(.) w**	**2 w**	**38 w**	**27 w**
Sub-Saharan Africa			**55 w**	**58 w**	**1 w**	**1 w**	**(.) w**	**3 w**	**44 w**	**40 w**
High-income oil exporters			**30 w**	**47 w**	**..**	**..**	**21 w**	**16 w**	**49 w**	**36 w**
97 Libya	7	*205*	57	..	(.)	..	(.)	..	43	..
98 Saudi Arabia	19	*888*	31	65	..	..	17	*3*	52	*32*
99 Kuwait	17	*364*	18	25	..	..	33	48	49	27
100 United Arab Emirates	..	*671*	..	23	..	..	..	20	..	57
Industrial market economies			**66 w**	**70 w**	**2 w**	**2 w**	**1 w**	**3 w**	**31 w**	**25 w**
101 Spain	382	17,227	57	64	9	5	(.)	3	34	28
102 Ireland	203	7,251	82	93	(.)	*(.)*	(.)	1	17	6
103 Italy	5,587	67,292	68	70	3	3	2	5	27	21
104 New Zealand	53	1,488	90	68	..	*(.)*	(.)	1	10	32
105 Belgium[c]	4,823	40,860	86	83	1	2	(.)	2	13	14
106 United Kingdom	11,346	68,392	61	71	2	1	1	5	36	24
107 Austria	1,204	14,628	67	72	12	7	(.)	2	21	18
108 Netherlands	3,586	35,149	81	84	2	1	1	2	17	13
109 France	7,139	72,242	64	69	2	2	1	3	33	26
110 Australia	432	4,548	57	43	(.)	*(.)*	(.)	1	43	56
111 Finland	815	10,499	63	63	23	26	(.)	1	14	10
112 Germany, Fed. Rep.	15,764	161,304	76	77	2	3	1	2	22	18
113 Denmark	967	9,599	79	78	3	1	(.)	2	17	19
114 Japan	7,704	171,144	47	58	3	2	2	4	49	36
115 Sweden	2,685	24,457	82	83	3	2	(.)	2	15	14
116 Canada	2,973	51,523	88	94	(.)	*(.)*	(.)	*(.)*	12	5
117 Norway	734	5,618	78	70	2	1	(.)	1	20	28
118 Switzerland	2,646	25,230	75	74	2	2	1	4	22	20
119 United States	17,833	158,517	58	61	(.)	*(.)*	1	3	40	35
Nonreporting nonmember economies			**..**	**..**	**..**	**..**	**..**	**..**	**..**	**..**
120 *Albania*	..	..	..	..	..	..	..	..	..	..
121 *Angola*	36	..	3	..	(.)	..	(.)	..	97	..
122 *Bulgaria*	..	..	..	..	..	..	..	..	..	..
123 *Cuba*	27	..	27	..	68	..	..	..	5	..
124 *Czechoslovakia*	..	*15,250*	..	*11*	..	60	..	2	..	27
125 *German Dem. Rep.*	..	..	..	..	..	..	..	..	..	..
126 *Korea, Dem. Rep.*	..	..	..	..	..	..	..	..	..	..
127 *Mongolia*	..	..	..	..	..	..	..	..	..	..
128 *USSR*	..	..	..	..	..	..	..	..	..	..

a. Includes unallocable data.   b. Figures are for the South African Customs Union comprising South Africa, Namibia, Lesotho, Botswana, and Swaziland; trade between the component territories is excluded.   c. Includes Luxembourg.

Table 15. Balance of payments and reserves

	Current account balance (millions of dollars)		Receipts of workers' remittances (millions of dollars)		Net direct private investment (millions of dollars)		Gross international reserves		In months of import coverage
	Millions of dollars						Millions of dollars		
	1970	1985	1970	1985	1970	1985	1970	1985	1985
Low-income economies							**3,243 t**	**32,441 t**	**4.1 w**
China and India							**..**	**26,375 t**	**5.1 w**
Other low-income							**3,219 t**	**6,066 t**	**2.1 w**
1 Ethiopia	−32	−130	..	..	4	..	72	217	1.2
2 Bangladesh	..	−543	..	421	..	−1	..	353	1.4
3 Burkina Faso	9	..	18	..	(.)	..	36	143	..
4 Mali	−2	−113	6	35	..	4	1	29	0.7
5 Bhutan	..	..	..	..	..	..	..	..	..
6 Mozambique	..	..	..	..	..	..	..	..	..
7 Nepal	..	−126	..	..	..	..	94	105	2.2
8 Malawi	−35	..	..	..	9	..	52	274	..
9 Zaire	−64	377	2	..	42	7	189	337	1.8
10 Burma	−63	−203	..	..	..	..	98	116	2.1
11 Burundi	..	..	..	..	..	..	15	36	..
12 Togo	3	−48	..	6	(.)	..	35	300	6.0
13 Madagascar	10	−151	..	8	10	..	37	48	1.1
14 Niger	(.)	−57	..	..	(.)	..	19	140	3.8
15 Benin	−1	..	2	..	7	..	16	7	..
16 Central African Rep.	−12	−31	..	..	1	5	1	53	2.8
17 India	−394	−2,481	113	2,291	6	..	1,023	9,494	5.4
18 Rwanda	7	−42	1	1	(.)	15	8	113	3.9
19 Somalia	−6	−97	..	..	5	−1	21	9	0.2
20 Kenya	−49	−208	..	..	14	77	220	417	2.7
21 Tanzania	−36	..	..	..	..	..	65	16	..
22 Sudan	−42	157	..	259	..	−3	22	12	0.1
23 China	..	−11,417	..	180	..	1,031	..	16,881	4.9
24 Haiti	2	−100	17	98	3	5	4	13	0.3
25 Guinea	..	..	..	..	..	..	..	..	..
26 Sierra Leone	−16	−23	..	..	8	6	39	11	0.4
27 Senegal	−16	−338	3	..	5	..	22	15	0.2
28 Ghana	−68	−166	..	1	68	6	43	554	6.8
29 Pakistan	−667	−1,092	86	2,526	23	124	195	1,429	2.2
30 Sri Lanka	−59	−559	3	296	(.)	30	43	471	2.2
31 Zambia	108	−98	..	..	−297	..	515	200	2.5
32 Afghanistan	..	..	..	..	..	..	50	612	..
33 Chad	2	7	..	..	1	9	2	37	2.5
34 Kampuchea, Dem.	..	..	..	..	..	..	..	..	..
35 Lao PDR	..	..	..	..	..	..	6	..	..
36 Uganda	20	..	..	..	4	..	57	..	..
37 Viet Nam	..	..	..	..	..	..	243	..	..
Middle-income economies							**15,704 t**	**124,507 t**	**3.3 w**
Lower middle-income							**4,907 t**	**35,895 t**	**2.6 w**
38 Mauritania	−5	−108	1	1	1	7	3	62	1.2
39 Bolivia	4	−282	..	(.)	−76	10	46	491	5.4
40 Lesotho	..	9	..	..	..	3	..	44	1.5
41 Liberia	..	76	..	..	..	−16	..	2	(.)
42 Indonesia	−310	−1,840	..	61	..	271	160	5,988	3.2
43 Yemen, PDR	−4	−368	60	494	..	..	59	261	3.0
44 Yemen, Arab Rep.	..	−335	..	897	..	3	..	297	2.3
45 Morocco	−124	−889	63	967	20	20	141	345	0.8
46 Philippines	−48	8	..	111	−29	−14	255	1,099	1.6
47 Egypt, Arab Rep.	−148	−1,895	29	3,212	..	1,175	165	1,587	1.5
48 Côte d'Ivoire	−38	105	..	..	31	..	119	18	0.1
49 Papua New Guinea	..	−325	..	..	..	114	..	462	3.6
50 Zimbabwe	..	−97	..	..	..	−2	60	345	2.1
51 Honduras	−64	−263	..	..	8	28	20	112	1.0
52 Nicaragua	−40	−444	..	..	15	..	49	220	2.7
53 Dominican Rep.	−102	−163	25	205	72	68	32	347	1.7
54 Nigeria	−368	1,242	..	..	205	341	223	1,893	2.0
55 Thailand	−250	−1,554	..	..	43	160	911	3,004	3.0
56 Cameroon	−30	−165	..	14	16	7	81	142	0.3
57 El Salvador	9	−54	..	114	4	12	64	333	2.8
58 Botswana	..	140	..	..	..	59	..	783	11.2
59 Paraguay	−16	−226	..	(.)	4	1	18	560	4.8
60 Jamaica	−153	−19	29	26	161	12	139	161	1.5
61 Peru	202	55	..	..	−70	−54	339	2,465	7.7
62 Turkey	−44	−1,030	273	1,714	58	99	440	2,318	1.9
63 Mauritius	8	−30	..	..	2	8	46	43	0.8
64 Congo, People's Rep.	..	210	..	..	..	35	9	7	0.1
65 Ecuador	−113	−85	..	..	89	60	76	852	3.0
66 Tunisia	−53	−536	29	271	16	107	60	295	1.0
67 Guatemala	−8	−240	..	..	29	61	79	471	3.9

Note: For data comparability and coverage, see the technical notes.   Figures in italics are for years other than those specified.

	Current account balance (millions of dollars)		Receipts of workers' remittances (millions of dollars)		Net direct private investment (millions of dollars)		Gross international reserves		
							Millions of dollars		In months of import coverage
	1970	1985	1970	1985	1970	1985	1970	1985	1985
68 Costa Rica	−74	−168	..	..	26	67	16	526	3.8
69 Colombia	−293	−1,390	6	117	39	729	207	2,197	3.9
70 Chile	−91	−1,307	..	..	−79	112	392	2,950	5.8
71 Jordan	−20	−252	..	1,022	..	23	258	769	2.4
72 Syrian Arab Rep.	−69	−952	7	293	..	..	57	356	0.9
73 *Lebanon*	..	..	..	..	..	..	405	4,089	..
Upper middle-income							**10,796** *t*	**88,612** *t*	**3.7** *w*
74 Brazil	−837	−273	..	2	407	1,267	1,190	11,618	4.7
75 Uruguay	−45	−108	..	..	..	−8	186	1,031	8.6
76 Hungary	−25	−52	..	..	..	..	..	3,880	4.4
77 Portugal	..	379	..	2,075	..	231	1,565	8,010	9.8
78 Malaysia	8	−723	..	..	94	685	667	5,677	3.7
79 South Africa	−1,215	2,615	..	..	318	21	1,057	1,897	1.4
80 Poland	..	..	..	..	..	..	..	..	..
81 Yugoslavia	−372	*275*	441	..	..	..	143	1,703	*1.3*
82 Mexico	−1,068	540	..	..	323	492	756	5,678	2.3
83 Panama	−64	272	..	..	33	60	16	98	0.2
84 Argentina	−163	−954	..	..	11	977	682	4,553	4.8
85 Korea, Rep. of	−623	−887	..	..	66	200	610	2,971	1.0
86 Algeria	−125	1,015	211	313	45	−2	352	4,644	4.3
87 Venezuela	−104	3,086	..	..	−23	106	1,047	13,998	12.3
88 Greece	−422	−3,276	333	775	50	447	318	2,215	2.2
89 Israel	−562	1,099	..	..	40	40	452	4,014	3.3
90 Trinidad and Tobago	−109	22	3	(.)	83	−36	43	1,145	5.5
91 Hong Kong	..	..	..	..	..	..	..	..	..
92 Oman	..	223	..	43	..	125	12	1,185	3.2
93 Singapore	−572	−253	..	..	93	1,076	1,012	12,847	5.2
94 *Iran, Islamic Rep.*	−507	−414	..	..	25	..	217	..	..
95 *Iraq*	105	..	..	..	24	..	472	..	..
96 *Romania*	..	1,239	..	..	..	..	..	1,448	1.5
Developing economies							**18,946** *t*	**156,948** *t*	**3.5** *w*
Oil exporters							**3,670** *t*	**37,476** *t*	**3.7** *w*
Exporters of manufactures							**5,995** *t*	**72,366** *t*	**3.9** *w*
Highly indebted countries							**5,935** *t*	**51,578** *t*	**4.3** *w*
Sub-Saharan Africa							**2,028** *t*	**6,306** *t*	**1.7** *w*
High-income oil exporters							**2,475** *t*	**43,363** *t*	**7.3** *w*
97 Libya	645	1,890	..	..	139	−316	1,596	7,081	11.1
98 Saudi Arabia	71	−12,967	..	..	20	2,513	670	26,508	6.7
99 Kuwait	..	5,617	..	..	..	−57	209	6,301	7.4
100 United Arab Emirates	..	..	..	..	..	..	..	3,472	..
Industrial market economies							**72,867** *t*	**505,748** *t*	**4.2** *w*
101 Spain	79	2,765	469	1,025	179	1,698	1,851	15,966	5.2
102 Ireland	−198	−919	..	..	32	*120*	698	3,058	2.3
103 Italy	902	−4,132	446	1,170	498	−892	5,548	37,316	4.0
104 New Zealand	−232	−1,461	40	321	137	94	258	1,602	2.3
105 Belgium	717	622	154	384	140	766	2,946	16,026	2.4
106 United Kingdom	1,910	5,155	..	..	−185	−4,254	2,918	19,083	1.2
107 Austria	−75	−229	13	182	104	187	1,806	11,680	4.7
108 Netherlands	−483	5,178	..	..	−15	−2,840	3,362	25,150	3.8
109 France	−203	749	130	230	248	325	5,199	53,354	4.2
110 Australia	−837	−8,684	..	..	790	−324	1,709	8,361	2.7
111 Finland	−239	−658	..	..	−41	−265	455	4,374	3.0
112 Germany, Fed. Rep.	852	13,500	..	..	−290	−2,946	13,879	75,504	4.6
113 Denmark	−544	−2,708	..	..	75	−86	488	5,962	2.7
114 Japan	1,980	49,170	..	..	−260	−5,810	4,876	34,642	2.5
115 Sweden	−265	−1,204	..	..	−104	−964	775	7,778	2.4
116 Canada	821	−432	..	..	566	−6,008	4,732	9,079	1.0
117 Norway	−242	2,926	..	11	32	−1,049	813	13,583	6.3
118 Switzerland	72	6,207	..	66	..	−2,378	5,317	45,249	10.9
119 United States	2320	−117,750	..	..	−6,130	−900	15,237	117,982	3.1
Nonreporting nonmember economies							..	..	..
120 *Albania*	..	..	..	..	..	..	..	..	..
121 *Angola*	..	..	..	..	..	..	..	..	..
122 *Bulgaria*	..	..	..	..	..	..	..	..	..
123 *Cuba*	..	..	..	..	..	..	..	..	..
124 *Czechoslovakia*	..	..	..	..	..	..	..	..	..
125 *German Dem. Rep.*	..	..	..	..	..	..	..	..	..
126 *Korea, Dem. Rep.*	..	..	..	..	..	..	..	..	..
127 *Mongolia*	..	..	..	..	..	..	..	..	..
128 *USSR*	..	..	..	..	..	..	..	..	..

Table 16. Total external debt

	Long-term debt (millions of dollars) Public and publicly guaranteed		Long-term debt (millions of dollars) Private nonguaranteed		Use of IMF credit (millions of dollars)		Short-term debt (millions of dollars)		Total external debt (millions of dollars)	
	1970	1985	1970	1985	1970	1985	1970	1985	1970	1985
Low-income economies										
China and India										
Other low-income										
1 Ethiopia	169	1,742	0	0	0	50	..	77	..	1,869
2 Bangladesh	..	5,968	..	0	..	424	..	135	..	6,526
3 Burkina Faso	21	496	0	0	0	0	..	43	..	539
4 Mali	241	1,327	0	0	9	81	..	61	..	1,469
5 Bhutan	..	..	..	..	0	0	..	..	..	..
6 Mozambique	..	..	..	..	0	0	..	..	..	..
7 Nepal	3	527	0	0	0	11	..	23	..	562
8 Malawi	125	775	0	0	0	134	..	79	..	988
9 Zaire	312	4,821	..	..	0	721	..	309	..	..
10 Burma	108	2,947	0	0	17	71	..	86	..	3,104
11 Burundi	7	415	0	0	8	0	..	31	..	446
12 Togo	40	787	0	0	0	63	..	74	..	924
13 Madagascar	90	2,340	0	0	0	162	..	86	..	2,588
14 Niger	32	791	..	199	0	67	..	98	..	1,155
15 Benin	41	677	0	0	0	0	..	99	..	776
16 Central African Rep.	24	296	0	0	0	28	..	17	..	341
17 India	8,109	26,650	100	3,093	10	4,202	..	1,516	..	35,460
18 Rwanda	2	324	0	0	3	0	..	27	..	351
19 Somalia	77	1,309	0	0	0	142	..	35	..	1,486
20 Kenya	333	2,857	88	406	0	486	..	470	..	4,219
21 Tanzania	257	2,982	15	6	0	21	..	600	..	3,609
22 Sudan	308	5,086	..	..	31	665	..	581	..	..
23 China	..	7,020	..	..	0	0	..	..	..	..
24 Haiti	40	534	..	..	2	82	..	88	..	..
25 Guinea	313	1,292	..	..	3	13	..	76	..	..
26 Sierra Leone	61	390	0	0	0	78	..	59	..	527
27 Senegal	101	1,989	31	13	0	241	..	211	..	2,454
28 Ghana	471	1,170	..	..	46	656	..	302	..	..
29 Pakistan	3,081	10,681	5	26	45	1,266	..	722	..	12,695
30 Sri Lanka	321	2,815	..	99	79	321	..	299	..	3,534
31 Zambia	627	3,214	30	0	0	762	..	507	..	4,483
32 *Afghanistan*	..	..	..	..	15	0	..	..	..	..
33 *Chad*	33	150	0	0	3	9	..	3	..	161
34 *Kampuchea, Dem.*	..	..	..	..	0	0	..	..	..	..
35 *Lao PDR*	..	..	..	..	0	0	..	..	..	..
36 *Uganda*	142	726	0	0	0	282	..	22	..	1,030
37 *Viet Nam*	..	..	..	..	..	..	..	..	..	..
Middle-income economies										
Lower middle-income										
38 Mauritania	27	1,363	0	0	0	30	..	84	..	1,477
39 Bolivia	482	3,259	11	314	6	51	..	347	..	3,972
40 Lesotho	8	172	0	0	0	0	..	4	..	176
41 Liberia	158	879	0	0	4	226	..	50	..	1,155
42 Indonesia	2,447	26,625	461	3,810	139	46	..	5,280	..	35,761
43 Yemen, PDR	1	1,446	0	0	0	15	..	70	..	1,531
44 Yemen, Arab Rep.	..	1,868	0	0	0	11	..	160	..	2,039
45 Morocco	716	11,231	..	..	28	1,190	..	1,664	..	..
46 Philippines	575	13,561	919	2,998	69	1,052	..	8,573	..	26,184
47 Egypt, Arab Rep.	1,760	17,751	..	750	49	41	..	5,800	..	24,342
48 Côte d'Ivoire	257	5,700	11	1,400	0	622	..	725	..	8,446
49 Papua New Guinea	39	1,061	173	1,020	0	11	..	146	..	2,239
50 Zimbabwe	239	1,526	..	45	0	264	..	308	..	2,143
51 Honduras	95	2,178	19	141	0	134	..	259	..	2,713
52 Nicaragua	147	4,753	0	0	8	0	..	862	..	5,615
53 Dominican Rep.	212	2,521	141	151	7	297	..	325	..	3,294
54 Nigeria	458	13,016	115	416	0	0	..	4,916	..	18,348
55 Thailand	326	9,898	402	3,370	0	1,020	..	3,200	..	17,489
56 Cameroon	132	1,975	9	381	0	0	..	515	..	2,871
57 El Salvador	88	1,460	88	104	7	89	..	82	..	1,736
58 Botswana	15	334	..	..	0	0	..	2	..	..
59 Paraguay	112	1,525	..	104	0	0	..	151	..	1,780
60 Jamaica	162	2,823	822	90	0	693	..	169	..	3,775
61 Peru	859	10,527	1,799	1,342	10	702	..	1,117	..	13,688
62 Turkey	1,875	17,821	42	359	74	1,326	..	6,617	..	26,124
63 Mauritius	33	404	0	15	0	159	..	51	..	629
64 Congo, People's Rep.	140	1,760	..	..	0	0	..	660	..	..
65 Ecuador	194	7,121	49	70	14	360	..	1,683	..	9,233
66 Tunisia	543	4,442	..	246	13	0	..	562	..	5,250
67 Guatemala	106	2,148	14	106	0	116	..	226	..	2,595

Note: For data comparability and coverage, see the technical notes.   Figures in italics are for years other than those specified.

| | Long-term debt (millions of dollars) | | | | Use of IMF credit (millions of dollars) | | Short-term debt (millions of dollars) | | Total external debt (millions of dollars) | |
| | Public and publicly guaranteed | | Private nonguaranteed | | | | | | | |
	1970	1985	1970	1985	1970	1985	1970	1985	1970	1985
68 Costa Rica	134	3,665	112	297	0	189	..	40	..	4,191
69 Colombia	1,299	9,377	283	1,568	55	0	..	3,099	..	14,044
70 Chile	2,075	12,735	501	4,731	2	1,088	..	1,668	..	20,221
71 Jordan	120	2,693	0	0	0	63	..	917	..	3,673
72 Syrian Arab Rep.	233	2,751	0	0	10	0	..	815	..	3,566
73 *Lebanon*	64	172	..	..	0	0	..	235	..	..
Upper middle-income										
74 Brazil	3,432	73,894	1,706	17,200	0	4,619	..	11,017	..	106,730
75 Uruguay	270	2,686	29	60	18	350	..	814	..	3,910
76 Hungary	..	10,138	0	0	0	971	..	1,881	..	12,990
77 Portugal	487	10,803	85	519	0	628	..	2,610	..	14,560
78 Malaysia	396	13,834	50	4,132	0	118	..	..	..	..
79 South Africa	..	..	..	..	0	911	..	..	..	..
80 Poland	..	..	..	..	0	0	..	..	..	..
81 Yugoslavia	1,204	9,919	854	6,383	0	2,108	..	972	..	19,382
82 Mexico	3,196	72,510	2,770	16,500	0	2,969	..	5,450	..	97,429
83 Panama	194	3,276	..	..	0	311	..	1,123	..	..
84 Argentina	1,891	35,604	3,291	4,575	0	2,312	..	5,953	..	48,444
85 Korea, Rep. of	1,844	29,126	175	6,630	0	1,508	..	10,732	..	47,996
86 Algeria	941	13,664	0	0	0	0	..	1,862	..	15,526
87 Venezuela	729	16,650	236	5,150	0	0	..	10,279	..	32,079
88 Greece	916	12,452	388	1,657	0	0	..	4,530	..	18,639
89 Israel	2,284	15,850	361	4,494	13	0	..	3,529	..	23,873
90 Trinidad and Tobago	102	1,087	..	..	0	0	..	149	..	..
91 Hong Kong	3	251	..	..	0	0	..	749	..	..
92 Oman	..	1,946	..	..	0	0	..	422	..	..
93 Singapore	154	1,791	..	..	0	0	..	262	..	..
94 *Iran, Islamic Rep.*	..	..	..	..	0	0	..	..	..	..
95 *Iraq*	..	..	..	..	0	0	..	..	..	..
96 *Romania*	..	5,801	0	0	0	660	..	516	..	6,977

Developing economies
  Oil exporters
  Exporters of manufactures
  Highly indebted countries
  Sub-Saharan Africa

High-income oil exporters

97 Libya
98 Saudi Arabia
99 Kuwait
100 United Arab Emirates

Industrial market economies

101 Spain
102 Ireland
103 Italy
104 New Zealand
105 Belgium

106 United Kingdom
107 Austria
108 Netherlands
109 France
110 Australia

111 Finland
112 Germany, Fed. Rep.
113 Denmark
114 Japan
115 Sweden

116 Canada
117 Norway
118 Switzerland
119 United States

Nonreporting nonmember economies

120 *Albania*
121 *Angola*
122 *Bulgaria*
123 *Cuba*
124 *Czechoslovakia*

125 *German Dem. Rep.*
126 *Korea, Dem. Rep.*
127 *Mongolia*
128 *USSR*

Table 17. Flow of public and private external capital

	Disbursements (millions of dollars)				Repayment of principal (millions of dollars)				Net flow[a] (millions of dollars)			
	Public and publicly guaranteed		Private nonguaranteed		Public and publicly guaranteed		Private nonguaranteed		Public and publicly guaranteed		Private nonguaranteed	
	1970	1985	1970	1985	1970	1985	1970	1985	1970	1985	1970	1985
Low-income economies												
China and India												
Other low-income												
1 Ethiopia	28	368	0	0	15	69	0	0	13	299	0	0
2 Bangladesh	..	581	..	0	..	126	..	0	..	455	..	0
3 Burkina Faso	2	55	0	0	2	17	0	0	(.)	38	0	0
4 Mali	22	106	0	0	(.)	25	0	0	22	80	0	0
5 Bhutan	..	..	..	..	..	..	..	..	..	..	..	..
6 Mozambique	..	..	..	..	..	..	..	..	..	..	..	..
7 Nepal	1	93	0	0	2	7	0	0	−2	86	0	0
8 Malawi	39	52	0	0	3	48	0	0	36	4	0	0
9 Zaire	32	149	..	..	28	122	..	..	3	27	..	..
10 Burma	22	311	0	0	20	126	0	0	2	184	0	0
11 Burundi	1	71	0	0	(.)	13	0	0	1	58	0	0
12 Togo	5	54	0	0	2	51	0	0	3	4	0	0
13 Madagascar	11	157	0	0	5	64	0	0	5	93	0	0
14 Niger	12	75	..	..	2	37	..	..	11	38	..	..
15 Benin	2	37	0	0	1	14	0	0	1	24	0	0
16 Central African Rep.	2	49	0	0	2	7	0	0	−1	42	0	0
17 India	922	3,449	25	1,135	340	1,084	25	653	583	2,364	0	482
18 Rwanda	(.)	64	0	0	(.)	11	0	0	(.)	53	0	0
19 Somalia	4	140	0	0	1	40	0	0	4	99	0	0
20 Kenya	34	271	..	..	17	244	..	..	17	27	..	..
21 Tanzania	50	161	..	..	10	40	..	..	40	121	..	..
22 Sudan	53	109	..	..	22	64	..	..	30	45	..	..
23 China	..	..	..	..	..	..	..	..	..	..	..	..
24 Haiti	4	62	..	..	4	13	..	..	1	49	..	..
25 Guinea	90	97	..	..	11	46	..	..	80	51	..	..
26 Sierra Leone	8	35	0	0	10	7	0	0	−3	28	0	0
27 Senegal	20	216	1	6	5	45	3	5	14	171	−2	2
28 Ghana	43	119	..	..	13	57	..	..	30	62	..	..
29 Pakistan	485	986	3	13	112	766	1	14	374	220	2	−1
30 Sri Lanka	64	359	..	55	29	119	..	8	36	240	..	47
31 Zambia	351	263	..	..	35	44	..	..	317	219	..	..
32 *Afghanistan*	..	..	..	..	..	..	..	..	..	..	..	..
33 *Chad*	6	8	0	0	3	6	0	0	3	2	0	0
34 *Kampuchea, Dem.*	..	..	..	..	..	..	..	..	..	..	..	..
35 *Lao PDR*	..	..	..	..	..	..	..	..	..	..	..	..
36 *Uganda*	27	139	0	0	4	79	0	0	23	60	0	0
37 *Viet Nam*	..	..	..	..	..	..	..	..	..	..	..	..
Middle-income economies												
Lower middle-income												
38 Mauritania	4	86	0	0	3	51	0	0	1	35	0	0
39 Bolivia	55	115	..	..	17	143	..	..	38	−28	..	..
40 Lesotho	(.)	39	0	0	(.)	14	0	0	(.)	24	0	0
41 Liberia	7	58	0	0	12	8	0	0	−4	50	0	0
42 Indonesia	442	3,502	195	770	59	2,360	61	760	383	1,142	134	10
43 Yemen, PDR	1	493	0	0	0	95	0	0	1	398	0	0
44 Yemen, Arab Rep.	..	246	0	0	..	107	0	0	..	139	0	0
45 Morocco	167	671	..	..	37	545	..	..	130	127	..	..
46 Philippines	128	1,277	276	285	73	426	186	151	56	851	90	134
47 Egypt, Arab Rep.	398	2,417	..	340	300	1,682	..	140	99	735	..	200
48 Côte d'Ivoire	78	306	..	..	28	147	..	..	50	159	..	..
49 Papua New Guinea	37	83	111	308	0	65	20	178	37	18	91	130
50 Zimbabwe	..	220	..	..	5	210	..	..	..	10	..	..
51 Honduras	30	358	10	12	4	74	3	15	26	284	7	−3
52 Nicaragua	44	563	0	0	16	22	0	0	28	541	0	0
53 Dominican Rep.	38	198	22	6	7	84	20	14	31	114	2	−7
54 Nigeria	56	1,560	25	90	37	2,748	30	125	18	−1,188	−5	−35
55 Thailand	51	2,449	169	784	23	896	107	786	28	1,553	62	−2
56 Cameroon	28	182	11	112	5	145	2	322	24	38	9	−210
57 El Salvador	8	179	24	0	6	128	16	10	2	51	8	−10
58 Botswana	3	67	..	..	(.)	26	..	..	3	41	..	..
59 Paraguay	15	244	..	0	7	73	..	6	8	171	..	−6
60 Jamaica	15	400	..	..	6	193	..	..	9	208	..	..
61 Peru	148	517	240	45	101	152	233	168	48	364	7	−123
62 Turkey	330	2,719	1	42	129	2,249	3	134	201	470	−2	−92
63 Mauritius	2	66	0	4	1	40	0	4	1	26	0	(.)
64 Congo, People's Rep.	21	269	..	..	6	216	..	..	15	53	..	..
65 Ecuador	41	605	7	13	16	228	11	120	26	377	−4	−107
66 Tunisia	88	751	..	..	47	437	..	..	42	314	..	..
67 Guatemala	37	259	6	1	20	148	2	3	17	111	4	−2

Note: For data comparablity and coverage, see the technical notes.   Figures in italics are for years other than those specified.

| | Disbursements (millions of dollars) | | | | Repayment of principal (millions of dollars) | | | | Net flow[a] (millions of dollars) | | | |
| | Public and publicly guaranteed | | Private nonguaranteed | | Public and publicly guaranteed | | Private nonguaranteed | | Public and publicly guaranteed | | Private nonguaranteed | |
	1970	1985	1970	1985	1970	1985	1970	1985	1970	1985	1970	1985
68 Costa Rica	30	286	30	0	21	131	20	20	9	155	10	−20
69 Colombia	254	1,784	0	235	78	647	59	104	176	1,137	−59	131
70 Chile	405	1,178	247	86	165	223	41	201	240	955	206	−115
71 Jordan	14	421	0	0	3	301	0	0	12	119	0	0
72 Syrian Arab Rep.	60	527	0	0	30	264	0	0	30	263	0	0
73 *Lebanon*	12	26	..	..	2	43	..	..	10	−16	..	..
Upper middle-income												
74 Brazil	892	2,503	900	0	256	1,497	200	757	635	1,006	700	−757
75 Uruguay	38	220	13	0	47	124	4	69	−10	96	9	−69
76 Hungary	..	4,192	0	0	..	2,183	0	0	..	2,009	0	0
77 Portugal	18	1,615	20	75	63	1,500	22	143	−45	115	−1	−68
78 Malaysia	45	3,393	12	735	47	2,839	9	603	−2	553	3	133
79 South Africa	..	..	..	..	..	..	..	..	..	..	..	..
80 Poland	..	..	..	..	..	..	..	..	..	..	..	..
81 Yugoslavia	180	382	465	389	170	433	204	960	10	−50	261	−571
82 Mexico	772	4,423	603	793	475	3,475	542	1,413	297	948	61	−620
83 Panama	67	139	..	..	24	132	..	..	44	8	..	..
84 Argentina	486	3,790	..	..	343	838	..	..	143	2,952	..	..
85 Korea, Rep. of	444	5,615	32	2,501	199	2,879	7	1,242	245	2,736	25	1,259
86 Algeria	303	3,354	0	0	34	3,286	0	0	270	68	0	0
87 Venezuela	225	100	..	..	42	788	..	..	183	−688	..	..
88 Greece	164	2,894	144	220	62	803	37	210	102	2,090	107	10
89 Israel	411	680	123	580	26	787	36	485	385	−107	87	95
90 Trinidad and Tobago	8	211	..	..	10	104	..	..	−2	107	..	..
91 Hong Kong	0	9	..	..	1	47	..	..	−1	−38	..	..
92 Oman	..	703	..	..	..	143	..	..	..	559	..	..
93 Singapore	60	331	..	..	6	567	..	..	54	−236	..	..
94 *Iran, Islamic Rep.*	..	..	..	..	..	..	..	..	..	..	..	..
95 *Iraq*	..	..	..	..	..	..	..	..	..	..	..	..
96 *Romania*	..	509	0	0	..	1,230	0	0	..	−721	0	0

Developing economies
  Oil exporters
  Exporters of manufactures
  Highly indebted countries
  Sub-Saharan Africa

High-income oil exporters

97 Libya
98 Saudi Arabia
99 Kuwait
100 United Arab Emirates

Industrial market economies

101 Spain
102 Ireland
103 Italy
104 New Zealand
105 Belgium

106 United Kingdom
107 Austria
108 Netherlands
109 France
110 Australia

111 Finland
112 Germany, Fed. Rep.
113 Denmark
114 Japan
115 Sweden

116 Canada
117 Norway
118 Switzerland
119 United States

Nonreporting nonmember economies

120 *Albania*
121 *Angola*
122 *Bulgaria*
123 *Cuba*
124 *Czechoslovakia*

125 *German Dem. Rep.*
126 *Korea, Dem. Rep.*
127 *Mongolia*
128 *USSR*

a. Disbursements less repayments of principal may not equal net flow because of rounding.

Table 18. Total external public and private debt and debt service ratios

	Total long-term debt disbursed and outstanding				Total interest payments on long-term debt (millions of dollars)		Total long-term debt service as percentage of:			
	Millions of dollars		As percentage of GNP				GNP		Exports of goods and services	
	1970	1985	1970	1985	1970	1985	1970	1985	1970	1985
Low-income economies										
China and India										
Other low-income										
1 Ethiopia	169	1,742	9.5	37.1	6	35	1.2	2.2	11.4	*10.9*
2 Bangladesh	. .	5,968	. .	37.2	. .	89	. .	1.3	. .	16.7
3 Burkina Faso	21	496	6.6	46.4	(.)	10	0.7	2.5	6.8	. .
4 Mali	241	1,327	70.7	122.1	(.)	13	0.2	3.5	1.4	16.6
5 Bhutan	. .	. .	. .	. .	. .	. .	. .	. .	. .	. .
6 Mozambique	. .	. .	. .	. .	. .	. .	. .	. .	. .	. .
7 Nepal	3	527	0.3	22.5	(.)	6	0.3	0.5	. .	4.0
8 Malawi	125	775	44.2	75.7	3	28	2.2	7.4	7.7	. .
9 Zaire	. .	. .	. .	. .	. .	. .	. .	. .	. .	. .
10 Burma	108	2,947	5.0	42.1	3	70	1.0	2.8	17.2	51.4
11 Burundi	7	415	3.1	39.7	(.)	9	0.3	2.0	2.3	16.6
12 Togo	40	787	16.2	121.0	1	39	0.9	13.7	3.0	27.5
13 Madagascar	90	2,340	10.5	105.4	2	53	0.8	5.3	3.7	*19.6*
14 Niger	. .	990	. .	64.4	. .	. .	. .	. .	. .	. .
15 Benin	41	677	15.2	66.9	(.)	9	0.6	2.2	2.3	. .
16 Central African Rep.	24	296	13.5	44.9	1	7	1.7	2.0	5.1	*11.8*
17 India	8,209	29,743	15.4	15.0	202	1,066	1.1	1.4	25.1	*12.7*
18 Rwanda	2	324	0.9	19.1	(.)	4	0.1	0.9	1.2	*4.3*
19 Somalia	77	1,309	24.5	53.5	(.)	17	0.3	2.3	2.1	44.8
20 Kenya	421	3,263	27.2	58.5	. .	. .	. .	. .	. .	. .
21 Tanzania	272	2,988	21.3	48.6	. .	. .	. .	. .	. .	. .
22 Sudan	. .	. .	. .	. .	. .	. .	. .	. .	. .	. .
23 China	. .	. .	. .	. .	. .	. .	. .	. .	. .	. .
24 Haiti	. .	. .	. .	. .	. .	. .	. .	. .	. .	. .
25 Guinea	. .	. .	. .	. .	. .	. .	. .	. .	. .	. .
26 Sierra Leone	61	390	14.5	32.6	2	3	3.1	0.8	10.4	*5.7*
27 Senegal	132	2,002	15.6	82.8	2	45	1.1	3.9	4.0	*9.4*
28 Ghana	. .	. .	. .	. .	. .	. .	. .	. .	. .	. .
29 Pakistan	3,086	10,707	30.8	31.7	77	308	1.9	3.2	23.5	30.0
30 Sri Lanka	. .	2,914	. .	49.2	. .	113	. .	4.1	. .	14.7
31 Zambia	657	3,214	37.7	150.8	. .	. .	. .	. .	. .	. .
32 *Afghanistan*	. .	. .	. .	. .	. .	. .	. .	. .	. .	. .
33 *Chad*	33	150	9.9	. .	(.)	2	0.9	. .	4.2	. .
34 *Kampuchea, Dem.*	. .	. .	. .	. .	. .	. .	. .	. .	. .	. .
35 *Lao PDR*	. .	. .	. .	. .	. .	. .	. .	. .	. .	. .
36 *Uganda*	142	726	7.5	. .	5	27	0.4	. .	2.9	. .
37 *Viet Nam*	. .	. .	. .	. .	. .	. .	. .	. .	. .	. .
Middle-income economies										
Lower middle-income										
38 Mauritania	27	1,363	13.9	208.2	(.)	28	1.8	12.0	3.3	19.0
39 Bolivia	493	3,574	47.3	136.8	. .	. .	. .	. .	. .	. .
40 Lesotho	8	172	7.8	30.1	(.)	4	0.5	3.2	. .	6.2
41 Liberia	158	879	39.4	85.3	6	10	4.4	1.7	. .	3.8
42 Indonesia	2,908	30,435	30.0	36.6	45	1,931	1.7	6.1	. .	25.1
43 Yemen, PDR	1	1,446	. .	134.7	0	19	. .	10.6	0.0	*42.3*
44 Yemen, Arab Rep.	. .	1,868	. .	45.6	. .	19	. .	3.1	. .	55.8
45 Morocco	. .	. .	. .	. .	. .	. .	. .	. .	. .	. .
46 Philippines	1,495	16,559	21.1	52.1	42	970	4.3	4.9	22.8	19.5
47 Egypt, Arab Rep.	. .	18,501	. .	64.5	. .	627	. .	8.5	. .	33.6
48 Côte d'Ivoire	268	7,100	19.6	110.2	. .	. .	. .	. .	. .	. .
49 Papua New Guinea	211	2,082	33.7	96.2	10	131	4.8	17.3	. .	*27.3*
50 Zimbabwe	. .	1,571	. .	32.2	. .	. .	. .	. .	. .	. .
51 Honduras	115	2,320	16.3	73.2	4	104	1.5	6.1	5.2	20.0
52 Nicaragua	147	4,753	19.5	185.2	7	19	3.0	1.6	10.5	. .
53 Dominican Rep.	353	2,672	24.2	62.2	13	146	2.7	5.7	15.2	*23.1*
54 Nigeria	573	13,432	5.7	17.8	28	1,298	0.9	5.5	7.1	32.1
55 Thailand	727	13,268	11.1	36.0	33	911	2.5	7.0	14.0	25.4
56 Cameroon	141	2,356	13.0	31.0	5	133	1.0	7.9	4.0	*15.0*
57 El Salvador	176	1,565	17.3	42.5	9	76	3.1	5.8	12.0	*18.6*
58 Botswana	. .	. .	. .	. .	. .	. .	. .	. .	. .	. .
59 Paraguay	. .	1,629	. .	59.6	. .	80	. .	5.8	. .	13.5
60 Jamaica	985	2,913	73.0	171.9	. .	. .	. .	. .	. .	. .
61 Peru	2,658	11,869	38.1	74.9	162	287	7.1	3.8	40.0	16.0
62 Turkey	1,917	18,180	15.2	35.4	45	1,277	1.4	7.1	22.8	32.1
63 Mauritius	33	419	14.7	41.3	2	27	1.4	7.0	3.2	12.3
64 Congo, People's Rep.	. .	. .	. .	. .	. .	. .	. .	. .	. .	. .
65 Ecuador	243	7,191	14.8	61.5	10	729	2.2	9.2	14.0	33.0
66 Tunisia	. .	4,688	. .	59.2	. .	. .	. .	. .	. .	. .
67 Guatemala	120	2,254	6.5	20.8	7	116	1.6	2.5	8.2	22.3

Note: For data comparability and coverage, see the technical notes.   Public and private debt includes public, publicly guaranteed, and private nonguaranteed debt; data are shown only when available for all the catagories.   Figures in italics are for years other than those specified.

| | Total long-term debt disbursed and outstanding | | | | Total interest payments on long-term debt (millions of dollars) | | Total long-term debt service as percentage of: | | | |
| | Millions of dollars | | As percentage of GNP | | | | GNP | | Exports of goods and services | |
	1970	1985	1970	1985	1970	1985	1970	1985	1970	1985
68 Costa Rica	246	3,962	25.3	113.6	14	353	5.7	14.5	19.9	39.8
69 Colombia	1,582	10,945	22.5	33.3	59	861	2.8	4.9	19.3	33.4
70 Chile	2,576	17,465	32.2	123.9	104	1,646	3.9	14.7	24.4	44.1
71 Jordan	120	2,693	23.8	70.9	2	153	0.9	12.0	3.6	22.1
72 Syrian Arab Rep.	233	2,751	10.8	16.9	6	96	1.7	2.2	11.2	14.8
73 *Lebanon*	. .	. .	. .	. .	. .	. .	. .	. .	. .	. .

Upper middle-income

	1970	1985	1970	1985	1970	1985	1970	1985	1970	1985
74 Brazil	5,138	91,094	12.2	43.8	224	7,950	1.6	4.9	21.8	34.8
75 Uruguay	298	2,746	12.5	58.4	17	291	2.9	10.3	23.6	36.5
76 Hungary	. .	10,138	. .	51.1	. .	792	. .	13.0	. .	25.0
77 Portugal	572	11,322	9.2	57.2	34	1,040	1.9	13.6	. .	33.8
78 Malaysia	446	17,966	10.9	62.0	25	1,461	2.0	16.9	4.4	27.5
79 South Africa	. .	. .	. .	. .	. .	. .	. .	. .	. .	. .
80 Poland	. .	. .	. .	. .	. .	. .	. .	. .	. .	. .
81 Yugoslavia	2,058	16,302	15.0	35.3	104	1,625	3.5	6.5	19.7	21.2
82 Mexico	5,966	89,010	17.0	52.8	283	9,436	3.7	8.5	44.3	48.2
83 Panama	. .	. .	. .	. .	. .	. .	. .	. .	. .	. .
84 Argentina	5,182	40,179	23.3	56.4	. .	. .	. .	. .	. .	. .
85 Korea, Rep. of	2,019	35,756	23.3	43.0	76	2,991	3.2	8.6	20.4	21.5
86 Algeria	941	13,664	19.4	24.0	10	1,297	0.9	8.1	3.9	33.3
87 Venezuela	965	21,800	8.7	46.1	. .	. .	. .	. .	. .	. .
88 Greece	1,304	14,109	12.8	43.4	64	1,072	1.6	6.4	14.7	29.3
89 Israel	2,645	20,344	48.1	105.8	34	1,790	1.7	15.9	6.8	28.6
90 Trinidad and Tobago	. .	. .	. .	. .	. .	. .	. .	. .	. .	. .
91 Hong Kong	. .	. .	. .	. .	. .	. .	. .	. .	. .	. .
92 Oman	. .	. .	. .	. .	. .	. .	. .	. .	. .	. .
93 Singapore	. .	. .	. .	. .	. .	. .	. .	. .	. .	. .
94 *Iran, Islamic Rep.*	. .	. .	. .	. .	. .	. .	. .	. .	. .	. .
95 *Iraq*	. .	. .	. .	. .	. .	. .	. .	. .	. .	. .
96 *Romania*	. .	5,801	. .	. .	. .	543	. .	. .	. .	13.6

Developing economies
  Oil exporters
  Exporters of manufactures
  Highly indebted countries
  Sub-Saharan Africa

High-income oil exporters

97 Libya
98 Saudi Arabia
99 Kuwait
100 United Arab Emirates

Industrial market economies

101 Spain
102 Ireland
103 Italy
104 New Zealand
105 Belgium

106 United Kingdom
107 Austria
108 Netherlands
109 France
110 Australia

111 Finland
112 Germany, Fed. Rep.
113 Denmark
114 Japan
115 Sweden

116 Canada
117 Norway
118 Switzerland
119 United States

Nonreporting nonmember economies

120 *Albania*
121 *Angola*
122 *Bulgaria*
123 *Cuba*
124 *Czechoslovakia*

125 *German Dem. Rep.*
126 *Korea, Dem. Rep.*
127 *Mongolia*
128 *USSR*

Table 19. External public debt and debt service ratios

	External public debt outstanding and disbursed				Interest payments on external public debt (millions of dollars)		Debt service as percentage of:			
	Millions of dollars		As percentage of GNP				GNP		Exports of goods and services	
	1970	1985	1970	1985	1970	1985	1970	1985	1970	1985
Low-income economies	**15,490 t**	**92,997 t**	**17.1 w**	**15.7 w**	**398 t**	**2,249 t**	**1.2 w**	**1.0 w**	**12.4 w**	**7.9 w**
China and India	..	33,670 t	..	7.3 w	..	..	..	0.5 w	..	3.7 w
Other low-income	7,381 t	59,327 t	19.7 w	46.5 w	202 t	1,448 t	1.5 w	2.9 w	8.4 w	18.4 w
1 Ethiopia	169	1,742	9.5	37.1	6	35	1.2	2.2	11.4	10.9
2 Bangladesh	..	5,968	..	37.2	..	89	..	1.3	..	16.7
3 Burkina Faso	21	496	6.6	46.4	(.)	10	0.7	2.5	6.8	..
4 Mali	241	1,327	70.7	122.1	(.)	13	0.2	3.5	1.4	16.6
5 Bhutan	..	..	..	..	..	..	..	..	..	..
6 Mozambique	..	..	..	..	..	..	..	..	..	..
7 Nepal	3	527	0.3	22.5	(.)	6	0.3	0.5	..	4.0
8 Malawi	125	775	44.2	75.7	3	28	2.2	7.4	7.7	..
9 Zaire	312	4,821	9.1	111.8	9	219	1.1	7.9	4.4	8.6
10 Burma	108	2,947	5.0	42.1	3	70	1.0	2.8	17.2	51.4
11 Burundi	7	415	3.1	39.7	(.)	9	0.3	2.0	2.3	16.6
12 Togo	40	787	16.2	121.0	1	39	0.9	13.7	3.0	27.5
13 Madagascar	90	2,340	10.5	105.4	2	53	0.8	5.3	3.7	19.6
14 Niger	32	791	5.0	51.5	1	30	0.4	4.4	4.0	26.7
15 Benin	41	677	15.2	66.9	(.)	9	0.6	2.2	2.3	..
16 Central African Rep.	24	296	13.5	44.9	1	7	1.7	2.0	5.1	11.8
17 India	8,109	26,650	15.2	13.5	196	801	1.0	1.0	23.7	9.3
18 Rwanda	2	324	0.9	19.1	(.)	4	0.1	0.9	1.2	4.3
19 Somalia	77	1,309	24.5	53.5	(.)	17	0.3	2.3	2.1	44.8
20 Kenya	333	2,857	21.6	51.2	13	142	1.9	6.9	5.8	25.5
21 Tanzania	257	2,982	20.1	48.5	7	21	1.3	1.0	5.2	16.7
22 Sudan	308	5,086	15.3	70.5	13	67	1.7	1.8	10.7	15.6
23 China	..	7,020	..	2.6	..	..	..	..	..	..
24 Haiti	40	534	10.3	27.8	(.)	7	1.0	1.1	7.7	5.8
25 Guinea	313	1,292	47.2	70.2	4	20	2.2	3.6	..	..
26 Sierra Leone	61	390	14.5	32.6	2	3	3.1	0.8	10.4	5.7
27 Senegal	101	1,989	12.0	82.3	2	44	0.8	3.7	2.9	9.0
28 Ghana	471	1,170	20.8	23.6	12	25	1.1	1.6	5.2	12.2
29 Pakistan	3,081	10,681	30.7	31.7	77	305	1.9	3.2	23.4	29.5
30 Sri Lanka	321	2,815	16.4	47.6	12	108	2.1	3.8	10.8	13.9
31 Zambia	627	3,214	36.0	150.8	28	42	3.6	4.0	6.3	10.2
32 Afghanistan	..	..	..	..	..	..	..	..	..	..
33 Chad	33	150	9.9	..	(.)	2	0.9	..	4.2	..
34 Kampuchea, Dem.	..	..	..	..	..	..	..	..	..	..
35 Lao PDR	..	..	..	..	..	..	..	..	..	..
36 Uganda	142	726	7.5	..	5	27	0.4	..	2.9	..
37 Viet Nam	..	..	..	..	..	..	..	..	..	..
Middle-income economies	**34,172 t**	**535,599 t**	**12.4 w**	**38.1 w**	**1,294 t**	**41,376 t**	**1.6 w**	**5.7 w**	**11.0 w**	**21.6 w**
Lower middle-income	16,131 t	202,541 t	15.8 w	41.4 w	488 t	11,835 t	1.7 w	5.7 w	11.3 w	22.9 w
38 Mauritania	27	1,363	13.9	208.2	(.)	28	1.8	12.0	3.3	19.0
39 Bolivia	482	3,259	46.3	124.8	7	72	2.2	6.5	11.3	29.1
40 Lesotho	8	172	7.8	30.1	(.)	4	0.5	3.2	..	6.2
41 Liberia	158	879	39.4	85.3	6	10	4.4	1.7	..	3.8
42 Indonesia	2,447	26,625	25.2	32.0	24	1,655	0.9	4.8	..	19.9
43 Yemen, PDR	1	1,446	..	134.7	0	19	..	10.6	0.0	42.3
44 Yemen, Arab Rep.	..	1,868	..	45.6	..	19	..	3.1	..	55.8
45 Morocco	716	11,231	18.3	101.3	24	490	1.6	9.3	8.6	32.7
46 Philippines	575	13,561	8.1	42.7	24	831	1.4	4.0	7.3	15.9
47 Egypt, Arab Rep.	1,760	17,751	23.1	61.9	54	567	4.6	7.8	36.8	30.9
48 Côte d'Ivoire	257	5,700	18.8	88.5	12	430	2.9	9.0	7.0	17.4
49 Papua New Guinea	39	1,061	6.2	49.0	1	66	0.2	6.0	..	10.4
50 Zimbabwe	239	1,526	16.1	31.3	5	115	0.6	6.7	..	32.2
51 Honduras	95	2,178	13.6	68.8	3	96	0.9	5.4	3.1	17.6
52 Nicaragua	147	4,753	19.5	185.2	7	19	3.0	1.6	10.5	..
53 Dominican Rep.	212	2,521	14.5	58.6	4	136	0.8	5.1	4.4	16.1
54 Nigeria	458	13,016	4.6	17.2	20	1,256	0.6	5.3	4.2	30.8
55 Thailand	326	9,898	5.0	26.8	16	603	0.6	4.1	3.4	14.7
56 Cameroon	132	1,975	12.2	26.0	4	93	0.8	3.1	3.2	10.0
57 El Salvador	88	1,460	8.6	39.6	4	68	0.9	5.3	3.6	16.3
58 Botswana	15	334	18.3	47.3	(.)	23	0.7	6.9	..	5.4
59 Paraguay	112	1,525	19.2	55.8	4	80	1.8	5.6	11.8	12.9
60 Jamaica	162	2,823	12.0	166.6	9	205	1.1	23.5	2.8	36.5
61 Peru	859	10,527	12.3	66.5	44	146	2.1	1.9	11.6	7.9
62 Turkey	1,875	17,821	14.9	34.7	43	1,253	1.4	6.8	22.1	30.8
63 Mauritius	33	404	14.7	39.8	2	26	1.4	6.6	3.2	11.5
64 Congo, People's Rep.	140	1,760	52.4	86.5	3	107	3.4	15.9	..	19.6
65 Ecuador	194	7,121	11.8	60.9	7	711	1.4	8.0	8.6	28.8
66 Tunisia	543	4,442	38.7	56.1	18	241	4.6	8.6	19.5	24.9
67 Guatemala	106	2,148	5.7	19.8	6	107	1.4	2.3	7.4	21.3

Note: For data comparability and coverage, see the technical notes. Figures in italics are for years other than those specified.

		External public debt outstanding and disbursed				Interest payments on external public debt (millions of dollars)		Debt service as percentage of:			
		Millions of dollars		As percentage of GNP				GNP		Exports of goods and services	
		1970	1985	1970	1985	1970	1985	1970	1985	1970	1985
68	Costa Rica	134	3,665	13.8	105.1	7	334	2.9	13.3	10.0	36.6
69	Colombia	1,299	9,377	18.5	28.5	44	760	1.7	4.3	12.0	29.2
70	Chile	2,075	12,735	25.9	90.3	78	1,006	3.0	8.7	19.1	26.2
71	Jordan	120	2,693	23.8	70.9	2	153	0.9	12.0	3.6	22.1
72	Syrian Arab Rep.	233	2,751	10.8	16.9	6	96	1.7	2.2	11.2	14.8
73	Lebanon	64	172	4.2	. .	1	12	0.2	. .	. .	. .
	Upper middle-income	**18,042** *t*	**333,057** *t*	**10.4** *w*	**36.3** *w*	**806** *t*	**29,541** *t*	**1.5** *w*	**5.7** *w*	**10.8** *w*	**21.0** *w*
74	Brazil	3,432	73,894	8.2	35.5	135	6,280	0.9	3.7	12.5	26.5
75	Uruguay	270	2,686	11.3	57.2	16	282	2.7	8.6	21.7	30.6
76	Hungary	. .	10,138	. .	51.1	. .	792	. .	13.0	. .	25.0
77	Portugal	487	10,803	7.8	54.6	29	1,003	1.5	12.7	. .	31.5
78	Malaysia	396	13,834	9.7	47.8	22	1,130	1.7	13.7	3.7	22.3
79	South Africa	. .	. .	. .	. .	. .	. .	. .	. .	. .	. .
80	Poland	. .	. .	. .	. .	. .	. .	. .	. .	. .	. .
81	Yugoslavia	1,204	9,919	8.8	21.5	73	738	1.8	2.5	10.0	8.2
82	Mexico	3,196	72,510	9.1	43.0	216	7,502	2.0	6.5	23.6	37.0
83	Panama	194	3,276	19.5	72.2	7	300	3.1	9.5	7.7	6.9
84	Argentina	1,891	35,604	8.5	50.0	121	3,476	2.1	6.1	21.6	41.8
85	Korea, Rep. of	1,844	29,126	21.2	35.0	71	2,151	3.1	6.1	19.5	15.2
86	Algeria	941	13,664	19.4	24.0	10	1,297	0.9	8.1	3.9	33.3
87	Venezuela	729	16,650	6.6	35.2	40	1,372	0.7	4.6	2.9	12.8
88	Greece	916	12,452	9.0	38.3	41	957	1.0	5.4	9.4	24.7
89	Israel	2,284	15,850	41.5	82.4	13	1,323	0.7	11.0	2.8	19.7
90	Trinidad and Tobago	102	1,087	12.4	15.1	6	80	1.9	2.6	4.5	7.1
91	Hong Kong	3	251	0.1	0.7	0	24	(.)	0.2	(.)	0.2
92	Oman		1,946	. .	24.1	. .	112	. .	3.2	. .	4.8
93	Singapore	154	1,791	8.0	10.1	7	155	0.6	4.1	0.6	2.4
94	*Iran, Islamic Rep.*	. .	. .	. .	. .	. .	. .	. .	. .	. .	. .
95	*Iraq*	. .	. .	. .	. .	. .	. .	. .	. .	. .	. .
96	*Romania*	. .	5,801	. .	. .	. .	543	. .	*4.3*	. .	13.6
	Developing economies	**49,662** *t*	**628,595** *t*	**13.5** *w*	**31.5** *w*	**1,692** *t*	**43,625** *t*	**1.5** *w*	**4.3** *w*	**11.2** *w*	**19.7** *w*
	Oil exporters	**10,331** *t*	**176,855** *t*	**12.2** *w*	**34.5** *w*	**391** *t*	**14,848** *t*	**1.7** *w*	**5.9** *w*	**12.6** *w*	**25.6** *w*
	Exporters of manufactures	**17,517** *t*	**193,019** *t*	**13.0** *w*	**20.3** *w*	**522** *t*	**13,835** *t*	**1.2** *w*	**2.7** *w*	**11.8** *w*	**13.6** *w*
	Highly indebted countries	**17,932** *t*	**304,276** *t*	**10.2** *w*	**40.3** *w*	**876** *t*	**25,889** *t*	**1.6** *w*	**5.1** *w*	**12.4** *w*	**27.8** *w*
	Sub-Saharan Africa	**5,294** *t*	**62,984** *t*	**14.2** *w*	**39.1** *w*	**163** *t*	**2,956** *t*	**1.2** *w*	**4.8** *w*	**5.3** *w*	**21.5** *w*
	High-income oil exporters										
97	Libya										
98	Saudi Arabia										
99	Kuwait										
100	United Arab Emirates										
	Industrial market economies										
101	Spain										
102	Ireland										
103	Italy										
104	New Zealand										
105	Belgium										
106	United Kingdom										
107	Austria										
108	Netherlands										
109	France										
110	Australia										
111	Finland										
112	Germany, Fed. Rep.										
113	Denmark										
114	Japan										
115	Sweden										
116	Canada										
117	Norway										
118	Switzerland										
119	United States										
	Nonreporting nonmember economies										
120	*Albania*										
121	*Angola*										
122	*Bulgaria*										
123	*Cuba*										
124	*Czechoslovakia*										
125	*German Dem. Rep.*										
126	*Korea, Dem. Rep.*										
127	*Mongolia*										
128	*USSR*										

Table 20. Terms of external public borrowing

	Commitments (millions of dollars)		Average interest rate (percent)		Average maturity (years)		Average grace period (years)		Public loans with variable interest rates, as percentage of public debt	
	1970	1985	1970	1985	1970	1985	1970	1985	1970	1985
Low-income economies	3,613 t	11,160 t	3.0 w	4.6 w	30 w	30 w	9 w	7 w	0.1 w	5.8 w
China and India	..	..	..	..	..	..	..	..	..	..
Other low-income	2,663 t	6,492 t	3.2 w	3.4 w	28 w	33 w	9 w	8 w	0.1 w	4.7 w
1 Ethiopia	21	487	4.4	3.4	32	19	7	4	0.1	5.4
2 Bangladesh	..	772	..	1.0	..	41	..	10	..	0.1
3 Burkina Faso	9	93	2.3	1.7	37	41	8	9	0.0	0.6
4 Mali	34	120	1.1	1.3	25	43	9	9	0.0	0.4
5 Bhutan	..	..	..	..	..	..	..	..	..	..
6 Mozambique	..	..	..	..	..	..	..	..	..	..
7 Nepal	17	196	2.8	0.9	27	44	6	9	0.0	0.0
8 Malawi	14	128	3.8	1.2	29	48	6	10	0.0	9.4
9 Zaire	259	202	6.5	3.1	12	36	4	8	0.0	7.7
10 Burma	50	410	4.1	3.2	17	29	5	8	0.0	0.6
11 Burundi	1	139	2.9	1.3	5	38	2	9	0.0	1.5
12 Togo	3	61	4.5	0.8	17	49	4	10	0.0	6.8
13 Madagascar	23	167	2.3	3.0	40	34	9	8	0.0	8.1
14 Niger	19	129	1.2	4.8	40	23	8	7	0.0	13.3
15 Benin	7	45	1.8	3.4	32	34	7	9	0.0	7.6
16 Central African Rep.	7	37	2.0	3.3	36	27	8	7	0.0	0.0
17 India	950	4,668	2.5	6.4	35	26	8	6	0.0	8.4
18 Rwanda	9	60	0.8	4.0	50	27	10	7	0.0	0.0
19 Somalia	2	47	0.0	0.7	4	43	4	9	0.0	0.0
20 Kenya	50	245	2.6	6.9	37	21	8	6	0.1	4.3
21 Tanzania	284	73	1.2	0.5	39	47	11	11	1.6	0.1
22 Sudan	95	53	1.8	0.8	17	50	9	10	0.0	2.0
23 China	..	..	..	..	..	..	..	..	..	..
24 Haiti	5	47	4.8	1.4	10	46	1	10	0.0	2.2
25 Guinea	67	136	2.9	3.1	13	27	5	8	0.0	0.5
26 Sierra Leone	25	21	2.9	0.6	27	26	6	8	10.7	0.6
27 Senegal	7	77	3.8	6.4	24	25	7	6	0.0	7.3
28 Ghana	56	275	2.1	1.6	37	43	10	9	0.0	0.0
29 Pakistan	943	1,776	2.8	5.6	32	27	12	6	0.0	4.9
30 Sri Lanka	80	394	3.0	2.9	27	36	5	9	0.0	11.4
31 Zambia	556	237	4.2	2.3	27	41	9	9	0.0	17.9
32 *Afghanistan*	..	..	..	..	..	..	..	..	..	..
33 *Chad*	10	4	5.7	3.5	8	17	1	6	0.0	0.2
34 *Kampuchea, Dem.*	..	..	..	..	..	..	..	..	..	..
35 *Lao PDR*	..	..	..	..	..	..	..	..	..	..
36 *Uganda*	12	62	3.7	1.7	28	41	7	9	0.0	0.5
37 *Viet Nam*	..	..	..	..	..	..	..	..	..	..
Middle-income economies	8,969 t	62,417 t	6.3 w	8.6 w	17 w	13 w	5 w	5 w	2.4 w	50.9 w
Lower middle-income	3,723 t	28,191 t	5.1 w	8.3 w	21 w	15 w	6 w	5 w	0.5 w	32.2 w
38 Mauritania	7	66	6.0	1.9	11	36	3	8	0.0	2.9
39 Bolivia	24	53	1.9	6.8	26	28	4	7	0.0	26.4
40 Lesotho	(.)	23	5.5	3.6	27	35	2	7	0.0	0.0
41 Liberia	12	43	6.7	5.1	19	33	5	7	0.0	13.5
42 Indonesia	520	4,016	2.6	8.1	34	16	9	6	0.0	21.7
43 Yemen, PDR	63	836	0.0	2.1	21	23	11	5	0.0	0.0
44 Yemen, Arab Rep.	..	87	..	3.4	..	23	..	5	..	0.0
45 Morocco	186	1,020	4.6	8.5	20	15	3	3	0.0	36.3
46 Philippines	158	1,418	7.4	9.1	11	11	2	4	0.9	35.2
47 Egypt, Arab Rep.	471	2,009	7.6	8.6	18	25	11	12	0.0	2.3
48 Côte d'Ivoire	72	486	5.8	10.3	19	15	5	5	9.1	47.6
49 Papua New Guinea	80	114	6.3	9.2	22	13	8	4	0.0	37.7
50 Zimbabwe	..	168	..	6.2	..	23	..	7	..	32.9
51 Honduras	23	263	4.1	6.6	30	20	7	5	0.0	17.7
52 Nicaragua	23	449	7.1	4.0	18	17	4	3	0.0	29.8
53 Dominican Rep.	20	322	2.4	8.1	28	17	5	7	0.0	28.8
54 Nigeria	65	1,253	6.0	9.3	14	13	4	4	2.8	41.7
55 Thailand	106	2,398	6.8	8.4	19	18	4	10	0.0	32.6
56 Cameroon	41	294	4.7	8.1	29	18	8	4	0.0	5.3
57 El Salvador	12	185	4.7	4.7	23	28	6	7	0.0	11.6
58 Botswana	37	85	0.6	8.4	39	19	10	4	0.0	10.0
59 Paraguay	14	234	5.7	8.5	25	15	6	4	0.0	15.8
60 Jamaica	24	444	6.0	7.7	16	16	3	10	0.0	18.8
61 Peru	125	348	7.4	9.4	11	16	3	4	0.0	40.3
62 Turkey	491	3,588	3.6	8.7	19	11	5	4	0.9	29.1
63 Mauritius	13	75	0.0	7.1	24	18	2	5	5.8	20.6
64 Congo, People's Rep.	34	253	2.6	9.4	18	10	7	3	0.0	17.7
65 Ecuador	78	845	6.2	9.4	20	13	4	3	0.0	71.7
66 Tunisia	143	475	3.5	7.8	27	16	6	5	0.0	16.7
67 Guatemala	50	395	5.5	8.3	26	11	6	3	10.3	36.9

Note: For data comparability and coverage, see the technical notes.   Figures in italics are for years other than those specified.

	Commitments (millions of dollars)		Average interest rate (percent)		Average maturity (years)		Average grace period (years)		Public loans with variable interest rates, as percentage of public debt	
	1970	1985	1970	1985	1970	1985	1970	1985	1970	1985
68 Costa Rica	58	469	5.7	6.7	28	17	6	6	7.5	56.8
69 Colombia	363	2,600	6.0	9.7	21	12	5	3	0.0	40.7
70 Chile	356	1,884	6.8	9.4	12	13	4	2	0.0	81.5
71 Jordan	34	757	3.8	8.9	12	12	5	2	0.0	18.4
72 Syrian Arab Rep.	14	236	4.4	5.3	9	13	2	3	0.0	1.2
73 *Lebanon*	7	0	2.9	0.0	22	0	1	0	0.0	0.0
Upper middle-income	**5,246** *t*	**34,226** *t*	**7.2** *w*	**8.9** *w*	**14** *w*	**12** *w*	**4** *w*	**5** *w*	**4.0** *w*	**62.3** *w*
74 Brazil	1,427	3,014	6.8	9.6	14	12	3	3	11.7	71.5
75 Uruguay	72	153	7.9	11.4	12	5	3	1	0.7	64.3
76 Hungary[a]	. .	4,011	. .	8.1	. .	9	. .	5	. .	65.4
77 Portugal	59	3,407	4.3	8.8	17	9	4	4	0.0	36.5
78 Malaysia	84	2,743	6.1	8.5	19	22	5	17	0.0	54.3
79 South Africa	. .	. .	. .	. .	. .	. .	. .	. .	. .	. .
80 Poland	. .	. .	. .	. .	. .	. .	. .	. .	. .	. .
81 Yugoslavia	199	258	7.1	9.1	17	15	6	3	3.3	61.0
82 Mexico	857	2,309	7.9	9.3	12	11	3	3	5.7	80.1
83 Panama	111	207	6.1	8.6	15	15	4	4	0.0	58.5
84 Argentina	494	3,934	7.3	9.9	12	10	3	4	0.0	60.2
85 Korea, Rep. of	687	5,898	5.8	8.6	19	12	6	5	1.1	49.7
86 Algeria	301	3,140	6.4	7.0	10	11	2	2	2.8	30.0
87 Venezuela	198	34	7.8	9.5	8	20	2	5	2.6	93.4
88 Greece	245	2,884	7.2	9.5	9	11	4	7	3.5	65.4
89 Israel	440	511	10.0	9.1	13	11	4	7	0.0	1.2
90 Trinidad and Tobago	3	266	7.4	8.7	10	7	1	4	0.0	47.5
91 Hong Kong	0	0	0.0	0.0	0	0	0	0	0.0	33.2
92 Oman	. .	886	. .	9.3	. .	10	. .	4	. .	15.5
93 Singapore	69	402	6.9	10.1	18	10	4	5	0.0	21.9
94 *Iran, Islamic Rep.*	. .	. .	. .	. .	. .	. .	. .	. .	. .	. .
95 *Iraq*	. .	. .	. .	. .	. .	. .	. .	. .	. .	. .
96 *Romania*	. .	345	. .	*9.1*	. .	*13*	. .	*3*	. .	46.4
Developing economies	**12,582** *t*	**73,577** *t*	**5.4** *w*	**8.0** *w*	**20** *w*	**16** *w*	**6** *w*	**6** *w*	**1.6** *w*	**44.6** *w*
Oil exporters	**2,582** *t*	**15,540** *t*	**6.4** *w*	**8.4** *w*	**18** *w*	**14** *w*	**6** *w*	**5** *w*	**2.3** *w*	**54.1** *w*
Exporters of manufactures	**3,831** *t*	**22,339** *t*	**5.9** *w*	**8.3** *w*	**20** *w*	**14** *w*	**5** *w*	**5** *w*	**2.6** *w*	**48.6** *w*
Highly indebted countries	**4,756** *t*	**20,521** *t*	**7.0** *w*	**9.4** *w*	**14** *w*	**12** *w*	**4** *w*	**3** *w*	**3.9** *w*	**65.6** *w*
Sub-Saharan Africa	**1,848** *t*	**5,643** *t*	**3.6** *w*	**5.8** *w*	**26** *w*	**25** *w*	**8** *w*	**6** *w*	**0.9** *w*	**17.8** *w*

High-income oil exporters

97 Libya
98 Saudi Arabia
99 Kuwait
100 United Arab Emirates

Industrial market economies

101 Spain
102 Ireland
103 Italy
104 New Zealand
105 Belgium

106 United Kingdom
107 Austria
108 Netherlands
109 France
110 Australia

111 Finland
112 Germany, Fed. Rep.
113 Denmark
114 Japan
115 Sweden

116 Canada
117 Norway
118 Switzerland
119 United States

Nonreporting nonmember economies

120 *Albania*
121 *Angola*
122 *Bulgaria*
123 *Cuba*
124 *Czechoslovakia*

125 *German Dem. Rep.*
126 *Korea, Dem. Rep.*
127 *Mongolia*
128 *USSR*

a. Includes only debt in convertible currencies.

Table 21. Official development assistance from OECD & OPEC members

	Amount									
	1965	1970	1975	1980	1981	1982	1983	1984	1985	1986[a]
OECD					Millions of US dollars					
102 Ireland	0	0	8	30	28	47	33	35	39	62
103 Italy	60	147	182	683	666	811	834	1,133	1,098	2,423
104 New Zealand	..	14	66	72	68	65	61	55	54	66
105 Belgium	102	120	378	595	575	499	477	442	440	542
106 United Kingdom	472	500	904	1,854	2,192	1,800	1,610	1,430	1,530	1,796
107 Austria	10	11	79	178	220	236	158	181	248	197
108 Netherlands	70	196	608	1,630	1,510	1,472	1,195	1,268	1,136	1,738
109 France	752	971	2,093	4,162	4,177	4,034	3,815	3,788	3,995	5,136
110 Australia	119	212	552	667	650	882	753	777	749	787
111 Finland	2	7	48	111	135	144	153	178	211	313
112 Germany, Fed. Rep.	456	599	1,689	3,567	3,181	3,152	3,176	2,782	2,942	3,879
113 Denmark	13	59	205	481	403	415	395	449	440	695
114 Japan	244	458	1,148	3,353	3,171	3,023	3,761	4,319	3,797	5,588
115 Sweden	38	117	566	962	919	987	754	741	840	1,128
116 Canada	96	337	880	1,075	1,189	1,197	1,429	1,625	1,631	1,700
117 Norway	11	37	184	486	467	559	584	540	575	797
118 Switzerland	12	30	104	253	237	252	320	286	303	429
119 United States	4,023	3,153	4,161	7,138	5,782	8,202	8,081	8,711	9,403	9,784
Total	6,480	6,968	13,847	27,267	25,542	27,777	27,589	28,739	29,429	37,060
OECD					As percentage of donor GNP					
102 Ireland	0.00	0.00	0.09	0.16	0.16	0.27	0.20	0.22	0.24	0.28
103 Italy	0.10	0.16	0.11	0.17	0.19	0.23	0.24	0.33	0.31	0.40
104 New Zealand	..	0.23	0.52	0.33	0.29	0.28	0.28	0.25	0.25	0.27
105 Belgium	0.60	0.46	0.59	0.50	0.59	0.58	0.58	0.57	0.55	0.48
106 United Kingdom	0.47	0.41	0.39	0.35	0.43	0.37	0.35	0.33	0.33	0.33
107 Austria	0.11	0.07	0.21	0.23	0.33	0.36	0.24	0.28	0.38	0.21
108 Netherlands	0.36	0.61	0.75	1.03	1.08	1.07	0.91	1.02	0.91	1.00
109 France	0.76	0.66	0.62	0.64	0.73	0.74	0.74	0.77	0.79	0.72
110 Australia	0.53	0.59	0.65	0.48	0.41	0.56	0.49	0.45	0.48	0.49
111 Finland	0.02	0.06	0.18	0.22	0.28	0.29	0.32	0.35	0.40	0.45
112 Germany, Fed. Rep.	0.40	0.32	0.40	0.44	0.47	0.48	0.48	0.45	0.47	0.43
113 Denmark	0.13	0.38	0.58	0.74	0.73	0.77	0.73	0.85	0.80	0.89
114 Japan	0.27	0.23	0.23	0.32	0.28	0.28	0.32	0.34	0.29	0.28
115 Sweden	0.19	0.38	0.82	0.79	0.83	1.02	0.84	0.80	0.86	0.88
116 Canada	0.19	0.41	0.54	0.43	0.43	0.41	0.45	0.50	0.49	0.48
117 Norway	0.16	0.32	0.66	0.85	0.82	1.03	1.10	1.03	1.01	1.20
118 Switzerland	0.09	0.15	0.19	0.24	0.24	0.25	0.31	0.30	0.31	0.30
119 United States	0.58	0.32	0.27	0.27	0.20	0.27	0.24	0.24	0.24	0.23
OECD					National currencies					
102 Ireland (millions of pounds)	0	0	4	15	17	33	26	32	37	47
103 Italy (billions of lire)	38	92	119	585	757	1,097	1,267	1,991	2,097	3,612
104 New Zealand (millions of dollars)	..	13	55	74	78	87	91	95	109	125
105 Belgium (millions of francs)	5,100	6,000	13,902	17,399	21,350	22,800	24,390	25,527	26,145	24,201
106 United Kingdom (millions of pounds)	169	208	409	798	1,091	1,031	1,062	1,070	1,180	1,224
107 Austria (millions of schillings)	260	286	1,376	2,303	3,504	4,026	2,838	3,622	5,132	3,014
108 Netherlands (millions of guilders)	253	710	1,538	3,241	3,768	3,931	3,411	4,069	3,773	4,257
109 France (millions of francs)	3,713	5,393	8,971	17,589	22,700	26,513	29,075	33,107	35,894	35,572
110 Australia (millions of dollars)	106	189	402	591	568	798	802	873	966	1,173
111 Finland (millions of markkaa)	6	29	177	414	583	694	852	1,070	1,308	1,587
112 Germany, Fed. Rep. (millions of deutsche marks)	1,824	2,192	4,155	6,484	7,189	7,649	8,109	7,917	8,661	8,424
113 Denmark (millions of kroner)	90	443	1,178	2,711	2,871	3,458	3,612	4,650	4,657	5,623
114 Japan (billions of yen)	88	165	341	760	699	753	893	1,026	906	942
115 Sweden (millions of kronor)	197	605	2,350	4,069	4,653	6,201	5,781	6,129	7,226	8,035
116 Canada (millions of dollars)	104	353	895	1,257	1,425	1,477	1,761	2,104	2,227	2,362
117 Norway (millions of kroner)	79	264	962	2,400	2,680	3,608	4,261	4,407	4,946	5,894
118 Switzerland (millions of francs)	52	131	268	424	466	512	672	672	743	772
119 United States (millions of dollars)	4,023	3,153	4,161	7,138	5,782	8,202	8,081	8,711	9,403	9,784
OECD					Summary					
ODA (billions of US dollars, nominal prices)	6.48	6.97	13.86	27.30	25.57	27.78	27.59	28.74	29.43	37.06
ODA as percentage of GNP	0.48	0.34	0.35	0.37	0.34	0.37	0.36	0.36	0.35	0.36
ODA (billions of US dollars, constant 1980 prices)	20.68	18.41	21.84	27.30	25.69	27.99	27.43	28.65	28.80	30.54
GNP (trillions of US dollars, nominal prices)	1.35	2.04	3.96	7.39	7.50	7.43	7.70	8.03	8.42	10.24
GDP deflator[b]	0.31	0.38	0.63	1.00	1.00	0.99	1.01	1.00	1.02	1.21

	Amount									
	1976	1977	1978	1979	1980	1981	1982	1983	1984	1985[a]
OPEC	**Millions of US dollars**									
54 Nigeria	80	51	27	29	34	143	58	35	51	45
86 Algeria	11	35	39	281	81	55	129	37	48	45
87 Venezuela	109	26	96	110	135	92	125	142	90	32
94 Iran, Islamic Rep. of	751	152	231	−20	−72	−141	−193	20	−13	−171
95 Iraq	123	103	123	658	864	207	52	−30	−33	−26
97 Libya	98	130	132	145	376	257	44	144	20	151
98 Saudi Arabia	2,791	2,900	5,250	3,941	5,682	5,514	3,854	3,304	3,212	2,646
99 Kuwait	706	1,302	1,001	971	1,140	1,163	1,161	997	1,018	749
100 United Arab Emirates	1,028	1,091	889	968	1,118	805	407	348	84	58
Qatar	180	127	95	282	277	246	139	20	10	−2
Total OAPEC	4,937	5,688	7,529	7,246	9,538	8,247	5,786	4,820	4,359	3,621
Total OPEC	5,877	5,917	7,883	7,365	9,635	8,341	5,776	5,017	4,487	3,527
OPEC	**As percentage of donor GNP**									
54 Nigeria	0.19	0.11	0.05	0.04	0.04	0.19	0.08	0.05	0.07	0.06
86 Algeria	0.07	0.18	0.15	0.90	0.20	0.13	0.31	0.08	0.10	0.08
87 Venezuela	0.35	0.07	0.24	0.23	0.23	0.14	0.19	0.22	0.19	0.07
94 Iran, Islamic Rep. of	1.16	0.20	0.33	−0.02	−0.08	−0.13	−0.15	0.01	−0.01	−0.11
95 Iraq	0.76	0.55	0.55	1.97	2.36	0.94	0.18	−0.09	−0.10	−0.08
97 Libya	0.66	0.73	0.75	0.60	1.16	0.81	0.15	0.51	0.08	0.59
98 Saudi Arabia	5.95	4.93	8.06	5.16	4.87	3.45	2.50	2.86	3.44	2.88
99 Kuwait	4.82	8.19	5.53	3.52	3.52	3.65	4.34	3.73	3.82	3.16
100 United Arab Emirates	8.95	7.50	6.38	5.08	4.06	2.57	1.39	1.30	0.32	0.24
Qatar	7.35	5.09	3.29	6.07	4.16	3.50	2.13	0.39	0.17	−0.03
Total OAPEC	4.23	3.95	4.51	3.31	3.22	2.52	1.81	1.70	1.60	1.60
Total OPEC	2.32	1.96	2.39	1.75	1.79	1.45	0.98	0.86	1.13	1.06

	Net bilateral flows to low-income economies									
	1965	1970	1975	1979	1980	1981	1982	1983	1984	1985
OECD	**As percentage of donor GNP**									
102 Ireland	. .	. .	. .	. .	. .	. .	0.02	0.03	0.03	0.05
103 Italy	0.04	0.06	0.01	0.01	0.01	0.02	0.04	0.05	0.09	0.12
104 New Zealand	. .	. .	0.14	0.01	0.01	0.01	0.00	0.00	0.00	0.00
105 Belgium	0.56	0.30	0.31	0.27	0.24	0.25	0.21	0.21	0.20	0.23
106 United Kingdom	0.23	0.15	0.11	0.16	0.11	0.13	0.07	0.10	0.09	0.09
107 Austria	0.06	0.05	0.02	0.03	0.03	0.03	0.01	0.02	0.01	0.02
108 Netherlands	0.08	0.24	0.24	0.26	0.30	0.37	0.31	0.26	0.29	0.27
109 France	0.12	0.09	0.10	0.07	0.08	0.11	0.10	0.09	0.14	0.14
110 Australia	0.08	0.09	0.10	0.06	0.04	0.06	0.07	0.05	0.06	0.05
111 Finland	. .	. .	0.06	0.06	0.08	0.09	0.09	0.12	0.13	0.17
112 Germany, Fed. Rep.	0.14	0.10	0.12	0.10	0.08	0.11	0.12	0.13	0.11	0.14
113 Denmark	0.02	0.10	0.20	0.28	0.28	0.21	0.26	0.31	0.28	0.32
114 Japan	0.13	0.11	0.08	0.09	0.08	0.06	0.11	0.09	0.07	0.09
115 Sweden	0.07	0.12	0.41	0.41	0.36	0.32	0.38	0.33	0.30	0.31
116 Canada	0.10	0.22	0.24	0.13	0.11	0.13	0.14	0.13	0.15	0.15
117 Norway	0.04	0.12	0.25	0.37	0.31	0.28	0.37	0.39	0.34	0.40
118 Switzerland	0.02	0.05	0.10	0.06	0.08	0.07	0.09	0.10	0.12	0.12
119 United States	0.26	0.14	0.08	0.02	0.03	0.03	0.02	0.03	0.03	0.04
Total	0.20	0.13	0.11	0.08	0.07	0.08	0.08	0.08	0.07	0.09

a. Preliminary estimates.   b. See the technical notes.

Table 22. Official development assistance: receipts

	Net disbursements of ODA from all sources								
	Millions of dollars							Per capita (dollars)	As percentage of GNP
	1979	1980	1981	1982	1983	1984	1985	1985	1985
Low-income economies	**9,680 *t***	**11,775 *t***	**11,258 *t***	**11,375 *t***	**11,064 *t***	**11,243 *t***	**12,674 *t***	**5.2 *w***	**2.1 *w***
China and India	**1,367 *t***	**2,213 *t***	**2,387 *t***	**2,069 *t***	**2,412 *t***	**2,340 *t***	**2,410 *t***	**1.3 *w***	**0.5 *w***
Other low-income	**8,313 *t***	**9,563 *t***	**8,871 *t***	**9,306 *t***	**8,651 *t***	**8,903 *t***	**10,264 *t***	**16.2 *w***	**7.8 *w***
1 Ethiopia	191	212	245	200	339	364	710	16.8	15.1
2 Bangladesh	1,166	1,283	1,104	1,346	1,067	1,201	1,142	11.4	7.1
3 Burkina Faso	198	212	217	213	184	189	197	25.0	18.4
4 Mali	193	267	230	210	215	320	380	50.6	34.9
5 Bhutan	6	8	10	11	13	18	24	19.4	12.9
6 Mozambique	146	169	144	208	211	259	300	21.8	9.2
7 Nepal	137	163	181	201	201	198	236	14.3	10.1
8 Malawi	142	143	138	121	117	159	113	16.0	11.0
9 Zaire	416	428	394	348	315	313	324	10.6	7.5
10 Burma	364	309	283	319	302	275	356	9.6	5.1
11 Burundi	95	117	122	127	140	141	143	30.4	13.7
12 Togo	110	91	63	77	112	110	114	37.5	17.5
13 Madagascar	138	230	234	242	179	151	182	17.8	8.2
14 Niger	174	170	193	258	175	162	305	47.7	19.8
15 Benin	85	91	82	81	86	78	96	23.7	9.5
16 Central African Rep.	84	111	102	90	93	114	105	40.5	15.9
17 India	1,350	2,147	1,910	1,545	1,743	1,542	1,470	1.9	0.7
18 Rwanda	148	155	154	151	149	165	181	30.1	10.7
19 Somalia	194	433	375	462	327	363	354	65.7	14.5
20 Kenya	351	397	449	485	401	411	439	21.5	7.9
21 Tanzania	589	679	703	684	594	558	487	21.9	7.9
22 Sudan	687	583	632	740	957	617	1,129	51.5	15.6
23 China	17	66	477	524	670	798	940	0.9	0.4
24 Haiti	93	105	107	128	134	135	153	25.8	8.0
25 Guinea	56	90	107	90	68	123	119	19.3	6.5
26 Sierra Leone	54	91	60	82	66	61	66	18.0	5.5
27 Senegal	307	262	397	285	322	368	295	44.9	12.2
28 Ghana	169	193	148	141	110	216	204	16.1	4.1
29 Pakistan	684	1,130	764	849	669	683	750	7.8	2.2
30 Sri Lanka	323	390	379	417	474	468	486	30.7	8.2
31 Zambia	278	318	232	317	217	240	329	49.1	15.4
32 *Afghanistan*	108	32	23	9	14	7	17	..	..
33 Chad	86	35	60	65	95	115	182	36.2	..
34 *Kampuchea, Dem.*	108	281	130	44	37	17	13	..	..
35 *Lao PDR*	54	41	35	38	30	34	37	10.3	2.7
36 *Uganda*	47	114	136	133	137	164	184	12.5	..
37 *Viet Nam*	336	229	242	136	106	109	114	1.8	..
Middle-income economies	**12,189 *t***	**13,811 *t***	**13,822 *t***	**12,069 *t***	**11,993 *t***	**12,134 *t***	**12,930 *t***	**11.4 *w***	**0.9 *w***
Lower middle-income	**10,005 *t***	**11,865 *t***	**11,609 *t***	**10,242 *t***	**9,758 *t***	**9,827 *t***	**9,867 *t***	**14.6 *w***	**2.0 *w***
38 Mauritania	167	176	234	187	176	172	205	120.8	31.2
39 Bolivia	161	170	169	147	174	172	202	31.7	6.2
40 Lesotho	66	94	104	93	108	101	94	61.1	16.5
41 Liberia	81	98	109	109	118	133	91	41.1	8.8
42 Indonesia	721	950	975	906	745	673	603	3.7	0.7
43 Yemen, PDR	77	100	87	143	107	84	112	53.7	10.4
44 Yemen, Arab Rep.	268	472	411	413	328	333	288	36.2	7.0
45 Morocco	472	894	1,034	771	396	351	834	38.0	7.5
46 Philippines	267	300	376	333	429	397	486	8.9	1.5
47 Egypt, Arab Rep.	1,450	1,387	1,292	1,417	1,438	1,768	1,759	36.3	6.1
48 Côte d'Ivoire	162	210	124	137	155	128	125	12.4	1.9
49 Papua New Guinea	284	326	336	311	333	322	259	73.7	12.0
50 Zimbabwe	13	164	212	216	209	298	237	28.2	4.9
51 Honduras	97	103	109	158	192	290	276	63.0	8.7
52 Nicaragua	115	223	172	121	120	114	102	31.3	4.0
53 Dominican Rep.	78	125	105	137	102	198	222	34.6	5.2
54 Nigeria	27	36	41	37	48	33	32	0.3	(.)
55 Thailand	393	418	407	389	432	475	481	9.3	1.3
56 Cameroon	277	265	199	212	129	187	160	15.7	2.1
57 El Salvador	60	97	167	223	295	263	345	72.4	9.4
58 Botswana	100	106	97	102	104	103	97	90.5	13.7
59 Paraguay	31	31	55	85	51	50	50	13.6	1.8
60 Jamaica	123	136	155	180	181	170	169	76.0	10.0
61 Peru	200	203	233	188	297	310	316	17.0	2.0
62 Turkey	594	952	724	644	353	241	176	3.5	0.3
63 Mauritius	32	33	58	48	41	36	29	28.2	2.8
64 Congo, People's Rep.	91	92	81	93	108	98	71	38.0	3.5
65 Ecuador	70	46	59	53	64	136	136	14.5	1.2
66 Tunisia	211	232	240	210	205	184	162	22.7	2.1
67 Guatemala	67	73	75	64	76	65	83	10.4	0.8

Note: For data comparability and coverage, see the technical notes.   Figures in italics are for years other than those specified.

	Net disbursements of ODA from all sources							Per capita (dollars)	As percentage of GNP
	Millions of dollars								
	1979	1980	1981	1982	1983	1984	1985	1985	1985
68 Costa Rica	56	65	55	80	252	218	280	107.7	8.0
69 Colombia	54	90	102	97	86	88	62	2.2	0.2
70 Chile	−27	−10	−7	−8	(.)	3	40	3.3	0.3
71 Jordan	1,299	1,275	1,065	799	788	697	550	156.8	14.5
72 Syrian Arab Rep.	1,773	1,697	1,500	962	998	863	639	60.8	3.9
73 *Lebanon*	101	237	455	187	123	78	94	35.3	. .
Upper middle-income	**2,184** *t*	**1,946** *t*	**2,213** *t*	**1,828** *t*	**2,235** *t*	**2,307** *t*	**3,062** *t*	**6.6** *w*	**0.4** *w*
74 Brazil	107	85	235	208	101	161	123	0.9	0.1
75 Uruguay	14	10	8	4	3	4	5	1.6	0.1
76 Hungary	. .	. .	. .	. .	. .	. .	. .	. .	. .
77 Portugal	136	113	82	49	45	98	103	10.0	0.5
78 Malaysia	125	135	143	135	177	327	229	14.7	0.8
79 South Africa	. .	. .	. .	. .	. .	. .	. .	. .	. .
80 Poland	. .	. .	. .	. .	. .	. .	. .	. .	. .
81 Yugoslavia	−29	−17	−15	−8	3	3	11	0.5	(.)
82 Mexico	75	56	100	140	132	83	145	1.8	0.1
83 Panama	35	46	39	41	47	72	69	31.7	1.5
84 Argentina	43	19	44	30	47	49	39	1.3	0.1
85 Korea, Rep. of	134	139	331	34	8	−37	−9	−0.2	(.)
86 Algeria	102	176	168	137	145	122	173	7.9	0.3
87 Venezuela	7	15	14	12	10	14	11	0.6	(.)
88 Greece	41	40	14	12	13	13	13	1.3	(.)
89 Israel	1,185	892	772	857	1,345	1,256	1,978	467.4	10.3
90 Trinidad and Tobago	4	5	−1	6	6	5	7	5.6	0.1
91 Hong Kong	12	11	10	8	9	14	21	3.8	0.1
92 Oman	165	168	231	132	71	67	78	62.8	1.0
93 Singapore	6	14	22	21	15	41	24	9.3	0.1
94 *Iran, Islamic Rep.*	6	31	9	3	48	13	17	0.4	. .
95 *Iraq*	18	8	9	6	13	4	26	1.6	. .
96 *Romania*	. .	. .	. .	. .	. .	. .	. .	. .	. .
Developing economies	**21,869** *t*	**25,586** *t*	**25,080** *t*	**23,445** *t*	**23,057** *t*	**23,377** *t*	**25,603** *t*	**7.2** *w*	**1.3** *w*
Oil exporters	**4,784** *t*	**4,931** *t*	**4,676** *t*	**4,116** *t*	**3,952** *t*	**4,065** *t*	**3,856** *t*	**7.4** *w*	**0.7** *w*
Exporters of manufactures	**2,917** *t*	**3,450** *t*	**3,824** *t*	**3,239** *t*	**3,938** *t*	**3,875** *t*	**4,660** *t*	**2.3** *w*	**0.5** *w*
Highly indebted countries	**1,778** *t*	**2,309** *t*	**2,725** *t*	**2,402** *t*	**2,376** *t*	**2,320** *t*	**3,016** *t*	**5.4** *w*	**0.4** *w*
Sub-Saharan Africa	**5,998** *t*	**6,919** *t*	**6,933** *t*	**7,103** *t*	**6,877** *t*	**7,140** *t*	**8,168** *t*	**19.5** *w*	**0.5** *w*
High-income oil exporters	**25**	**47**	**50**	**80**	**59**	**49**	**42**	**2.3** *w*	**(.)** *w*
97 Libya	5	17	11	12	6	5	5	1.4	(.)
98 Saudi Arabia	11	16	30	57	44	36	29	2.5	(.)
99 Kuwait	2	10	9	6	5	5	4	2.5	(.)
100 United Arab Emirates	7	4	1	5	4	3	3	2.3	(.)
Industrial market economies									
101 Spain									
102 Ireland									
103 Italy									
104 New Zealand									
105 Belgium									
106 United Kingdom									
107 Austria									
108 Netherlands									
109 France									
110 Australia									
111 Finland									
112 Germany, Fed. Rep.									
113 Denmark									
114 Japan									
115 Sweden									
116 Canada									
117 Norway									
118 Switzerland									
119 United States									
Nonreporting nonmember economies	. .	. .	. .	. .	. .	. .	. .	. .	. .
120 *Albania*									
121 *Angola*	47	53	61	60	75	95	92	10.5	. .
122 *Bulgaria*									
123 *Cuba*	49	32	14	17	13	12	18	1.8	. .
124 *Czechoslovakia*									
125 *German Dem. Rep.*									
126 *Korea, Dem. Rep.*									
127 *Mongolia*									
128 *USSR*									

Table 23. Central government expenditure

	Defense		Education		Health		Housing, amenities; social security and welfare		Economic services		Other[a]		Total expenditure (percentage of GNP)		Overall surplus/deficit (percentage of GNP)	
	1972	1985	1972	1985	1972	1985	1972	1985	1972	1985	1972	1985	1972	1985	1972	1985
Low-income economies	..	..	..	..	..	..	..	..	..	..	..	..	..	..	..	..
China and India	..	..	..	..	..	..	..	..	..	..	..	..	..	..	..	..
Other low-income	17.2 w	18.6 w	13.2 w	7.6 w	4.9 w	3.7 w	5.4 w	7.2 w	23.1 w	23.9 w	36.2 w	39.1 w	18.0 w	20.3 w	−4.6 w	−5.3 w
1 Ethiopia	14.3	..	14.4	..	5.7	..	4.4	..	22.9	..	38.3	..	13.7	..	−1.4	..
2 Bangladesh	5.1	..	14.8	..	5.0	..	9.8	..	39.3	..	25.9	..	9.4	..	−1.9	..
3 Burkina Faso	11.5	18.2	20.6	16.9	8.2	5.5	6.6	7.0	15.5	14.4	37.6	37.9	11.1	14.8	0.3	−0.9
4 Mali	..	..	..	..	..	..	..	..	..	..	..	..	..	..	..	..
5 Bhutan	..	..	..	..	..	..	..	..	..	..	..	..	..	..	..	..
6 Mozambique	..	..	..	..	..	..	..	..	..	..	..	..	..	..	..	..
7 Nepal	7.2	6.2	7.2	12.1	4.7	5.0	0.7	6.8	57.2	48.5	23.0	21.5	8.5	19.7	−1.2	−8.1
8 Malawi	3.1	5.7	15.8	12.3	5.5	7.9	5.8	2.5	33.1	35.1	36.7	36.4	22.1	29.5	−6.2	−5.5
9 Zaire	11.1	5.2	15.2	0.8	2.3	1.8	2.0	0.6	13.3	5.3	56.1	86.2	19.8	23.3	−3.8	−2.4
10 Burma	31.6	18.5	15.0	11.7	6.1	7.3	7.5	9.3	20.1	35.2	19.7	17.8	20.0	15.9	−7.3	−0.2
11 Burundi	10.3	..	23.4	..	6.0	..	2.7	..	33.9	..	23.8	..	19.9	..	(.)	..
12 Togo	..	6.9	..	11.7	..	3.6	..	9.2	..	23.5	..	45.2	..	42.0	..	−2.1
13 Madagascar	3.6	..	9.1	..	4.2	..	9.9	..	40.5	..	32.7	..	20.8	..	−2.5	..
14 Niger	..	..	..	..	..	..	..	..	..	..	..	..	..	..	..	..
15 Benin	..	..	..	..	..	..	..	..	..	..	..	..	..	..	..	..
16 Central African Rep.	..	..	..	..	..	..	..	..	..	..	..	..	..	..	..	..
17 India	..	18.8	..	1.9	..	2.4	..	4.4	..	27.0	..	45.5	..	16.7	..	−8.4
18 Rwanda	25.6	..	22.2	..	5.7	..	2.6	..	22.0	..	21.9	..	12.5	..	−2.7	..
19 Somalia	23.3	..	5.5	..	7.2	..	1.9	..	21.6	..	40.5	..	13.5	..	0.6	..
20 Kenya	6.0	12.9	21.9	19.8	7.9	6.7	3.9	0.6	30.1	24.8	30.2	35.3	21.0	26.6	−3.9	−5.2
21 Tanzania	11.9	13.8	17.3	7.2	7.2	4.9	2.1	1.4	39.0	24.0	22.6	48.6	19.7	24.7	−5.0	..
22 Sudan	24.1	..	9.3	..	5.4	..	1.4	..	15.8	..	44.1	..	19.2	..	−0.8	..
23 China	..	..	..	..	..	..	..	..	..	..	..	..	..	..	..	..
24 Haiti	..	8.4	..	6.0	..	5.7	..	1.7	..	11.4	..	66.8	14.5	18.8	..	..
25 Guinea	..	..	..	..	..	..	..	..	..	..	..	..	..	..	..	..
26 Sierra Leone	..	4.4	..	16.5	..	7.5	..	2.6	..	19.8	..	49.2	..	15.4	..	−10.0
27 Senegal	..	..	..	..	..	..	..	..	..	..	..	..	18.8	..	−2.8	..
28 Ghana	7.9	7.5	20.1	18.0	6.3	9.8	4.1	7.0	15.1	23.8	46.6	33.9	19.5	12.5	−5.8	−2.1
29 Pakistan	39.9	32.3	1.2	2.9	1.1	1.1	3.2	10.2	21.4	27.8	33.2	25.7	16.5	19.0	−6.8	−7.2
30 Sri Lanka	3.1	2.6	13.0	6.4	6.4	3.6	19.5	11.1	20.2	10.2	37.7	66.2	25.4	32.6	−5.3	−6.8
31 Zambia	(.)	..	19.0	..	7.4	..	1.3	..	26.7	..	45.7	..	34.0	30.3	−13.8	−7.0
32 Afghanistan	..	..	..	..	..	..	..	..	..	..	..	..	..	..	..	..
33 Chad	24.6	..	14.8	..	4.4	..	1.7	..	21.8	..	32.7	..	12.0	..	−2.7	..
34 Kampuchea, Dem.	..	..	..	..	..	..	..	..	..	..	..	..	..	..	..	..
35 Lao PDR	..	..	..	..	..	..	..	..	..	..	..	..	..	..	..	..
36 Uganda	23.1	16.7	15.3	11.7	5.3	2.5	7.3	2.8	12.4	8.6	36.6	57.7	21.8	..	−8.1	..
37 Viet Nam	..	..	..	..	..	..	..	..	..	..	..	..	..	..	..	..
Middle-income economies	14.4 w	11.0 w	14.0 w	11.5 w	6.8 w	4.4 w	19.4 w	16.2 w	24.7 w	23.6 w	20.0 w	33.3 w	19.6 w	23.4 w	−2.8 w	−3.5 w
Lower middle-income	15.7 w	14.2 w	16.4 w	13.8 w	5.2 w	3.8 w	12.7 w	8.9 w	25.9 w	23.2 w	24.0 w	36.1 w	19.4 w	24.8 w	−3.3 w	−4.0 w
38 Mauritania	..	..	..	..	..	..	..	..	..	..	..	..	..	..	..	..
39 Bolivia	18.8	5.4	31.3	12.2	6.2	1.5	(.)	5.4	12.5	5.3	31.2	70.2	9.6	39.9	−1.8	−35.4
40 Lesotho	(.)	11.8	22.4	14.8	7.4	5.8	6.0	3.4	21.6	45.6	42.7	18.7	14.5	22.7	3.5	−0.9
41 Liberia	..	9.5	..	16.5	..	5.5	..	1.5	..	31.8	..	35.2	..	28.2	..	−8.4
42 Indonesia	18.6	12.9	7.4	11.3	1.4	2.5	0.9	1.4	30.5	37.9	41.2	33.9	15.1	20.2	−2.5	1.5
43 Yemen, PDR	..	..	..	..	..	..	..	..	..	..	..	..	..	..	..	..
44 Yemen Arab Rep.	..	30.1	..	20.6	..	4.4	..	..	..	8.7	..	36.1	..	33.3	..	−19.1
45 Morocco	12.3	14.9	19.2	19.2	4.8	3.1	8.4	7.0	25.6	25.8	29.7	30.1	22.8	33.5	−3.9	−6.8
46 Philippines	10.9	11.9	16.3	20.1	3.2	6.0	4.3	4.0	17.6	44.9	47.7	13.2	13.4	10.8	−2.0	−1.9
47 Egypt, Arab Rep.	..	17.5	..	10.6	..	2.4	..	14.4	..	7.9	..	47.1	..	48.1	..	−10.4
48 Côte d'Ivoire	..	..	..	..	..	..	..	..	..	..	..	..	..	..	..	..
49 Papua New Guinea	..	4.7	..	19.1	..	9.0	..	1.4	..	20.5	..	45.2	..	35.8	..	−1.0
50 Zimbabwe	..	16.2	..	20.4	..	6.2	..	4.8	..	26.0	..	26.5	..	39.1	..	−9.9
51 Honduras	12.4	..	22.3	..	10.2	..	8.7	..	28.3	..	18.1	..	15.4	..	−2.7	..
52 Nicaragua	12.3	..	16.6	..	4.0	..	16.4	..	27.2	..	23.4	..	15.5	..	−3.9	..
53 Dominican Rep.	8.5	8.4	14.2	15.1	11.7	10.3	11.8	15.2	35.4	35.2	18.4	15.8	18.5	14.2	−0.2	−1.2
54 Nigeria	40.2	..	4.5	..	3.6	..	0.8	..	19.6	..	31.4	..	10.2	..	−0.9	..
55 Thailand	20.2	20.2	19.9	19.5	3.7	5.7	7.0	4.6	25.6	22.6	23.5	27.4	17.2	21.8	−4.3	−5.6
56 Cameroon	..	8.8	..	14.4	..	5.1	..	11.4	..	33.8	..	26.6	..	22.8	..	0.9
57 El Salvador	6.6	20.3	21.4	14.5	10.9	5.9	7.6	3.4	14.4	12.6	39.0	43.3	12.8	19.8	−1.0	−0.8
58 Botswana	(.)	6.8	10.0	17.5	6.0	4.8	21.7	9.0	28.0	29.9	34.5	32.0	33.7	48.2	−23.8	17.2
59 Paraguay	13.8	10.2	12.1	10.7	3.5	5.8	18.3	32.9	19.6	22.2	32.7	18.1	13.1	10.8	−1.7	−1.7
60 Jamaica	..	..	..	..	..	..	..	..	..	..	..	..	..	..	..	..
61 Peru	14.8	..	22.6	..	6.1	..	2.9	..	30.6	..	23.0	..	16.7	12.9	−1.0	..
62 Turkey	15.5	10.9	18.1	10.0	3.2	1.8	3.1	3.6	41.8	19.6	18.3	54.1	22.7	25.7	−2.2	−7.6
63 Mauritius	0.8	0.8	13.5	13.8	10.3	7.6	18.0	17.3	13.9	12.8	43.4	47.6	16.3	27.3	−1.2	−5.3
64 Congo, People's Rep.	..	..	..	..	..	..	..	..	..	..	..	..	..	..	..	..
65 Ecuador	15.7	11.3	27.5	27.7	4.5	8.3	0.8	1.1	28.9	16.6	22.6	35.0	13.4	14.5	0.2	−0.9
66 Tunisia	4.9	7.9	30.5	14.3	7.4	6.5	8.8	12.4	23.3	33.1	25.1	25.7	23.1	40.4	−0.9	−5.1
67 Guatemala	11.0	..	19.4	..	9.5	..	10.4	..	23.8	..	25.8	..	9.9	..	−2.2	..

Note: For data comparability and coverage, see the technical notes. Figures in italics are for years other than those specified.

	Defense		Education		Health		Housing, amenities; social security and welfare		Economic services		Other[a]		Total expenditure (percentage of GNP)		Overall surplus/deficit (percentage of GNP)	
	1972	1985	1972	1985	1972	1985	1972	1985	1972	1985	1972	1985	1972	1985	1972	1985
68 Costa Rica	2.8	3.0	28.3	19.4	3.8	22.5	26.7	17.1	21.8	20.2	16.7	17.8	18.9	24.5	−4.5	−1.4
69 Colombia	..	..	..	..	..	..	..	..	..	..	..	..	13.0	..	−2.5	..
70 Chile	10.0	11.5	20.0	13.2	10.0	6.1	40.0	43.8	22.5	7.1	20.0	18.4	43.2	35.5	−13.0	−2.7
71 Jordan	..	27.7	..	11.3	..	4.2	..	14.5	..	24.8	..	17.5	..	42.9	..	−9.9
72 Syrian Arab Rep.	37.2	..	11.3	..	1.4	..	3.6	..	39.9	..	6.7	..	28.8	..	−3.5	..
73 *Lebanon*	..	..	..	..	..	..	..	..	..	..	..	..	..	..	..	..
Upper middle-income	**14.4 w**	**9.7 w**	**12.3 w**	**10.6 w**	**7.9 w**	**4.6 w**	**23.0 w**	**19.0 w**	**24.1 w**	**23.8 w**	**18.3 w**	**32.3 w**	**19.7 w**	**22.7 w**	**−2.5 w**	**−3.3 w**
74 Brazil	8.3	4.0	8.3	3.2	6.7	7.6	35.0	32.7	23.3	14.5	18.3	38.0	17.6	21.1	−0.3	−4.4
75 Uruguay	5.6	10.8	9.5	6.4	1.6	4.1	52.3	48.6	9.8	8.1	21.2	21.9	25.0	24.8	−2.5	−2.4
76 Hungary	..	6.9	..	1.6	..	3.6	..	25.7	..	38.8	..	23.4	..	55.3	..	−1.0
77 Portugal	..	..	..	..	..	..	..	..	..	..	..	..	..	..	..	..
78 Malaysia	18.5	..	23.4	..	6.8	..	4.4	..	14.2	..	32.7	..	26.5	..	−9.4	..
79 South Africa	..	..	..	..	..	..	..	..	..	..	..	..	21.8	..	−4.2	..
80 Poland	..	..	..	..	..	..	..	..	..	..	..	..	..	..	..	..
81 Yugoslavia	20.5	54.8	(.)	(.)	24.8	(.)	35.6	6.8	12.0	17.3	7.0	21.1	21.1	6.7	−0.4	−0.1
82 Mexico	4.2	2.7	16.4	12.4	5.1	1.5	25.0	11.9	34.2	27.2	15.2	44.4	12.0	24.9	−3.0	−7.7
83 Panama	(.)	..	20.7	..	15.1	..	10.8	..	24.2	..	29.1	..	27.6	..	−6.5	..
84 Argentina	10.0	8.8	20.0	9.5	(.)	1.8	20.0	38.3	30.0	20.3	20.0	21.3	19.6	18.0	−4.9	−5.4
85 Korea, Rep. of	25.8	29.7	15.9	18.4	1.2	1.4	5.8	6.7	25.6	17.5	25.7	26.3	18.3	18.4	−3.9	−1.3
86 Algeria	..	..	..	..	..	..	..	..	..	..	..	..	..	..	..	..
87 Venezuela	10.3	6.1	18.6	17.7	11.7	7.6	9.2	14.7	25.4	22.8	24.8	31.1	21.3	25.6	−0.3	3.3
88 Greece	14.9	..	9.1	..	7.4	..	30.6	..	26.4	..	11.7	..	27.5	..	−1.7	..
89 Israel	40.0	27.8	7.1	7.1	3.6	3.5	7.1	20.3	7.1	5.4	35.1	36.0	43.9	97.6	−15.7	−20.7
90 Trinidad and Tobago	..	..	..	..	..	..	..	..	..	..	..	..	..	..	..	..
91 Hong Kong	..	..	..	..	..	..	..	..	..	..	..	..	..	..	..	..
92 Oman	39.3	43.0	3.7	7.7	5.9	4.2	3.0	1.5	24.4	23.3	23.6	20.3	62.1	62.1	−15.3	−13.1
93 Singapore	35.3	20.1	15.7	20.2	7.8	6.2	3.9	6.5	9.9	15.0	27.3	32.0	16.8	26.3	1.3	4.1
94 *Iran, Islamic Rep.*	24.1	10.2	10.4	16.2	3.6	7.4	6.1	13.3	30.6	25.0	25.2	28.0	30.8	..	−4.6	..
95 *Iraq*	..	..	..	..	..	..	..	..	..	..	..	..	..	..	..	..
96 *Romania*	..	..	..	..	..	..	..	..	..	..	..	..	..	..	..	..
Developing economies	**15.1 w**	**12.1 w**	**13.8 w**	**10.4 w**	**6.6 w**	**4.2 w**	**18.2 w**	**14.6 w**	**21.7 w**	**34.7 w**	**24.6 w**	**23.9 w**	**19.3 w**	**22.3 w**	**−2.9 w**	**−4.3 w**
Oil exporters	**17.2 w**	**9.8 w**	**12.7 w**	**13.7 w**	**4.9 w**	**4.3 w**	**10.6 w**	**11.0 w**	**30.7 w**	**25.2 w**	**24.4 w**	**36.1 w**	**16.9 w**	**26.4 w**	**−7.6 w**	**−4.0 w**
Exporters of manufactures	**13.7 w**	**13.4 w**	**9.6 w**	**5.3 w**	**9.7 w**	**4.2 w**	**30.3 w**	**18.4 w**	**20.6 w**	**23.7 w**	**16.0 w**	**34.9 w**	**18.7 w**	**20.1 w**	**−0.7 w**	**−3.7 w**
Highly indebted countries	**12.0 w**	**6.4 w**	**14.0 w**	**9.9 w**	**8.5 w**	**4.6 w**	**25.5 w**	**22.4 w**	**22.0 w**	**20.4 w**	**17.9 w**	**36.6 w**	**17.8 w**	**20.8 w**	**−2.4 w**	**−4.4 w**
Sub-Saharan Africa	**20.2 w**	**11.2 w**	**13.2 w**	**14.5 w**	**5.1 w**	**5.7 w**	**3.1 w**	**5.0 w**	**21.2 w**	**24.9 w**	**37.2 w**	**38.8 w**	**16.4 w**	**23.7 w**	**−3.1 w**	**−3.3 w**
High-income oil exporters	**9.0 w**	**23.6 w**	**15.2 w**	**11.1 w**	**5.5 w**	**6.4 w**	**14.1 w**	**14.1 w**	**16.8 w**	**20.3 w**	**39.5 w**	**24.5 w**	**21.1 w**	**29.1 w**	**10.5 w**	**7.0 w**
97 *Libya*	..	..	..	..	..	..	..	..	..	..	..	..	..	..	..	..
98 *Saudi Arabia*	..	..	..	..	..	..	..	..	..	..	..	..	..	..	..	..
99 Kuwait	8.4	14.6	15.0	11.6	5.5	6.5	14.2	17.9	16.6	26.6	40.1	22.8	34.4	43.1	17.4	7.0
100 United Arab Emirates	24.4	45.3	16.5	9.7	4.3	6.2	6.1	5.0	18.3	5.1	30.5	28.7	4.3	16.3	0.3	(.)
Industrial market economies	**20.9 w**	**16.8 w**	**5.4 w**	**3.8 w**	**10.0 w**	**11.4 w**	**36.6 w**	**35.5 w**	**12.1 w**	**9.1 w**	**15.1 w**	**23.4 w**	**22.9 w**	**29.1 w**	**−1.6 w**	**−5.4 w**
101 Spain	6.5	4.4	8.3	6.0	0.9	0.6	49.8	64.2	17.5	10.1	17.0	14.8	19.8	31.5	−0.5	−6.3
102 Ireland	..	3.1	..	11.7	..	13.2	..	30.1	..	15.0	..	26.9	33.0	57.1	−5.5	−12.1
103 Italy	6.3	3.5	16.1	7.7	13.5	12.1	44.8	32.5	18.4	7.5	0.9	36.8	31.8	55.3	−9.4	−15.9
104 New Zealand	5.8	4.7	16.9	10.9	14.8	12.5	25.6	32.3	16.5	12.3	20.4	27.3	28.5	42.9	−3.8	−4.9
105 Belgium	6.7	5.1	15.5	12.9	1.5	1.7	41.0	42.7	18.9	13.8	16.4	23.8	39.2	55.9	−4.3	−10.6
106 United Kingdom	16.7	..	2.6	..	12.2	..	26.5	..	11.1	..	30.8	..	32.7	41.1	−2.7	−3.1
107 Austria	3.3	3.0	10.2	9.6	10.1	11.7	53.7	47.7	11.3	13.4	11.4	14.6	29.6	39.8	−0.2	−4.5
108 Netherlands	..	5.3	..	10.9	..	11.0	..	41.0	..	9.9	..	21.9	40.8	56.6	(.)	−5.5
109 France	..	..	..	..	..	..	..	..	..	..	..	..	32.5	45.2	0.7	−3.1
110 Australia	14.1	9.3	4.2	7.5	7.0	9.5	20.8	29.4	14.3	8.3	39.6	36.0	22.5	31.6	−0.5	−3.2
111 Finland	6.1	5.1	15.3	13.8	10.6	10.4	28.4	35.0	27.9	21.6	11.6	14.0	24.8	30.0	1.3	−1.0
112 Germany, Fed. Rep.	12.4	9.2	1.5	0.7	17.5	18.7	46.9	50.5	11.3	7.1	10.4	13.8	24.2	30.7	0.7	−1.7
113 Denmark	7.3	..	16.0	..	10.0	..	41.6	..	11.3	..	13.7	..	32.7	43.7	2.7	−4.2
114 Japan	..	..	..	..	..	..	..	..	..	..	..	..	12.7	17.8	−1.9	−6.0
115 Sweden	12.5	6.4	14.8	8.6	3.6	1.2	44.3	50.1	10.6	6.8	14.3	26.9	28.0	46.5	−1.2	−7.0
116 Canada	..	7.9	..	3.5	..	6.4	..	35.8	..	17.2	..	29.2	..	26.6	..	−6.9
117 Norway	9.7	8.2	9.9	8.9	12.3	10.8	39.9	36.3	20.2	20.1	8.0	15.7	35.0	38.2	−1.5	(.)
118 Switzerland	15.1	10.3	4.2	3.1	10.0	13.1	39.5	50.6	18.4	12.2	12.8	10.8	13.3	19.9	0.9	−0.1
119 United States	32.2	24.9	3.2	1.8	8.6	11.3	35.3	31.6	10.6	8.3	10.1	22.1	19.4	24.5	−1.6	−5.3
Nonreporting nonmember economies																
120 *Albania*																
121 *Angola*																
122 *Bulgaria*																
123 *Cuba*																
124 *Czechoslovakia*																
125 *German Dem. Rep.*																
126 *Korea, Dem. Rep.*																
127 *Mongolia*																
128 *USSR*																

Percentage of total expenditure

a. See the technical notes.

Table 24. Central government current revenue

	Percentage of total current revenue												Total current revenue (percentage of GNP)	
	Tax revenue													
	Taxes on income, profit, and capital gain		Social security contributions		Domestic taxes on goods and services		Taxes on international trade and transactions		Other taxes[a]		Nontax revenue			
	1972	1985	1972	1985	1972	1985	1972	1985	1972	1985	1972	1985	1972	1985
Low-income economies	..	..	..	..	..	..	..	..	..	..	..	..	..	..
China and India	..	..	..	..	..	..	..	..	..	..	..	..	..	..
Other low-income	21.0 w	16.8 w	0.5 w	0.2 w	26.8 w	34.9 w	33.1 w	29.0 w	2.3 w	0.9 w	16.3 w	18.2 w	13.8 w	15.6 w
1 Ethiopia	23.0	..	(.)	..	29.8	..	30.4	..	5.6	..	11.1	..	10.5	..
2 Bangladesh	3.7	..	..	..	22.4	..	18.0	..	3.8	..	52.2	..	8.6	..
3 Burkina Faso	16.8	17.4	(.)	8.5	18.0	16.2	51.8	30.0	3.2	18.5	10.2	9.5	11.4	14.3
4 Mali	..	..	..	..	..	..	..	..	..	..	..	..	..	..
5 Bhutan	..	..	..	..	..	..	..	..	..	..	..	..	..	..
6 Mozambique	..	..	..	..	..	..	..	..	..	..	..	..	..	..
7 Nepal	4.1	8.0	(.)	(.)	26.5	40.7	36.7	27.7	19.0	6.2	13.7	17.4	5.2	9.2
8 Malawi	31.4	34.6	(.)	(.)	24.2	32.6	20.0	19.6	0.5	0.5	23.8	12.7	16.0	21.1
9 Zaire	22.2	29.3	2.2	0.9	12.7	24.2	57.9	31.2	1.4	3.3	3.7	11.2	14.3	16.8
10 Burma	28.7	4.0	(.)	(.)	34.2	40.5	13.4	14.9	(.)	(.)	23.8	40.5	12.4	14.4
11 Burundi	18.1	..	1.2	..	18.3	..	40.3	..	15.6	..	6.5	..	11.5	..
12 Togo	..	33.2	..	6.0	..	8.3	..	29.2	..	0.8	..	22.5	..	36.5
13 Madagascar	13.1	..	7.2	..	29.9	..	33.6	..	5.5	..	10.8	..	18.3	..
14 Niger	..	..	..	..	..	..	..	..	..	..	..	..	..	..
15 Benin	..	..	..	..	..	..	..	..	..	..	..	..	..	..
16 Central African Rep.	..	..	..	..	..	..	..	..	..	..	..	..	..	..
17 India	..	16.2	..	(.)	..	38.9	..	24.4	..	0.5	..	19.9	..	14.0
18 Rwanda	17.9	..	4.4	..	14.1	..	41.7	..	13.8	..	8.1	..	9.8	..
19 Somalia	10.7	..	(.)	..	24.7	..	45.3	..	5.2	..	14.0	..	13.7	..
20 Kenya	35.6	28.3	(.)	(.)	19.9	40.8	24.3	20.4	1.4	0.5	18.8	10.0	18.0	21.7
21 Tanzania	29.9	..	(.)	..	29.1	..	21.7	..	0.5	..	18.8	..	15.8	..
22 Sudan	11.8	..	(.)	..	30.4	..	40.5	..	1.5	..	15.7	..	18.0	..
23 China	..	..	..	..	..	..	..	..	..	..	..	..	..	..
24 Haiti	..	..	..	..	..	..	..	..	..	..	..	..	..	..
25 Guinea	..	..	..	..	..	..	..	..	..	..	..	..	..	..
26 Sierra Leone	..	28.0	..	(.)	..	25.0	..	40.4	..	1.0	..	5.6	..	7.3
27 Senegal	20.0	..	(.)	..	25.9	..	42.7	..	7.5	..	3.8	..	17.0	..
28 Ghana	18.4	19.2	(.)	(.)	29.4	22.2	40.6	40.9	0.2	0.2	11.5	17.5	15.1	10.5
29 Pakistan	13.6	12.2	(.)	(.)	35.9	35.0	34.2	30.9	0.5	0.3	15.8	21.6	12.3	15.7
30 Sri Lanka	19.1	15.3	(.)	(.)	34.7	39.5	35.4	32.3	2.1	1.4	8.7	11.5	20.1	23.8
31 Zambia	49.7	29.5	(.)	(.)	20.2	45.9	14.3	16.3	0.1	1.6	15.6	6.6	23.2	23.9
32 Afghanistan	..	..	..	..	..	..	..	..	..	..	..	..	..	..
33 Chad	16.7	..	(.)	..	12.3	..	45.2	..	20.5	..	5.3	..	10.8	..
34 Kampuchea, Dem.	..	..	..	..	..	..	..	..	..	..	..	..	..	..
35 Lao PDR	..	..	..	..	..	..	..	..	..	..	..	..	..	..
36 Uganda	22.1	6.9	(.)	(.)	32.8	24.9	36.3	66.2	0.3	(.)	8.5	2.0	13.7	..
37 Viet Nam	..	..	..	..	..	..	..	..	..	..	..	..	..	..
Middle-income economies	26.1 w	24.4 w	12.4 w	10.6 w	27.0 w	25.6 w	12.7 w	9.8 w	5.2 w	4.2 w	16.6 w	25.4 w	18.0 w	22.7 w
Lower middle-income	23.8 w	34.8 w	7.0 w	3.6 w	28.9 w	22.9 w	19.1 w	14.3 w	6.4 w	4.9 w	14.8 w	19.7 w	16.5 w	20.9 w
38 Mauritania	..	..	..	..	..	..	..	..	..	..	..	..	..	..
39 Bolivia	13.7	6.1	(.)	20.9	27.4	17.4	41.1	30.0	9.8	2.4	8.0	23.1	7.8	4.3
40 Lesotho	10.2	9.5	(.)	(.)	2.3	8.0	73.7	70.8	5.9	0.2	7.8	11.4	15.4	20.5
41 Liberia	..	38.1	..	(.)	..	27.3	..	28.4	..	3.3	..	2.9	..	20.0
42 Indonesia	45.5	67.0	..	(.)	22.8	9.4	17.6	3.3	3.5	1.6	10.6	18.7	13.4	22.5
43 Yemen, PDR	..	..	..	..	..	..	..	..	..	..	..	..	..	..
44 Yemen Arab Rep.	..	13.3	..	(.)	..	8.1	..	49.4	..	13.3	..	15.9	..	19.6
45 Morocco	16.4	18.8	5.9	4.9	45.7	37.7	13.2	17.9	6.1	7.6	12.6	13.1	18.5	26.5
46 Philippines	13.8	26.6	(.)	(.)	24.3	36.4	23.0	23.7	29.7	2.5	9.3	10.8	12.4	11.5
47 Egypt, Arab Rep.	..	15.2	..	13.6	..	12.1	..	15.7	..	6.5	..	37.0	..	39.4
48 Côte d'Ivoire	..	..	..	..	..	..	..	..	..	..	..	..	..	..
49 Papua New Guinea	..	49.2	..	(.)	..	12.8	..	23.1	..	1.6	..	13.2	..	23.8
50 Zimbabwe	..	42.1	..	(.)	..	31.9	..	14.8	..	1.1	..	10.1	..	31.2
51 Honduras	19.2	..	3.0	..	33.8	..	28.2	..	2.3	..	13.5	..	12.6	..
52 Nicaragua	9.5	..	14.0	..	37.3	..	24.4	..	9.0	..	5.8	..	12.6	..
53 Dominican Rep.	17.9	19.4	3.9	3.8	19.0	33.8	40.3	28.4	1.8	2.5	17.0	12.1	17.9	12.7
54 Nigeria	43.0	..	(.)	..	26.3	..	17.5	..	0.2	..	13.0	..	11.6	..
55 Thailand	12.1	20.7	(.)	(.)	46.3	43.9	28.7	22.2	1.8	2.0	11.2	11.1	12.9	16.3
56 Cameroon	..	57.2	..	5.4	..	10.9	..	15.2	..	3.3	..	8.0	..	24.8
57 El Salvador	15.2	16.3	(.)	(.)	25.6	37.9	36.1	27.5	17.2	7.8	6.0	10.3	11.6	14.3
58 Botswana	19.9	33.7	(.)	(.)	2.4	1.1	47.2	20.9	0.4	0.1	30.0	44.2	30.7	68.4
59 Paraguay	8.8	12.6	10.4	10.8	26.2	25.9	24.8	11.3	17.0	23.6	12.8	15.8	11.5	9.8
60 Jamaica	..	..	..	..	..	..	..	..	..	..	..	..	..	..
61 Peru	17.2	..	(.)	..	32.2	..	15.9	..	22.1	..	12.6	..	15.5	..
62 Turkey	30.8	38.0	(.)	(.)	31.0	27.3	14.6	7.5	5.9	9.8	17.7	17.4	20.6	18.0
63 Mauritius	22.7	11.8	(.)	(.)	23.3	20.8	40.2	51.4	5.5	4.2	8.2	11.9	15.6	21.7
64 Congo, People's Rep.	19.4	..	(.)	..	40.3	..	26.5	..	6.3	..	7.5	..	18.4	..
65 Ecuador	19.6	53.5	(.)	(.)	19.1	17.7	52.4	21.4	5.1	3.4	3.8	4.1	13.6	13.6
66 Tunisia	15.9	12.2	7.1	7.9	31.6	19.8	21.8	28.5	7.8	5.5	15.7	26.2	23.6	37.7
67 Guatemala	12.7	..	(.)	..	36.1	..	26.2	..	15.6	..	9.4	..	8.9	..

Note: For data comparability and coverage, see the technical notes. Figures in italics are for years other than those specified.

	Percentage of total current revenue												
	Tax revenue												Total current revenue (percentage of GNP)
	Taxes on income, profit, and capital gain		Social security contributions		Domestic taxes on goods and services		Taxes on international trade and transactions		Other taxes[a]		Nontax revenue		
	1972	1985	1972	1985	1972	1985	1972	1985	1972	1985	1972	1985	1972	1985
68 Costa Rica	17.7	16.9	13.4	25.2	38.1	31.0	18.0	22.4	1.6	−0.2	11.2	4.7	15.8	23.3
69 Colombia	37.2	..	13.9	..	16.0	..	20.3	..	7.2	..	5.5	..	10.6	..
70 Chile	14.3	11.4	28.6	7.3	28.6	39.9	14.3	10.9	..	7.0	14.3	23.5	30.2	32.8
71 Jordan	..	12.4	..	(.)	..	11.3	..	35.2	..	13.9	..	27.1	..	27.7
72 Syrian Arab Rep.	6.8	..	(.)	..	10.4	..	17.3	..	12.1	..	53.4	..	25.1	..
73 *Lebanon*	..	..	..	..	..	..	..	..	..	..	..	..	..	..
Upper middle-income	**27.3 w**	**20.3 w**	**15.2 w**	**13.6 w**	**26.0 w**	**26.7 w**	**9.4 w**	**7.9 w**	**4.5 w**	**3.8 w**	**17.6 w**	**27.7 w**	**18.7 w**	**23.6 w**
74 Brazil	20.0	17.9	27.7	23.3	35.4	18.0	7.7	4.3	3.1	3.9	6.2	32.6	19.1	24.7
75 Uruguay	4.7	7.9	30.0	25.6	24.5	44.7	6.1	12.2	22.0	5.2	12.6	4.4	22.7	22.9
76 Hungary	..	13.0	..	24.9	..	31.8	..	5.9	..	9.1	..	15.3	..	54.2
77 Portugal	..	..	..	..	..	..	..	..	..	..	..	..	..	..
78 Malaysia	25.2	..	0.1	..	24.2	..	27.9	..	1.4	..	21.2	..	20.3	..
79 South Africa	54.8	..	1.2	..	21.5	..	4.6	..	5.0	..	12.8	..	21.2	..
80 Poland	..	..	..	..	..	..	..	..	..	..	..	..	..	..
81 Yugoslavia	(.)	(.)	52.3	(.)	24.5	62.0	19.5	35.9	(.)	(.)	3.7	2.1	20.7	6.7
82 Mexico	36.4	24.7	19.4	12.1	32.1	70.2	13.2	2.7	−9.8	−18.8	8.6	9.1	10.4	17.6
83 Panama	23.3	..	22.4	..	13.2	..	16.0	..	7.7	..	17.3	..	21.8	..
84 Argentina	12.5	3.1	25.0	24.1	25.0	42.6	12.5	13.3	(.)	6.9	25.0	9.9	14.7	15.9
85 Korea, Rep. of	29.2	25.3	0.8	1.5	41.7	43.2	10.7	14.2	5.2	3.9	12.3	11.9	13.4	19.0
86 Algeria	..	..	..	..	..	..	..	..	..	..	..	..	..	..
87 Venezuela	54.2	59.2	6.0	3.2	6.7	4.3	6.1	18.0	1.1	1.6	25.9	13.7	21.8	31.0
88 Greece	12.2	..	24.5	..	35.5	..	6.7	..	12.0	..	9.2	..	25.4	..
89 Israel	40.0	36.7	(.)	9.0	20.0	27.4	20.0	4.4	10.0	2.7	10.0	19.7	31.3	0.1
90 Trinidad and Tobago	..	..	..	..	..	..	..	..	..	..	..	..	..	..
91 Hong Kong	..	..	..	..	..	..	..	..	..	..	..	..	..	..
92 Oman	71.1	26.6	(.)	(.)	(.)	0.8	3.0	3.1	2.3	0.6	23.6	69.0	47.4	47.8
93 Singapore	24.4	30.1	(.)	(.)	17.6	14.0	11.1	4.6	15.5	15.7	31.4	35.6	21.6	28.7
94 Iran, Islamic Rep.	7.9	9.5	2.7	8.8	6.4	5.1	14.6	11.5	4.9	4.8	63.6	60.2	26.2	..
95 *Iraq*	..	..	..	..	..	..	..	..	..	..	..	..	..	..
96 *Romania*	..	..	..	..	..	..	..	..	..	..	..	..	..	..
Developing economies	**25.4 w**	**23.4 w**	**11.4 w**	**9.3 w**	**27.0 w**	**27.1 w**	**14.7 w**	**11.8 w**	**4.9 w**	**3.7 w**	**16.6 w**	**24.7 w**	**17.5 w**	**21.1 w**
Oil exporters	**30.7 w**	**30.2 w**	**7.1 w**	**7.2 w**	**17.4 w**	**21.9 w**	**13.7 w**	**8.7 w**	**3.2 w**	**2.6 w**	**27.9 w**	**29.4 w**	**15.9 w**	**24.8 w**
Exporters of manufactures	**21.2 w**	**18.8 w**	**23.6 w**	**13.7 w**	**35.2 w**	**28.0 w**	**8.2 w**	**10.7 w**	**3.8 w**	**3.8 w**	**8.0 w**	**25.0 w**	**18.8 w**	**20.9 w**
Highly indebted countries	**26.0 w**	**22.2 w**	**16.2 w**	**15.1 w**	**29.0 w**	**32.4 w**	**11.7 w**	**8.0 w**	**4.2 w**	**3.3 w**	**10.5 w**	**19.0 w**	**16.6 w**	**20.8 w**
Sub-Saharan Africa	**30.0 w**	**36.2 w**	**0.6 w**	**1.5 w**	**24.6 w**	**24.4 w**	**30.8 w**	**23.9 w**	**1.9 w**	**1.7 w**	**12.1 w**	**12.3 w**	**14.2 w**	**19.3 w**
High-income oil exporters														
97 *Libya*	..	..	..	..	..	..	..	..	..	..	..	..	..	..
98 *Saudi Arabia*	..	..	..	..	..	..	..	..	..	..	..	..	..	..
99 Kuwait	68.8	0.9	(.)	(.)	19.7	0.7	1.5	1.6	0.2	0.1	9.9	96.7	55.2	53.2
100 United Arab Emirates	..	..	..	..	..	..	..	..	..	..	..	..	..	..
Industrial market economies	**40.4 w**	**40.8 w**	**26.9 w**	**30.5 w**	**21.4 w**	**16.8 w**	**1.8 w**	**1.3 w**	**3.3 w**	**2.1 w**	**6.2 w**	**8.5 w**	**22.1 w**	**24.5 w**
101 Spain	15.9	21.7	38.9	46.2	23.4	15.4	10.0	4.2	0.7	3.1	11.1	9.5	20.0	26.4
102 Ireland	28.1	31.9	8.9	13.5	32.6	32.1	16.6	7.2	3.2	3.9	10.5	11.5	30.6	47.4
103 Italy	16.6	36.5	39.2	33.1	31.7	23.9	0.4	0.2	4.3	2.0	7.7	4.2	26.9	40.7
104 New Zealand	61.4	61.9	(.)	(.)	19.9	17.5	4.1	3.5	4.5	1.9	10.0	15.2	27.3	39.5
105 Belgium	31.3	38.0	32.4	32.9	28.9	23.1	1.0	(.)	3.3	1.9	3.1	4.1	35.0	45.8
106 United Kingdom	39.4	38.5	15.1	18.3	27.1	29.5	1.7	(.)	5.5	2.5	11.2	11.2	33.5	37.9
107 Austria	20.7	20.2	30.0	33.3	28.3	27.0	5.4	1.4	10.2	7.9	5.5	8.1	29.7	35.6
108 Netherlands	32.5	23.0	36.7	39.4	22.3	20.0	0.5	(.)	3.4	2.1	4.7	15.4	43.2	51.7
109 France	16.9	16.8	37.1	44.5	37.9	30.0	0.3	(.)	2.9	3.7	4.9	4.9	33.5	42.2
110 Australia	58.3	60.4	(.)	(.)	21.9	24.0	5.2	5.2	2.1	0.5	12.5	9.9	24.4	28.8
111 Finland	30.0	30.7	7.8	9.0	47.7	47.1	3.1	1.2	5.8	3.9	5.5	8.0	27.1	29.0
112 Germany, Fed. Rep.	19.7	17.0	46.6	55.5	28.1	21.6	0.8	(.)	0.8	0.1	4.0	5.7	25.2	29.2
113 Denmark	40.0	37.1	5.1	4.6	42.1	41.3	3.1	0.7	2.8	3.1	6.8	13.3	35.5	42.7
114 Japan	64.8	68.8	(.)	(.)	22.6	16.7	3.5	2.0	6.8	7.5	2.4	5.0	11.2	11.9
115 Sweden	27.0	19.4	21.6	30.2	34.0	29.2	1.5	0.5	4.7	5.0	11.3	15.6	32.5	41.7
116 Canada	..	48.5	..	13.4	..	19.5	..	5.3	..	0.1	..	13.3	..	20.4
117 Norway	22.5	25.6	20.5	21.0	47.9	37.8	1.6	0.5	1.0	0.8	6.6	14.2	37.0	44.0
118 Switzerland	13.9	15.4	37.3	49.2	21.5	19.0	16.7	7.7	2.6	3.3	8.0	5.5	14.5	19.6
119 United States	59.4	50.0	23.6	32.9	7.1	4.5	1.6	1.6	2.5	0.8	5.7	10.2	18.0	19.8
Nonreporting nonmember economies														
120 *Albania*														
121 *Angola*														
122 *Bulgaria*														
123 *Cuba*														
124 *Czechoslovakia*														
125 *German Dem. Rep.*														
126 *Korea, Dem. Rep.*														
127 *Mongolia*														
128 *USSR*														

a. See the technical notes.

Table 25. Money and interest rate

		Monetary holdings, broadly defined					Average annual inflation (GDP deflator)	Nominal interest rates of banks (average annual percentage)			
		Average annual nominal growth rate (percent)		Average outstanding (percentage of GDP)				Deposit rate		Lending rate	
		1965–80	1980–85	1965	1980	1985	1980–85	1980	1985	1980	1985
	Low-income economies **China and India** **Other low-income**										
1	Ethiopia	12.7	12.8	12.5	25.3	38.0	2.6	..	..	..	..
2	Bangladesh	..	25.0	..	18.6	25.7	11.5	8.25	12.00	11.33	12.00
3	Burkina Faso	..	..	..	..	..	7.2	6.25	7.25	9.38	10.00
4	Mali	14.4	17.1	..	17.4	23.8	7.4	7.50	7.25	9.38	10.00
5	Bhutan	..	..	..	..	..	..	..	..	..	..
6	Mozambique	..	..	..	..	..	25.8	..	..	..	..
7	Nepal	17.9	18.6	8.4	21.9	28.6	8.4	4.00	4.50	14.00	17.00
8	Malawi	15.4	16.0	17.6	20.3	24.3	11.4	7.92	12.50	16.67	18.38
9	Zaire	28.2	58.5	11.7	9.4	9.6	55.3	..	..	..	..
10	Burma	11.5	13.5	29.0	23.9	31.7	2.6	..	..	..	..
11	Burundi	32.8	12.8	10.1	12.7	16.6	6.6	2.50	4.50	12.00	12.00
12	Togo	20.3	13.1	10.9	29.0	44.6	6.9	6.25	7.25	9.38	10.00
13	Madagascar	12.0	13.1	19.6	27.6	23.9	19.4	..	..	..	..
14	Niger	18.3	5.4	3.8	13.3	14.8	8.5	6.25	7.25	9.38	10.00
15	Benin	17.3	12.5	10.6	21.1	24.2	9.7	6.25	7.25	9.38	10.00
16	Central African Rep.	12.7	7.8	13.5	18.9	17.8	10.8	5.50	7.50	10.50	12.50
17	India	15.3	16.7	25.7	38.4	44.3	7.8	..	..	16.50	16.50
18	Rwanda	19.0	8.7	15.8	13.8	11.9	7.6	6.25	6.25	13.50	13.88
19	Somalia	20.4	25.6	12.8	31.0	22.8	45.4	4.50	14.00	7.50	19.00
20	Kenya	18.6	14.1	..	37.7	39.5	10.0	5.75	11.25	10.58	14.00
21	Tanzania	20.1	..	..	37.2	..	19.6	6.25	4.50	11.50	12.29
22	Sudan	21.0	28.7	14.2	28.2	29.0	31.7	..	..	..	..
23	China	..	23.0	..	30.1	46.7	2.4	..	..	..	..
24	Haiti	20.3	7.3	9.9	26.1	27.5	7.0	..	..	..	..
25	Guinea	..	..	..	..	..	8.3	..	..	..	..
26	Sierra Leone	15.9	36.5	11.7	20.6	22.6	25.0	9.17	11.33	11.00	15.00
27	Senegal	15.6	10.5	15.3	27.0	25.5	9.7	6.25	7.25	9.38	10.00
28	Ghana	25.9	41.4	20.3	16.2	10.5	57.0	11.50	15.00	19.00	20.00
29	Pakistan	14.7	15.0	40.8	38.2	37.6	8.1	..	..	..	..
30	Sri Lanka	15.1	20.3	31.4	32.9	35.6	14.7	14.50	17.33	19.00	13.00
31	Zambia	12.7	17.6	..	32.6	33.4	14.7	7.00	7.71	9.50	18.60
32	Afghanistan	14.1	14.5	14.4	26.8	..	..	..	..	..	..
33	Chad	12.5	22.3	9.3	20.0	..	..	5.50	5.50	11.00	11.50
34	Kampuchea, Dem.	..	..	..	..	..	..	..	..	..	..
35	Lao PDR	..	..	..	..	..	..	..	..	..	..
36	Uganda	23.1	58.8	..	7.4	..	..	6.80	20.00	10.80	24.00
37	Viet Nam	30.1	..	..	..	..	..	..	..	..	..
	Middle-income economies **Lower middle-income**										
38	Mauritania	20.7	12.0	5.7	20.5	23.6	8.1	5.50	5.50	12.00	12.00
39	Bolivia	24.7	507.3	11.8	16.2	6.2	569.1	18.00	140.00	28.00	150.00
40	Lesotho	..	21.1	..	..	48.8	11.4	9.60	14.80	11.00	19.70
41	Liberia	..	..	..	..	..	1.6	10.30	9.34	18.40	19.34
42	Indonesia	54.9	23.6	..	13.7	22.7	10.7	6.00	18.00	9.00	12.00
43	Yemen, PDR	15.2	16.0	..	114.8	148.2	5.7	..	..	..	..
44	Yemen, Arab Rep.	..	..	..	..	..	9.7	..	..	..	..
45	Morocco	16.1	12.4	29.4	46.7	50.7	7.8	4.90	..	7.00	..
46	Philippines	17.7	18.0	19.9	19.0	19.2	19.3	..	..	..	..
47	Egypt, Arab Rep.	17.7	24.4	35.3	47.4	76.0	11.0	..	..	..	..
48	Côte d'Ivoire	20.4	9.6	21.8	25.8	27.3	10.0	6.25	7.25	9.38	10.00
49	Papua New Guinea	..	9.0	..	33.1	34.4	5.5	6.90	9.49	11.15	10.64
50	Zimbabwe	..	12.1	..	54.6	45.2	13.2	3.52	10.04	17.54	17.17
51	Honduras	14.6	12.2	15.4	23.3	30.3	5.4	..	..	..	..
52	Nicaragua	15.0	36.9	15.4	21.0	35.2	33.8	7.50	..	..	..
53	Dominican Rep.	18.5	17.4	16.7	23.4	24.6	14.6	..	..	..	..
54	Nigeria	28.5	10.5	13.9	25.1	34.7	11.4	5.27	9.12	8.43	9.52
55	Thailand	17.8	20.3	25.6	35.9	58.9	3.2	12.00	13.00	18.00	19.00
56	Cameroon	19.1	22.4	12.5	20.4	21.4	11.8	7.50	7.50	13.00	14.50
57	El Salvador	14.3	16.2	21.6	28.1	34.9	11.6	..	..	..	..
58	Botswana	..	18.7	..	31.1	29.5	5.2	..	..	..	..
59	Paraguay	44.0	15.1	12.0	20.4	20.2	15.8	..	..	..	..
60	Jamaica	17.3	26.5	24.2	35.6	47.8	18.3	10.29	21.31	13.00	21.90
61	Peru	25.9	102.5	18.7	16.3	16.4	98.6	..	8.30	..	60.00
62	Turkey	27.4	51.9	23.0	16.7	24.4	37.1	10.00	49.20	25.67	52.33
63	Mauritius	21.8	14.3	27.3	41.1	42.5	8.5	9.25	9.46	12.19	13.83
64	Congo, People's Rep.	14.2	16.1	16.5	14.8	16.2	12.6	6.50	8.25	11.00	12.00
65	Ecuador	22.6	26.1	15.6	20.2	17.8	29.7	..	17.20	..	20.20
66	Tunisia	17.4	16.9	30.2	42.1	48.6	10.0	2.50	5.25	7.25	9.63
67	Guatemala	16.3	11.6	15.2	20.5	25.4	7.4	..	..	..	..

Note: For data comparability and coverage, see the technical notes. Figures in italics are for years other than those specified.

| | Monetary holdings, broadly defined | | | | | Average annual inflation (GDP deflator) | Nominal interest rates of banks (average annual percentage) | | | |
| | Average annual nominal growth rate (percent) | | Average outstanding (percentage of GDP) | | | | Deposit rate | | Lending rate | |
	1965-80	1980-85	1965	1980	1985	1980-85	1980	1985	1980	1985
68 Costa Rica	24.6	31.1	19.3	38.8	38.6	36.4	..	16.50	..	20.92
69 Colombia	26.5	27.2	19.8	23.7	28.1	22.5	31.30	29.10	19.00	..
70 Chile	165.8	22.6	..	17.6	25.6	19.3	37.50	..	47.14	38.33
71 Jordan	19.1	14.0	..	89.2	115.2	3.9	..	..	..	..
72 Syrian Arab Rep.	21.9	22.3	24.6	40.5	63.6	6.1	5.00	7.00	..	..
73 Lebanon	16.2	26.7	83.4	176.1	..	..	..	..	..	..

Upper middle-income

	1965-80	1980-85	1965	1980	1985	1980-85	1980	1985	1980	1985
74 Brazil	43.4	175.6	20.8	17.3	21.8	147.7	..	..	..	..
75 Uruguay	65.3	44.2	28.6	30.5	38.3	44.6	50.30	81.90	66.60	94.60
76 Hungary	11.3	6.3	..	46.5	45.2	5.6	3.00	5.00	9.00	12.00
77 Portugal	18.4	21.1	77.7	82.4	78.9	22.7	18.20	26.80	18.50	25.50
78 Malaysia	21.5	15.5	26.3	69.5	104.5	3.1	6.23	8.56	7.75	11.38
79 South Africa	14.0	15.7	56.6	49.5	55.3	13.0	6.00	14.00	9.50	16.50
80 Poland	..	..	..	..	..	35.2	..	..	..	..
81 Yugoslavia	25.7	40.9	43.5	59.1	47.8	45.1	5.88	30.75	11.50	48.00
82 Mexico	21.7	61.4	27.0	28.3	26.6	62.2	26.15	59.48	28.10	54.73
83 Panama	..	..	..	..	..	3.7	..	..	..	..
84 Argentina	86.3	316.0	..	22.2	12.7	342.8	88.00	510.50	..	..
85 Korea, Rep. of	35.5	18.4	11.1	31.8	40.0	6.0	14.80	6.00	18.00	11.50
86 Algeria	22.1	19.7	32.1	58.5	79.7	6.9	..	..	..	..
87 Venezuela	22.3	16.5	20.5	42.6	65.4	9.2	..	10.52	..	9.33
88 Greece	21.4	26.6	..	..	..	20.6	14.50	15.50	21.30	20.50
89 Israel	40.1	..	30.2	52.6	..	196.3	..	178.80	176.90	496.30
90 Trinidad and Tobago	23.1	15.8	22.3	29.7	55.0	7.6	6.57	6.76	10.00	12.69
91 Hong Kong	..	..	..	69.3	..	7.9	..	..	..	..
92 Oman	29.4	21.7	..	13.8	23.7	4.9	..	..	..	..
93 Singapore	17.6	15.2	58.4	75.8	104.5	3.1	9.37	4.99	11.72	7.93
94 Iran, Islamic Rep.	27.0	20.7	21.6	52.1	..	..	..	..	..	..
95 Iraq	16.3	..	19.7	..	..	..	..	..	..	..
96 Romania	..	7.8	..	..	..	..	..	..	..	..

Developing economies
Oil exporters
Exporters of manufactures
Highly indebted countries
Sub-Saharan Africa

High-income oil exporters

	1965-80	1980-85	1965	1980	1985	1980-85	1980	1985	1980	1985
97 Libya	..	..	..	..	..	−0.3	5.13	5.50	7.00	7.00
98 Saudi Arabia	32.1	13.2	16.4	18.6	43.1	−3.2	..	..	..	..
99 Kuwait	17.8	8.0	28.1	34.4	68.8	−3.6	4.50	4.50	6.80	6.80
100 United Arab Emirates	..	16.2	..	19.0	52.1	−1.4	..	..	..	..

Industrial market economies

	1965-80	1980-85	1965	1980	1985	1980-85	1980	1985	1980	1985
101 Spain	19.7	7.7	60.3	75.3	62.3	12.6	13.05	10.53	16.85	13.52
102 Ireland	16.1	7.6	66.0	58.1	48.7	10.8	12.00	6.98	15.96	12.44
103 Italy	17.9	12.9	69.2	88.1	79.8	14.2	12.70	10.90	19.03	18.51
104 New Zealand	12.8	15.7	55.4	48.0	51.7	9.8	11.00	14.71	12.63	12.53
105 Belgium	10.4	6.2	58.3	56.0	54.8	5.9	7.69	6.69	..	12.54
106 United Kingdom	13.8	13.5	49.0	46.4	61.0	6.4	14.08	8.87	16.17	12.29
107 Austria	13.3	7.6	49.0	72.6	79.0	4.9	5.00	3.75	..	..
108 Netherlands	14.7	6.0	55.0	79.0	86.9	3.5	5.96	4.10	13.50	9.25
109 France	15.0	10.4	54.5	70.7	69.9	9.5	6.25	6.80	18.73	17.77
110 Australia	13.1	11.7	53.5	51.5	51.3	9.1	8.58	10.46	10.58	15.96
111 Finland	14.7	14.9	39.7	39.5	45.7	8.6	9.00	8.75	9.77	10.41
112 Germany, Fed. Rep.	10.1	5.6	46.1	60.3	63.6	3.2	7.95	4.44	12.04	9.53
113 Denmark	11.5	17.4	45.8	42.6	55.7	8.1	10.80	8.20	17.20	14.70
114 Japan	17.2	8.7	98.9	134.0	157.3	1.2	5.50	3.50	8.32	6.52
115 Sweden	10.5	9.0	55.7	54.6	53.1	8.6	11.25	11.83	15.12	16.72
116 Canada	15.4	6.8	41.3	65.8	63.0	6.3	12.86	8.46	18.25	10.00
117 Norway	12.8	14.0	51.9	52.9	58.8	8.5	5.08	5.35	12.63	13.46
118 Switzerland	7.0	10.2	102.3	105.6	122.8	4.5	7.75	4.36	5.56	5.43
119 United States	9.2	10.6	65.0	60.6	67.4	5.3	13.07	8.05	15.27	9.93

Nonreporting nonmember economies

120 Albania
121 Angola
122 Bulgaria
123 Cuba
124 Czechoslovakia

125 German Dem. Rep.
126 Korea, Dem. Rep.
127 Mongolia
128 USSR

a. See the technical notes.

Table 26. Income distribution

	Year	Lowest 20 percent	Second quintile	Third quintile	Fourth quintile	Highest 20 percent	Highest 10 percent
Low-income economies							
China and India							
Other low-income							
1 Ethiopia		..	..	..	..	..	..
2 Bangladesh	1981–82	6.6	10.7	15.3	22.1	45.3	29.5
3 Burkina Faso		..	..	..	..	..	..
4 Mali		..	..	..	..	..	..
5 Bhutan		..	..	..	..	..	..
6 Mozambique		..	..	..	..	..	..
7 Nepal		..	..	..	..	..	..
8 Malawi		..	..	..	..	..	..
9 Zaire		..	..	..	..	..	..
10 Burma		..	..	..	..	..	..
11 Burundi		..	..	..	..	..	..
12 Togo		..	..	..	..	..	..
13 Madagascar		..	..	..	..	..	..
14 Niger		..	..	..	..	..	..
15 Benin		..	..	..	..	..	..
16 Central African Rep.		..	..	..	..	..	..
17 India	1975–76	7.0	9.2	13.9	20.5	49.4	33.6
18 Rwanda		..	..	..	..	..	..
19 Somalia		..	..	..	..	..	..
20 Kenya	1976	2.6	6.3	11.5	19.2	60.4	45.8
21 Tanzania		..	..	..	..	..	..
22 Sudan		..	..	..	..	..	..
23 China		..	..	..	..	..	..
24 Haiti		..	..	..	..	..	..
25 Guinea		..	..	..	..	..	..
26 Sierra Leone		..	..	..	..	..	..
27 Senegal		..	..	..	..	..	..
28 Ghana		..	..	..	..	..	..
29 Pakistan		..	..	..	..	..	..
30 Sri Lanka	1980–81	5.8	10.1	14.1	20.3	49.8	34.7
31 Zambia	1976	3.4	7.4	11.2	16.9	61.1	46.4
32 *Afghanistan*		..	..	..	..	..	..
33 *Chad*		..	..	..	..	..	..
34 *Kampuchea, Dem.*		..	..	..	..	..	..
35 *Lao PDR*		..	..	..	..	..	..
36 *Uganda*		..	..	..	..	..	..
37 *Viet Nam*		..	..	..	..	..	..
Middle-income economies							
Lower middle-income							
38 Mauritania		..	..	..	..	..	..
39 Bolivia		..	..	..	..	..	..
40 Lesotho		..	..	..	..	..	..
41 Liberia		..	..	..	..	..	..
42 Indonesia	1976	6.6	7.8	12.6	23.6	49.4	34.0
43 Yemen, PDR		..	..	..	..	..	..
44 Yemen Arab Rep.		..	..	..	..	..	..
45 Morocco		..	..	..	..	..	..
46 Philippines	1985	5.2	8.9	13.2	20.2	52.5	37.0
47 Egypt, Arab Rep.	1974	5.8	10.7	14.7	20.8	48.0	33.2
48 Côte d'Ivoire	1985–86	2.4	6.2	10.9	19.1	61.4	43.7
49 Papua New Guinea		..	..	..	..	..	..
50 Zimbabwe		..	..	..	..	..	..
51 Honduras		..	..	..	..	..	..
52 Nicaragua		..	..	..	..	..	..
53 Dominican Rep.		..	..	..	..	..	..
54 Nigeria		..	..	..	..	..	..
55 Thailand	1975–76	5.6	9.6	13.9	21.1	49.8	34.1
56 Cameroon		..	..	..	..	..	..
57 El Salvador	1976–77	5.5	10.0	14.8	22.4	47.3	29.5
58 Botswana		..	..	..	..	..	..
59 Paraguay		..	..	..	..	..	..
60 Jamaica		..	..	..	..	..	..
61 Peru	1972	1.9	5.1	11.0	21.0	61.0	42.9
62 Turkey	1973	3.5	8.0	12.5	19.5	56.5	40.7
63 Mauritius	1980–81	4.0	7.5	11.0	17.0	60.5	46.7
64 Congo, People's Rep.		..	..	..	..	..	..
65 Ecuador		..	..	..	..	..	..
66 Tunisia		..	..	..	..	..	..
67 Guatemala		..	..	..	..	..	..

Note: For data comparability and coverage, see the technical notes.   Figures in italics are for years other than those specified.

252

	Year	Percentage share of household income, by percentile groups of households[a]					
		Lowest 20 percent	Second quintile	Third quintile	Fourth quintile	Highest 20 percent	Highest 10 percent
68 Costa Rica	1971	3.3	8.7	13.3	19.8	54.8	39.5
69 Colombia		..	..	..	..	..	..
70 Chile		..	..	..	..	..	..
71 Jordan		..	..	..	..	..	..
72 Syrian Arab Rep.		..	..	..	..	..	..
73 Lebanon		..	..	..	..	..	..

Upper middle-income

	Year	Lowest 20 percent	Second quintile	Third quintile	Fourth quintile	Highest 20 percent	Highest 10 percent
74 Brazil	1972	2.0	5.0	9.4	17.0	66.6	50.6
75 Uruguay		..	..	..	..	..	..
76 Hungary	1982	6.9	13.6	19.2	24.5	35.8	20.5
77 Portugal	1973–74	5.2	10.0	14.4	21.3	49.1	33.4
78 Malaysia	1973	3.5	7.7	12.4	20.3	56.1	39.8
79 South Africa		..	..	..	..	..	..
80 Poland		..	..	..	..	..	..
81 Yugoslavia	1978	6.6	12.1	18.7	23.9	38.7	22.9
82 Mexico	1977	2.9	7.0	12.0	20.4	57.7	40.6
83 Panama	1973	2.0	5.2	11.0	20.0	61.8	44.2
84 Argentina	1970	4.4	9.7	14.1	21.5	50.3	35.2
85 Korea, Rep. of	1976	5.7	11.2	15.4	22.4	45.3	27.5
86 Algeria		..	..	..	..	..	..
87 Venezuela	1970	3.0	7.3	12.9	22.8	54.0	35.7
88 Greece							
89 Israel	1979–80	6.0	12.0	17.7	24.4	39.9	22.6
90 Trinidad and Tobago	1975–76	4.2	9.1	13.9	22.8	50.0	31.8
91 Hong Kong	1980	5.4	10.8	15.2	21.6	47.0	31.3
92 Oman		..	..	..	..	..	..
93 Singapore		..	..	..	..	..	..
94 *Iran, Islamic Rep.*		..	..	..	..	..	..
95 *Iraq*		..	..	..	..	..	..
96 *Romania*		..	..	..	..	..	..

Developing economies
  Oil exporters
  Exporters of manufactures
  Highly indebted countries
  Sub-Saharan Africa

High-income oil exporters

	Year	Lowest 20 percent	Second quintile	Third quintile	Fourth quintile	Highest 20 percent	Highest 10 percent
97 Libya		..	..	..	..	..	..
98 Saudi Arabia		..	..	..	..	..	..
99 Kuwait		..	..	..	..	..	..
100 United Arab Emirates		..	..	..	..	..	..

Industrial market economies

	Year	Lowest 20 percent	Second quintile	Third quintile	Fourth quintile	Highest 20 percent	Highest 10 percent
101 Spain	1980–81	6.9	12.5	17.3	23.2	40.0	24.5
102 Ireland	1973	7.2	13.1	16.6	23.7	39.4	25.1
103 Italy	1977	6.2	11.3	15.9	22.7	43.9	28.1
104 New Zealand	1981–82	5.1	10.8	16.2	23.2	44.7	28.7
105 Belgium	1978–79	7.9	13.7	18.6	23.8	36.0	21.5
106 United Kingdom	1979	7.0	11.5	17.0	24.8	39.7	23.4
107 Austria		..	..	..	..	..	..
108 Netherlands	1981	8.3	14.1	18.2	23.2	36.2	21.5
109 France	1975	5.5	11.5	17.1	23.7	42.2	26.4
110 Australia	1975–76	5.4	10.0	15.0	22.5	47.1	30.5
111 Finland	1981	6.3	12.1	18.4	25.5	37.6	21.7
112 Germany, Fed. Rep.	1978	7.9	12.5	17.0	23.1	39.5	24.0
113 Denmark	1981	5.4	12.0	18.4	25.6	38.6	22.3
114 Japan	1979	8.7	13.2	17.5	23.1	37.5	22.4
115 Sweden	1981	7.4	13.1	16.8	21.0	41.7	28.1
116 Canada	1981	5.3	11.8	18.0	24.9	40.0	23.8
117 Norway	1982	6.0	12.9	18.3	24.6	38.2	22.8
118 Switzerland	1978	6.6	13.5	18.5	23.4	38.0	23.7
119 United States	1980	5.3	11.9	17.9	25.0	39.9	23.3

Nonreporting nonmember economies

	Year	Lowest 20 percent	Second quintile	Third quintile	Fourth quintile	Highest 20 percent	Highest 10 percent
120 *Albania*		..	..	..	..	..	..
121 *Angola*		..	..	..	..	..	..
122 *Bulgaria*		..	..	..	..	..	..
123 *Cuba*		..	..	..	..	..	..
124 *Czechoslovakia*		..	..	..	..	..	..
125 *German Dem. Rep.*		..	..	..	..	..	..
126 *Korea, Dem. Rep.*		..	..	..	..	..	..
127 *Mongolia*		..	..	..	..	..	..
128 *USSR*		..	..	..	..	..	..

a. These estimates should be treated with caution; see the technical notes.

Table 27. Population growth and projections

	Average annual growth of population (percent)			Population (millions)			Hypothetical size of stationary population (millions)	Assumed year of reaching net reproduction rate of 1	Population momentum 1985
	1965–80	1980–85	1985–2000	1985	1990[a]	2000[a]			
Low-income economies	**2.3 w**	**1.9 w**	**1.9 w**	**2,439 t**	**2,662 t**	**3,177 t**			
China and India	**2.2 w**	**1.6 w**	**1.5 w**	**1,805 t**	**1,959 t**	**2,270 t**			
Other low-income	**2.7 w**	**2.7 w**	**2.7 w**	**634 t**	**730 t**	**945 t**			
1 Ethiopia	2.7	2.5	2.9	42	49	65	204	2040	1.9
2 Bangladesh	2.7	2.6	2.3	101	114	141	305	2030	1.9
3 Burkina Faso	2.0	2.6	2.9	8	9	12	42	2040	1.9
4 Mali	2.6	2.3	2.7	8	9	11	36	2035	1.8
5 Bhutan	1.5	2.2	2.3	1	1	2	4	2035	1.7
6 Mozambique	2.5	2.6	3.1	14	16	21	68	2035	1.8
7 Nepal	2.4	2.4	2.7	17	19	24	73	2040	1.8
8 Malawi	2.9	3.1	3.3	7	8	11	38	2040	1.9
9 Zaire	2.8	3.0	3.0	31	36	47	130	2030	1.9
10 Burma	2.2	2.0	1.9	37	41	49	87	2020	1.7
11 Burundi	1.9	2.7	3.1	5	5	7	24	2035	1.8
12 Togo	3.0	3.3	3.2	3	4	5	15	2045	2.0
13 Madagascar	2.5	3.2	3.0	10	12	16	48	2035	1.9
14 Niger	2.7	3.0	3.2	6	7	10	36	2040	1.9
15 Benin	2.7	3.1	3.2	4	5	6	20	2035	2.0
16 Central African Rep.	1.8	2.5	2.9	3	3	4	12	2035	1.8
17 India	2.3	2.2	1.8	765	843	996	1,678	2010	1.7
18 Rwanda	3.3	3.2	3.7	6	7	10	40	2040	1.8
19 Somalia	3.3	2.9	3.1	5	6	8	30	2040	1.9
20 Kenya	3.9	4.1	4.0	20	25	36	121	2030	2.0
21 Tanzania	3.3	3.5	3.5	22	27	37	123	2035	1.9
22 Sudan	3.0	2.7	2.9	22	25	34	101	2035	1.8
23 China	2.2	1.2	1.3	1,040	1,116	1,274	1,683	2000	1.6
24 Haiti	2.0	1.8	1.9	6	7	8	16	2025	1.7
25 Guinea	1.9	2.4	1.9	6	7	8	21	2045	1.3
26 Sierra Leone	1.7	2.2	2.6	4	4	5	18	2045	1.8
27 Senegal	2.5	2.9	3.1	7	8	10	31	2035	1.9
28 Ghana	2.2	3.3	3.0	13	15	20	53	2030	1.9
29 Pakistan	3.1	3.1	2.7	96	112	146	395	2035	1.8
30 Sri Lanka	1.8	1.4	1.6	16	17	20	31	2005	1.7
31 Zambia	3.1	3.5	3.5	7	8	11	37	2035	2.0
32 *Afghanistan*	2.4	..	..	..	..	..	..	..	..
33 *Chad*	2.0	2.3	2.5	5	6	7	22	2040	1.8
34 *Kampuchea, Dem.*	0.3	..	..	..	..	..	..	..	..
35 Lao PDR	1.4	2.0	2.8	4	4	5	17	2040	1.8
36 *Uganda*	2.9	3.0	3.2	15	17	23	74	2035	1.9
37 *Viet Nam*	..	2.6	2.4	62	70	88	167	2015	1.8
Middle-income economies	**2.4 w**	**2.3 w**	**2.1 w**	**1,242 t**	**1,365 t**	**1,663 t**			
Lower middle-income	**2.5 w**	**2.5 w**	**2.3 w**	**675 t**	**761 t**	**947 t**			
38 Mauritania	2.2	2.1	2.8	2	2	3	8	2035	1.8
39 Bolivia	2.5	2.8	2.5	6	7	9	22	2030	1.8
40 Lesotho	2.3	2.7	2.7	2	2	2	6	2030	1.8
41 Liberia	3.0	3.4	3.2	2	3	4	11	2035	1.9
42 Indonesia	2.3	2.1	1.8	162	179	212	363	2010	1.8
43 Yemen, PDR	2.0	2.6	2.3	2	2	3	7	2035	1.9
44 Yemen, Arab Rep.	2.8	2.5	3.0	8	9	12	39	2040	1.9
45 Morocco	2.5	2.5	2.4	22	25	31	66	2025	1.8
46 Philippines	2.8	2.5	2.2	55	62	75	140	2015	1.8
47 Egypt, Arab Rep.	2.4	2.8	2.2	49	55	67	132	2020	1.8
48 Côte d'Ivoire	5.0	3.8	3.1	10	12	16	42	2035	1.9
49 Papua New Guinea	2.4	2.6	2.2	4	4	5	11	2030	1.7
50 Zimbabwe	3.1	3.7	3.1	8	10	13	33	2025	2.0
51 Honduras	3.2	3.5	3.0	4	5	7	15	2020	1.9
52 Nicaragua	3.1	3.4	2.9	3	4	5	12	2025	2.0
53 Dominican Rep.	2.7	2.4	2.0	6	7	9	15	2010	1.8
54 Nigeria	2.5	3.3	3.4	100	118	163	529	2035	1.9
55 Thailand	2.7	2.1	1.6	52	57	66	99	2000	1.7
56 Cameroon	2.7	3.2	3.4	10	12	17	51	2030	1.9
57 El Salvador	2.7	1.0	2.0	5	5	6	13	2015	1.7
58 Botswana	4.2	3.5	3.2	1	1	2	5	2025	2.0
59 Paraguay	2.9	3.3	2.5	4	4	5	10	2020	1.8
60 Jamaica	1.1	1.6	1.5	2	2	3	4	2005	1.7
61 Peru	2.7	2.3	2.0	19	21	25	45	2015	1.7
62 Turkey	2.4	2.5	1.9	50	56	67	111	2010	1.7
63 Mauritius	1.7	1.3	1.2	1	1	1	2	2000	1.7
64 Congo, People's Rep.	2.7	3.1	3.6	2	2	3	9	2025	1.9
65 Ecuador	3.1	2.9	2.5	9	11	14	26	2015	1.8
66 Tunisia	2.1	2.3	2.2	7	8	10	18	2015	1.8
67 Guatemala	2.8	2.9	2.5	8	9	12	26	2020	1.8

Note: For data comparability and coverage, see the technical notes.   Figures in italics are for years other than those specified.

	Average annual growth of population (percent)			Population (millions)			Hypothetical size of stationary population (millions)	Assumed year of reaching net reproduction rate of 1	Population momentum 1985
	1965–80	1980–85	1985–2000	1985	1990ᵃ	2000ᵃ			
68 Costa Rica	2.8	2.7	1.9	3	3	3	5	2005	1.8
69 Colombia	2.2	1.9	1.7	28	31	37	59	2010	1.7
70 Chile	1.8	1.7	1.2	12	13	15	20	2000	1.6
71 Jordan	2.6	3.7	3.1	4	4	6	12	2020	1.9
72 Syrian Arab Rep.	3.4	3.6	3.1	11	12	17	39	2020	1.9
73 *Lebanon*	1.6	..	..	..	..	..	..	..	..
Upper middle-income	**2.2 w**	**2.0 w**	**1.8 w**	**567 t**	**604 t**	**716 t**			
74 Brazil	2.5	2.3	1.8	136	150	178	292	2010	1.7
75 Uruguay	0.4	0.7	0.7	3	3	3	4	2000	1.3
76 Hungary	0.4	−0.1	−0.1	11	11	11	10	2020	1.1
77 Portugal	0.6	0.7	0.5	10	11	11	12	2020	1.3
78 Malaysia	2.5	2.5	1.9	16	17	21	33	2005	1.8
79 South Africa	2.3	2.5	2.2	32	37	45	95	2025	1.8
80 Poland	0.8	0.9	0.6	37	38	41	48	2020	1.3
81 Yugoslavia	0.9	0.7	0.5	23	24	25	26	2020	1.3
82 Mexico	3.2	2.6	2.2	79	89	110	197	2010	1.8
83 Panama	2.6	2.2	1.6	2	2	3	4	2000	1.8
84 Argentina	1.6	1.6	1.2	31	33	37	53	2010	1.5
85 Korea, Rep. of	1.9	1.5	1.2	41	44	49	65	2000	1.6
86 Algeria	3.0	3.3	2.9	22	26	34	81	2025	1.8
87 Venezuela	3.5	2.9	2.6	17	20	24	39	2005	1.8
88 Greece	0.7	0.6	0.3	10	10	10	11	2020	1.2
89 Israel	2.8	1.8	1.4	4	5	5	7	2005	1.6
90 Trinidad and Tobago	1.3	1.6	1.5	1	1	1	2	2005	1.7
91 Hong Kong	2.2	1.4	1.0	5	6	6	7	2010	1.4
92 Oman	3.6	4.8	3.1	1	1	2	5	2030	1.9
93 Singapore	1.6	1.2	0.9	3	3	3	3	2010	1.4
94 *Iran, Islamic Rep.*	3.2	2.9	3.0	45	52	69	157	2020	1.8
95 *Iraq*	3.4	3.6	3.7	16	19	27	75	2025	1.9
96 *Romania*	1.1	0.5	0.6	23	23	25	28	2020	1.3
Developing economies	**2.3 w**	**2.0 w**	**1.9 w**	**3,681 t**	**4,027 t**	**4,840 t**			
Oil exporters	**2.7 w**	**2.7 w**	**2.5 w**	**523 t**	**578 t**	**736 t**			
Exporters of manufactures	**2.2 w**	**1.6 w**	**1.4 w**	**2,098 t**	**2,272 t**	**2,624 t**			
Highly indebted countries	**2.5 w**	**2.4 w**	**2.2 w**	**554 t**	**603 t**	**745 t**			
Sub-Saharan Africa	**2.7 w**	**3.3 w**	**3.3 w**	**418 t**	**491 t**	**666 t**			
High-income oil exporters	**5.2 w**	**4.3 w**	**3.7 w**	**18 t**	**22 t**	**31 t**			
97 Libya	4.5	3.9	3.8	4	5	7	18	2025	1.9
98 Saudi Arabia	4.6	4.2	3.8	12	14	20	61	2030	1.8
99 Kuwait	7.0	4.5	2.9	2	2	3	4	2010	1.8
100 United Arab Emirates	15.9	6.2	2.8	1	2	2	3	2010	1.4
Industrial market economies	**0.9 w**	**0.6 w**	**0.4 w**	**737 t**	**755 t**	**781 t**			
101 Spain	1.0	0.7	0.6	39	40	42	46	2020	1.3
102 Ireland	1.4	0.9	0.8	4	4	4	5	2020	1.4
103 Italy	0.6	0.3	0.1	57	57	58	50	2020	1.1
104 New Zealand	1.3	0.9	0.6	3	3	4	4	2020	1.3
105 Belgium	0.3	0.1	0.1	10	10	10	9	2020	1.1
106 United Kingdom	0.2	0.1	0.1	57	57	57	55	2020	1.1
107 Austria	0.3	0.0	0.1	8	8	8	8	2020	1.1
108 Netherlands	0.9	0.4	0.3	14	15	15	14	2020	1.2
109 France	0.7	0.6	0.4	55	56	59	60	2020	1.2
110 Australia	1.8	1.4	0.9	16	17	18	20	2020	1.4
111 Finland	0.3	0.5	0.3	5	5	5	5	2020	1.1
112 Germany, Fed. Rep.	0.3	−0.2	−0.2	61	60	59	44	2020	1.0
113 Denmark	0.5	0.1	−0.1	5	5	5	4	2020	1.1
114 Japan	1.2	0.7	0.4	121	124	129	124	2020	1.1
115 Sweden	0.5	0.1	0.0	8	8	8	7	2020	1.0
116 Canada	1.3	1.1	0.7	25	27	28	29	2020	1.3
117 Norway	0.6	0.3	0.2	4	4	4	4	2020	1.2
118 Switzerland	0.5	0.2	0.1	6	6	7	6	2020	1.1
119 United States	1.0	1.0	0.6	239	249	262	277	2020	1.3
Nonreporting nonmember economies	**1.0 w**	**0.9 w**	**0.8 w**	**363 t**	**379 t**	**409 t**			
120 *Albania*	2.5	2.1	1.8	3	3	4	6	2005	1.7
121 *Angola*	2.8	2.5	2.9	9	10	13	43	2040	1.9
122 *Bulgaria*	0.5	0.2	0.2	9	9	9	10	2020	1.1
123 *Cuba*	1.5	0.8	1.1	10	11	12	14	2010	1.5
124 *Czechoslovakia*	0.5	0.3	0.4	15	16	16	18	2020	1.2
125 *German Dem. Rep.*	−0.2	−0.1	0.0	17	17	17	16	2020	1.1
126 *Korea, Dem. Rep.*	2.7	2.5	2.0	20	23	28	46	2010	1.8
127 *Mongolia*	3.0	2.6	2.5	2	2	3	5	2020	1.8
128 *USSR*	0.9	0.9	0.7	277	289	308	384	2020	1.3

a. For the assumptions used in the projections, see the technical notes.

Table 28. Demography and fertility

	Crude birth rate per thousand population		Crude death rate per thousand population		Percentage change in: Crude birth rate 1965-85	Crude death rate 1965-85	Total fertility rate		Percentage of married women of childbearing age using contraception[a]	
	1965	1985	1965	1985	1965-85	1965-85	1985	2000	1970	1984
Low-income economies	**43** *w*	**29** *w*	**17** *w*	**10** *w*	**−35.0** *w*	**−41.8** *w*	**3.9** *w*	**3.2** *w*		
China and India	**42** *w*	**24** *w*	**16** *w*	**9** *w*	**−43.3** *w*	**−46.4** *w*	**3.2** *w*	**2.5** *w*		
Other low-income	**46** *w*	**43** *w*	**21** *w*	**15** *w*	**−8.3** *w*	**−28.6** *w*	**5.9** *w*	**4.7** *w*		
1 Ethiopia	43	46	20	19	5.1	−4.0	6.2	5.5	..	*2*
2 Bangladesh	47	40	21	15	−14.6	−29.0	5.7	3.7	..	25
3 Burkina Faso	46	49	24	21	5.6	−13.9	6.5	6.0	..	*1*
4 Mali	56	48	26	20	−14.6	−25.5	6.5	5.9	..	*1*
5 Bhutan	43	43	31	21	−0.7	−34.7	6.2	5.3	..	..
6 Mozambique	49	45	27	18	−6.8	−33.0	6.3	5.8	..	..
7 Nepal	46	43	24	18	−5.5	−25.3	6.3	5.4	..	7
8 Malawi	56	54	29	22	−4.3	−23.7	7.6	6.4	..	*1*
9 Zaire	47	45	21	15	−4.2	−28.3	6.1	5.0	..	*1*
10 Burma	40	30	18	11	−24.7	−40.1	3.9	3.0	..	5
11 Burundi	47	47	24	18	0.4	−24.0	6.5	5.9	..	*1*
12 Togo	50	49	22	16	−1.8	−26.3	6.5	5.4	..	..
13 Madagascar	44	47	21	15	7.1	−29.2	6.5	4.8	..	..
14 Niger	48	51	29	21	7.2	−26.5	7.0	6.4	..	*1*
15 Benin	49	49	24	17	0.4	−29.5	6.5	5.4	..	6
16 Central African Rep.	34	42	24	16	22.4	−32.8	5.6	5.5	..	..
17 India	45	33	20	12	−27.2	−41.0	4.5	3.0	12	35
18 Rwanda	52	52	17	19	1.0	8.1	8.0	6.7	..	*1*
19 Somalia	50	49	26	20	−1.4	−23.5	6.8	6.2	..	(.)
20 Kenya	51	54	21	13	4.7	−37.7	7.8	6.1	6	17
21 Tanzania	49	50	22	15	2.5	−30.3	7.0	5.8	..	*1*
22 Sudan	47	45	24	17	−3.8	−28.3	6.6	5.5	..	5
23 China	39	18	13	7	−53.8	−61.1	2.3	2.1	..	69
24 Haiti	43	35	20	13	−16.3	−36.6	4.7	3.6	..	7
25 Guinea	46	50	29	24	8.5	−17.2	6.0	5.6	..	*1*
26 Sierra Leone	48	48	33	25	0.8	−23.0	6.5	6.1	..	4
27 Senegal	47	46	23	19	−1.5	−18.9	6.7	5.6	..	12
28 Ghana	49	46	20	14	−5.8	−29.0	6.4	4.5	..	*10*
29 Pakistan	48	44	21	15	−12.5	−30.1	6.1	4.6	6	8
30 Sri Lanka	33	25	8	6	−21.7	−26.8	3.2	2.3	6	57
31 Zambia	49	49	20	15	−0.8	−26.5	6.8	5.6	..	*1*
32 *Afghanistan*	54	..	29	..	..	..	..	..	2	..
33 *Chad*	45	44	28	21	−4.0	−25.8	5.7	5.5	..	*1*
34 *Kampuchea, Dem.*	44	..	20	..	..	..	..	..	..	..
35 *Lao PDR*	..	42	..	19	..	..	6.4	5.5	..	..
36 *Uganda*	49	50	19	17	3.0	−11.7	6.9	5.7	..	*1*
37 *Viet Nam*	44	34	17	8	−22.6	−54.2	4.6	3.1	..	..
Middle-income economies	**40** *w*	**32** *w*	**15** *w*	**10** *w*	**−22.2** *w*	**−30.6** *w*	**4.3** *w*	**3.3** *w*		
Lower middle-income	**44** *w*	**36** *w*	**17** *w*	**11** *w*	**−20.6** *w*	**−36.7** *w*	**4.8** *w*	**3.6** *w*		
38 Mauritania	44	45	25	19	2.0	−25.1	6.3	5.9	..	*1*
39 Bolivia	46	42	21	15	−8.1	−29.9	5.9	4.2	..	26
40 Lesotho	42	41	18	14	−2.4	−22.2	5.8	4.8	..	5
41 Liberia	46	49	22	16	6.6	−25.0	6.9	5.7	..	*1*
42 Indonesia	43	32	20	12	−24.4	−39.5	4.1	2.8	0	40
43 Yemen, PDR	50	46	26	19	−7.5	−29.4	6.0	4.4	..	..
44 Yemen, Arab Rep.	49	48	27	21	−1.4	−23.5	6.8	5.8	..	*1*
45 Morocco	49	36	18	11	−27.1	−41.5	4.9	3.6	1	27
46 Philippines	42	33	12	8	−21.3	−34.0	4.3	3.0	2	32
47 Egypt, Arab Rep.	43	36	19	10	−17.7	−47.2	4.7	3.3	10	32
48 Côte d'Ivoire	44	45	22	14	2.0	−36.3	6.5	5.2	..	*3*
49 Papua New Guinea	43	37	20	13	−13.3	−34.9	5.4	4.0	..	*4*
50 Zimbabwe	55	47	17	12	−15.1	−31.6	6.2	4.2	..	40
51 Honduras	50	42	17	9	−16.6	−45.8	6.0	3.8	..	35
52 Nicaragua	49	42	16	10	−13.5	−34.2	5.6	3.9	..	9
53 Dominican Rep.	46	32	14	7	−30.1	−48.6	4.0	2.7	..	50
54 Nigeria	51	50	23	16	−3.3	−28.4	6.9	5.7	..	5
55 Thailand	41	26	10	8	−37.4	−24.2	3.2	2.2	15	65
56 Cameroon	40	47	20	14	18.1	−29.5	6.8	5.6	..	*3*
57 El Salvador	46	38	13	10	−17.7	−23.1	5.2	3.3	..	48
58 Botswana	53	46	19	12	−14.2	−33.7	6.7	4.8	..	29
59 Paraguay	41	35	8	7	−17.1	−13.8	4.4	3.0	..	39
60 Jamaica	38	25	8	6	−34.2	−32.5	2.8	2.2	..	52
61 Peru	45	33	16	11	−26.1	−34.8	4.3	3.0	..	43
62 Turkey	41	30	14	8	−26.7	−40.9	3.9	2.7	32	62
63 Mauritius	36	20	8	7	−44.4	−14.7	2.5	2.1	..	78
64 Congo, People's Rep.	42	45	18	12	7.7	−32.0	6.3	5.7	..	..
65 Ecuador	45	35	13	7	−21.9	−48.5	4.7	3.1	..	40
66 Tunisia	44	32	16	9	−27.0	−45.3	4.6	3.1	10	42
67 Guatemala	46	40	17	10	−13.1	−43.7	5.7	3.7	..	25

Note: For data comparability and coverage, see the technical notes.   Figures in italics are for years other than those specified.

	Crude birth rate per thousand population		Crude death rate per thousand population		Percentage change in:		Total fertility rate		Percentage of married women of childbearing age using contraception[a]	
					Crude birth rate	Crude death rate				
	1965	1985	1965	1985	1965–85	1965–85	1985	2000	1970	1984
68 Costa Rica	45	29	8	4	−36.5	−47.4	3.3	2.3	..	66
69 Colombia	45	27	14	7	−38.7	−48.5	3.3	2.5	34	55
70 Chile	32	22	11	7	−33.1	−38.0	2.5	2.1	..	43
71 Jordan	..	39	17	7	..	−57.1	6.2	3.9	22	26
72 Syrian Arab Rep.	48	44	16	8	−7.2	−49.4	6.7	4.1	..	30
73 *Lebanon*	40	..	12	..	..	..	..	..	55	..
Upper middle-income	**36 w**	**28 w**	**11 w**	**8 w**	**−24.0 w**	**−23.3 w**	**3.7 w**	**2.9 w**		
74 Brazil	39	29	11	8	−24.3	−30.5	3.6	2.6	..	65
75 Uruguay	21	19	10	10	−12.1	3.2	2.6	2.1	..	..
76 Hungary	13	12	11	14	−12.2	27.2	1.7	1.8	67	74
77 Portugal	23	14	10	9	−39.1	−13.5	2.0	1.9	..	70
78 Malaysia	40	30	12	6	−26.2	−45.5	3.7	2.4	33	51
79 South Africa	41	37	19	13	−9.9	−32.1	4.9	3.6	..	..
80 Poland	42	19	7	10	−54.8	28.4	2.3	2.1	60	75
81 Yugoslavia	21	16	9	9	−23.8	(.)	2.1	2.1	59	55
82 Mexico	44	33	11	7	−26.0	−39.0	4.3	2.8	..	48
83 Panama	40	26	9	5	−33.3	−41.4	3.2	2.2	..	61
84 Argentina	22	23	9	9	7.8	(.)	3.3	2.5	..	74
85 Korea, Rep. of	35	21	11	6	−40.0	−44.8	2.4	2.1	32	70
86 Algeria	50	41	18	10	−18.1	−45.1	6.3	4.2	..	7
87 Venezuela	42	31	8	5	−26.0	−37.0	3.9	2.4	..	49
88 Greece	18	13	8	9	−27.8	12.5	2.0	1.9	..	..
89 Israel	26	23	6	7	−12.8	7.9	2.9	2.3	..	..
90 Trinidad and Tobago	33	25	7	7	−18.2	(.)	2.8	2.2	44	55
91 Hong Kong	27	14	6	5	−48.1	−16.7	1.8	2.0	50	72
92 Oman	50	44	24	13	−12.5	−45.8	6.7	4.6	..	..
93 Singapore	31	17	6	5	−44.0	−16.7	1.7	1.9	45	74
94 *Iran, Islamic Rep.*	50	41	17	11	−18.6	−35.2	5.6	4.3	3	23
95 *Iraq*	49	44	18	8	−9.4	−55.5	6.7	5.2	14	..
96 *Romania*	15	14	9	10	−6.7	11.1	2.1	2.0	..	58
Developing economies	**42 w**	**30 w**	**16 w**	**10 w**	**−30.8 w**	**−38.0 w**	**4.0 w**	**3.2 w**		
Oil exporters	**46 w**	**38 w**	**18 w**	**11 w**	**−17.7 w**	**−38.6 w**	**5.1 w**	**3.9 w**		
Exporters of manufactures	**40 w**	**24 w**	**15 w**	**9 w**	**−41.3 w**	**−42.0 w**	**3.1 w**	**2.5 w**		
Highly indebted countries	**41 w**	**34 w**	**14 w**	**9 w**	**−19.2 w**	**−32.8 w**	**4.4 w**	**3.4 w**		
Sub-Saharan Africa	**48 w**	**48 w**	**22 w**	**17 w**	**−0.4 w**	**−24.8 w**	**6.7 w**	**5.6 w**		
High-income oil exporters	**48 w**	**41 w**	**18 w**	**8 w**	**−12.7 w**	**−56.6 w**	**6.9 w**	**5.3 w**		
97 Libya	49	45	17	10	−7.9	−45.4	7.2	5.5	..	..
98 Saudi Arabia	48	42	20	8	−12.4	−58.1	7.1	5.7	..	..
99 Kuwait	48	34	7	3	−28.5	−56.6	5.2	3.0	..	..
100 United Arab Emirates	41	30	14	4	−25.9	−74.8	5.9	3.7	..	..
Industrial market economies	**20 w**	**13 w**	**9 w**	**9 w**	**−33.8 w**	**−7.0 w**	**1.8 w**	**1.9 w**		
101 Spain	21	13	8	7	−38.1	−12.5	2.0	1.9	..	51
102 Ireland	22	19	12	9	−13.6	−21.7	2.6	2.0	60	..
103 Italy	19	10	10	9	−47.4	−10.0	1.5	1.7	..	78
104 New Zealand	23	16	9	8	−30.4	−4.6	2.1	2.0	..	..
105 Belgium	17	12	12	11	−27.9	−7.4	1.6	1.7	..	85
106 United Kingdom	18	13	12	12	−29.3	3.4	1.8	1.8	69	77
107 Austria	18	12	13	12	−31.8	−4.6	2.1	1.7	..	..
108 Netherlands	20	12	8	8	−40.2	(.)	1.5	1.7	..	78
109 France	18	14	11	10	−22.2	−9.1	2.0	2.1	64	79
110 Australia	20	15	9	7	−25.0	−22.2	2.0	2.1	67	..
111 Finland	17	13	10	9	−22.8	−5.2	1.7	1.8	77	80
112 Germany, Fed. Rep.	18	10	12	11	−45.2	−8.3	1.3	1.5	..	..
113 Denmark	18	10	10	11	−42.2	11.9	1.4	1.6	67	..
114 Japan	19	13	7	6	−33.2	−14.3	1.8	1.9	56	57
115 Sweden	16	11	10	11	−28.9	10.0	1.7	1.8	..	78
116 Canada	23	15	8	7	−37.2	−12.5	1.7	1.8	..	73
117 Norway	18	12	10	10	−31.5	(.)	1.7	1.8	..	71
118 Switzerland	19	11	10	9	−40.3	−10.0	1.5	1.7	..	70
119 United States	22	16	9	9	−27.3	−3.6	1.8	1.9	65	68
Nonreporting nonmember economies	**20 w**	**19 w**	**8 w**	**10 w**	**−3.4 w**	**25.1 w**	**2.5 w**	**2.3 w**		
120 *Albania*	35	27	9	6	−23.0	−34.8	3.4	2.4	..	..
121 *Angola*	49	48	29	22	−3.5	−25.7	6.4	5.9	..	1
122 *Bulgaria*	15	14	8	11	−9.2	39.0	2.0	2.0	..	76
123 *Cuba*	34	17	8	5	−50.0	−37.5	2.0	2.0	..	60
124 *Czechoslovakia*	16	15	10	12	−10.4	18.0	2.1	2.0	..	95
125 *German Dem. Rep.*	17	14	14	13	−17.0	−7.1	1.8	1.9	..	..
126 *Korea, Dem. Rep.*	39	30	12	6	−24.5	−47.4	3.8	2.7	..	..
127 *Mongolia*	42	35	12	8	−16.4	−34.6	4.9	3.4	..	..
128 *USSR*	18	19	7	10	1.1	37.0	2.3	2.2	..	..

a. Figures include women whose husbands practice contraception; see the technical notes.

Table 29. Life expectancy and related indicators

	Life expectancy at birth (years)				Infant mortality rate (aged under 1)		Child death rate (aged 1–4)	
	Male		Female					
	1965	1985	1965	1985	1965	1985	1965	1985
Low-income economies	47 w	60 w	50 w	61 w	127 w	72 w	19 w	9 w
China and India	48 w	63 w	51 w	64 w	116 w	58 w	16 w	6 w
Other low-income	44 w	51 w	45 w	53 w	150 w	112 w	27 w	19 w
1 Ethiopia	42	43	43	47	165	168	37	38
2 Bangladesh	45	50	44	51	153	123	24	18
3 Burkina Faso	40	44	42	47	193	144	52	29
4 Mali	38	45	40	48	200	174	47	43
5 Bhutan	30	44	32	43	184	133	30	20
6 Mozambique	36	45	39	48	171	123	31	22
7 Nepal	41	47	40	46	184	133	30	20
8 Malawi	37	44	40	46	199	156	55	35
9 Zaire	42	50	45	53	135	102	30	20
10 Burma	46	57	49	61	122	66	21	..
11 Burundi	42	46	45	49	142	118	38	23
12 Togo	40	49	44	52	153	97	36	12
13 Madagascar	41	51	45	54	..	109	18	21
14 Niger	35	42	38	45	180	140	46	28
15 Benin	41	48	43	51	166	115	52	19
16 Central African Rep.	40	47	41	50	167	137	47	27
17 India	46	57	44	56	151	89	23	11
18 Rwanda	47	46	51	49	141	127	35	26
19 Somalia	37	44	40	48	165	152	37	33
20 Kenya	43	52	46	56	112	91	25	16
21 Tanzania	41	50	45	54	138	110	29	22
22 Sudan	39	47	41	50	160	112	37	18
23 China	54	68	55	70	90	35	11	2
24 Haiti	44	53	47	56	158	123	37	22
25 Guinea	34	39	36	41	196	153	53	34
26 Sierra Leone	32	39	33	40	220	175	69	43
27 Senegal	40	45	42	48	171	137	42	27
28 Ghana	46	51	49	55	120	94	25	11
29 Pakistan	46	52	44	50	149	115	23	16
30 Sri Lanka	63	68	64	72	63	36	6	2
31 Zambia	43	50	46	54	121	84	29	15
32 *Afghanistan*	35	..	35	..	..	..	..	..
33 *Chad*	35	43	38	46	183	138	47	27
34 *Kampuchea, Dem.*	43	..	46	..	134	..	20	..
35 *Lao PDR*	..	44	..	46	..	151	34	23
36 *Uganda*	43	45	47	49	121	108	26	21
37 *Viet Nam*	48	63	51	67	..	49	8	4
Middle-income economies	53 w	60 w	56 w	64 w	104 w	68 w	17 w	8 w
Lower middle-income	47 w	56 w	50 w	60 w	132 w	82 w	22 w	11 w
38 Mauritania	39	45	42	48	170	132	41	25
39 Bolivia	42	51	47	54	160	117	37	20
40 Lesotho	47	53	50	56	142	106	20	14
41 Liberia	41	49	44	52	171	127	32	23
42 Indonesia	43	53	45	57	138	96	20	12
43 Yemen, PDR	38	45	39	47	194	145	52	30
44 Yemen, Arab Rep.	37	44	38	46	200	154	55	34
45 Morocco	48	57	51	61	145	90	32	10
46 Philippines	54	61	57	65	72	48	11	4
47 Egypt, Arab Rep.	48	59	50	63	172	93	21	11
48 Côte d'Ivoire	43	51	45	55	174	105	37	15
49 Papua New Guinea	44	51	44	54	140	68	22	7
50 Zimbabwe	46	55	50	59	103	77	15	7
51 Honduras	48	60	52	64	128	76	24	7
52 Nicaragua	49	57	52	61	121	69	24	6
53 Dominican Rep.	53	63	56	66	102	70	14	6
54 Nigeria	40	48	43	52	177	109	33	21
55 Thailand	54	62	58	66	88	43	11	3
56 Cameroon	44	53	47	57	143	89	34	10
57 El Salvador	53	60	56	67	120	65	20	5
58 Botswana	46	54	49	60	107	71	21	11
59 Paraguay	63	64	67	68	60	43	7	2
60 Jamaica	63	71	67	76	49	20	4	1
61 Peru	49	57	52	60	131	94	24	11
62 Turkey	52	62	55	67	152	84	35	9
63 Mauritius	59	62	63	69	65	25	9	1
64 Congo, People's Rep.	48	56	51	59	118	77	19	7
65 Ecuador	55	64	57	68	112	67	21	5
66 Tunisia	51	61	52	64	145	78	30	8
67 Guatemala	48	58	50	63	112	65	16	5

Note: For data comparability and coverage; see the technical notes.   Figures in italics are for years other than those specified.

	Life expectancy at birth (years)				Infant mortality rate (aged under 1)		Child death rate (aged 1–4)	
	Male		Female					
	1965	1985	1965	1985	1965	1985	1965	1985
68 Costa Rica	63	71	66	76	72	19	8	(.)
69 Colombia	54	63	59	67	96	48	8	3
70 Chile	57	67	62	74	107	22	14	1
71 Jordan	49	63	52	66	115	49	19	3
72 Syrian Arab Rep.	51	62	54	65	114	54	18	4
73 *Lebanon*	60	..	64	..	56	..	4	..
Upper middle-income	**58 w**	**64 w**	**62 w**	**69 w**	**84 w**	**52 w**	**11 w**	**4 w**
74 Brazil	55	62	59	67	104	67	15	5
75 Uruguay	65	70	72	75	47	29	3	1
76 Hungary	67	67	72	74	39	20	3	1
77 Portugal	63	71	69	77	65	19	6	1
78 Malaysia	56	66	60	70	55	28	5	2
79 South Africa	45	53	48	57	124	78	22	7
80 Poland	66	67	72	76	42	19	3	1
81 Yugoslavia	64	69	68	75	72	27	7	2
82 Mexico	58	64	61	69	82	50	8	3
83 Panama	62	70	65	74	56	25	4	1
84 Argentina	63	67	69	74	58	34	4	1
85 Korea, Rep. of	55	65	58	72	63	27	6	2
86 Algeria	49	59	51	63	154	81	34	8
87 Venezuela	61	66	65	73	65	37	6	2
88 Greece	69	72	72	78	34	16	2	1
89 Israel	71	73	74	77	27	14	2	(.)
90 Trinidad and Tobago	63	67	67	72	42	22	3	1
91 Hong Kong	64	73	71	79	28	9	2	(.)
92 Oman	40	52	42	55	173	109	43	17
93 Singapore	64	70	68	75	26	9	1	(.)
94 *Iran, Islamic Rep.*	52	60	52	60	157	111	32	17
95 *Iraq*	51	59	53	63	119	73	21	7
96 *Romania*	66	69	70	74	44	24	3	1
Developing economies	**49 w**	**60 w**	**52 w**	**62 w**	**118 w**	**71 w**	**18 w**	**9 w**
Oil exporters	**47 w**	**56 w**	**50 w**	**60 w**	**140 w**	**88 w**	**22 w**	**12 w**
Exporters of manufactures	**50 w**	**63 w**	**53 w**	**65 w**	**87 w**	**56 w**	**15 w**	**5 w**
Highly indebted countries	**53 w**	**60 w**	**57 w**	**65 w**	**107 w**	**66 w**	**16 w**	**7 w**
Sub-Saharan Africa	**41 w**	**49 w**	**44 w**	**53 w**	**167 w**	**104 w**	**32 w**	**18 w**
High-income oil exporters	**48 w**	**61 w**	**51 w**	**65 w**	**115 w**	**61 w**	**33 w**	**5 w**
97 Libya	48	59	51	62	138	90	29	10
98 Saudi Arabia	47	60	50	64	148	61	38	4
99 Kuwait	61	69	65	74	43	22	5	1
100 United Arab Emirates	56	68	59	73	100	35	14	1
Industrial market economies	**68 w**	**73 w**	**74 w**	**79 w**	**23 w**	**9 w**	**1 w**	**(.) w**
101 Spain	68	74	73	80	38	10	3	(.)
102 Ireland	69	71	73	76	25	10	1	(.)
103 Italy	68	74	73	79	36	12	3	(.)
104 New Zealand	68	71	74	77	20	11	1	(.)
105 Belgium	68	72	74	78	24	11	1	(.)
106 United Kingdom	68	72	74	77	20	9	1	(.)
107 Austria	66	70	73	77	28	11	2	(.)
108 Netherlands	71	73	76	80	14	8	1	(.)
109 France	68	75	75	81	22	8	1	(.)
110 Australia	68	75	74	80	19	9	1	(.)
111 Finland	66	72	73	79	17	6	1	(.)
112 Germany, Fed. Rep.	67	72	73	78	24	10	1	(.)
113 Denmark	71	72	75	78	19	7	1	(.)
114 Japan	68	75	73	80	18	6	1	(.)
115 Sweden	72	74	76	80	13	6	1	(.)
116 Canada	69	72	75	80	23	8	1	(.)
117 Norway	71	74	76	80	17	8	1	(.)
118 Switzerland	69	73	75	80	18	8	1	(.)
119 United States	68	72	74	80	22	11	1	(.)
Nonreporting nonmember economies	**65 w**	**65 w**	**72 w**	**72 w**	**33 w**	**32 w**	**3 w**	**4 w**
120 *Albania*	65	67	67	73	87	43	10	3
121 *Angola*	34	43	37	45	192	143	52	30
122 *Bulgaria*	66	68	73	74	31	16	2	1
123 *Cuba*	65	73	69	77	38	16	4	(.)
124 *Czechoslovakia*	64	66	73	74	26	15	1	1
125 *German Dem. Rep.*	67	68	74	75	25	10	1	(.)
126 *Korea, Dem. Rep.*	55	65	58	71	63	27	6	2
127 *Mongolia*	55	61	58	65	88	49	10	4
128 *USSR*	66	65	74	74	28	29	2	(.)

Table 30. Health-related indicators

	Population per:				Daily calorie supply per capita	
	Physician		Nursing person			
	1965	1981	1965	1981	1965	1985
Low-income economies	**8,390** w	**5,770** w	**4,880** w	**3,880** w	**2,046** w	**2,339** w
China and India	**4,230** w	**2,530** w	**4,440** w	**2,890** w	**2,061** w	**2,428** w
Other low-income	**26,110** w	**17,350** w	**7,350** w	**7,620** w	**1,997** w	**2,073** w
1 Ethiopia	70,190	88,120	5,970	5,000	1,832	1,681
2 Bangladesh	8,400	9,700	..	19,400	1,964	1,899
3 Burkina Faso	74,100	55,860	4,170	3,070	2,009	1,924
4 Mali	49,200	26,450	3,200	2,320	1,860	1,788
5 Bhutan	..	18,200	..	7,960	2,904	2,571
6 Mozambique	17,990	37,000	5,370	5,610	1,982	1,678
7 Nepal	46,200	28,770	..	33,430	1,931	2,034
8 Malawi	46,900	53,000	49,240	2,980	2,132	2,448
9 Zaire	35,100	..	..	..	2,188	2,154
10 Burma	11,900	4,900	11,410	4,890	1,928	2,547
11 Burundi	56,320	..	7,310	..	2,391	2,116
12 Togo	23,200	21,200	4,990	1,640	2,378	2,236
13 Madagascar	10,540	9,940	3,620	1,090	2,486	2,469
14 Niger	65,460	..	6,210	..	1,996	2,250
15 Benin	32,390	17,000	2,540	1,660	2,008	2,173
16 Central African Rep.	34,250	22,430	3,000	2,120	2,130	2,050
17 India	4,880	3,700	6,500	4,670	2,100	2,189
18 Rwanda	72,330	32,100	7,450	10,260	1,665	1,919
19 Somalia	33,900	17,500	3,630	2,550	2,145	2,072
20 Kenya	12,820	10,140	1,860	990	2,287	2,151
21 Tanzania	21,700	..	2,100	..	1,970	2,335
22 Sudan	23,500	9,800	3,360	1,440	1,874	1,737
23 China	3,780	1,730	3,040	1,670	2,034	2,602
24 Haiti	14,000	820	12,870	..	2,007	1,855
25 Guinea	54,610	..	4,750	..	1,899	1,728
26 Sierra Leone	17,700	19,300	4,700	2,110	1,836	1,817
27 Senegal	21,100	14,200	2,640	1,990	2,474	2,342
28 Ghana	13,670	7,250	3,710	630	1,949	1,747
29 Pakistan	..	2,910	9,910	5,870	1,747	2,159
30 Sri Lanka	5,800	7,460	3,210	1,260	2,155	2,385
31 Zambia	11,400	7,800	5,820	1,660	2,073	2,137
32 Afghanistan	15,770	..	24,450	..	2,203	..
33 Chad	72,440	..	13,620	..	2,393	1,504
34 Kampuchea, Dem.	22,400	..	3,670	..	2,276	..
35 Lao PDR	26,500	..	5,320	..	1,958	2,228
36 Uganda	11,100	24,500	3,130	2,000	2,383	2,083
37 Viet Nam	..	4,310	..	1,040	2,031	2,240
Middle-income economies	**11,240** w	**5,080** w	**3,300** w	**1,380** w	**2,357** w	**2,731** w
Lower middle-income	**20,800** w	**8,230** w	**4,790** w	**1,810** w	**2,115** w	**2,514** w
38 Mauritania	36,890	..	..	..	2,070	2,078
39 Bolivia	3,300	2,000	3,990	..	1,868	2,146
40 Lesotho	19,880	..	4,700	..	2,065	2,358
41 Liberia	12,400	9,400	2,300	2,940	2,155	2,311
42 Indonesia	31,740	12,300	9,500	..	1,792	2,533
43 Yemen, PDR	12,870	7,120	1,850	820	1,999	2,337
44 Yemen, Arab Rep.	58,200	7,100	..	3,440	2,002	2,250
45 Morocco	12,120	18,600	2,290	900	2,182	2,678
46 Philippines	..	6,710	1,130	2,590	1,936	2,341
47 Egypt, Arab Rep.	2,300	760	2,030	790	2,435	3,263
48 Côte d'Ivoire	19,080	..	1,850	..	2,357	2,505
49 Papua New Guinea	12,600	16,070	620	960	1,908	2,181
50 Zimbabwe	8,000	7,100	990	1,000	2,089	2,054
51 Honduras	5,400	3,120	1,540	..	1,963	2,211
52 Nicaragua	2,560	2,230	1,390	590	2,398	2,425
53 Dominican Rep.	1,700	1,400	1,640	1,240	1,870	2,461
54 Nigeria	44,230	12,000	5,780	2,420	2,185	2,038
55 Thailand	7,230	6,870	5,020	2,140	2,200	2,462
56 Cameroon	26,680	..	1,970	..	2,043	2,089
57 El Salvador	..	2,720	1,300	..	1,859	2,148
58 Botswana	24,300	7,380	16,210	700	2,015	2,219
59 Paraguay	1,850	1,750	1,550	650	2,627	2,796
60 Jamaica	1,980	2,700	340	..	2,232	2,585
61 Peru	1,620	..	880	..	2,324	2,171
62 Turkey	2,900	1,530	2,290	1,240	2,636	3,167
63 Mauritius	3,860	1,800	1,990	570	2,272	2,740
64 Congo, People's Rep.	14,210	..	950	..	2,255	2,549
65 Ecuador	3,000	..	2,320	..	1,942	2,054
66 Tunisia	8,000	3,900	1,150	950	2,296	2,836
67 Guatemala	3,690	..	8,250	1,360	2,028	2,294

Note: For data comparability and coverage, see the technical notes.   Figures in italics are for years other than those specified.

	Population per:				Daily calorie supply per capita	
	Physician		Nursing person			
	1965	1981	1965	1981	1965	1985
68 Costa Rica	2,000	. .	630	. .	2,366	2,803
69 Colombia	2,500	. .	890	. .	2,174	2,574
70 Chile	2,100	. .	600	. .	2,591	2,602
71 Jordan	4,700	1,200	1,810	1,170	2,282	2,947
72 Syrian Arab Rep.	5,400	2,240	11,760	1,370	2,144	3,168
73 Lebanon	1,240	640	2,500	. .	. .	. .
Upper middle-income	**2,170 w**	**1,340 w**	**1,690 w**	**900 w**	**2,622 w**	**2,987 w**
74 Brazil	2,500	1,300	1,550	1,140	2,405	2,633
75 Uruguay	880	500	590	. .	2,811	2,695
76 Hungary	630	300	240	140	3,186	3,482
77 Portugal	1,240	500	1,160	. .	2,531	3,161
78 Malaysia	6,220	3,920	1,320	1,390	2,249	2,684
79 South Africa	2,100	. .	500	. .	2,643	2,979
80 Poland	800	550	410	. .	3,238	3,280
81 Yugoslavia	1,200	700	850	300	3,287	3,602
82 Mexico	2,020	1,200	950	. .	2,643	3,177
83 Panama	2,130	1,010	680	. .	2,255	2,419
84 Argentina	600	. .	610	. .	3,209	3,221
85 Korea, Rep. of	2,700	1,390	2,990	350	2,255	2,841
86 Algeria	8,590	. .	11,770	. .	1,682	2,677
87 Venezuela	1,210	1,000	560	. .	2,321	2,583
88 Greece	710	400	600	370	3,086	3,721
89 Israel	400	400	300	130	2,795	3,060
90 Trinidad and Tobago	3,820	1,500	560	390	2,497	3,006
91 Hong Kong	2,460	1,300	1,220	800	2,502	2,698
92 Oman	23,790	1,410	6,380	440	. .	. .
93 Singapore	1,900	1,100	600	340	2,214	2,771
94 Iran, Islamic Rep.	3,800	2,900	4,170	1,160	2,140	3,122
95 Iraq	5,000	2,000	2,910	2,250	2,138	2,926
96 Romania	760	700	400	280	2,994	3,385
Developing economies	**9,310 w**	**5,560 w**	**4,320 w**	**3,300 w**	**2,150 w**	**2,470 w**
Oil exporters	**21,250 w**	**7,370 w**	**5,830 w**	**1,720 w**	**2,113 w**	**2,671 w**
Exporters of manufactures	**3,870 w**	**2,330 w**	**3,980 w**	**2,650 w**	**2,155 w**	**2,499 w**
Highly indebted countries	**10,710 w**	**5,020 w**	**2,010 w**	**1,670 w**	**2,424 w**	**2,613 w**
Sub-Saharan Africa	**36,570 w**	**26,760 w**	**5,340 w**	**2,570 w**	**2,094 w**	**2,024 w**
High-income oil exporters	**7,530 w**	**1,380 w**	**4,440 w**	**620 w**	**1,969 w**	**3,265 w**
97 Libya	3,950	620	850	360	1,923	3,612
98 Saudi Arabia	9,400	1,800	6,060	730	1,866	3,128
99 Kuwait	800	700	270	180	2,963	3,138
100 United Arab Emirates	. .	720	. .	390	2,672	3,625
Industrial market economies	**860 w**	**530 w**	**460 w**	**180 w**	**3,114 w**	**3,417 w**
101 Spain	800	360	1,220	280	2,844	3,358
102 Ireland	950	780	170	120	3,530	3,831
103 Italy	1,850	750	790	250	3,113	3,538
104 New Zealand	820	610	980	110	3,311	3,386
105 Belgium	700	370	590	130	. .	3,679
106 United Kingdom	870	680	200	120	3,346	3,131
107 Austria	720	440	350	170	3,303	3,514
108 Netherlands	860	480	270	. .	3,149	3,343
109 France	830	460	. .	110	3,303	3,359
110 Australia	720	500	110	100	3,174	3,389
111 Finland	1,300	460	180	100	3,119	3,026
112 Germany, Fed. Rep.	640	420	500	170	3,143	3,474
113 Denmark	740	420	190	140	3,417	3,547
114 Japan	970	740	410	210	2,669	2,856
115 Sweden	910	410	310	100	2,922	3,097
116 Canada	770	550	190	120	3,289	3,432
117 Norway	790	460	340	70	3,047	3,239
118 Switzerland	710	390	270	130	3,413	3,432
119 United States	670	500	310	180	3,292	3,663
Nonreporting nonmember economies	**760 w**	**330 w**	**640 w**	**. .**	**3,152 w**	**3,389 w**
120 Albania	2,100	. .	550	. .	2,398	2,726
121 Angola	13,140	. .	3,820	. .	1,912	1,969
122 Bulgaria	600	400	410	190	3,434	3,663
123 Cuba	1,150	720	820	. .	2,371	3,122
124 Czechoslovakia	540	350	200	130	3,406	3,465
125 German Dem. Rep.	870	490	. .	. .	3,222	3,791
126 Korea, Dem. Rep.	. .	. .	. .	. .	2,255	3,151
127 Mongolia	710	400	310	240	2,594	2,807
128 USSR	480	270	280	. .	3,231	3,440

Table 31. Education

Number enrolled in school as percentage of age group

	Primary						Secondary						Higher education	
	Total		Male		Female		Total		Male		Female		Total	
	1965	1984	1965	1984	1965	1984	1965	1984	1965	1984	1965	1984	1965	1984
Low-income economies	74 w	97 w	76 w	109 w	46 w	84 w	21 w	32 w	29 w	41 w	10 w	25 w	4 w	4 w
China and India	83 w	106 w	..	119 w	..	93 w	25 w	36 w	41 w	43 w	13 w	28 w	5 w	4 w
Other low-income	44 w	70 w	58 w	77 w	31 w	59 w	9 w	23 w	13 w	27 w	4 w	15 w	1 w	3 w
1 Ethiopia	11	32	16	..	6	..	2	12	3	14	1	8	(.)	(.)
2 Bangladesh	49	62	67	67	31	55	13	19	23	26	3	11	1	5
3 Burkina Faso	12	29	16	37	8	22	1	4	2	6	1	3	(.)	1
4 Mali	24	..	32	..	16	..	4	..	5	..	2	..	(.)	1
5 Bhutan	7	25	13	32	1	17	(.)	4	1	6	(.)	1	(.)	(.)
6 Mozambique	37	83	48	94	26	71	3	6	3	8	2	4	(.)	(.)
7 Nepal	20	77	36	104	4	47	5	23	9	35	2	11	1	5
8 Malawi	44	62	55	71	32	53	2	4	3	6	1	2	(.)	1
9 Zaire	70	98	95	112	45	84	5	57	8	81	2	33	(.)	1
10 Burma	71	102	76	..	65	..	15	24	20	..	11	..	1	5
11 Burundi	26	49	36	58	15	40	1	4	2	5	1	3	(.)	1
12 Togo	55	97	78	118	32	75	5	21	8	32	2	10	(.)	2
13 Madagascar	65	121	70	125	59	118	8	36	10	43	5	30	1	5
14 Niger	11	28	15	34	7	19	1	7	1	..	(.)	..	..	1
15 Benin	34	64	48	86	21	42	3	19	5	28	2	11	(.)	2
16 Central African Rep.	56	77	84	98	28	51	2	16	4	..	1	..	..	1
17 India	74	90	89	105	57	73	27	34	41	44	13	23	5	9
18 Rwanda	53	62	64	64	43	60	2	2	3	3	1	1	(.)	(.)
19 Somalia	10	25	16	32	4	18	2	17	4	23	1	12	.)	1
20 Kenya	54	97	69	101	40	94	4	19	6	22	2	16	(.)	1
21 Tanzania	32	87	40	91	25	84	2	3	3	4	1	2	(.)	(.)
22 Sudan	29	49	37	57	21	41	4	19	6	23	2	16	1	2
23 China	89	118	..	129	..	107	24	37	..	43	..	31	(.)	1
24 Haiti	50	76	56	81	44	72	5	16	6	16	3	16	(.)	1
25 Guinea	31	32	44	44	19	20	5	13	9	20	2	7	(.)	2
26 Sierra Leone	29	45	37	..	21	..	5	14	8	..	3	..	(.)	1
27 Senegal	40	55	52	66	29	44	7	13	10	17	3	8	1	2
28 Ghana	69	67	82	75	57	59	13	36	19	45	7	27	1	2
29 Pakistan	40	42	59	54	20	29	12	15	18	..	5	..	2	2
30 Sri Lanka	93	103	98	105	86	101	35	61	34	58	35	64	2	4
31 Zambia	53	100	59	105	46	95	7	17	11	22	3	12	..	2
32 Afghanistan	16	..	26	..	5	..	2	..	4	..	1	..	(.)	..
33 Chad	34	38	56	55	13	21	1	6	3	11	(.)	2	..	(.)
34 Kampuchea, Dem.	77	..	98	..	56	..	9	..	14	..	4	..	1	..
35 Lao PDR	40	90	50	103	30	77	2	19	2	22	1	15	(.)	1
36 Uganda	67	57	83	65	50	49	4	8	6	..	2	..	(.)	1
37 Viet Nam	..	113	..	120	..	105	..	48	..	..	..	..	..	..
Middle-income economies	85 w	104 w	92 w	109 w	79 w	99 w	22 w	47 w	25 w	56 w	19 w	49 w	6 w	13 w
Lower middle-income	75 w	103 w	83 w	110 w	66 w	97 w	16 w	40 w	20 w	48 w	12 w	39 w	5 w	12 w
38 Mauritania	13	37	19	45	6	29	1	12	2	..	(.)	..	..	..
39 Bolivia	73	91	86	96	60	85	18	37	21	40	15	34	5	16
40 Lesotho	94	111	74	97	114	126	4	21	4	17	4	26	(.)	2
41 Liberia	41	76	59	95	23	57	5	23	8	..	3	..	1	2
42 Indonesia	72	118	79	121	65	116	12	39	18	45	7	34	1	7
43 Yemen, PDR	23	66	35	96	10	35	11	19	17	26	5	11	..	..
44 Yemen, Arab Rep.	9	67	16	112	1	22	(.)	10	..	17	..	3	..	1
45 Morocco	57	80	78	97	35	62	11	31	16	37	5	25	1	8
46 Philippines	113	107	115	106	111	107	41	68	42	65	40	71	19	29
47 Egypt, Arab Rep.	75	84	90	94	60	72	26	58	37	70	15	46	7	21
48 Côte d'Ivoire	60	77	80	91	41	63	6	20	10	28	2	12	(.)	2
49 Papua New Guinea	44	61	53	68	35	55	4	11	6	..	2	..	..	2
50 Zimbabwe	110	131	128	135	92	127	6	39	8	46	5	31	(.)	3
51 Honduras	80	102	81	102	79	101	10	33	11	31	9	36	1	9
52 Nicaragua	69	99	68	100	69	106	14	43	15	39	13	48	2	11
53 Dominican Rep.	87	112	87	107	87	117	12	45	11	..	12	..	2	10
54 Nigeria	32	92	39	103	24	81	5	29	7	..	3	..	(.)	3
55 Thailand	78	97	82	..	74	..	14	30	16	..	11	..	2	23
56 Cameroon	94	107	114	116	75	97	5	23	8	29	2	18	(.)	2
57 El Salvador	82	70	85	69	79	70	17	24	18	23	17	26	2	12
58 Botswana	65	97	59	91	71	103	3	25	5	23	3	27	..	2
59 Paraguay	102	101	109	107	96	99	13	31	13	..	13	..	4	10
60 Jamaica	109	106	112	106	106	107	51	58	53	56	50	60	3	6
61 Peru	99	116	108	120	90	112	25	61	29	..	21	..	8	22
62 Turkey	101	113	118	116	83	109	16	38	22	47	9	28	4	9
63 Mauritius	101	106	105	105	97	106	26	51	34	54	18	48	3	1
64 Congo, People's Rep.	114	..	134	..	94	..	10	..	15	..	5	..	1	6
65 Ecuador	91	114	94	117	88	117	17	55	19	51	16	53	3	33
66 Tunisia	91	116	116	127	65	105	16	32	23	37	9	26	2	6
67 Guatemala	50	76	55	80	45	69	8	17	10	17	7	16	2	7

Note: For data comparability and coverage; see the technical notes. Figures in italics refer to years other than those specified.

	Primary						Secondary						Higher education	
	Total		Male		Female		Total		Male		Female		Total	
	1965	1984	1965	1984	1965	1984	1965	1984	1965	1984	1965	1984	1965	1984
68 Costa Rica	106	101	107	102	105	100	24	42	23	40	25	45	6	22
69 Colombia	84	119	83	119	86	119	17	49	18	48	16	49	3	13
70 Chile	124	107	125	108	122	106	34	66	31	63	36	69	6	15
71 Jordan	95	99	105	98	83	99	38	79	52	80	23	78	2	37
72 Syrian Arab Rep.	78	107	103	115	52	98	28	59	43	70	13	47	8	16
73 Lebanon	106	..	118	..	93	..	26	..	..	..	..	..	14	..
Upper middle-income	**96 w**	**105 w**	**100 w**	**108 w**	**92 w**	**101 w**	**29 w**	**56 w**	**31 w**	**64 w**	**26 w**	**61 w**	**7 w**	**15 w**
74 Brazil	108	103	109	108	108	99	16	35	16	..	16	..	2	11
75 Uruguay	106	109	106	110	106	107	44	67	42	..	46	..	8	26
76 Hungary	101	99	102	98	100	99	..	73	..	73	..	73	13	15
77 Portugal	84	120	84	120	83	119	42	47	49	43	34	51	5	12
78 Malaysia	90	97	96	98	84	97	28	53	34	53	22	53	2	6
79 South Africa	90	..	91	..	88	..	15	..	16	..	14	..	4	..
80 Poland	104	101	106	102	102	100	58	77	52	75	64	80	18	16
81 Yugoslavia	106	98	108	98	103	98	65	82	70	84	59	80	13	20
82 Mexico	92	116	94	118	90	115	17	55	21	56	13	53	4	15
83 Panama	102	105	104	107	99	102	34	59	32	56	36	63	7	25
84 Argentina	101	107	101	107	102	107	28	65	26	62	31	69	14	29
85 Korea, Rep. of	101	99	103	99	99	99	35	91	44	94	25	88	6	26
86 Algeria	68	94	81	106	53	83	7	47	10	54	5	39	1	6
87 Venezuela	94	109	93	109	94	108	27	45	27	40	28	49	7	23
88 Greece	110	105	111	105	109	105	49	82	57	..	41	..	10	17
89 Israel	95	98	95	97	95	99	48	74	46	70	51	78	20	34
90 Trinidad and Tobago	93	96	97	94	90	98	36	76	39	75	34	78	2	4
91 Hong Kong	103	105	106	106	99	104	29	69	32	66	25	72	5	13
92 Oman	..	83	..	93	..	72	..	30	..	40	..	19	..	..
93 Singapore	105	115	110	118	100	113	45	71	49	70	41	73	10	12
94 Iran, Islamic Rep.	63	107	85	117	40	95	18	43	24	51	11	35	2	4
95 Iraq	74	104	102	111	45	98	28	53	42	67	14	37	4	10
96 Romania	101	98	102	99	100	98	39	73	44	72	32	74	10	12
Developing economies	**78 w**	**99 w**	**84 w**	**109 w**	**62 w**	**90 w**	**22 w**	**38 w**	**28 w**	**45 w**	**14 w**	**32 w**	**5 w**	**7 w**
Oil exporters	**72 w**	**93 w**	**85 w**	**106 w**	**56 w**	**79 w**	**12 w**	**37 w**	**35 w**	**47 w**	**12 w**	**28 w**	**5 w**	**10 w**
Exporters of manufactures	**86 w**	**106 w**	**94 w**	**117 w**	**71 w**	**94 w**	**9 w**	**39 w**	**40 w**	**46 w**	**18 w**	**32 w**	**6 w**	**6 w**
Highly indebted countries	**88 w**	**104 w**	**91 w**	**108 w**	**84 w**	**99 w**	**20 w**	**47 w**	**23 w**	**56 w**	**20 w**	**56 w**	**7 w**	**14 w**
Sub-Saharan Africa	**41 w**	**77 w**	**52 w**	**87 w**	**30 w**	**68 w**	**2 w**	**21 w**	**6 w**	**27 w**	**3 w**	**14 w**	**1 w**	**2 w**
High-income oil exporters	**43 w**	**75 w**	**60 w**	**82 w**	**25 w**	**67 w**	**10 w**	**45 w**	**14 w**	**52 w**	**5 w**	**38 w**	**1 w**	**10 w**
97 Libya	78	..	111	..	44	..	14	..	24	..	4	..	1	11
98 Saudi Arabia	24	68	36	77	11	58	4	38	7	47	1	29	1	10
99 Kuwait	116	103	129	105	103	102	52	82	59	85	43	79	..	16
100 United Arab Emirates	..	97	..	97	..	97	..	58	..	52	..	65	(.)	8
Industrial market economies	**107 w**	**102 w**	**107 w**	**102 w**	**106 w**	**101 w**	**63 w**	**90 w**	**64 w**	**89 w**	**60 w**	**91 w**	**21 w**	**38 w**
101 Spain	115	108	117	108	114	107	38	89	46	88	29	91	6	26
102 Ireland	108	97	107	97	108	97	51	93	53	..	50	..	12	22
103 Italy	112	99	113	99	110	99	47	74	53	74	41	73	11	26
104 New Zealand	106	106	107	107	104	105	75	85	76	84	74	86	15	29
105 Belgium	109	98	110	98	108	99	75	91	..	..	..	..	15	31
106 United Kingdom	92	101	92	101	92	101	66	83	67	..	66	..	12	20
107 Austria	106	97	106	97	105	97	52	76	52	73	52	79	9	26
108 Netherlands	104	95	104	94	104	96	61	102	64	103	57	100	17	31
109 France	134	108	135	109	133	107	56	90	53	84	59	96	18	27
110 Australia	99	107	99	107	99	106	62	94	63	92	61	95	16	27
111 Finland	92	103	95	104	89	103	76	101	72	94	80	109	11	31
112 Germany, Fed. Rep.	..	99	..	100	..	99	..	74	..	72	..	76	9	29
113 Denmark	98	101	97	101	99	101	83	104	98	105	67	104	14	29
114 Japan	100	100	100	100	100	101	82	95	82	94	81	94	13	30
115 Sweden	95	98	94	98	96	98	62	83	63	79	60	88	13	38
116 Canada	105	106	106	107	104	105	56	102	57	102	55	102	26	44
117 Norway	97	97	97	98	98	98	64	96	66	..	62	..	11	29
118 Switzerland	87	..	87	..	87	..	37	..	38	..	35	..	8	21
119 United States	..	101	..	102	..	100	..	95	..	95	..	95	40	57
Nonreporting nonmember economies	**102 w**	**105 w**	**103 w**	**104 w**	**102 w**	**100 w**	**66 w**	**93 w**	**61 w**	**60 w**	**73 w**	**71 w**	**14 w**	**21 w**
120 Albania	92	98	97	100	87	96	33	63	40	67	26	58	8	7
121 Angola	39	134	53	146	26	121	5	12	..	..	..	..	(.)	2
122 Bulgaria	103	102	104	102	102	101	54	90	54	90	55	91	17	17
123 Cuba	121	106	123	110	119	102	23	75	23	71	24	79	3	20
124 Czechoslovakia	99	87	100	87	97	88	29	42	23	31	35	54	14	16
125 German Dem. Rep.	109	98	107	97	111	98	60	87	62	..	57	..	19	30
126 Korea, Dem. Rep.	..	..	..	..	..	..	..	..	..	..	..	..	..	..
127 Mongolia	98	105	98	104	97	106	66	88	65	84	66	92	8	26
128 USSR	103	106	103	..	103	..	72	100	65	..	79	..	..	21

Table 32. Labor force

	Percentage of population of working age (15–64 years)		Agriculture		Industry		Services		Average annual growth of labor force (percent)		
	1965	1985	1965	1980	1965	1980	1965	1980	1965–80	1980–85	1985–2000
Low-income economies	**54 w**	**59 w**	**77 w**	**72 w**	**9 w**	**13 w**	**14 w**	**15 w**	**2.1 w**	**2.3 w**	**1.9 w**
China and India	**55 w**	**61 w**	**77 w**	**72 w**	**9 w**	**14 w**	**14 w**	**14 w**	**2.1 w**	**2.3 w**	**1.6 w**
Other low-income	**52 w**	**52 w**	**79 w**	**71 w**	**8 w**	**10 w**	**13 w**	**19 w**	**2.2 w**	**2.5 w**	**2.6 w**
1 Ethiopia	52	51	86	80	5	8	9	12	2.1	1.7	2.2
2 Bangladesh	51	53	84	75	5	6	11	19	1.9	2.8	3.0
3 Burkina Faso	48	44	89	87	3	4	7	9	1.6	1.9	2.2
4 Mali	53	50	90	86	1	2	8	13	1.7	2.5	2.7
5 Bhutan	55	55	95	92	2	3	4	5	1.8	1.9	1.9
6 Mozambique	55	51	87	85	6	7	7	8	3.2	..	..
7 Nepal	56	54	94	93	2	1	4	7	1.6	2.3	2.3
8 Malawi	51	47	92	83	3	7	5	9	2.2	2.6	2.6
9 Zaire	52	51	82	72	9	13	9	16	1.7	2.3	2.5
10 Burma	57	54	64	53	14	19	23	28	2.2	1.9	1.8
11 Burundi	53	52	94	93	2	2	4	5	1.2	2.0	2.4
12 Togo	52	50	78	73	9	10	13	17	2.7	2.3	2.5
13 Madagascar	54	51	85	81	4	6	11	13	2.1	1.9	2.3
14 Niger	51	51	95	91	1	2	4	7	1.8	2.3	2.6
15 Benin	52	49	83	70	5	7	12	23	1.9	2.0	2.5
16 Central African Rep.	57	55	88	72	3	6	9	21	1.2	1.3	1.8
17 India	54	56	73	70	12	13	15	17	1.7	2.0	1.8
18 Rwanda	51	49	94	93	2	3	3	4	2.9	2.8	2.9
19 Somalia	49	53	81	76	6	8	13	16	3.1	2.0	1.7
20 Kenya	48	45	86	81	5	7	9	12	3.6	3.5	3.7
21 Tanzania	53	50	92	86	3	5	6	10	2.8	2.8	3.0
22 Sudan	53	52	82	71	5	8	14	21	2.4	2.8	3.1
23 China	55	65	81	74	8	14	11	12	2.4	2.5	1.4
24 Haiti	52	51	77	70	7	8	16	22	1.0	2.0	2.2
25 Guinea	55	52	87	81	6	9	7	10	1.7	1.6	1.8
26 Sierra Leone	54	55	78	70	11	14	11	16	0.9	1.1	1.4
27 Senegal	53	52	83	81	6	6	11	13	3.1	1.9	2.1
28 Ghana	52	48	61	56	15	18	24	26	1.9	2.7	2.9
29 Pakistan	50	53	60	55	18	16	22	30	2.6	3.2	2.8
30 Sri Lanka	54	62	56	53	14	14	30	33	2.2	1.6	1.6
31 Zambia	51	48	79	73	8	10	13	17	2.7	3.2	3.5
32 *Afghanistan*	55	..	69	..	11	..	20	..	1.7	..	..
33 *Chad*	55	55	92	83	3	5	5	12	1.6	1.8	2.1
34 *Kampuchea, Dem.*	52	..	80	..	4	..	16	..	1.2	..	..
35 *Lao PDR*	56	53	81	76	5	7	15	17	1.6	1.8	2.2
36 *Uganda*	52	52	91	86	3	4	6	10	3.0	2.7	3.0
37 *Viet Nam*	..	55	79	68	6	12	15	21	1.8	..	..
Middle-income economies	**54 w**	**57 w**	**56 w**	**43 w**	**17 w**	**23 w**	**27 w**	**34 w**	**2.5 w**	**2.5 w**	**2.4 w**
Lower middle-income	**52 w**	**55 w**	**65 w**	**55 w**	**12 w**	**16 w**	**23 w**	**29 w**	**2.4 w**	**2.6 w**	**2.5 w**
38 Mauritania	52	53	89	69	3	9	8	22	1.8	2.7	3.1
39 Bolivia	53	53	54	46	20	20	26	34	2.0	2.7	2.7
40 Lesotho	56	52	92	86	3	4	6	10	1.8	2.0	2.1
41 Liberia	51	52	79	74	10	9	11	16	2.6	2.2	2.7
42 Indonesia	53	56	71	57	9	13	21	30	2.1	2.4	2.2
43 Yemen, PDR	52	51	54	41	12	18	33	41	1.6	2.8	3.1
44 Yemen, Arab Rep.	54	51	79	69	7	9	14	22	0.7	2.6	3.4
45 Morocco	50	52	61	46	15	25	24	29	2.9	3.3	3.1
46 Philippines	52	56	58	52	16	16	26	33	2.5	2.5	2.4
47 Egypt, Arab Rep.	54	55	55	46	15	20	30	34	2.2	2.6	2.7
48 Côte d'Ivoire	54	54	81	65	5	8	15	27	2.7	2.7	2.6
49 Papua New Guinea	55	54	87	76	6	10	7	14	1.9	2.2	2.0
50 Zimbabwe	51	45	79	73	8	11	13	17	3.0	2.7	3.0
51 Honduras	50	50	68	61	12	16	20	23	2.8	3.9	3.9
52 Nicaragua	48	50	57	47	16	16	28	38	2.9	3.8	3.9
53 Dominican Rep.	47	53	59	46	14	15	27	39	2.8	3.5	2.9
54 Nigeria	51	49	72	68	10	12	18	20	3.0	2.6	2.9
55 Thailand	51	59	82	71	5	10	13	19	2.8	2.5	1.7
56 Cameroon	55	50	86	70	4	8	9	22	1.7	1.8	2.2
57 El Salvador	50	60	59	43	16	19	26	37	3.3	2.9	3.3
58 Botswana	50	48	89	70	4	13	8	17	2.4	3.5	3.4
59 Paraguay	49	51	55	49	20	21	26	31	3.2	3.1	2.8
60 Jamaica	51	56	37	31	20	16	43	52	2.0	2.9	2.4
61 Peru	51	56	50	40	19	18	32	42	2.9	2.9	2.8
62 Turkey	53	57	75	58	11	17	14	25	1.7	2.3	2.0
63 Mauritius	52	63	37	28	25	24	38	48	2.6	3.3	2.1
64 Congo, People's Rep.	55	51	66	62	11	12	23	26	2.0	1.8	2.2
65 Ecuador	50	53	55	39	19	20	26	42	2.7	3.1	2.9
66 Tunisia	50	56	49	35	21	36	29	29	2.8	3.1	2.8
67 Guatemala	50	53	64	57	15	17	21	26	2.3	2.8	3.3

Note: For data comparability and coverage; see the technical notes. Figures in italics are for years other than those specified.

	Percentage of population of working age (15-64 years)		Percentage of labor force in:						Average annual growth of labor force (percent)		
			Agriculture		Industry		Services				
	1965	1985	1965	1980	1965	1980	1965	1980	1965–80	1980–85	1985–2000
68 Costa Rica	49	59	47	31	19	23	34	46	3.8	3.1	2.4
69 Colombia	49	59	45	34	21	24	34	42	2.6	2.8	2.3
70 Chile	56	63	27	17	29	25	44	58	2.2	2.6	1.7
71 Jordan	27	49	37	10	26	26	37	64	1.7	4.4	4.2
72 Syrian Arab Rep.	46	48	52	32	20	32	28	36	3.3	3.5	4.0
73 *Lebanon*	51	..	29	..	24	..	47	..	1.7	..	..
Upper middle-income	**56 w**	**59 w**	**45 w**	**29 w**	**23 w**	**31 w**	**32 w**	**40 w**	**2.6 w**	**2.3 w**	**2.3 w**
74 Brazil	53	59	49	31	20	27	31	42	3.3	2.3	2.1
75 Uruguay	63	63	20	16	29	29	51	55	0.4	0.6	0.9
76 Hungary	66	66	32	18	40	44	29	38	0.1	0.0	0.3
77 Portugal	62	64	38	26	30	37	32	38	1.2	1.0	0.8
78 Malaysia	50	59	59	42	13	19	29	39	3.4	2.9	2.6
79 South Africa	54	55	32	17	30	35	39	49	1.8	2.8	2.8
80 Poland	62	66	44	29	32	39	25	33	1.1	0.7	0.7
81 Yugoslavia	63	68	57	32	26	33	17	34	0.9	1.0	0.7
82 Mexico	49	54	50	37	22	29	29	35	3.9	3.2	3.0
83 Panama	51	58	46	32	16	18	38	50	2.7	3.0	2.6
84 Argentina	63	60	18	13	34	34	48	53	1.1	1.1	1.5
85 Korea, Rep. of	53	64	55	36	15	27	30	37	2.8	2.7	1.9
86 Algeria	50	49	57	31	17	27	26	42	2.2	3.6	3.7
87 Venezuela	49	56	30	16	24	28	47	56	4.2	3.5	3.0
88 Greece	65	65	47	31	24	29	29	40	0.5	0.6	0.3
89 Israel	59	60	12	6	35	32	53	62	3.0	2.2	2.1
90 Trinidad and Tobago	53	61	20	10	35	39	45	51	1.9	2.5	2.1
91 Hong Kong	56	68	6	2	53	51	41	47	3.9	2.5	1.4
92 Oman	53	50	62	50	15	22	23	28	3.8	5.2	2.7
93 Singapore	53	67	6	2	27	38	68	61	4.2	1.9	0.8
94 *Iran, Islamic Rep.*	50	53	49	36	26	33	25	31	3.2	3.3	3.2
95 *Iraq*	51	50	50	30	20	22	30	48	3.6	3.7	4.0
96 *Romania*	65	66	57	31	26	44	18	26	0.2	0.7	0.7
Developing economies	**54 w**	**58 w**	**70 w**	**62 w**	**12 w**	**16 w**	**18 w**	**22 w**	**2.3 w**	**2.4 w**	**2.1 w**
Oil exporters	**52 w**	**53 w**	**61 w**	**49 w**	**15 w**	**19 w**	**24 w**	**31 w**	**2.8 w**	**2.8 w**	**2.8 w**
Exporters of manufactures	**55 w**	**61 w**	**71 w**	**66 w**	**11 w**	**16 w**	**16 w**	**17 w**	**2.2 w**	**2.2 w**	**1.6 w**
Highly indebted countries	**53 w**	**56 w**	**51 w**	**40 w**	**18 w**	**23 w**	**31 w**	**37 w**	**2.9 w**	**2.5 w**	**2.5 w**
Sub-Saharan Africa	**52 w**	**50 w**	**79 w**	**75 w**	**8 w**	**9 w**	**13 w**	**16 w**	**2.5 w**	**2.4 w**	**2.7 w**
High-income oil exporters	**53 w**	**54 w**	**58 w**	**35 w**	**15 w**	**21 w**	**28 w**	**44 w**	**5.6 w**	**4.4 w**	**3.4 w**
97 Libya	53	50	41	18	21	29	38	53	3.6	3.7	3.5
98 Saudi Arabia	53	54	68	48	11	14	21	37	4.9	4.4	3.5
99 Kuwait	60	58	2	2	34	32	64	67	6.9	6.2	3.5
100 United Arab Emirates	..	67	21	5	32	38	47	57	..	5.2	2.1
Industrial market economies	**63 w**	**67 w**	**14 w**	**7 w**	**38 w**	**35 w**	**48 w**	**58 w**	**1.3 w**	**1.0 w**	**0.5 w**
101 Spain	64	65	34	17	35	37	32	46	0.6	1.3	0.8
102 Ireland	57	60	31	19	28	34	41	48	0.8	1.6	1.6
103 Italy	66	67	25	12	42	41	34	48	0.3	0.7	0.2
104 New Zealand	59	65	13	11	36	33	51	56	1.9	1.8	1.2
105 Belgium	63	68	6	3	46	36	48	61	0.7	0.7	0.1
106 United Kingdom	65	65	3	3	47	38	50	59	0.3	0.5	0.2
107 Austria	63	67	19	9	45	41	36	50	0.2	0.8	0.1
108 Netherlands	62	69	9	6	41	32	51	63	1.4	1.4	0.5
109 France	62	66	18	9	39	35	43	56	0.8	0.9	0.5
110 Australia	62	66	10	7	38	32	52	61	2.4	1.8	1.3
111 Finland	65	67	24	12	35	35	41	53	0.7	0.9	0.3
112 Germany, Fed. Rep.	65	70	11	6	48	44	41	50	0.3	0.7	−0.5
113 Denmark	65	66	14	7	37	32	49	61	1.2	0.6	0.2
114 Japan	67	68	26	11	32	34	42	55	1.0	0.9	0.5
115 Sweden	66	65	11	6	43	33	46	62	1.1	0.3	0.3
116 Canada	59	68	10	5	33	29	57	65	3.2	1.4	0.9
117 Norway	63	64	16	8	37	29	48	62	1.8	0.8	0.7
118 Switzerland	65	67	9	6	49	39	41	55	0.8	0.7	−0.1
119 United States	60	66	5	4	35	31	60	66	2.2	1.2	0.8
Nonreporting nonmember economies	**61 w**	**65 w**	**34 w**	**22 w**	**34 w**	**39 w**	**32 w**	**39 w**	**1.3 w**	**1.1 w**	**0.8 w**
120 *Albania*	52	59	69	56	19	26	12	18	2.8	2.9	2.4
121 *Angola*	55	52	79	74	8	10	13	17	2.2	1.7	2.1
122 *Bulgaria*	67	67	46	18	31	45	23	37	0.2	0.0	0.2
123 *Cuba*	59	66	33	24	25	29	41	48	2.3	2.3	1.7
124 *Czechoslovakia*	65	64	21	13	47	49	31	37	0.9	0.4	0.7
125 *German Dem. Rep.*	61	67	15	11	49	50	36	39	0.5	0.9	0.2
126 *Korea, Dem. Rep.*	52	58	57	43	23	30	20	27	2.7	3.0	2.8
127 *Mongolia*	54	56	54	40	20	21	26	39	2.7	3.0	2.8
128 *USSR*	62	66	34	20	33	39	33	41	1.2	0.9	0.5

Table 33. Urbanization

	Urban population				Percentage of urban population				Number of cities of over 500,000 persons	
	As percentage of total population		Average annual growth rate (percent)		In largest city		In cities of over 500,000 persons			
	1965	1985	1965-80	1980-85	1960	1980	1960	1980	1960	1980
Low-income economies	**17** *w*	**22** *w*	**3.6** *w*	**4.0** *w*	**10** *w*	**16** *w*	**31** *w*	**55** *w*	**55** *t*	**148** *t*
China and India	**18** *w*	**23** *w*	**3.0** *w*	**3.6** *w*	**7** *w*	**6** *w*	**33** *w*	**59** *w*	**49** *t*	**114** *t*
Other low-income	**13** *w*	**20** *w*	**4.9** *w*	**5.4** *w*	**26** *w*	**30** *w*	**19** *w*	**40** *w*	**6** *t*	**34** *t*
1 Ethiopia	8	15	6.6	3.7	30	37	0	37	0	1
2 Bangladesh	6	18	8.0	7.9	20	30	20	51	1	3
3 Burkina Faso	6	8	3.4	5.3	. .	41	0	0	0	0
4 Mali	13	20	4.9	4.5	32	24	0	0	0	0
5 Bhutan	3	4	3.7	5.2	. .	. .	0	0	0	0
6 Mozambique	5	19	11.8	5.3	75	83	0	83	0	1
7 Nepal	4	7	5.1	5.6	41	27	0	0	0	0
8 Malawi	5	. .	7.8	. .	. .	19	0	0	0	0
9 Zaire	19	39	7.2	8.4	14	28	14	38	1	2
10 Burma	21	24	2.8	2.8	23	23	23	23	1	2
11 Burundi	2	2	1.8	2.7	. .	. .	0	0	0	0
12 Togo	11	23	7.2	6.4	. .	60	0	0	0	0
13 Madagascar	12	21	5.7	5.3	44	36	0	36	0	1
14 Niger	7	15	6.9	7.0	. .	31	0	0	0	0
15 Benin	11	35	10.2	4.4	. .	63	0	63	0	1
16 Central African Rep.	27	45	4.8	3.9	40	36	0	0	0	0
17 India	19	25	3.6	3.9	7	6	26	39	11	36
18 Rwanda	3	5	6.3	6.7	. .	. .	0	0	0	0
19 Somalia	20	34	6.1	5.4	. .	34	0	0	0	0
20 Kenya	9	20	9.0	6.3	40	57	0	57	0	1
21 Tanzania	6	14	8.7	8.3	34	50	0	50	0	1
22 Sudan	13	21	5.1	4.8	30	31	0	31	0	1
23 China	18	22	2.6	3.3	6	6	42	45	38	78
24 Haiti	18	27	4.0	4.1	42	56	0	56	0	1
25 Guinea	12	22	6.6	4.3	37	80	0	80	0	1
26 Sierra Leone	15	25	4.3	5.1	37	47	0	0	0	0
27 Senegal	27	36	4.1	4.0	53	65	0	65	0	1
28 Ghana	26	32	3.4	3.9	25	35	0	48	0	2
29 Pakistan	24	29	4.3	4.8	20	21	33	51	2	7
30 Sri Lanka	20	21	2.3	8.4	28	16	0	16	0	1
31 Zambia	24	48	7.1	5.5	. .	35	0	35	0	1
32 *Afghanistan*	9	. .	6.0	. .	33	17	0	17	0	1
33 *Chad*	9	27	9.2	3.9	. .	39	0	0	0	0
34 *Kampuchea, Dem.*	11	. .	1.9	. .	. .	. .	. .	. .	. .	. .
35 *Lao PDR*	8	15	4.8	5.6	69	48	0	0	0	0
36 *Uganda*	6	7	4.1	3.0	38	52	0	52	0	1
37 *Viet Nam*	16	20	4.1	3.4	32	21	32	50	1	4
Middle-income economies	**37** *w*	**48** *w*	**4.4** *w*	**3.5** *w*	**28** *w*	**27** *w*	**37** *w*	**49** *w*	**59** *t*	**131** *t*
Lower middle-income	**27** *w*	**36** *w*	**4.5** *w*	**3.7** *w*	**29** *w*	**31** *w*	**31** *w*	**46** *w*	**22** *t*	**55** *t*
38 Mauritania	7	31	12.4	3.4	. .	39	0	0	0	0
39 Bolivia	40	44	2.9	5.6	47	44	0	44	0	1
40 Lesotho	2	17	14.6	5.3	. .	. .	0	0	0	0
41 Liberia	23	37	6.2	4.3	. .	. .	0	0	0	0
42 Indonesia	16	25	4.7	2.3	20	23	34	50	3	9
43 Yemen, PDR	30	37	3.2	4.9	61	49	0	0	0	0
44 Yemen, Arab Rep.	5	19	10.7	7.3	. .	25	0	0	0	0
45 Morocco	32	44	4.2	4.2	16	26	16	50	1	4
46 Philippines	32	39	4.0	3.2	27	30	27	34	1	2
47 Egypt, Arab Rep.	41	46	2.9	3.4	38	39	53	53	2	2
48 Côte d'Ivoire	23	45	8.7	6.9	27	34	0	34	0	1
49 Papua New Guinea	5	14	8.4	4.9	. .	25	0	0	0	0
50 Zimbabwe	14	27	7.5	5.0	40	50	0	50	0	1
51 Honduras	26	39	5.5	5.2	31	33	0	0	0	0
52 Nicaragua	43	56	4.6	4.5	41	47	0	47	0	1
53 Dominican Rep.	35	56	5.3	4.2	50	54	0	54	0	1
54 Nigeria	15	30	4.8	5.2	13	17	22	58	2	9
55 Thailand	13	18	4.6	3.2	65	69	65	69	1	1
56 Cameroon	16	42	8.1	7.0	26	21	0	21	0	1
57 El Salvador	39	43	3.5	4.0	26	22	0	0	0	0
58 Botswana	4	20	15.4	4.5	. .	. .	. .	. .	. .	. .
59 Paraguay	36	41	3.2	3.7	44	44	0	44	0	1
60 Jamaica	38	53	3.4	3.2	77	66	0	66	0	1
61 Peru	52	68	4.1	3.8	38	39	38	44	1	2
62 Turkey	32	46	4.3	4.4	18	24	32	42	3	4
63 Mauritius	37	54	4.0	2.1	. .	. .	. .	. .	. .	. .
64 Congo, People's Rep.	35	40	3.5	3.6	77	56	0	0	0	0
65 Ecuador	37	52	5.1	3.7	31	29	0	51	0	2
66 Tunisia	40	56	4.2	3.7	40	30	40	30	1	1
67 Guatemala	34	41	3.6	4.2	41	36	41	36	1	1

Note: For data comparability and coverage; see the technical notes.   Figures in italics are for years other than those specified.

	Urban population				Percentage of urban population				Number of cities of over 500,000 persons	
	As percentage of total population		Average annual growth rate (percent)		In largest city		In cities of over 500,000 persons			
	1965	1985	1965–80	1980–85	1960	1980	1960	1980	1960	1980
68 Costa Rica	38	45	3.7	3.8	67	64	0	64	0	1
69 Colombia	54	67	3.5	2.8	17	26	28	51	3	4
70 Chile	72	83	2.6	2.1	38	44	38	44	1	1
71 Jordan	47	69	5.3	4.0	31	37	0	37	0	1
72 Syrian Arab Rep.	40	49	4.5	5.5	35	33	35	55	1	2
73 *Lebanon*	49	. .	4.6	. .	64	79	64	79	1	1
Upper middle-income	**49** *w*	**65** *w*	**3.8** *w*	**3.2** *w*	**27** *w*	**26** *w*	**39** *w*	**50** *w*	**37** *t*	**76** *t*
74 Brazil	50	73	4.5	4.0	14	15	35	52	6	14
75 Uruguay	81	85	0.7	0.9	56	52	56	52	1	1
76 Hungary	43	55	1.8	1.3	45	37	45	37	1	1
77 Portugal	24	31	2.0	3.3	47	44	47	44	1	1
78 Malaysia	26	38	4.5	4.0	19	27	0	27	0	1
79 South Africa	47	56	2.6	3.3	16	13	44	53	4	7
80 Poland	50	60	1.8	1.6	17	15	41	47	5	8
81 Yugoslavia	31	45	3.0	2.5	11	10	11	23	1	3
82 Mexico	55	69	4.5	3.6	28	32	36	48	3	7
83 Panama	44	50	3.4	2.6	61	66	0	66	0	1
84 Argentina	76	84	2.2	1.9	46	45	54	60	3	5
85 Korea, Rep. of	32	64	5.7	2.5	35	41	61	77	3	7
86 Algeria	38	43	3.8	3.7	27	12	27	12	1	1
87 Venezuela	72	85	4.5	3.5	26	26	26	44	1	4
88 Greece	48	65	2.5	1.9	51	57	51	70	1	2
89 Israel	81	90	3.5	2.4	46	35	46	35	1	1
90 Trinidad and Tobago	30	64	5.0	3.3	. .	. .	0	0	0	0
91 Hong Kong	89	93	2.3	1.3	100	100	100	100	1	1
92 Oman	4	9	8.1	7.3	. .	. .	. .	. .	. .	. .
93 Singapore	100	100	1.6	1.2	100	100	100	100	1	1
94 *Iran, Islamic Rep.*	37	54	5.5	4.6	26	28	26	47	1	6
95 *Iraq*	51	70	5.3	6.3	35	55	35	70	1	3
96 *Romania*	34	51	3.4	1.0	22	17	22	17	1	1
Developing economies	**24** *w*	**31** *w*	**3.9** *w*	**3.8** *w*	**19** *w*	**21** *w*	**34** *w*	**46** *w*	**114** *t*	**279** *t*
Oil exporters	**29** *w*	**41** *w*	**4.3** *w*	**3.5** *w*	**24** *w*	**24** *w*	**34** *w*	**48** *w*	**17** *t*	**47** *t*
Exporters of manufactures	**23** *w*	**29** *w*	**3.2** *w*	**3.5** *w*	**12** *w*	**12** *w*	**37** *w*	**46** *w*	**70** *t*	**154** *t*
Highly indebted countries	**44** *w*	**57** *w*	**3.5** *w*	**3.5** *w*	**23** *w*	**23** *w*	**35** *w*	**50** *w*	**29** *t*	**67** *t*
Sub-Saharan Africa	**13** *w*	**25** *w*	**6.2** *w*	**5.7** *w*	**22** *w*	**32** *w*	**8** *w*	**42** *w*	**2** *t*	**14** *t*
High-income oil exporters	**40** *w*	**73** *w*	**9.5** *w*	**6.0** *w*	**29** *w*	**28** *w*	**0** *w*	**34** *w*	**0** *t*	**3** *t*
97 Libya	29	60	9.7	6.7	57	64	0	64	0	1
98 Saudi Arabia	39	72	8.5	6.1	15	18	0	33	0	2
99 Kuwait	78	92	8.2	5.1	75	30	0	0	0	0
100 United Arab Emirates	56	79	18.9	5.5	. .	. .	. .	. .	. .	. .
Industrial market economies	**70** *w*	**75** *w*	**1.4** *w*	**1.5** *w*	**18** *w*	**18** *w*	**48** *w*	**55** *w*	**104** *t*	**152** *t*
101 Spain	61	77	2.4	1.6	13	17	37	44	5	6
102 Ireland	49	57	2.2	2.7	51	48	51	48	1	1
103 Italy	62	67	1.0	0.9	13	17	46	52	7	9
104 New Zealand	79	83	1.5	0.9	25	30	0	30	0	1
105 Belgium	93	96	0.5	0.4	17	14	28	24	2	2
106 United Kingdom	87	92	0.5	0.3	24	20	61	55	15	17
107 Austria	51	56	0.1	0.7	51	39	51	39	1	1
108 Netherlands	86	88	1.5	0.9	9	9	27	24	3	3
109 France	67	73	2.7	1.0	25	23	34	34	4	6
110 Australia	83	86	0.2	1.4	26	24	62	68	4	5
111 Finland	44	60	2.5	2.9	28	27	0	27	0	1
112 Germany, Fed. Rep.	79	86	0.8	0.1	20	18	48	45	11	11
113 Denmark	77	86	1.1	0.3	40	32	40	32	1	1
114 Japan	67	76	2.1	1.8	18	22	35	42	5	9
115 Sweden	77	86	1.0	1.2	15	15	15	35	1	3
116 Canada	73	77	1.5	1.7	50	32	50	32	1	1
117 Norway	37	73	5.0	0.9	14	18	31	62	2	9
118 Switzerland	53	60	1.2	0.9	19	22	19	22	1	1
119 United States	72	74	1.2	2.3	13	12	61	77	40	65
Nonreporting nonmember economies	**52** *w*	**65** *w*	**2.4** *w*	**1.8** *w*	**9** *w*	**8** *w*	**23** *w*	**32** *w*	**31** *t*	**59** *t*
120 *Albania*	32	34	3.4	3.3	27	25	0	0	0	0
121 *Angola*	13	25	6.4	5.8	44	64	0	64	0	1
122 *Bulgaria*	46	68	2.8	1.7	23	18	23	18	1	1
123 *Cuba*	58	71	2.7	0.8	32	38	32	38	1	1
124 *Czechoslovakia*	51	66	1.9	1.4	17	12	17	12	1	1
125 *German Dem. Rep.*	73	76	0.1	0.6	9	9	14	17	2	3
126 *Korea, Dem. Rep.*	45	63	4.6	3.8	15	12	15	19	1	2
127 *Mongolia*	42	55	4.5	3.3	53	52	0	0	0	0
128 *USSR*	52	66	2.2	1.6	6	4	21	33	25	50

Technical notes

This tenth edition of the World Development Indicators provides economic and social indicators for periods or selected years in a form suitable for comparing economies and groups of economies. It contains two new tables, one presenting a picture of industrial output and earnings, the other introducing a number of monetary indicators. This makes a total of 33 main tables. The statistics and measures have been carefully chosen to give an extensive picture of development. Considerable effort has been made to standardize the data; nevertheless, statistical methods, coverage, practices, and definitions differ widely. In addition, the statistical systems in many developing economies are still weak, and this affects the availability and reliability of the data. Readers are urged to take these limitations into account in interpreting the indicators, particularly when making comparisons across economies.

All growth rates shown are in constant prices and, unless otherwise noted, have been computed by using the least-squares method. The least-squares growth rate, r, is estimated by fitting a least-squares linear trend line to the logarithmic annual values of the variable in the relevant period. More specifically, the regression equation takes the form of $\log X_t = a + bt + e_t$, where this is equivalent to the logarithmic transformation of the compound growth rate equation, $X_t = X_o (1 + r)^t$. In these equations, X is the variable, t is time, and $a = \log X_o$ and $b = \log (1 + r)$ are the parameters to be estimated; e is the error term. If b^* is the least-squares estimate of b, then the annual average growth rate, r, is obtained as [antilog (b^*)] -1.

Table 1. Basic indicators

The estimates of *population* for mid-1985 are based on data from the U.N. Population Division or from World Bank sources. In many cases the data take into account the results of recent population censuses. Note that refugees not permanently settled in the country of asylum are generally considered to be part of the population of their country of origin. The data on *area* are from the FAO *Production Yearbook, 1985*. For basic indicators for U.N. and World Bank member countries with populations of less than 1 million, see the table in *Box A.1*.

Gross national product (GNP) measures the total domestic and foreign output claimed by residents and is calculated without making deductions for depreciation. It comprises gross domestic product (see the note for Table 2) adjusted by net factor income from abroad. That income comprises the income residents receive from abroad for factor services (labor and capital) less similar payments made to nonresidents who contributed to the domestic economy.

The *GNP per capita* figures are calculated according to the *World Bank Atlas* method. The Bank recognizes that perfect cross-country comparability of GNP per capita estimates cannot be achieved. Beyond the classic, strictly intractable "index number problem," two obstacles stand in the way of adequate comparability. One concerns GNP numbers themselves. There are differences in the national accounting systems and in the coverage and reliability of underlying statistical information between various countries. The other relates to the conversion of GNP data, expressed in different national currencies, to a common numeraire—conventionally the U.S. dollar—to compare them across countries. The Bank's procedure for converting GNP to U.S. dollars generally uses a three-year average of the official exchange rate. For a few countries, however, the prevailing official exchange rate does not fully reflect the rate effectively applied to actual foreign exchange transactions and in these cases an alternative conversion factor is used.

Recognizing that these shortcomings affect the comparability of the GNP per capita estimates, the World Bank has introduced several improvements in the estimation procedures. Through its regular review of member countries' national accounts, the Bank systematically evaluates the GNP estimates, focusing on the coverage and concepts employed and, where appropriate, making adjustments to improve comparability. The Bank also undertakes a systematic review to assess the appropriateness of the exchange rates as conversion factors. An alternative conversion factor is used when the official exchange rate is judged to diverge by an exceptionally large margin from the rate effectively applied to foreign transactions. This applies to only a small number of countries.

The estimates of 1985 GNP and 1985 GNP per capita are calculated on the basis of the 1983–85 base period. With this method the first step is to calculate the conversion factor. This is done by tak-

ing the simple arithmetic average of the actual exchange rate for 1985 and of adjusted exchange rates for 1983 and 1984. To obtain the deflated exchange rate for 1983, the actual exchange rate for 1983 is multiplied by the relative rate of inflation for the country and the United States between 1983 and 1985. For 1984, the actual exchange rate is multiplied by the relative rate of inflation for the country and the United States between 1984 and 1985.

This averaging of the actual and deflated exchange rates is intended to smooth the impact of

Box A.1 Basic indicators for U.N. and World Bank member countries with populations of less than 1 million

U.N./World Bank member	Population (thousands) mid-1985	Area (thousands of square kilometers)	GNP per capita[a] Dollars 1985	GNP per capita[a] Average annual growth rate (percent) 1965–85[b]	Average annual rate of inflation[a] (percent) 1965–80	Average annual rate of inflation[a] (percent) 1980–85[b]	Life expectancy at birth (years) 1985
Guinea-Bissau	886	36	180	−1.5	. .	30.4	39
Gambia, The	748	11	230	1.1	8.3	8.8	43
Comoros	454	2	240	−0.3	. .	. .	55
Maldives	182	(.)	290	1.9	. .	. .	53
São Tomé and Principe	108	1	320	0.8	. .	5.8	65
Cape Verde	325	4	430	5.0	. .	17.6	63
Guyana	790	215	500	−0.2	8.0	9.4	65
Solomon Islands	267	28	510	3.5	7.1	10.9	58
Western Samoa	163	3	660	. .	. .	15.9	65
Swaziland	757	17	670	2.7	9.1	9.6	54
Tonga	97	1	730	. .	. .	. .	64
St. Vincent and the Grenadines	119	(.)	850	1.2	10.8	5.9	69
Vanuatu	134	15	880	. .	. .	. .	56
Grenada	96	(.)	970	−0.1	11.2	6.6	68
Dominica	78	1	1,150	0.4	12.7	4.8	75
Belize	159	23	1,190	2.7	7.2	1.2	66
St. Lucia	136	1	1,240	2.8	9.3	3.8	70
St. Kitts and Nevis	43	(.)	1,550	2.4	9.8	5.0	64
Fiji	696	18	1,710	2.9	10.4	5.2	65
Antigua and Barbuda	79	(.)	2,020	0.2	9.1	4.0	73
Suriname	393	163	2,580	3.4	11.8	4.2	66
Malta	358	(.)	3,310	8.1	3.5	1.7	73
Gabon	997	268	3,670	1.5	12.7	10.1	51
Cyprus	665	9	3,790	. .	−2.1	8.1	74
Barbados	254	(.)	4,630	2.3	11.3	8.4	73
Bahamas, The	231	14	7,070	−0.5	6.4	5.2	70
Bahrain	417	1	9,420	. .	. .	0.2	69
Iceland	241	103	10,710	2.4	27.1	49.2	77
Luxembourg	366	3	14,260	4.0	6.3	10.0	74
Qatar	315	11	16,270	−7.0	. .	. .	72
Brunei	224	6	17,570	−1.2	. .	−2.7	74
Djibouti	362	22	. .	. .	. .	. .	48
Equatorial Guinea	373	28	. .	. .	. .	. .	45
Kiribati	64	1	. .	. .	. .	6.9	53
Seychelles	65	(.)	. .	. .	12.1	. .	69

Note: Countries with italicized names are those for which no GNP per capita can be calculated.
a. See the technical notes.   b. Figures in italics are for years other than those specified.

Box A.2 Gross product per capita by ICP and *Atlas* methods
(*United States = 100*)

Economy	1980		1984		1985	
	ICP	Atlas	ICP	Atlas	ICP	Atlas
Argentina	33.5	17.1	27.9	14.0	25.9	13.0
Austria	75.4	86.6	74.6	58.9	75.5	55.8
Belgium	82.4	103.9	78.5	55.5	78.3	51.5
Bolivia	14.2	4.4	10.0	3.2	9.5	2.9
Botswana	13.9	8.0	17.8	6.0	18.7	5.1
Brazil	29.3	17.2	25.3	11.1	26.4	10.0
Cameroon	7.9	6.5	9.4	5.2	9.8	4.9
Canada	101.5	90.3	98.4	85.6	99.8	83.4
Chile	31.9	20.6	26.9	11.0	26.6	8.8
Colombia	24.8	11.0	23.4	9.1	23.3	8.0
Costa Rica	27.7	17.3	23.5	7.7	22.8	7.9
Côte d'Ivoire	12.0	9.5	8.7	4.1	8.7	3.8
Denmark	85.9	108.4	87.5	72.1	88.3	68.5
Dominican Rep.	17.3	9.2	16.0	6.2	15.2	4.9
Ecuador	22.6	11.8	20.2	7.4	20.0	7.1
El Salvador	12.4	6.3	9.9	4.6	9.8	4.3
Ethiopia	2.4	0.9	2.2	0.7	2.0	0.7
Finland	75.5	91.2	77.3	69.5	78.5	66.3
France	85.4	105.4	82.0	63.1	81.3	58.2
Germany, Fed. Rep.	89.1	114.1	86.6	71.8	87.4	66.7
Greece	44.5	36.9	41.9	24.3	42.0	21.6
Guatemala	20.3	9.7	16.3	7.7	15.4	7.6
Honduras	10.6	5.5	8.8	4.5	8.7	4.5
Hong Kong	62.4	47.0	72.3	41.0	70.9	37.9
Hungary	40.4	16.7	41.8	13.3	41.0	11.8
India	5.0	2.1	5.3	1.7	5.4	1.5
Indonesia	9.6	4.4	9.7	3.6	9.6	3.2
Ireland	47.9	46.7	47.7	32.0	46.8	29.5
Israel	59.4	40.9	55.8	32.8	55.1	30.0
Italy	68.0	60.3	64.5	41.4	64.7	39.8
Japan	73.4	77.9	79.0	68.5	81.1	69.1
Kenya	5.6	3.5	4.9	2.0	4.8	1.8
Korea, Rep. of	22.5	13.6	27.3	13.8	27.9	13.3
Luxembourg	92.8	131.9	86.6	84.9	87.4	81.6
Madagascar	5.0	3.2	3.8	1.7	3.7	1.5
Malawi	3.7	1.6	3.1	1.2	3.0	1.0
Mali	3.0	1.7	2.4	0.9	2.3	0.9
Morocco	10.5	8.1	9.8	4.3	9.8	3.7
Netherlands	81.4	102.5	75.5	61.4	75.5	56.0
Nigeria	7.8	8.8	5.3	4.8	5.2	4.6
Norway	99.0	117.1	100.4	89.9	101.5	84.7
Pakistan	9.6	2.7	10.0	2.4	10.3	2.3
Panama	27.9	14.6	26.4	12.7	26.4	12.3
Paraguay	18.6	12.6	16.6	7.0	16.5	5.7
Peru	21.9	9.6	17.9	6.6	17.5	5.9
Philippines	15.2	6.3	13.2	4.2	12.1	3.7
Poland	37.7	..	33.4	13.6	33.2	12.9
Portugal	33.4	20.8	31.4	12.7	31.7	12.0
Senegal	6.0	4.3	5.7	2.4	5.6	2.3
Spain	55.5	48.2	52.4	28.6	52.2	26.6
Sri Lanka	10.7	2.3	11.7	2.3	11.7	2.3
Tanzania	3.1	2.4	2.6	1.9	2.5	1.6
Tunisia	17.4	11.8	17.4	8.2	17.6	7.4
United Kingdom	72.1	81.3	71.2	55.3	72.3	51.2
United States	100.0	100.0	100.0	100.0	100.0	100.0
Uruguay	37.2	29.6	28.9	12.4	28.4	10.1
Venezuela	47.4	33.6	37.2	22.4	35.7	19.0
Yugoslavia	35.3	27.9	33.3	14.6	32.7	12.6
Zambia	6.4	5.5	5.3	3.1	5.2	2.4
Zimbabwe	7.8	6.4	7.5	4.9	7.7	4.0
United States (US$)	11,450	11,650	15,330	15,540	16,160	16,400

Note: ICP values for 1980 are actual Phase IV results; for other years they are extrapolated from the 1980 values. *Atlas* estimates are based on the current *Atlas* method applied to current data and are GNP per capita. ICP values relate to GDP per capita.

fluctuations in prices and exchange rates. The second step is to convert the GNP at current purchaser values and in national currencies of the year 1985 by means of the conversion factor as derived above. Then the resulting GNP in U.S. dollars is divided by the midyear population to derive the 1985 per capita GNP. The estimates of GNP per capita for 1985 are shown in this table.

The following formulas describe the procedures for computing the conversion factor for year t:

$$(e^*_{t-2,t}) = \frac{1}{3} \left[e_{t-2} \left(\frac{P_t}{P_{t-2}} \middle| \frac{P^\$_t}{P^\$_{t-2}} \right) + e_{t-1} \left(\frac{P_t}{P_{t-1}} \middle| \frac{P^\$_t}{P^\$_{t-1}} \right) + e_t \right]$$

and for calculating per capita GNP in U.S. dollars for year t:

$$(Y^\$_t) = Y_t / N_t \div e^*_{t-2,t}$$

where,

Y_t = current GNP (local currency) for year t
P_t = GNP deflator for year t
e_t = annual average exchange rate (local currency/U.S. dollars) for year t
N_t = mid-year population for year t
$P^\$_t$ = U.S. GNP deflator for year t

Because of problems associated with the availability of data and the determination of conversion factors, information on GNP per capita is not shown for nonreporting nonmarket economies.

The use of official exchange rates to convert national currency figures to the U.S. dollar does not attempt to measure the relative domestic purchasing powers of currencies. The United Nations International Comparison Project (ICP) has developed measures of real gross domestic product (GDP) on an internationally comparable scale by using purchasing power parities (PPP) instead of exchange rates as conversion factors. This project has covered 60 countries in four phases, at 5-year intervals. Phase V, now underway, is expected to cover about 70 countries. The United Nations, the U.N. Economic Commissions for Europe, for Latin America, and for Asia and the Pacific, and other international agencies such as the European Community, the Organisation for Economic Co-operation and Development, the Asian Development Bank, the Inter-American Development Bank, and the World Bank are engaged in research on improving the methodology and extending annual purchasing power comparisons to all countries. Until such coverage is complete, exchange rates remain the only generally available means of converting GNP from national currencies to U.S. dollars. The table in Box A.2 gives examples of gross product per capita as computed by the *Atlas* method and the ICP method. The ICP data for 1980

are actual results of the ICP Phase IV; those for 1984 and 1985 are estimated by adjusting the 1980 PPPs by relative rates of inflation in the country and the U.S., and using the estimated PPPs as conversion factors.

Information on ICP has been published in four reports, which are listed in the bibliography to this report.

The *average annual rate of inflation* is that measured by the growth rate of the GDP implicit deflator, for each of the periods shown. The GDP deflator is first calculated by dividing, for each year of the period, the value of GDP at current purchaser values by the value of GDP at constant purchaser values, both in national currency. The least-squares method is then used to calculate the growth rate of the GDP deflator for the period. This measure of inflation, like any other, has limitations. For some purposes, however, it is used as an indicator of inflation because it is the most broadly based deflator, showing annual price movements for all goods and services produced in an economy.

Life expectancy at birth indicates the number of years a newborn infant would live if patterns of mortality prevailing for all people at the time of its birth were to stay the same throughout its life. Data are from the U.N. Population Division, supplemented by World Bank estimates.

The *summary measures* for GNP per capita and life expectancy in this table are weighted by population. Those for average annual rates of inflation are weighted by the share of country GDP valued in current U.S. dollars.

Tables 2 and 3. Growth and structure of production

Most of the definitions used are those of the U.N. *System of National Accounts*, series F, no. 2, revision 3.

GDP measures the total final output of goods and services produced by an economy—that is, by residents and nonresidents—regardless of the allocation to domestic and foreign claims. It is calculated without making deductions for depreciation. For most countries, GDP by industrial origin is measured at producer prices; for some countries, purchaser values series are used. GDP at producer prices is equal to GDP at purchaser values, less import duties. Note that in editions before 1986 GDP at producer prices and GDP at purchaser values were referred to as GDP at factor cost and GDP at market prices, respectively. The figures for GDP are dollar values converted from domestic currency by using the single-year official exchange rates. For a few countries where the official exchange rate does not reflect the rate effectively applied to actual foreign exchange transactions, an alternative conversion factor is used. Note that this procedure does not use the three-year averaging computation used for calculating GNP per capita in Table 1.

The *agricultural sector* comprises agriculture, forestry, hunting, and fishing. In developing countries with high levels of subsistence farming, much of the agricultural production is either not exchanged or not exchanged for money. This increases the difficulties of measuring the contribution of agriculture to GDP. *Industry* comprises mining, *manufacturing* (for which subgroup, data are entered in a separate column), construction, and electricity, water, and gas. All other branches of economic activity are categorized as *services*.

National accounts series in domestic currency units were used to compute the indicators in these tables. The growth rates in Table 2 were calculated from constant price series; the sectoral shares of GDP in Table 3, from current price series.

In calculating the *summary measures* for each indicator in Table 2, rescaled constant 1980 U.S. dollar values for each country are first calculated for each of the years of the periods covered, the values aggregated for each year, and the least-squares procedure used to compute the summary measure. The average sectoral percentage shares in Table 3 are computed from group aggregates of sectoral GDP in current U.S. dollars. In this year's edition, for many of the economic indicators, the summary measures include an overall estimate for countries against which the ''n.a.'' symbol is shown. This gives a more consistent aggregate measure by standardizing country coverage for each time period shown.

Tables 4 and 5. Growth of consumption and investment; structure of demand

GDP is defined in the note for Table 2.

General government consumption includes all current expenditure for purchases of goods and services by all levels of government. Capital expenditure on national defense and security is regarded as consumption expenditure.

Private consumption is the market value of all goods and services purchased or received as income in kind by households and nonprofit institutions. It excludes purchases of dwellings, but includes imputed rent for owner-occupied dwellings.

Gross domestic investment consists of the outlays for additions to the fixed assets of the economy, plus net changes in the value of inventories.

Gross domestic savings are calculated by deducting total consumption from gross domestic product.

Exports of goods and nonfactor services represent the value of all goods and nonfactor services sold to the rest of the world; they include merchandise, freight, insurance, travel, and other nonfactor services. The value of factor services, such as investment income, interest, and labor income, is excluded.

The *resource balance* is the difference between exports of goods and nonfactor services and imports of goods and nonfactor services.

National accounts series in national currency units were used to compute the indicators in these tables. The growth rates in Table 4 were calculated from constant price series; the shares of GDP in Table 5, from current price series.

The *summary measures* are calculated by the method explained in the notes for Tables 2 and 3.

Table 6. Agriculture and food

The basic data for *value added in agriculture* are from the World Bank's national accounts series in national currencies. The 1980 value added in current prices in national currencies is converted to U.S. dollars by applying the single-year conversion procedure, as described in the technical notes for Tables 2 and 3. The growth rates of the constant price series in national currencies are applied to the 1980 value added in U.S. dollars to derive the values, in 1980 U.S. dollars, for 1970 and 1985.

The figures for the remainder of this table are from the Food and Agriculture Organization (FAO).

Cereal imports and *food aid in cereals* are measured in grain equivalents and defined as comprising all cereals under the *Standard International Trade Classification* (SITC), Revision 1, Groups 041–046. The figures are not directly comparable since cereal imports are based on calendar-year and recipient-country data, whereas food aid in cereals is based on data for crop years from donor countries and international organizations. The earliest available food aid data are for 1974.

Fertilizer consumption is measured in relation to arable land. This includes land under temporary crops (double-cropped areas are counted once), temporary meadows for mowing or pastures, land under market or kitchen gardens, land temporarily fallow or lying idle, as well as land under permanent crops.

The *index of food production per capita* shows the average annual quantity of food produced per capita in 1983–85 in relation to that in 1979–81. The estimates are derived by dividing the quantity of food production by total population. For this index, food is defined as comprising cereals, starchy roots, sugar cane, sugar beet, pulses, edible oils, nuts, fruits, vegetables, livestock, and livestock products. Quantities of food production are measured net of animal feed, seeds for use in agriculture, and food lost in processsing and distribution.

The *summary measures* for fertilizer consumption are weighted by total arable land area; the *summary measures* for food production are weighted by population.

Table 7. Structure of manufacturing

The basic data for *value added in manufacturing* are from the World Bank's national accounts series in national currencies. The 1980 value added in current prices in national currencies is converted to U.S. dollars by applying the conversion procedure described in the notes for Tables 2 and 3. The growth rates of the constant price series in national currencies are applied to the 1980 value added in U.S. dollars to derive the values, in 1980 U.S. dollars, for 1970 and 1984.

The percentage *distribution of value added* among manufacturing industries is provided by United Nations Industrial Development Organization (UNIDO). UNIDO industrial statistics are used for calculating the shares, with the base values expressed in 1980 dollars.

The classification of manufacturing industries is in accord with the U.N. *International Standard Industrial Classification of All Economic Activities* (ISIC). *Food and agriculture* comprise *ISIC* Division 31; *textiles and clothing* Division 32; *machinery and transport equipment* Major Group 382–384; and *chemicals* Major Group 351 and 352. *Other* comprises wood and related products (Division 33), paper and related products (Division 34), petroleum and related products (Major Group 353–356), basic metals and mineral products (Division 36–37), fabricated metal products and professional goods (Major Group 381 and 385), and other industries (Major Group 390). When data for textiles, machinery or chemicals are not available, they are included in *other*.

Table 8. Manufacturing earnings and output

In this new table, four indicators are shown—two relate to real earnings per employee, one to labor's share in total value added generated, and one to labor productivity in the manufacturing sector; all based on data from the UNIDO database.

Earnings per employee are in constant prices and are derived by deflating nominal earnings per employee from UNIDO by the consumer price index (CPI). The CPI is from the IMF *International Financial Statistics* (IFS). *Total earnings as percentage of value added* are derived by dividing total nominal earnings of employees by nominal value added, to show labor's share in income generated in the manufacturing sector. *Gross output per employee* is also in constant prices and is presented as a measure of labor productivity. To derive this indicator, UNIDO data on *gross output per employee* in current prices are deflated by implicit deflators for value added in manufacturing or in industry, which are from the World Bank's data files.

To improve cross-country comparability UNIDO has, where possible, standardized the coverage of establishments to a cutoff point of those with 5 or more employees.

The concepts and definitions are in accordance with the *International Recommendations for Industrial Statistics*, published by the United Nations. *Earnings* (wages and salaries) cover all payments in cash or kind made by the employer during the year, in connection with the work done. The payments include (a) all regular and overtime cash payments and bonuses and cost of living allowances; (b) wages and salaries paid during vacation and sick leave; (c) taxes and social insurance contributions and the like, payable by the employees and deducted by the employer and (d) payments in kind. The value of *gross output* is estimated on the basis of either production or shipments. On the production basis it consists of (a) the value of all products of the establishment; (b) the value of industrial services rendered to others; (c) the value of goods shipped in the same condition as received; (d) the value of electricity sold; (e) the net change between the value of work-in-progress at the beginning and the end of the reference period. In the case of estimates compiled on a shipment basis, the net change between the beginning and the end of the reference period in the value of stocks of finished goods is also included. *Value added* is defined as the current value of gross output less the current cost of (a) materials, fuels and other supplies consumed; (b) contract and commission work done by others; (c) repair and maintenance work done by others; (d) goods shipped in the same condition as received. The term *employees* in this table combines two categories defined by the U.N.: *regular employees* and *persons engaged*. Together these groups comprise regular employees, working proprietors, active business partners, and unpaid family workers; they exclude homeworkers. The data refer to the average number of employees during the year.

Table 9. Commercial energy

The data on energy are from U.N. sources. They refer to commercial forms of primary energy: petroleum and natural gas liquids, natural gas, solid fuels (coal, lignite, and so on), and primary electricity (nuclear, geothermal, and hydroelectric power)—all converted into oil equivalents. Figures on liquid fuel consumption include petroleum derivatives that have been consumed in nonenergy uses. For converting primary electricity into oil equivalents, a notional thermal efficiency of 34 percent has been assumed. The use of firewood and other traditional fuels, though substantial in some developing countries, is not taken into account because reliable and comprehensive data are not available.

Energy imports refer to the dollar value of energy imports—Section 3 in the *Standard International Trade Classification* (SITC), Revision 1—and are expressed as a percentage of earnings from merchandise exports.

Because data on energy imports do not permit a distinction between petroleum imports for fuel and for use in the petrochemicals industry, these percentages may overestimate the dependence on imported energy.

The *summary measures* of *energy production* and *consumption* are computed by aggregating the respective volumes for each of the years covered by the time periods, and then applying the least-squares growth rate procedure. For *energy consumption per capita*, population weights are used to compute summary measures for the specified years.

The *summary measures* of *energy imports as a percentage of merchandise exports* are computed from group aggregates for energy imports and merchandise exports in current dollars.

Table 10. Growth of merchandise trade

The statistics on merchandise trade, Tables 10 through 14, are primarily from the U.N. trade data system, which accords with the U.N. *Yearbook of International Trade Statistics*—that is, the data are based on countries' customs returns. Values in these tables are in current U.S. dollars.

For the value data in Table 10, however, statistics are also used from the International Monetary Fund (IMF), and in a few (footnoted) cases, World Bank estimates are reported. Secondary sources and World Bank estimates are based on aggregated reports that become available before the detailed reports that are submitted to the U.N. In some cases, they also permit coverage adjustments for significant components of a country's foreign trade that do not pass through customs.

Merchandise exports and imports, with some exceptions, cover international movements of goods across customs borders. Exports are valued f.o.b. (free on board), imports c.i.f. (cost, insurance, and freight), unless otherwise specified in the foregoing sources. These values are in current dollars; note that they do not include trade in services.

The *growth rates of merchandise exports and imports* are in constant terms and are calculated from quantum indexes of exports and imports. Quantum indexes are obtained from the export or import value index as deflated by the corresponding price index. To calculate these quantum indexes for developing countries, the World Bank uses its own price indexes, which are based on international prices for primary commodities and unit value indexes for manufactures. These price indexes are both country-specific and disaggregated by broad commodity groups, which ensures consistency between data for a group of countries and those for individual countries. Such data consistency will increase as the World Bank continues to improve its trade price indexes for an increasing number of countries. For industrial economies the indexes are from the U.N. *Yearbook of International Trade Statistics* and *Monthly Bulletin of Statistics*, and the IMF *International Financial Statistics*.

The *terms of trade*, or the net barter terms of trade, measure the relative level of export prices compared with import prices. Calculated as the ratio of a country's index of average export price to the average import price index, this indicator shows changes over a base year in the level of export prices as a percentage of import prices. The terms-of-trade index numbers are shown for 1983 and 1985, where 1980 = 100. The price indexes are from the sources cited above for the growth rates of exports and imports.

The *summary measures* are calculated by aggregating the 1980 constant U.S. dollar price series for each year, and then applying the least-squares growth rate procedure for the periods shown. Note again that these values do not include trade in services.

Tables 11 and 12. Structure of merchandise trade

The shares in these tables are derived from trade values in current dollars reported in the U.N. trade data system and the U.N. *Yearbook of International Trade Statistics,* supplemented by other regular statistical publications of the U.N. and the IMF. Note that, unlike Table 10, no World Bank estimates are used in these tables.

Merchandise exports and imports are defined in the note for Table 10.

The categorization of exports and imports follows the *Standard International Trade Classification* (SITC), series M, no. 34, Revision 1.

In Table 11, *fuels, minerals, and metals* are the commodities in *SITC* Section 3 (mineral fuels, lubricants and related materials), Divisions 27 and 28 (minerals and crude fertilizers, and metalliferous ores) and Division 68 (nonferrous metals). *Other primary commodities* comprise *SITC* Sections 0, 1, 2, and 4 (food and live animals, beverages and tobacco, inedible crude materials, oils, fats, and waxes) less Divisions 27 and 28. *Machinery and transport equipment* are the commodities in *SITC* Section 7. *Other manufactures* represent *SITC* Sections 5 through 9 less Section 7 and Division 68. In this edition *textiles and clothing,* representing *SITC* Divisions 65 and 84 (textiles, yarns, fabrics, and clothing), are shown as a subgroup of *other manufactures*. Note that because of a lack of detailed information for many countries, this definition is not the same as that used for exporters of manufactures defined on page xi.

In Table 12, *food* commodities are those in *SITC* Sections 0, 1, and 4 and Division 22 (food and live animals, beverages, oils and fats, and oilseeds and nuts), less Division 12 (tobacco). *Fuels* are the commodities in *SITC* Section 3 (mineral fuels, lubricants and related materials). *Other primary commodities* comprise *SITC* Section 2 (crude materials, excluding fuels), less Division 22 (oilseeds and nuts) plus Division 12 (tobacco) and Division 68 (nonferrous metals). *Machinery and transport equipment* are the commodities in *SITC* Section 7. *Other manufactures,* calculated as the residual from the total value of manufactured imports, represent *SITC* Sections 5 through 9 less Section 7 and Division 68.

The *summary measures* in Table 11 are weighted by total merchandise exports of individual countries in current dollars; those in Table 12, by total merchandise imports of individual countries in current dollars. (See note to Table 10.)

Table 13. Origin and destination of merchandise exports

Merchandise exports are defined in the note for Table 10. Trade shares in this table are based on statistics from the U.N. and the IMF on the value of trade in current dollars. *Industrial market economies* also include Gibraltar, Iceland, and Luxembourg; *high-income oil exporters* also include Bahrain, Brunei, and Qatar.

The *summary measures* are weighted by the value of total merchandise exports of individual countries in current dollars.

Table 14. Origin and destination of manufactured exports

The data in this table are from the U.N. and are among those used to compute Special Table B in the U.N. *Yearbook of International Trade Statistics. Manufactured goods* are the commodities in *SITC,* Revision 1, Sections 5 through 9 (chemicals and related products, basic manufactures, manufactured articles, machinery and transport equipment, and other manufactured articles and goods not elsewhere classified) excluding Division 68 (nonferrous metals). Note, again, that because of a lack of detailed information for many countries, this definition is not the same as that used for exporters of manufactures defined on page xi.

The country groups are the same as those in Table 13. The *summary measures* are weighted by manufactured exports of individual countries in current dollars.

Table 15. Balance of payments and reserves

Values in this table are in current U.S. dollars.

The *current account balance* is the difference between (a) exports of goods and services plus inflows of unrequited official and private transfers and (b) imports of goods and services plus unrequited transfers to the rest of the world. The current account balance estimates are primarily from IMF data files and conform to the *IMF Balance of Payments Manual* definitions.

Workers' remittances cover remittances of income by migrants who are employed or expect to be employed for more than a year in their new economy, where they are considered residents. Those derived from shorter-term stays are included in private transfers.

Net direct private investment is the net amount invested or reinvested by nonresidents in enterprises in which they or other nonresidents exercise significant managerial control. Including equity capital, reinvested earnings, and other capital, these net figures also take into account the value of direct investment abroad by residents of the reporting country. These estimates were compiled primarily from IMF data files.

Gross international reserves comprise holdings of monetary gold, special drawing rights (SDRs), the reserve position of IMF members in the Fund, and holdings of foreign exchange under the control of monetary authorities. The data on holdings of international reserves are from IMF data files. The gold component of these reserves is valued throughout at year-end London prices: that is, $37.37 an ounce in 1970 and $327.30 an ounce in 1985. The reserve levels for 1970 and 1985 refer to the end of the year indicated and are in current dollars at prevailing exchange rates. Due to differences in the definition of international reserves, in the valuation of gold, and in reserve management practices, the levels of reserve holdings published in national sources do not have strictly comparable significance. Reserve holdings at the end of 1985 are also expressed in terms of the number of months of imports of goods and services they could pay for, with imports at the average level for 1985.

The *summary measures* are computed from group aggregates for gross international reserves and total imports of goods and services in current dollars.

Table 16. Total external debt

The data on debt in this and successive tables are from the World Bank Debtor Reporting System, supplemented by World Bank estimates. That system is concerned solely with developing economies and does not collect data on external debt for other groups of borrowers, nor from economies that are not members of the World Bank. The dollar figures on debt shown in Tables 16 through 21 are in U.S. dollars converted at official exchange rates.

In this edition, the data on debt include private nonguaranteed debt reported by twenty developing countries and complete or partial estimates (depending on the reliability of information) for an additional twenty-nine countries.

Public loans are external obligations of public debtors, including the national government, its agencies, and autonomous public bodies. *Publicly guaranteed loans* are external obligations of private debtors that are guaranteed for repayment by a public entity. These two categories are aggregated in the tables. *Private nonguaranteed loans* are external obligations of private debtors that are not guaranteed for repayment by a public entity.

Use of IMF credit denotes repurchase obligations to the IMF for all uses of IMF resources, excluding those resulting from drawings in the reserve tranche and on the IMF Trust Fund. It is shown for the end of the year specified. It comprises purchases outstanding under the credit tranches, including enlarged access resources, and all of the special facilities (the buffer stock, compensatory financing, extended Fund, and oil facilities). Trust Fund loans are included individually in the Debtor Reporting System and are thus shown within the total of public long-term debt. Use of IMF credit outstanding at year-end (a stock) is converted to U.S. dollars at the dollar-SDR exchange rate in effect at year-end.

Short-term external debt is debt with an original maturity of one year or less. Available data permit no distinctions between public and private nonguaranteed short-term debt.

Total external debt is defined for the purpose of this report as the sum of public, publicly guaranteed, and private nonguaranteed long-term debt, use of IMF credit, and short-term debt.

Table 17. Flow of public and private external capital

Data on *disbursements* and *repayment of principal* (amortization) are for public, publicly guaranteed, and private nonguaranteed long-term loans. The *net flow* estimates are disbursements less the repayment of principal.

Table 18. Total external public and private debt and debt service ratios

Total long-term debt data in this table cover public and publicly guaranteed debt and private nonguaranteed debt. The ratio of debt service to exports of goods and services is one of several conventional measures used to assess the ability to service debt. The average ratios of debt service to GNP for the economy groups are weighted by

GNP in current dollars. The average ratios of debt service to exports of goods and services are weighted by exports of goods and services in current dollars.

Table 19. External public debt and debt service ratios

External public debt outstanding and disbursed represents public and publicly guaranteed loans drawn at year-end, net of repayments of principal and write-offs. For estimating external public debt as a percentage of GNP, the debt figures are converted into U.S. dollars from currencies of repayment at end-of-year official exchange rates. GNP is converted from national currencies to U.S. dollars by applying the conversion procedure described in the technical notes for Tables 2 and 3.

Interest payments are actual payments made on the outstanding and disbursed public and publicly guaranteed debt in foreign currencies, goods, or services; they include commitment charges on undisbursed debt if information on those charges is available.

Debt service is the sum of actual repayments of principal (amortization) and actual payments of interest made in foreign currencies, goods, or services on external public and publicly guaranteed debt. Procedures for estimating total long-term debt as a percentage of GNP, average ratios of debt service to GNP, and average ratios of debt service to exports of goods and services are the same as those described in the notes for Table 18.

The *summary measures* are computed from group aggregates of debt service and GNP in current dollars.

Table 20. Terms of external public borrowing

Commitments refer to the public and publicly guaranteed loans for which contracts were signed in the year specified. They are reported in currencies of repayment and converted into U.S. dollars at average annual official exchange rates.

Figures for *interest rates, maturities,* and *grace periods* are averages weighted by the amounts of the loans. Interest is the major charge levied on a loan and is usually computed on the amount of principal drawn and outstanding. The maturity of a loan is the interval between the agreement date, when a loan agreement is signed or bonds are issued, and the date of final repayment of principal. The grace period is the interval between the agreement date

and the date of the first repayment of principal.

Public loans with variable interest rates, as a percentage of public debt, refer to interest rates that float with movements in a key market rate; for example, the London interbank offered rate (LIBOR) or the U.S. prime rate. This column shows the borrower's exposure to changes in international interest rates.

The *summary measures* in this table are weighted by the amounts of the loans.

Table 21. Official development assistance from OECD and OPEC members

Official development assistance (ODA) consists of net disbursements of loans and grants made on concessional financial terms by official agencies of the members of the Development Assistance Committee (DAC) of the Organisation for Economic Cooperation and Development (OECD) and members of the Organization of Petroleum Exporting Countries (OPEC), with the object of promoting economic development and welfare. It includes the value of technical cooperation and assistance. All data shown are supplied by the OECD, and all U.S. dollar values converted at official exchange rates.

Amounts shown are net disbursements to developing countries and multilateral institutions. The disbursements to multilateral institutions are now reported for all DAC members on the basis of the date of issue of notes; some DAC members previously reported on the basis of the date of encashment. *Net bilateral flows to low-income economies* exclude unallocated bilateral flows and all disbursements to multilateral institutions.

The nominal values shown in the summary for ODA from OECD countries are converted into 1980 prices using the dollar GDP deflator. This deflator is based on price increases in OECD countries (excluding Greece, Portugal, and Turkey) measured in dollars. It takes into account the parity changes between the dollar and national currencies. For example, when the dollar appreciates, price changes measured in national currencies have to be adjusted downward by the amount of the appreciation to obtain price changes in dollars.

The table, in addition to showing totals for OPEC, shows totals for the Organization of Arab Petroleum Exporting Countries (OAPEC). The donor members of OAPEC are Algeria, Iraq, Kuwait, Libya, Qatar, Saudi Arabia, and United Arab Emirates. ODA data for OPEC and OAPEC are also obtained from the OECD.

Table 22. Official development assistance: receipts

Net disbursements of ODA from all sources consist of loans and grants made on concessional financial terms by all bilateral official agencies and multilateral sources, with the object of promoting economic development and welfare. The disbursements shown in this table are not strictly comparable with those shown in Table 21 since the receipts are from all sources; disbursements in Table 21 refer to those made by members of the OECD and OPEC only. Net disbursements equal gross disbursements less payments to donors for amortization. Net disbursements of ODA are shown per capita and as a percentage of GNP.

The *summary measures* of per capita ODA are computed from group aggregates for population and for ODA. *Summary measures* for ODA as a percentage of GNP are computed from group totals for ODA and for GNP in current U.S. dollars.

Table 23. Central government expenditure

The data on central government finance in Tables 23 and 24 are from the IMF *Government Finance Statistics Yearbook, 1986,* and IMF data files. The accounts of each country are reported using the system of common definitions and classifications found in the IMF *Manual on Government Finance Statistics* (1986). Due to differences in coverage of available data, the individual components of central government expenditure and current revenue shown in these tables may not be strictly comparable across all economies. The shares of total expenditure and revenue by category are calculated from national currencies.

The inadequate statistical coverage of state, provincial, and local governments has dictated the use of central government data only. This may seriously understate or distort the statistical portrayal of the allocation of resources for various purposes, especially in large countries where lower levels of government have considerable autonomy and are responsible for many social services.

It must be emphasized that the data presented, especially those for education and health, are not comparable for a number of reasons. In many economies private health and education services are substantial; in others public services represent the major component of total expenditure but may be financed by lower levels of government. Great caution should therefore be exercised in using the data for cross-country comparisons.

Central government expenditure comprises the expenditure by all government offices, departments, establishments, and other bodies that are agencies or instruments of the central authority of a country. It includes both current and capital (development) expenditure.

Defense comprises all expenditure, whether by defense or other departments, on the maintenance of military forces, including the purchase of military supplies and equipment, construction, recruiting, and training. Also in this category is expenditure on strengthening public services to meet wartime emergencies, on training civil defense personnel, on supporting research and development, and on funding administration of military aid and programs.

Education comprises expenditure on the provision, management, inspection, and support of pre-primary, primary, and secondary schools; of universities and colleges; and of vocational, technical, and other training institutions by central governments. Also included is expenditure on the general administration and regulation of the education system; on research into its objectives, organization, administration, and methods; and on such subsidiary services as transport, school meals, and medical and dental services in schools.

Health covers public expenditure on hospitals, medical and dental centers, and clinics with a major medical component; on national health and medical insurance schemes, and on family planning and preventive care. Also included is expenditure on the general administration and regulation of relevant government departments, hospitals and clinics, health and sanitation, and national health and medical insurance schemes; and on research and development.

Housing and community amenities and social security and welfare cover public expenditure on housing, such as income-related schemes, on provision and support of housing and slum clearance activities, on community development, and on sanitary services; and public expenditure on compensation to the sick and temporarily disabled, for loss of income on payments to the elderly, the permanently disabled, and the unemployed, and on family, maternity, and child allowances. They also include the cost of welfare services such as care of the aged, the disabled, and children, as well as the cost of general administration, regulation, and research associated with social security and welfare services.

Economic services comprise public expenditure associated with the regulation, support, and more efficient operation of business, economic development, redress of regional imbalances, and creation of employment opportunities. Research, trade promotion, geological surveys, and inspection and regulation of particular industry groups are among the activities included. The five major categories of economic services are industry, agriculture, fuel and energy, transportation and communication, and other economic affairs and services.

Other covers expenditure on the general administration of government not included elsewhere; for a few economies it also includes amounts that could not be allocated to other components.

Overall surplus/deficit is defined as current and capital revenue and grants received, less total expenditure less lending minus repayments.

The *summary measures* for the components of central government expenditure are computed from group totals for expenditure components and central government expenditure in current dollars. Those for total expenditure as a percentage of GNP and for overall surplus/deficit as a percentage of GNP are computed from group totals for the above total expenditures and overall surplus/deficit in current dollars, and GNP in current dollars, respectively.

Table 24. Central government current revenue

Information on data sources and comparability is given in the note for Table 23. Current revenue by source is expressed as a percentage of total current revenue, which is the sum of tax revenue and nontax revenue and is calculated from national currencies.

Tax revenue is defined as all government revenue from compulsory, unrequited, nonrepayable receipts for public purposes, including interest collected on tax arrears and penalties collected on nonpayment or late payment of taxes. Tax revenue is shown net of refunds and other corrective transactions. *Taxes on income, profit, and capital gain* are taxes levied on the actual or presumptive net income of individuals, on the profits of enterprises, and on capital gains, whether realized on land sales, securities, or other assets. *Social Security contributions* include employers' and employees' social security contributions as well as those of self-employed and unemployed persons. *Domestic taxes on goods and services* include general sales, turnover, or value added taxes, selective excises on goods, selective taxes on services, taxes on the use of goods or property, and profits of fiscal monopolies. *Taxes on international trade and transactions* in-

clude import duties, export duties, profits of export or import monopolies, exchange profits, and exchange taxes. *Other taxes* include employers' payroll or manpower taxes, taxes on property, and other taxes not allocable to other categories.

Nontax revenue comprises all government revenue that is not a compulsory nonrepayable payment for public purposes. Receipts from public enterprises and property income are included in this category. Proceeds of grants and borrowing, funds arising from the repayment of previous lending by governments, incurrence of liabilities, and proceeds from the sale of capital assets are not included.

The *summary measures* for the components of current revenue are computed from group totals for revenue components and total current revenue in current dollars; those for current revenue as a percentage of GNP are computed from group totals for total current revenue and GNP in current dollars.

Table 25. Money and interest rates

The data on monetary holdings are based on data reported in the IMF's *International Financial Statistics (IFS)*. *Monetary holdings, broadly defined,* comprise the monetary and quasi-monetary liabilities of a country's financial institutions to residents other than the central government. For most countries, monetary holdings are the sum of *money (IFS line 34)* and *quasi-money (IFS line 35)*. *Money* comprises the economy's means of payment: currency outside banks and demand deposits. *Quasi-money* comprises time and savings deposits and similar bank accounts that the issuer will readily exchange for money. Where nonmonetary financial institutions are important issuers of quasi-monetary liabilities, these are also included in the measure of monetary holdings.

The growth rates for monetary holdings are calculated from year-end figures while the ratios of monetary holdings to GDP are based on the midpoint between the year-end figures for the specified year and the preceding year.

The *nominal interest rates of banks*, also from *IFS*, are representative of the rates paid by commercial or similar banks to holders of their quasi-monetary liabilities (deposit rates) and charged by the banks on loans to prime customers (lending rate). They are, however, of limited international comparability partly because coverage and definitions vary, but also because countries differ in the scope available to banks for adjusting interest rates to reflect market conditions.

Since interest rates (and growth rates for monetary holdings) are expressed in nominal terms, much of the variation between countries stems from differences in inflation. For ease of reference, the Table 1 indicator of recent inflation is repeated in this table.

Table 26. Income distribution

The data in this table refer to the distribution of total disposable household income accruing to percentile groups of households ranked by total household income. The distributions cover rural and urban areas and refer to different years between 1970 and 1985.

The data for income distribution are drawn from a variety of sources, including the Economic Commission for Latin America and the Caribbean (ECLAC), Economic and Social Commission for Asia and the Pacific (ESCAP), International Labour Organisation (ILO), the Organisation for Economic Co-operation and Development (OECD), the U.N. *National Account Statistics: Compendium of Income Distribution Statistics, 1985,* the World Bank, and national sources.

Collection of income distribution data is not systematically organized or integrated with the official statistical system in many countries, and the data are derived from surveys designed for other purposes, most often consumer expenditure surveys, that also collect some information on income. These surveys use a variety of income concepts and sample designs, and in many cases their geographic coverage is too limited to provide reliable nationwide estimates of income distribution. Therefore, while the estimates shown are considered the best available, they do not avoid all these problems and should be interpreted with extreme caution.

The scope of the indicator is similarly limited. Because households vary in size, a distribution in which households are ranked according to per capita household income, rather than according to total household income, is superior for many purposes. The distinction is important because households with low per capita incomes frequently are large households, whose total income may be high, and conversely many households with low household incomes may be small households with high per capita incomes. Information on the distribution of per capita household income exists for only a few countries. The World Bank's Living Standards Measurement Study is assisting a few selected countries to improve their collection and analysis of data on income distribution. Some of the data is used in this table.

Table 27. Population growth and projections

The *growth rates of population* are period averages calculated from midyear populations.

The estimates of *population* for mid-1985 are based on data from the U.N. Population Division and from World Bank sources. In many cases the data take into account the results of recent population censuses. Note again that refugees not permanently settled in the country of asylum are generally considered to be part of the population of their country of origin.

The *projections of population* for 1990 and 2000, and to the year in which the population will eventually become stationary, are made for each economy separately. Starting with information on total population by age and sex, fertility rates, mortality rates, and international migration in the base year 1985, these parameters are projected at five-year intervals on the basis of generalized assumptions until the population becomes stationary. The base-year estimates are from updated computer printouts of the U.N. *World Population Prospects as Assessed in 1984,* from the most recent issues of the U.N. *Population and Vital Statistics Report,* from World Bank country data, and from national censuses.

The *net reproduction rate* (NRR) indicates the number of daughters a newborn girl will bear during her lifetime, assuming fixed age-specific fertility and mortality rates. The NRR thus measures the extent to which a cohort of newborn girls will reproduce themselves under given schedules of fertility and mortality. An NRR of 1 indicates that fertility is at replacement level: at this rate child-bearing women, on average, bear only enough daughters to replace themselves in the population.

A *stationary population* is one in which age- and sex-specific mortality rates have not changed over a long period, while age-specific fertility rates have simultaneously remained at replacement level (NRR=1). In such a population, the birth rate is constant and equal to the death rate, the age structure is constant, and the growth rate is zero.

Population momentum is the tendency for population growth to continue beyond the time that replacement-level fertility has been achieved; that is, even after NRR has reached 1. The momentum of a population in a given year is measured as a ratio of the ultimate stationary population to the population of that year, given the assumption that fertility remains at replacement level. For example, the 1985 population of India is estimated at 765 million. If NRR was 1 in 1985, the projected stationary population would be 1,349 million—reached in the middle of the 22nd century—and the population momentum would be 1.8.

A population tends to grow even after fertility has declined to replacement level because past high growth rates will have produced an age distribution with a relatively high proportion of women in, or still to enter, the reproductive ages. Consequently, the birth rate will remain higher than the death rate and the growth rate will remain positive for several decades. It takes at least 50–75 years, depending on the initial conditions, for a population's age distribution to adjust fully to changed fertility rates.

To make the projections, assumptions about future mortality rates are made in terms of female life expectancy at birth (that is, the number of years a newborn girl would live if subject to the mortality risks prevailing for the cross-section of population at the time of her birth). Economies are divided according to whether their primary school enrollment ratio for females is above or below 70 percent. In each group a set of annual increments in female life expectancy is assumed, depending on the female life expectancy in 1980–85. For a given life expectancy at birth, the annual increments during the projection period are larger in economies with a higher primary school enrollment ratio and a life expectancy of up to 62.5 years. At higher life expectancies, the increments are the same.

To project fertility rates, the year in which fertility will reach replacement level is estimated. These estimates are speculative and are based on information on trends in crude birth rates (defined in the note for Table 28), total fertility rates (also defined in the note for Table 28), female life expectancy at birth, and the performance of family planning programs. For most economies it is assumed that the total fertility rate will decline between 1985 and the year of reaching a net reproduction rate of 1, after which fertility will remain at replacement level. For most countries in Sub-Saharan Africa, and for a few countries in Asia and the Middle East, total fertility rates are assumed to remain constant for some time and then to decline until replacement level is reached; for a few countries they are assumed to increase and then to decline.

In some countries, fertility is already below replacement level or will decline to below replacement level during the next 5 to 10 years. Because a population will not remain stationary if its net reproduction rate is other than 1, it is assumed that fertility rates in these economies will regain replacement levels in order to make estimates of the stationary population for them. For the sake of consistency with the other estimates, the total fertility rates in industrial economies are assumed to remain constant until 1985–90 and then to increase to replacement level by 2010.

International migration rates are based on past and present trends in migration flow. The estimates of future net migration are speculative. For most economies the net migration rates are assumed to be zero by 2000, but for a few they are assumed to be zero by 2025.

The estimates of the hypothetical size of the stationary population and the assumed year of reaching replacement-level fertility are speculative. *They should not be regarded as predictions.* They are included to show the long-run implications of recent fertility and mortality trends on the basis of highly stylized assumptions. A fuller description of the methods and assumptions used to calculate the estimates is available from the World Bank publication: *World Population Projections 1985—Short- and Long-term Estimates by Age and Sex with Related Demographic Statistics.*

Table 28. Demography and fertility

The *crude birth and death rates* indicate the number of live births and deaths per thousand population in a year. They come from the sources mentioned in the note for Table 27. Percentage changes are computed from unrounded data.

The *total fertility rate* represents the number of children that would be born per woman, if she were to live to the end of her childbearing years and bear children at each age in accordance with prevailing age-specific fertility rates. The rates given are from the sources mentioned in the note for Table 27.

The *percentage of married women of childbearing age using contraception* refers to women who are practicing, or whose husbands are practicing, any form of contraception. These generally comprise condoms, diaphragms, spermicides, intrauterine devices (IUDs), injectable and oral contraceptives, female and male sterilization, rhythm, withdrawal and abstinence. *Women of childbearing age* are generally women aged 15–44, although for some countries contraceptive usage is measured for other age groups: 18–44, 15–49, and 19–49.

Data are mainly derived from the World Fertility

Survey, the Contraceptive Prevalence Survey, World Bank country data, and the U.N. report *Recent Levels and Trends of Contraceptive Use as Assessed in 1983*. For a few countries for which no survey data are available, program statistics are used: these include Bangladesh, India, Indonesia, and several African countries. Program statistics may understate contraceptive prevalence because they do not measure use of methods such as rhythm, withdrawal, or abstinence, or contraceptives not obtained through the official family planning program. The data refer to a variety of years, generally not more than three years distant from those specified.

All *summary measures* are country data weighted by each country's share in the aggregate population.

Table 29. Life expectancy and related indicators

Life expectancy at birth is defined in the note for Table 1.

The *infant mortality rate* is the number of infants who die before reaching one year of age, per thousand live births in a given year. The data are from a variety of U.N. sources—"Infant Mortality: World Estimates and Projections, 1950-2025" in *Population Bulletin of the United Nations* (1983), recent issues of U.N. *Demographic Yearbook*, and *Population and Vital Statistics Report*—and from the World Bank.

The *child death rate* is the number of deaths of children aged 1-4 per thousand children in the same age group in a given year. Estimates are based on the data on infant mortality and on the relationship between the infant mortality rate and the child death rate implicit in the appropriate Coale-Demeny model life tables; see Ansley J. Coale and Paul Demeny, *Regional Model Life Tables and Stable Populations* (Princeton, NJ: Princeton University Press, 1966).

The *summary measures* in this table are country figures weighted by each country's share in the aggregate population.

Table 30. Health-related indicators

The estimates of *population per physician and nursing person* are derived from World Health Organization (WHO) data. They take into account more recent estimates of population. Nursing persons include graduate, practical, assistant, and auxiliary nurses; the inclusion of auxiliary nurses allows for a better estimation of the availability of nursing care. Be-

cause definitions of nursing personnel vary—and because the data shown are for a variety of years, generally not more than three years distant from those specified—the data for these two indicators are not strictly comparable across countries.

The *daily calorie supply per capita* is calculated by dividing the calorie equivalent of the food supplies in an economy by the population. Food supplies comprise domestic production, imports less exports, and changes in stocks; they exclude animal feed, seeds for use in agriculture, and food lost in processing and distribution. These estimates are from the Food and Agriculture Organization (FAO).

The *summary measures* in this table are country figures weighted by each country's share in the aggregate population.

Table 31. Education

The data in this table refer to a variety of years, generally not more than three years distant from those specified, and are mostly from Unesco.

The data on *number enrolled in primary school* are estimates of children of *all* ages enrolled in primary school. Figures are expressed as the ratio of pupils to the population of school-age children. While many countries consider primary school age to be 6-11 years, others do not. The differences in country practices in the ages and duration of schooling are reflected in the ratios given. For some countries with universal primary education, the gross enrollment ratios may exceed or fall below 100 percent because some pupils are younger or older than the country's standard primary school age. The data on *number enrolled in secondary school* are calculated in the same manner, but again the definition of secondary school age differs among countries. It is most commonly considered to be 12-17 years.

The estimates of *number enrolled in higher education* are calculated similarly, using the 20-24 age cohort.

The *summary measures* in this table are country enrollment rates weighted by each country's share in the aggregate population.

Table 32. Labor force

The *population of working age* refers to the population aged 15-64. The estimates are from the International Labour Organisation (ILO) based on U.N. population estimates.

The *summary measures* are weighted by population.

The *labor force* comprises economically active persons aged 10 years and over, including the armed forces and the unemployed, but excluding housewives, students, and other economically inactive groups. *Agriculture, industry, and services* are defined as in Table 2. The estimates of the sectoral distribution of the labor force are from the ILO, *Labour Force Estimates and Projections, 1950–2000,* 1986.

The *summary measures* are weighted by labor force.

The *labor force growth rates* are from ILO data and are based on age-specific activity rates reported in the source cited above.

The application of ILO activity rates to the Bank's latest population estimates may be inappropriate for some economies in which there are important changes in unemployment and underemployment, in international and internal migration, or in both. The labor force projections for 1985–2000 should thus be treated with caution.

The *summary measures* are country growth rates weighted by each country's share in the aggregate labor force in 1980.

Table 33. Urbanization

The data on *urban population as a percentage of total population* are from the U.N. *Estimates and Projections of Urban, Rural and City Populations 1950–2025: The 1982 Assessment,* 1985, supplemented by data from various issues of the U.N. *Demographic Yearbook* and from the World Bank.

The *growth rates of urban population* are calculated from the World Bank's population estimates; the estimates of urban population shares are calculated from the sources cited above. Data on urban agglomeration are from the U.N. *Patterns of Urban and Rural Population Growth, 1980.*

Because the estimates in this table are based on different national definitions of what is "urban," cross-country comparisons should be interpreted with caution.

The *summary measures* for urban population as a percentage of total population are calculated from country percentages weighted by each country's share in the aggregate population; the other summary measures in this table are weighted in the same fashion, using urban population.

Bibliography

National accounts and economic indicators	International Monetary Fund. 1986. *Government Finance Statistics Yearbook*. Vol. 9. Washington, D.C.. U.N. Department of International Economic and Social Affairs. Various years. *Statistical Yearbook*. New York. ———. 1985. *National Accounts Statistics: Compendium of Income Distribution Statistics*. Statistical Papers, series M, no. 79. New York. FAO, IMF, and UNIDO data files. National sources. World Bank country documentation. World Bank data files.
Energy	U.N. Department of International Economic and Social Affairs. Various years. *World Energy Supplies*. Statistical Papers, series J. New York. World Bank data files.
Trade	International Monetary Fund. Various years. *Direction of Trade Statistics*. Washington, D.C.. ———. Various years. *International Financial Statistics*. Washington, D.C.. U.N. Conference on Trade and Development. Various years. *Handbook of International Trade and Development Statistics*. Geneva. U.N. Department of International Economic and Social Affairs. Various years. *Monthly Bulletin of Statistics*. New York. ———. Various years. *Yearbook of International Trade Statistics*. New York. FAO, IMF, and World Bank data files. U.N. trade tapes. World Bank country documentation.
Balance of payments, capital flows, and debt	The Organisation for Economic Co-operation and Development. Various years. *Development Co-operation*. Paris. ———. 1986. *Geographical Distribution of Financial Flows to Developing Countries*. Paris. IMF balance of payments data files. World Bank Debtor Reporting System.
Labor force	International Labour Office. 1986. *Labour Force Estimates and Projections, 1950–2000*. 3rd ed. Geneva. International Labour Organisation tapes.
Population	U.N. Department of International Economic and Social Affairs. Various years. *Demographic Yearbook*. New York. ———. Various years. *Population and Vital Statistics Report*. New York. ———. 1980. *Patterns of Urban and Rural Population Growth*. New York. ———. 1982. "Infant Mortality: World Estimates and Projections, 1950–2025." *Population Bulletin of the United Nations*, no. 14. New York. ———. Updated printouts. *World Population Prospects as Assessed in 1982*. New York. ———. 1983. *World Population Trends and Policies: 1983 Monitoring Report*. New York. ———. 1984. *Recent Levels and Trends of Contraceptive Use as Assessed in 1983*. New York. ———. 1985. *Estimates and Projections of Urban, Rural and City Populations, 1950–2025; The 1982 Assessment*. New York. World Bank data files.
Social indicators	Food and Agriculture Organization. 1986. *Food Aid Bulletin* (April). Rome. ———. 1981. *Fertilizer Yearbook 1982*. Rome. ———. 1983. *Food Aid in Figures* (December). Rome. ———. 1985a. *Fertilizer Yearbook 1984*. Rome. ———. 1985b. *Trade Yearbook 1984*. Rome. ———. 1986. *Production Yearbook 1985*. Rome. U.N. Department of International Economic and Social Affairs. Various years. *Demographic Yearbook*. New York. ———. Various years. *Statistical Yearbook*. New York. U.N. Educational Scientific and Cultural Organization. Various years. *Statistical Yearbook*. Paris. World Health Organization. Various years. *World Health Statistics Annual*. Geneva. ———. Various years. *World Health Statistics Report*. Geneva. FAO and World Bank data files.

International Comparison Project reports

Kravis, Irving B., Zoltan Kenessey, Alan Heston, Robert Summers. 1975. *Phase I: A System of International Comparisons of Gross Product and Purchasing Power.* Baltimore, Md.: Johns Hopkins University Press.

Kravis, Irving B., Alan Heston, Robert Summers. 1978. *Phase II: International Comparisons of Real Product and Purchasing Power.* Baltimore, Md.: Johns Hopkins University Press.

———. 1982. *Phase III: World Product and Income: International Comparisons of Real Gross Product.* Baltimore, Md.: Johns Hopkins University Press.

———. 1986. *Phase IV: World Comparisons of Purchasing Power and Real Product for 1980.* New York: United Nations.